Dictionary of Literary Biography

Documentary Series

Wright, edited by Margaret A. Van Antwerp (1982)

3 *Saul Bellow, Jack Kerouac, Norman Mailer, Vladimir Nabokov, John Updike, Kurt Vonnegut,* edited by Mary Bruccoli (1983)

4 *Tennessee Williams,* edited by Margaret A. Van Antwerp and Sally Johns (1984)

5 *American Transcendentalists,* edited by Joel Myerson (1988)

6 *Hardboiled Mystery Writers: Raymond Chandler, Dashiell Hammett, Ross Macdonald,* edited by Matthew J. Bruccoli and Richard Layman (1989)

7 *Modern American Poets: James Dickey, Robert Frost, Marianne Moore,* edited by Karen L. Rood (1989)

8 *The Black Aesthetic Movement,* edited by Jeffrey Louis Decker (1991)

9 *American Writers of the Vietnam War: W. D. Ehrhart, Larry Heinemann, Tim O'Brien, Walter McDonald, John M. Del Vecchio,* edited by Ronald Baughman (1991)

10 *The Bloomsbury Group,* edited by Edward L. Bishop (1992)

11 *American Proletarian Culture: The Twenties and The Thirties,* edited by Jon Christian Suggs (1993)

12 *Southern Women Writers: Flannery O'Connor, Katherine Anne Porter, Eudora Welty,* edited by Mary Ann Wimsatt and Karen L. Rood (1994)

13 *The House of Scribner, 1846-1904,* edited by John Delaney (1996)

14 *Four Women Writers for Children, 1868-1918,* edited by Caroline C. Hunt (1996)

15 *American Expatriate Writers: Paris in the Twenties,* edited by Matthew J. Bruccoli and Robert W. Trogdon (1997)

16 *The House of Scribner, 1905-1930,* edited by John Delaney (1997)

Yearbooks

1980 edited by Karen L. Rood, Jean W. Ross, and Richard Ziegfeld (1981)

1981 edited by Karen L. Rood, Jean W. Ross, and Richard Ziegfeld (1982)

1982 edited by Richard Ziegfeld; associate editors: Jean W. Ross and Lynne C. Zeigler (1983)

1983 edited by Mary Bruccoli and Jean W. Ross; associate editor: Richard Ziegfeld (1984)

1984 edited by Jean W. Ross (1985)

1985 edited by Jean W. Ross (1986)

1986 edited by J. M. Brook (1987)

1987 edited by J. M. Brook (1988)

1988 edited by J. M. Brook (1989)

1989 edited by J. M. Brook (1990)

1990 edited by James W. Hipp (1991)

1991 edited by James W. Hipp (1992)

1992 edited by James W. Hipp (1993)

1993 edited by James W. Hipp, contributing editor George Garrett (1994)

1994 edited by James W. Hipp, contributing editor George Garrett (1995)

1995 edited by James W. Hipp, contributing editor George Garrett (1996)

1996 edited by Samuel W. Bruce and L. Kay Webster, contributing editor George Garrett (1997)

1997 edited by Matthew J. Bruccoli and George Garrett, with the assistance of L. Kay Webster (1998)

Concise Series

Concise Dictionary of American Literary Biography, 6 volumes (1988-1989): *The New Consciousness, 1941-1968; Colonization to the American Renaissance, 1640-1865; Realism, Naturalism, and Local Color, 1865-1917; The Twenties, 1917-1929; The Age of Maturity, 1929-1941; Broadening Views, 1968-1988.*

Concise Dictionary of British Literary Biography, 8 volumes (1991-1992): *Writers of the Middle Ages and Renaissance Before 1660; Writers of the Restoration and Eighteenth Century, 1660-1789; Writers of the Romantic Period, 1789-1832; Victorian Writers, 1832-1890; Late Victorian and Edwardian Writers, 1890-1914; Modern Writers, 1914-1945; Writers After World War II, 1945-1960; Contemporary Writers, 1960 to Present.*

American Poets Since World War II
Sixth Series

Dictionary of Literary Biography® • Volume One Hundred Ninety-Three

American Poets Since World War II
Sixth Series

Edited by
Joseph Conte
State University of New York, Buffalo

A Bruccoli Clark Layman Book
Gale Research
Detroit, Washington, D.C., London

Printed in the United States of America

The paper used in this publication meets the minimum requirements
of American National Standard for Information Sciences–Permanence
Paper for Printed Library Materials, ANSI Z39.48-1984.∞ ™

Library of Congress Cataloging-in-Publication Data

American poets since World War II. Sixth series / edited by Joseph Conte.
   p. cm.–(Dictionary of literary biography; v. 193)
"A Bruccoli Clark Layman book."
Includes bibliographical references and index.
ISBN 0-7876-1848-9 (alk. paper)
1. American poetry–20th century–Bio-bibliography–Dictionaries. 2. Poets, American–
20th century–Biography–Dictionaries. 3. American poetry–20th century–History and
criticism. I. Conte, Joseph Mark, 1960- . II. Series.
PS323.5.A5 1998
811'.5409–dc21   98-3658
[B]   CIP

10 9 8 7 6 5 4 3 2 1

In Memory of Constance Coiner

Contents

Plan of the Series

. . . Almost the most prodigious asset of a country, and perhaps its most precious possession, is its native literary product — when that product is fine and noble and enduring.

Mark Twain*

The advisory board, the editors, and the publisher of the *Dictionary of Literary Biography* are joined in endorsing Mark Twain's declaration. The literature of a nation provides an inexhaustible resource of permanent worth. We intend to make literature and its creators better understood and more accessible to students and the reading public, while satisfying the standards of teachers and scholars.

To meet these requirements, *literary biography* has been construed in terms of the author's achievement. The most important thing about a writer is his writing. Accordingly, the entries in *DLB* are career biographies, tracing the development of the author's canon and the evolution of his reputation.

The purpose of *DLB* is not only to provide reliable information in a convenient format but also to place the figures in the larger perspective of literary history and to offer appraisals of their accomplishments by qualified scholars.

The publication plan for *DLB* resulted from two years of preparation. The project was proposed to Bruccoli Clark by Frederick C. Ruffner, president of the Gale Research Company, in November 1975. After specimen entries were prepared and typeset, an advisory board was formed to refine the entry format and develop the series rationale. In meetings held during 1976, the publisher, series editors, and advisory board approved the scheme for a comprehensive biographical dictionary of persons who contributed to North American literature. Editorial work on the first volume began in January 1977, and it was published in 1978. In order to make *DLB* more than a reference tool and to compile volumes that individually have claim to status as literary history, it was decided to organize volumes by

From an unpublished section of Mark Twain's autobiography, copyright by the Mark Twain Company

topic, period, or genre. Each of these freestanding volumes provides a biographical-bibliographical guide and overview for a particular area of literature. We are convinced that this organization—as opposed to a single alphabet method—constitutes a valuable innovation in the presentation of reference material. The volume plan necessarily requires many decisions for the placement and treatment of authors who might properly be included in two or three volumes. In some instances a major figure will be included in separate volumes, but with different entries emphasizing the aspect of his career appropriate to each volume. Ernest Hemingway, for example, is represented in *American Writers in Paris, 1920–1939* by an entry focusing on his expatriate apprenticeship; he is also in *American Novelists, 1910–1945* with an entry surveying his entire career, as well as in *American Short-Story Writers, 1910–1945, Second Series* with an entry concentrating on his short stories. Each volume includes a cumulative index of the subject authors and articles. Comprehensive indexes to the entire series are planned.

Since 1981 the series has been further augmented by the *DLB Yearbooks,* which update published entries and add new entries to keep the *DLB* current with contemporary activity. There have also been *DLB Documentary Series* volumes which provide biographical and critical source materials for figures whose work is judged to have particular interest for students. One of these companion volumes is entirely devoted to Tennessee Williams.

We define literature as the *intellectual commerce of a nation:* not merely as belles lettres but as that ample and complex process by which ideas are generated, shaped, and transmitted. *DLB* entries are not limited to "creative writers" but extend to other figures who in their time and in their way influenced the mind of a people. Thus the series encompasses historians, journalists, publishers, book collectors, and screenwriters. By this means readers of *DLB* may be aided to perceive literature not as cult scripture in the keeping of intellectual high priests but firmly positioned at the center of a nation's life.

DLB includes the major writers appropriate to each volume and those standing in the ranks behind them. Scholarly and critical counsel has been sought in deciding which minor figures to include and how full their entries should be. Wherever possible, useful references are made to figures who do not warrant separate entries.

Each *DLB* volume has an expert volume editor responsible for planning the volume, selecting the figures for inclusion, and assigning the entries. Volume editors are also responsible for preparing, where appropriate, appendices surveying the major periodicals and literary and intellectual movements for their volumes, as well as lists of further readings. Work on the series as a whole is coordinated at the Bruccoli Clark Layman editorial center in Columbia, South Carolina, where the editorial staff is responsible for accuracy and utility of the published volumes.

One feature that distinguishes *DLB* is the illustration policy—its concern with the iconography of literature. Just as an author is influenced by his surroundings, so is the reader's understanding of the author enhanced by a knowledge of his environment. Therefore *DLB* volumes include not only drawings, paintings, and photographs of authors, often depicting them at various stages in their careers, but also illustrations of their families and places where they lived. Title pages are regularly reproduced in facsimile along with dust jackets for modern authors. The dust jackets are a special feature of *DLB* because they often document better than anything else the way in which an author's work was perceived in its own time. Specimens of the writers' manuscripts and letters are included when feasible.

Samuel Johnson rightly decreed that "The chief glory of every people arises from its authors." The purpose of the *Dictionary of Literary Biography* is to compile literary history in the surest way available to us—by accurate and comprehensive treatment of the lives and work of those who contributed to it.

The *DLB* Advisory Board

Introduction

A suitable discussion has taken place during the past century regarding the dominant mode of the literary arts. Although poetry might once have made undisputed claim to being the most precious form of writing, the modern prose of Gustave Flaubert, Henry James, Marcel Proust, James Joyce, and Virginia Woolf gave substance to Stendhal's assertion that "prose was the higher art." Responding to the challenge issued by modern fiction, Ezra Pound, in his essay "The Prose Tradition in Verse" (1914), resigns himself to arguing, following the English poet and novelist Ford Madox Ford, that "poetry should be written at least as well as prose." One part concession and one part exhortation, Pound's advice to the poets of his day was to practice the "clarity and precision" that he observed in the best prose. Such writing was culturally astute and not sentimental, efficient and not prolix, a work of "serious art" and not a pastime. Though the style of writing in any period undergoes continual change, Pound's preeminent concern was that verse was losing its grip on the cultural and intellectual bearings of the age. This problem—more than discussions of a marginal readership and the near exclusion from commercial publication venues—has special relevance in our postindustrial society. The challenge to modernist poetry came from the psychological novel, whose protagonists expressed the anxieties and disruptions (the fragmentation) of life during a traumatic epoch. As a theorist of postmodernism, Jean-François Lyotard states succinctly in *The Postmodern Condition* (1979), "It seems to me that the essay (Montaigne) is postmodern, while the fragment (*The Athaeneum*) is modern." The ascendancy of the critical essay in postmodernism—whether it is the theoretical and philosophical treatise of the sort practiced by Lyotard and published in *Diacritics* or the essay of social and political commentary that one finds in nationally circulated journals such as *The New Republic*—would be difficult to dispute. But before poetry is consigned to permanent marginality, one must examine the ways in which it continues to challenge the "serious" reader. It remains the genre of writing in which the subtlest combinations of intellect and affect are promoted. Poetry (although it is accompanied by fiction in this regard) serves as a proving ground for stylistic innovations that are not generally permitted in the relatively "unmarked"

voice of the essay. Especially as jargon and neologism clot many of the expressions of critical theory, poetry retains the capacity to use the precise word in its context so that there can be no doubt as to its appropriateness or definition. The radical or "field" coherence of poetry allows for an associative discovery of meaning that is often restricted by the "vector" of causal argumentation and narrative exposition in prose. Lastly, poetry is a virtual engine sufficiently supple in its form to treat the complexities of the postmodern (information) age; less bound now by tradition than other genres, the writing of poetry has become an adaptive system that is always capable of generating new meaning. As the abundant differences in the modes of writing represented in this volume suggest, the availability of poetry to all manner of cultural material and organizational methods allows it to contend—socially and intellectually—with critical prose and fiction whose reliance on academic and commercial publication venues restricts their expression.

Dictionary of Literary Biography 193: American Poets Since World War II, Sixth Series is devoted to American poets who have made a significant contribution to their art after 1945. Such a criterion allows for the inclusion of poets of different age groups, diverse styles, and competing poetic principles. Some of the poets presented here had already established their careers by the close of World War II; others have only recently begun to attract—or provoke—the critical attention that their talents deserve. The presence of poets accomplished in traditional forms and familiar genres alongside those practiced in a resolutely avant-garde approach is not an accident of this volume but its intention. Readers of *DLB* volumes can choose to read according to their inclinations, but the juxtapositions of poetic careers that either reinforce or contend with one another is perhaps the chief advantage of a book with such variety of subjects and contributors. The poets included all have a strong claim for their importance in the period; however, the thorough critical appraisal, biographical information, and bibliographical support provided by the contributors will enable readers to judge each case for themselves.

The selection of entries for this volume gives special consideration to its relation to those prior volumes in the *DLB* series that address American poetry after 1945. *DLB 193* extends the selection of contemporary poets made by this editor in *DLB 169: American Poets Since World War II, Fifth Series* (1996) and *DLB 165: American Poets Since World War II, Fourth Series* (1996). A continuing concern was to review the treatment of poets included in the two-volume *DLB 5: American Poets Since World War II* (1980). In the eighteen years since the publication of *DLB 5* several of the poets included there have produced major new works or have since been the beneficiaries of extensive critical studies. Such changes called for an entirely fresh appraisal. In other instances it has been deemed sufficient to update and revise the treatment originally afforded the poet to account for less-dramatic shifts in a career. The passage of eighteen years has naturally seen the decline of interest in certain mid-century authors, but it also brings a demand for a reassessment of postmodern poetry with entries devoted to previously overlooked—but by no means minor—poets. And finally, this volume presents several poets whose work was still in a gestatory stage in 1980 and who thus appear in the *DLB* for the first time. Such poets may well introduce the poetics that will carry us into the next century.

From this vantage point near the close of the twentieth century, the history of postmodern poetry can broadly be described in three generational clusters. The first generation of postmodern poets are those born shortly after the turn of the century. The milestones of high modernism, such as the publication of T. S. Eliot's *The Waste Land* (1922), were written while they were still quite young. In a literal manner they regard the modern poets of their day—Wallace Stevens, Pound, Eliot, Robert Frost, Gertrude Stein, Marianne Moore, and William Carlos Williams—as both their elders (by some twenty or more years) and as their mentors. With these mentors they carry on an extensive personal and epistolary contact. Their early mature work appears between 1929 and 1944, marked by the grinding demands of the Great Depression and often inflected by leftist politics and economic theory. They are well aware that their writing follows upon the dramatic breach with the genteel aesthetic of late-nineteenth-century poetry as found in Eliot's "The Love Song of J. Alfred Prufrock" (1917), Pound's first gathering of his epic in *A Draft of XXX Cantos* (1930), or Stein's cubist poetry in *Tender Buttons* (1914). In one sense they are late-modernists; they regard their work as an extension of the modernist campaign to "make it new." But they also struggle "to witness / and adjust" (adapting Williams's phrase) to the modern condition, interjecting

within the revolutionary aesthetic the social, political, and personal concerns of their generation.

Louis Zukofsky (1904–1978) is a representative type of the first postmodernist, embarking upon his career under the close and sought-after tutelage of Ezra Pound (chronicled in their extensive correspondence between 1927 and 1963). The first half of Zukofsky's own eight-hundred-page epic poem, *"A,"* written during the years 1928 to 1974, resembles the canto structure of Pound's "poem including history." After 1951, however, Zukofsky's work becomes increasingly hermetic, procedural in form, and language oriented. In short the latter part of his career represents a departure from his modernist mentor and his hortatory manner and culminates in such distinctively postmodern achievements as *80 Flowers* (1978). However different in style and biography, other members of this first generation follow a similar pattern that realizes a slow sundering of the mentor-disciple relationship. Among poets in this volume, Carl Rakosi (1903–) began his career among the "Objectivist" group headed by Zukofsky, but after a long silence resumed writing poetry in a plain-spoken style that drew upon his experiences as a social worker. The vast majority of his work was produced after 1965. Louise Bogan (1897–1970) immersed herself in the New York avant-garde of the 1920s that included Williams, Lola Ridge, Mina Loy, and Edmund Wilson before crafting her own formal lyric style. The meeting of Elizabeth Bishop (1911–1979) and Moore on the steps of the New York Public Library in 1934 initiated yet another lasting friendship and tutelage of a literary career, though Bishop's poetry assumed a more personal idiom than Moore's. The presence of first-generation postmodern poets in this series is justified not only by the substantial work they completed after 1945 but also by their continued influence on contemporary poets. Their careers serve as instructive graphs of the transition between a modern and postmodern poetics. In some cases the first postmoderns worked in relative obscurity until discovered, published, and in turn adopted as mentors by members of the postwar generation. Essays on several important poets born in the first decade of this century—including Charles Reznikoff, Edward Dahlberg, Laura Riding Jackson, Langston Hughes, and Stanley Kunitz—can be found in *DLB 45: American Poets, 1880–1945, First Series* and *DLB 48: American Poets, 1880–1945, Second Series.*

Several recent studies, among them Albert Gelpi's *Coherent Splendor* (1987) and Cary Nelson's *Repression and Recovery* (1989), have shown that modern American poetry was hardly the monolithic program that the New Critical canon had suggested.

Fissures arising from differing relationships with Romanticism, in the test of domestic or expatriate affiliations, and in the conflicting political allegiances of the 1930s and 1940s suggest that the spate of movements and groupings that were identified or actively promoted after 1950 were an inevitable result of such disagreements.

The postwar generation of postmodern poets are those born in the second quarter of the century, with a particularly distinguished class of 1926–1927 that includes A. R. Ammons, John Ashbery, Robert Bly, Robert Creeley, Allen Ginsberg, James Merrill, W. S. Merwin, Frank O'Hara, and James Wright. Their notable early works appeared between 1955 and 1970. It may be judicious to describe the attitude of postwar poets to their modernist forebears as ambivalent—that is, capable of registering strongly positive or negative responses in separate cases. Creeley, for example, rejects the symbolist mode of Eliot for the immediate contact with the real he finds in Williams. This shift from a poetics of transcendence to one of immanence becomes a defining characteristic of mid-century poetry, as Charles Altieri has argued in *Self and Sensibility in Contemporary American Poetry* (1984). Charles Olson (1910–1970), who was the first poet to identify himself as "postmodern" in "The Present is Prologue" (1950), espouses a posthumanism and posthistoricism that runs counter to the romantic ideology found in Stevens. His essay "Projective Verse" (1950) serves to define the poetics of immediate apprehension practiced by poets of the Black Mountain School, including Robert Duncan (1919–1988) and Joel Oppenheimer (1930–1988). But Ammons, Ashbery, and James Schuyler have retained a closer affinity for the romantic imagination expressed in Stevens's "poem of the act of the mind." Robert Lowell's first three volumes emulated the dense symbolic language and impersonal registers of Eliot only to follow Ginsberg's *Howl* (1956) into a confessional mode in *Life Studies* (1959) that made a virtue of traumatic personal revelation. As M. L. Rosenthal and others have noted, the shift from an impersonal to a personal register and the disclosure of the self in the poem are distinguishing aspects of postwar poetry. In the end the postwar poets neither denied the continuing relevance of the modernist writers nor pledged absolute fealty to their principles.

An additional source of generational tension stems from the longevity of the modernist poets whose major late works appear simultaneously with the important early works of the postwar poets. Thus one finds Creeley's landmark *For Love* published in the same year as Williams's remarkable *Pictures from Brueghel* (1962). Ashbery's *Some Trees* (1956) closely follows Stevens's *Collected Poems,* published on his seventy-fifth birthday in 1954. Bishop, who was slow to publish and whose reputation accrued gradually, arrives at her *Selected Poems* in the same year as Moore's meticulous edition of her *Complete Poems* (1967).

One finds in the work of these postwar poets many acts of homage to their still-productive modernist predecessors. But these homages are accompanied by profuse statements on poetics that suggest their project was not merely to extend modernism but to advance from it. Olson's "Projective Verse," Denise Levertov's "Some Notes on Organic Form," Ginsberg's "First thought best thought," Robert Kelly's "Notes on the Poetry of the Deep Image," O'Hara's "Personism: A Manifesto," Lowell's autobiographical essay "91 Revere Street," and Adrienne Rich's politically charged "When We Dead Awaken" are among the landmark documents that challenge modernist precepts, add new concepts to the encyclopedia of poetics, and found postmodern schools of poetry. The proliferation of movements and manifestoes at mid century can be read as an attempt by second-generation postmodernists to accentuate their differences from and exploit the fissures within the dominant mode of modernism. Each school challenges the New Critical emphasis on an ironic and distant voice, the mastery of a well-wrought form, and the limiting of poetic language and subject matter to the decorous. The proposition of an organic process in poetry by the members of the Black Mountain School, the chatty casualness of the New York School, the reliance upon the intuition among the Beats, and the confessional provocations of a psyche-in-distress contribute to the expansive modulations of postwar poetry.

If the poets of the 1950s and 1960s suffered somewhat from the anxiety of influence, they also enjoyed the largest and broadest readership for poetry in this century: unofficial tabulation from royalty statements, course enrollments, political rallies in public parks, and the burgeoning popularity of poetry readings in academic lecture halls and bohemian clubs suggest that the cachet of poetry reached its peak in this countercultural era. Individual volumes of poetry by Bly, Creeley, Ginsberg, Sylvia Plath, Anne Sexton, and Gary Snyder sold tens of thousands of copies. Like many other aspects of American life at mid century, poetry enjoyed a period of unbridled expansion.

Third-generation postmodern poets are most likely the contemporaries of many readers of this volume. Born during the twenty years after World War II, they count themselves among the Baby Boomers. Their numbers are legion; their achievements are still under evaluation. They are college graduates for whom "Modern Poetry" was a three-credit course in their major; most hold graduate degrees in literature or creative writing; and many teach their craft in university writing programs. They have had the opportunity of sitting at a seminar table with acclaimed members of the postwar movements who have been the holders of distinguished professorships and whose papers fetch large sums from special collections. But contemporary poets do not identify themselves with postwar movements beyond an acknowledgment of their historical importance. They often feel only slight indebtedness to the prior generation for the battles fought—mostly between the academics and the bohemians, the "cooked" and the "raw" poetries—that are now largely resolved. Few marvel that the renegade poets of the 1960s are now ensconced in the university or in textbook anthologies or that open and closed forms cohabit in little magazines or in the latest volume by Ashbery.

The field of contemporary poetry cannot be solely described in terms of movements and schools. Instead one finds a four-sided mandala of less tightly bonded interest groups or PACs (Poetry Action Committees). In one quarter reside the traditionalists, who have assumed the mantle of the academic poets of the postwar generation, though in a more discursive and less intricate language. Aided by recent collections—such as *The Direction of Poetry: An Anthology of Rhymed and Metered Verse Written in the English Language Since 1975* (1988), *Expansive Poetry: Essays on the New Narrative and the New Formalism* (1989), and *A Formal Feeling Comes: Poems in Form by Contemporary Women* (1994)—an alliance of New Formalists calls for a return to traditional rhyme and meter (to recoup what they view as the slack practice of the 1960s and 1970s) and a renewed emphasis on narrative to foster a general, educated audience for poetry (which the diffuse poetries of the counterculture had supposedly lost). Alfred Corn (1943–), Timothy Steele (1948–), Vikram Seth (1952–), Brad Leithauser (1953–), and Gjertrud Schnackenberg (1953–) revive stanzaic forms and metrical devices fallen into disuse. Though some among their group combine neoconservativism with a return to traditional forms, one should note that the lesbian formalist Marilyn Hacker (1942–) addresses the milieu of homosexual life in her sonnets, and businessman-poet Dana Gioia (1950–) has successfully resisted both an academic appointment and the republicanism of the management class. Entries on all of the New Formalists mentioned here can be found in *DLB 120: American Poets Since World War II, Third Series;* a fresh assessment of the career of an important mentor and sponsor of the formalists, Anthony Hecht (1923–), can be found in *DLB 169.*

In the opposite quarter reside the experimentalists, whose antiestablishment convictions preclude participation in the "professional verse culture." They are widely published (in small-press books, financially precarious but daring magazines, and on always-warm laser-jet printers) but poorly distributed. They form an underground wholly ignored by the Associated Writing Programs and by the prize-selection committees that announce the winners of the latest competitions in their newsletters. The Language Poets are the most identifiable of this group, attacking the conventions of the personal voice and transparent, "absorptive" language in the lyric. Important poets of the Language movement included in this volume are Rae Armantrout (1947–), Carla Harryman (1952–), and Bob Perelman (1947–); others appearing in recent *DLB* volumes are Charles Bernstein (1950–), Kathleen Fraser (1935–), Lyn Hejinian (1941–), Susan Howe (1937–), Bernadette Mayer (1945–), Michael Palmer (1943–), Ron Silliman (1946–), and Barrett Watten (1948–). These poets muster an array of antiabsorptive techniques that provoke self-consciousness about the reading process. Blatant artifice, syntactical disruptions, phonetic play, typographical anomalies, impermeability, splicing and co-opting of itinerant texts, and popular iterations combine to assert what Bernstein in *A Poetics* (1992) calls the "skepticism, doubt, noise, [and] resistance" of postmodern culture. The Language Poets' elaboration of poststructuralist theories of language and their recourse to Marxist attacks on a publishing industry that commodifies referential language have heightened their appeal to a theoretically aware university readership. A few Language Poets, such as Bernstein, Howe, and Perelman, have in fact entered the professoriat. In contrast to the foregrounding of textuality in Language writing, performance poetry—such as the shamanistic songs and Yiddish vaudeville of Jerome Rothenberg (1931–) in this volume, the parodic lectures of the scholar-translator in Armand Schwerner's (1927–) *The Tablets* (1971–), and the free-form "talk poems" of David Antin (1932–)—stresses the improvisation of an oral performance incorporating autobiographical, ethnographic, musical, or other nonliterary sources.

In a third quarter reside poets for whom identity politics are a prominent consideration. Issues of race, gender, ethnicity, and sexual preference constitute the subject matter of their work, which ranges from the most intimate personal revelation to broad public pronouncements. They are less concerned than either traditionalists or experimentalists by debates over poetic form though they pursue styles that differentiate their work from the speech and experience of white Middle America. The espousal of an opaque or overly literary language runs counter to the political statements they feel compelled to make. Their charge is to give voice to those previously repressed segments of American society and therefore to introduce a pluralist concept of community. They speak first to an audience with whom they share their experience of alterity and marginality, but they consequently seek the understanding of a larger readership. In the gender and hemispheric politics of Carolyn Forché (1950–), in the pan-African rituals and the tonalities of jazz as recorded by Nathaniel Mackey (1947–) and the ever-combative Ishmael Reed (1938–), in the reconciliation of Asian tradition and modern Hawaiian life in Cathy Song (1955–) and the Native American incantations of Mary TallMountain (1918–1994), in the bilingual culture of Simon Ortiz (1941–), American poetry overcomes its monochromatic and monotonal historical origins.

The fourth quarter is occupied by the practitioners of the most pervasive mode in American poetry today, the personal (or postconfessional) lyric. These poets extend the confessional mode of Lowell, Plath, Sexton, W. D. Snodgrass, and John Berryman, though they are less strident in their attack on decorum and perhaps no longer able to shock through autobiographical revelation in the era of tabloid journalism. Despite the moderation in tone, these poets continue to explore the psyche and emotions in poems that test the propositions of the self against the experience of the world. They exhibit a general disregard for formalist techniques (including meter) that might impede immediate expression, and they refuse to distract from the presentation of the self by calling attention to the language-as-object. Poets such as Louise Glück (1943–), Robert Hass (1941–), Jonathan Holden (1941–), Sharon Olds (1942–), James Tate (1943–), and James Wright (1927–1980) have pursued the family drama and childhood's traumatic incidents, psychic distress and substance abuse, and sexual adventuring and marital strife as their common subjects. Beyond the immediate relation to confessionalism, these poets share an exploration of subjectivity that is the legacy of the romantic lyric. Like the odes of William Wordsworth or John Keats—in a language only slightly heightened from the American vernacular and soothing to the contemporary ear—these poems call upon remembrance within a dramatic setting and often reveal the poet's sensibility and identity.

Despite Olson's mid-century warning against "the lyrical interference of the individual as ego" in "Projective Verse," the self in the postconfessional lyric once again assumes the role of arbiter of meaningful experience. These are the poems that dominate such verse magazines as *American Poetry Review* (with its author photographs accompanying poems), *Shenandoah, Prairie Schooner,* and the *Denver Quarterly.* And these poems represent the majority of those discussed in writing workshops where the dynamics of group therapy now reigns. The prevalence of the postconfessional lyric raises the questions of what the reader turns to poetry for and what he does not turn to poetry for. The apparent antipathy among writing programs for speculative thought and cultural argument has left the field of social and intellectual critique open to the critical essay. In contending with millennial shifts in postmodern culture, a renewed emphasis on "the self" in the lyric may signal one form of retreat on the part of poetry. If our present media culture seems depersonalized, or at best artificially personal, poetry's return to the intimate voice may be considered as pharmaceutical for those who are overtaxed by the information age. But the contemporary personal lyric seems insufficiently concerned with how the self might presently be constructed, linguistically or socially, as if the laying bare of some inner psychodrama (as in the "tranquilized Fifties") were an unmediated act that had stood without being commented upon by theorists such as Jacques Lacan, Gilles Deleuze, or Michel Foucault during the past three decades.

The four-part mandala of contemporary poetry here described is not intended to locate poets permanently or exclusively in particular quarters. Adrienne Rich (1929–), for example, began her career as a formalist in the school of W. H. Auden and underwent a conversion to become one of the foremost exponents (in poetry and prose) of feminist politics. One observes among recent writers a more flexible alliance not permitted by the close-knit movements of mid century. Poets are often not responsible for the labels attached to their work, and contemporary poets frequently resist the scholar's restrictive and ultimately reductive labels. While LeRoi Jones/Amiri Baraka (1934–) abandoned his association with the New York bohemian schools to lead the Black Arts movement, Reed, Lorenzo Thomas (1944–), and Nathaniel Mackey now move more easily between an African American poetics and an experimental mode. Similarly, female poets such as Levertov (1923–1997), Fraser, and Forché have worked to correlate the terms of lyric poetry and political activism.

The third generation of postmodern poets may also be characterized by outright resistance to the aesthetic and political program of modernism. In this regard the poets are in alignment with much that has transpired in literary criticism and theory in the past twenty years. The poets of identity politics have been especially critical of the Eurocentric and masculinist bias that permeated modernism. The pluralism that espouses the equal validity and aesthetic worth of disparate cultural experience directly challenges the elitist, sexist, and discriminatory attitudes implicit in modernism. The postmodern lyric's renewed emphasis on personal expression serves as repudiation of the impersonal and objectivist slant of modern verse and reinstates the individual to authority over totalizing systems. Whereas the modernists held the word as sacred and symbolic *Logos,* with intrinsic and incantatory meaning, the postmodern avant-garde regards language as a plastic medium that can be reshaped without lingering impressions. Rather than aspire to a pure, refined art, the postmodern poet appropriates theoretical jargon and demotic speech, the embedded phraseology of commerce and the free signifier. Lastly, there exists a reactionary postmodernism that dubs the modernist revolt against nineteenth-century aesthetics a failure because of its disregard for the general audience and urges a return to traditional forms, public statement, and coherence of narration and setting. On all fronts there is little doubt that the contemporary poet now disdains many of the precepts of modernism. A new literary period has begun.

Contemporary poetry has been even more agitated by debates about the canon than other fields of literary endeavor. Popular acclaim and satisfied booksellers temper judgments as Susan Sontag displaces E. B. White in essay collections or as Toni Morrison captures the Nobel Prize that eluded Vladimir Nabokov. But because poetry continues to operate within a limited economy and an eroding readership outside of the university—only a few volumes are published by trade houses, and reviews of poetry in major newspapers and magazines have virtually vanished—arguments as to who the important figures are, how they are identified, and why they should be taught preoccupy the field. The literary canon demands selectivity. It should guide the reader toward works that are significant or rewarding. In the past decade especially, pluralists have argued that such "guides to reading" are neither benign nor impartial. The canon creates a hierarchy of writers, and it traditionally reinforces the dominant culture at the expense of the marginal or disenfranchised. Literary history has a greater obligation to

inclusivity in an attempt to establish a thorough cultural record and to recover unjustly neglected or repressed works. Thus the canon-reinforcing process of evaluation sometimes clashes with the politics of inclusion and efforts at suitable representation of the diversity of American voices.

In 1929 Pound asserted in his own effort at canon formation, "How to Read," that poetry should be chosen for an anthology "because it contained an invention, a definite contribution to the art of verbal expression." He argues that one should not "sub-divide the elements in literature according to some non-literary categoric division. You do not divide physics or chemistry according to racial or religious categories." Although Pound deplored the conservatism of the anthologist, he nevertheless equates the terms of literary selection with the supposedly impersonal and universal truths of science. That equation is precisely the object of complaint among today's pluralists: the universal category too often turned out to be male and white.

In their efforts to expand the canon, pluralists have introduced a remarkable number of special-interest anthologies that identify poets by gender, race, ethnicity, sexual preference, and nationality, or some combination thereof. Among these are *Breaking Silence: An Anthology of Contemporary Asian American Poets* (1983), *Harper's Anthology of 20th Century Native American Poetry* (1987), and *Gay and Lesbian Poetry in Our Time* (1988). As Alan Golding points out in "American Poetry Anthologies," an essay in *Canons* (1984), such collections have the notable virtue of preserving a specific tradition and rehistoricizing our understanding of literary heritage. But they are also symptoms of an increasing literary balkanization through which one reader's familiar figures of contemporary poetry escape the notice of another. And as Bernstein in his 1992 essay "State of the Art" points out, "Too often, the works selected to represent cultural diversity are those that accept the model of representation assumed by the dominant culture in the first place" (*A Poetics*).

Pound's premise about anthologies should not be considered invalid, but the criteria he posits must evolve as the tradition advances. Inventive writers of all descriptions continue to be neglected by the canon in favor of aesthetically conservative writers. Cultivating those works that include, as Pound says, "an invention, a definite contribution to the art of verbal expression" is crucial to the survival of poetry in America. The canon of contemporary poetry persists because one must finally discriminate between inventive and stale work. New critiques that persuasively describe daring work to a skeptical readership, in tandem with the poetics of inclusion that represent a panoply of American traditions, make a revised and expanded canon essentially beneficial to American poetry. One recent anthology that proposes a multicultural and international solution to the dilemma of representation is *Poems for the Millennium* (1995). In the first of two volumes, extending "From Fin-de-Siècle to Negritude," editors Rothenberg and Pierre Joris offer a capacious gathering that embraces a wide cultural heritage and delineates the innovative contributions to twentieth-century poetry.

The entries in *DLB 193: American Poets Since World War II, Sixth Series* are substantial enough to supply biographical and literary-historical context in addition to an extensive evaluation of the poet's body of works. At the same time the entry length limits the number of poets that can be treated. Although each volume contributes to a thorough understanding of the literary history of the genre and period, it cannot offer a complete representation of the work in the field. One should regard this volume as a companion and supplement to entries in the earlier volumes of the series. Readers will also find entries on important poets writing after World War II in *DLB 16: The Beats: Literary Bohemians in Postwar America* (1983), *DLB 41: Afro-American Poets Since 1955* (1985), *DLB 82: Chicano Writers, First Series* (1989), and *DLB 122: Chicano Writers, Second Series* (1992). As an incremental series these volumes combine critical selection and comprehensive literary history.

The movements and schools that were so prevalent at mid century partially depended on the personal association of the poets. The New York School poets were fellow students at Harvard before relocating to the art community of lower Manhattan. Olson and Creeley kept up a voluminous correspondence before they met at Black Mountain in North Carolina. With the institutionalization of creative-writing programs, contemporary poets move singly to jobs at colleges and universities across the country. Among the results of this distribution of talent are the affiliation of poets by publishing venues and by their practice in certain genres and forms. While the personal lyric is the most prevalent contemporary type of poem in terms of quantity, the meditative poem appears to be growing in importance. The lyric devotes itself to the physical and the passionate; in its intimate voice the lyric provokes an emotional response. The meditative poem retreats from the turbulent desires of the ego; it is cognitive rather than sensual, abstract rather than particular. The lyric is hot; the meditative poem is cool. The chief modernist predecessor in the meditative mode is Stevens, who sought to define modern poetry as "the act of the mind." The major exponents of the meditative mode are now Ashbery and Ammons. Their excursions of thought find a comfortable rhythm in longer works such as "Self-Portrait in a Convex Mirror" (1975), "A Wave" (1984), and *Flow Chart* (1991) by Ashbery; and *Tape for the Turn of the Year* (1965), *Sphere: The Form of a Motion* (1974), *Garbage* (1994), and *Glare* (1997) by Ammons. Younger poets at work in meditative poetry include Robert Hass and, in this volume, Ann Lauterbach (1942–). James Schuyler's long impromptus, such as "The Morning of the Poem" (1980) and "A Few Days" (1985), combine the Stevensian "act of the mind" with the casual conversational style that one encounters among other members of the New York School such as O'Hara and Ted Berrigan (1934–1983).

The appeal of the meditative poem resides in the patience with which the mind of the poet deploys, maps, and inscribes itself. As a reaction to the abstract language and indeterminacy of scene in meditative poetry, there have been several recent exponents of a return to narrative verse. With James Merrill's elegant masque *The Changing Light at Sandover* (1983) now completed, poetic works deploying many characters and eventful linear narratives followed. Vikram Seth chronicles the foibles of Bay Area yuppies in his 307-page novel-in-verse, *The Golden Gate* (1986). Frederick Turner and Frederick Feirstein publish a manifesto on behalf of the New Narrative in *Expansive Poetry* (1989).

The fizzling of several modernist epic poems and a distaste for the hierarchical structures and belief systems that frame them has led many postmodern poets to serial composition. Poems written in many loosely associated parts also signify the impatience of poets with the short personal lyric demanded by journals. The series is a modular form in which individual sections are both discontinuous and capable of multiple orderings. In contrast to the linear causality of most narrative forms, the serial poem is desultory and polyvalent, accommodating an expanding and heterodox universe. Among the first postmodern examples is George Oppen's *Discrete Series* (1934). Mid-century practice includes the open-ended "Passages" of Robert Duncan, published through several volumes; Robert Creeley's *Pieces* (1969); *The Journals* (1975) of Paul Blackburn (1926–1971); and the later books of Jack Spicer (1925–1965). Among contemporary poets included in this volume, Leslie Scalapino (1948–) has prolifically explored the shifting and combinatorial form of seriality in such works as *Way* (1988) and *The Return of Painting, The Pearl, and Orion: A Trilogy* (1997). As Lynn Keller observes in *Forms of Expansion: Recent*

Long Poems by Women (1997), poets such as Rachel Blau DuPlessis and Beverly Dahlen have turned to feminist serial poems as an alternative to the patriarchal assumptions of culture prevalent in male-dominated epic poetry. The serial poem represents the most innovative contribution of postmodern poetry to the long form.

In contrast to the return to traditional poetic forms espoused by the New Formalists, some postmodern poets have invented their own constricting formal devices. These procedural forms consist of predetermined and arbitrary constraints that are relied upon to generate the context and direction of the poem during composition. Unconvinced by the presence of any grand order in the world, the poet discretely enacts a personal order. Procedural forms present themselves as alternatives to the well-made metaphorical lyric once touted by the New Criticism. Louis Zukofsky composes the densely recorded *80 Flowers* (1978) in honor of an eightieth birthday he did not live to see; each "flower" is comprised of eight five-word lines. In such books as *Themes and Variations* (1982) and his Norton "lectures" *I–VI* (1990), John Cage (1912–1992) invents the mesostic, a form of acrostic poem in which he "writes through," or across, a proper name or aesthetic term centered vertically in the text. Jackson Mac Low (1922–) has adapted both the word-count technique in his ongoing composition *Twenties* (1991) and the acrostic writing method based on *The Cantos* of Pound in *Words nd Ends for Ez* (1989). Silliman (1946–) employs a mathematical sequence known as the Fibonacci series to determine the number of sentences in each paragraph of his book-length prose poem, *Tjanting* (1981). These poets advocate constraint for its paradoxically liberating and generative effect.

Many critics and poets have lamented the increasing marginalization of poetry in American culture and intellectual life, with the postmortem examination performed in essays such as Joseph Epstein's "Who Killed Poetry?" in *Commentary* (1988). Few were disturbed by Epstein's declaration that there were no longer any great poets who spoke of language as an "exalted thing" and went forth as "a kind of priest." The passage of such romantic postures was not lamented because neither American poets nor their readers were any longer comfortable with the production or consumption of a cultural artifact in an elitist or quasi-religious vein. Few contemporary poets wish to see themselves as so detached from the secular and egalitarian American experience; few readers wish to worship much of anything.

Epstein scored more heavily when he attacked poets where they live, challenging the cultural efficacy of "poetry professionals" who are wholly supported as teachers in creative-writing programs and whose publications are largely endowed by grants and foundations. Poetry became irrelevant—or at least marginal—to American life when poets needed only to perform their academic obligations of workshops, readings, and the publication of a quadrennial volume to secure their careers. Epstein's accusations hurt because he pointed to the most prestigious institutions among the society of poets as the culprits of the genre's decline. Responses that prescribed solutions rather than merely denying that the patient had expired include Dana Gioia's "Can Poetry Matter?" in *The Atlantic Monthly* (1991), Jonathan Holden's *The Fate of American Poetry* (1991), and Vernon Shetley's *After the Death of Poetry* (1993). All stop short of suggesting that poets resign their tenured positions. These essays contend that the intensive and self-absorbed "difficulty" of poetry—promoted by modernists as a required response to the complexities of their world and in disdain for the common reader—has increasingly repelled a general audience. Poetry, these commentators argue, must appeal to and engage the intellectual and cultural concerns of the general reader whose attentions have been captured by prose.

While critics argue over the death of poetry, the writing of poetry has never been more democratically practiced. Gioia estimates that writing programs "will produce about 20,000 accredited professional poets over the next decade." The quantity alone is impressive, but these poets—whether professional or freelance laborers—will surely be more diverse in their backgrounds than their predecessors. The result of American pluralism is that there are now many more types of poets and poetry than there were in the homogenized, New Critical 1940s. The absence of a "major" poet may be the price paid for the gradual dissolution of the dominant culture that would have identified and rewarded him. Furthermore, production has increased with the workforce. As Rochelle Ratner observed with a touch of weariness in an essay for *American Book Review* titled "Superfluous?" in 1994, "a recent 'Poetry Showcase' at Poets House in New York City had nearly 1000 books on display, all published in 1993." As readership erodes in the relentless surf of popular broadcast media, one wonders whether the chapbooks and small-press publications have not already outnumbered the people who purchase them. But the almost tenfold growth in noncommercial literary presses between 1965 and 1990 documented by Loss Pequeño Glazier in

Small Press (1992) suggests something important: even as poetry appears to decline in prestige and in the attention paid to it by major markets, there is a thriving "back channel" of writing and exchange that escapes the notice of culturally conservative institutions. This alternative ferment, separate from the résumé stuffing of some eminent poets and critics, may yet provide the next significant advance in poetics and speak to the role of poetry in the next century.

—Joseph Conte

Acknowledgments

This book was produced by Bruccoli Clark Layman, Inc. Karen L. Rood is senior editor for the *Dictionary of Literary Biography* series. Penelope M. Hope was the in-house editor.

Administrative support was provided by Ann M. Cheschi and Brenda A. Gillie.

Bookkeeper is Joyce Fowler.

Copyediting supervisor is Samuel W. Bruce. The copyediting staff includes Phyllis A. Avant, Patricia Coate, Christine Copeland, Thom Harman, and William L. Thomas Jr. Freelance copyeditors are Charles Brower, Leslie Haynsworth, Rebecca Mayo, and Jennie Williamson.

Editorial associate is Jeff Miller.

Layout and graphics staff includes Janet E. Hill and Mark J. McEwan.

Office manager is Kathy Lawler Merlette.

Photography editors are Margaret Meriwether and Paul Talbot. Photographic copy work was performed by Joseph M. Bruccoli.

Production manager is Philip B. Dematteis.

Systems manager is Marie L. Parker.

Typesetting supervisor is Kathleen M. Flanagan. The typesetting staff includes Pamela D. Norton and Patricia Flanagan Salisbury. Freelance typesetters include Deidre Murphy and Delores Plastow.

Walter W. Ross, Steven Gross, and Ronald Aikman did library research. They were assisted by the following librarians at the Thomas Cooper Library of the University of South Carolina: Linda Holderfield and the interlibrary-loan staff; reference-department head Virginia Weathers; reference librarians Marilee Birchfield, Stefanie Buck, Stefanie DuBose, Rebecca Feind, Karen Joseph, Donna Lehman, Charlene Loope, Anthony McKissick, Jean Rhyne, and Kwamine Simpson; circulation-department head Caroline Taylor; and acquisitions-searching supervisor David Haggard.

The editor would like to acknowledge the Dean of Arts and Letters, Kerry Grant, and the Chair of the Department of English, Kenneth Dauber, at the State University of New York at Buffalo for providing research support that contributed to the timely completion of this volume. The Poetry Collection at the University at Buffalo has proved an invaluable resource for materials and information related to contemporary poets; the curator, Robert J. Bertholf, and assistant curator, Michael D. Basinski, deserve gratitude for their assistance. I am dedicating this volume to the memory of Constance Coiner, my colleague at the State University of New York at Binghamton. Constance completed her essay on Carolyn Forché only a month or two before her death on the ill-fated TWA Flight 800. I enjoyed our intense and animated conversations by telephone and the E-mail that we exchanged on the *DLB* project, Forché's poetry, and life in academia. Her loss will be deeply felt by the profession and by all those who knew her. Special thanks are due to the friends who tolerated an editor's irritability in reaching after fact and reason, especially Joy Leighton and Robert Basil. Several colleagues and contributors served as unofficial consultants to the project, taking time away from their own work to offer invaluable advice, particularly Ronald Baughman, Elisabeth Frost, Burt Kimmelman, James McCorkle, Patrick Meanor, Diane Middlebrook, and Mark Scroggins. Finally, Penny Hope at Bruccoli Clark Layman, Inc. deserves gratitude and praise for her skillful editing of the text and preparation of the materials for the volume.

American Poets Since World War II
Sixth Series

Dictionary of Literary Biography

Michael Anania
(5 August 1939 –)

Robert Archambeau
Lake Forest College

BOOKS: *The Color of Dust* (Chicago: Swallow Press, 1970);
Set/Sorts (Chicago: Wine Press, 1974);
The Fall (Chicago: Editions du Grenier, 1977);
Aesthetique du Râle (Chicago: Editions du Grenier, 1977);
Riversongs (Urbana & London: University of Illinois Press, 1978);
The Red Menace (New York: Thunder's Mouth, 1984);
Constructions/Variations (Peoria, Ill.: Spoon River Poetry, 1985);
The Sky at Ashland: On the Conditions of Place: Two Poems (New York: Haybarn Press, 1985);
The Sky at Ashland (Mount Kisco, N.Y.: Mayer Bell, 1986);
In Plain Sight: Obsessions, Morals and Domestic Laughter (Mount Kisco, N.Y.: Asphodel Press, 1991);
Selected Poems (Wakefield, R.I.: Asphodel Press, 1994).

OTHER: *New Poetry Anthology,* edited by Anania (Chicago: Swallow Press, 1969);
Gardening the Skies, edited by Anania (Springfield: Southwest Missouri State University Press, 1988).

In the afterword to his first book, the 1969 *New Poetry Anthology,* Michael Anania wrote, "There is little evidence that modernism is dead or even dying. The tradition of Pound, Eliot, Williams, Stevens and their contemporaries is very much alive." Anania's importance as a poet lies in how he preserves and develops this modernist tradition in American poetry. A deep commitment to modernism and the tradition of experimental, often difficult, poetry that flows from modernism has informed Anania's career as poet, editor, essayist, and novelist from its beginning to the

Michael Anania

present day. Anania's poetry draws its energies from a wide range of modernist sources; it shows the influence of William Carlos Williams in its emphasis on concrete particulars and American places and the influence of Wallace Stevens in its speculative, philosophical lyricism. Anania has also shown a strong commitment to modernism and its traditions as an editor with *Audit* (later *Audit/Poetry*) from 1962 to 1967, *Partisan Review* from 1974 to 1975, the Swallow Press from 1967 to 1974, and *Tri-Quarterly* since 1976. His essays, many of which are collected in *In Plain Sight: Obsessions, Morals and Domestic Laughter* (1991), include some of the most insightful insider's views of American literary publishing available today as well as sensitive treatments of many poets whose work lies outside the American mainstream. The 1984 autobiographical novel *The Red Menace* also shows Anania's modernist and experimentalist allegiances in its deliberately disjointed and digressive narrative structure.

Michael Anania was born in Omaha, Nebraska, on 5 August 1939. His mother, Dora, was born in Oldenburg, Germany, and his father, Angelo, who died when Anania was nine, was born in Omaha to parents from the southern Italian province of Calabria. Tuberculosis made it impossible for Angelo to hold a steady job, and Anania grew up in an Omaha housing project. Anania's fascination with his father, who survived by odd jobs, card dealing, and street wisdom and who never left the house without a gun, is reflected in *The Red Menace*. Both the father and the gun make repeated appearances in Anania's poetry, notably in "Temper" in *The Color of Dust* (1970) and "Reeving" in *Riversongs* (1978). "Reeving" depicts Angelo as "the dying gambler in black / coughing into his cards / or oiling the blue sheen / of his stub revolver."

Of the inner-city Omaha schools where he was educated Anania has said, "Standing up and saying you were a poet would be a little bit like standing up and saying you were a target." Nevertheless, Anania developed an interest in poetry early and carried it with him first to the University of Nebraska at Lincoln, where he studied from 1957 to 1958, and later to the Municipal University of Omaha (now the Omaha campus of the University of Nebraska), where he completed his undergraduate studies. As an undergraduate Anania wrote poetry as well as plays and stories modeled on Jean-Paul Sartre, edited the campus literary magazine (the first step on a distinguished editorial career), admired existentialism, and was, in his own words, "thrilled by anything complicated and remote." He also became what he calls a "sentimental Communist"; he documented his failed attempt to join the Communist Party in his novel *The Red Menace*. While an undergraduate Anania also clashed with one of his teachers at Nebraska, the poet Karl Shapiro, who was later to become a friend and influence. The clash itself was an instance of unfortunate timing: Shapiro was then writing an important series of articles attacking the more retrograde political and social views of Pound and Eliot while Anania, entranced with their "complicated and remote" cosmopolitan modernism, was just coming to appreciate them.

Before leaving Omaha for graduate school Anania attended a *Poetry* magazine gala in Chicago that was to prove important in two ways. Here Anania met W. H. Auden, whom he was to see on several occasions in later years, and their association helped form Anania's deep attachment to English poetry. Here, too, Anania met Louis Untermeyer and Oscar Williams, the leading anthologists of the day, a meeting that becomes significant in light of Anania's later achievements as an anthologist and editor of books and journals.

After marrying Joanne Oliver in December 1960 Anania arrived at SUNY at Buffalo in 1961 with the goal of using its extensive modern poetry archive to write a dissertation on Wallace Stevens or William Butler Yeats. Anania was still feeling the lure of the remote and complicated when he arrived in Buffalo, but the simple fact of leaving his home state soon gave him the impetus to attempt a poetry that was not remote but grounded in the very things with which he was most intimately familiar. As Anania puts it, "Leaving Nebraska made it clear that writing about Nebraska was like writing about Rome or Florence—it was tangible, real, nobody knew it, there were concrete things in it for poems and what had absolute familiarity for me was unknown to others." This sense of the value of the tangible and familiar was reinforced by Anania's discovery of William Carlos Williams. While Anania had read some of Williams's poetry before coming to Buffalo, he now had access to an astonishing archive of material and came to see the possibilities of Williams's poetics for the first time.

A dissertation on Williams's early poetry was already under way when Albert Cook, then chairman of the English department at Buffalo, brought together an unprecedented group of poets and critics concerned with contemporary poetry, including at one time or another such luminaries as Charles Olson, Robert Creeley, Gregory Corso, Ed Dorn, Leroi Jones, Diane Wakowski, Leslie Fiedler, and Hugh Kenner. Soon Cook had transformed Buffalo into a vortex of creative energy, a vortex hospitable to both the modernism and the regionalism that had become so important to Anania. In this company Anania wrote many of the poems included in *The Color of Dust*, the manuscript of which was largely complete by the time Anania left Buffalo in 1964 to teach at nearby Fredonia.

Anania's work on the manuscript for *The Color of Dust* was in no small way facilitated by the confidence and camaraderie that came from this gathering of poets who wrote outside the American mainstream. Describing the democratic atmosphere of Buffalo in the early 1960s, Anania has said that "all poets of any stripe other than the kind of Snodgrass-Roethke-Dickey official American poetry were all ridiculous outsiders, so we were all strangely equal." To be treated like a peer by poets twenty years his senior was a great boon to an aspiring poet such as Anania.

Anania left upstate New York in 1965 to teach for three years at Northwestern University before taking a position at the Chicago campus of the University of Illinois. Editorial and teaching duties along with work on the never-finished Williams dissertation delayed the publication of *The Color of Dust,* but when the book came out in 1970, it was well received and widely reviewed. The book is made up of four sections, the first of which, "Stops Along the Western Bank of the Missouri River," consists of nine linked poems that return again and again to the urban and rural landscapes Anania had known in Nebraska and to themes about the relation of landscape to history and to language. The first section begins with the four-part poem "A Journey," the most successful poem in the volume and the most indicative of the direction Anania's career was to follow. It foreshadowed the poetics of place that informs "The Riversongs of Arion," the major series in Anania's next book of poems, *Riversongs.*

The landscapes of "A Journey" are primarily urban and reflect that, while Anania is very much a Midwestern poet, he can also be a profoundly urban poet. These landscapes, saturated with detail, can have the dry, quiet, uncanny quality of a Giorgio de Chirico painting:

> an old black fisherman
> wrinkles the shadows of a doorway,
> dreams of bullheads, long horns.
> Clark Street at the silent turning
> of shadows in the dust of August,
> a passing car rearranges the atmosphere
> raising a cloud of fine curb dust,
> a carp breaks water in a swirl of scum
> then slips back into the ages of mud
> as the dust sifts through sunlight
> into heavy air.

This passage is one of many that show how one of the things Anania learned from his intense study of William Carlos Williams was how to love the details of a place, right down to the particularities of the sidewalks ("cracked by the roots of elms / that hang over the walks") and the proper nouns by which places are known ("Cecil's Barber Shop, Mason Street, Rees Street"). Williams's work also taught Anania how to get those particularities into his poems without romanticizing or idealizing them. In fact, the distance between the ideal and the real is one of the themes of "A Journey," which begins by ironically juxtaposing the name of Grace Street in Omaha and the aspirations of those who named that street with the reality of the street itself as it drops "down to the yards, / to the open sewer that / swills into the river."

The mythical and historical only begin to be layered onto the intimate geography of "A Journey" at the end. Here, in a section significantly titled "Afterthoughts," Anania sees Omaha in the quasi-mythic context of the landscapes of the American West and sees "At the flats where the river bends / a

MICHAEL ANANIA

Riversongs

University of Illinois Press / *Urbana Chicago London*

Title page for Anania's 1978 book, the first in which he employs his poetics of place

party of white men, / a dark woman standing apart / looking to round hills." This unnamed group is Meriwether Lewis and William Clark's expedition, the woman Sacagawea, who is transformed into the river's spirit of place in the final, epiphanic lines where the ordinary world fuses with the world of mythic history:

> We move through intersections
> capable of history.
> Birdwoman, bronze lady of the river,
> figurehead of keelboats,
> steel lady of bridges,
> we pass in the dead of August.

The association of the quotidian place with these figures of American myth and history comes only late in the poem, however, and this epiphany remains secondary to the evocation of the physical details of the city itself. They are "Afterthoughts. First, // the city in dust."

Among the other poems from "Stops Along the Western Bank of the Missouri River" that stress themes of the connections and distances between place and the language and stories through which readers understand place are "Shear Face," "Arbor Lodge," and "Missouri Among the Rivers," which ends with the lines "Bluff crests in Fontenelle are quiet, / give no emblem, figured name." Herein lies the paradox of place and language that so fascinates Anania: the place bears no natural relation to language for it; yet even to speak of this disjunction between place and language the poet finds himself using a proper name (that of Logan Fontenelle, last chief of the Omahas) that is redolent with the history of the region.

Another poem from this section, "Of the River Itself," addresses the dichotomy of permanence and change, a theme that is to haunt Anania's work for the rest of his career. "This is my advice to foreigners," the poem begins, "call it simply—*the river* / . . . and except when it is necessary / ignore the fact that it moves." There is a kind of will to stability and permanence here despite the poet's knowing such stability to be illusory. The poem ends with a bold assertion—"We are not confused, / we do not lose our place"—but in the context of the poem this statement must be taken not as certainty but as a wish for, or will to, certainty, a desire for an impossibly unchanging world. The river, despite what the reader may want to believe, is in constant flux, and what is dramatized in this poem is the impossible wish to turn it into an emblem of permanence.

The second section of *The Color of Dust* is untitled and consists of short lyric and dramatic poems notable for the casualness with which they mix references to high and popular culture: William Butler Yeats, the classical Japanese printmaker Hokusai, Lois Lane, and Grace Slick of Jefferson Airplane all make their appearances. Anania's casualness in this regard shows the influence of Frank O'Hara, whose poetry Anania selected for a special issue of *Audit/Poetry* and whose work influenced Anania in many of his early poems, "Nemesis to Lois Lane" showing the influence most clearly. This section of *The Color of Dust* is also notable for its sympathetic but unromanticized portraits of society's outsiders (as in "Valeeta" and the three "Songs From an Institution").

The third and fourth sections of *The Color of Dust* consist primarily of meditative poems. When Anania returns to the past in these poems, his concerns are less with the particularities of place and more with his own ancestry. In "The Temper," for example, Anania remembers his father and uses this memory as an occasion to reflect once again on the question of permanence and change. Anania first evokes his father's sense of what is reliable in this world by showing him in one of his characteristic poses:

holding the revolver in his hand,
tapping the butt on the table,
saying, that is solid,
more than this table, solid,
tempered blue sheen thunk
reflected on the table top
snubnosed, hammerless real McCoy.

In contrast to his father's faith in the solidity and reliability of the gun is Anania's recurrent sense of a world in flux, a world where "the steam gathers into droplets / that run through us," where "we are no barrier / to the gathering in, changes in the weather." In "Document," an elegy for his grandfather that follows "Temper" in *The Color of Dust,* Anania comes to embrace this sense of flux and impermanence. Near the end of that poem Anania has his grandfather accept his own impermanence, saying "I flow, / to goldenrod and sunflower, / flower of my hands, color of dust."

Riversongs, Anania's second major collection, appeared in 1978 and includes the poems "Set/ Sorts" and "Esthetique du Râle," both of which had appeared under separate cover in limited editions. The book begins with the ten-poem series "The Riversongs of Arion," which intentionally recalls "Stops Along the Western Bank of the Missouri River" and was first drafted in 1970 as a development of the earlier poems. The poems in "The Riversongs of Arion" echo the earlier poems in both their series form and their concern with the geography of the Missouri River near Omaha. The series is particularly reminiscent of Anania's concern in "A Journey" with showing how the world of our daily lives is "capable of history." However, while myth and history come only as afterthoughts to a cataloguing of particulars in "A Journey," they are at the center of "The Riversongs of Arion," beginning with the identity of the speaker himself. The Arion of Greek legend is a man captured by pirates who is allowed to sing one last song before his execution. This song summons a dolphin that carries him to freedom. The Arion of Anania's sequence is a contemporary man who, while rafting down the Missouri, gets stuck just south of Omaha at a spot he imagines is just across the river from the place where the Lewis and Clark expedition camped. While the Arion of Greek legend is literally delivered from captivity by his song, the Arion of Anania's sequence delivers the reader from his captivity in the present world of historyless phenomena through his evocation of a mythic, regional past in song.

The first poem in the sequence begins with the evocation of the present-day world, a world of immediate sensations in which the speaker is, literally and figuratively, stranded: "Adrift on an oil-drum raft / I have traveled this river south / past packinghouse spills // with split-bellied watermelons / and castaway

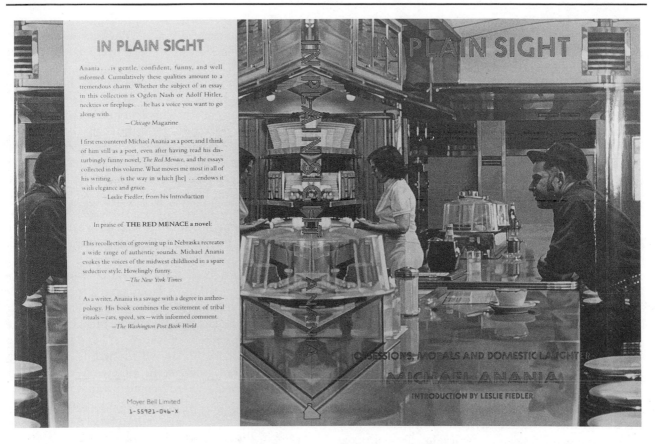

Dust jacket for Anania's 1991 collection of essays, including his views on fellow poets outside the mainstream

chicken heads." The series continues this presentation of a despoiled world until a random detail, the movement of catfish upstream, brings to mind first the oral lore of those who have worked the river and then a memory of the explorers who traveled this same river generations ago:

> . . . Rivermen call this
> the catfish dance because
> from the banks they seem
>
> stationary, bobbing up
> and down in the dark foam.
> Marquette feared the thud
>
> of their bodies against his canoe.

Soon Arion wills himself to believe that the point where he is stranded is a spot across from the camp of the Lewis and Clark expedition, and the series becomes a rich blend of Arion's song and material from Captain Clark's journals. As in Anania's earlier poem "A Journey," Sacagawea seems to become Omaha's spirit of place—"the city squats above the river, / as an Indian woman at her / day's work might squat"—but the vision here is a tentative one, tempered by Anania's sense of impermanence and flux. The idea of

Sacagawea transformed into Omaha's spirit of place relies on the notion that these riverbanks are the same shores on which Sacagawea stood, but as Anania's Arion acknowledges, "In time / the river sidewinds its banks. / Never the same soil."

In the end, though, the series of poems offers two affirmations. The first of these takes the form of embracing the process by which the world of observed phenomena seems to invite and accept imaginative leaps like that Arion takes in envisioning Sacagawea as the local spirit of Omaha: "Light play and murmur acquiesce / to image and parable, that tongue // flicking, our incessant song." The second affirmation is an acceptance of change itself, which comes in the final song, in which the flow of the river is transformed into the flow of fluids through "the delicate tubes that feed and drain" a man in a hospital. Here, in a development of a theme announced in "Document" from *The Color of Dust,* the river's flux and flow becomes emblematic of the cycle of life itself.

Memory, the passage of time, and the image of the river come up repeatedly in sections 2 and 3 of *Riversongs,* but these sections also invoke a strong sense of the urban world of social unrest, the world of activism and protest and riots that surrounded Anania at the Chicago campus of the University of Illinois where he taught. Chicago's urban landscapes and the tension of the Cold War find their way into such poems as "Tracings" and "Blind Pew," and the milieu of urban riot and protest is the subject of "News Notes, 1970," the immediate occasion of which was a riot in the Chicago Loop following a concert by Sly and the Family Stone. This last poem is important not only for the way it documents the experience of urban unrest but also for its exploding of certain romantic notions of how one can escape from such unrest. The last of the four parts of the poem turns suddenly from a city with "cars / overturned and burning" to a calm and apparently changeless pastoral landscape. Anania refuses the easy romantic notion of nature as a timeless retreat from historical strife and change, however; he sees the processes of change in nature itself in "the sounding fall / as ice moved a millennium." Even at a time when the need for stability became a psychological necessity, Anania remained fundamentally a poet of transience and change.

The fourth section of *Riversongs* consists of a series of poems called "Set/Sorts," which in their spare, short-lined tercets show the influence of Robert Creeley, a poet Anania had known at Buffalo. While the series deals with love intimately and beautifully, its lyricism is matched by Anania's typical intellectual rigor. The poem includes some of his finest images of the mind trying and failing to grasp stable patterns in the world, such as the following from "Sorts: I": "how // soon the sense fails / like crystal husking / its facets into some // dazzle without weight or shape."

The fifth and final section of *Riversongs* develops Anania's concerns with transience, perception, and landscape in new ways. In "A Hanging Screen" Anania wishes for his poetry to be an art which embodies in its very form the transience he had celebrated in so many of his earlier poems: "I wanted to make this poem / of silk," he says, "stretched tight / and polished, an ink wash / drifting ambiguous mountains, // words gathered like momentary details." He longs for an art "alive and painting a surface / of perceptual change, the eye's / return always at odds with / memory." Two other poems from this section, "Interstate 80" and "Return," develop Anania's concern with how the world is perceived by taking as their subject the automobile as an instrument not of transportation but of perception, marking the ways rapid linear movement down the highways affects our perception of landscape and time.

Like *Riversongs,* Anania's 1986 book, *The Sky at Ashland,* includes many poems previously published under separate covers in limited editions: "Constructions," "Such Summers," and "Variations for a Summer Evening" initially appeared as *Constructions/Variations* (1985), while "The Sky at Ashland" and "On the Conditions of Place" were first printed as *The Sky at Ashland: On the Conditions of Place: Two Poems* (1985). The world of urban disturbance has receded in this book, along with the activist furor that surrounded Anania at the University of Illinois–Chicago in the 1970s. Here, as the critic Robert Bray says, "The landscape is natural, not cultural: a single implication of roads, one lonely image of farming ('gray silos'); the rest is a wild garden place whose 'natural' literary genre is the pastoral."

The book opens with a section consisting of the six-part title poem and many shorter works, many of which use the terse, Creeleyesque tercets of "Set/Sorts," and all of which revisit tropes and themes familiar to readers of Anania's earlier work. Meditations on the relation of language to the world are found in the title poem ("If words extend themselves from place / to place, are their movements less // determined than the course of water . . . ") and in "The Fair Maid of Ribblesdale," in which "words, like waves, define the shore," making the merely physical into human experience. There are also differences in Anania's use of the recurring symbol of permanence and change, the river. In "Mt. Vernon Gardens, 1978," for example, the river becomes a symbol not of historical change and duration but of individual identity and the ever-changing current of consciousness and emotion that somehow makes up a life. The river here

> . . . seems to slide
> through us, not
>
> in the blood,
> strumming, but
> in the under-
>
> current of feeling
> bulging like dense
> water, moment to
>
> moment, this dry
> season, all these
> years beneath our skin

The second and third sections of *The Sky at Ashland,* by contrast, mark a departure from Anania's previous work. The second section, with such poems as "Song Vert(e)," "Motet," and "Canticle," uses music as both metaphor and formal guide as do some of the jazz-influenced poems from the third section, such as "Cantilena" and "Variations for a Summer Evening." Other poems from the third section exploit the energy of demotic American speech, which Anania rightly sees as heavily mannered and rhetorical.

(In his essay "O Lana Turner We Love You Get Up" he has written that what is "plain" is "not the least bit like talk," with its "lovely slouch and exaggeration.") "A Pastoral," which is dedicated to Anania's friend Chicago novelist Nelson Algren, shows Anania's marvelous ear for the structure of speech with lines such as "Hilda used to live on Milwaukee Avenue, and now, who knows, if ya get my drift." While this kind of demotic language is one of the primary idioms of Anania's novel *The Red Menace,* poems such as "A Pastoral" and "Lucy to the Driver" from the third section of *The Sky at Ashland* are among the few poems in which Anania makes extended use of the energies of demotic speech. The section ends with another rarity in Anania's work, an occasional poem. "Fortieth Anniversary Poem, August 6, 1985," written for the fortieth anniversary of the dropping of the atomic bomb on Hiroshima, makes powerful use of chantlike repetition (a rare device in Anania's spare, even fastidious, poetics) to stress the incomprehensible power of the blast, "this light and its forty-year shadow."

Each of the final two sections in *The Sky at Ashland* consists of a single poem of several parts: "Borrowed Music" (dedicated to Objectivist poet Ralph Mills Jr., Anania's colleague at the University of Illinois–Chicago) and "Constructions," an elegiac poem in twelve parts. While distinct in both form and thematic concern, both poems end by confronting the artifice of poetry and "the limits of words / all they cannot touch." In this sense they can be seen as a continuation of Anania's long meditation on the relation of language to the world.

Among the many previously uncollected poems that appear in Anania's *Selected Poems* (1994), the most important, "Factum, Chansons, Etc.," also takes up the question of language and its relation to physical things. The poem begins with a quotation from Amethe Smeaton's 1937 translation of the book by Vienna-circle linguistic philosopher Rudolph Carnap, *The Logical Syntax of Language,* in which Carnap makes a distinction between determined and undetermined names: "In a name / language, in / addition to // names with / determined / meanings, such // as Prague" there are also "names with / undetermined // meanings, such / as *a* and *b*." In the sections of the poem that follow, Anania takes this abstruse statement and plays with it, as in this passage in which he

watches an old film of Carnap's Prague and proposes that

If *a* is the city, gray
and somewhat out of focus,
and *b*, the sharp trolley lines,

or if the foreground
is scattered with mulberries
and pin-cherry is a tree

whose gnarled branches shine
. . . .
the residue of decaying fruit seems reliable[.]

The mock-logic of Anania's proposition and the juxtaposition of the arid language of Carnap's philosophy with the lush world of pin cherries and mulberries show both the limitations of our philosophical frameworks as descriptions of the world and the poverty of linguistic theory. For Anania, "what there is at hand demands / the more attention always."

Nearly twenty-five years after "A Journey," in which Anania wrote of abstractions as afterthoughts secondary to the power of physical particulars, Anania states again in "Factum, Chansons, Etc." an affirmation of the world of things, and in this the reader can sense the underlying consistency of Anania's sensibility, a sensibility as rooted in the concrete as that of William Carlos Williams and as speculative as that of Wallace Stevens. While the difficulty of Anania's work will always limit its audience, the work rewards the effort it demands, and his projected second novel and new volume of poetry promise to carry the modernist tradition in American prose and poetry into the next century.

Interview:
Illinois Reads: Talks with Illinois Authors: Michael Anania, videotape, Library Cable Network, 1986.

References:
Robert Bray, "The Regionalist Tradition in Midwestern Poetry," in *Studies in Illinois Poetry,* edited by John E. Hallwas (Urbana, Ill.: Stormline Press, 1989), pp. 117–143;
Daniel L. Guillory, "Tradition and Innovation in Twentieth-Century Illinois Poetry," in *Studies in Illinois Poetry,* edited by Hallwas (Urbana, Ill.: Stormline Press, 1989), pp. 43–60.

Rae Armantrout
(13 April 1947 –   )

Ann Vickery
University of Melbourne

BOOKS: *Extremities* (Great Barrington, Mass.: The Figures, 1978);
The Invention of Hunger (Berkeley, Cal.: Tuumba, 1979);
Precedence (Providence, R.I.: Burning Deck, 1985);
Necromance (Los Angeles: Sun & Moon Press, 1991);
Couverture, translated by Denis Dormoy (Asnières-sur-Oise: Les Cahiers de Royaumont, 1991);
Made to Seem (Los Angeles: Sun & Moon Press, 1995).

OTHER: "Why Don't Women Do Language-Oriented Writing?," *L=A=N=G=U=A=G=E,* 1 (1978);
Ron Silliman, ed., *In the American Tree,* includes a contribution by Armantrout (Orono, Maine: National Poetry Foundation, 1986), pp. 147–157;
Douglas Messerli, ed., *"Language" Poetries,* includes a contribution by Armantrout (New York: New Directions, 1987), pp. 101–107;
Paul Hoover, ed., *Postmodern American Poetry,* includes a contribution by Armantrout (New York: Norton, 1994), pp. 514–517;
Messerli, ed., *From the Other Side of the Century: A New American Poetry 1960–1990,* includes a contribution by Armantrout (Los Angeles: Sun & Moon Press, 1994), pp. 722–731;
Maggie O'Sullivan, ed., *Out of Everywhere: Linguistically Innovative Poetry by Women in North America & the UK,* includes a contribution by Armantrout (London: Reality Street Editions, 1996), pp. 92–99.

SELECTED PERIODICAL PUBLICATIONS–
UNCOLLECTED: "Poetic Silence," in *Writing/Talks,* edited by Bob Perelman (Carbondale: Southern Illinois University Press, 1985), pp. 31–47;
"Chains," *Poetics Journal,* 5 (May 1985): 93–94;
"Mainstream Marginality," *Poetics Journal,* 6 (1986): 141–144;
"The Person in My Work," *Poetics Journal,* 9 (June 1991): 69–70;
"Feminist Poetics and the Meaning of Clarity," *Sagetrieb,* 11 (Winter 1992): 7–16;

Rae Armantrout

"About" and "Part of It," *Salt,* 10 (1997): 140–142;
"It," *Boxkite,* 1 (1997): 135–136.

Rae Armantrout's poetry is renowned for its sharp social observation combined with an eloquent and often sparse lyricism. Armantrout was a key member of the West Coast poetry community that emerged in the 1970s and later became associated with Language poetry. She worked closely with a dynamic group of writers including Ron Silliman, Lyn Hejinian, Bob Perelman, Steve Benson, Barrett Watten, Tom Mandel, and Carla Harryman. Although Language writing has been viewed as advocating a poetics of nonreferentiality, Armantrout's writing immediately undercuts such sweeping definitions. Her poetry continues to explore the pull between the familiar and the unknown in which meaning is often translated as shifting somewhere between private thought and social process. She is suspicious of the term *language-oriented* because "it seems to imply division between language and experience, thought and feeling, inner and outer." Strongly influenced by George Oppen's attention to detail, Armantrout agrees with him that "however elusive, sincerity is the measure and goal of the poem." Although she does not believe that truth or sincerity can ever be arrived at, she says, "I think we'd better keep trying." This ethical approach is apparent in her poetic practice, which consistently draws the reader to a heightened awareness of the structures underlying his or her own perceptions.

While other Language writers such as Silliman and Watten turned their attention to the political and discursive economies of capitalism, Armantrout's focus was primarily on the local. Her writing "homes in" on the cultural banalities of everyday life, revealing them in an often comic and ironic light. "I like ending a poem with a statement which is satisfactory at first," she admits, yet "troubling on second thought." In foregrounding and then unsettling the habitual patterns of thought, she forces a reappraisal of the self. As one of her poems states, "I can't seem to get comfortable." She specifically developed her interest in this relation between subjectivity and culture in terms of a feminist poetics, although one based less on unity than on disjunction and contradiction. Wary of definitions, she saw the expressive, self-determining poetry of early second-wave feminism as reproducing the same limitations as more-mainstream verse—inevitably eliding or appropriating the voices of those pushed to a marginal position and manipulating material in order to produce an illusion of intimacy.

Born in Vallejo, California, on 13 April 1947 to John William and Hazel Hackett Armantrout, Mary Rae Armantrout grew up in San Diego. Her father was a chief in the U.S. Navy for most of his life, and her mother managed candy stores. As an undergraduate Armantrout majored in English. She studied for a couple of years at San Diego State University before transferring to the University of California, Berkeley, where she completed a B.A. degree in 1970. She received a master's degree in creative writing at San Francisco State University in 1975. In 1971 Armantrout married Charles Korkegian. Their son, Aaron, was born in 1979, less than a year after they moved back to San Diego. Many of her poems evocatively describe the minutiae of family life, both its rites and its vicissitudes. Armantrout has taught at California State

University and is currently teaching at the University of California, San Diego. In 1989 she received a California Arts Council Fellowship, and in 1993 she received the Fund for Poetry Award. She has coordinated the New Writing series at the University of California, San Diego, and been coeditor of *The Archive Newsletter*.

Her first book, *Extremities* (1978), explores the tensions, edges, and conjunctions between history and story. Having been brought up in a fundamentalist Christian household, Armantrout constantly returns to the Bible and theological questions. She also interrogates the grounding of narrative through mythic plots or fairy tales. Susan Howe has stated that the poems in *Extremities* are like riddles: they present terse but subtle puzzles. "The novelty of a riddle," she comments, "is that by depriving something of its name, we render it unrecognizable." A good example of such a riddle is "Generation," which fractures the folktale of Hansel and Gretel, giving it a feminist slant:

We know the story.

She turns
back to find her trail
devoured by birds.
The years; the
undergrowth.

Like British fiction writer Angela Carter, Armantrout's revision of the fairy tale is rather sinister in its psychology. The story is more about degeneration, about the inability to find one's way back to an earlier, familiar place. The opening line, "We know the story," links the female character to all women who have heard about and dread the effects of aging.

The logic of history is also explored in "Special Theory of Relativity":

You know those ladies
in old photographs? Well,
say one stares into your room
as if into the void
beyond her death in 1913.

Photographic images hold traces of an alternative history, a history not spoken or written. The poem reflects Armantrout's interest in critical projects of feminist recovery, such as Ann Douglas's *The Feminization of American Culture* (1977). In Armantrout's poem, the woman who looks out of the photograph defies the erasure of women from history. She also challenges (as well as reverses) the subject-object distinction by becoming both the watched and the watcher. Armantrout hypothesizes this event, "Well, say one . . . ," but leaves the implications of the woman's gaze open.

*Armantrout with her parents, Hazel and John Armantrout,
in 1949*

The open-ended nature of "Special Theory of Relativity" can be found in other poems in *Extremities*. "Tone" is a poem in which the six parts are connected only through their performative analyses of particular types of tone. The poem is an early example of the level of abstraction that Armantrout reaches in her work. While the second part is parodic and dark—"But the bouquet you made of / doorknobs, long nails for / their stems sometimes / brings happiness"—the next stanza is reflective and anxious: "Is it bourgeois to dwell on nuance? Or effeminate? Or should we attend to it the way a careful animal sniffs the wind?" Armantrout also borrows sentences overheard in the street: "But Mama's saying she's alright / 'as far as breathing and all that.'" Such attention to the idiosyncrasy of speech patterns recalls William Carlos Williams, an early but important influence for Armantrout. The poem's final line, "Sound that represents the end of lack," suggests that audible variation is part of poetic

meaning and that it should be recognized as another form of presence.

In a talk given at Intersection (and later published as "Poetic Silence" in *Writing/Talks,* 1985), Armantrout points out that the new prose poem (such as "Tone") is often composed of nonnarrative declarative sentences. Such poems, she believes, "tend to create a tone of certainty, of resolution and completeness which leaves little room for the experience of silence." The relationships between the nonnarrative sentences are dense and problematic—the reader is left more with a puzzle than a pause. In such poetry the reader seeks to fit the part to the whole. A characteristic aspect of Armantrout's work is this consideration of the form and function of poetic silence. She is concerned with the constant shifting between cessation and the impulse of response. Within emptiness, she believes that voices may be received subliminally or that questions may arise. Silence around the word, then, holds further meaning about the world.

For Armantrout silence may be accommodated by ending a poem abruptly or unexpectedly. It may be created through "extremely tenuous connections between parts of a poem" or through ellipsis, self-contradiction, and retraction. Armantrout further notes that she "may deliberately create the effect of inconsequence" or place "the existent in perceptible relation to the non-existent, the absent or the outside." The title poem, "Extremities," thus traces the desert as a space "of zeros." In such a landscape "the glitter of edges / again catches the eye" along "lines across which beings vanish / flare / the charmed verges of presence." She cites Frederic Jameson, saying that silence can perhaps enable "the unthinkable and conceptually paradoxical, that which cannot be unknotted by the operation of pure thought."

A year after *Extremities* Armantrout's second volume, *The Invention of Hunger* (1979), was published by Tuumba Press. It is a slim volume charting the themes of pregnancy ("Natural History," "You Float"), childbirth ("The Dark"), and the effects of motherhood on the boundaries of female subjectivity ("Fiction"). Here, she is not merely presenting a record of her experience (Armantrout gave birth to her son, Aaron, in the same year as the volume was published). Rather, *The Invention of Hunger* is strongly meditative—circling round the impossible connections between thought and body, individual and family. As the title suggests, the volume reflects on errant desires, maternal anxieties, and the process of constant discovery. The centerpiece of the volume, "Fiction," is a long nineteen-part piece combining prose sentences and poetic fragments—the brevity of each section heightening the effect of a private world being presented. The intimate framework of the poem automatically belies its understated title. Fiction usually presents a sequential narrative of beginning, middle, and end. The details of life, however, may but may not necessarily have such a pattern. The title, then, has a certain ironic resonance. Armantrout explores childbirth and parenting as another kind of textuality, another way of "furthering the story."

As she says in "Chains," a short piece written for a symposium on narrative (later published by *Poetics Journal* in May 1985), poetry has uncertainty about it. It is a kind of antinarrative. This form makes it more open to exploring the experiences of the everyday. In its destabilizing effects, motherhood is more poetic than fiction. The poem works through a series of clusters, a concentrated image or thought (or what might best be thought of as a meaning-complex) that is not necessarily linked to the cluster before or after it. In "Fictions" the narrator, or the "I," stands at an unstable center while the reader proceeds through "effort, wonder and argument." This structure informs the thematic focus—doubt mixed with resemblance between self and other, particularly across generations.

The narrator's elderly father predicts the child will be male and "look Irish as he did—himself reborn in a form she must love." The narrator wonders if resemblance is only a matter of fate when her father's prophecy is borne out. The "month old son" also orients himself through recognition and imitation. Language is an integral part of this process: "A sense of self starts in the mouth and spreads slowly." The home of language, the tongue, has an "old architecture." His crying, however, is empty and, like a vacuum, can be filled with meaning:

> "He's just a baby."
> "He's just hungry."
> "He's just scared."

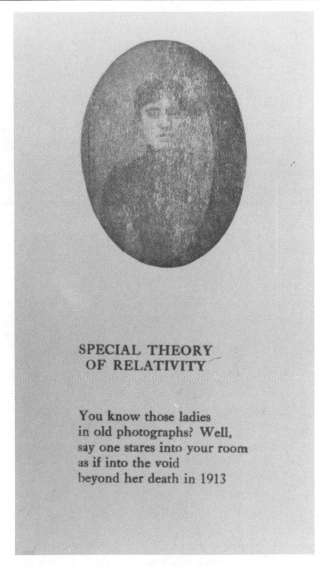

SPECIAL THEORY
OF RELATIVITY

You know those ladies
in old photographs? Well,
say one stares into your room
as if into the void
beyond her death in 1913

Poem from Extremities *(1978), in which Armantrout explores the logic of history (by permission of Rae Armantrout)*

As Armantrout points out, there is little difference between the hollowness of a child's cry and the clamor of the old. "In his old age he went mad," she writes of her father. Time becomes circular, and senility produces a comic effect: "Any stress, including the imminent operation, returns him to an incident that occurred during WWII. The 'Japs' had torpedoed his ship and it had almost sunk. Now, whenever he got agitated, he would yell, 'We're taking on water.'" The melodrama of such moments, as with the woman's first labor pains, seem like something out of a movie, confirming "the set trajectory of fictions." Each event, "each new crisis," is like a "complication in the plot of a comedy, a mere detour en route to the happy resolution she was still expecting 'after this.'"

Another poem called "Fiction" appeared in the subsequent volume, *Precedence* (1985). Whereas the combination of prose and poem of the first "Fiction" recalls similar early pieces by Carla Harryman—*Animal Instincts* (1989), for instance— the series of aphorisms of the second "Fiction" recalls Hejinian's later work in "The Person," published in *The Cold of Poetry* (1944); parts of *Legend* (1980) by Bruce Andrews, Charles Bernstein, Ray Di Palma, Steve McCaffery, and Ron Silliman; or Bob Perelman's "China," published in *Primer* (1981). The thirteen sentences appear unconnected, but all focus on some aspect concerning the *effect* of an idea or form of knowledge. Thus, the first sentence, "Excitement of being someone else about whom a remark was imagined dominated her morning," suggests the excitement caused by gossip, while another sentence "Being young, he drew weather and taped it on the walls" describes the painted or drawn response of a young boy to his natu-

Armantrout in Texas, circa 1960, visiting a ranch that belonged to family friends, Ronald and Mary Cox

ral environment. Responses range from habit ("The new television perched upon the console of the old") to political incomprehension ("A Black man in a Union Jack t-shirt was yelling, 'Do you have any idea *what I mean*?'") to daily incomprehension ("What did the bitter green nodules say to the smeared glass?").

Description, Armantrout suggests, is limited and requires the reader to bring his or her own experiential associations into the frame. In an interview she noted, "What I am most interested in are complex, oblique relations between stanzas or sections. Typically one of my poems would deal with an abstract subject in a series of discrete and concrete ways." Her poems are composed by what she sees and hears, "and then, immediately, what those sights and sounds cause her to think about." In this manner, her "personal (home and neighborhood) experience is very much part" of her poems.

Other poems in *Precedence* explore this process of orientation, of locating one's self in a world. They concentrate on aspects of home and place, particularly the permeable consciousness of suburban life in America. Poems such as "Double" view the "hazy" tiers of "pale houses" lining the hill through a double vision,

where one can almost "hear bad puns delivered with a wink." In "Postcards" Armantrout also presents two mundane snapshots:

> Man in
> the eye clinic
> rubbing his
> eye—
>
> too convincing. Like
> memory.
>
> My parents' neighbors' house,
> backlit,
> at the end of their street.

While postcards generally promise exciting glimpses of the foreign or exotic, the messages that accompany the picture are often dull and predictable. Here the second stanza comments on the images that precede and follow it. They are "too convincing" in their vision; they present a reality where "to *look* / reveals no more."

In the 1980s Armantrout's writing began to appear regularly in national and international journals.

Her works were also published in two anthologies: *In the American Tree* (1986) and *"Language" Poetries* (1987). During this time the collective phenomenon of Language poetry was continually attacked—with individual writers often selected as representative of the movement's methods and intent. In one particular article published in *Contact II* Kenneth Warren focused on Rae Armantrout's "Single Most," a poem which later appeared in her third volume, *Precedence*. He characterized it as animation out of control. Although both Bruce Andrews's and Lynne Dreyer's works were also castigated, it was this McCarthy-like "naming names" that paradoxically felt like a personal attack to Armantrout. At such times she found herself automatically positioned and neutralized in terms of other people's placements of poetry into categories.

In the year following *Precedence* Armantrout responded more directly to the marginalizing practices of verse and criticism that was more in the mainstream than her own. Taking *The Morrow Anthology of Younger American Poets* (1985) as emblematic of the poetic practice contested by Language writing, she highlighted both its naturalizing presumptions of selection and subsequent limitations. Her comments were authoritatively referred to in "Aesthetic Tendency and the Politics of Poetry," a 1988 collaboration by Ron Silliman, Lyn Hejinian, Steve Benson, Carla Harryman, Bob Perelman, and Barrett Watten that contrasted the poetics of Language writing as oppositional to the poetry often found in such collections. In her review Armantrout argues that the lack of detail regarding the editors' methodology renders invisible the politics informing the eventual selection. However, she believed that an editorial pattern could be discerned. The typical anthologized or prizewinning poem usually privileged a single, unified, first-person narrative. It was written in a traditional, identifiable form. Generally, it moved away from song toward a more anecdotal form of storytelling, which Armantrout sees as causing a "radical narrowing of poetic possibility." The poem positions the writer physically in some particular setting, often rustic or isolated. Furthermore, the poet is conferred with a special aura of authority over the events that he relays. "For me," Armantrout adds, "there is an oppressive machismo in all this."

Even in the poetry by women writers, the language is merely instrumental, often used for "ulterior purposes, not appreciated and explored." The epiphanic closure to such poems seeks to share an emotional insight, but one which presumes a commonality of experience. Not only does it deny change but it also veils an impulse to make its subject into a fetish and to use it simply as a garment in a narrative ultimately grounded on poetic control.

In "Traveling through the Yard" Armantrout satirizes a well-known example of such narrative poetry, William Stafford's "Traveling through the Dark." As Michael Leddy has pointed out, this poem is prominent in many introductory literature textbooks. Stafford's poem is about a driver who, upon finding a dead deer "on the edge of the Wilson River Road," hesitates from rolling it into the canyon when he realizes that the deer is still carrying a live but as yet unborn fawn. Thinking "hard for us all," he eventually pushes the deer "over the edge into the river." In Armantrout's version the narrator finds a dove corpse lying near her back porch:

> It was lying near my back porch
> in the gaudy light of morning—
> a dove's corpse, oddly featherless,
> alive with flies.
> I stopped,
> dustpan in hand, and heard
> them purr over their feast.
> To leave that there would make some stink!
> So thinking hard for all of us,
> I scooped it up, heaved it
> across the marriage counselor's fence.

The moment of ethical crisis foregrounded in Stafford's version is defused in Armantrout's by an underlying whiff of black humor. The dove, "oddly featherless," seems to be the unfortunate victim of the cat, whose guilty trace is heard in the flies which "purr over their feast." Like Stafford's narrator, Armantrout's narrator mentally toughens herself to dispose of the body. Faced with similar emotional traumas, the marriage counselor seems a fitting neighbor for such a poet. The perverse domesticity of Armantrout's poem is reminiscent of Lorine Niedecker's writing—which likewise presents condensed images and rejects any easy or sentimental resolution.

In "Feminist Poetics and the Meaning of Clarity," a paper originally presented at the American Literature Association conference in 1992, Armantrout addresses the argument that women require a conventional poetic form to represent their social position most effectively. Such models of clarity (poems based on a single narrative or extended metaphor) are viewed by Armantrout as "fenced yards": "Is this the kind of control we should aspire to?" she asks. "What's on the other side of the fence?" For Armantrout the "usual tone of trustworthy casualness" that Alicia Ostriker praises in her reading of Elizabeth Bishop's poetry is a sign of a monologic and bounded world. As she says, "There is no outside to this . . . system, no acknowledged division within it. It is imperialistic."

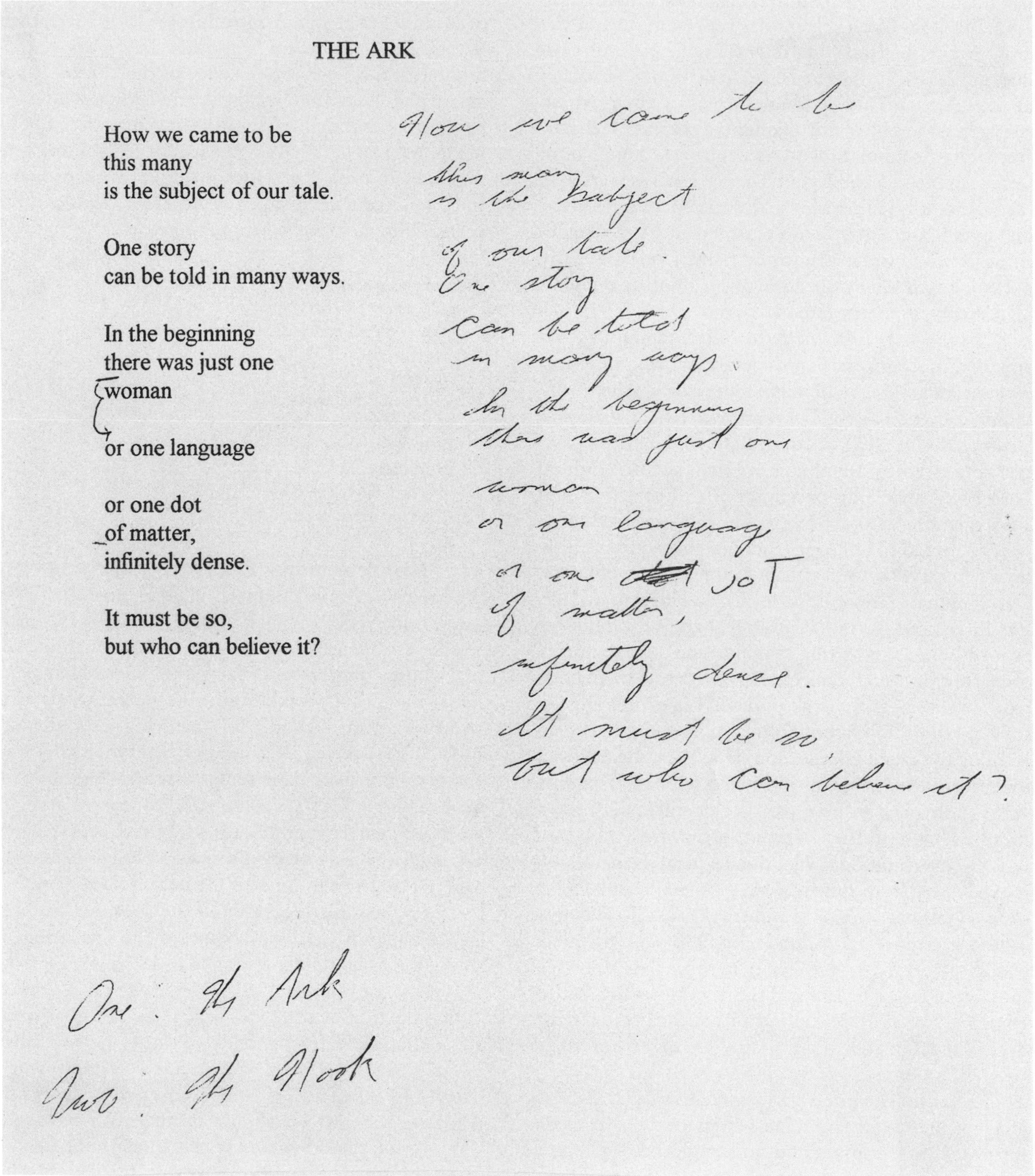

THE ARK

How we came to be
this many
is the subject of our tale.

One story
can be told in many ways.

In the beginning
there was just one
woman

or one language

or one dot
of matter,
infinitely dense.

It must be so,
but who can believe it?

How we came to be
this many
is the subject
of our tale.
One story
can be told
in many ways.
In the beginning
there was just one
woman
or one language
or one ~~dot~~ JOT
of matter,
infinitely dense.
It must be so
but who can believe it?

One: The Ark

Two: The Hook

Two early versions of the first section of Armantrout's "It" (Collection of Rae Armantrout)

IT

1. THE ARK

How we came to be

this many
is the subject

of our tale.
One story

must ~~can~~ be told
in many ways.

In the beginning
there was just one

woman
or one language

or one jot
of matter,

infinitely dense.

It must be so,
but who can believe it?

2. THE HOOK

"But what about...?"
she asks

and stops,
shrunken

to the impulse
to formulate

Armantrout also challenges the related argument that women are largely absent or marginal figures within the field of formal innovation in America. In her own case Armantrout sees herself as writing out of a strong tradition of both male and female poets, including figures such as Gertrude Stein, William Carlos Williams, Laura Riding, George Oppen, and Niedecker. Furthermore, she believes that many women are turning to unconventional forms precisely in order to redefine textually or challenge the limitations of the feminine. On one level this means opening one's work up to comment and debate. Practicing a dialogic poetics, Armantrout has long shared her work in progress with other writers. She collaborated with Ron Silliman on a piece called "Engines" that later appeared in his book *Demo to Ink* (1992). When she moved to San Diego, the writers of the San Francisco Bay area marked the occasion by putting together *Return Ticket,* a special unpublished volume of poems dedicated to Armantrout and responding to her work.

Removing the guard of solitary authorship is but one strategy of transforming poetic orthodoxy. In arguing for a re-visioning of poetic subjectivity, Armantrout addresses French psychoanalytic and feminist thought. While she is attracted to the idea of a writing that eschews logic or which offers a "limitless sensuosity," she distrusts categorical definitions such as "masculine" and "feminine." However, she does admit to feeling "most female when . . . resisting or subverting systems." For Armantrout the condition of being a woman is to be divided internally, always divided against the self. Systematic thinking tends to have a comedic function in her work. Her writing becomes "compelled by starts and stops, silences, and (the trappings of) logic." Yet, it is always mixing (as she remarks of Niedecker's poetry) "social fact (problem) with epistemological question."

The dark comic touch found in "Traveling through the Yard" becomes even more apparent in *Necromance.* Published by Sun and Moon Press in 1991, the collection takes its title from the opening poem. "Necromance" appears in three important anthologies in the 1990s—the Norton *Postmodern American Poetry* (1994), *From the Other Side of the Century: A New American Poetry 1960–1990* (1994), and a cross-Atlantic collection of innovative women's poetry, *Out of Everywhere* (1996). The poem is an ironic meditation on individualism, specifically the relationship between consciousness and freedom. The first part of "Necromance" powerfully demonstrates the conceptual disturbance of Armantrout's poetics:

> Poppy under a young
> pepper tree, she thinks.
> The Siren always sings

> like this. Morbid
> glamour of the singular.
> Emphasizing correct names
> as if making amends.
> Ideal
> republic of the separate
> dust motes
> afloat in abeyance.
> Here the sullen
> come to see their grudge
> as pose, modeling.

> The flame trees tip themselves
> with flame.
> But in that land
> men prized
> virginity. She washed
> dishes in a black liquid
> with islands of froth—
> and sang.

The poem is an ironic meditation on individualism, specifically the relationship between consciousness and freedom. In the opening section of "Necromance" the association of female sexuality with the flower is joined to the more specific symbolism of the poppy as a sign of remembrance for those soldiers who have fallen. "The Siren always sings / like this" not only recalls its warning sound during wartime, but more importantly, the articulation of desire itself. Both the Siren and the poppy represent the negative pull of social prescriptions, signaling death through man's loss of control. Recalling Plato's republic, which banished the poets and elided the role of women, the second stanza forms a critique of the "morbid glamour of the singular." An alternative, Armantrout suggests, is for the person to be viewed as "dust motes," elements floating "in abeyance."

According to Plato, the feminine is dangerous because it is a "pose," a representation. Like poetry, the feminine is a medium of artifice and seduction. While the "young" pepper tree matures, it ignites into flame, recalling the vivid colors of the poppy in bloom. Here, the "flame trees tip themselves with flame," suggesting an autoerotic sexuality in excess of the cultural logic. The republic, however, still recuperates the cultural value of femininity as virgin and pure through the sign of Woman.

In her own rite of passage the female character learns the art of necromancy. Necromancy is both the art of magic and communication with the dead. "She" thus aligns herself with the Other of femininity, performing the feminine domestic duties but subverting them in the process. While dishes are washed in black liquid, she finds her own voice and sings. Armantrout therefore maps out an ambivalent female position, as "she" is seen to exist between the dead of the presymbolic (with song being viewed as communication beyond the symbolic) and the symbolic (as "she" implicitly still sings from the kitchen). While "she" can only repeat the cultural feminine, there is the possibility of performative subversion via imitation. Yet this possibility remains "The mermaid's privacy." Such privacy is an area of mystery, "Hard to say where / It occurs," but always "just a bit further" from definition.

"Are our thoughts our own?" Armantrout asks. "We are discrete genetic entities and yet each of us had her first words put in her mouth by her parents and grew up to join the pre-existing discourse of the time." As she states in "Attention": "Ventriloquy / is the mother tongue." The song in that poem repeats the refrain "I'm not a baby. / Wa, wa, wa." The assertion of womanhood, "I'm not a baby," is contradicted by the "Wa, wa, wa" that immediately follows it. The baby doll of femininity is performatively reinforced but, as Armantrout suggests later, possibly "feigned." Armantrout's playfulness destabilizes the relations of power produced by gender through foregrounding the slipperiness of the very rhetoric that gender relies on. In an interview with Manuel Brito, Armantrout notes, "There is a pleasure in encountering an impasse (emotional or otherwise)." Elsewhere she writes:

Until I see beauty
in disinterest, in digression! Juggling
vs. cathexis.

Hejinian is among the many who view Armantrout's oxymoronic technique as a particularly powerful strategy of subversion. In pairing words with opposite connotations, she suggests that "Endless reflection is possible afterwards."

The title of Armantrout's fifth volume of poetry, *Made to Seem* (1995), continues her fascination with image and the real, which is interwoven with a more direct treatment of sexuality. "A Story" follows the "Fiction" poems of earlier volumes yet has the good mother saying, "I love you, but I don't / like the way you lie there / pinching your nipples." The story the mother eventually tells is about an old lady who believes that she is still menstruating. When told by a doctor that there are only two forms of infractions to the rule of age, exceptions and spite, the old lady argues, "When names perform a function, / that's fiction." Both listener and central character of the narrative reflect one another's refusal to repress their sexuality in order to satisfy the reason of others. And by having the story told, the "stubborn old woman" gets "away" with defining herself. As Armantrout announces in another poem, "it is attractive to be deceived."

Poems such as "Covers" also reflect upon subversive performance and masquerade, of acting out a role or covering up to avoid exposure. Others such as "States" undercut the recognition of sexual states such as transvestism—what appears to be one thing is revealed to be possibly another. Models exemplified in classics such as Louisa May Alcott's *Little Women* (1868–1869) and *Little Men* (1871) diminish actual relationships, forcing "lists of objects, lists of attributes." In "Sets" Armantrout presents generic characters—the extraterrestrial, the ballerina, the flamenco dancer, the disco stud, and the flustered magician—sequentially performing for an unseen judge. Such images, Armantrout notes, came from a cartoon she happened to be watching with her son. The contestants' anxiety for the particular moment is contrasted against the pattern of the known and the familiar. As she states, "A vivid memory / is frightening / because it makes time / short, being one of few."

In *Made to Seem* the constant replay of events and signs leads to a tiredness of routine. There is a sense of things "winding down" or "wearing off." Even Death is viewed as "stylized," a fashionable ally. Whereas "The Garden" in *Necromance* had found a new threat of violence in the "outworn" knowledge associated with the oleander tree, in "Turn of Events" the oleanders are "the same as before . . . plants someone might call exotic if anybody called." As the narrator states, "Perpetuation and stasis. / She wanted to deal with the basics—though what this scene might be the basis for she didn't know." Armantrout notes that the lengthy and difficult illnesses of her mother and mother-in-law form the basis of part of the collection. She also returns to such experiences in poems from her manuscript "The Pretext," which will be published by Sun and Moon Press in a year or so. "What's the worst that could happen?" she asks in her poem "About." One's family becomes an inimical reference, a presage for one's own future, which is "trapped / In these pools."

In other recent work Armantrout continues to concentrate on the implications of the intrinsic familial framework. In a departure from her poetry to date, Armantrout has just completed a narrative detailing her girlhood memoirs. This is to be published by Atelos Press, a newly formed press run by Lyn Hejinian. In a further piece titled "It," she contrasts an embodied subjectivity with a broader communal story, the story of the ark:

How we came to be

this many
is the subject

of our tale
One story

has been told
in many ways

In the beginning
there was just one

woman
or one language

or one jot
of matter

infinitely dense

It must be so,
but who can believe it?

In this first section Armantrout returns to the singular—the one woman, the one language, the one jot of matter. Through voicing her apprehension about such immanence, Armantrout raises the question of belief. Can there be both a gnostic faith in the world as well as a continuing critical interrogation of its knowledges? The archetypal story of origins that she focuses on is paradoxically also a story of migration, evolution, and survival. This invariable contradiction is what makes Armantrout's poetry so provocative and valuable. In its reflective density her poetry continues to articulate the ineffable.

Interview:
Manuel Brito, "Interview with Rae Armantrout," in *A Suite of Poetic Voices: Interviews with Contemporary American Poets* (Santa Brigida, Canary Islands: Kadle Books, 1992), pp. 13–22.

References:
Susan Howe, Review of *Extremities,* in *The L=A=N=G=U=A=G=E Book,* edited by Bruce Andrews and Charles Bernstein (Carbondale: Southern Illinois University Press, 1984), pp. 208–211;

Michael Leddy, "'See Armantrout for an Alternate View': Narrative and Counternarrative in the Poetry of Rae Armantrout," *Contemporary Literature,* 35 (Winter 1994): 739–760;

Bob Perelman, *The Marginalization of Poetry: Language Writing and Literary History* (Princeton: Princeton University Press, 1996), pp. 21–23, 136–140;

Jeffrey Peterson, "The Siren Song of the Singular: Armantrout, Oppen, and the Ethics of Representation," *Sagetrieb,* 12 (Winter 1993): 89–104;

Ron Silliman and others, "Aesthetic Tendency and the Politics of Poetry," *Social Text,* 19–20 (Fall 1988): 261–275.

Papers:
Although Armantrout has kept most of her papers private, a correspondence with Lyn Hejinian may be found in the Lyn Hejinian Papers, Archive for New Poetry, Mandeville Department of Special Collections, Central University Library, University of California, San Diego. The Mandeville Department of Special Collections at the University of California, San Diego, also has some production material—administrative files, manuscripts, typescripts, and publishing proofs—about *Necromance* and *Precedence* in its Sun and Moon Press Archive.

David Bromige
(22 October 1933 –)

Charla Howard
Long Beach City College

BOOKS: *The Gathering* (Buffalo, N.Y.: Sumbooks, 1965);

The Ends of the Earth (Los Angeles: Black Sparrow Press, 1968);

Please, Like Me (Los Angeles: Black Sparrow Press, 1968);

The Quivering Roadway: Poems (Berkeley, Cal.: Archangel, 1969);

Threads (Los Angeles: Black Sparrow Press, 1971);

Birds of the West (Toronto: Coach House Books, 1973);

Ten Years in the Making: Selected Poems, Songs & Stories, 1961–1970 (Vancouver: Vancouver Community Press, 1973);

Three Stories (Los Angeles: Black Sparrow Press, 1973);

Out of My Hands (Los Angeles: Black Sparrow Press, 1974);

Spells & Blessings (Vancouver: Talon Books, 1974);

Tight Corners & What's Around Them (Being the Brief & Endless Adventures of Some Pronouns in the Sentences of 1972–1973), Prose and Poems (Los Angeles: Black Sparrow Press, 1974);

Credences of Winter (Santa Barbara, Cal.: Black Sparrow Press, 1976);

Living in Advance, by Bromige, Barry Gifford, Paul DeBarros, and others (Cotati, Cal.: Open Reading Books, 1976);

My Poetry (Berkeley, Cal.: The Figures, 1980);

P-E-A-C-E (Berkeley, Cal.: Tuumba, 1981);

In the Uneven Steps of Hung Chow: First Flight (Berkeley, Cal.: Little Dinosaur, 1981);

The Melancholy Owed Categories (Weymouth, U.K.: Last Straw Press, 1984);

You See, Parts I & II, by Bromige and Opal Nations (San Francisco: e. g. press, 1986);

Red Hats (Atwood, Ohio: Tonsure Press, 1986);

Desire: Selected Poems, 1963–1987 (Santa Rosa, Cal.: Black Sparrow Press, 1988);

Men, Women and Vehicles: Prose Works (Santa Rosa, Cal.: Black Sparrow Press, 1990);

Tiny Courts in a World without Scales (London, Ont.: Brick Books, 1991);

photograph by Sam Jaffe

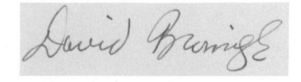

They Ate (Sebastopol, Cal.: X Press Editions, 1992);

The Harbormaster of Hong Kong (Los Angeles: Sun & Moon Press, 1993);

Romantic Traceries (Elmwood, Conn.: Abacus, 1993);

A Cast of Tens (Penngrove, Cal.: Avec Books, 1993);

From the First Century (Elmwood, Conn.: Cricket Press, 1995);

Piccolo Mondo, by Bromige, Angela Bowering, George Bowering, and Mike Matthews (Toronto: Coach House Books, 1998).

OTHER: "Philosophy and Poetry," *Poetics Journal,* no. 3 (1983): 20–24;

"On Mimesis and Society," in *Patterns/Contexts/Time* (Santa Fe, N.M.: Tyuoni Editions, 1990), pp. 30–31;

"A Collaboration," in *A Night at the Palace: Poets & Painters* (San Francisco: Cups Magazine, 1994), pp. 3–6;

"& Moon," in *Fifty* (Los Angeles: Sun & Moon Press, 1996).

SELECTED PERIODICAL PUBLICATIONS–
UNCOLLECTED: "For Joan," *Raven,* no. 7 (1958);

"A Nightmare" and "Swung Clockwise on Your Dreams and Fears," *Raven,* no. 8 (1960): 16;

"Her Face Is Small and Whiter than the Waves," *Raven,* no. 9 (1961): 55;

"Song of the Geek," *Raven,* no. 10 (1962): 20–22;

"Robert Creeley's *For Love,*" *Northwest Review,* 6, no. 2 (1963): 110–122;

"Marlene Heimach," *This,* no. 2 (1972);

"A Form of Confession," *Open Reading,* no. 1 (1972): 31–32;

"Single-Mindedness & Three Brains," *Open Reading,* no. 2 (1972): 53–54;

"Beyond Prediction," *Credences,* no. 2 (1974): 101–113;

"The Poetry of Edward Dorn," *San Francisco Review of Books* (1976): 21–22;

"Talking at the Boundaries," *American Book Review* (1977): 11–12;

"Ken Irby's *Catalpa,*" *Credences,* no. 7 (1979): 101–103;

"Intention & Poetry," *Hills,* no. 6/7, "Talks" issue (1980): 25–47;

"Joy Cones," *Hills,* no. 9 (1981): 1–16;

"Allen Fisher's Residency," *80 Langton Street Residence Program for 1982* (1983): 19–46;

"Alternatives of Exposition," *Poetics Journal,* no. 5 (1985): 155–158;

"A Note on *Tjanting,*" *Difficulties,* no. 2 (1985): 66–70;

"You See, Part 3," by Bromige and Opal Nations, *Paper Air,* 3, no. 3 (1986): 32–41;

"Interview," and "Grenier's *Oakland,*" *Jimmy & Lucy's House of K,* no. 6 (1986);

"What Keeps Me Interested," *Jimmy & Lucy's House of K,* no. 7 (1986): 4–5;

"Jackfish City Days," *Writing,* no. 15 (1986): 32–43;

"The Automobile Our Narrative," *Gallery Works,* no. 7 (1987);

"American Testament" and "Interview," *Difficulties,* no. 3 (1987): 1–45;

"War in Heaven," *Arshile,* no. 3 (1994): 79–97;

"Voices Seeking You," by Bromige and Steve Benson, *Interruptions* (1994): 45–50;

"Around Corners," *Tight,* 5, no. 2 (1994): 57;

"Deliberate" and "Symptomatic," *Avec,* no. 10 (1995): 81–90;

"Replica," *Dickens,* no. 1 (1997);

"Hide the Poor," *Tinfish,* no. 5 (1997): 21–22;

"Four Poems from 'Initializing,'" *Boo,* no. 7 (1997);

"Jackson Mac Low's Lifetime," *Crayon,* no. 1 (1997): 5–15;

"The Bridge as Obstacle," *Antenym,* no. 14 (1998): 1.

The nature of David Bromige's work is paradoxical, by turn highly personal and extremely impersonal. In the words of Bromige's mentor and friend, Robert Duncan, written to the John Simon Guggenheim Foundation in 1977,

> He has gained the art and language in which he brings his readers deeper than any consideration of a personality to the awareness of a living man (hence in reading these recent books of his I find myself in a solitude and a–"Tight Corner," he might call it–edge or risk of Being, that seems even as it is most his to be speaking for a depth of my own inner being).

This response echoes in Marjorie Perloff's words on the back cover of Bromige's *Desire: Selected Poems, 1963–1987* (1988) when, after noting it is "a truly original book" in which "narrative and lyric fuse to create configurations of great density" in language that "is extremely rich and elliptical," she observes that "his images take us into a world where things happen mysteriously and often frighteningly–and it is to us that they happen!"

Duncan and Perloff finger the pulse of Bromige's poetry and give an accurate reading. The dynamic throughout Bromige's body of work may be summarized as follows: the figure of a man the reader glimpses throughout, in whatever putative circumstance, is always aware of his actual existence as embodied in a poem–embodied in one and, moreover, *created* through one. In a lithograph by M. C. Escher, "Drawing Hands," one hand holds a pencil as it draws into existence the other hand–that is drawing the first hand into existence! In the conflict this lithograph presents between the flat and the spatial, one senses, as in Bromige's poetry, the same coincidence of process and product, of artifice and the real; the same wonder at the act of creation; the same laughter at the illusory quality in representation; and the same forlornness at reality in art being forever unreachable though seemingly so near.

But there is also another quality. The more engaging and confidential Bromige's personae become, the more keenly readers may sense the insurmountable distance between themselves and the text, or between themselves and another. The words that promise so much come between reader and writer like "a bridge that is also an obstacle," as Bromige writes (in "The Bridge as Obstacle" published in *Antenym,* no. 14). It is no different, he implies, when people actually speak with one another. There may be a *feeling* of mutuality, but how much does the feeling have to do with the communicative faculty? One hears what one wants to hear and yet wants what is real. And that double image *is* reality. As Bromige writes in the opening of the title poem of *The Quivering Roadway: Poems* (1969),

> only an illusion yet warning of the heat to be
> prepared against, or for, that day
> I locate you where you've gone to wander
> under the dingy fir trees with the smoking
> huts behind them, the ruined stalls, the creek
> flowing past with a sluggish melancholy exactly
> as befits a sluggish melancholy creek
> as aimlessly as if, being a poet & lost
> because your book was finished, you'd published it

In "From Home so Far," a poem from *Threads* (1971), he writes,

> The pass
> our task had brought us to was wooded, in a landscape
> seductive & unending—the words
> refer to pre-verbal images nonetheless post-verbal, since,
>   last evening,
>
> I had a vocabulary—yet are entities in themselves if I but let
>   them
> "take me"—who am I fooling?—seized
> by my own head within its landscape! why not be
> seized, what else so pleases. . . .
> or otherwise creating overruling passions
> to disappear into—there were dizzying glimpses down, adjective
> wedded to noun, despite the rules, language to mind despite
> unwedded to consciousness, I didn't care
> what was for tea, or if we missed it.

This unremitting focus upon the language act of the poem means that Bromige's poetry is a far cry from Confessional poetry. In that, the frame is carefully preserved. The putative authenticity of the utterance depends upon it. Bromige's authentic gestures constantly break the frame, reminding the

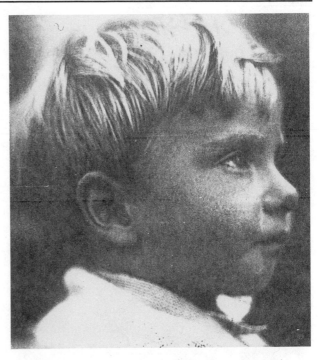

Bromige in 1935 (photograph by Harold Bromige)

readers that they are reading, that they are reading a poem, and that they know little about the author and less of the author's intentions. This work is novel in Bromige's work because of the seductive performance of the candid and the immediate. One feels that one is (at last) in the hands of a poet who *understands*. Then suddenly this impression is revealed as an illusion.

There is one further turn. This analysis suggests that the reader is the one who feels abandoned, bereft. But in Bromige's work, more commonly the reader infers that it is the poet who has found himself isolated, alienated, misunderstood, or spurned. And somehow, this ability to sense another's alienation and forlornness along with one's own, this ability which Bromige's poetry reveals as existing, is the transcendence to which Robert Duncan alludes, the mystery Marjorie Perloff speaks of—a poetry that "even as it is most his" seems "to be speaking for a depth" of the reader's "own inner being."

The sense of isolation that is one of the chief elements in Bromige's poetry, this "loner" quality, has made Bromige difficult to categorize. He has appeared in anthologies associated with Language writing. Readers feel the distance in his poetry through devices that constantly call attention to the poem as a language act. They are asked to attend to the quality of glass in the window, so to speak, as much as the nature of the view it reveals or obscures. Bromige himself has said in an unpublished

DAVID BROMIGE
THREADS

BLACK SPARROW PRESS
LOS ANGELES 1971

Title page for Bromige's fifth book, which he dedicated to his father, Harold Bromige: "Those chromosomes, I / yearned to be / as you"

interview with Christopher Reiner that many Language writers have been of "inestimable help."

Unlike the majority of the Language writers' works, however, Bromige's essays on poetics carry their theory implicitly and do not speak to a program or declare manifestos. Unlike their works, also, his early books display an affinity for the authors known as Projectivist, or Black Mountain, poets. But in his early books, although he uses a web of technical effects that sound and look to be Projectivist, he not so much furthers Projectivist poetics as he confounds them, bringing them up against limits hitherto unacknowledged (save on occasion by Creeley) and showing how the idea of the authentic voice to which they would conform meets its inevitable nemesis when rendered in print. The Language writers, who had their own bone to pick with the Black Mountain poets, were among the first to see what Bromige was about, so their subsequent

support of his endeavors, despite surface dissimilarities and his unsettling likeness to Projectivism, makes sense. His is, after all, an art made out of epistemological slippage, with an implicit critique of reference.

His art, as he says in the Reiner interview, is nothing new: "Shakespeare is the star exploiter of such slippage, and, relevant to that, he is our genius of the pun," a device used by Bromige throughout his work. In the same interview he equates the pun both with marriage and with a poem, as "two voices protecting a finite space from erasure-by-identity." These voices, often conflicting or indifferent to one another, "prevent his poems from being destroyed by understanding."

Perhaps one cause of Bromige's mindfulness concerning the propensity of language to mislead lies in his triple nationality, in his being British, Canadian, and American—three peoples, to paraphrase Winston Churchill, kept apart by a common tongue. He grew up in England and on the Canadian prairies, attended the University of British Columbia, then immigrated to the United States to take up a graduate fellowship at the University of California, Berkeley, and has resided in California ever since. He has been married four times: to an Englishwoman, a Canadian, a Californian, and a New Yorker. And, as a further likely cause of his keen ear for the resonance of English words, he has, by his own account in his unpublished memoir, "been in and out of a number of much scribbled-over social castes."

David Bromige was born on West End Lane, West Hampstead, to Harold Thomas Bromige, a cinematographer, and Ada Cann Bromige, a housewife. (His single sibling, Dora Margaret, is ten years his senior.) His family was moving from the working class into the middle class. He was to undergo in infancy a trauma that accounts for (as he maintains in his article in volume twenty-six of Gale Research's *Contemporary Authors' Autobiography Series*) the multiple voicings and the cognitive emphasis of his work. Suspected of being tubercular, at the age of eighteen months he was placed in an isolation hospital where his family was not permitted to visit him. In the four months he was there three shifts of nurses ("of various dialect groups no doubt," as he reports in his unpublished memoir) replaced his natural caregivers. He had to negotiate for nurturing with each of these, and they were "full of surprises, I imagine or remember, both linguistic and sexual."

Four years later he suffered the common displacements of his generation caused by World War II, surviving the Blitz (an account of which he gives in his child's-eye story "Finders Keepers" in *The Gathering*, 1965), the buzz bombs, and the rockets. But for him the war was not all terror and anxiety. People put themselves out for one another; there was a great sense of unity, of civic ability to respond. Cousins from Canada and the United States, enlisted in the military, often filled the Bromige household during their furloughs, so he grew up among transatlantic hijinks, youth mindful that this could be its final fling. At the end of the war Bromige's sister married one of these soldiers, Matthew Meredith, and immigrated to Canada, settling in Saskatchewan. About this time Bromige, at age eleven, won a scholarship to attend Haberdashers' Aske's (Hampstead) School for Boys, an ancient and, at that time, distinctly minor public school, where through boredom he ceased to shine academically. Athletics proved more attractive, and he ran cross-country for the school, where he also played cricket, tennis, rugby, and soccer. "Writing is an athletic event," he asserts in his memoir, "dependent upon rules, chance, and improvisatory skill, and on endurance, attentiveness, the memory of your opponents' (your poem's) strong and weak points, and, ultimately, blind faith."

In the summer of 1949 Bromige's parents separated, and his mother took him to North Battleford, Saskatchewan, where he was to live with his sister and her husband. (His mother subsequently returned to England where she reconciled with her husband.) Bromige made several trips back and forth during his adolescence, at various times working on farms in Saskatchewan and in England and at one point attending the Berkshire College of Agriculture, prior to a year as dairyman on a farm in Bjuv, Sweden.

In 1953, back in Saskatchewan, he went to work at the Provincial Mental Hospital as a student psychiatric nurse. Something of this time of his life in North Battleford ("Jackfish City") is depicted in "Robbing Peter," a novel begun in 1986, chapters of which have been published in *Writing*, no. 15. Realistic in style, this, Bromige's first novel, consists of a series of letters between two school chums now grown up: Peter, who immigrates to Canada, and Paul, who stays in England, kept there in part by Peter's horror stories of prairie life, a calculation on the part of Peter, who wants Paul to stay put in order to give Peter a tie to his homeland so that he himself may continue his transatlantic adventures and yet have a sense of being tethered to home.

Boredom and curiosity caused Bromige to hitch rides in the spring to Windsor and Toronto via Chicago and Detroit and to take a string of odd jobs, as he details in "In the Steps of the Master"

from *In the Uneven Steps of Hung Chow: First Flight* (1981). These jobs continued after he had hitched back west headed for Vancouver but had stopped instead in Edmonton, where he had been offered construction work but instead took a job at Oliver—another provincial mental hospital. In another year he had scraped the money together for train fare to the coast, where his sister and her family were now living. Once there, a chance meeting with the registrar of the University of British Columbia, who believed the patchily educated but well-read high-school dropout could hold his own there, led to Bromige's getting into the university.

There Bromige found himself in his element. He studied poetry with Earle Birney and Louis Dudek and playwriting with Tony Friedson; edited the campus literary magazine, *Raven,* and the critics page of the weekly newspaper; and won prizes for journalism, playwriting, and poetry. He reviewed on the air for the Canadian Broadcasting Corporation and toured the province with the University of British Columbia Players Theater. In his senior year he won a Woodrow Wilson Fellowship and went to study at the University of California, Berkeley, in 1962.

Bromige had interrupted his course of studies in 1957 when he met an actress, Ann Livingston, who was about to return to England to attend drama school. She did return; they corresponded, and he joined her. They married and lived for a year in London in his parents' house. Bromige worked as a supply teacher—at one point he replaced one of his former teachers at Mora Road Elementary—and later as a solicitor's clerk in Lincoln's Inn Fields. During the evenings, while Ann Livingston rehearsed at the London Academy of Music and Dramatic Art, Bromige rehearsed at the Tavistock Theatre and was in plays by Clifford Odets, Eugene O'Neill, and William Shakespeare. Her course of studies over, the young couple returned to British Columbia but soon parted. The story "Love Would Make It All Come True" in *Out of My Hands* (1974) touches on this relationship, which also informs his second, also epistolary and as yet unpublished, novel, "The Love Is in the Letters," written in the early 1990s but set in the 1950s. The story is told entirely through the woman's half of a correspondence; her handwriting is poor, and the man constantly has to guess at what she is saying to him.

Joan Peacock, of a Vancouver family, had studied law at the University of British Columbia, graduating about the time Bromige first enrolled. Introduced by friends, they began to live together in 1959, married in 1961, and moved to Berkeley together the next year. After Bromige earned his mas-

*Photomontage designed by Bromige to illustrate "Six of One, Half-a-Dozen of the
Other," a poem in which he carries himself on his back as Aeneas carried his
father, Anchises (Bromige as Aeneas: photograph by James Garrahan, 1975;
Bromige as Anchises: photograph by Andy Ross, 1977; from*
The Falcon, *1977)*

ter's degree, the couple returned to Vancouver for
six months so that their son, Christopher, could be
born at the hospital where Joan's parents were doc-
tors. It was then that Bromige learned he had diabetes (he has been insulin dependent ever since).
Put on the wagon, as he says in the memoir, "the
DB Joan married had ceased to exist." In 1966
they separated; they stayed in touch, however, so
that their child could be with each parent every
week.

In his last year at the University of British
Columbia, Bromige had rubbed elbows with the
writers who launched or were to carry on the poetry newsletter *This*. They encouraged him to read

Charles Olson, Robert Creeley, Robert Duncan,
Denise Levertov, Allen Ginsberg, Philip Whalen,
and others in the *New American Poetry* (1960).

At Berkeley, Bromige became teaching assistant in turn to Thom Gunn, Thomas Parkinson, Stephen Booth, John Montague, and Levertov. "From
Stephen Booth I learned the crucial importance of
sequence—he would always make clear what Shakespeare's characters knew or didn't know at any
point in the action. I worked out then how to make
poems whose lines could change direction with the
'knowledge' imparted by succeeding lines," he said
in a letter dated 27 November 1997. Bromige met
Duncan and began a friendship that lasted decades.

Duncan was instrumental in getting Bromige's first book, *The Gathering,* published by Fred Wah's Sumbooks Press in Buffalo in 1965 and in recommending him to John Martin of the newly formed Black Sparrow Press Press, then of Los Angeles, which published three of Bromige's next four books–*Please, Like Me* (1968), *The Ends of the Earth* (1968), and *Threads.*

The undercutting or reframing that stamps all Bromige's writing is present in *The Gathering,* and there is another common thread. Whatever interposes between the experiencing subject and the objective immediacy gets noticed, as in "With Someone Like You":

> "I tell you" who'd not inquired "I've forgotten John, Arvids,
>   Charlie, Ken, Walter &
> that fascinating guy I met in
> the Cosmopolitan Restaurant,"
>
> the wedding ring isn't dry on her finger
> as they sit down to her albums
> the fire bright on her first
> husband, arms akimbo in the Lake
> District, & other pictures
>
> she tears out & throws in the coals
> fiercely as she embraces the present
> seen in that light, representativ [*sic*].

The newlywed burns snapshots of her previous lovers to demonstrate the strength of her affection for her husband; however, he sees that her act places him in a class with these others. Immediacy is lost to a habit of thought. This fact is sad but also funny. Such epistemological slippage, when humans treat it as though it did not exist, when they act, in short, like machines, is often comic and sad by turns, and such comedy is a mark of Bromige's writing.

His next four books–*Please, Like Me; The Ends of the Earth; The Quivering Roadway;* and *Threads*–through various approaches embody Bromige's concerns, while the material derives almost exclusively from events of that time and place. Berkeley in those years was a petri dish of dissenting ideas, a fact which Bromige found stimulating. In "David's Rod" from *Men, Women and Vehicles: Prose Works* (1990) Bromige writes: "All hell was breaking loose–aye, and heaven too." To cope with radical alterations, moralities were being invented, not without conflict. In "Part of All You Need" in *The Ends of the Earth* a young couple turn the apartment of the poet's housemate (who has had to go to the mental hospital thanks to "betrayal") into their "squat," and the woman begins to take up the victim's clothes on her sewing machine; when the narrator catches her at this, he meets "the black unabashedness of her de-

Cover for Bromige's 1991 book, a collection of brief political poems that reviewer Iain Higgins described as "formal as well as moral heirs to Blake's Songs of Innocence *and* Songs of Experience"

nial, the straight stare / Yes, you want to get this in there, how it felt, the forktness of Fuck you / She said, Dont ask me to find reasons for my actions."

In 1970 Bromige started teaching full-time at Sonoma State University. With the writer Sherril Jaffe he moved from Berkeley to Sebastopol, a town (then) of some four thousand inhabitants, set among apple orchards. Their hilltop home became a hangout for poets on brief rustications, and from the many discussions that arose he distilled his "Tight Corners"–a radical change of technique for him: composed on three-by-five-inch file cards, these were short pieces consisting of two or three declarative sentences. In one of these the poet writes, "I say everything you're thinking. I have no thoughts of my own." The statement delineates the instant of both writing and reading—bearing in mind that the referent of "I" may have shifted between the two sentences. It is like a pun in that it has—is made of—two "voices," but it presents its information in such a way as to still their conflict. It is like a snapshot of a confrontation that, revealing each is ground to the other's figure, shows how each depends upon the other, shows how the situation can never be other than what it is, a question that distance and presence pose to each other. It offers thereby a means to reconciliation; it is entirely about reading.

Tight Corners, which appeared in 1974, established Bromige (in the words of Robert Duncan's 1977 letter recommending Bromige to the John Simon Guggenheim Foundation) as "a leading spirit of a new consciousness of the thrust of poetic language." In a 1986 retrospective article in *The Difficulties,* no. 3, Ron Silliman wrote:

> There is little in Bromige's earlier books that would seem to hint toward the title sequence of *Tight Corners* . . . and, through it, to the full range of his mature writing.
> . . . .
> In 1972, the paradigm of "New American Poetry," which had dominated the non- (or anti-) academic verse scene for 20 years, was transforming itself literally out of existence, breaking apart from within and without. . . . Bromige's place, and that of "Tight Corners," within this ferment is worth noting.

Silliman demonstrates this by analyzing a typical "Tight Corner": "The truck had nearly struck their car. He had screamed. She had asked him not to." As Silliman comments,

> the effect it creates is radically different from the one it depicts. Rather than being intimately intertwined, each of these sentences is composed so as to convey a maximum of distance from the others. . . . This narrative points to . . . the chasm that opens between sentences . . . and between presence and representation.

Silliman concludes by placing Bromige's "Tight Corners"—"the first work to open up the question of language's cognitive domain"—on a par with Jackson Mac Low's attention to process and Cid Coolidge and Robert Grenier's investigations of form, at the cutting edge of American poetry. Bromige meanwhile had already met and become friends with Grenier, and through publishing in Grenier's magazine *This,* whose coeditor was the young poet Barrett Watten, was encountering the poetry of these writers.

Coincident with *Tight Corners,* Bromige published a collection of similar size with Coach House Press in Toronto. *Birds of the West* (1973) is thoroughly imbued with the Sonoma landscape. One section, "Pond" (which appears to function as a part of the verb *ponder*), replicates in its form the casual, relaxed immediacies of the rural counterculture. Another, a serial poem titled "White-Tail Kite," is devoted to a bird that often hovered over a meadow next to the log cabin. The poet is enthralled with the kite's riveting attentiveness to the field it lives by, air currents its medium as writing is his own: "I will, I won't— / a kind of nothingness / I guess, although I know // it's air, seeing / how it buffets you / by your adjustments // in the face of / or force of it, / supports you there & // thus you hover / & will have to / plunge through // & into it, / to verify / your hope."

One striking poem from "Pond" again encapsulates the moment of reading during which writer and reader are one—

If Wants to Be the Same

The mounting excitement
as we move
step by step
of difference
off the same

if wants to be the same

the same as *is*

—where, as Jerome McGann remarks in *Black Riders: The Visible Language of Modernism* (1993), even the letters appear to be speaking. It is also a poem of great longing that suggests several situations found in Greek mythology, without any overt recourse to anything but the most everyday of words.

In this, his fortieth year, Bromige was awarded academic tenure. His writing now in some demand in the small-press world, he had other books brought out in the middle 1970s: *Ten Years in the Making: Selected Poems, Songs & Stories, 1961–1970* (1973) by Vancouver Community Press; *Spells & Blessings* (1974), poems about the interdependence of the known and the unknown, by another Vancouver house, Talon Books; and three pamphlets from Black Sparrow Press—*Credences of Winter* (1976), *Out of My Hands,* and *Three Stories* (1973). This latter pair show Bromige as an accomplished storyteller. *Out of My Hands* is a compact tour de force, three intimate pieces inspired by a sentence from Michael Polanyi's *Knowing and Being* (1969): "But in the language of Azande it is self-contradictory to doubt the efficacy of oracles, and this only proves that Zande lan-

VULNERABLE BLUNDERS VENERABLE BUNDLES VENERABLE
BUMBLES VULNERABLE BLUNDERS VENERABLE BUNGLERS
VULNERABLE PUNTERS VENERABLE BLINDERS VULNERABLE
BUNDLES VULNERABLE NUMBERS VENERABLE TRUNDLERS
VENERABLE BUNGLES VULNERABLE WONDERS VULNERABLE
LUMBERS VULNERABLE PLUNDERER VENERABLE BUMBLERS
VULNERABLE VENERABLE VERSUS VENERABLE VULNERABLE
DUMBBELLS VULNERABLE BUNDLES VENERABLE BUNGLES
VENERABLE BUMBLES VULNERABLE DANDLERS VENERABLE
MANTLES VULNERABLE BLUNDERS VENERABLE STUMBLERS
VULNERABLE BINDLE VULNERABLE BANGLES VENERABLEST
BUNDLES VENERABLE NUMBINGS VULNERABLE HUMMING
VENERABLE TANGLES VENERABLE MUMBLINGS VENERABLE
SANDALS VULNERABLE BUNDLES VENERABLE DRUMMINGS
VULNERABLE JUNGLE VULNERABLE NUMBINGS VENERABLE
BAUBLES VENEREAL COMINGS VULNERABLE BUNDLINGERS
VENERABLE CRUMBLES VERIFIABLE NUMBERS VULNERABLE
BUNDLES VULNERABLE BUMMERS VENERABLE GRUMBLERS
VERIFIABLE STUNNERS VENEREAL GRINDERS VULNERABLE
BINDERS VENERABLE WONDERS VENERABLE STUMBLEBUM
VULNERABLE UNDONE VULNERABLE ANYONE VULNERABLE
UNCLE VENERABLE ANKLE VULNERABLE ANGLE VENERABLE
VENDIBLES VULNERABLE UPFROMUNDERS VULNERABLEST
DUNCE INANES VENERABLE SHAMBLES VULNO VENERABLE
VULNERARY VESTIBULES VULNERABLE NOONE VENERABLE
DUNDERHEADS VULNERABLE FUMBLETHUMBIANIARISMS
VULNERABLE THUNDERHEADS VENERABLE BLUNDERS ON
BUNDLES VENERABLE MANGLES VENERATABLE PLUNGERS
VULNERABLE BUNDLES VULNERABLE RUMMIES VENERABLE
TUMMIES VULNERABLE NUMBER VENERATED STUMBLERS
VENERABLE BUNDLE VENERABLE EVERYBODY VULNERABLE
LUNGS VULNERABLE LUNGERS VENERABLE VERBALIZINGS
VULNERABLE RUMBLES VENERABLE DANGLES VULNERABLE

"Of Vulnerable Bundles," the cover Bromige wrote and designed for From the First
Century *(1995)*

guage cannot be trusted in respect of oracles." Two other books Bromige had a hand in appeared in these years: a book of songs, *Living in Advance* (1976), he had written with friends—the novelist Barry Gifford and the musicologist Paul DeBarros, among others; and Jaffe's brief pieces of satirical prose, *Scars Make Your Body More Interesting* (1975), which he illustrated and got Black Sparrow Press to publish.

A Canada Council Fellowship allowed Bromige to spend the 1976–1977 school year composing. The book that emerged, *My Poetry* (1980), was hailed by Ron Silliman, in his article "Modes of Autobiography" published in the magazine *Soup,* no. 2, as essential reading for anyone who wanted to be in touch with recent developments in American poetry. This book earned Bromige an award from the National Endowment for the Arts for 1980. The piece "One Spring," a collage of items (mostly from a local newspaper) that offers an overview of a small California town, won a Pushcart Prize when it was published in Watten's magazine *This* (Winter 1979–1980).

Bromige's marriage to Jaffe had ended in 1978, and he had relocated to San Francisco, commuting to Sonoma State. With Cecelia Belle he rented an apartment in the Haight-Ashbury neighborhood. It was a time of ferment in the poetic community, with weekly talks and readings and a stack of manuscripts circulating among some dozen poets or more. When the stack came back to Bromige after three months with many suggestions scribbled on his own manuscript, he incorporated some of these suggestions into the final version of *My Poetry*. "By

My," he has said, "I meant to say 'my kind of poetry, no matter by whom.'"

Now Belle and Bromige were looking for somewhere affordable to settle down and raise a child. They spent six years in the Sonoma County center, Santa Rosa, where in 1982 their daughter Margaret was born; in 1987 they moved to Sebastopol. Caring for an infant in the straitened circumstances of the 1980s with Cecelia both working and attending graduate school meant that Bromige published—and wrote—less. Before this happened, though, Lyn Hejinian published in her Tuumba series the chapbook *P-E-A-C-E* (1981), a vision of the present as seen from a deteriorated future. Other small books published during the middle 1980s are equally curious and engaging: *In the Uneven Steps of Hung Chow,* three hilarious tales about a misguiding sage as told by his gullible disciple; *The Melancholy Owed Categories* (1984), Bromige's first book to be published in England with three variations on a poem made from the rhyme words of a poem by John Keats; and *You See, Parts I & II* (1985), a collaboration with the "pataphysically" humorist-poet Opal Nations, a densely musical poem filled with conflicts among foresight, perception, and presence. Published in small editions, these books had scant circulation.

When he was in his early fifties Bromige's work enjoyed a renaissance. *Red Hats* (1986), a book of poetic prose, is generally considered on a par with the groundbreaking books *Tight Corners* and *My Poetry.* Because each of the sentences in *Red Hats* may or may not lead to the next, surprises are frequent, and constant vigilance is both the requisite and the reward:

> These indentations were made by a hammer. How many born-again Christians have read Foxe's *Book of Martyrs?* Channel swimmers smear themselves with grease. The mailman who delivered the telegram laid his hand on her shoulder. Will we die out for want of simplicity? These tufts might be thought decorative or practical or nuisances. She had a cock and huge balls into which he was to stick his dreaming prick. Let's note the rigid will with which will-lessness is advocated. Individuals in the absolute sense are nowhere found in Nature or society. Swarm, hive, shoal, flock, herd, family.

In 1987 a 120-page issue of a journal called *The Difficulties* and edited by Tom Beckett was devoted to articles and interviews with and about Bromige. It remains, together with Stephen Fredman's *Poets' Prose: The Crisis in American Verse* (1983), the best source for the scholar. In 1988, Black Sparrow Press published selected poems,

Desire, which won the Western States Poetry Award and, at more than three thousand copies sold, is Bromige's best-known book. The Western States jury, chaired by Robert Hass, said of Bromige:

> Very few poets have watched their own poems unfold with such mordant and skeptical intelligence. *Desire* is nervy and bracing work, not easy to enter, and deeply suspicious of easy entry, but it is that suspicion, impatient, ironic, amused, that gives the book its originality and edge. . . . At their best the poems make . . . epistemological comedy of a high order, prickly, caustic, rueful, painful, and funny.

Two years after *Desire* Black Sparrow Press published Bromige's selected prose, *Men, Women and Vehicles.* None of Bromige's books demonstrates better the variety of his means. But whatever his approach, the focus is maintained on linguistic and semantic elements as engines of the plot.

In 1991 Bromige published *Tiny Courts in a World without Scales,* fifty brief poems consisting mainly of political commentary, local and global, from the desk of a "language mechanic," which was now how Bromige identified himself in his frequent letters to the editor. This book went into a second printing in 1993. In *The Poetry Review (Canada)* Iain Higgins remarks that "the tossed-off feel of Bromige's poems is deceptive. The poems are anything but tossed-off; their demotic ease typically overshadows an artistry that makes them formal as well as moral heirs to Blake's *Songs of Innocence* and *Songs of Experience.*"

They Ate (1992) is a comic novella, detective spoof, and political satire, set in England in 1914. In 1993 a long-awaited book of poetry, *The Harbormaster of Hong Kong,* appeared from Sun and Moon Press in Los Angeles. Writing about this volume for *The American Book Review,* Rochelle Owens noted that "Bromige has created a poetics of derivations marked with an irresistibly funny style. His is a sensibility that reconstitutes the personal, social and political with the sophistication of a congenial terrorist equipped with a smart bomb." In it he shows a "minute awareness of the function of discourse."

Writing in *The Washington Review,* Mark Wallace found that the poems in *A Cast of Tens* (1993) "concern the very nature of attention itself. They call on us to notice what we, as readers of the signs thrown at us from every direction, bring into our attention or ignore, choose to make significant or pretend does not affect us. These poems show how we can ignore even the most blatant necessi-

Bromige in 1996 (photograph by James Garrahan)

ties of living in a time 'when truth and justice / leave the dictionary / sanitized.'"

Romantic Traceries, which appeared slightly earlier, consists of poems that extend the formal ideas of *The Melancholy Owed Categories* by using the rhyme words of several poems by Keats and Percy Bysshe Shelley to compose odes whose mixed dictions (English Romantic/American Present) are each other's critique, with hilarious and ennobling results:

My Fanny

Re your generous support which has always been capable
Of enduring long though unnoticed-by-me hours in a cold
Study in a lifetime like anyone's one step from the tomb
When you'd sooner have been pumping away nights

Celebrating the furnace & the motion of our blood
To be flush (& not via poesy) with time: again,
'Twas me or you! For you show me what is
Unvarnished, & say, I've wasted you.

From the First Century (1995) includes sixty-four of the first one hundred poems from a series Bromige calls "Vulnerable Bundles" in his unpublished memoir, "the poem as strobe and as waterfall (in Hoelderlin's sense)." His latest published book, the collaborative novel written with George and Angela Bowering and Mike Matthews, set at the University of British Columbia in 1961 when they were students there, *Piccolo Mondo* (1998) is at once a deconstruction and a reconstruction of that historical moment. A, D, G, and M—the principal characters—and their creators, chapter by chapter in turnabout, expose the untruths by which each lives in the past and in the present they would compose.

In 1998 Bromige received an award from the Fund for Poetry for his "contribution to the art," as well as a Stein Award for innovative writing. David Bromige's works have consistently been a working-through of several cruces puzzling and attractive also to other minds in his time: the ways in which language both creates and obscures reality; the relation of language to perception; the multiple and differing registrations of phenomena; the impact of these socially and politically; and the role that poetry has to play in these apparent givens.

A Bromige poem rethinks and refeels pre-existing formulae in a great range of modes. The work is by turns skeptical, slapstick, sentimental, sincere, and subtle, and replete with the humor that arises from cognitive dissonance. As a craftsman he has made himself capable of many modes, in a manner akin to Stuart Davis in the world of painting. As an artist and a "language mechanic," he is always discovering something of what actually transpires among reader, author, and page.

References:

Difficulties, special Bromige issue, edited by Tom Beckett, 3 (1987);

Stephen Fredman, *Poet's Prose: The Crisis in American Verse* (Cambridge: Cambridge University Press, 1983);

Jerome McGann, *Black Riders: The Visible Language of Modernism* (Princeton, N.J.: Princeton University Press, 1993).

Papers:

The Mandeville Special Collections Library of the Geisel Library at the University of California, San Diego, holds a collection of Bromige's correspondence that includes materials from Robert Creeley, Robert Duncan, and others: Calgary, Canadian Literary Archives, Special Collections, University of Alberta has a collection of correspondence from 1961 to 1973 including many letters from George Bowering. Burnaby, Special Collections, Simon Fraser University has correspondence in the files of *The Northwest Review* from the 1960s. Special Collections, University of British Columbia, has correspondence in the files of *Prism International* from the 1960s. The electronic archives of the Buffalo Poetics List (EPC, State University of New York at Buffalo) holds many letters and some poems, centering on discussions of contemporary poetics, from 1996 to the present.

John Cage
(5 September 1912 – 12 August 1992)

Rod Smith

BOOKS: *Silence: Lectures and Writings* (Middletown, Conn.: Wesleyan University Press, 1961);

A Year from Monday: New Lectures and Writings (Middletown, Conn.: Wesleyan University Press, 1967);

M: Writings '67–'72 (Middletown, Conn.: Wesleyan University Press, 1973);

Empty Words: Writings '73–'78 (Middletown, Conn.: Wesleyan University Press, 1979);

Themes & Variations (Barrytown, N.Y.: Station Hill Press, 1982); reprinted with additional material in *Composition in Retrospect* (Cambridge, Mass.: Exact Change, 1993);

X: Writings '79–'82 (Middletown, Conn.: Wesleyan University Press, 1983);

I–VI (Cambridge, Mass. & London: Harvard University Press, 1990);

John Cage: Writer, Previously Uncollected Pieces, edited by Richard Kostelanetz (New York: Limelight Editions, 1993).

OTHER: Cage and others, *Rolywholyover: A Circus,* an exhibition catalogue (Los Angeles: Museum of Contemporary Art, 1993).

John Cage is perhaps unique in the range and depth of his influence on post-1945 artistic practice. John Rockwell wrote in *The New York Times,* "As the unchallenged father figure of American experimental music, Mr. Cage wields an influence that extends far beyond sound alone. . . . Indeed, the entire American avant-garde would be unthinkable without Mr. Cage's music, writings, and genially patriarchal personality." Cage discouraged such pronouncements, considering that ideas were contextual, were "in the air," citing the example of inventors in different places coming up with the same idea at virtually the same time. Nevertheless, Cage's enthusiasm and openness to experimentation, his genius and humor, and his collaborative mind-set have led a strikingly large variety of artists and thinkers—including Laurie Anderson, Joseph Beuys, Norman O. Brown, Merce Cunningham, Allen

John Cage, early 1970s (photograph by James Klosty)

Ginsberg, Jasper Johns, Olivier Messiaen, Robert Rauschenberg, John Zorn, and many others—to acknowledge his influence and inspiration. Cage's writings and his musical career are closely linked. As Jackson Mac Low says in *Writings about John Cage* (1993), "Writing about John Cage is like writing about the ocean. Writing about any aspect inevitably involves writing about most of the others."

John Milton Cage Jr. was born on 5 September 1912 in Los Angeles, California, to Lucretia Harvey and John Milton Cage. John Milton Cage Sr. was an inventor involved in a great variety of fields, including early submarine and radio technologies. John Sr.'s example of optimistic devotion to his work was

Cage in California, circa 1918

later carried on by his son. Lucretia Cage, in her son's words, "was never happy." She wrote for the *Los Angeles Times* in the 1920s, was involved with women's clubs, and held various secretarial positions.

Cage was an "A" student throughout his school years, becoming interested in music at an early age. At age twelve he initiated and hosted a radio program for the Boy Scouts of America in Hollywood. Cage graduated class valedictorian from Los Angeles High School in 1928. One of his earliest extended writings, "Other People Think," included in *John Cage: An Anthology* (1970), won the Southern California Oratorical Contest held at the Hollywood Bowl. In this youthful expression of his belief in the necessity of nonintention Cage wrote, "One of the greatest blessings that the United States could receive in the near future would be to have her industries halted, her people speechless, a great pause in her world affairs created, and finally to have everything stopped that runs . . . . Then, in that moment of complete intermission, of undisturbed calm . . . we should have the opportunity to learn that other people think."

Cage attended Pomona College in Claremont, California. After two years he left, expressing dislike for the educational practice of having everyone read the same book. He went to Europe, where he studied architecture and piano, painted, wrote poetry, and in Majorca first composed music. He re-

turned to the United States at the height of the Great Depression, supporting himself by gardening in return for a room and by giving weekly lectures to Santa Monica housewives on contemporary music and painting: "You could have ten lectures for two dollars and a half." His lecture on Arnold Schoenberg led him to contact the pianist Richard Buhlig, who eventually took a serious interest in Cage's compositions. Pursuing his interest in composition, Cage went to New York in 1933 to study with Henry Cowell and Adolph Weiss, returning to Los Angeles in 1934 for three years of study with Schoenberg. Cage was a quintessential storyteller, and many of his anecdotes date from his years with Schoenberg. The following paragraph, from the lecture "Indeterminacy," included in his first book, *Silence: Lectures and Writings* (1961), is an example of his Zen-influenced style of storytelling. "Indeterminacy" was recorded in 1958 with Cage's recitation; David Tudor provided the music. This recording is an excellent starting point for those who have no experience of Cage's art.

During a counterpoint class at UCLA, Schoenberg sent everybody to the blackboard. We were to solve a particular problem he had given and to turn around when finished so he could check on the correctness of the solution. I did as directed. He said, "That's good. Now find another solution." I did. He said, "Another." And so on. Finally, I said, "There are no more solutions." He said, "What is the principle underlying all of the solutions?"

Cage came to believe years later that the answer Schoenberg had sought was "The question is the principle underlying all of the solutions," and this conclusion only increased Cage's estimation of Schoenberg.

Cage married Xenia Andreyevna Kashevaroff in 1935. They moved in 1937 to Seattle, where he served as composer-accompanist at the Cornish School. He met dancer Merce Cunningham while in Seattle and reconnected with him in New York in 1942 after living and working in California and Chicago. Cage and Cunningham were to become the most widely recognized composer-choreographer team of the postwar era. In New York between 1942 and 1952 Cage made the acquaintance of a wide number of artists who would become important to his work in various ways; among the most important were Marcel Duchamp (French painter and conceptual artist), Morton Feldman (composer), Robert Rauschenberg (artist), Daisetz Teitaro Suzuki (Zen scholar), and David Tudor (pianist and composer). Cage's marriage ended in 1945. He did not remarry, living and often working with Cunningham for the rest of his life.

Silence, Cage's first book, collects lectures and articles, the earliest of which, "The Future of Music: Credo," dates from 1937. As James Pritchett wrote in *The Music of John Cage* (1993), *Silence* was perhaps Cage's greatest commercial success and possibly "the most important event in Cage's career as a composer. . . . The audience for the book was wider than for his recordings or concerts." *Silence* is now in its eleventh printing.

While *Silence* is not a book of poems, it is a poetic book. Cage's earliest writings were strongly informed by his musical concerns. Many of the texts use non-normative discursive devices, often analogous to musical composition. "Lecture on Nothing" was written in the same rhythmic structure as his *Sonatas and Interludes for Prepared Piano* (1946–1948) and other musical compositions of that time. In the introduction Cage states, "When M. C. Richards asked me why I didn't one day give a conventional informative lecture, adding that that would be the most shocking thing I could do, I said, 'I don't give these lectures to surprise people, but out of a need for poetry.' . . . As I see it, poetry is not prose simply because poetry is in one way or another formalized. It is not poetry by reason of its content or ambiguity but by reason of its allowing musical elements (time, sound) to be introduced into the world of words."

This emphasis on the formal aspect of poetry is apparent in virtually every poetic text Cage published.

"Lecture on Nothing" is one of the most striking articulations of his early aesthetic. It is also one of his most widely cited and anthologized texts. Toward the beginning of "Lecture on Nothing" he states, "I have nothing to say and I am saying it and that is poetry as I need it."

Cage's musical compositions had been informed since the late 1930s by the statement in "The Future of Music: Credo" in *Silence:* "Wherever we are, what we hear is mostly noise. When we ignore it, it disturbs us. When we listen to it, we find it fascinating." During the 1940s and throughout the 1950s Cage's music and thought underwent many changes. His approach to composition evolved from the use of a complex micro-macrocosmic rhythmic structure, among other things, toward the use of chance operations and indeterminacy. This change was also a philosophical one. Cage was interested in Indian, Buddhist, and Zen Buddhist philosophies. Two of his most important teachers were Gita Sarabhai, an Indian woman who had come to the United States to learn about Western music to combat more effectively its influence on her own traditions, and the influential author Suzuki. It was from Sarabhai that Cage learned that in Indian musical traditions "The purpose of music is to sober and quiet the mind, thus making it susceptible to divine influences." Cage decided that this was indeed the purpose of music. His compositions of the late 1940s and early 1950s such as *Sonatas and Interludes for Prepared Piano, String Quartet in Four Parts* (1950), and *Sixteen Dances* (1951) reflect this reconception in a movement away from a belief in the composer's role as "organizer of sounds" in order to express an emotional state toward "composition as process" to open the mind to the complexity of life.

Composer Christian Woolf had introduced Cage to *The I Ching or Book of Changes,* and, inspired by the graphic notation of composer Feldman, Cage invented a method of composition using *The I Ching. The I Ching* is an ancient Chinese text used in divination. It is based on principles of mutually embracing opposites, the interactions of yin (the weak) and yang (the strong). The method of divination in the book is to relate the tossing of three coins six times (there is also a method using yarrow-stalks) to one of sixty-four hexagrams, each of which is accompanied by poetic descriptions of life situations. Cage found a method of relating any number to sixty-four, allowing him to use *The I Ching* not as an oracle but as chance operations that he said allowed him to free himself of his likes and dislikes. This method gave him a new perspective from which to produce art; the asking of questions and the construction of contexts in which those questions would be asked became his role as artist. In *Conversing with Cage* (1988) he remarks with respect to his compositions, "Instead of representing my control, they represent questions that I've asked and the answers that have been given by means of chance operations. I've merely changed my responsibility from making choices to asking questions. It's not easy to ask questions."

Cage first used *I Ching* chance operations in the third movement of his *Concerto for Prepared Piano and Chamber Orchestra* (1951), although *Music of Changes,* which pianist David Tudor premiered on New Year's Day 1952, is often cited as his first major work using chance operations. The article "To Describe the Process of Composition Used in Music of Changes and Imaginary Landscape No. 4" appears in *Silence.* Cage used chance operations in his music, writing, and visual art for the rest of his life. Although he used many other methods of composition, *I Ching* chance operations became "the ground" of his artistic practice to which he constantly returned.

Cage had questioned the conventional belief that the noises of everyday life were separate from those of music; now he would question the idea that silence existed separate from sound. He wrote his "silent piece," *4'33",* using chance operations in 1952, although it was conceived at least five years earlier. In a talk given in 1948 Cage mentioned an idea "to compose a piece of uninterrupted silence and sell it to the Muzak Co. It will be 4 1/2 minutes long—these being the standard lengths of 'canned' music, and its title will be 'Silent Prayer.'" Cage said on many occasions that it was the all-black and particularly the all-white paintings of Rauschenberg that "gave him the courage" to compose *4'33".* The composition was a watershed. It is at once conceptual art, theater, and music. The piece consists of three movements in which no notes are played. Sometime in the late 1940s or early 1950s Cage had visited an anechoic chamber at Harvard University; he sat down in the chamber expecting complete silence yet heard two noises. When he asked the engineer what they were, the engineer said that the high one was the nervous system in operation and the low one was the blood circulating. Cage writes in "45' for a Speaker," "Whether I make them or not there are always sounds to be heard and all of them are excellent." Cage tried to avoid having favorites—"If I have favorites I'll be disappointed when I don't find them"—so it is entirely sensible that he considered *4'33",* in which no sounds are intentionally produced by the performer, his most important piece. "No day goes by without my making use of that piece in my life and work. . . . I always think of it before I write the next piece."

4'33" was, to say the least, controversial; as Cage said at Harvard in 1989, "I lost friends over it." It is not surprising that the musical establishment would be troubled by Cage's aesthetic; however, it is also important to note that Cage was not in accord, aesthetically, with many others associated with the avant-garde. While Cage valued the work of many of the Abstract Expressionists, his work certainly did not take the heroic stance easily associated with that aesthetic. A useful anecdote in this respect is a dinner conversation Cage had with Abstract Expressionist Willem de Kooning, described in *Conversing with Cage.* De Kooning said, "'If I put a frame around these crumbs on the table that's not art.' And what I'm saying is that it is. He was saying that it wasn't because he connects art with his activity—he connects with himself as an artist whereas I would want art to slip out of us into the world in which we live." Following the performance instructions, the score for the three parts of *4'33"* reads simply:

I

TACET

II

TACET

III

TACET[.]

Cage writes in "Composition as Process," included in *Silence,* "WHEN ONE SAYS THAT THERE IS NO CAUSE AND EFFECT, WHAT IS MEANT IS THAT THERE ARE AN INCALCULABLE INFINITY OF CAUSES AND EFFECTS, THAT IN FACT EACH AND EVERY THING IN ALL OF TIME AND SPACE IS RELATED TO EACH AND EVERY OTHER THING IN ALL OF TIME AND SPACE." This statement is an expression of the Buddhist concept of "dependence arising," or the term Cage preferred, "interpenetration." It means that nothing exists of itself but only in relation to other things and that "all things are the buddha." There is no center, but rather each person or thing is a center among other centers, all of which interpenetrate, and none of which is more significant than any other. In 1952 on his second visit to Black Mountain College (he had visited in 1948 with Cunningham, teaching and organizing a Satie Festival), Cage instigated what has come into common art history parlance as "the first happening." The audience was seated facing each other, and around and among them, sometimes simultaneously, sometimes in sequence, Cunningham danced, Charles Olson and M. C. Richards read poetry, Cage lectured, Rauschenberg played scratchy records, his white paintings were displayed, and a movie and slides were shown; all in all a multiplicity of experiences was offered. This circuslike theatricality is a Cagean affirmation of life, of the complexity of nature, of anarchy, of the need to "move from zero." It is one of four interpenetrating elements, chance and silence being two other elements, in a reasonable understanding of Cage's aesthetic. The fourth element is "indeterminacy." All four relate not only to his interest in Buddhism but also to his anarchist social ideas. Cage was not only a complex artist but also an artist of complexity. He wished to affirm life, to discover it by opening his eyes with his audience, not for them.

Pritchett discusses in *The Music of John Cage* the distinction between chance and indeterminacy, "In Cage's terminology, 'chance' refers to the use of some sort of random procedure in the act of composition. . . . 'Indeterminacy,' on the other hand, refers to the ability of a piece to be performed in substantially different ways—that is, the work exists in such a form that the performer is given a variety of unique ways to play it."

In discussing chance operations with Joan Retallack in *Aerial 6/7* (1991) Cage explained: "I try in general to use the chance operations—each number that I use, I try to have it do one thing, rather than two things . . . to get an event divided into all the different aspects that bring it into existence and then to ask as many questions as there are aspects of an event . . . so that one number won't bring two parameters into being, but only one. That is toward a kind of confidence in the uniqueness of happenings, hmm? And then taking what happens." While Cage used chance to emphasize the uniqueness of events in the process of composition, indeterminacy allowed him to emphasize the uniqueness of each performance. Only after 1957 did he begin to explore indeterminacy fully in his work.

Also in the 1950s Cage carried on a correspondence with the French composer Pierre Boulez. Cage worked closely with Earle Brown, Woolf, Feldman, and Tudor—the five of them becoming known in music as the "New York School." He composed *Williams Mix* for magnetic tape; *Music for Piano*, a series of "time-length pieces" such as *34' 46.776": For a Pianist* (1954); *Winter Music* (1957); *Music Walk* (1958); and many others. He taught at the New School for Social Research, where he met Allan Kaprow and Mac Low. In 1955 he and Jasper Johns were introduced and quickly became close friends.

Cage working on Sonatas and Interludes, *1947*

Cage toured with and composed for the Cunningham Dance Company. His interest in mycology grew, and in 1958 in Italy he won $6,000 answering questions about mushrooms on a quiz show. Also in 1958 Johns, Rauschenberg, and painter Emile de Antonio organized *The 25-Year Retrospective Concert of the Music of John Cage* at Town Hall in New York, which included the premiere of his *Concert for Piano and Orchestra*.

In the early 1960s Cage became increasingly well-known, even notorious. This notoriety affected the time he had to compose; he was called upon to travel, to lecture, and to perform more than he ever had. Cage was able to combine his interest in indeterminacy with the new circumstances of his life in the 1962 composition *0'00" (4' 33" No. 2)*. A logical extension of *4'33"*, its score, which was later expanded, consisted of this sentence: "In a situation provided with maximum amplification (no feedback), perform a disciplined action." This piece literally allowed him to break the barriers between his life and art. Performances included such acts as drinking a glass of water or typing letters. George Maciunas, the major instigator of the international group of artists and musicians known as Fluxus, considered Cage central to the avant-garde of his time. In the exhibition catalogue *In the Spirit of Fluxus* Maciunas is quoted as saying, "Wherever John Cage went he left a little John Cage group, which some admit, some not admit his influence. But the fact is there, that those groups formed after his visits."

A Year from Monday: New Lectures and Writings, Cage's second book, appeared in 1967. While many of the concerns of *Silence* remain, it also includes an increasing concern with the social, expressed through Cage's optimistic and individualist anarchism. In the introduction to his "Diary: How to Improve the World (You Will Only Make Matters Worse)" Cage explains that it "was written for publication by Clark Coolidge in his magazine *Joglars,* Providence, R.I. It is a mosaic of ideas, statements, words, and stories. It is also a diary. For each day, I determined by chance operations how many parts of the mosaic I would write and how many words would be in each. The number of words per day was to equal, or, by the last statement written, to exceed one hundred words. . . . I used twelve different type faces, letting chance operations determine which face would be used for which statement." Arguably, given the method, concerns, and context of original publication (a literary magazine), this is Cage's first mature "poem" (though works which appear in *Silence,* particularly "Lecture on Nothing," "Lecture on Something," and "Where Are We Going? and What Are We Doing?," might also qualify for that epithet). The "Diary" continued, on and off, through 1982. Additional sections can be found in the books *M: Writings '67–'72* (1973) and *X: Writings '79–'82* (1983).

The method of composition for the "Diary" is telling and is of use in tracing Cage's evolution as a poet. Cage notes in discussing the "Diary" with Joan Retallack in *MUSICAGE/CAGE MUSES on Words. Art. Music.* (1995), "I would frequently write near the beginning, and near the end, and then in the middle, and so on until I got the whole thing filled up." So, while the "content" of the piece is largely observation and opinion, the method involved a chance-generated multiplicity. This method is analogous to Cage's descriptions of Johns's painting process. Johns would work at multiple points on a canvas, not privileging one area over another. Multiplicity of source material remained an important aspect of Cage's writing; however, in his later writings, such as *Themes & Variations* (1982) and *I–VI* (1990), his relationship to and use of source material altered radically.

In the fourth section of the "Diary" Cage wrote, "When Gandhi was asked what / he thought of Western Civilization, he / said, 'It would be nice.'" Stimulated by the thought of Buckminster Fuller (engineer, writer, and lecturer) and Marshall McLuhan (Canadian educator and writer), during the 1960s Cage became increasingly interested in "improving the world."

George J. Leonard in *Into the Light of Things: The Art of the Commonplace from Wordsworth to John Cage* (1994) writes, "There are two Cages, and the second one is the best critic of the first." While of course there were many more than two Cages, Leonard writes convincingly, and in fact Cage himself corroborated Leonard's ideas by turning them into a performance at Hofstra University in 1990. Cage sat before Leonard as though in judgment, with his back to the audience, while Leonard delivered the section titled "The Two Cages" "at him, like a trial attorney's summation."

The first Cage is the Cage of Eastern quietude, of the oft-cited remark from *Silence:* "Our intention is to affirm life, not to bring order out of chaos nor to suggest improvements in creation, but simply to wake up to the life we're living, which is so excellent once one gets one's mind and one's desires out of its way and lets it act of its own accord." The second Cage, in Leonard's words, "was the first to recognize the paradox in his giving people new ears, new eyes, then sending them out to experience global pollution." However, "The second Cage never wholly replaced the first one; if he had fully converted [to social activism], Cage might have been happier, but he would be less interesting."

In 1961 Cage composed the orchestral work *Atlas Eclipticalis,* his first composition using star charts. He founded the New York Mycological Society in 1962 with several others. Also in 1962 he toured Japan with Tudor. Throughout the 1960s his involvement with the Cunningham Dance Foundation continued. He directed the first performance of Erik Satie's *Vexations* in 1963; the performance lasted eighteen hours and forty minutes. He continued his *Variations* series, begun in 1958. From 1967 to 1969 he composed his, and perhaps the first, piece of computer music, with Lejaren Hiller at the University of Illinois. David Revill describes the premiere of the piece, *HPSCHD,* in his biography of Cage, *The Roaring Silence, John Cage: A Life* (1992). Seven live performers were accompanied by an equipment list that consisted of "Seven pre-amplifiers, 208 computer-generated tapes, fifty-two projectors, sixty-four slide projectors, eight movie projectors, 6,400 slides, forty movies, a 340-foot circular screen and several eleven by forty foot rectangular screens"— all in an arena capable of holding sixteen thousand people.

Mac Low, in his essay "Something About the Writings of John Cage" in *Writings about John Cage,* explains that in 1967 Cage "began writing two kinds of texts which are avowedly poems: (1) asyntactical

Cage in Japan, 1962, with Daisetz T. Suzuki, whose Zen teachings had a major influence on Cage's music and poetry (photograph by Yasuhiro Yoshioka)

sequences . . . drawn from the *Journal* of the American philosopher and naturalist Henry David Thoreau and arranged by *I Ching* chance operations; and (2) poems in which the capitalized letters of a name run down the center of each strophe, for which Cage adopted the term mesostics." These texts constitute the large part of Cage's third book, *M.* Up to this point, with the "Diary" being something of an exception, Cage's writing had tended to use methods similar to his musical composition. As he told Daniel Charles in *For the Birds* (1981), "my essays . . . didn't deal with the question of the impossibility or possibility of meaning. They took for granted that meaning exists." It was with *M* and following the lead, as he said, of such writers as Coolidge and Mac Low that he began to write a poetry which, literally, took nothing for granted.

In 1967 poet and essayist Wendel Berry introduced Cage to Thoreau's *Journal;* Cage wrote in the introduction to *Empty Words: Writings '73–'78* (1979) that in Thoreau he had discovered "any idea I've ever had worth its salt." In Thoreau, the iconoclastic celebrator of the natural world and author of "On the Duty of Civil Disobedience," Cage had found a place in which, for him, East met West. Cage dived into Thoreau, producing a great variety of texts and compositions, including the beautiful

"Mureau" included in *M,* which is one of his most successful poems. The title "Mureau" comes from combining the words *music* and *Thoreau.* Cage wrote it by subjecting all the remarks about music, sound, and silence in the Dover edition of Thoreau's *Journal* to chance operations. "Mureau," like the later "Empty Words," is a mix of letters, syllables, phrases, and sentences. The West German S-Press released a sixty-five-minute recording of Cage reading "Mureau" in 1972. The movement of the spoken text "suggests what perpetual flow of spirit would produce A thrumming beyond and through important." It is not a paradox that a text produced via stringent prearranged constraints should have such complex and musical meaning. It is a gauge of Cage's mastery of a method which he invented.

The term *mesostic* was given to Cage by philosopher Norman O. Brown. It would become by the late 1970s his preferred poetic form. As Cage had come to the most basic elements of music, sound and silence, he would come to the most basic element in writing, the letter. As he wrote in his "Diary": "To raise language's temperature we not only remove syntax: we give each letter undivided attention, setting it in unique face and size; *to read* becomes the verb *to sing.*" "The first series of mesostics Cage wrote were for the multimedia composition *Song Books* (1970), which grew from the sentence "We connect Satie with Thoreau." The next were "36 Mesostics Re and Not Re Duchamp," which appear in *M*. They are normatively syntactic, expressing stories and ideas about (and not about) Duchamp, whom Cage had come to know well in the 1960s. He had asked Duchamp to teach him chess, and they spent a great deal of time together. The final two mesostics in the series are about Duchamp's death in 1968:

> questions i Might
>   hAve
>   leaRned
>   to ask Can
>   no longEr
>   receive repLies.
>
>   the telegraM
>   cAme.
>   i Read it.
>   death we expeCt,
>   but all wE get
>   is Life.

While the back cover of *M* (the title of which was arrived at by subjecting the alphabet to chance operations) tells booksellers it is "Philosophy & Music," and certainly those concerns are present, it is more aptly identified as "Poetry," or perhaps "Poetry & Politics." *M* continues the optimistic search for social alternatives, begun in *A Year from Monday*, in the celebration of such figures as Fuller and McLuhan; however, Cage adds a new figure, that of Mao Tse-tung. Norman O. Brown had written Cage that "China maybe has stepped into the future" and advised Cage to look into Mao's writings. Cage did so with enthusiasm. It was a mistake many Western intellectuals made at that time. Cage often spoke of Mao's China with enthusiasm in the early and mid 1970s; however, after Mao's death, as the many crimes of the Cultural Revolution and Tibetan genocide became known in the United States, and known to Cage, he dropped this interest. Cage mentions Mao many times in *M*. But Mao is absent from his next collection, *Empty Words*.

Empty Words continues the investigations, begun in *M*, of Thoreau's *Journal* in the title piece, and of the mesostic form in many pieces, most notably in "Writing for the Second Time Through *Finnegans Wake*." "Empty Words" is broken into four parts and has four elements of composition—phrases, words, syllables, and letters; the second part omits phrases; the third is just syllables and letters; the fourth part is just letters—or, as Cage says in his introduction to the piece, just "letters and silences." It is one of the most radical texts in an already radical body of work. Each section of "Empty Words" is written to last two and a half hours in recitation. Cage often performed from "Empty Words." A 1977 performance in Milan, which Cage describes in *I–VI*, is of particular note. Cage had been billed as "a kind of rock star." During the performance the "full house" at the Teatro Lyrico for part 3 of "Empty Words" became "very busy"; they were talking, whistling, singing, playing instruments, and "presently they came up on the stage." Then "the stage was full of people" to whom Cage paid no attention, and "gradually it all subsided and they left the stage." Through it all Cage just continued his reading; when he finished and rose from the table, "it was like an acclamation they were so enthusiastic." The audience came back on the stage, showering him with flowers and adoration. Cage concludes the story by saying, "Now I don't know what part of that requires explanation but it seems to me all of it does." The following passage from a 1985 interview of Cage by Linda Low is included in *Conversing with Cage*:

Q: But isn't it important for a poet to make sense?
A: Just the opposite. A poet should make nonsense.
Q: Why?
A: Well, for example, if you open *Finnegans Wake*, which is I think without doubt the most important book of the twentieth century, you will see that it's just nonsense. Why is it nonsense? So that it can make a multiplicity of sense, and you can choose your own path, rather than being forced down Joyce's. Joyce had an anarchic attitude toward the reader so the reader could do his own work.
Q: Do you write with intent?
A: People read thinking I'm doing something to them with my books. I'm not. They're doing something to themselves. . . . What intention could I possibly have had in writing "Empty Words"?. . . I don't want my reader to experience "Empty Words" except in his own way.

In 1975 the Canadian Broadcasting Corporation commissioned a piece from Cage to mark the U.S. bicentennial. He responded with *Lecture on the Weather* for twelve speakers. *Lecture on the Weather* is composed of texts by Thoreau accompanied by recordings of weather sounds and, in the third of three sections, projections of drawings by Thoreau. The effect is of a storm brewing, a catastrophe on the way. The preface to *Lecture on the Weather*, which is to be read at every performance, is included in *Empty Words*. The final three paragraphs read:

The desire for the best and most effective in connection with the highest profits and the greatest power has led to the fall of nations before us: Rome, Britain, Hitler's Germany. Those were not chance operations. We would do well to give up the notion that we alone can keep the world in line, that only we can solve its problems.

More than anything else we need communion with everyone. Struggles for power have nothing to do with communion. Communion extends beyond borders: it is with one's enemies also. Thoreau said: "The best communion men have is in silence."

Our political structures no longer fit the circumstances of our lives. Outside the bankrupt cities we live in Megalopolis which has no geographical limits. Wilderness is global park. I dedicate this work to the U.S.A. that it may become just another part of the world, no more, no less.

Cage generally preferred to make suggestions for improvement rather than to criticize. His compositional activities of the 1970s included works that illustrated his belief in Thoreau's words "The best form of government is no government at all." These included chamber and orchestral works with no conductor or with a conductor which the performers could choose to follow or not. Also at this time he wrote three series for solo virtuosos–*Etudes Australes* (1975) for piano, *Etudes Boreales* (1978) for solo cello, and *Freeman Etudes* for violin (not completed until shortly before his death in 1992)–in which he wanted to make a music that was considered impossible to play in order to show "the impracticality of the impossible." For each of these pieces he worked closely with a virtuoso to learn the limits of what was considered possible to do on his particular instrument and then to write a music that called upon the performer to exceed those limits. In the mid 1970s Cage suffered from acute arthritis, which had plagued him for many years. With the help of Yoko Ono and Shizuku Yamamoto he adopted the macrobiotic diet. Within a few weeks his arthritis was cured.

In 1975 *Triquarterly* requested from Cage a contribution to a special issue called "In the Wake of the Wake," which led to a reawakening of Cage's interest in James Joyce. "Writing for the Second Time Through *Finnegans Wake*" was written using mesostics on the name James Joyce. It begins:

> wroth with twone nathandJoe
> A
> Malt
> jhEm
> Shen
>
> pftJschute
> sOlid
> hat the humptYhillhead of humself
> is a knoCk out
> in thE park[.]

The mesostic rule used in the work is that, for example, in the word *JOYCE*, no *O* may be used on the lines between the *J* and the *O*, and no *Y* between

the *O* and the *Y*. Cage also kept a list of the syllables and did not permit repetition of syllables for any given letter in the mesostic string.

The "string," in this case Joyce's name, was a term Cage adopted for the vertical word or words around which a mesostic was organized. The words not attached directly to the string he referred to as "wing words." These words were included, or not, following the rule stated above, according to taste. In her essay "Music for Words Perhaps: Reading/Hearing/Seeing John Cage's *Roaratorio*," in *Postmodern Genres* (1988), Marjorie Perloff discusses Cage's composition of "Writing for the Second Time Through *Finnegans Wake*"; she points out that "Commentary on Cage is usually so preoccupied with his use of self-imposed rules and chance operations that it slights the role the poet-composer's extraordinary art plays." In a detailed discussion Perloff examines the first page of *Finnegans Wake* and describes the choices Cage made relative to the "wing words" of his text. These choices reveal not only a substantial knowledge of Joyce but also a powerful poetic sensibility.

In 1978 Klaus Schoning asked Cage if he would write some music to go with his "Writing for the Second Time Through *Finnegans Wake*." Cage composed *Roaratorio, an Irish Circus on Finnegans Wake*. The work consists of recordings of the sounds and places mentioned in *Finnegans Wake*, Cage's recitation, and a selection of traditional Irish music.

Another genre Cage explored thoroughly was that of the interview. *Conversing with Cage,* edited by Richard Kostelanetz, constitutes a kind of ur-interview with Cage, covering his aesthetic, personal, and social concerns in a collage of statements from interviews across the breadth of his career. Kostelanetz edited the book in such a way that what Cage said relative to a particular subject in 1967, for example, is followed by his thoughts on it in 1984. Two additional books, *For the Birds,* and *MUSICAGE/CAGE MUSES on Words. Art. Music.,* constitute lengthy conversations from specific eras. *For the Birds* dates from the early 1970s, while the last conversation in the Retallack book took place just twelve days prior to Cage's death.

Cage's last Wesleyan University Press collection, *X: Writings '79–'82,* includes his fourth and fifth writings through *Finnegans Wake*. The first and third remain unpublished; the fifth, titled "Muoyce" (music-Joyce), does with the name Joyce what he had done with the name Thoreau in "Mureau." *X* also includes the eighth and final installment of "Diary: How to Improve the World (You Will Only Make Matters Worse)."

Comments about composer Charles Ives on the last page of Cage's 7 April 1964 letter to Michael O. Zahn (from Cage's A Year from Monday, *1967)*

Two of the texts in *X* are departures: "James Joyce, Marcel Duchamp, Erik Satie: An Alphabet" and "Composition in Retrospect." Both are largely discursive texts in mesostic form. "Composition in Retrospect" is at once a poem and an explanation of Cage's evolution as a thinker and philosopher. Various aspects of his composition—such as method, structure, notation, interpenetration, and discipline—are discussed. One of the mesostics on the word *discipline* reads: "Devote myself / to askIng / queStions / Chance / determIned / answers'll oPen / my mind to worLd around / at the same tIme / chaNging my music / sElf-alteration not self-expression." "James Joyce, Marcel Duchamp, Erik Satie: An Alphabet" is actually an imaginative script or highly unusual fiction in which the ghosts of the names in the title and others interact in the most unexpected ways.

> in a teMple
> just outside cAlcutta inhabited by the ghost
> of sRi ramakrishna that has been
> standing on one hand in eCstasy
> for ovEr ninety-three years
> duchamp picks up an inhaLator and breathes philadelphia[.]

In the 1980s Cage's fame continued to grow; every birthday, particularly those with a zero or five attached, was occasion for a round of international festivals of his music, art, and poetry, including appearances and performances by him. Yet his artistic output did not wane; if anything, it increased. In 1978 he began making prints and continued to do so yearly until

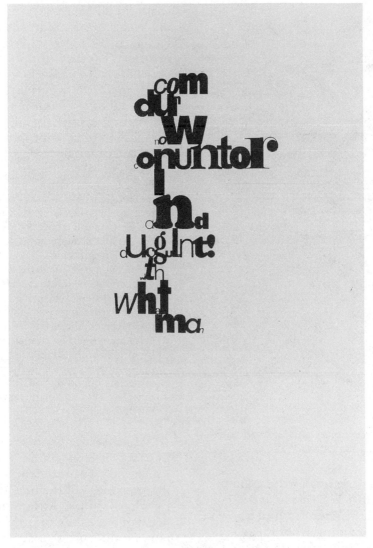

Page from Cage's "Diary: How to Improve the World (You Will Only Make Matters Worse) Continued 1969 (Part V)," in his M: Writings *'67–72 (1973)*

his death, branching out into other visual arts, including painting and drawing. His "composition for museum," *Rolywholyover: A Circus* (1993), which uses chance operations to determine the placement and duration of the hanging of his own and many other visual works, is at the time of this writing touring major museums around the world. His musical output was extensive, including many songs composed using mesostics. He also composed a series of five *Europeras* (1985–1991) that subjected the opera tradition to chance operations. Another significant composition dating from this time is *Ryoanji* (1983–1985), which takes as its inspiration the Zen garden in Japan of the same name. Many of Cage's last compositions are in a series of "number pieces" written using time brackets for each sound in which the decision when to play was left to the per-

former—their titles are simply the number of performers in a given ensemble. Cage used a superscript for the number of the composition. For example, Two^6 is the sixth composition for two performers. Pritchett writes in *The Music of John Cage,* "These works are so beautiful because they return to John Cage's compositional strengths: concentration, spaciousness, simplicity. Because each bracket contains a single sound, there is an intensity to each note, a focused concentration to every event."

In 1982 Cage published *Themes & Variations.* In the introduction he writes, "I used my library of mesostics on one hundred and ten different subjects [all aspects of Cage's work, listed in the introduction] and fifteen different names [people important to Cage's work such as Duchamp, Cunningham, Suzuki] to make a chance-determined renga-like mix." *Themes*

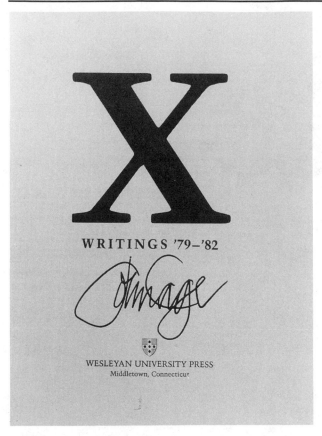

*Title page for Cage's 1983 book, which includes poems inspired
by James Joyce's* Finnegans Wake

& *Variations* is the first in a series of writings, most in mesostic form, many of which made use of computer facility, in which he tried "to find a way of writing which though coming from ideas is not about them; or is not about ideas but produces them." This series of texts includes "Anarchy," published in *John Cage at Seventy-Five* (1989); "Art is Either a Complaint or Do Something Else," written from statements by Johns and published in *Aerial 6/7*; and the voluminous Norton Lectures, *I–VI*. In many of these texts Cage used a "global" method of writing through in which an entire text or mix of texts would be subjected to chance via computer. *I–VI* is his longest effort in this regard.

Referring to its six sections, *I–VI* is the pragmatic title for his longest poem, which was delivered at Harvard University as the Charles Eliot Norton Lectures of 1988–1989. The actual title of the piece is *MethodStructureIntentionDisciplineNotationIndeterminacyInterpenetrationImitationDevotionCircumstancesVariableStructureNounderstandingContingencyInconsistencyPerformance*. These fifteen aspects of his work in musical composition are from the extended version of his *Composition in Retrospect* (1993). Aiming for nonhomogeneity in source material, Cage created fifteen files to be subjected to chance operations, one for each aspect, into which he inserted, in the following order: quotations from *Composition in Retrospect,* Ludwig Wittgenstein, Thoreau, Ralph Waldo Emerson, daily newspapers, L. C. Beckett (writer), Fuller, McLuhan, and *Themes & Variations*. The files are printed at the end of *I–VI* and in themselves constitute a fascinating essay on and of his aesthetics. This paragraph from the introduction to *I–VI* describes the poem concisely:

In the language of these lectures, syntax may appear or not. Generally it doesn't. Words, in fact, can appear by themselves. The have-nots of language, what the Chinese call empty words, particles, connectives, etc., have a position equal to that of the full words. Repetition is a characteristic of this work, as it is, Schoenberg said, of music. Even variation, he said, is repetition, some things changed and others not. Repetition is extreme when the source material is slight. But it occurs unpredictably between lectures, between parts of them, and within a single part. The lectures are written to be read aloud. A space followed by an apostrophe indicates a new breath. Syllables that would not normally be accented but should be are printed in bold type. It was after giving three of these lectures that I made up this notation for facilitating their delivery.

In reading this work the reader's attention hovers between sound and sense, never sure which will take precedence on the next line or how the "meaning" of the line just read will be altered by what follows. Although to give a sense of a poem of more than four hundred pages in short citation is difficult, this quote is from section V:

> we aRe
> to oUst the
> was ' neCessary
> in The
> woUld be
> woRds in
> dEath '
> haVe
> begAn
> a centeR of
> It **life ' or**

as is this:

> feeT
> likE **this** the first time
> to be liviNg all
> the atmosphere of Clouds
> emploYed
> Is thought of as
> uNited
> deep or touCh

```
the human impOssibility of
        aNd that '
    alwayS[.]
```

John Cage died 12 August 1992, less than a month short of his eightieth birthday. In his late writings he is no longer interested in "nonsense" nor in "sense" in any conventional understanding of those terms. Rather he has achieved a poetry which mimics the process-of-meaning creation in that while the form (as of any language) is already constituted, the possibilities for almost infinite recombination are such that the ideas already exist. It is the poet's task not to have them but to find them, already extant, in the material of language. As he wrote in *Composition in Retrospect:*

```
the past must be Invented
    the future Must be
        revIsed
        doing boTh
            mAkes
            whaT
    the present Is
        discOvery
            Never stops[.]
```

Letters:

Julie Lazar, ed., "Correspondence," *Grand Street,* 45 (1993): 101–131;

Jean-Jacques Nattiez, ed., *The Boulez-Cage Correspondence* (Cambridge, New York & Melbourne: Cambridge University Press, 1993).

Interviews:

Daniel Charles, *For the Birds: John Cage in Conversation with Daniel Charles* (Salem: Marion Boyars, 1981);

Conversing with Cage, edited by Richard Kostelanetz (New York: Limelight Editions / Toronto: Fitzhugh & Whiteside, 1988);

Joan Retallack, *MUSICAGE/CAGE MUSES on Words. Art. Music.* (Hanover, N.H. & London:

Wesleyan University Press & University Press of New England, 1995).

Biography:

David Revill, *The Roaring Silence, John Cage: A Life* (New York: Arcade, 1992).

References:

Richard Fleming and William Duckworth, eds., *John Cage at Seventy-Five* (Lewisberg, Pa.: Bucknell University Press / London & Toronto: Associated University Press, 1989);

Peter Gena and Jonathan Brent, eds., *A John Cage Reader* (New York, London & Frankfurt: C. F. Peters, 1982);

Richard Kostelanetz, ed., *John Cage* (New York: Praeger, 1970; London: Allen Lane/Penguin, 1971); revised and enlarged as *John Cage: An Anthology* (New York: Da Capo, 1991);

Kostelanetz, ed., *Writings about John Cage* (Ann Arbor: University of Michigan Press, 1993);

George J. Leonard, *Into the Light of Things: The Art of the Commonplace from Wordsworth to John Cage* (Chicago & London: University of Chicago Press, 1994);

Marjorie Perloff, "Music for Words Perhaps: Reading/Hearing/Seeing John Cage's *Roaratorio,*" in *Postmodern Genres,* edited by Perloff (Norman: University of Oklahoma Press, 1988);

Perloff and Charles Junkerman, eds., *John Cage: Composed in America* (Chicago & London: University of Chicago Press, 1994);

James Pritchett, *The Music of John Cage* (New York, London & Melbourne: Cambridge University Press, 1993);

Rod Smith, ed., *Aerial 6/7* (Washington, D.C.: Edge Books, 1991);

Nicholas Zurbrugg, *The Parameters of Postmodernism* (Carbondale & Edwardsville: Southern Illinois University Press, 1993).

Anne Carson
(21 June 1950 –)

Steven Marks

BOOKS: *Eros the Bittersweet: An Essay* (Princeton: Princeton University Press, 1986);
Short Talks (London, Ont.: Brick Books, 1992);
Plainwater: Essays and Poetry (New York: Knopf, 1995);
Glass, Irony, and God (New York: New Directions, 1995);
Autobiography of Red (New York: Knopf, 1998).

OTHER: "Kinds of Water," in *Best American Essays of 1988,* edited by Annie Dillard (New York: Ticknor & Fields, 1988);
"Chex l'Oxymoron," in *The Best of Grand Street,* edited by Ben Sonnenberg (New York: Random House, 1989);
"The Life of Towns," in *The Best American Poetry of 1990,* edited by Jorie Graham (New York: Ticknor & Fields, 1990), pp. 252–258;
"Water Margins," in *The Journey Prize Anthology,* edited by Douglas Glover (Toronto: McLelland & Stuart, 1994).

SELECTED PERIODICAL PUBLICATIONS–
UNCOLLECTED: "Conversations with the Confused," *New Muses* (1984): 4;
"The Autobiography of Red: Chapters 1–4," *Columbia Magazine,* 89 (1994): 53–70;
"Economy," *Village Voice Literary Supplement* (June 1995): 28;
"Short Talks on Chromoluminism," *New York Times,* 22 June 1995, p. A27;
"Shoes: An Essay On How Plato's *Symposium* Begins," *Iowa Review,* 25 (1995): 47–52;
"Old Home," *Parnassus,* 45 (1996): 22–27;
"The Jaget," *Chicago Review,* 13 (1997): 20–34;
"Ice Blink," *Raritan,* 17 (1997): 12;
"Economy, Its Fragrance," *Threepenny Review* (March 1997): 20–37;
"Lines" and "Despite Her Pain," *New Yorker* (31 March 1997): 61, 78.

Albert Einstein credited his discovery of fundamental laws of the universe to his ability to ask

Anne Carson (photograph © Allen McInnis)

the simple questions. Much the same can be said of Anne Carson, who in her poetry and essays asks questions about gender, desire, anger, self, and language that allow the reader to see the world afresh. Her intent is not to push a narrative down a linear path but to plant a field with "instant[s] of nature" that gradually grow into a story present not only in the reader's consciousness, but in some preverbal consciousness as well. She points to a new direction for postmodernism, one that is unafraid of turning back to the discussion of the metaphysical, although not a metaphysics of the logo-centric variety—that is, a metaphysics with rationality at its center.

Carson sees her work as "an irritant." She questions the accepted convention of *sophrosyne* (self-control) at the base of Western civilization and the self it engendered, a self whose civil behavior and speech create edges that restrict the flow of consciousness between the internal and external worlds. One of the principal questions behind her writing appears in her essay "The Gender of Sound" from *Glass, Irony, and God* (1995). She asks whether there is "another kind of human self than one based on disassociation of inside and outside. Or indeed, another human essence than self."

Guy Davenport, in his introduction to *Glass, Irony, and God,* a collection of poems and essays, has recognized this revamping of poetic vision that characterizes her poetry. In fact, he says, many readers will find it "unpoetic, or joltingly new," as readers once had difficulty with Walt Whitman and Emily Dickinson. James Laughlin, founder and publisher of New Directions Books, also recognizes her new voice and direction, describing her as one of the most important younger poets now writing.

Anne Carson was born in Toronto, Canada, on 21 June 1950, the daughter of Robert and Margaret Ryerson Carson. Currently Carson teaches classics at McGill University in Montreal. Prior to this she taught at Princeton and Emory. Throughout her career she has published scholarly essays in the field of classics as well as poetry. There is a strong autobiographical element in many of her poems, although it cannot be entirely trusted for accuracy. Carson uses autobiography in a slanted, often playful manner. The intent is to make the reader focus less on the "penny-dreadful" facts and more on the larger truths that come out of personal revelations. For example, the long poem "Canicula di Anna," which appears in *Plainwater: Essays and Poetry* (1995), is a chronicle of a present-day phenomenology conference written either by or to Anna. Quite naturally, the reader of the poem wonders whether Anna is Carson herself and whether the poem is about an actual event that she attended. The same can be said of the Anna Xenia who appears in her poem "The Fall of Rome: A Traveller's Guide" from *Glass, Irony, and God.* Although the speaker seems to be addressing a native of Rome by the name of Anna Xenia, there are many other and stronger indications that the speaker is addressing the part of herself that brushes against the outside world, the "Rome" of consciousness, contact, and engagement.

If all of Carson's poetry is strongly autobiographical, then she has traveled rather extensively and with purpose (a pilgrimage by foot across Spain and one by car across the United States); she has a brother with a similar rebellious and wandering

bent, a father with dementia, and a mother with whom she has typical generational differences. Carson, as evidenced in her poems, has also had her share of failed romantic relationships. All of this matters and none of it matters in her poetry. What is true autobiography and what is not is of little consequence since Carson uses the particulars to step from a universe of ordered space-time coordinates to one of multiplicity and simultaneity with regard to space and time. This biographical uncertainty makes sense, too, since she studies authors from antiquity. The biographical details of their lives have varying degrees of reliability.

In one respect all of Carson's poetry is a response to a major shift in the perception of consciousness that took place in the Greece of the seventh century B.C. This particular span of time in this particular corner of the world saw the concurrent arrival of lyric poems, a fascination with the trigonometry of eros, and a phonetic alphabet in which the written consonant reinforced the notion of an edge to the continuous stream of self that characterizes spoken language. This sense of edge was further reinforced by the triangulation of forces between the lover, the beloved, and desire itself, which characterizes eros. The lyric poets, Carson says in *Eros the Bittersweet* (1986), "record this struggle from within a consciousness—perhaps new in the world—of the body as a unity of limbs, sense and self, amazed at its own vulnerability."

Carson's poetry in its postmodern shadings is not so certain about that unified sense of self. Commenting upon the notion of an illusory self posited by classical Chinese masters in her poem/essay "The Anthropology of Water," included in *Plainwater,* she agrees with them that "there is no self." The difference, however, between a postmodernism that merely borrows allusions to the past and her own version is quite distinct. Not content with borrowing, but insistent upon owning the entire process and product of making connections, Carson repeatedly roots her aphorisms in concrete details and experienced events. She can make a statement on the questionability of self because she has been witness to her father's losing his mind, as this example also from "The Anthropology of Water" demonstrates:

He was falling away from himself in shreds, the inside became visible like bones hanging black and loose in the glare of an X ray. He would look down at himself and smile. Lips always moving. And I drew close, he was saying, "You bastard, you stupid bastard you goddamn stupid bastard you goddamn stupid useless bastard you."

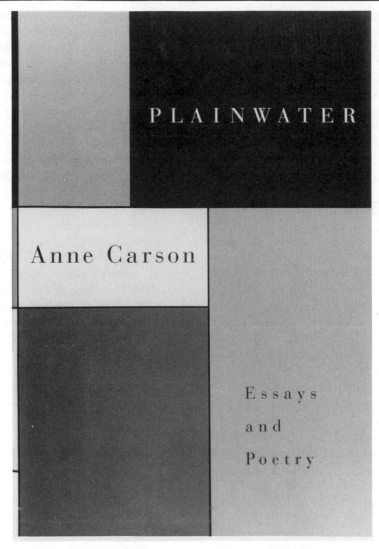

PLAINWATER

Anne Carson

Essays
and
Poetry

*Dust jacket for one of Carson's 1995 books, which illustrates the bitterness
of gaining the object of desire*

Building upon Socrates' beliefs about madness, Carson also explores being outside one's self or losing one's self as an entrance into deeper realities. One of those deeper realities is that writing, reading—any pursuit of knowledge (self or otherwise)— is an erotic act. The inability to completely map the outside world on the mind and the mind on the outside world creates desire in the same manner in which eros creates a triangle between the ideal, the actual, and the lover. Plato says that falling in love or seeing a thing of beauty is remembering the realm of the gods, collapsing the legs of the triangle. The bittersweet nature of this memory is the pain and pleasure of souls sprouting wings that carry them away from their divided consciousness. Carson also evokes William Blake's notion that man lives in a world that he has constructed so as to limit his perception to just five windows, or senses.

The architecture of Carson's work is the superimposition of fanciful structures one upon the other. The layers, however, are not fixed in place: Classical formations intrude into the modern world; Asian nuances appear in medieval European pilgrimages; and Chicago pops up in the Greece of the seventh century B.C. If one can imagine the surface of a ruffled lake becoming smooth and reflecting the trees and clouds above and then the roiled water below the surface clearing and revealing the underwater landscape, one can gain some sense of what Carson does with her poetry and lyric essays. But the turbulent surface and the spinning flecks of pyrite and mica from the disturbed lake bed are also a part of the architecture of her poetry. Movement toward meaning that partially reveals and then hides itself is the intellectual, and visceral, pleasure of her poetry.

Carson can also be called an anthropological poet. Describing how she will write about love, Carson says in the introduction to a section of "The Anthropology of Water" titled "Just for the Thrill: An Essay on the Difference Between Men and Women": "I traveled into it like a foreign country, noted its behavior, transcribed its idioms. . . . " Indeed, much of her poetry has to do with travel and travelers. In this way she is similar to the seventeenth-century Japanese poet Matsuo Bashō in both form and content. In *The Roaring Stream: A New Zen Reader* (1996) editors Nelson Foster and Jack Shoemaker describe Bashō's work as "travelogues, in which he alternates prose passages with haiku." The same can be said of Carson's work. Furthermore, a description in *The Roaring Stream* of Bashō's masterpiece, "Narrow Road to the Interior," applies equally well to Carson's longer poems, especially "Kinds of Water: An Essay on the Road to Compostela": both poems "treat readers to an extended tour through a landscape simultaneously physical, emotional, historical, and cultural, especially literary and religious."

In 1986 Princeton University Press published a book-length essay by Carson titled *Eros the Bittersweet.* On one level the book is a depiction of eros in seventh-century B.C. Greek poetry. On another level it is emblematic of how her writing is interpreted by a reader. Carson uses a sensual and precise language, but her sure use of words does not lend itself to an easy summary. Much of her poetry and prose is just slightly out of reach, so she examines the situation again and again, and from all angles, in *Eros the Bittersweet.* The classical demonstration of this reaching for meaning is included in a fragment of a poem by the Greek poet Sappho in which the most beautiful and delicious apple remains high up in the tree, beyond the reach of the apple picker. He is below, and what is between him and the apple is a third element—a longing, a desire for something he lacks. And the longing is not one of greed or avarice but of a need to possess what is, or once was, a part of the self. Readers will experience that same triangulation (to use her word) as they read her work. There is the self; there are the words; and there is the work's collective meaning; they all seem to shift ever so slightly and pleasingly as soon as the reader thinks he has them surrounded. The pleasure comes not from the apprehension but from the trying.

The overall structure of this book, which often exists in a borderland between poetry and essay, is to show that falling in love and coming to know are similar. Citing many works from antiquity, Carson notes in *Eros the Bittersweet:* "Wings and breath transport Eros as wings and breath convey words: an ancient analogy between language and love is here apparent." The argument in her book begins with the poetry of Sappho, who "first called eros 'bittersweet.'" Carson then proceeds to explain the three-part structure of eros noted above and how the lover believes he loses part of himself as desire grows. What is actually happening, according to Carson's essay, is that the lover is becoming aware of where the self ends as a result of his intense desire to become one with his beloved. Of course, if his desire is ever truly enacted, his beloved will be annihilated. Thus, a lack is necessary in order for eros to be active. The desire is sweet but contingent upon the bitterness of division. Carson goes on to say in a section of her book titled "Losing the Edge" that the "self forms at the edge of desire." Eros reminds that a boundary prevents one person from dissolving into another. That very pain keeps desire alive. Carson concludes that the real subject of most love poems is the lack felt by the lover.

A paragraph does not go by in this intelligent and challenging book that does not invite long contemplation. In the next part of the essay Carson moves to a discussion of language and how its edges help to define the self. The introduction of the Greek phonetic alphabet marks edges of sound just as eros marks edges of self. Consonants, in particular, symbolize the very production of sounds used "to construct speech" by means of a letter that is an abstraction since it only marks the edge of a sound and is not sounded itself. What eros and language do is to keep this "difference visible." In doing so, the lover or reader gets to feel the edge between the actual and the possible. What the lover/reader wants to feel is the edge and connections.

In the act of reading, the mind shifts between narrative and exegesis as each exerts its pull. The result, says Carson in *Eros the Bittersweet,* is that

> your mind is unwilling to let go of either level of activity, and remains arrested at a point of stereoscopy between the two. They compose one meaning. The novelist who constructs this moment of emotional and cognitive interception is making love, and you are the object of his wooing.

In 1995 Knopf published a collection of essays and poetry by Carson titled *Plainwater.* Some of the material in this collection had appeared in literary journals prior to 1990. "Kinds of Water" and selections from "Short Talks" were published in *The Best American Essays of 1988* and *The Best American Poetry of 1992,* respectively. The poems originally appeared in *Grand Street, Bomb, Planetarium Station, The South-*

Anne Carson
GLASS, IRONY
AND GOD

Introduction by Guy Davenport

*Cover for Carson's 1995 book that won the 1996 QSPELL
Book Award*

in no way does this concept mean that aesthetic and existential desires are not met in this book.

In this respect Carson's work is similar to that of both Jeanette Winterson and Carole Maso. In Maso's *Ava* (1993), for instance, the narrator's lucidity waxes and wanes as many different memories, stories, images, and people come in and out of focus on the last day of her life. Meaning comes out of movement. And in Winterson's *Sexing the Cherry* (1990) sixteenth-century London gradually dissolves, although not completely, into the modern world, with islands of fantasy making their appearance during the novel's journey. Maso defined this narrative method best in an essay published in *American Poetry Review* (March/April 1995):

> I must admit that conventional storytelling bores me silly. The analytic bits, the dreary descriptive impulse, the cause and effect linearity, the manufactured social circumstances.

> To create whole worlds through implication, suggestion, in a few bold strokes. Not to tyrannize with the narrative. Allow a place for the reader to live, to dream.

Since in *Plainwater* Carson does not tyrannize to make meaning, a reader can, by discussing the structure and language of the essay or poem, let what manifests itself at the moment arise, because that constellation of images, thoughts, and feelings may or may not appear in subsequent readings.

Carson has written in "Short Talks," the second section of *Plainwater,* "I will do anything to avoid boredom. . . . It is the task of a lifetime. You can never know enough, never work enough, never use the infinitives and participles oddly enough, never impede the movement harshly enough, never leave the mind quickly enough." "Short Talks," for example, consists of brief paragraphs that have the intention of making the reader slip out of rational thought to "construct an instant of nature gradually, without the boredom of a story." These prose pieces are not only about being in a moment but also about creating the moment, moment by moment. Or, as Carson in "Short Talks" puts it in a description of pouring water from one vessel to another:

> There is a moment when the water is not in one vessel nor in the other—what a thirst it was. . . .

In the structure of the third section, "Canicula di Anna," the superimposition of times and places is readily apparent. "Canicula di Anna" is at once a chronicle of a present-day phenomenology conference, a fifteenth-century painting, and a story about its painter, among other layers. At the same time,

west Review, The Yale Review, and *Brick Books. Plainwater* received a starred review (given to books of notable merit) in *Publishers Weekly* and was favorably reviewed elsewhere. Eric Murphy Selinger in a *Boston Phoenix* review said that "Carson is the most elusive, reflective, intriguing new poet I have read all year."

In *Plainwater* Carson has written a small library that, in great measure, takes the thesis of *Eros the Bittersweet* and puts it into action. This thesis states that the bittersweet nature of eros takes the course of moving from the sweetness of the chase to the bitterness of gaining the object of desire and thereby losing desire. Carson uses a parable by Franz Kafka to make her point. A man chasing children's tops is unfulfilled by the capture of one of the tops. His joy only comes from running after the spinning tops. Capture is understanding; the chase is desire. In *Plainwater* Carson and the reader go on merry chases after tops maddeningly, pleasingly spinning just beyond rational comprehension. But

Dust jacket for Carson's 1998 book, which emphasizes "truth and observation"

the narrator is creating the narrative as she views a painting which is simultaneously in the present and in the fifteenth century:

> Two things happened
> (in the painting, a superposition of colors)
> at once, both impossible.

This section, like all of the others, has a commentary; in "Canicula di Anna" it appears as an afterword. Now that her story is over, the narrator in the commentary says that she fears the reader will want more, want her to fill out her story. What happens when a story ends? The reader can be pleased and not ask any questions. He can ask for another story. He can discuss the one just heard, but he can never experience the phenomenon of hearing it again for the first time.

Carson's emphasis on structure is Pythagorean, a combination of the geometries of physical and metaphysical worlds:

> You will see the edges cut away from you, back into a world of another kind—back into real emptiness, some would say.

Ultimately, this observation in the introduction to "The Life of Towns" brings the question of how to define the self, which Carson poses as the question "Can you punctuate yourself as silence?" The thirty-six short poems that follow are memories and resonances that assemble loosely to create a "town." The punctuation of the poems reinforces the notion of the edge between what the reader perceives as a unity and all that is outside of that unity, whether that is a town or the self.

Every line of these poems ends with a period, whether a thought has come to an end or has been interrupted. If being is born out of language, then recompartmentalizing language (as Carson does) can dissolve one self (the self in which "normal" grammar and syntax prevail) into another self–a self, furthermore, which was always there but never seen until the narrative was punctuated differently. The old self (or unity) has been silenced by the new punctuation. What this idea brings to mind is the belief of some people that the Torah is written in black fire on white fire and that its true meaning will only be understood when the white space is understood as an unknown letter.

Late in 1995 New Directions published another book of poems and essays by Carson. *Glass, Irony, and God* won the Ninth Annual QSPELL Book Award (1996) for the best book written in English by a Québec resident. Carson was also awarded a Lannan Literary Award in 1996, an award given to "writers who have made a significant contribution to English-language literature and to emerging writers of distinctive literary merit who demonstrate potential."

As a collection *Glass, Irony, and God* includes the same assortment of verse, prose, and essay that is found in *Plainwater*. The last selection of *Glass, Irony, and God,* for example, reminds the reader of the essays that punctuate *Plainwater* and include the same well-articulated images and literary examples that one finds in *Eros the Bittersweet.* "The Gender of Sound" is about how culture, society, and history have been "putting a door on the female mouth" by fostering an "association of female sound with monstrosity, disorder and death." Basically, she argues that men's use of sound is perceived as regulated and under control. The female sound, however, is perceived as coming from craziness or possessing the ability to make the hearer crazy. Although this analysis does not encapsulate the whole of the argument (nor could it), Carson's essay concludes, among other things, that the still-current notion that women are out of control–as exemplified by their crying, laughter, and chatter–has ancient roots. Men, on the other hand, use *logos* (rational speech) as both a bulwark and fence against this female speech that makes no sharp distinction between the inside and the outside.

"The Fall of Rome: A Traveller's Guide" is another selection in *Glass, Irony, and God* that resembles one in *Plainwater,* particularly "Canicula di Anna." Yet another poem of many layers and complexities, "The Fall of Rome" is at the core a meditation on the way to gain some mastery over death by remaining in conversation. One of these conversations,

says Carson, is the creation of art. She uses the example of a Renaissance Italian painter, Luca Signorelli, to make her point.

> Signorelli is painting late in his studio
> when they carry in his son,
>
> killed in a riot.
> He sits up all night with the body,
> making sketch after sketch.
>
> and throwing them into a pile.
> From that time
> all his angels
>
> have the one
> same
> face.

"The Glass Essay," another particularly strong selection in *Glass, Irony, and God,* Davenport says in his introduction to the book is "a poem richer than most novels nowadays." About the end of a relationship with a man Carson names Law, "The Glass Essay" uses the work and life of Emily Brontë to search for the source of the narrator's anger and pain. Carson wants to look beyond the conventional interpretation of anger seen in Brontë's poetry and novel *Wuthering Heights* (1847) as an "act of revenge / for all that life withheld from Emily." Somehow, Carson says, anger seems to be something Brontë was born with, "as if anger could be a kind of vocation for some women." Richard Silberg, writing in *Poetry Flash,* says of "The Glass Essay": "The voice of the narrator is so nakedly honest–she comes across rather the way she describes Emily Brontë, 'The little raw soul'–so humorous, both ironic and piercing, so clear and intelligent."

Two of the selections in *Glass, Irony, and God,* although of the same fabric as all her work, are so differently and strangely woven as to deserve special attention. The first selection, "The Truth About God," evokes an image of God that recalls William Blake's Urizen at the beginning of his work of creation. "God had the book of life open at PLEASURE," Carson explains in one section that proceeds to make a list of things, liquid or liquidlike, that man and woman have difficulty holding because their flesh is like a sieve. The "pleasure" she describes is not the grace taught in religious institutions but a coming-on that is violent. One of the sections, for example, titled "The God Coup," alludes to a hit made during battle. An allusion that comes to mind is to the sonnet by John Donne that begins: "Batter my heart, three personed God." In the selection "My Religion," which appears as the first poem in

"The Truth About God," Carson speaks of the simplicity of the real truth of religion as

> a creature
> let loose in a room
> and battering
>
> to get out.
> It batters my soul
> with its rifle butt.

Nor does Carson avoid spelling out the power-based authority of a patriarch who, because he gets to say what nature is, also gets to say what is natural. When in the section "God's Woman" he asks her whether she is angry at nature, she replies:

> Yes I am angry at nature I do not want nature stuck
> up between my legs on your pink baton
>
> or ladled out like geography whenever
> your buckle needs a lick.
> What do you mean *Creation?*
>
> God circled her.
> Fire. Time. Fire.
> Choose, said God.

The discussion of a God new at his job is also at the center of "The Book of Isaiah," which includes Carson's story of the contract between God and his prophet. Like any contract-making, there are negotiations and battles to gain advantage and power. The opening give-and-take in Carson's poem may be summarized thus.

Prior to the instances related in the poem, Isaiah and God have been on good terms, speaking often with each other. One morning, however, Isaiah wakes up angry because God has "filled Isaiah's ears with stingers." Isaiah interprets his pain as sin, which he then projects upon the nation of Judah. God, explains the poem's unnamed narrator, "saw things differently." God sees the "worldsheet" (history, society, culture, now, place) as burning in Isaiah. Isaiah then begins to address the nation, but they do not hear. Not until God has "shattered Isaiah's indifference" to the true source of his power to prophesy and "washed Isaiah's hair in fire" does the nation wake out of its sleep and listen.

Isaiah then calls upon God, who, when he finally arrives, once again smashes "Isaiah like glass through every socket of his nation" and calls his prophet a liar. Isaiah argues that he may be "a small man," but he is no liar. And the first section of the poem then concludes with the following exchange:

> God paused.
> And so that was their contract.
> Brittle on both sides, no lying.
> Isaiah's wife came to the doorway, the doorposts had moved.
> What's that sound? said Isaiah's wife.
> The fear of the Lord, said Isaiah.
> He grinned in the dark, she went back inside.

Even this small section gives the reader a sense of examining sacred source material before the editors and theologians came along with their emendations. "Book of Isaiah" is more about Isaiah and his relation to God than it is about what God wants to reveal to the world through his prophet. The text clearly shows that Isaiah is getting some personal satisfaction as well from his arrangement with God. That is why he grins in the dark after telling his wife that the sound she heard was the fear of God.

If the forthcoming books of Carson are any indication, Davenport believes she will continue to write "in a kind of mathematics of emotions, with daring equations and recurring sets and subsets of images." He adds that in her poetry "truth and observation are more important than lyric effect or coloring." In 1998, in addition to *Autobiography of Red* (Knopf), the following books by Carson are scheduled to be published: *Sophokles Elektra: Translation with Commentary and Notes* (Oxford University), *Wild Workshop* (Faber and Faber), *Economy of the Unlost: Poetry of Simonides and Celan* (Princeton University), and a reprint of *Eros the Bittersweet* (Dalkey Archive).

A *Booklist* review of *Glass, Irony, and God* describes her work as not only displaying "mental acuity," but as being "emotionally accessible" as well. Most important, says the review, it is poetry for "those wanting to be overcome, in a grand way, by an intense, urgent, new kind of poetry."

References:

Nelson Foster and Jack Shoemaker, *The Roaring Stream: A New Zen Reader* (Hopewell, N. J.: Ecco Press, 1996);

Carole Maso, "An Essay," *American Poetry Review,* 62 (March/April 1995): 26–31;

Janet St. John, *Booklist* (1 November 1995): 450;

Eric Murphy Selinger, *Boston Phoenix* (23 December 1995).

Clark Coolidge
(26 February 1939 –   )

Bruce Campbell
University of California, Riverside

BOOKS: *Flag Flutter & U.S. Electric* (New York: Lines Books, 1966);

Clark Coolidge (New York: Lines Books, 1967);

Ing (New York: Angel Hair Books, 1968);

Space (New York: Harper & Row, 1970);

To Obtain the Value of the Cake Measure from Zero: A Play in One Act, by Coolidge and Tom Veitch (San Francisco: Pants Press, 1970);

The So: Poems 1966 (New York: Adventures in Poetry, 1971);

Suite V (New York: Adventures in Poetry, 1973);

The Maintains (San Francisco: This Press, 1974);

Polaroid (New York: Adventures in Poetry / Bolinas, Cal.: Big Sky, 1975);

Quartz Hearts (San Francisco: This Press, 1978);

Own Face (Lenox, Mass.: Angel Hair Books, 1978);

Smithsonian Depositions Subject to a Film (New York: Vehicle Editions, 1980);

A Geology (Needham, Mass.: Potes & Poets, 1981);

American Ones: (Noise & Presentiments) (Bolinas, Cal.: Tombouctou Books, 1981);

Research (Berkeley, Cal.: Tuumba, 1982);

Mine: The One That Enters the Stories (Berkeley, Cal.: Figures, 1982);

The Crystal Text (Great Barrington, Mass.: Figures, 1986);

Solution Passage: Poems 1978–1981 (Los Angeles: Sun & Moon Press, 1986);

Melencolia (Great Barrington, Mass.: Figures, 1987);

Mesh (Detroit: In Camera, 1988);

At Egypt (Great Barrington, Mass.: Figures, 1988);

Sound As Thought: Poems 1982–1984 (Los Angeles: Sun & Moon Press, 1990);

Supernatural Overtones, by Coolidge and Ron Padgett (Great Barrington, Mass.: Figures, 1990);

Baffling Means: Writings/Drawings, by Coolidge and Philip Guston (Stockbridge, Mass.: o.blēk, 1991);

Odes of Roba (Great Barrington, Mass.: Figures, 1991);

The Book of During (Great Barrington, Mass.: Figures, 1991);

Clark Coolidge (photograph by Peeter Vilms)

On the Pumice of Morons: The Unaugural Poem, by Coolidge and Larry Fagin (Great Barrington, Mass.: Figures, 1993);

Lowell Connector: Lines & Shots from Kerouac's Town, by Coolidge and Michael Gizzi, John Yau, and others (West Stockbridge, Mass.: Hard Press, 1993);

The Rova Improvisations (Los Angeles: Sun & Moon Press, 1994);

Registers (People in All) (Bolinas, Cal.: Avenue B, 1994);

For Kurt Cobain (Great Barrington, Mass.: Figures, 1995);

Keys to Caverns (Grand Canary, Spain: Zasterle Press, 1995);

The Names (Brightlingsea, Essex, U.K.: Active in Airtime, 1997);

This Time We Are Both/City in Regard (Los Angeles: Sun & Moon Press, forthcoming).

OTHER: "Arrangement," in *Talking Poetics from the Naropa Institute: Annals of the Jack Kerouac School of Disembodied Poetics,* volume 1, edited by Anne Waldman and Marilyn Webb (Boulder, Colo. & London: Shambala, 1978);

"Weathers," in *In the American Tree,* edited by Ron Silliman (Orono, Me.: National Poetry Foundation at the University of Maine, 1986);

Jim Brodey, *Heart of the Breath: Poems, 1979–1992,* edited by Coolidge (West Stockbridge, Mass.: Hard Press, 1996).

SELECTED PERIODICAL PUBLICATIONS–UNCOLLECTED: "Oflengths," *Tottel's,* 11 (Fall 1973): entire issue;

"Words," *Friction,* 7 (Summer 1984): 45–48;

"The Symphony," *Abacus,* no. 40 (1989), entire issue;

"A First Reading of *On The Road* and *Later,*" *Talisman,* 3 (Fall 1989): 100–102.

Given the changes in Coolidge's body of works, readers will likely have decided preferences. Coolidge begins as a gestural poet in the tradition of the New York poets and the painters of Abstract Expressionism (or gestural painting), becomes in the mid 1970s more of a Constructivist poet, only to resemble, since the early 1980s, a meditative-philosophical poet. These changes do not mean that Coolidge's work, taken as a whole, is incoherent; rather, they mean that Coolidge discloses poetic, linguistic, and rhetorical possibilities he does not himself choose to follow. In other words, Coolidge's influence spreads well beyond his most recent phase.

Born in Providence, Rhode Island, on 26 February 1939 to Arlan Ralph and Sylvia Clark Coolidge, Clark Coolidge attended Brown University from 1956 to 1958 (where his father was a professor of music). His major was geology, not English. Music may well have been a keener influence on Coolidge than any of the literature usually taught in universities in the 1950s. In the summer of 1958 he moved to Los Angeles where he "began writing long letters of what was happening," according to the chronology in *Stations* (1978). Still, not until he lived in New York in the West Village (from the fall of 1958 to the summer of 1959) when he took "long walks around the city" did he begin "to scribble for myself." In addition to the peripatetic charms of the city, Coolidge was stimulated by the music, art, and "Beat mags"—and, of course, by meeting other artists. In 1960, according to the chronology, he returned to Providence, where he "worked as searcher" in the order department of the Brown University Library. He married in 1962 and "began experimenting with cut-ups/chance etc." In 1964 Coolidge and Michael Palmer began editing a literary magazine, *Joglars.* After three issues it ceased publication in 1966. Coolidge was also divorced in 1966 and returned to New York, where he met many poets, thus explaining his early attribution as a New York School poet. Later that year his first book was published by Aram Saroyan's Lines Books: *Flag Flutter & U.S. Electric,* twenty-two pages of stapled mimeograph sporting the author's cover photograph of an owl with wings spread in flight.

This first publication set a pattern Coolidge has diverged from only once. The little magazine/small press community has nurtured and sustained Coolidge. To date only one book, *Space* (1970), has been published by a major trade publisher (Harper and Row). His earliest books are stapled affairs, often mimeographed, with print runs in the hundreds. For the most part they have never been reprinted. But of course this is an old story: for more than a century much of the most important American poetry has had to survive without the support of major publishers, sometimes self-published, sometimes even published abroad.

Coolidge is a prolific writer—even counting books to the exclusion of his periodical contributions (to say nothing of work that remains in manuscript). One book alone, *Solution Passage: Poems 1978–1981* (1986), admittedly his longest to date, is roughly equivalent in size to the collected poems of most poets (that is, nearly four hundred pages). That Coolidge's work has also undergone tremendous changes makes a short overview dealing with the body of his work all the more difficult.

The work by Coolidge that first gained attention, both through his own books and through contributions to anthologies—particularly Paul Carroll's *The Young American Poets* (1968) and Ron Padgett and David Shapiro's *An Anthology of New York Poets* (1970)—has been characterized as Steinian: a reduced syntax has allowed him to foreground the *form* of language. His work is essentially analytical. This writing first marks the initial reputation of Coolidge, in part because it is so different from what other writers of the time were doing. The difference explains its impact but not its significance.

Coolidge's first book opens with the allure of urban space. That Coolidge explicitly uses mobility is not accidental, considering the amalgam of experiences and influences acknowledged in the chronology composed in 1970. His early impulse is one of excitement, movement, even openness. In "Acid," the first poem in *Flag Flutter,* Coolidge

*Cover for Coolidge's 1970 book, the only collection of his poems
published by a major house*

gives notations of urban space with its different levels, street calls, signage, and continuing drama that one is always catching in medias res; thus, he intersperses bits of narrative. The effect parallels that of the "all-over" paintings of Abstract Expressionism. The first definition offered for "space" in *Space* is "that which is characterized by extension in all directions, boundlessness, infinite divisibility." Yet all the events impinge, however implicitly, upon a consciousness. (Only in his third phase, beginning with *Mine: The One That Enters the Stories* in 1982, does Coolidge explicate this consciousness and ground it in an important way.) The last poem of *Flag Flutter,* "The Tab" (one of only six poems from this volume also included in *Space*), moves to a nounal density:

"mica flask moves layout hasty / bunkum geode olive lion candle." It moves past a "layout hasty" to the compression of a lexical landscape. This is the kind of writing which antagonists of the later Language writers often call (incorrectly) nonreferential. Each word refers, but these references are not generally found together. Here each word puts the next into a context.

In April 1967 Coolidge traveled to San Francisco to play drums in poet David Meltzer's Serpent Power band, which in May cut an album for Vanguard. When coming across the varied musical references in Coolidge one should recall that Coolidge was a "'society' 'jazz' 'rock' drummer/Classical Percussionist," according to his own words in his biographical note in *An Anthology of New York Poets*. This musical background may account for the varied rhythms in Coolidge's poems. In December 1967 Coolidge married again. His wife Susan the next year bore a daughter, Celia Elizabeth, now a painter and photographer. Coolidge's stay in San Francisco was short, a matter of three years.

Though Coolidge was still living in San Francisco at the time, his third book was published in 1968 in a run of five hundred copies by Anne Waldman and Lewis Warsh's Angel Hair Books, then located in New York City. The book sported a Philip Guston cover. (Guston later became an important friend to Coolidge, and although Guston had died in 1980, the collaboration *Baffling Means: Writings/Drawings* appeared in 1991.) The title *Ing* (1968) indicates how much closer to his material Coolidge was now working. *Ing* foregrounds the continuing activity of writing. In consequence, *Ing* is suggestive of a lexical space rather than a geographic one. But space cannot be divorced from time—the fifth definition for *space* is duration. The intensely active morpheme of the title represents a presencing of the act made concrete in the language. The opening poem (minus the proper spacing) states: "these / ing / those // one." Through the activity (here any "ing"), this becomes that. The activity becomes a thing. Thus, the opening poem of *Ing* can be contrasted with "been / tion / balance // anole," which comes up halfway through the book. Here the past tense, turned into a state of being (that is, "tion"), achieves a momentary balance through what might be called a "nounifying" act. Yet, as can be seen through the morphemic thrust, Coolidge is working so close to the medium that he is dealing with parts of parts of speech. He is particularly doing this by the end of *Ing:* "a ture / the ing." Yet with the grounding of the morphemes, sound homologies claim more weight than usual. The "ture" may be part of an "aperture," but sounded out it seems "sure." The morphemes may call to mind several words at once or even a grammatical category.

With the end of *Ing* Coolidge also reached the end of *Space*. The poem "A D" closes both books. (There are five poems from *Ing* included in *Space*.) *Space* is the end of Coolidge's first phase, although the poems in *The So: Poems 1966* (1971) belong to this phase. Indeed, eleven poems in *The So* appear in *Space*. More important, *Space* respects the order of the other books. In this way *Space* represents a kind of selected poems directed toward the potentially larger audience for a book by a major trade publisher. Thus, the first phase of Coolidge's career is given focus by *Space*. Further, given the low-tech productions of Coolidge's other early works, *Space,*

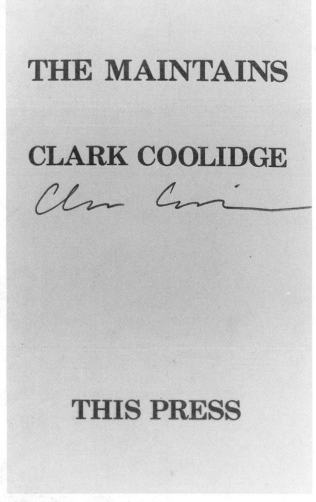

THE MAINTAINS

CLARK COOLIDGE

THIS PRESS

Title page for Coolidge's 1974 book, which connected him with the Language poets

considered as a physical product, is a significant departure. It sports a cover by Jasper Johns: stenciled letters spell out "SPACE" alongside a ruler with Clark Coolidge's name woodburned in the center. Johns's cover suggests that Coolidge's work in his first phase is concerned not only with space but also with scale (or measurement).

In this first phase Coolidge places an unusual stress on the words, manifested in part through the reduction of syntax. The effect is to treat "words as objects" as the dust-jacket blurb on *Space* says. Coolidge's writing is not *about* something; it *is* something. This fact necessitates the reader's paying close attention to the words of Coolidge rather than to the ideas. Perhaps on this level Coolidge's work bears a close resemblance to that of Gertrude Stein, although taken over the length of all his work, the resemblance is misleading. Like a nature photographer, Coolidge focuses in tight on his object. The

mine: the one that enters the stories   clark coolidge

*Cover for Coolidge's 1982 book, in which he wrote: "This world is certainly
unstable of language, not to speak of deed. The entrance to the ground
is not everywhere."*

reader must then see the object in a new light, unfiltered by the habitual thoughts of precedence. Language becomes a source of experience rather than solely a recording mechanism.

The same year that saw the publication of *Space,* 1970, saw Coolidge's move to the Berkshires in western Massachusetts, where he has lived since. The return occasioned Coolidge's "The Road Log (Out West to Back East Again)," a poem in *Big Sky,* volume three, an important source for uncollected Coolidge. Never has Coolidge been quite so explicitly notational nor quite so personal. The influence of Ted Berrigan has never been more pervasive. Coolidge was not to pursue this path, although it was interesting. The year 1970 was also important for Coolidge because June marked the inclusion of

his poetry in *An Anthology of New York Poets,* edited by Padgett and Shapiro and published by Random House Vintage Books. Under "Statement" Coolidge wrote, "This is a sentence."

Coolidge's second stage begins in 1974 with the publication of *The Maintains* by Barrett Watten's This Press. This book sports an austere cover, white background with black lettering, and had a run of one thousand copies. This publication also represents a new connection for Coolidge with a younger group of writers, the Language writers. The sound and to some extent even the effect of *The Maintains* are developed on the basis of earlier work such as "The Tab." (The line "oxide thought unit organs lyric" may be compared to the line quoted earlier from "The Tab.") This intense involvement with

THE CRYSTAL TEXT
CLARK COOLIDGE

Cover for Coolidge's 1986 book, a meditation inspired by a piece of crystal on his writing desk

the words, which led Coolidge to move from noun to noun without the usual syntactic or grammatical links, led Barrett Watten to suggest that Coolidge was building up a syntax out of the rhythm of the words. The length of *The Maintains* is certainly significant in terms of such a buildup. And *The Maintains* is the first (but certainly not the last) long work for Coolidge. Coolidge achieves in it a density of verbal expression reminiscent of the denser passages of Louis Zukofsky. Whereas in *Ing* Coolidge emphasizes the moment of activity best expressed in a morpheme, in *The Maintains* he realizes that immediacy is not sufficient. The emphasis on the thing, on words as things, gives rise in Coolidge to something else. There must also be "a hither / a matrice."

The "matrice" here is of a "cognate realm." Coolidge is moving into and through the dictionary rather than staying at the denotative level as in the page definitions for *Space*. But there is also the sense that the words (and later the things) are the means of something else: the activity of *making* is a way of being, "being as the than by which things / may thing by." This is, then, the ontological ground to Coolidge. Furthermore, Coolidge's most abiding influences and connections are with Jack Kerouac and the Beats. In fact, since 1977 Coolidge has been an adjunct faculty member of the Naropa Institute's poetics department, a department operating under the banner of the Jack Kerouac School for Disembodied Poetics.

SOLUTION PASSAGE

POEMS 1978-1981

CLARK COOLIDGE

Los Angeles
Sun & Moon Press

*Title page for Coolidge's 1986 collection of poems suggesting the
paradox of moving and staying*

Coolidge's next book, *Polaroid* (1975), unlike
The Maintains, was published by Adventures in Poetry, which had published earlier work. It begins
with the stanzaic pattern of *The Maintains,* but after
fifty pages the words start to separate so that the visual quality is similar to that in Coolidge's earlier
works. By page 69 Coolidge is dealing with blocks
of texts, the lines lengthening toward a "prosodic"
quality. *Polaroid* encapsulates Coolidge's development into longer forms. The prosodic effect is somewhat analogous to what Ron Silliman calls "the new
sentence" although Silliman draws a distinction between the two. *Polaroid,* however, is a different work
from *The Maintains.* Not only does Coolidge place a
lesser burden on the nouns, but he also uses fewer of
them. Phrases proliferate. Thus, one must examine
longer passages. In part, this is owing to the concern
with the means of expression: "means that such this
will as where only means itself evens still both,"
where the "evens" can be read as a balance between
"means" and "will." Most simply, "means does."

The proliferation of phrases opens up another dimension, still but faintly seen in *Polaroid* though pursued in later works. Reflections on the process are
taking place within the process itself. A concern
with "means" becomes a concern with "meaning."
"Meaning into come willing out." There is an implicit connection here of meaning with orgasm, a
connection that underwrites the later *Book of During*
(1991). By the end of *Polaroid* the reader sees meaning as another thing; thus, "point seem thing." In
this realm things and meanings are cosubstantial.
And Coolidge's procedure has worked to reveal the
thingness of the point.

These two works represent the height of Coolidge's synthetic or constructivist mode. The other
important work of this mode, "Weathers," has
never been collected into book form although four
sections of it can be read in Silliman's anthology of
Language writing, *In the American Tree* (1986). Coolidge is building up a language, but the nature of the
world built up in this manner depends upon its constituent parts. To begin with prepositions (as in
Coolidge's "Oflengths") brings one result, and to
begin with poetic diction and/or metaphors brings
another. The result depends upon the choice of language. Perhaps Coolidge's own dissatisfaction with
a prepositional world leads him to note, "There is
nothing *of* here" (*Baffling Means*).

At the time Coolidge was publishing these
works he was keeping a notebook, selections of
which comprise the later *Crystal Text* as well as *Baffling Means.* Here the publication dates (1986 and
1991, respectively) can be particularly misleading.
Yet the distinction between the kind of works Coolidge chose to publish at this time and the notebook
entries which he published years later is instructive.
The characterizations or pronouncements about art
that Coolidge sometimes writes in the notebooks are
hardly to be found in the works published at the
same time. He says in *Baffling Means,* "Art is no
longer / having to make a move." The notebook allowed him to think about what he was doing. It was
this space of "about" that Coolidge disallowed in his
writing at the time and yet later moved toward. But
the notebook can be seen as important beyond its
content. Evidently Coolidge took seriously Samuel
Beckett's 1961 statement in *Beckett by the Madeleine*
by Tom Driver that "to find a form that accommo-
dates the mess, / that is the task of the artist now,"
since Coolidge says in the notebook that Beckett's
statement "seems / pointed exactly at our condition
now" and has quoted it many times. The notebook
becomes a form for dealing with the mess although
the form becomes as loose as the mess.

Participants in a poetry conference in Wansee, Germany, May 1992; (standing) Leslie Scalapino, Charles Bernstein, Kathleen Fraser, Clark Coolidge, Susan Coolidge, Hans Joachim Rieke, and (seated) Hannah Mockel-Rieke

The passages collected in *Baffling Means* from notebooks written between 1972 and 1976 have the additional support of Guston's drawings, which go far beyond illustration, even if they are captioned; often a single drawing will sprout up about several different lines. Coolidge's title is provocative. In his preface he explains the title by saying, "because we wouldn't know what we'd get." But this explanation scarcely touches the provocation, especially if considered in light of the "means" of the contemporaneous *Polaroid*. *Baffling Means* displays a reflexivity characteristic of Coolidge: the baffling means and the means baffle; or between the means and the meaning is the baffling. The individual is caught in the "baffling," turning between the means and the meaning. The concept is located on this same dividing line (between means and meaning) if "Concept of object / gives us outside and inside." The often remarked upon quality of words as objects in early Coolidge led him beyond the object to the concept of object. The object, therefore, is where inside and outside meet.

In 1978 Coolidge published two important works—*Quartz Hearts,* published by This Press in an edition of five hundred copies; and *Own Face,* published in a run of 750 copies and dedicated to its publisher, Bernadette Mayer. A work of 1972–1973, according to the end of the text, *Quartz Hearts* is a

"hinge-work." According to Coolidge in the "Notes" section, *Quartz Hearts* links the last section of *Polaroid,* "completed August 1973," with "the beginning of my long (as yet untitled) 'prosoid' work (first section completed November 1973)." However, as the last half of the hinge has never been published complete (nor in book form), *Quartz Hearts* has provided a different hinge from the one Coolidge imagined. In *Quartz Hearts* Coolidge allows himself some of the latitude he claims in his notebook ruminations, "meditations on the state(s) of things, in other words words." *Quartz Hearts* thus extends a line of development from William Carlos Williams's "No ideas but in things" in *Paterson* (1992) and Robert Creeley's "and things are made of words." Coolidge's contribution might be phrased as "and words are right here." *Quartz Hearts* is then a book of "things first placed." Having burrowed through the dictionary, Coolidge comes upon the landscape of language: "A definition is as the end of its string."

As a meditation the work demands a distance and consequently a different attention from that Coolidge had brought to his earlier productions. Thus, in *Quartz Hearts* for the first time Coolidge has discovered the singular form of the personal pronoun—for example, "I like to see / the change I think I can't hear." Thinking is pitched against the senses

Cover for one of Coolidge's 1994 books, poems inspired by the music of the Rova Saxophone Quartet

part of it (or reads his heart there). "The / language inside is going to make forms / harder?"

If Coolidge's language has reminded readers of things, it is because his words are resistant. But the longer he mined this area the more the thing became a concept: "I've got no idea about but write it." The resistance once posited in the word (the means) leaches back into the concept where another level of resistance is registered: it does not mean anything. Consequently, the thingness of words becomes the nothingness of meaning. Or as Coolidge puts it in the first poem in *Own Face,* "But it says nothing." All the same, the work will not be dismissed so nonchalantly as nothing, for "the time it says nothing one moves." Time and movement will not be stayed, stalled, or stilled by nothing. "And somehow the set of things has you again, / a fascination in love of self." "The set of things," then, is literally fascinating. Fascination becomes the term for the engagement with the object, an engagement grounded "in love of self." For this reason, "I goal out of the mess." Beginning with this phase of his career, one of the recurring themes of Coolidge's work is that of beginning again. The effort is one of continual balance and struggle: "the crank to maintain, the balance / of static laws to fizz." Still, not only is *Own Face* the most lyrical of Coolidge's books to date, but it also establishes the path he will take in *Solution Passage, Sound As Thought: Poems 1982–1984* (1990), and *Odes of Roba* (1991). That this is the path he had been searching for may be inferred from the advantage he took of it once he found it. The three books comprise roughly 750 pages and were written in a little more than seven years.

The third phase of Coolidge's career began in 1982. This phase is marked by greater critical acceptance: *Mine* was the first of Coolidge's works to be published by Geoffrey Young's The Figures (in an edition of 750 copies). The Figures was still located in Berkeley but within two years would move to Great Barrington in the Berkshires of western Massachusetts. Doubtless the move helped strengthen the poet-publisher relationship, for The Figures has gone on to publish seven of Coolidge's subsequent books, including in 1986 *The Crystal Text* (in an edition of one thousand copies). These are the last prose books Coolidge has published (excepting *Baffling Means,* though it had been written years earlier). Why are they the last prose works? If, as he writes in *Mine,* "This world is certainly unstable of language, not to speak of deed. The entrance to the ground is not everywhere," then in these two works a form of knowledge secures "the entrance to the ground." Was this what Coolidge was interested in all along? In *The Crystal Text* there is a passage which

to determine the change otherwise unavailable. Where does this change come from? It comes from the leverage thought purchases against sight, concept purchases against object, and "I" purchases against words. But, like a teeter-totter, in time the purchase will go the other way. Purchase is reciprocal. As he writes in *Mine,* "Writing is impossible, the words are all there. . . . Thought, the words have changed." Most simply, thought is used to change the words; the benefit that accrues is that of being able to continue. Coolidge must write himself into and out of thought. This demand also registers Coolidge's distance from a poetics built on the senses: "I / don't sense I state," as he says in *Quartz Hearts.* Does a sense then come out of the stating? It does if one sees the point. Yet, by grafting nouns, as in "quartz hearts," Coolidge is able to create a figure for the concept of the object in which the inside and the outside, emotion and observation, measurement and bodily organ are fused. This fusion lends itself to a classically romantic reading: the quartz (that is, the thing) is understood when the reader becomes

suggests this: "Interest in structure only in the terms that a / language exists. Exists and or languages, / entrances and exits." Coolidge's interest in structure, then, had always been oriented toward the entrance to the ground of language; which is also to say it was never, as Coolidge here characterizes it, an end in itself. This is why he does not choose to continue with writing as a form of knowledge. Instead, Coolidge appears to have written off his debts to the poetics of knowledge: "Knowing has / nothing to do with any of this." Knowledge is something codified and transmitted; it "is only cast shards of a certain fascination" but a fascination that cannot admit it is fascinated, for to do so would be to lose all objective reliability. All the same, Coolidge is not aiming for ignorance. What then can his answer be? In *Crystal Text* he writes, "What I discover in writing comes out of the / mess, the mix. I know no nodes before." It is in the process of writing that the conjunctions are found. At the same time, there is no guarantee that the nodes will remain. This is one reason the poet must continue to write. As he says in *Solution Passage,* "I let myself out of the marry by learning / the sentence never to complete."

Mine builds on the "prosoidic" base of earlier Coolidge works such as *Smithsonian Depositions Subject to a Film* (1980), *American Ones: (Noise & Presentiments)* (1981), and *A Geology* (1981). At the same time, *Mine* appears to share more of the critical focus of the notebook works. The personal pronoun leads Coolidge into process, for "I live in composition. In other words, confusion, will, and doubt." Not only is the poet "in composition," but also things themselves are "events"—much as Whitehead argues in *Process and Reality*. It underscores the nature of Coolidge's poetics as process, consonant with a new emphasis on time (over space), which, according to the readings of philosopher Henri Lefevbre, means a turn from the public space to the private time. Ironically, in *The Crystal Text* Coolidge writes that "I only *have* time when I / move off each mark." It is in the moving off that time is allied with the private, particularly (here) in its wayward sense. But if "Things may be better understood as events" in *Mine, The Crystal Text* butts heads with the solidity (or resistance) of the object. It is in this resistance, after all, that the American philosopher Charles Sanders Peirce had located the meaning of reality.

Written from 25 August 1982 to 9 June 1983, *The Crystal Text* is a meditation provoked by a piece of crystal on the poet's writing desk. The choice of object is scarcely innocent; Coolidge not only uses "crystal" to recall "quartz" (as in *Quartz Hearts*) but also states in *The Crystal Text,* "Quartz is the original untampered word." "Quartz," then, is foundational in terms of a language. Furthermore, *The Crystal Text* confronts the reader with the question "How can one speak from within the thought / of the thing, . . . from / the heart?" The processual act of knowing, confronted by and sliding off the blockages of thought, is basically a sensual prospect. What is implicit becomes explicit in Coolidge's *The Book of During* (1991) and its shorter offshoot, *Mesh* (1988), in which sex is more than "holding up the head. Exactitude of lock." Exactitude it may be, but the poet cannot remain locked. Coolidge after all is trying to engender an experience which has not already been codified by thought or knowledge, and getting there has taken a great deal of writing. The challenge, however, is that each openness tends to become closed through habituation. The linguistic connections previously formed come too readily to mind. And so the poet fights himself. As he writes in *Sound As Thought,* "Amiss, A lock. / Matchable opens and the world is strayed." In other words, Coolidge is a poet who prizes the surprise. This is why forgetting has always been as important to Coolidge as insight. "Forgetfulness allows me to move," according to Coolidge in *The Crystal Text*. As the jazz composer Henry Threadgill has remarked, "You do something you know too well, you're not going to get excited. You'll do what you know." Coolidge's answer can be inferred from the title of his major collection, *Solution Passage*. The solution lies in the movement, lies also in the paradox of movement; for "The sensation that to move is to stay / in the sensation of moving." And "Writing means motion," as Coolidge says in *Sound As Thought*. For Charles Olson the trick was to learn to dance sitting down. For Clark Coolidge the trick is move and stay, stay the moves (and stray the moves) by writing. Given the realities of a subatomic world, of how science manifests its own paradoxes—for even crystal is not solid—perhaps it is not surprising if Coolidge is forced to grapple with a lyricism of change and deflection.

As things now stand, it seems the second stage of Coolidge's work has been crucial in providing a framework for the improvisatory leap of the later work. Improvisation is one way in which jazz has influenced Coolidge; but there is another. It has taught him to attend to the noise; in this case the lyric noise in writing. "The mate of a book is its mind's din / the truth its eventual slake," according to *Solution Passage*. This "slake" is something each reader must work through. Coolidge's texts seem to invite reflection and comment perhaps as much as they brook them. In other words, the "slake" is demanded as much as postponed. For "There is nothing here in words but what you know / Nothing then but trouble in the bidden."

Interviews:

Barrett Watten, "Conversation with Clark Coolidge," *This,* 4 (1973): unpaginated;

Watten, "Conversation with Clark Coolidge 10/16/75," *Stations,* 5 (1978): 11–15;

Jim Cohn and Laurie Price, "An Interview with Clark Coolidge," *Friction,* 7 (1984): 7–44;

Laurel LaPlante and Fred Covitz, "An Interview with Clark Coolidge," *Environs,* 3 (1986): unpaginated;

Anne Waldman, "*Research* Interview with Clark Coolidge," *Jimmy & Lucy's House of 'K,'* 6 (1986): 123–127;

Lee Bartlett, "Clark Coolidge: 'A Constant Retrogression,' and 'This Is Not Memory,'" in *Talking Poetry,* edited by Bartlett (Albuquerque: University of New Mexico Press, 1987);

Lydia Tomkiw, "Clark Coolidge Interview," *B City,* 5 (1988): 18–25.

Bibliography:

"Clark Coolidge: A Selected Bibliography," *Talisman,* 3 (Fall 1989): 125–128.

References:

Charles Bernstein, "Maintaining Space: Clark Coolidge's Early Works," *Stations,* 5 (Winter 1978): 4–6;

Big Sky, special issue on Coolidge, no. 3 (1972);

Bruce Campbell, "'All the Movement Still My Own': Clark Coolidge's *Mesh,*" *Sagetrieb,* 10 (Spring & Fall 1991): 133–144;

Campbell, "'The Place Between the Name and the Thing': Clark Coolidge's *Crystal Text,*" *Temblor,* 7 (1988): 143–145;

Anne Mack and Jay Rome, "Truth in the Body of Falsehood," *Parnassus,* 15, no. 1 (1989): 257–280;

Aldon J. Nielson, "Clark Coolidge and a Jazz Aesthetic," *Pacific Coast Philology,* 1 (28 September 1993): 94–112;

Ron Silliman, "Ubeity," *Stations,* 5 (Winter 1978): 19–23;

Barrett Watten, *Total Syntax* (Carbondale & Edwardsville: Southern Illinois University Press, 1985);

Krysztof Ziarek, "Word for Sign: Poetic Language in Coolidge's *The Crystal Text,*" *Sagetrieb,* 10 (Spring & Fall 1991): 145–166.

Cid Corman
(29 June 1924 –   )

William Walsh
Miami University (Ohio)

BOOKS: *subluna* (Dorchester, Mass.: Privately printed, 1944);

The Precisions (Corona, N.Y.: Sparrow Magazine, 1955);

The Responses (Ashland, Mass.: Origin Press, 1956);

The Marches & Other Poems (Ashland, Mass.: Origin Press, 1957);

Stances and Distances (Ashland, Mass.: Origin Press, 1957);

A Table in Provence (Ashland, Mass.: Origin Press, 1959);

The Descent from Daimonji (Ashland, Mass.: Origin Press, 1959);

Cool Gong (Ashland, Mass.: Origin Press, 1959);

Clocked Stone (Ashland, Mass.: Origin Press, 1959);

For Sure (Ashland, Mass.: Origin Press, 1959);

Invitation to Primavera (Toronto: Contact Press, 1960);

For Instance (Ashland, Mass.: Origin Press, 1962);

Sun Rock Man (Kyoto, Japan: Origin Press, 1962);

In No Time (Kyoto, Japan: Origin Press, 1963);

In Good Time (Kyoto, Japan: Origin Press, 1964);

All in All (Kyoto, Japan: Origin Press, 1964; New Rochelle, N.Y.: Elizabeth Press, 1974);

For Good (Kyoto, Japan: Origin Press, 1964);

Nonce (New Rochelle, N.Y.: Elizabeth Press, 1965);

Stead (New Rochelle, N.Y.: Elizabeth Press, 1966);

At: Bottom (Bloomington, Ind.: Caterpillar, 1966);

For You (Kyoto, Japan: Origin Press, 1966);

For Granted (New Rochelle, N.Y.: Elizabeth Press, 1967);

Words for Each Other (London: Rapp & Carroll, 1967);

& Without End (New Rochelle, N.Y.: Elizabeth Press, 1968; London: Villiers Publications, 1968);

Hearth (Kyoto, Japan: Origin Press, 1968);

No Less (New Rochelle, N.Y.: Elizabeth Press, 1968);

The World as University (Kyoto, Japan: Origin Press, 1968);

No More (New Rochelle, N.Y: Elizabeth Press, 1969);

Plight (New Rochelle, N.Y: Elizabeth Press, 1969);

For Keeps (Kyoto, Japan: Origin Press, 1970);

Cid Corman on Boston Common, early 1940s

Nigh (New Rochelle, N.Y: Elizabeth Press, 1970);

Livingdying (New York: New Directions, 1970);

Of the Breath Of (San Francisco: Maya, 1970);

For Now (Kyoto, Japan: Origin Press, 1971);

Cicadas (Amherst, N.Y: Slow Loris Press, 1971);

Out & Out (New Rochelle, N.Y: Elizabeth Press, 1972);

Be Quest (New Rochelle, N.Y: Elizabeth Press, 1972);

A Language Without Words (Arkesden, Saffron Walden, Essex, U.K.: Hedda's Cottage/Byways, 1972);

Poems: Thanks to Zuckerkandl (Rushden, Northamptonshire, U.K.: Sceptre Press, 1973);

So Far (New Rochelle, N.Y: Elizabeth Press, 1973);

Three Poems (Rushden, Northamptonshire, U.K.: Sceptre Press, 1973);

RSVP (Knotting, Bedfordshire, U.K.: Sceptre Press, 1974);

Yet (New Rochelle, N.Y: Elizabeth Press, 1974);

0/1 (New Rochelle, N.Y: Elizabeth Press, 1974);

For Dear Life (Los Angeles: Black Sparrow Press, 1975);

Once and For All: Poems for William Bronk (New Rochelle, N.Y: Elizabeth Press, 1975);

Unless (Kyoto, Japan: Origin Press, 1975);

Any How (Japan: Kisetsusha, 1976);

Leda & the Swan (Paris: Emmanuel Hozguard, 1976);

The Art of Poetry and Two Other Essays (Santa Barbara: Black Sparrow Press, 1976);

For the Asking (Los Angeles: Black Sparrow Press, 1976);

's (New Rochelle, N.Y.: Elizabeth Press, 1976);

William Bronk: An Essay (Carrboro, N.C.: Truck Press, 1976);

Meed (Kyoto, Japan: Origin Press, 1976);

Belongings (Boston: Origin Press, 1977);

Gratis (Boston: Origin Press, 1977);

Antics (Boston: Origin Press, 1977);

Word for Word: Essays on the Arts of Language (Santa Barbara: Black Sparrow Press, 1977);

At Their Word: Essays on the Arts of Language (Santa Barbara: Black Sparrow Press, 1978);

So (Boston: Origin Press, 1978);

Of Course (Boston: Origin Press, 1978);

Auspices (Milwaukee: Pentagram Press, 1979);

In the Event (Bangor, Maine: Theodore Press, 1979);

Tabernacle (Boston: Origin Press, 1980);

Manna (West Branch, Iowa: Toothpaste Press, 1981);

Identities (Vineyard, Maine: Salt-Works Press, 1981);

At Least (Iowa City: Corycian Press, 1982);

Projectile, Percussive, Prospective: The Making of a Voice (Portree, Isle of Skye, Scotland: Aquila, 1982);

Tu: Poems (West Branch, Iowa: Toothpaste Press, 1983);

Aegis: Selected Poems, 1970–1980 (Barrytown, N.Y: Station Hill Press, 1983);

At A Loss (Brattleboro, Vt.: Longhouse, 1984);

At Once (Kyoto, Japan: Origin Press, 1985);

Essay on Poetry (Elmwood, Conn.: Potes & Poets Press, 1985);

Three Poems (Minneapolis: Coffee House Press & the MCBA 'Dirty Works' Class, 1985);

In Particular: Poems New and Selected (Dunvegan, Ontario: Cormorant Books, 1986);

The Promise The Premise (London: Northern Lights, 1986);

Root Song (Elmwood, Conn.: Potes and Poets Press, 1986);

And the Word (Minneapolis: Coffee House Press, 1987);

No News (Tokyo: Tels Press, 1987);

Tel 2 Let (Charleston, Ill.: Tel-Let, 1988);

The Faith of Poetry (Green River, Vt.: Longhouse, 1989);

Yea (Los Angeles: Lapis, 1989);

Of, 2 volumes (Venice, Cal.: Lapis, 1990);

All Yours (New York: Cooper Union for the Advancement of Science & Art, 1991);

Nothing to Nothing (Charleston, Ill.: Tel-Let, 1991);

Afterword as Preface (Green River, Vt.: Longhouse, 1991);

Where Were We Now: Essays and Postscriptum (Seattle: Broken Moon, 1991);

No News (Sedona, Ariz.: Saru Press, 1992);

How Now: Poems (Boulder, Colo.: Cityful Press, 1995);

Tributary, by Corman and Beauford Delaney (New York: Edgewise Press, 1998).

OTHER: Theocritus, *A Thanksgiving Eclogue* (Corona, N.Y.: Sparrow Magazine, 1954);

Ferrini and Others, by Corman and others (Berlin: Gerhardt, 1955);

Matsuo Bashō, *Cool Melon*, translated by Corman (Ashland, Mass.: Origin Press, 1959);

Kusano Shimpei, *Selected Frogs*, translated by Corman and Kamaike Susumu (Kyoto, Japan: Origin Press, 1963);

Translations from the Spanish, translated by Corman and Clayton Eshleman (Reno, Nev.: Richard Morris, 1967);

Bashō, *Back Roads to Far Towns*, translated by Corman and Kamaike Susumu (New York: Grossman, 1968);

Shimpei, *Frogs & Others*, translated by Corman (New York: Grossman, 1969);

Francis Ponge, *Things*, translated by Corman (New York: Grossman, 1971);

Rene Char, *Leaves of Hypnos*, translated by Corman (New York: Grossman, 1973);

Phillippe Jaccottet, *Breathings*, translated by Corman (New York: Grossman, 1974);

The Gist of Origin, edited by Corman (New York: Grossman, 1975);

Peerless Mirror: Twenty Tanka from The Manyoshu,
  translated by Corman (Cambridge, Mass.:
  Firefly Press, 1981);
One Man's Moon: Fifty Haiku by Bashō, Buson, Issa, Ha-
  kuin, Shiki, Santoka, translated by Corman
  (Frankfort, Ky.: Gnomon Press, 1984);
Shimpei, *Asking Myself/Answering Myself,* translated
  by Corman and Susumu Kamaike (New York:
  New Directions, 1984);
Lorine Niedecker, *The Granite Pail: The Selected Poems*
  of Lorine Niedecker, edited, with a preface, by
  Corman (San Francisco: North Point Press,
  1985);
Ryunosuke Akutagawa, *Hell Screen, Cogwheels and a*
  Fool's Life, translated by Corman, Takashi Ko-
  jiba, and Will Petersen (New York: Eridanos
  Library/Marsilio Publishers, 1988);
Born of a Dream: Fifty Haiku by Bashō, Buson, Taigi,
  Issa, Shiki, translated by Corman (Frankfort,
  Ky.: Gnomon Press, 1989);
Bashō, *Little Enough: Forty-Nine Haiku,* translated by
  Corman (Frankfort, Ky.: Gnomon Press,
  1991);
Kusano, *Mt. Fuji: Selected Poems 1943–1986,* intro-
  duction by Corman (Rochester, Minn.: Katy-
  did Books, 1991);
Santoka Taneda, *Walking into the Wind,* translated by
  Corman (Tiburon, Cal.: Cadmus, 1994);
Marcel Cohen, *The Peacock Emperor Moth,* translated
  by Corman (Providence, R.I.: Burning Deck,
  1995);
Bashō, *Back Roads to Far Towns,* translation and notes
  by Corman and Kamaike Susumu (Hopewell,
  N.J.: Ecco Press, 1996).

Cid (Sidney) Corman is adamant about some
things. One is that he is the most prolific writer in
human history. And one would have to think long
and hard to find a writer of equal output. More than
one hundred titles now exist—poetry, prose, and
translations—and dozens of other manuscripts sit in
his house in Kyoto, Japan, books for which he explains he has neither the time, means, nor interest in
looking for a publisher. Corman's prolificness is the
result of writing *literally* every day—even ill—for fifty
years now. Whereas Corman's output borders on
the legendary, he is perhaps better known for his
launching and editorship of *Origin,* a magazine instrumental in nurturing a community of writers in
the Ezra Pound/William Carlos Williams line
whose high commitment to poetry did not necessarily translate into high visibility. Charles Olson, William Bronk, Louis Zukofsky, and Robert Creeley
are but some of the key figures who benefited from
the forum that *Origin* provided. For fifty years Cid

Corman has figured as an important model of con-
stancy, integrity, and gritty decorum, an attractive
alternative to the often self-serving excesses and
fads that punctuate twentieth-century American poetry.

Born in Boston in 1924, Cid Corman attended
Boston Latin School, "a tough competitive scene,"
as he recalls, and entered Tufts University in 1941
with the vague idea of following his uncle "in the direction of law and perhaps diplomacy." It was, however, as he puts it, "a combination of a growing interest in poetry and the reading of all of Ruskin's
Modern Painters (with its glowing descriptions of the
Campagna and of Turner) that turned me on." Ex-
empted from the draft due to poor eyesight and a
kidney ailment, Corman graduated magna cum
laude in 1945 with the conviction that writing was to
be his life's work:

> I knew at once, though the writing I did was wretched
> even when publishable, that this was my world–my
> thing: not only what I could do and intended to do ex-
> tremely well, but what I most wanted: work that was a
> constant and was play also.

Steered to the University of Michigan by John
Ciardi, Corman studied under Roy W. Cowden but
had little patience with the "stubborn stupidities" of
the academy and "opted out" of the prescribed
path–a job on the faculty after completion of his
master of arts degree: "Poetry was my work–not
playing teacher." What followed was a disappoint-
ing stint at the University of North Carolina at
Chapel Hill (where he had gone to fulfill his dream
of writing verse drama) and brief stays in New Orleans and Los Angeles before he returned to Boston
in 1948 bent on forging a poetic community.

Wanting "poetry out in the community," Corman organized discussion groups in the local public
libraries and, through his friend Nat Hentoff, "the
voice of jazz in Boston" for radio station WMEX,
acquired a fifteen-minute poetry slot that aired
every Saturday evening from 1949 to 1951. Among
those who read their work on "This Is Poetry" were
Creeley, Archibald MacLeish, John Crowe Ransom,
Richard Wilbur, John Ciardi, Theodore Roethke,
Stephen Spender, Richard Eberhart, and Vincent
Ferrini. Corman also played recordings of Olson,
Pound, T. S. Eliot, and James Joyce.

By this time, 1949–1950, Creeley had commissioned Corman to gather material for a magazine he
proposed to begin. From this process the work of
Bronk came to their attention. At this time Olson
was also winning a reputation: the first Maximus
poem was circulating, and Creeley spoke glowingly

*Cover for Corman's 1965 book, poems influenced by Objectivism
and the Japanese Noh tradition*

When Corman left America in 1954 to study at the Sorbonne on a Fulbright grant, he had between five hundred and seven hundred poems published in more than one hundred magazines. Individual volumes of his work began to appear regularly in the mid 1950s under the Origin Press imprint. Of these early volumes, perhaps the most important is *Sun Rock Man* (1962), the product of an eighteen-month teaching assignment in Matera, Italy, that followed his stay in Paris.

Sun Rock Man is the volume in which Corman emerges into his own and finds what he calls "a confident vein of poetry, which didn't occur until Europe essentially." Therein he clarifies certain themes that are to dominate his subsequent collections. The pervading theme of the mature work is the struggle of the individual to reconcile self to the human predicament. This reconciliation, in Corman's terms, requires the negotiation of seeming opposites: on the one hand, an acceptance of humankind's powerlessness to impose a satisfactory order or meaning on an unresponsive and indifferent universe, and on the other, the need for humankind to confirm its place and its worth. In this existential quest, the poet probes notions of identity, time, and death in an attempt to delineate more clearly the human situation and offer fleeting insights as compensations that allay what might otherwise become a suffocating nihilism.

Corman had transplanted himself from Matera (via Florence) to Kyoto when *Sun Rock Man* came out, though it was written entirely in Italy. There, through Gary Snyder and Will Petersen, he had landed a university teaching position. He was also busy publishing the first collections of Theodore Enslin and Snyder, and Zukofsky's *"A" 1–12* under the Origin Press imprint. Perhaps most significant to his own poetry, however, was his introduction to Kamaike Susumu, with whom he was later to translate such Japanese poets as Bashō and Kusano Shimpei. Corman notes that "What seemed at first—before I began to probe—an easy task ended up requiring eight years." The volume includes keen observations of people going about their daily routines, routines that, as individual poems progress, become situated within larger philosophical questions of time and place, as is the case in "The Labors":

Men work. Usually
hardly at all. In the hills
they lazy about in gangs,
let machines grind rock to gravel.

In tandem, but freely,
they shovel buckets full and

of the ideas in "Objective Verse," then near completion. However, when Corman returned from a monthlong stay at Yaddo that summer, he learned of the collapse of Creeley's plans for the magazine and decided that it was "time for a fresh effort in the little mag world." Encouraged by Evelyn Shoolman, a wealthy local patron of the arts who promised funds to get him started, Corman used some of the material gathered for the Creeley venture to launch *Origin*. The first series ran for twenty numbers over five years (spring 1951 through winter 1957) and included the work of such individuals as Olson, Creeley, Bronk, Robert Duncan, Paul Blackburn, Larry Eigner, Denise Levertov, Theodore Enslin, Irving Layton, Gael Turnbull, as well as Corman.

heave them up to the shoulder
and up into the truck beside.

Slowly rock is eaten
away. Slowly the men eat
up the day. Slowly the day
dies. The truck pulls out. Rock remains.

On a ridge above them
a shepherd crowding some grass
lets his flock browse corralled by
only a barking bounding dog.

Beyond them clouds go on
covering sky. Somewhere the
sun descends. A dog sheep men
rock hills collect between them night.

However, the poem is more than a tourist's jottings, its power emerging from such astute rhythmical decisions as the announcement of the "lazy" pace by the initial line break and the acceleration and gathering of the players into the viewer's collective vision by the unpunctuated final lines.

There are also poems that, in their brevity and suggestiveness, reflect the confluence of Objectivist and Japanese influence. The shorter lines increase the white space around the poem so that individual words—particularly prepositions and participles—emerge renewed and demand attention. For instance, in "The Incident":

on the train
coming down

reaching a bag
down from the rack
on my shoulder
the hand

naturally
of a priest[.]

Or in "The Transaction":

an old woman
holding her black
neckerchief out

an old man
picking the two
loose ends up

pours walnuts
out of his brass
pan into a

sack[.]

In a 1990 article for *Shadow Play* Jan Bender associates the emphasis on white space in Corman's work

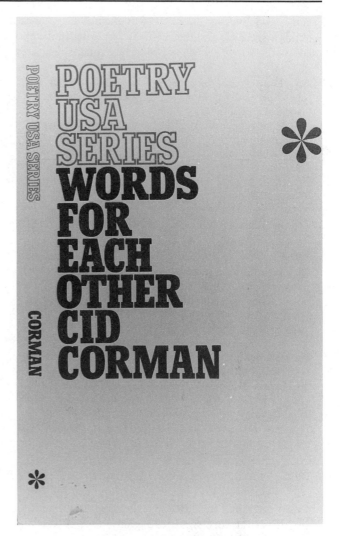

Dust jacket for one of Corman's 1967 books, the first collection of his poetry published in Great Britain

with the role of silence in Japanese Noh theater: "The blank part, the silence, the *ma,* where nothing is sounded, that is, where the nothing is sounded, is thought to be the core of the expression and where the true interest lies." The association of Corman's poems with the oral Noh is an important one, because Corman has championed the oral poem since the mid 1950s. He is adamant that all his poems are meant to be voiced, because the oral delivery underscores the transience of our experience. As he puts it in "The Genitive Case" from *Word for Word: Essays on the Arts of Language* (1977), "We are dying. . . . The very words here imply that continually and ARE as instruments of that fact and act and only." However, acceptance of this fact or plight functions as a necessary prelude to a heightened experiencing of the relational quality of life and the interpenetration of all things sentient and nonsentient. As is the case in "The Incident" and "The Transaction," the poems are often satori poems, recording fleeting moments of insight into this mysterious oneness, and their oral delivery is intended to evoke in the audience a similar awareness and the requisite response. In the preface to *Words for Each Other* (1967), he explains:

> The poems of this book, insofar as they succeed, will need no explanation, will find themselves in you as resourceful breath.
> Something in them, in the sounded meanings joined here, should feed something in you that merits sharing—a little life that feels beyond itself the dying implied in every word, in every thing, in every legend man has devised, in ache in ache in ache, invoking the only judgement man is worthy of: love.

And in "Art as Center" (1966), also in *Word for Word,* he writes,

> Art is the most endurable projection of realization given man to feel more fully what he is and what he is of.
> This may not be much, but it is all and enough that man is given and is possible: such nature as stays open to all else that shares the predicament.
> So the man making art is the man making life come alive more truly for others; he knows what all men come to know with more or less acuteness: that each day and each night he is dying. And he is that one who steeped in the dying finding song, enduring sound of sense, can and does put out himself beyond himself for the only meaning: you.

The poems testify to the need to expand beyond the self, to the realization that, as he insists in "Beckett" (1966), "The situation is OF, the genitive case. . . . One is never out of—just as one is always and eternally a part of and interpenetrable, wholly, egregiously, penetrable." It is therefore significant that *Sun Rock Man* concludes with "La Cantina," wherein the peasants' endurance is ennobled and celebrated in the drinking and singing that allow a transcendence of their dismal situations. The old men turn the passing of a friend into a pronouncement of a collective spirit that expands to include their scattered brethren:

> An old friend has gone, a dear friend.
> They gather in the back room in the cantina
> with roast lamb, tomatoes, olives
> and a huge loaf of brown bread.
>
> There are no women. Only a pale angel
> in ancient papier-mâché,
> the trumpet faintly gold at the lips,
> leans over them from destruction.
>
> They drain their pitchers of coarse red wine,
> the wine breaks into and fills their hearts,
> their voices as one burst from their mouths
> ascending. The angel does not hear,
>
> but the men in the central hall, they hear
> the cheer and the beat beaten
> along the long table. And the men,

> old men, old peasants from the backlands,
>
> old men come out of the rock,
> recognize the cry for a friend who has gone
> and they, out of the same wine, the same bread,
> break forth in mountainous song.

Having found his main thematic concerns early in his career, Corman gradually refined his development as a poet toward the essentials of experience, identity, and language. *0/1* (1974) is comprised of poems that record the difficulty of forging relations; for instance, "The Con":

> It doesn't matter
> the money I gave
> him, he got from me,
>
> weeping at the door
> unanswered elsewhere
> wanting help, he claimed,
>
> a boy, tinct of black,
> promising return,
> providing a name
>
> and address, but that
> he never allowed
> himself to hear what
>
> I was trying to
> get across to him,
> that even my life
>
> was his, as a friend,
> if he wanted one.
> He wanted money.

Other poems exhibit the struggle to escape polarization toward a synthesis of the subject-object position:

> What you are
> I am. As if
> to admit
>
> the look in the
> mirror of
> the mirror. Not
>
> nature to
> be upheld—but
> seen for what
>
> it is: unseen
> unless as
> an edifice.

And still others recount the tendencies toward the figurative with which the poet wrestles:

VENELLES

The sky appears, far back at first,
hanging behind the mountain ridge
piled up by trees whose green persists,

though the land left fallow through fall
burns yellow. The great air opens
gradually parcels of blue,

but as if that were too modern
clouds come on like tumbling wagons
windily widening crowding

West. Such steady vast progressions,
mowing and mown, suggests a barn
whose bins will never swell too high

with hay. But just then, beyond me,
a friend shouts up: "Hey! it's going
to rain!" And I look out again.

In this poem, which is reminiscent of both Wilbur's
"Praise in Summer" and Creeley's "I Know A Man,"
the mellifluous description attests to man's propensity to interpret and frame and regulate his experience of the indecipherable other, a propensity that
necessitates that he "look out again" with clearer
eyes and with language made so spare that it includes nothing but the essentials. That this is a difficult, if not impossible, prospect is perhaps nowhere
evidenced more clearly than in "The Gem":

> Morion. The stone
> that looks black, made smooth
> age after age and
>
> small, as if some smoke
> were embedded in
> crystal, ash water
>
> Apache tear. As
> nearly Arp as Arp
> is. Nothing extra,
>
> all edge and no edge,
> solid heart. What one
> offers another.

That the stone itself not only operates as a metaphor
for the poem but also requires the further comparisons to achieve definition is illustrative of the inherent difficulties Corman investigates. Corman's
skeletal poems typically enact this distrust of rhetoric, the reliance on brief lines and pared-down vocabulary reminiscent of Williams, but also of Oppen, Creeley, and Bronk.

   The 1980s witnessed no ebbing in the flow of
volumes appearing under Corman's name. The bet-

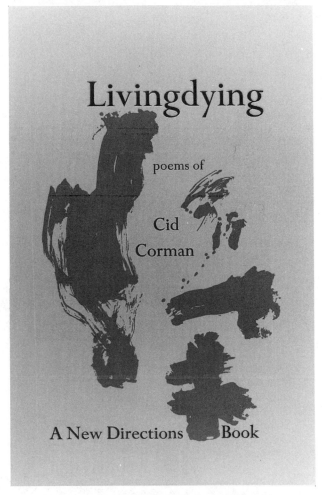

*Title page for Corman's 1970 collection of minimalist poems,
which Alicia Ostriker called reminiscent "of other arts in
their purity"*

ter poems continue to investigate the major themes
but include a refreshing degree of self-examination,
as is the case in these two examples from *Root Song*
(1986):

> So much more
> than this is
> this. And yet
>
> how say it,
> how expect
> it to stand
>
> beyond self
> within this
> emptiness?
>
> . . . .
>
> What the hell
> do we think

we're doing

What am I–
to be clear–
up to here?

The Spirit
binds us and
releases

us. I am
trying to
say no more

than that I'm
trying to
say no more.

It is, perhaps, only natural that during the last few years Corman has written more poems that reflect over a life and a career in poetry. In "Nationality" from *All Yours* (1991), the theme of anonymity versus arbitrary categorizations is delivered in a retrospective mood:

I suppose I am
American though
most of my life now

has been in Japan.
I feel a little
of both and a lot

of Neither. I like
to believe I am
a human being

without being too
proud of that–knowing
something too much of

our history–and
another creature
of this planet whose

unique nature and
situation has
permitted my fact.

"The Testing," from the same volume, takes on a similar cast:

I have never felt
any need to prove
myself a man. The

fact has been much too
obvious–more an
embarrassment than

a pride. and to test
myself or any

one else not only

has seemed futile and
mean but meaningless–
for living is such

a dying and just
to be human in
any helpful sense

miraculous–what
we credit God with
or even this sky.

To conclude, however, that Corman has reached a point of retirement would be naive. When asked recently what he is currently up to, Corman responded that at age seventy he is working full time at poetry, turning out a volume a day. The first two volumes of *Of,* his magnum opus, appeared under the Lapis Press imprint in 1990, and the remaining three volumes await a publisher. *Of* is one book in five volumes, each volume comprising about 750 poems. The first two volumes exhibit a clarity of expression that is stunningly challenging. The major concerns persist but are delivered so cleanly and simply that one is startled into recognition of a writer so at one with his craft that the poems seem to well up of their own accord. The relationship among language-speaker-listener-existence throbs into life as the particulars of speech–noun, article, verb, and pronoun–unhinge and remake themselves in "The Disappearing Act":

You repeat a word–
a–word–long enough–
long–enough–and it

insists on being
nothing–the nothing
it is. And the word–

whatever it is–
is another–word–
repeating you. *You.*

In "Speaking of Yesterday" the distinction between reader-writer is collapsed as fixed notions of time dissolve in the writing-reading process:

Tomorrow
promises
never to

come–but who
can trust what
today says?

The aptly titled "Syntax" elevates what might have been a mere descriptive noticing to a plumbing of the interpenetration of objects, Corman's deft syntactical sense exploding notions of cause and effect and luring the reader-listener into the mystery of event:

> Wind
> the window shakes
> and rattles
>
> Each
> objecting to
> the other.

The inanimate becomes an enlivened microcosm as the active intelligence registers it as both "piece / and all of" in "The Puzzle":

> You merely
> touch the piece
> and all of
>
> a sudden
> it seems to
> have a place
>
> in the whole
> or so it seems
> to want to.

If Corman's poetic output over the years testifies to a single-minded, dogged pursuit, his editorship of *Origin* does nothing to contradict such a picture. The introduction to *The Gist of Origin* (1975) is instructive as to the struggles of this little magazine from its inception in 1951 to the end of the third series in January 1971. Two subsequent series have since emerged, although the fifth series was aborted after six issues. Economic and organizational problems plagued the magazine from the outset. However, Corman was never easily deterred. If in Florence in the late 1950s his regular two-hour meditations on a late self-portrait by Rembrandt convinced him that he, like the artist, "could live, in the face of whatever might come," then his editorship of *Origin* gave him ample opportunity to test his resolve. The difficulties with the first series are representative of how many balls Corman had in the air at any given time. Unforeseen medical expenses prevented the early patron Shoolman from continuing funding beyond an initial $550. The "fabulous list of potential subscribers and supporters" subsequently compiled by Olson to remedy the situation, a list which included "amongst his friends and acquaintances, Charlie Chaplin, a number of well-known senators and congressmen, composers, artists, dancers, and one of Hemingway's wives," produced little in the way of assistance. Corman's answer was to find a cheaper mode of production: he abandoned "regular printing for varitype and photo offset." When even this switch proved too costly, Corman was forced to look elsewhere for printers, first to Villiers Press in London and later to a local printer Creeley had discovered in Mallorca. These maneuverings were not without their pitfalls, however. At one point a friend of Creeley absconded with the funds, an episode that delayed the appearance of the issue and, as Corman tells it, "aged me rapidly." Subsequent strategies for keeping the magazine in print included negotiating deals with university libraries. The second series was financed by selling manuscripts and letters from the first series to the University of Texas and Indiana University. This sale enabled Corman to "give away the magazine." As he put it in 1960:

> *Origin* is not for sale; it can be had for love, as it happens, not for money. Not that anyone wanting to offer money to help, coming with love also, will be repulsed. But anyone who wishes to receive the magazine may have it by writing me and letting me know. But anyone must write me, concernedly, for him or herself only. What sharing occurs upon receipt is one's private affair. Requests will be honored for a year . . . and then must be renewed. Priority will be given to those who demonstrate concern for the material, which doesn't mean, of necessity, agreement with it.

However, the importance of *Origin* extends beyond its testimony to Corman's perseverance. The agenda of the magazine Corman spelled out as follows in the initial issue of *Origin:*

> ORIGIN
>
> is devoted to giving adequate outlet
>   to those new/unknown writers
> who have shown maturity/insight
>   into their medium
>
>   to giving
>   the push to creative minds, to
>   demonstrate the going concerns, di-
>   rections of contemporary
>   creativity.

Among those who benefited from this "adequate outlet" was Zukofsky. Corman met Zukofsky for the first time in Florence in the summer of 1957, and a correspondence ensued. As Corman explains in the introduction to *The Gist of Origin,* his subsequent decision to feature Zukofsky in the second series of the magazine was designed to remedy the fact that although Zukofsky "had already produced a remarkable body of work, most of it was hard to come by and unknown." Corman wanted "to bring his work to the attention of his peers and other younger poets." Nor was Zukofsky the sole recipient of such benevolence:

Cover for a special Corman issue of the little magazine Madrona *(December 1975)*

"There were others, like Snyder and Lorine Niedecker, who also warranted more ample presentation." Olson, Zukofsky, Creeley, Bronk, Duncan,
Niedecker, and Eigner, to name but a few, made significant appearances in *Origin*. This is not to say, however, that relations were always easy among the contributors. Corman explains that "much of the fiercest
criticism I've received as an editor has come from
those I published objecting to other work I've published." However, the emphasis was on "the continuity and relation of writers," and Corman industriously
kept the switchboard humming:

> As on my radio show I had made a point of transmitting
> all comments that came in and seemed to me of any use to
> the poets involved, so with the magazine I copied out com-
> ments on contributors to pass them on to them. I made a
> conscious effort to bring many of the writers into active re-
> lation with each other—not as a school or group, but for
> mutual stimulation, exchange of thoughts, community of
> feeling. Most were at considerable distance from one an-

other, so that direct contact was either infrequent or
quite unlikely.

To trace and assess the development of Cid Corman's career is a precarious and potentially giddy
proposition, given his fifty-year insistence on escaping
restrictive notions of progression and evaluation in his
poetry. Writers of short reviews have typically emphasized the overt associations with Japanese art
forms (and not without good reason), often simultaneously contextualizing the work within a tradition of
what Robert J. Griffin in a 1970 article for *The Nation*
calls "the skinny poem." Alicia Ostricker's appraisal of
Livingdying (1970) in a 1972 article for *Partisan Review* is
representative: "The pure language, in minimal lines
like those of Williams or Creeley, makes one think of
other arts in their purity: a clean tone of harpsichord
music, or flute, or lute, or Matisse colors, or *sumi* painting, or the Zen archer, shooting well." Those with a
little more space to fill have unraveled some of the

subtleties of those associations. Michael Heller in a 1976 article for *Parnassus* extends Corman's revised notion of selfhood and its relation to the "nothing" into a discussion of the parallels between Corman's geographical self-exile and the universal human exile at the center of the poems. Jan Bender in a 1990 article for *Shadow Play* elucidates the structural and thematic echoes of the Noh program in the poems, paying particular attention to the role of the voiced event and the importance of *Yūgen,* that suggestiveness and mystery "causing us to feel something." Clive Faust, also writing for the 1990 issue of *Shadow Play* dedicated to Corman's work, attends to the religious element in the poems, suggesting an affinity between Corman's "concentration on minute detail," his reluctance to resort to commentary, and the Objectivists' concept of poem as event, the attempt "to trace the act of the world upon the consciousness," as Oppen explains it in his notebooks.

Each Corman volume is a record of a life lived in and of the world, and no secondhand account can adequately trace that fact. Each volume is such a refusal to separate and judge that assessment is akin to squeezing the ball so tightly that it squirts from our grasp or watching it so closely that we forget to catch it. Corman would have us see it for a moment with our fingertips.

Early in his fifty-year career Corman found his subject—the plight of the individual—and his progress has been one of paring in pursuit of the essentials. To plot a chronology of influences would be reductive. Imagist, Objectivist, New American, Eastern—traces of these traditions surface in the poems—but Corman's importance rests finally on what he has done with them. Williams's keen eye for the small revealing detail; Oppen's scrupulous attention to the line break, syntactical maneuver, and the smallest of words; and Bronk's persistent probing of the human situation converge with Corman's study of Eastern forms and his belief in the primacy of the voiced word.

In a world where spectacle and self-promotion too often mute meditation and sincerity, Corman has resisted fads. It is perhaps a sign of our times that the final three volumes of *Of* currently await a publisher at his home in Kyoto; it is certainly a testimony to what is remarkably healthy in twentieth-century letters that Corman's persistent voice refuses to roll over and die in an extended confessional whine. Hayden Carruth contends that Corman hits about 10 percent of the time, a conservative estimate. Nonetheless, considering Corman's output, even that seems an impressive average. The magnitude of Corman's life work is certainly a challenge for the reader, but a challenge that rewards the careful reader.

Letters:

Charles Olson and Cid Corman: Complete Correspondence 1950–1964, 2 volumes, edited by George Evans (Orono, Maine: National Poetry Foundation, University of Maine, 1987).

Bibliography:

John Taggart, *A Bibliography of Works by Cid Corman* (New Rochelle, N.Y.: Elizabeth Press, 1975).

References:

Jan Bender, "The Experience of Poetry," *Shadow Play,* special issue on Corman, 1 (Spring 1990): 58–66;

Hayden Carruth, "Once and for All," *New York Times Book Review,* 16 May 1976, p. 12;

Clive Faust, "Minims and Semi-breves on Corman," *Shadow Play,* special issue on Corman, 1 (Spring 1990): 71–77;

Robert J. Griffin, "They Lick the Platter Clean," *Nation* (20 July 1970): 53–55;

Michael Heller, "Sounding Toward a Greater Speechlessness," *Parnassus,* 4 (Spring/Summer 1976): 96–110;

Madrona, special issue on Corman, 3 (December 1975);

Alicia Ostricker, "Of Being Numerous," *Partisan Review,* 39 (Spring 1972): 270–271.

Papers:

Collections of Corman's papers are housed at the University of Texas, Austin; Kent State University; Indiana University, Bloomington; New York University; Syracuse University; Boston University; Simon Fraser University, Burnaby, British Columbia; State University of New York, Buffalo; and the Berg Collection of the New York Public Library.

James Dickey

(2 February 1923 – 19 January 1997)

Ronald Baughman
University of South Carolina

See also the Dickey entries in *DLB 5: American Poets Since World War II; DLB Yearbook: 1982; DLB Yearbook: 1993; and DS 7: Modern American Poets: James Dickey, Robert Frost, Marianne Moore.*

BOOKS: *Into the Stone and Other Poems,* in *Poets of Today VII,* edited by John Hall Wheelock (New York: Scribners, 1960), pp. 33–92;

Drowning with Others (Middletown, Conn.: Wesleyan University Press, 1962);

Helmets (Middletown, Conn.: Wesleyan University Press, 1964; London: Longmans, Green, 1964);

The Suspect in Poetry (Madison, Minn.: Sixties Press, 1964);

Two Poems of the Air (Portland, Ore.: Centicore Press, 1964);

Buckdancer's Choice (Middletown, Conn.: Wesleyan University Press, 1965);

Poems 1957–1967 (Middletown, Conn.: Wesleyan University Press, 1967; London: Rapp & Carroll, 1967);

Spinning the Crystal Ball (Washington, D.C.: Library of Congress, 1967);

Babel to Byzantium: Poets and Poetry Now (New York: Farrar, Straus & Giroux, 1968);

Metaphor as Pure Adventure (Washington, D.C.: Library of Congress, 1968);

Deliverance (Boston: Houghton Mifflin, 1970; London: Hamilton, 1970);

The Eye-Beaters, Blood, Victory, Madness, Buckhead and Mercy (Garden City, N.Y.: Doubleday, 1970; London: Hamilton, 1971);

Self-Interviews, recorded and edited by Barbara and James Reiss (Garden City, N.Y.: Doubleday, 1970);

Exchanges (Bloomfield Hills, Mich.: Bruccoli Clark, 1971);

Sorties (Garden City, N.Y.: Doubleday, 1971);

Jericho: The South Beheld, text by Dickey, illustrations by Hubert Shuptrine (Birmingham, Ala.: Oxmoor House, 1974);

James Dickey (photograph © Terry Parke)

The Zodiac (limited edition, Bloomfield Hills, Mich. & Columbia, S.C.: Bruccoli Clark, 1976; trade edition, Garden City, N.Y.: Doubleday, 1976);

The Strength of Fields [single poem] (Bloomfield Hills, Mich. & Columbia, S.C.: Bruccoli Clark, 1977);

God's Images: The Bible, a New Vision, text by Dickey, etchings by Marvin Hayes (Birmingham, Ala.: Oxmoor House, 1977);

The Enemy from Eden (Northridge, Cal.: Lord John Press, 1978);

Tucky the Hunter, text by Dickey, illustrations by Marie Angel (New York: Crown, 1978; London: Macmillan, 1979);

Veteran Birth: The Gadfly Poems 1947–1949 (Winston-Salem, N.C.: Palaemon Press, 1978);

In Pursuit of the Grey Soul (Bloomfield Hills, Mich. & Columbia, S.C.: Bruccoli Clark, 1978);

Head-Deep in Strange Sounds (Winston-Salem, N.C.: Palaemon Press, 1978);

The Water-Bug's Mittens: Ezra Pound: What We Can Use (Moscow: University of Idaho, 1979; Bloomfield Hills, Mich. & Columbia, S.C.: Bruccoli Clark, 1980);

The Strength of Fields [collection] (Garden City, N.Y.: Doubleday, 1979);

Scion (Deerfield, Mass.: Deerfield Press / Dublin, Ireland: Deerfield Press/Gallery Press, 1980);

The Early Motion (Middletown, Conn.: Wesleyan University Press, 1981);

Falling, May Day Sermon, and Other Poems (Middletown, Conn.: Wesleyan University Press, 1981);

The Starry Place Between the Antlers: Why I Live in South Carolina (Bloomfield Hills, Mich. & Columbia, S.C.: Bruccoli Clark, 1981);

Deliverance [screenplay] (Carbondale & Edwardsville: Southern Illinois University Press, 1982);

Puella (Garden City, N.Y.: Doubleday, 1982);

Värmland (Winston-Salem, N.C.: Palaemon Press, 1982);

The Central Motion: Poems, 1968–1979 (Middletown, Conn.: Wesleyan University Press, 1983);

False Youth: Four Seasons (Dallas: Pressworks, 1983);

Night Hurdling: Poems, Essays, Conversations, Commencements, and Afterwords (Bloomfield Hills, Mich. & Columbia, S.C.: Bruccoli Clark, 1983);

Bronwen, the Traw, and the Shape-Shifter, text by Dickey, illustrations by Richard Jesse Watson (San Diego, New York & London: Bruccoli Clark/Harcourt Brace Jovanovich, 1986);

Alnilam (Garden City, N.Y.: Doubleday, 1987);

Wayfarer: A Voice from the Southern Mountains, text by Dickey, photographs by William A. Bake (Birmingham, Ala.: Oxmoor House, 1988);

The Eagle's Mile (Hanover, N.H. & London: Wesleyan University Press/University Press of New England, 1990);

Southern Light, text by Dickey, photographs by James Valentine (Birmingham, Ala.: Oxmoor House, 1991);

The Whole Motion: Collected Poems, 1945–1992 (Hanover, N.H. & London: Wesleyan University Press/University Press of New England, 1992);

To the White Sea (Boston & New York: Houghton Mifflin, 1993);

Striking In: The Early Notebooks of James Dickey, edited by Gordon Van Ness (Columbia & London: University of Missouri Press, 1996).

MOTION PICTURES: *Deliverance,* screenplay by Dickey, Warner Bros., 1972;

Call of the Wild, screenplay by Dickey, Charles Fries, 1976.

VIDEOS: *Writer's Workshop,* videocassette including interview with Dickey, produced by University of South Carolina and the South Carolina ETV Network, 1992;

"The Sacred Words: The Elements of Poetry," *Literary Visions,* videocassette including interview with Dickey, produced by Maryland Public Television, 1992;

James Dickey at 70: A Tribute, script and narration by Ronald Baughman, photographs by Gene Crediford, produced by University of South Carolina Department of Media Arts, September 1993.

OTHER: Yevgeny Yevtushenko, *Stolen Apples,* includes twelve poems adapted by Dickey (Garden City, N.Y.: Doubleday, 1971);

Ronald Baughman, "James Dickey," in *Dictionary of Literary Biography Documentary Series,* volume 7: *Modern American Poets,* edited by Karen Rood (Detroit, New York, Fort Lauderdale & London: Bruccoli Clark Layman/Gale, 1989), pp. 3–126–includes excerpts from Dickey's journals, letters, and other private papers;

"Lightnings or Visuals," *South Atlantic Review,* 57 (January 1992): 1–14.

James Dickey was a visionary poet who sought transformation of the Self in order to live as fully as possible. Immersed in death encounters, he formulated a poetic vision dramatizing his heightened sense of renewal to experience, to life. At the same time he recognized that death and the dead were his constant companions, and he consequently tried to maintain a balance between life and death by connecting with the Other. He attempted to transcend his station as a human being through an "exchange of identities," as H. L. Weatherby notes in his *Sewanee Review* essay "The Way of Exchange in James Dickey's Poetry." This exchange of identities–with other people, with animals, and with inanimate objects–became a means of acquiring their knowledge, of absorbing new and more-expansive points of view. These concerns and this process were central

Dickey as a football player at Clemson A&M, fall 1942

first semester he enlisted in the U.S. Army Air Corps. From 1943 to 1945 he participated in approximately 100 combat missions as a member of the 418th Night Fighter Squadron in the South Pacific.

After the war Dickey enrolled at Vanderbilt University, a change in schools that marked his shift in interest from athletics to academics. At Vanderbilt, Dickey soon came to the attention of English professor Monroe Spears, who recognized his student's literary talent and guided him to major in English and philosophy and minor in astronomy. On 4 November 1948 Dickey married Maxine Syerson, with whom he would have two sons, Christopher and Kevin. In 1949 Dickey earned a B.A. degree in English, graduating magna cum laude, and in 1950 an M.A. His thesis was titled "Symbol and Image in the Short Poems of Herman Melville."

Dickey began his teaching career at Rice Institute in September 1950, but four months later he was recalled to active military duty in the training command of the U.S. Air Force during the Korean War. After completing his military obligations, he returned to Rice and began making journal entries toward a novel that thirty-six years later he would publish as *Alnilam* (1987).

In 1954 Dickey received a *Sewanee Review* Fellowship, with which he traveled to Europe and concentrated on writing poetry. A year later he moved to the University of Florida where, with the help of novelist and historian Andrew Lytle, he had obtained a teaching appointment. He resigned this position, however, in the spring of 1956 following a controversy arising from his reading of his poem "The Father's Body." Dickey then left Florida for New York; there he established a successful advertising career, first as a copywriter and later as an executive with McCann-Erickson. During the next three years Dickey was associated with a series of advertising agencies. He eventually returned to Atlanta where he created advertisements for such companies as Coca-Cola and Delta Air Lines.

While writing ad copy Dickey also added to his growing list of poetry publications and awards. In 1958 he received the Union League's Civic and Arts Foundation Prize from the Union League Club of Chicago for poems published in *Poetry: A Magazine of Verse*. A year later he won the Vachel Lindsay Prize and the Longview Foundation Award. A collection of his poetry was published as *Into the Stone and Other Poems* with work by Jon Swan and Paris Leary in *Poets of Today VII* (1960), and the following year he permanently abandoned his career in advertising. During 1961–1962 a Guggenheim Fellowship allowed Dickey to travel to Positano, Italy, where

to Dickey's poetry throughout his more than thirty-five years as a writer.

Born in Buckhead, Georgia, an affluent community then on the outskirts of Atlanta, James Lafayette Dickey, the second son of lawyer Eugene Dickey and Maibelle Swift Dickey, grew up with the knowledge that he was a "replacement child" for Eugene Jr., a brother who had died of meningitis. This early awareness of the relationship between death and life, reinforced by his combat experiences in early adulthood, contributed to his later poetic theme of living the Energized Life.

Dickey's high-school interests centered on athletics, particularly football and track. After graduating from North Fulton High in 1941, he attended Darlington School in Rome, Georgia, from 1941 to 1942. In the fall of 1942 he entered Clemson A & M (now Clemson University) where he played tailback on the freshman football squad, but at the end of his

he composed *Drowning with Others* (1962). In Positano, as he noted in his January 1992 *South Atlantic Review* essay "Lightnings or Visuals," his 1970 novel *Deliverance* also had its origins: "the whole of my novel *Deliverance* came from an image that appeared to me when I was half asleep in full sunlight after a picnic in Italy, where I was living at the time. . . . The image was that of a man standing at the top of a cliff: that, and no more. The picture was powerful and urgent, but I had no clue as to any meaning, if there was or could be one: one discovered, one assigned."

Dickey returned to the United States in 1962 and spent the next four years as a poet-in-residence at such schools as Reed College (1963–1964), San Fernando Valley State College (1964–1965), and the University of Wisconsin–Madison (1966). His collection *Helmets* appeared in 1964, and his recognition as a poet was heightened when he received the 1966 National Book Award for *Buckdancer's Choice* (1965), the Melville Cane Award from the Poetry Society of America, and a National Institute of Arts and Letters Award. Between 1966 and 1968 Dickey served as consultant in poetry for the Library of Congress. During that time his *Poems 1957–1967* (1967) and his collection of reviews and essays *Babel to Byzantium: Poets and Poetry Now* (1968) were published. In 1968 he was appointed poet-in-residence at the University of South Carolina, but because of contractual requirements with the Library of Congress, he did not begin his teaching position until the fall of 1969. In 1970 he was named First Carolina Professor of English at the University of South Carolina.

Dickey lived in Columbia, South Carolina, and taught at the University of South Carolina from 1969 to 1997. In this setting he produced many of his major works, including his popularly and critically acclaimed first novel, *Deliverance,* for which he also wrote the screenplay, suggested the musical theme "Duellin' Banjos," and acted the role of Sheriff Bullard in the Academy Award–nominated 1972 Warner Brothers movie. Other major Dickey works appearing during the early to mid 1970s were a poetry collection, *The Eye-Beaters, Blood, Victory, Madness, Buckhead and Mercy* (1970); two books on writing and the creative process, *Self-Interviews* (1970) and *Sorties* (1971); and a long poem, *The Zodiac* (1976). Dickey's first wife, Maxine, died in 1976, and that same year he married Deborah Dodson, with whom he had a daughter, Bronwen. Jimmy Carter invited Dickey to write and read a poem for the 1977 inaugural celebration in Washington, D.C. "The Strength of Fields," the poem Dickey wrote for that occasion, served as the title poem of his

Dickey in the South Pacific during World War II

1979 collection. *The Strength of Fields* was followed in 1982 by *Puella,* one of Dickey's most experimental poetry volumes, and in 1987 by *Alnilam,* his most ambitious novel. On 18 May 1988 Dickey was inducted into the fifty-member American Academy of Arts and Letters, and in 1989 he was selected a judge for the Yale Series of Younger Poets, a clear indication of his continuing importance to and influence on American writers. During his seventies Dickey remained a prolific, energetic writer: he produced his final collection of poetry, *The Eagle's Mile* (1990), and his third novel, *To the White Sea* (1993). From November 1994 to the time of his death in early 1997, Dickey endured serious health problems but continued writing and conducting classes at the University of South Carolina. He taught his last class on 14 January and on the following day was hospitalized for the last time. At the time of his death he was at work on *Crux,* a novel set during World War II, and was overseeing preliminary work on a movie adaptation of his novel *To the White Sea.*

Dickey explored consistent themes throughout his career, though these themes were addressed through an increasing complexity of vision. Simi-

Dickey reading to his sons, Kevin and Christopher, circa 1960

larly, his poetic techniques evolved from the polished "closed" forms (often encompassing a narrative thrust) of his first volumes to the looser, "associational," "open" forms (predominantly lyrical in nature) of his later works. Dickey's first three collections—*Into the Stone, Drowning with Others,* and *Helmets*—are notable for their narrative power and careful metrical structures. To emphasize the dramatic element central to the poems in these collections, Dickey often employed a three-beat, anapestic line with trochaic and iambic substitutions; he aimed at memorable statements in individual lines and stanzas. In the poems of these collections Dickey used recognizable stanzaic forms, sometimes with a refrain that reinforced the unity in the individual works. Later, however, the poet evolved new forms to reflect his deepening vision. In *Buckdancer's Choice,* for example, Dickey began radical experiments with

the appearance of the poem on the page and with speech rhythms in an attempt to avoid "artificiality." As he stated in "The Poet Turns on Himself," first published in 1966 and later collected in *Babel to Byzantium:*

> I had in the beginning a strong dislike of rhyming poems, for the element of artificiality is one of the characteristics of poetry I most distrust, and I have always had trouble distinguishing between artificiality and the traditional modes and methods of verse; for a long time I was convinced that craft and artifice were the same thing. . . . Although I didn't care for rhyme and the "packaged" quality which it gives even the best poems, I did care very much for meter, or at least rhythm.

> I began to conceive of something I called—doubtless misleadingly—the "open" poem: a poem which would have none of the neatness of most of those poems we call "works of art" but would have the capacity to in-

volve the reader in it, in all its imperfections and impurities, rather than offering him a (supposedly) perfected and perfect work for contemplation, judgment, and evaluation.

The "open" poem was intended to reflect the workings of the mind by clustering images and ideas in short bursts. As its name implies, this form creates open spaces on the page that work against the confining appearance of conventional poetry. The form allows a layering of dramatic relationships among images, events, and wording. For example, when the voyeur in "The Fiend" (collected in the *Buckdancer's Choice*) moves from the secrecy of tree-filled shadows back onto the sidewalk, he tries to appear an ordinary public man again:

> At the sidewalk he changes   gains weight   a solid citizen
> Once more.

Dickey's language turns on dramatically ironic wordplay—the shadowy figure "gains weight" to become a "solid" (flesh-and-blood/respectable) "citizen" (member of a group/insider) "Once more" (momentarily/again). Moreover, the clusters of phrases and images with their caesuras (or breaks) suggest thought patterns and speech rhythms of both the voyeur and his poet-observer.

For Dickey the "open" poem invited the use of what he called "associational" imagery, though he did not fully define the special qualities of this imagery. In "Pine" (collected in *The Eye-Beaters*) the wind in the pine tree is described through a series of breath images that encompass clouds, trees, and the whole of nature:

> How hard to hold and shape head-round.
> So any hard hold
> Now loses; form breathes near. Close to forest-form
> By ear, so landscape is eyelessly
> Sighing through needle-eyes.

The imagery here depends on the sounds of words laid side by side in short phrases and clauses, not on traditional figurative devices—simile or metaphor—that define relationships. Clearly, "associational" imagery accompanied Dickey's developing interest in a lyrical, rather than narrative, emphasis in his poetry.

Drawing upon Gerard Manley Hopkins and Hart Crane as models, Dickey further developed his lyrical language experiments in *Puella* and *The Eagle's Mile*. In these two collections his language became increasingly abstract, increasingly difficult, as "In Lace and Whalebone" from *Puella* illustrates: *"Blood into light //* Is possible: lamp, lace and tackle   paired

bones of the deep / Rapture." Though in *Puella* such language veers precariously close to inaccessibility, in *The Eagle's Mile* it achieves compelling results.

The literary Self, which is at the technical and thematic center of Dickey's poetry, is presented as his "writing instrument . . . which has the quality of [the poet's] personality as an informing principle," he states in "The Second Birth," an essay collected in *The Suspect in Poetry* (1964). The Self responds to and tries to comprehend experience, his own and that of the Other. Dickey's central character is often a solitary figure placed in a natural landscape, a location that allows transcendence from the ordinary into an enriched understanding of existence. The dynamic relationship between the Self and the Other—human or nonhuman—transforms both through an exchange of interiors. Once the connection is broken, the protagonist is changed, having experienced the thoughts or feelings of the Other, and he returns to his original state, though now renewed by the exchange. In this sense, Dickey's poetry can be described as thematically and psychologically circular in structure.

The quest for transcendence takes various forms but is often expressed as a desire to achieve a kind of heaven on earth. The Self's attempts to attain this version of heaven—a state of living the fully energized life or, at least, of striking a harmonious balance between life and death—can succeed or fail. If the effort is successful, the speaker gains an almost Christ-like sense of "enthrallment"; if the connection falters, the protagonist's sense of loss is emphatic and he becomes an earthbound, fallen angel.

Dickey's early volumes—*Into the Stone, Drowning with Others,* and *Helmets*—define his primary themes and subjects—family, love, war, nature. Much of Dickey's work treats human relationships, particularly those involving the family; the relationships are potentially joyous but are also filled with painful complications, either because human beings fail to connect fully or because they are immersed in death. Dickey's early history provides a source for his complex relationship with the dead. As he declares in *Self-Interviews:*

> I did have an older brother, Eugene, who died before I was born, and I did gather by implication and hints of family relatives that my mother, an invalid with angina pectoris, would not have dared to have another child if Gene had lived. I was the child who was born as a result of this situation. And I have always felt a sense of guilt that my birth depended on my brother's death.

In the collection *Into the Stone* Eugene dominates "The String," "The Underground Stream," and "The Other." In these poems he is variously described as an

"WE CAN no longer doubt that we are in the presence of a major talent, a true art."

So said the *Hudson Review* of James Dickey's previous book, *Drowning With Others*. This new collection, presenting his best work of the past three years, shows the poet at the height of his powers, his vision deepened and extended, his individual voice even more certain and more powerful. Here is the world of James Dickey in its fullest expression: a world where the flow of a river, the still-sensed aura of a dead man, the wild lunge of a hunted buck through a laurel slick, each carries its particular revelation and adds its own dimension to our view of man and the universe in which he lives. *Helmets* is truly an outstanding work.

James Dickey, poet, sportsman and soldier, moved from his Atlanta home in 1963 to become poet-in-residence at Reed College, Portland, Oregon.

Of the poems brought together in this volume, the great majority have previously been printed in periodicals: *Poetry, Virginia Quarterly Review, Yale Review, Sewanee Review, Hudson Review, Paris Review,* and especially *The New Yorker,* in which not less than fifteen of them first appeared.

WESLEYAN UNIVERSITY PRESS
Middletown, Connecticut

poems by JAMES DICKEY

HELMETS

Dust jacket for the American edition of Dickey's third collection of poems (1964), his first book to have been published in Great Britain

"incredible child" who, as Dickey states in "The String," is "in my mind and on my hands." In "The Other" Eugene is portrayed as "king-sized" and god-like, and the speaker takes an ax to a tree in an attempt to transform his own insufficient body into the ideal proportions of his brother. As the speaker chops, Eugene plays a "great harp" and sings "Of the hero, withheld by its body." Through his brother's music, the speaker gains an awareness that his life is dependent upon and haunted by his brother's death. "In that music come down from the branches / In utter, unseasonable glory, // . . . coming to sing in the wood / Of what love still might give, / Could I turn wholly mortal in my mind, / My body-building angel give me rest, / This tree cast down its foliage with the years." The angel-like figure of the dead brother becomes an object to which Dickey's speakers aspire throughout his poetry. Yet they confront this figure with ambivalence since they cannot hope to measure up to, fully connect with, or exorcise this larger-than-life specter.

Dickey's war poetry, also introduced in his first three collections, further expands upon his complex relationship to the dead, particularly as a combat survivor. He senses that he has been given a second opportunity for life, that he has been singled out for a special purpose, but that he cannot fully escape the death-immersion to which war has subjected him. The stages in the process of moving from painful memories to a renewal of life are constant in Dickey's war poetry. His speakers first manifest self-lacerating anguish brought on by the harrowing combat deaths they have witnessed. To overcome such torments they confront the horrors of war through detailed re-creations of combat memories: "The Performance" in *Into the Stone* and "Between Two Prisoners" in *Drowning with Others* are two well-known early examples of confrontation through the dramatically re-created scene. Next, Dickey's speakers reevaluate or reorder their understanding of the meaning of their experiences with death, as in "The Firebombing," collected in *Two Poems of the Air* (1964), and *Buckdancer's Choice*. This process of experiencing anguish, confronting and re-creating the horrors that have produced this anguish, and re-ordering their understanding of their

Dust jacket for Dickey's 1965 book, which won the 1966 National Book Award for Poetry

war experiences becomes the basis for his protagonists' renewal to life.

"The Jewel" in *Into the Stone* is a powerful expression of the process that Dickey's combat survivors undergo in attempting to comprehend the war and its effects on them. While camping with his sons, the middle-aged speaker realizes that he is "A man doubled strangely in time," for the setting–the night, the tent, the reflection in his coffee cup of "a smile I was issued"–moves him in his mind back to that period when he went through "his amazing procedure" inside a cockpit to prepare for nighttime bombing missions during the war. "Forgetting I am alive," he imaginatively re-enters the "great, stressed jewel," his airplane. In this setting he must remain a technically minded operator who is not allowed to question what he is doing, who "Has taken his own vow of silence, / *Alone, in late night.*" In the final stanza of the poem, however, the speaker returns to the present and expresses what has haunted him through all the years since the war: "Truly, do I live? Or shall I die, at last, / Of waiting? Why should the fear grow loud / With the years, of being the first to give in / To the matched, priceless glow of the engines, / *Alone, in late night?*" The speaker

recognizes that he may be a casualty of war in two senses: by being seduced by the drama and opportunities for glory in war and by being haunted by his fear of his own death and his guilt at causing the deaths of others. He thus cannot be completely certain that he is truly alive, that he is not dying through his ambiguity-ridden memories. Yet he is making an effort to come to terms with these memories.

To escape the often painful world of man, Dickey often moves toward the nonhuman world of nature that seems to promise solace and edification. For the poet, nature is a powerful vehicle for transcending the world and moving into a realm beyond himself. Yet he fully realizes that nature often conceals its secrets–its wonders and its horrors–behind a mask that is only partially penetrable by man. "Walking on Water" in *Into the Stone* is an early statement of Dickey's view of man's relationship with nature. The young speaker rides a plank that he poles across "the shining topsoil of the bay," through "the sun / Where it lay on the sea." This single human being–a diminutive figure on a fragile piece of wood–contrasts with the broad expanse of sky overhead and the vast power of the ocean underfoot:

"Later, it came to be said / That I was seen walking on water, / . . . A child who leaned on a staff, A curious pilgrim hiking / Between two open blue worlds." The boy-"pilgrim" is suddenly threatened in this watery Edenic garden by a shark (rather than a serpent), changing the idyllic scene into one fraught with possibilities of danger. The speaker evades the shark by stepping on shore and pushing the plank out to sea, while a chorus of sea birds "nodding their heads" celebrate his escape from death "until I return / In my ghost, which shall have become, then, // A boy with a staff, / To loose them, beak and feather, from the spell / Laid down by a balancing child. . . ." Yet "under their place of enthrallment, / A huge, hammer-headed spirit / Shall pass, as if led by the nose into Heaven." The child figure serves as a Christ-like median between heaven and the underworld, between eternal life and death. Nature's heavenly creatures, the birds, affirm the boy's power, but nature's emissary of death's underworld, the shark, demonstrates how vulnerable the living are to death's forces.

That the natural world may reveal either benevolent or savage secrets is even more fully explored in "Kudzu," a poem collected in *Helmets*. Kudzu, a vine imported from Japan to the American South for the beneficial purpose of preventing soil erosion, becomes as well a ubiquitous, suffocating Japanese invasion upon the Georgia countryside: "In Georgia, the legend says / That you must close your windows // At night to keep it out of the house." The kudzu covers and protects the surface of the earth but also conceals another of nature's harbingers of death, the snake: "For when the kudzu comes, // The snakes do, and weave themselves / Among its lengthening vines, / Their spade heads resting on leaves, / Growing also, in earthly power / And the huge circumstance of concealment." To rid themselves of the dangers posed by the snakes, Georgia farmers release their hogs into the tangled mass of vines, where the hogs brutally tear snakes apart, to the accompaniment of a "sound" that is "intense, subhuman, / Nearly human with purposive rage." Yet the pigs finally cannot eradicate the seething fusion of vines and snakes, "growing insanely," which remains a danger but also, ironically, a source of energy and exhilaration to man. Dickey's speaker, recording a kind of exchange between vegetable life and himself, declares:

> From them, though they killed
> Your cattle, such energy also flowed

> To you from the knee-high meadow
> (It was as though you had

A green sword twined among
The veins of your growing right arm—
Such strength as you would not believe
If you stood alone in a proper
Shaved field among your safe cows—):
Came in through your closed

Leafy windows and almighty sleep
And prospered, till rooted out.

Like the child in "Walking on Water," the protagonist of "Kudzu" becomes energized by the potential danger beneath nature's calm surface. But the danger is real, and the speaker in "Kudzu" recognizes the inevitability of his being ultimately "rooted out."

In "Hunting Civil War Relics at Nimblewill Creek," collected in *Drowning with Others,* Dickey brings together many of his central concerns—family (which here involves his Southern heritage as well as a younger brother), love, war, and nature. The Civil War–battlefield setting of the poem allows the speaker to dramatize his relationship with his living brother while discovering a deeper connection with the Confederate dead of the past. While his brother searches the battleground with a "mine detector," the speaker watches his face—"For I can tell / If we enter the buried battle / Of Nimblewill / Only by his expression." The brother's facial responses—his silent smiles, the "faint light" that "glows / On my brother's mouth"—become the means of communication between the two brothers and between the living and the dead. As they walk through the battleground, the speaker observes that "underfoot I feel / The dead regroup, / The burst metals all in place, / The battle lines be drawn / Anew to include us" and that his brother—"a long-buried light on his lips"—"smiles as if / He rose from the dead within / Green Nimblewill / And stood in his grandson's shape."

Here the dead and the living are symbolically united, and as the brothers joyously hear "the dead outsinging two birds" that have accompanied them onto the battlefield, they also celebrate their own relationship as brothers, "Not breathing 'Father,' / At Nimblewill, / But saying, 'Fathers! Fathers!'" The brothers are thus transformed through their spiritual connection with each other and with their dead Southern countrymen. The war-torn battlefield has been claimed by nature—here portrayed as an unusually benevolent force—which facilitates the connection of the speaker and his brother with the Other, whether living or dead.

Dickey reached full maturity as a poet in his National Book Award–winning volume *Buckdancer's Choice,* which collects some of his most celebrated

The 1966 National Book Award winners—Arthur M. Schlesinger Jr., Janet Flanner, Katherine Anne Porter, and James Dickey—with New York mayor John V. Lindsay (third from left), who gave the welcoming speech at the awards dinner

and discussed works, including "The Firebombing," "The Fiend," and "Slave Quarters." In this volume Dickey further probes his major subjects—war, the Self, the family, the natural environment. Both "The Firebombing" and "Slave Quarters" treat the issue of guilt (about combat involvement and slavery, respectively) and brilliantly employ the process of recognition, re-creation, and encounter found in "The Jewel." In both poems the threat of death and destruction, literal or symbolic, remains powerful, just as it does in "The Fiend," with its voyeur protagonist who simultaneously celebrates and stalks his female victims.

Yet in certain poems of *Buckdancer's Choice,* death becomes a force for transformation, which can be either positive or negative. In the title poem of the collection the approach to death of the speaker's mother becomes a model of creativity and courage. As she suffers in bed from angina pectoris, her antidote to dying is to whistle "all day to herself / The thousand variations of one song; // It is called Buckdancer's Choice." Her "prone music" conjures up in the child-speaker's mind the image of the "Freed black, with cymbals at heel, / An ex-slave who thrivingly danced," one of the traveling minstrels, "the classic buck-and-wing men." The dancer flaps his arms and elbows in a heroic if doomed attempt to transform them into angel wings, and these two performers—the mother and the black dancer, both "slaves / Of death"—unite in the child's mind as embodiments of the individual's courageous efforts not to give in. The mother's song rises

Through stratum after stratum of a tone
Proclaiming what choices there are
For the last dancers of their kind,

For ill women and for all slaves
Of death, and children enchanted at walls
With a brass-beating glow underfoot,

Not dancing but nearly risen
Through barnlike, theatrelike houses
On the wings of the buck and wing.

Thus the mother's whistling, the buck-and-wing man's dance, and the poet's own dancelike, three-beat anapestic lines in their three-line stanzas combine to produce an art that can to a large extent transcend the ravages of death (the song and its subject are "nearly risen").

To transcend the realities of this world and to transform one's Self through connection with another being are clearly related to the concept of reincarnation. In *Self-Interviews* Dickey notes:

Reincarnation is one religious idea I have always loved believing in. I don't know whether the soul passes from one kind of creature to another; I hope it does. I would live this human life gladly if I knew I was going to be a bird—next time—or have any kind of consciousness at all. . . . I'd like to be some sort of bird, a migratory sea bird like a tern or a wandering albatross, but until death, until this either happens or doesn't happen, I'll have to keep trying to do it, to die and fly, by words.

The poem "Reincarnation," which was first collected in *Buckdancer's Choice* under that title and was

Maxine and James Dickey, May 1968

then retitled "Reincarnation (I)" for *Poems 1957–1967*, centers on a dead Southern judge who is reborn as a diamondback rattlesnake, a comic but illuminating comment on Southern justice. The snake, a symbol of evil and death, winds around the hub of a discarded wheel, a symbol of the life and death cycle, in wait "for the first man to walk by the gentle river." The diamondback has been so transformed that it has lost all traces of its previous existence as a human: "Fallen from that estate, he has gone down on his knees / And beyond, disappearing into the egg buried under the sand // And wakened to the low world being born, consisting now / Of the wheel on its side not turning, but leaning to rot away / In the sun a few feet farther off than it is for any man." This man-snake travels backward to a lower form of existence than he has enjoyed previously: "It is in the new / Life of resurrection that one can come in one's own time / To a place like a rotting wheel, . . . stopped / By a just administration of light and dark over the diamonds / Of the body." The poet suggests here that the human judge has through reincarnation descended the chain of being, or perhaps simply confirmed the true position he occupied as a man.

In "Falling," a section of *Poems 1957–1967* composed primarily of previously uncollected works, rising to and falling from great heights becomes a central motif in examining the human capacity for transformation, whether the mystical changes undergone by a stewardess as she falls from an airplane in "Falling" or the evolutions in character revealed by a lineman as he ascends and descends light poles in "Power and Light." "Reincarnation (II)," first collected in *Two Poems of the Air,* is perhaps the fullest explication of Dickey's theme of transformation. In this poem a desk-bound, sedentary office worker who has lived with a "clean desktop" in a "hell of thumbs" discovers, upon his death and reincarnation as a migratory sea bird, that "I always had / These wings buried deep in my back: / There is a wing-growing motion / Half-alive in every creature." He thus achieves in this new life a consequence that he did not have in his previous life, and he acutely perceives the nature and reality of his experience. As Dickey states in *Self-Interviews,* "In this poem I wanted to show the voyage of a man who discovers himself reborn as a sea bird . . . and comes to realize that this is not a dream he's having, that he really is a bird circling in a completely void

Dickey and his second wife, Deborah Dodson Dickey, on the deck at their home in Columbia, South Carolina (photograph by Steve Hunt, Columbia Newspapers)

area where there are no ships or birds. He realizes that this is not an hallucination; he really does have wings and a long beak." Reincarnated as an albatross, he circles toward the Southern Cross, "not to be taken in / By the False Cross as in / Another life," but to fly from the artificial heaven fabricated by man into the truer paradise of physical instinct known only by birds and animals. Yet ahead of the bird lic still further deaths and rebirths: "to be dead / In one life is to enter / Another to break out to rise above the clouds / Fail pull back their rain // Dissolve." For Dickey, reincarnation achieves only a qualified triumph over death, since rebirth is itself followed by succeeding deaths and rebirths in a never-ending cycle. However, reincarnation, the most dramatic expression of an exchange of identity with the Other, does provide an intense but momentary communion between the human and the nonhuman.

A major shift in Dickey's focus occurs in *The Eye-Beaters, Blood, Victory, Madness, Buckhead and Mercy.*

Before *The Eye-Beaters* most of the poet's works began with the Self and then moved outward to connect the Self with another animate or inanimate being. In *The Eye-Beaters* the direction of the poems is inward rather than outward, and the Self becomes the principal concern as the speaker takes stock of who and what he has become. The protagonist in many of these poems is aging and physically ill, a condition that forces him to internalize the possibility of death rather than to examine it primarily in relation to others. Moreover, many of the poems focus upon relationships with family, friends, and lovers—relationships that are subject to the destructive powers of time. *"Variations on Estrangement,"* the subtitle of the final poem, "Turning Away," suggests the central subject matter of the collection. The speaker's increased awareness of his own inability to defeat time and death produces an unusually somber tone in *The Eye-Beaters.*

"The Cancer Match" dramatizes a physical breakdown of the Self. Recently released from a hospital, the cancer-ridden speaker concedes that he does not have "all the time / In the world, but I have all night." During this one dark night he wrestles with his soul by pitting bourbon against "this thing growing" inside, and like "judo masters," the bourbon and cancer war against each other—"Or are they dancing?" Although he has been told that there is no hope for recovery, the protagonist asserts an aggressive optimism: "Internally, I rise like my old self / To watch . . . . / We are looking at this match / From the standpoint // Of tonight / Alone."

As the struggle between cancer and bourbon rages within, the speaker cries out for his "Basic Life / Force!"—his joy, my laughter—to defeat death, to "win / Big, win big" in this struggle. But no matter how he calls on his inner resources of youthful strength—"O Self / Like a beloved son!"—the outcome is predetermined. Significantly, during his confrontation with death, he does not seek transformation into another form of life, a snake or a sea bird, but instead calls for the Self to evolve into what it was in youth. The younger Self cannot rescue or aid the older Self, though the speaker strikes a brave, defiant tone.

The realization of the protagonist of "The Cancer Match" that his life is infused by death is shared by the central character in "Victory," the single war poem in *The Eye-Beaters*. "Victory" is set immediately after V-J Day as the speaker, on his birthday, celebrates the Allied victory over Japan, exulting in the survival of both his nation and himself. As he stacks ammunition crates, the narrator has a *V* sunburned onto his skin, an emblem of victory but also a harbinger of the dramatic transformation he will undergo. He suddenly feels his navel burn "like an entry-wound," a sensation that causes him to go "South in my mind" into memories of home. He then drinks himself into a whiskey stupor, attains a vision of his combat survival, and hallucinates a snake's head coming out of the bottle and biting him. Though he has lived through the war, he is imprinted with death delivered by the snake, ironically but accurately identified as "the angel / Of peace." To symbolize his recognition that peace, like war, is dominated by death, the protagonist is compelled to go—"I can't help it"—to a Yokohama tattoo parlor where he has a snake design emblazoned on his skin. Coiling from his throat through the *V* on his chest, the snake tattoo dominates the speaker, and he returns home in the form and color of "the new prince of peace." He finds a renewed life, but this life is marked by the emblem of death. The protagonist, like the speaker in "The Cancer Match," bears sobering intimations of his own mortality.

Dickey's reassessment of the Self in *The Eye-Beaters* leads to his mid-career review of his beliefs concerning the source and nature of poetry. His long poem *The Zodiac* is an extended drama focusing on the quarrel between imagination and pure reason, personified respectively by his versions of the poet Henrik Marsman and the ancient philosopher Pythagoras. Dickey asserts that the secrets of the creative process and of the universe itself can best be penetrated by the poet's imagination—incorporating, as it does, instinct, memory, and unbound intellect—rather than by the mathematical, rigidly rational system of the philosopher.

Dickey based *The Zodiac* on a work of the same title by Dutch poet Henrik Marsman, a poet-sailor who was killed in a 1940 North Atlantic torpedo attack. Marsman personifies the artist—restless, questing, often drunken, often on the verge of madness—who wrestles with the nature of creativity. Though the reader initially suspects that the twelve-part division of the narrative corresponds with the twelve signs of the zodiac, the poet develops no such structural arrangement. Instead, Marsman's thoughts and experiences direct the structure of the poem. His is the primary voice of *The Zodiac*, though his point of view is fused with that of a second speaker, an omniscient "I" who is engaged with and reacts to Marsman's struggles with the universe, time, and history in Part I of the poem—a section that occupies nearly half of its length. Parts II through VI focus on Marsman's belief that philosophy and mathematics, espoused by Pythagoras, cannot grasp or explain human or divine mysteries. Parts VIII through XI reveal Marsman's turning to his own life—his memories, dreams, fantasies, drunken hallucinations—as the source for both his understanding and his creativity. Part XII examines his final stance growing out of what he has learned through his tortured quest.

Marsman believes that his conception of life embodies what is missing in Pythagoras's theory of the music of the spheres. According to Marsman, Pythagoras has drawn exclusively upon the tools of human reason—philosophy and mathematics—to define a three-part connection among the stars, moon, and sun that becomes a paradigm for the harmony—the creativity—of the universe. Marsman pays homage to the philosopher's idea but asserts that it does not allow for a key ingredient of creativity—the human imagination—to complete the equation. Marsman thus adopts an expansive, even excessive, approach to life in order to assert the power of the imagination for good or ill. He lives in a single room—"a priest's failed prison-cell"—unmarried and childless and drunken on whiskey, intellect, and madness. Embodying the Platonic concept of "seizure" or inspiration, Marsman as a visionary poet probes his own personal history in an effort to comprehend human history.

In the final section of *The Zodiac* Marsman resolves to steer his "craft"—his ship and his poetry—through art: "The instrument   the tuning-fork— / He'll flick it with his bandless wedding-finger— / . . . / And shall vibrate through the western world / So long as the hand can hold its island / Of blazing paper, and bleed for its images: / Make what it can of what is: // So long as the spirit hurls on space / The star-beasts of intellect and madness." Marsman's course leads him to certain death, but his power to fuse memory, imagination, intellect, and madness into art suggests a kind of triumph over death. He remains, however, like his creator, a poet not only of elation but also of darkness. As Dickey states in *Sorties,* "I am a haunted artist like the others. I know what the monsters know, and shall know more, and more than any of them if I can survive myself for a little while longer."

The tone of Dickey's next collection, *The Strength of Fields,* contrasts decidedly with that of *The Zodiac,* partly because the title poem of the 1979 collection was written as a celebration of Jimmy Carter's inauguration, partly because half of the volume is composed of Dickey's "translations"—"Free-flight Improvisations from the UnEnglish"—of other writers, and partly because he seems to have exorcised himself of certain demons through his treatment of Marsman.

Two poems, "The Voyage of the Needle" and "The Strength of Fields," typify the serenity and sense of connectedness that dominate the collection. "The Voyage of the Needle" recalls a trick taught to the speaker by his mother when he was a child: a tissue supporting a needle is placed on top of water; when the tissue becomes saturated and dissolves, the needle floats as if by magic. The adult speaker repeats this "magic" trick as he bathes; the needle points toward his heart; and the recollection of his mother showing him the trick pierces his heart and mind. A device for mending, for joining two parts into a whole, the needle serves as a means of connecting the living speaker with his dead mother: "It is her brimming otherworld / That rides on the needle's frail lake, on death's precarious membrane." The poet's relationship with his mother, previously dramatized as a mixture of guilt and love, is transformed through memory into a mended wholeness conveying "joy and glory." In "The Strength of Fields" a man, presumably the president-elect, is burdened with heavy responsibilities yet approaches these tasks with optimism. As a

Dickey and his daughter, Bronwen (photograph by Leonard Copeland)

Southerner, the speaker gains an inner peace from his close kinship to his native soil. As he walks his farmland at night, he appeals to the "Dear Lord of all the fields" for strength to fulfill his duties. He variously entreats the dead beneath the ground, the heavens, and the natural world around him—his "source / Of the power"—for guidance. His appeals are answered as he perceives that he must respond to the pressures of his office with "More kindness," an ideal of Southern conduct. The speaker's perception suggests that he has achieved harmony with his surroundings, himself, and his obligations; this feeling infuses the poem, and *The Strength of Fields* in general, with a tranquility unusual for Dickey.

His next collection, *Puella,* is the most complete embodiment of both Dickey's experimentation with lyrical language and his quest for transformation of the Self as an informing principle. In *Puella* Dickey adopts the identity and voice—"male-imagined"—of Deborah, his second wife, to examine key events in a young woman's coming of age, in her ever-increasing physical and imaginative aware-

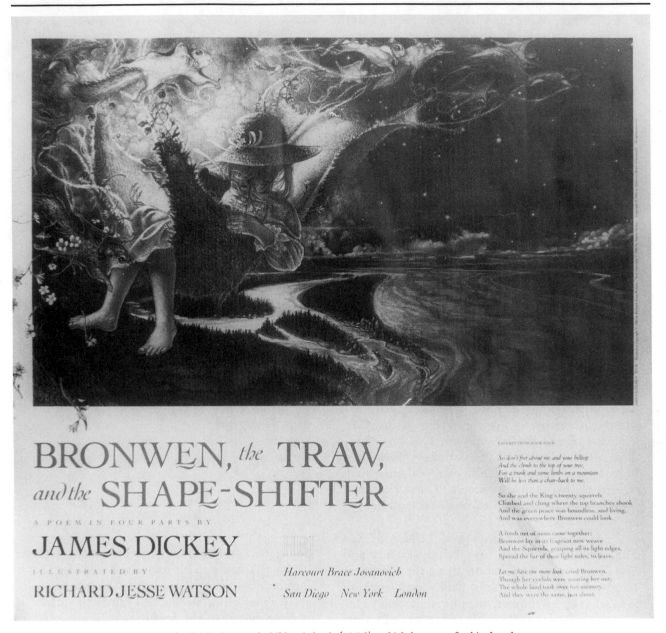

Poster for Dickey's second children's book (1986), which he wrote for his daughter

ness of her own Selfhood. In this collection the poet employs imagery related to sound and the four ancient elements of life—air, fire, water, and earth—and requires the reader to discover imagistic relationships suggested but not explicitly drawn by Dickey.

Puella is organized around a journey of discovery, a quest for identity. In the initial poem, "Deborah Burning a Doll Made of House Wood," the young protagonist watches her childhood doll being consumed by flame, and she announces, "I am leaving," thereby beginning her journey into womanhood. She rises from the ashes of her childhood to examine her heritage, her personal being, her artistic potential. In "Doorstep, Lightning, Waif-Dreaming"

she sits on the front step of strangers and asks if she is their child; but instead of being welcomed into their family, she receives a vision of fire coursing through her body and mind. She thus realizes that she is not a child of ordinary mortals but rather a creature created by inner lightning from her own "root-system of fire." Her internal fire gains artistic expression in other poems of the collection through her individual sound in playing the piano or her startling appearance in the wedding costume of her ancestors. The conclusion of the volume and of the speaker's journey occurs in the final poem, "Summons," which presents a series of surreally conflated images culminating in Deborah's pregnancy.

In "Summons" she repeatedly calls, *"Have someone be nearing,"* evoking not only her unborn child but also her husband, a three-way union that is nearly complete when she is "With half of my first child / With invention unending." In the course of her journey Deborah becomes an archetypal figure of natural creativity that will be whole and *"unending."*

Like *Puella, The Eagle's Mile,* Dickey's final collection, employs the ancient philosophers' elements—earth, water, and air—to convey his speaker's visionary transformations. In this volume these elements become crucial symbols of man's state and of his efforts to transcend that state. Moreover, they affirm the role of the imagination—the most crucial weapon in Dickey's arsenal—in confronting and recreating the realities that he perceives.

In *The Eagle's Mile* the earth is invested with contrasting characteristics: the speaker recognizes that he is a living being through his connection with the earth, but he also acknowledges that the earth contains his final prison, the grave. As an isolated, contemplative wanderer, the narrator celebrates his connection with the solidity of earth in "Earth," the first section of "Immortals": "Always as it holds us in one place, the earth / Grows as it moves, exhaling / Its rooted joy. . . . // I cannot be anything / But alive, in a place as far // From the blank and stark, as this." Yet as he moves across the surface of land, he also longs to transcend its hold on him. He endeavors to be released into the freedom of the air but reluctantly resigns himself to his place on earth, the location of the grave. He perceives, while visiting the grave of a loved one in "Tomb Stone," that "deep enough / In death, the earth becomes / Absolute earth." The living stand breathing in the "rectangular solitude // Risen over" the dead. Furthermore, in "Gila Bend," as the protagonist revisits the aerial gunnery range over which he flew more than forty years earlier as a World War II trainee, he walks the fiercely hot earth as "a cadaver / On foot," almost willing to be branded by the searing sand as penance for those who trained here and died later during battle. On this scorched earth, "no man could get / To his feet, even to rise face-out // Full-force from the grave." The "Absolute earth" of this site is comparable to hell—the hell of war and death in which one is trapped forever.

In contrast to the immobile earth, the sea is constantly in a state of flux. The land-bound speaker in "Expanses" walks upon the beach, watching the "chopped soft road" of the ocean, which creates in him a sense of "Joy." Yet he asserts that one should not "confuse the sea / With any kind of heart: never to mix blood with something // As free as foam." The ocean can either grant man a limited "trouble-free" release from the earth or provide a setting for possibly greater liberation. The speaker in "Moon Flock" notes the desire for man "to grow wings," yearning to "leap // Leap till he's nearly forever // Overhead: overhead floating" in air. But instead of looking up into the night sky at the moon where human flight would occur, one more likely looks "straight // Straight // Straight out over the night sea / As it comes in. Do that. / Do it and think of your death, too, as a white world // Struggling for wings." The sea, particularly the night sea, functions as a darkly fluid locale in which flight from or into the "white world" of death can at least be contemplated.

The most exalted element in *The Eagle's Mile* is the air, the element in which Dickey experienced and survived combat during World War II, thereby achieving a "saved, shaken life," as he describes it in "A View of Fujiyama After the War," collected in *Drowning with Others.* In "Air," the second section of "Immortals," the poet asserts that "Air, much greater than the sea— / More basic, more human than the sea," contains the "high lucidity / Of vigil." At some point the earth will receive man in death, "but the air / You can never keep doesn't know / When it lived in your chest: / Mindless, nerveless, breathless, / The air glitters / All the outside, and keeps carrying // You from within." The literal life-sustaining capability of air has its equivalence in its capacity to grant symbolic freedom to those who are earthbound. For Dickey, air is consistently associated with potential escape, with the possibility of liberation from the earth's—and death's—hold on its creatures.

The large, soaring birds in "Eagles" make "of air a thing that would be liberty / Enough for any world but this one." The speaker acknowledges that he "used to know the circular truth / Of the void" but that he now stands on solid earth aspiring for a spiritual connection with the eagles' flight: "Go up without anything // Of me in your wings, but remember me in your feet // . . . / Where you take hold, I will take // That stand in my mind." The speaker's momentary release from his earthly perspective occurs through creatures of the air, as he longs to transcend permanently the "rooted joy" of earth into the cold, stark void above the land. Similarly in "Night Bird," the protagonist exults inwardly as he imagines a large bird's flight through darkness, rising and falling above the earth. Though blinded by darkness, the speaker shares the eagle's transcendent moment as it flies: "You are sure that like a curving grave / It must be able to fall, // and rise // . . . and suddenly there is no limit // To what a man can get out of / His failure to see: // this gleam //

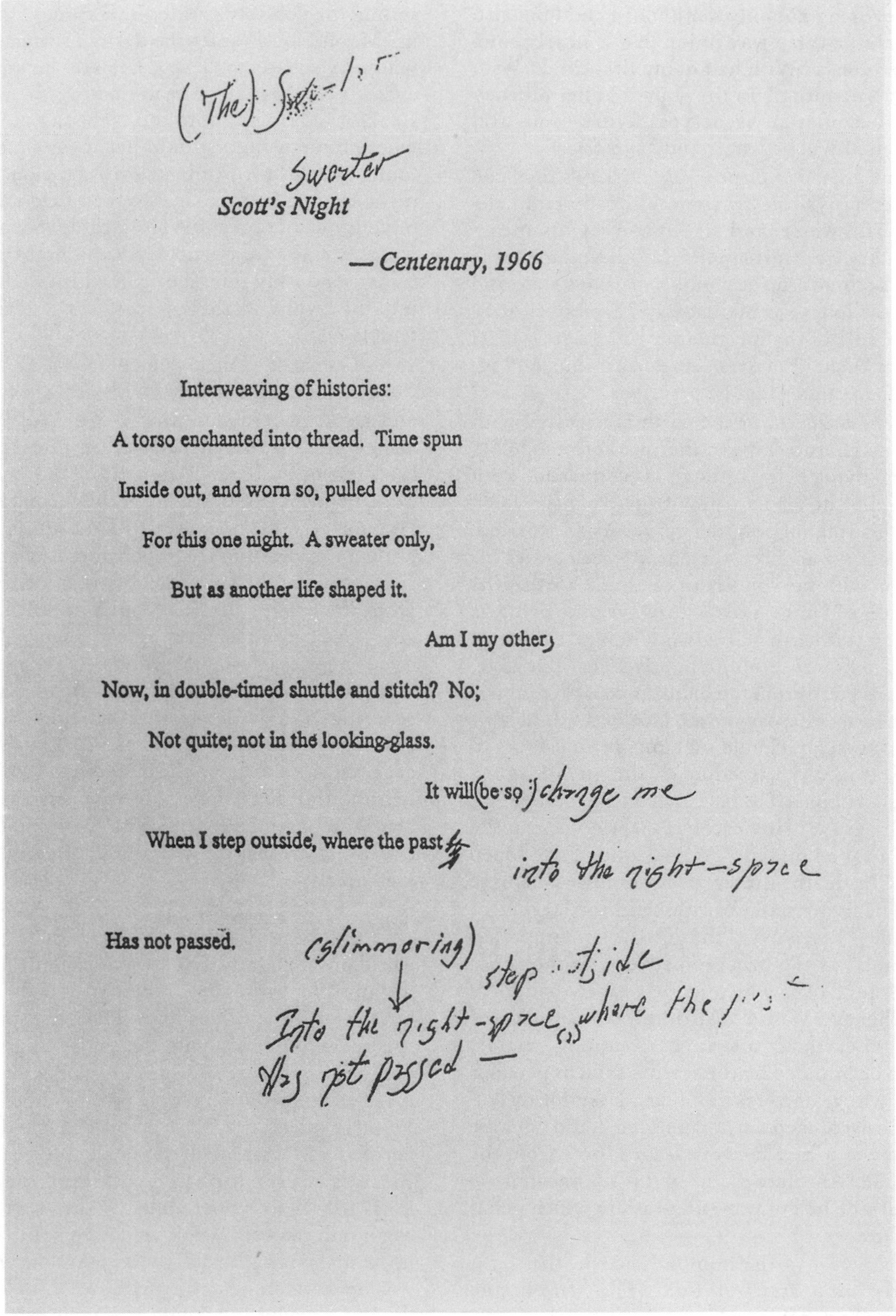

(The) ~~Sixte-125~~

Sweater

Scott's Night

— *Centenary, 1966*

Interweaving of histories:

A torso enchanted into thread. Time spun

Inside out, and worn so, pulled overhead

For this one night. A sweater only,

But as another life shaped it.

Am I my other,

Now, in double-timed shuttle and stitch? No;

Not quite; not in the looking-glass.

It will(be so) *j change me*

When I step outside, where the past *into the night-space*

Has not passed. *(glimmering)*

step outside

Into the night-space, where the p's

has not passed —

Revised draft for the poem Dickey wrote to commemorate the F. Scott Fitzgerald Centenary (Bruccoli Collection)

Of air." The perception of the bird's rising and falling in the night air with its equation to man's rising and falling as he confronts the grave depends upon the imagination rather than upon actual, everyday vision. In this regard, Dickey's speaker in *The Eagle's Mile,* like Marsman, makes use of the creative artistic imagination to transcend man's ordinary existence on "Absolute earth." As Dickey advises the dead and living dead in "Sleepers": "Sound off. / Not knowing where your tombs / Already lie, assemble, sail through // The lifted spaces, unburied."

Throughout his career Dickey pursued new forms, new voices in order to keep his vision engaging to himself and to his readers. He evolved in his poetry from an early emphasis on narrative to a mid-career experimentation with lyric language. In his last collection Dickey retracted slightly from the pure lyricism of *Puella* to create a more accessible poetry. A similar process occurs within the author's three novels. The highly dramatic *Deliverance* became a critical and popular success in part because of its narrative accessibility. *Alnilam,* on the other hand, is quite static, finding its power not in narrative drive but in lyrical set pieces that depend in part on structural experiments involving the printed page. *To the White Sea* parallels Dickey's most recent poetry in the sense that the novel has a renewed narrative impulse combined with highly lyrical language. Throughout his career as poet and novelist, Dickey drove himself to fulfill Ezra Pound's dictum to "Make it new." Because his works are not only "new" but also compelling and engaging, James Dickey will be remembered as one of the most important literary voices in America.

Interviews:

The Voiced Connections of James Dickey: Interviews and Conversations, edited by Ronald Baughman (Columbia: University of South Carolina Press, 1989).

Bibliographies:

Jim Elledge, *James Dickey: A Bibliography: 1947–1974* (Metuchen, N.J.: Scarecrow Press, 1979);

Elledge, "James Dickey: A Supplementary Bibliography, 1975–1980: Part I," *Bulletin of Bibliography,* 38 (April–June 1981): 92–100, 104;

Elledge, "James Dickey: A Supplementary Bibliography, 1975–1980: Part II," *Bulletin of Bibliography,* 38 (July–September 1981): 150–155;

"Continuing Bibliography," *James Dickey Newsletter* (Fall 1984–);

Ronald Baughman, "James Dickey," *Contemporary Authors Bibliographical Series, Volume 2: American Poets,* edited by Baughman (Detroit: Bruccoli Clark/Gale Research, 1986), pp. 71–105;

Matthew J. Bruccoli and Judith S. Baughman, *James Dickey: A Descriptive Bibliography* (Pittsburgh: University of Pittsburgh Press, 1990).

References:

George L. Alexander, "A Psychoanalytic Observation on the Scopophilic Imagery in James Dickey's *Deliverance,*" *James Dickey Newsletter,* 11 (Fall 1994): 2–11;

Lee Bartlett and Hugh Witemeyer, "Ezra Pound and James Dickey: A Correspondence and a Kinship," *Paideuma,* 2 (Fall 1982): 290–312;

Ronald Baughman, "James Dickey's *Alnilam:* Toward a True Center Point," *South Carolina Review,* 26 (Spring 1994): 173–179;

Baughman, *Understanding James Dickey* (Columbia: University of South Carolina Press, 1985);

Ross Bennett, "The Firebombing: A Reappraisal," *American Literature,* 52 (November 1980): 430–448;

David C. Berry Jr., "Harmony with the Dead: James Dickey's Descent into the Underworld," *Southern Quarterly,* 12 (April 1974): 233–244;

Harold Bloom, ed., *James Dickey: Modern Critical Views* (New York: Chelsea House, 1987);

Robert (Crunk) Bly, "The Collapse of James Dickey," *Sixties,* 9 (Spring 1967): 70–79;

Neal Bowers, *James Dickey: The Poet as Pitchman* (Columbia: University of Missouri Press, 1985);

Richard J. Calhoun, ed., *James Dickey: The Expansive Imagination: A Collection of Critical Essays* (DeLand, Fla.: Everett/Edwards, 1973);

Calhoun and Robert W. Hill, *James Dickey* (Boston: Twayne, 1983);

Peter Davison, "The Difficulties of Being Major: The Poetry of Robert Lowell and James Dickey," *Atlantic Monthly,* 220 (October 1967): 116–121;

Donald J. Greiner, "The Harmony of Bestiality in James Dickey's *Deliverance,*" *South Carolina Review,* 5 (December 1972): 43–49;

Greiner, "The Iron of English: An Interview with James Dickey," *South Carolina Review,* 26 (Spring 1994): 9–20;

Daniel L. Guillory, "Water Magic in the Poetry of James Dickey," *English Language Notes,* 8 (December 1970): 131–137;

Paul G. Italia, "Love and Lust in James Dickey's *Deliverance,*" *Modern Fiction Studies,* 21 (Summer 1975): 203–213;

Robert Kirschten, *James Dickey and the Gentle Ecstasy of Earth: A Reading of the Poems* (Baton Rouge: Louisiana State University Press, 1988);

Kirschten, *"Struggling for Wings": The Art of James Dickey* (Columbia, S.C.: University of South Carolina Press, 1997);

Kirschten, ed., *Critical Essays on James Dickey* (New York: G. K. Hall, 1994);

Richard Kostelanetz, "Flyswatter and Gadfly," *Shenandoah,* 16 (Spring 1965): 92–95;

Patricia Laurence, "James Dickey's *Puella* in Flight," *South Carolina Review,* 26 (Spring 1994): 61–71;

Anthony Libby, "Fire and Light: Four Poets to the End and Beyond," *Iowa Review,* 4 (Spring 1973): 111–126;

Laurence Lieberman, *The Achievement of James Dickey: A Comprehensive Selection of His Poems With a Critical Introduction* (Glenview, Ill.: Scott, Foresman, 1968);

Lieberman, "Erotic Pantheism in James Dickey's Madness," *South Carolina Review,* 26 (Spring 1994): 72–86;

Michael Mesic, "A Note on James Dickey," in *American Poetry Since 1960,* edited by Robert B. Shaw (Chester Springs, Pa.: Dufour, 1974), pp. 145–153;

N. Michael Niflis, "A Special Kind of Fantasy: James Dickey on the Razor's Edge," *Southwest Review,* 57 (Autumn 1972): 311–317;

Joyce Carol Oates, "Out of Stone, Into Flesh: The Imagination of James Dickey," *Modern Poetry Studies,* 5 (Autumn 1974): 97–144;

Paul O'Neill, "The Unlikeliest Poet," *Life,* 61 (22 July 1966): 68–70;

Joyce M. Pair, "The Peace of the Pure Predator: Dickey's Energized Man in *To the White Sea*," *James Dickey Newsletter,* 10 (Spring 1994): 15–27;

Louis D. Rubin Jr., "Understanding The Buckhead Boys," *South Carolina Review,* 26 (Spring 1994): 196–197;

Dave Smith, "James Dickey's Motions," *South Carolina Review,* 26 (Spring 1994): 41–60;

Smith, "The Strength of James Dickey," *Poetry,* 137 (March 1981): 349–358;

William C. Strange, "To Dream, To Remember: James Dickey's *Buckdancer's Choice*," *Northwest Review,* 7 (Fall/Winter 1965/1966): 33–42;

Ernest Suarez, *James Dickey and the Politics of Canon: Assessing the Savage Ideal* (Columbia: University of Missouri Press, 1993);

Suarez, "Roll God, Roll: Muldrow's Primitive Creed," *James Dickey Newsletter,* 10 (Spring 1994): 3–14;

Henry Taylor, "Going for Broke: A Strategy in James Dickey's Poetry," *South Carolina Review,* 26 (Spring 1994): 27–39;

The Texas Review, Special Issue: The Fiction of James Dickey, 17 (Fall/Winter 1996/1997);

Arthur Gordon Van Ness, *Outbelieving Existence: The Measured Motion of James Dickey* (Columbia, S.C.: Camden House, 1992);

H. L. Weatherby, "The Way of Exchange in James Dickey's Poetry," *Sewanee Review,* 74 (July–September 1966): 669–680;

Bruce Weigl and T. R. Hummer, eds., *The Imagination as Glory: The Poetry of James Dickey* (Urbana: University of Illinois Press, 1984).

Papers:

The Special Collections Department of the Emory University Libraries in Atlanta, Georgia, holds manuscripts, letters, and substantial amounts of other Dickey materials. Washington University Libraries in Saint Louis, Missouri, and the Library of Congress in Washington, D.C., also hold manuscripts.

Robert Duncan
(7 January 1919 – 3 February 1988)

George F. Butterick
University of Connecticut

and

Robert J. Bertholf
State University of New York at Buffalo

See also the Duncan entries in *DLB 5: American Poets Since World War II* and *DLB 16: The Beats: Literary Bohemians in Postwar America.*

BOOKS: *Heavenly City Earthly City* (Berkeley, Cal.: Bern Porter, 1947);

Poems 1948–49 (Berkeley, Cal.: Berkeley Miscellany Editions, 1949);

Medieval Scenes (San Francisco: Centaur Press, 1950; revised, with a preface by Duncan, Kent, Ohio: Kent State University Libraries, 1978);

Fragments of a Disordered Devotion (San Francisco: Privately printed, 1952; San Francisco: Gnomon Press / Toronto: Island Press, 1966);

Caesar's Gate Poems 1949–1950 (Mallorca: Divers Press, 1955; revised with an introduction, poems, and a closing essay by Duncan, Berkeley, Cal.: Sand Dollar, 1972);

Letters Poems MCMLIII–MCMLVI (Highlands, N.C.: Jargon, 1958);

Faust Foutu: An Entertainment in Four Parts (Stinson Beach, Cal.: Enkidu Surrogate, 1959);

Selected Poems (San Francisco: City Lights Books, 1959);

The Opening of the Field (New York: Grove, 1960; London: Cape, 1969);

Roots and Branches (New York: Scribners, 1964; London: Cape, 1970);

As Testimony: The Poem & The Scene (San Francisco: White Rabbit Press, 1964);

Writing Writing A Composition Book Stein Imitations (Albuquerque: Sumbooks, 1964);

Medea at Kolchis: The Maiden Head (Berkeley, Cal.: Oyez, 1965);

The Sweetness and Greatness of Dante's Divine Comedy (San Francisco: Open Space, 1965);

A Book of Resemblances Poems: 1950–1953 (New Haven: Henry Wenning, 1966);

Robert Duncan (photograph by Pat Bazalon)

Of the War: Passages 22–27 (Berkeley, Cal.: Oyez, 1966);

The Years as Catches: First Poems (1939–1946) (Berkeley, Cal.: Oyez, 1966);

The Cat and the Blackbird (San Francisco: White Rabbit Press, 1967);

Bending the Bow (New York: New Directions, 1968; London: Cape, 1971);

The First Decade: Selected Poems 1940–1950 (London: Fulcrum Press, 1968);

Derivations: Selected Poems 1950–1956 (London: Fulcrum Press, 1968);

Names of People (Los Angeles: Black Sparrow Press, 1968);

The Truth & Life of Myth (New York: House of Books, 1968);

Play Time Pseudo Stein (New York: Poets Press, 1969); revised, with a preface by Duncan (San Francisco: Tenth Muse, 1969);

Poetic Disturbances (San Francisco: Maya, 1970);

65 Drawings, A Selection . . . from One Drawing Book, 1952–1956 (Los Angeles: Black Sparrow Press, 1970);

Tribunals: Passages 31–35 (Los Angeles: Black Sparrow Press, 1970);

A Prospectus for . . . Ground Work (San Francisco: Privately printed, 1971);

Poems from the Margins of Thom Gunn's Moly (San Francisco: Privately printed, 1972);

A Seventeenth Century Suite (San Francisco: Privately printed, 1973);

An Ode and Arcadia, by Duncan and Jack Spicer (Berkeley, Cal.: Ark Press, 1974);

Dante (Canton, N.Y.: Institute of Further Studies, 1974);

Fictive Certainties: Essays (New York: New Directions, 1979);

Ground Work: Before the War (New York: New Directions, 1984);

Ground Work II: In the Dark (New York: New Directions, 1987);

Selected Poems, edited by Robert J. Bertholf (New York: New Directions, 1993; revised and enlarged, 1977);

A Selected Prose, edited by Bertholf (New York: New Directions, 1995).

Robert Duncan's poetry established the San Francisco Bay area as a major center for poetry in the United States. There were other poets—Kenneth Rexroth, James Broughton, Jack Spicer, and Robin Blaser—but it was Duncan's authority as a poet that struck the attention of other poets and readers. Together with Charles Olson and Robert Creeley, Duncan is also known as one of the principal Black Mountain Poets, having taught briefly at the experimental Black Mountain College (March–August 1956) in western North Carolina. Duncan was born in Oakland, California. His mother, Marguerite Wesley Duncan, died shortly after giving birth, and his father, Edward Howard Duncan, a day laborer,

was unable to keep the child. He was adopted by a couple who were "orthodox theosophists" and who chose the baby on the basis of the astrological chart they drew. He grew up as Robert Edward Symmes, and his first poems were published under that name. He was raised in Bakersfield, California, where his adopted father was an architect. His grandmother had been an elder in a Hermetic order similar to William Butler Yeats's Order of the Golden Dawn. The tales told and read to him as a child by his parents and the appropriately named Aunt Fay (the theosophists' world was marked by correspondences) were as lasting and important as any later influences and establish a constant world of reference in the poems. Duncan grew into a spiritualist who looked on experiences in the world as keys to be read and deciphered for hidden mysteries inherent in them. Spiritualist Madam Helena Petrovna Blavatsky played as important a part in his later life as she did earlier in the lives of the members of his adopted family. Edna Keough, his high school English teacher, revealed the world of poetry to him first through the work of the American poet H. D. He explained later: "She saw poetry not as cultural commodity or an exercise to improve sensibility, but as a vital process of the spirit." By the time he was eighteen he had already taken the orders, accepted poetry as his commitment for life: "I recognized in poetry my sole and ruling vocation."

Duncan attended the University of California at Berkeley for two years from 1936 to 1938, publishing his first poems in school magazines, before leaving for New York, where he became part of the circle of Anaïs Nin that included Kenneth Patchen, Henry Miller, and British poet George Barker. He was influenced by these writers early in his career as well as by Edith Sitwell, Jean Cocteau, Gertrude Stein, James Joyce, and the French Surrealists. In New York he followed exhibitions in art galleries and museums and witnessed the emergence of Abstract Expressionism. Throughout his writing life his poems were dominated by an intense attention to artistic form that came from his life within artists' circles and museums. His article "The Homosexual in Society" appeared in the magazine *Politics* in 1944; the essay was an honest call for sexual freedom and individual rights. He eventually returned to the San Francisco area in 1945. Moving to Berkeley in the spring of 1946, he soon met Spicer and Blaser and launched "the Berkeley Renaissance." He again attended the university (1948–1950), studying medieval and Renaissance civilization under the noted scholar Ernst Kantorowicz. In 1951 Duncan began his long-standing relationship with the painter Jess Collins, and in 1952 he joined the group of poets publishing in *Origin* magazine, after responding to a poem by Denise Levertov published there.

Duncan's association with the *Black Mountain Review* then followed, as did a regular correspondence with Olson. Following Olson's death, Duncan became the leading spokesman for the poetry of open form in America, gaining its impetus from Olson's theoretical essay "Projective Verse," first published in 1950. Duncan received a series of awards in the 1950s and 1960s: the Union League Civic and Arts Foundation Prize (*Poetry* magazine), 1957; the Harriet Monroe Memorial Prize (*Poetry* magazine), 1961; a Guggenheim Fellowship, 1963; the Levinson Prize (*Poetry* magazine), 1964; and National Endowment for the Arts grants, 1966–1967. Few poets have written more articulately and self-consciously about their own intentions and understanding of poetry. In the 1972 reprint of *Caesar's Gate,* at what seemed the height of his prestige, Duncan did a curious and courageous thing, announcing he would not publish another collection for fifteen years (although poems occasionally appeared singly or in small separate publications), when a volume to be called *Ground Work: Before the War* would prepare the way for the work of his final years. That volume appeared in 1984, and for it Duncan received the National Poetry Award in 1985. Also in 1985 he received the American Book Award from the Before Columbus Foundation. *Ground Work II: In the Dark* (1987) appeared just two months before Duncan's death in 1988.

Duncan's early poems have been collected in two volumes, *The First Decade: Selected Poems 1940–1950* (1968) and *Derivations: Selected Poems 1950–1956* (1968), and his earliest work has been published as *The Years as Catches: First Poems (1939–1946)* (1966). Apart from early poems of enormous promise—"A Spring Memorandum: Fort Knox" and "An African Elegy"—his first most important poem is "The Venice Poem." Consciously structured after Igor Stravinsky's music, this poem uses a complicated symphonic form to articulate the nexus of his psychological traumas, the engagement of his poems with the traditons of art and literature, and his determined drive to create new forms for poetry. His set of poems written in 1947, published as *Medieval Scenes* (1950), is Duncan's contribution to "the serial poem," which established the organizational principles of a series of poems on a common subject which are not necessarily tied together by narrative links. This early series led to the major poems in "The Structure of Rime" and "the Passages Poems." From "Passage Over Water" (1939), which he called his "first poem," to the lucid "Spring Memorandum," written in 1940 while he was at military training

camp after his induction into the army (he would be released shortly on psychological grounds), to "An African Elegy" and "The Years as Catches" (both of 1942), and "Among my friends love is a great sorrow" and "An Elegiac Fragment" (both of 1946), the tone of the poems is elegiac. Failures at love, personal deficiencies, and defeats at writing are haunting themes of these early poems. In "Heavenly City, Earthly City" these themes appear along with the evidence of his allegiances to Ezra Pound, D. H. Lawrence, and Wallace Stevens. The poem concludes:

> There is a wisdom of night and day,
> older than that proud blaze of sun,
> in which we rest, a passion, primitive to love,
> of perishing, a praise and recreation of the sun.
> My earthly city is reveald in its beauty.

The larger presences, Platonic—almost Blakean—of his later poems appear in the work of this early period (though it was not until 1953, after hearing a reading of William Blake by the Scottish-born balladeer Helen Adam, that Duncan gave himself over to Blake, whom he later called "the divine"):

> Enormous Worm, turning upon Himself in His cyst,
> disturbing the night with His love, who
> has seen Him? I found at the roots of a tree
> where Randlett and I were lying in the late afternoon
> an Imago, like dried paper, that we
> as children called Child-of-the-Earth. . . .

The wondering eyes of childhood, which persist as a theme in Duncan's poetry, appear here, too—the continual awe at majesty that makes Duncan himself so majestic (some, however, will say aggrandized, portentous, overly romantic). In "An African Elegy" and "Heavenly City, Earthly City" this quality is called "the marvelous" and gives an indication of Duncan's prophetic stance in his later "The Passages Poems."

But it is with "The Venice Poem" of 1948, a long poem patterned after Stravinsky's *Symphony in Three Movements,* that Duncan displays the extent of his powers. The setting is not the Italian Venice, despite the title, but Berkeley of the late 1940s, specifically a house or cooperative on Hearst Street that Duncan shared with others—writers and students, including poets Spicer and Blaser ("We formed a table, a round table in our own minds"). The campanile on the Berkeley campus becomes the bell tower of San Marco, and it rings the close or coda of the poem. Berkeley, because of specific events in the shared household, is a "Carnal City," not the Venice of art and imagination. It is Venus's Venice and

Duncan at age five with his sister, both adopted by Edwin and Minnehaha Symmes (Literary Estate of Robert Duncan)

provides the stage for the action of the present. The poem is about the betrayal of love but also about the love that is poetry—"Music, magic," poetry itself, emerging like Venus "out of the shell-coil ear." It is the Venice also of *Othello*: there is lust, deception, jealousy, rage, and the taint of adultery, although the child subsequently born and cared for at the end, and celebrated by the campanile's bells, is as much the poet himself, the "Little cross-eyed king held / secure in the center of all things." Duncan's own cross-eyed condition, of which he freely and frequently speaks, may readily be taken as emblematic of his ability, or insistence, to create a twin vision in his work—the simultaneous experience of the metaphysical in the physical, the ideal in the real. This poem is unabashedly Platonic ("Who has waited in Love's cave / watching the shadows of real things . . ."), especially in the face of the nominalism of Pound—whose presence in the poem is felt via di-

rectives that continued to guide Duncan ("the melodic coherence, the tone leading of vowels")—and of William Carlos Williams and Olson. It is also, like so many of Duncan's poems, about poetry itself, its nature and creation.

After a period of personal uncertainty, 1949–1950, during which the poems in *Caesar's Gate* (1955) were written, described in his 1972 introduction as "a period of irresolution . . . a feverish realm illustrated by the soul's fears and hopes, claims and illusions, in which the soul is haunted by what it is," Duncan established a household with Collins (known simply as Jess). He wrote "The Song of the Borderguard" in December 1950 in the spirit that the new relationship, lasting until Duncan's death in 1988, had given him. The poet himself is the border guard, "the Poet on Guard," because he scans the musicality of the advancing lines, the array of words as they fall into the formation of syntax. It is another poem seeking a metaphor for the act of poetry itself. In it "The borderlines of sense in the morning light / are naked as a line of poetry in a war." And, as Duncan says in excerpts from a notebook, "I make poetry as other men make war . . . to exercise my faculties at large." Elsewhere, the border is a "field" or "bounds," the metaphor a dance, a meadow, or even a moose. From this time on, Duncan was again immersed in a world of art. Like Jess's explorations of collage in images, Duncan's poems take on the aspect of a collage in words; images and ideas enter the poems in nonhierarchical structures—an idea Duncan had taken from Olson.

"An Essay at War," the introductory poem in the retrospective volume *Derivations,* provides the transition between the early and middle work. This poem follows after another poem, "The Effort," which remained unpublished in Duncan's lifetime. In both, Duncan attempts to honor his modernist masters—mainly Pound, Williams, Stein, and Lawrence—to assert his own poetics and to work out the poetics of collage. He says in "The Effort," "I have a high-flown / hermetic, rhapsodic diction / poet's delirium." Both poems are about poetics or the creative process itself, and they mark a transition from a delirium of the highly rhetorical lines of "The Venice Poem" period to the lyrical forms of *Letters Poems MCMLIII–MCMLVI* (1958) and, most successfully, *The Opening of the Field* (1960). "An Essay at War" begins self-consciously enough with the admission that the design of a poem is "constantly / under reconstruction." Already the commitment to process is evident; the poem is "the mind dance / wherein thot shows its pattern: / a proposition / in movement"— though here it is the naturally unfolding organicism of associations, without the instantaneity of projective process. Amid images of light and fire, war intrudes—the Korean conflict raging at the time. "An Essay at War" is exactly that—an essay, an attempt, to resolve conflicting emotions and methods. Weakly discursive, never seeming to settle on its topic—first poetics, then love, then the war again (the poet writes, "I have no idea of what is going on / A single verity might outlast the idea")—it nevertheless is an important poem for Duncan, constantly seeking as it does a plan, which he begins to realize in *Letters*. Meanwhile, it is exploratory and advancing, as seen in the concluding section, which begins with these questions:

> When does the poem end?   Why
> does it go on? to exhaust
> what possibilities?   Why does the war
> go on?
>
>   He conceives the poem
> as a shattered pitcher of rock crystal

With *Letters* Duncan joins his own generation. He steps beyond the influence of modernists Pound, Stravinsky, Stein, and others and becomes a true contemporary of Olson, Levertov, Creeley, Broughton—to whom many of the poems are dedicated. With this book, Duncan began to conceive of a book of poems as a whole book, not simply as a collection of poems. The poems of 1950–1953, which included "An Essay at War," were published in 1966 as *A Book of Resemblances*. The whole book was a version of the serial poem, so the poems in *Letters* (the title means letters of the alphabet) were written from 1953 to 1956 and were inspired in part by the Hebrew mystical text, the *Zohar*, with its "new picture of language" in which "the letters of the Logos dance." In the introduction Duncan announces his intention to enter "the process which sets self-creation and self-consciousness in constant interplay . . . a process of re-vision and disorganization to keep creation of the poem and consciousness of the poem in interplay." He unhesitatingly embraces "the discontinuities of poetry." His success may be measured by "An Owl Is an Only Bird of Poetry," with the sheer certainty of its end:

> This is an owl as he flies out of himself
> into the heart that reflects all owl.
>
> Who gives his hoot for joy as he flies.
>
>   Alights.

It is a poem that embodies poetry as no metaphor alone could—only an identity, the exchange of consciousness and creation that Duncan writes of in

Self-portrait by Duncan in an early journal (Bancroft Library, University of California, Berkeley; Literary Estate of Robert Duncan)

"Nests," prefatory to the flight of the book. The poem creates its own form, just as the owl "flies thru a time which his wing creates." The themes continue to be Romantic ones—the immanence of poetry-in-things rising as readily as man's perception falls upon them, states of mind, and the apperception of correspondences. But this new freedom of form, the opening field, allows far greater simultaneity than even the old Modernist collage. Ideas about the process of the poem appear throughout the volume. Duncan is now moving toward the principle of writing in which the form of the poem is an enactment of thought and feeling in words: the experience itself and not a record or a commentary about the experience. The poet himself has said the book "reflects the impact of what's called Black Mountain," and he identifies specifically his discovery in *Origin* magazine of Levertov's poem "The Shifting" that opened to him this new possibility for poetry in America. Although maintaining ties to the traditons of art, music, and literature, he joined his contemporaries in a community of poets reaching for the possibilities of poetry realized by Pound and Williams and Stein, and then made new by Olson's essays and poems. After living with Jess on Mallorca from February 1955 to March 1956 (where he read Blake and Joyce extensively), Duncan taught at Black Mountain College through August 1956, where his *Medea at Kolchis: The Maiden Head,* later published in 1965, was performed. Duncan returned to San Francisco as the assistant director of the Poetry Center at San Francisco State University to continue explorations in theater with a group of Black Mountain students, joining the poets active in the area since the 1940s and recent Beat arrivals from the road, all adding to the San Francisco Renaissance then underway. Olson arrived in the spring of 1957 to offer a series of lectures titled "The Special View of History," which introduced Duncan to Alfred North Whitehead and the philosophy of process. With this sense of process, together with previous openings provided by Levertov and other *Origin* poets, as well as poets in the *Black Mountain Review,* Duncan proposed for himself a book, an entrance into the new field of the poem, called first "The Field" and finally *The Opening of the Field,* his most widely read book. He had begun the book on a visit to London in January 1956, but it was Olson's lectures that stimulated the formation of the whole book. It begins with a title page collage by Jess and includes some of Duncan's finest poems: "Often I Am Permitted to Return to a Meadow"; "The Dance"; the beginnings of the "Structure of Rime" series; "This Place Rumord to Have Been Sodom"; "Poetry, a Natural Thing"; "A Poem Beginning with a Line by Pindar" (known also as "the Pindar poem"), which is, along with some of the later "Passages Poems," against the Vietnam War; "My Mother Would Be a Falconress"; and "Food for Fire, Food for Thought."

Throughout the volume there is a consistent theme of new beginnings, or dancing the old beginnings anew, and it appears immediately in the opening poem, "Often I Am Permitted to Return to a Meadow." To Duncan poetry is a "permission," granted by forces larger than the poet, to observe forces larger than one would ever wish to become. The poet inhabits a thoroughly Platonic world, Romantic and Transcendental. He is a direct successor not only of Ralph Waldo Emerson and Walt Whitman but also of Samuel Taylor Coleridge, William Wordsworth, and Percy Bysshe Shelley. His meadow is the same "meadow, grove, and stream," his grass the same "splendour in the grass" that Wordsworth sighted in his ode "Intimations of Immortality from Recollections of Early Childhood." Duncan's poem draws, literally, upon a dream, an "Atlantean" drama recurrent from childhood. He describes it in a published excerpt from his "The H. D. Book": "First there was the upward rise of a hill that filled the whole horizon of what was seen. A field of grass rippled as if by the life of the grass itself, yet I was told there was no wind. When I saw that there was no wind it was a fearful thing, where blade by blade the grass so bowed of its own accord to the West. . . . Then, in a sudden almost blurred act of the play, there was a circle of children . . .

dancing in the field." The children dance a round dance such as "ring-around-a-rosy," and the dreamer is in the center of them. In the next episode the dreamer is shown an underground throne room, which gets flooded by a great wave. "The open field, the dance and the presumption, the seeing the dark throne and the flooding of the underworld . . . seem now a prediction of what life will be, now a showing forth of some content of what life is, as in the Orphic mysteries the story of Persephone was shown in scenes. The restless dead, the impending past life, what had been cast away—a seed—sprouts and in the vital impulse would speak to us. The head of a giant woman rises from the ground."

The subject of Duncan's poems is often poetry itself, though in no tedious or programmatic way, because the process of seeing or envisioning assimilates the things seen or envisioned. The meadow is the poem itself, the "field" of the poem (and of the book's title), according to Olson's sense of "open" poetry or "composition by field" theory, as described in "Projective Verse." The poem is a field of action (as Williams also wrote), in which the dream occurs and can occur time and again. The open field can be understood also as the field, or canvas, of a painting, say of Clyfford Still or Jackson Pollock. Its boundary is one ultimately staked by the sounds of language, a necessary and provocative limitation. The careful recurrence, the correspondences of "mind" and "mine," the light appearance of "all" followed by the more definite "hall" and concluded, decisively, by "fall"—the lines are delicately yet deliberately linked. Like the children in their dance or ring, the words join hands and swing, roundly, successively, a true *versus* with echoes and shadows of echoes, like the dream itself and related memories from the past, all echoes and "rhymes." The poem participates fully and eagerly in the Platonic theory of forms—the "shadows," as the poet says, "likenesses" of "the First Beloved." "She it is Queen Under The Hill" might be hyphenated throughout the poem like some of the other primal figures throughout Duncan's poetry ("She-it-is," "Queen Under-The-Hill"). She can be Brigit, the Celtic muse. She is his own lost mother, the eternal feminine anywhere, whatever rules the poem, this "disturbance of words within words / that is a field folded"—itself a most perfect definition of the postmodern poem. She is also the Muse, or perhaps Mary. It is, as in most of Duncan's poems, a question of art (or appearance) and reality, but not art versus reality: always the near contraries, holding their bounds "against chaos," until the field is defined. But never finally: the ambiguity is seen, among other places, in the "given property of the mind"—*property* both as a

Duncan in the 1940s, when he was part of a group of poets and artists who began "the Berkeley Renaissance" (Estate of Helen Adam)

thing possessed (a tract of land, even, a meadow in that sense) and a quality, an abstraction. The process of mythopoetics creates a field of action, a meadow of thought and feeling, that provides a place of habitation for the poet. The meadow or the poem remains, although "everlasting," only an "omen" of what is, so that it, too, remains an open possibility—as the book, as the life. The presence of children, no matter how precocious, in the poem reminds one of Duncan's comment in his "Pages from a Notebook," first published in 1953: "To be a child is not an affair of how old one is. 'Child' like 'angel' is a concept, a realm of possible being."

"The Dance," also written in 1956, includes the same meadow, the same tireless children in their round dance. Structurally, the poem is just as crafted, only differently. New syncopations are explored, and before rounding out the poem, so that it too is a dance, Duncan interposes a prose passage of a remembered experience of dancing from his own past, during the summer of 1945 while staying among a colony of artists and writers in Woodstock, New York. Again the title serves as the first line so

that no gesture is wasted—a sweeping away into the circulation of sounds that is the dance of the poem. The precise placement of the poetic feet, the careful spacing, is mimetically a dance—almost "heel-toe, heel-toe"—the rocking motion seen also in its oxymoronic fourth line:

> The Dance
>
> from its dancers circulates among the other
>   dancers. This
> would-have-been feverish cool excess of
>   movement makes
> each man hit the pitch co-
>   ordinate.

Akin to the Yeatsian dancer-in-the-dance, the dance of the title exists beyond the turns of the poem, which in its turn participates utterly in the dance (Williams's "The Dance" is no different). The poem is the embodiment of Creeley's essential proposition and the basic principle of Olson's "Projective Verse" that "form is never more than an extension of content." Like Olson and Pound before him,

*Cover for Duncan's 1960 book, which was inspired by Charles Olson's lectures
on "open" poetry or "composition by field"*

Duncan makes this dance one of the intellect and of the syllables on the page. Here in Duncan's poem, Olson's hero Maximus, who in his first address to Gloucester announces as his purpose to tell "who obeys the figures of / the present dance," is praised:

> Maximus calld us to dance the Man.
> We calld *him* to call
>   season   out of season-
> d mind!

Duncan writes in his important essay "Towards an Open Universe": "The dancer comes into the dance when he loses his consciousness of his own initiative, what *he* is doing, feeling or thinking, and enters the consciousness of the dance's initiative, taking feeling and thought there." Just as the words mimic dancers, the dancers "mimic flowers," until the whole poem is aflower, with the heavier prose stanza toward the end the roots of all, rooted in experience, grounded in the past. The dance itself has been suspended with the simple lines, appropriately short as if intended for one out of breath, echoing Wordsworth and Whitman as well as suggesting a Platonic emanation:

> I see now a radiance.
> The dancers are gone.
> They lie in heaps, exhausted,
> dead tired we say.
> They'll sleep until noon.

The stanza in the prose of memory is then injected, and the poem picks up in promise as it ends. The whole is a masterful control of measure, the pace or rate, or what Duncan elsewhere repeatedly calls "ratio." In that conclusion, the past memory ("That was my job that summer . . .") is continued into the future (*"I'll slip away before they're up"*) as it appears in the present ("and see the dew shining") in typical postmodern simultaneity. Later, in his "Prospectus" for the forthcoming "Ground Work," the poet elaborates on his sense of dance, how reading in the *Zohar,* "it was the letters of the Logos I saw dancing there—and then I was to come to see these in turn as the members of the Life Code, the configurations of chemical probabilities, and that that dance was the Spirit that haunted all dancing orders." But first the motif of the dance continues into "The Poem Beginning with a Line by Pindar."

This most important poem begins amid an anagogic vision, of which Duncan gives an account in his *The Truth & Life of Myth* (1968): "Reading late at night the third line of the first Pythian Ode in the translation by Wade-Gery and Bowra, my mind lost the hold of Pindar's sense and was faced with certain puns, so that the words *light, feet, hears, you, brightness, begins* moved in a world beyond my reading, . . . no longer words alone but also powers in a theogony, having resonances in Hesiodic and Orphic cosmogonies where the foot that moves in the dance of the poem appears as the pulse of measures in first things." The opening lines call into play the relationship of heart and mind:

> The light foot hears you and the brightness begins
> god-step at the margins of thought,
>   quick adulterous tread at the heart.
> Who is it that goes there?
>   Where I see your quick face
> notes of an old music pace the air,
> torso-reverberations of a Grecian lyre.

The poem then immediately moves to the myth of Cupid and Psyche, who illustrate the struggle of thought (or the soul) and heart, as represented in *Cupid and Psyche,* a painting by Goya that Duncan had seen in Barcelona. As the associations flow, they gradually advance the poem from the beauty of the youthful lovers to the beauty of age and of older poets who have led the way for Duncan with their "faltering, / their unaltering wrongness that has style, / their variable truth." Duncan invokes the "variable foot" poetics of Williams, recent victim of apoplexy like Dwight D. Eisenhower, then president, who had suffered a mild stroke in November 1957, resulting in a slight temporary difficulty in speaking:

> A stroke. These little strokes. A chill. . . .
>   The old man, feeble, does not recoil.

> Recall. A phase so minute,
>   only a part of the world in-jerred.

> The Thundermakers descend,
> damerginf a nuv. A nerb.
>   The present dented of the U
> nighted stayd.

> damaging a nuv. A nerb.
>   The present dented of the U
> nighted stayd. . . .

Duncan goes on to questions of the state of contemporary politics, the nation's health in the midst of the Cold War. He invokes Whitman's America for comparison, quoting from "When Lilacs Last in the Dooryard Bloom'd," and includes a catalog of the presidents since Lincoln's time, as critical of their spirit and influence as he later was in his denunciation of Lyndon Johnson for leading the nation deeper into war, concluding with a passage of the highest order of political poetry:

> I see always the under side turning,
> fumes that injure the tender landscape.
>   From which up break
> lilac blossoms of courage in daily act
>   striving to meet a natural measure.

The third of the four sections of the poem is dedicated to Charles Olson, whose "Projective Verse" and *Maximus Poems* (1953) Duncan had come to find most valuable, and returns to the Cupid and Psyche legend, this time as it is told in Apuleius's *The Golden Ass.* Psyche's fate brings to mind Pound's (reflected in the *Pisan Cantos,* 1948) in the prison camp at Pisa:

>   Psyche
> must despair, be brought to her
>   insect instructor;
> must obey the counsels of the green reed;
> saved from suicide by a tower speaking,
>   must follow to the letter
>   freakish instructions.

> . . . .

> In the story the ants help. The old man at Pisa
>   . . . was
>   upheld by a lizard . . . [.]

Consideration of Pound, chief of the modernists, leads in turn to associations with the West, including the poet's own family history—early settlers in the American West as well as members of the Hermetic Order of the Golden Dawn (encouraging, in part, the dawn imagery in the poem), followers of another quest. His personal history, including his

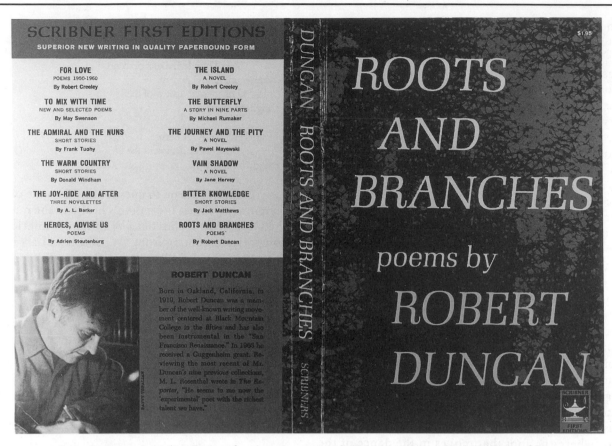

Cover for Duncan's 1964 collection of mythopoeic poems, including his autobiographical "Sequence of Poems for H. D.'s Birthday"

dream life, and that of the race are attractively intermingled, beginning with "the hero who struggles east / widdershins," counterclockwise, "to free the dawn." Above all is the sense of continuance, persistence. One of these "solitary first riders" advancing into legend is his own grandfather (about whom more is revealed in "Apprehensions" to come—how he made the trek into the Oregon Territory after the Civil War while his grandmother in her turn "entered the dragon West"):

> This land, where I stand, was all legend
> in my grandfathers' time: cattle raiders,
>   animal tribes, priests, gold.
> It was the West.

It is a land where "Snakes lurkd / guarding secrets"—a fact which leads, in turn, once more back to the Cupid and Psyche legend: Psyche is now "Scientia / holding the lamp, driven by doubt," while Cupid or Eros is "naked in foreknowledge / smiling in his sleep," and ultimately, taking advantage of the pun, "Cupidinous Death! / that will not take no for an answer."

It is not, however, Duncan's answer. Section 4, joined to the preceding one by the exclamation "Oh yes!" in response to the previous line "that will not take no for an answer," returns the poet to the meadow of the earliest poems in the book, including memories of his stay at Woodstock ("in Maverick Road the snow / thud by thud, from the roof / circling the house . . .") and the familiar ring of dancing children. The "light foot" of the opening line of the poem is picked up by the "footfall" of "the boundary walker" (recalling the "bounds" of "Often I Am Permitted") and, although "light," the foot is "informed / by the weight of all things." But the poetic feet continue to make the syllabic dance of the poem, and the "light foot" continues to push back the "dark"—

> The Indians give way, the clearing falls.
> Great Death gives way and unprepares us.
>   Lust gives way. The Moon gives way.
> Night gives way. Minutely, the Day gains.

—leading at last, once more, to Duncan's Atlantis dream persisting in his consciousness since childhood:

On the hill before the wind came
the grass moved toward the one sea,
    blade after blade dancing in waves.

There the children turn the ring to the left.
There the children turn the ring to the right.
    Dancing . . . Dancing . . .

Legends of the past continue into the present life:

We have come so far that all the old stories
whisper once more.
Mount Segur, Mount Vinoire, Mount Tamalpais . . .

Montsegur, Albigensian stronghold in Provence, figures also in Pound's *Cantos;* this poem was written in San Francisco with Mount Tamalpais to the north. The loftiness here requires a raised voice—duly supplied by the line from the hymn in the poet's reading, leading in turn, like the original line from Pindar, to the poet's more prosaic interjection or direct commentary. The method all along has been "a mosaic, an accumulation of metaphor," until yielding the final lines:

In the dawn that is nowhere
    I have seen the willful children

clockwise and counter-clockwise turning.

The poem is about, finally, the perpetuity of process itself, not of final or totalizing love, but the yearning for such love (and light)—the Love which activates love, as modeled by Cupid and Psyche, the heart and mind forever poised in their eternal relationship. It is a culminating image, the willful children dancing in a circle—first clockwise, then counterclockwise, or maybe both directions together, because they are willful—but not a foredoomed, closed, or even disclosing one. No finality is allowed other than the vision; it is a *perpetuum mobile,* still elusive and "no more than a nearness to the mind"—a single image not of completion but continuity. "The Structure of Rime," begun in *The Opening of the Field,* is an open-ended series of prose poems "in the shamanistic genre, of psychic double-talk," also "trance-projections" inspired by French poet St. John Perse, that have reference to "a constantly changing theory of rime, measure, correspondences." "Rime" for Duncan, as defined in his "Notes on the Structure of Rime" from 1961, is "the doctrine of correspondences" on the larger order, in "life feeling." It is by no means limited to recurrent sound patterns, what are commonly and narrowly known as rhyme; rather, as he says in an interview, it is like Arnold Schoenberg's observations about harmony, "simply a sense of measure being present. And while meas-

ure may be like a ruler—12 marks, and all of them equal—a measure actually means you're feeling something did happen before or did not happen before. Any sense of resemblance or any sense of disresemblance indicates the presence of rime. . . . There are rimes of sentence structure. There are rimes of gender." Presiding over all is the Master of Rime, identified as being on the order of "Primary fictions," like Nietzsche's Zarathustra or the Christ of the Romantic imagination. The subject the Master teaches is language, as is true for so many of Duncan's poems, on a cosmic scale: "Of *and* Or *are snails, repeat vegetable lessons, roaring a new will that lifts its horns into the heart of Man.*" The same poem, "Structure of Rime VIII," concludes:

Grammarian! from your side the never
healing! Undo the bindings of immutable syntax!

The eyes that are horns of the moon feast on the leaves of
    trampled sentences.

These "structures" persist despite the beginning of a new series titled "the Passages Poems" in the mid 1960s.

    Images other than the dance or meadow or owl are symbols of the ideal poem. In "Poetry, a Natural Thing" the symbol is, humorously perhaps, a moose. The subject is actually beauty, natural beauty—and so the ending of the poem (including a quotation from a rejection by John Crowe Ransom of some of Duncan's poems) is not purely comic:

The forlorn moosey-faced poem wears
    new antler-buds,
      the same,

"a little heavy, a little contrived,"

his only beauty to be
    all moose.

Perfection lies in fulfillment of the essential nature, whether of poem, poet, or moose.

    The self-consciousness of the book, of the collection proposed as an interconnected whole, is seen in the final poem, "Food for Fire, Food for Thought." "This is what I wanted for the last poem," the poet writes in the poem itself, "a loosening of conventions and return to open form." At the same time, there is a perfect fit, an appropriateness that can only be attributed to masterliness of control and attention. And always the renewal at the end: "Flamey threads of firstness go out from your touch, / Flickers of unlikely heat / at the edge of our belief bud forth." Olson had early criticized Duncan in "Against Wisdom as Such" for too readily seek-

```
ROOTS AND BRANCHES

    Sail, Monarchs, rising and falling
orange merchants in spring's flowery markets!
messengers of March in warm currents of news floating!
    flitting into areas of aroma,
tracing out of air unseen roots and branches of sense
    I share in thought,
filaments woven and broken where the world might light
casual certainties of me.   There are
    echoes of what I am in what you perform
this morning.  How you perfect my spirit!
    almost restore
an imaginary tree of the living in all its doctrines,
    by fluttering about,
intent and easy as you are --the profusion of you--
awakening transports of an inner view of things.



        .  .  .  .  .  .  .  .


    WHAT DO I KNOW OF THE OLD LORE?

A young editor wants me to write on Kabbalah for his magazine.

What do I know of the left and the right, of the Shekinah, of the
    Metatron?
It is an old book lying on the velvet cloth, the color of olive
    under-leaf and plumstain in the velvet;
it is a romance of pain and relief from pain, a tale told of the
    Lord of the Hour of Midnight,
the changing over that is a going down into Day from the Mountain.

Ah! the seed that lies in the sweetness of the Kabbalah
is the thot of those rabbis rejoicing in their common devotion,
of the thousand threads of their threnodies, praises, wisdoms,
    shared loves and curses interwoven.

There are terrible things in the design they weave, fair and
    unfair establishd in one.
How all righteousness is founded upon Jacob's cheat upon cheat,
    and the devout
pray continually for the humiliation and defeat of Esau,
for everlasting terror and pain to eat at the nephilim.

The waves of the old jews talking
persist at the shores.

Oh I know nothing of the left and the right.

The moon that moves the waters
comes clear from the earth's shadow.

All the old fears have been drawn up into the mountain that comes
    of knowing.

It is an old book of stories, the Bible is an old book of stories
    --a mirror made by goblins for that Ice-Queen, the Shekinah--
a likelihood of our hearts withheld from healing.

A young editor wants me to write on Kabbalah for his magazine.

Yes, for I too loved the scene of dark magic, the sorceror's
    sending up clouds of empire and martyrdom;
the Gem made by goblins yielding its secret gold to the knowing;
enchantresses coming in to the lodestone;  the star
```

Page from the final draft of Roots and Branches *(Henry W. and Albert A. Berg Collection, New York Public Library, Astor, Lenox and Tilden Foundations; Literary Estate of Robert Duncan)*

ing "wisdom" ahead of language, saying "heat, all but heat, is symbolic, and thus all but heat is reductive." It was perhaps the most valuable direct criticism Duncan ever received, and here he convincingly offers fire for touch to complete the book.

In 1961 Duncan began writing a tribute to H. D. Duncan read parts of H. D.'s *War Trilogy* as a student and then became a devoted student of her writing. The tribute developed into an exploration of the great masters of modernism–Williams, Pound, Joyce, and H. D.–but it also turned into an autobiographical meditation. Duncan explored the ways in which he discovered himself and found his derivations in the spiritualism of these writers, and in doing so he wrote the most important document of literary autobiography since Coleridge's *Biographia Literaria* (1817). The book was published chapter by chapter in magazines.

In Duncan's next collection, *Roots and Branches* (1964), poems continue on the largest, mythopoeic scale–soon to be called the "scales of the marvelous." Hermetic lore is a constantly guiding current; Dante and Blake rarely leave his side. There is the important autobiographical "Sequence of Poems for H. D.'s Birthday," the admirably sustained and measured "Apprehensions" similar in structure to the Pindar poem and also "The Dance"; there are also grand poems like "The Continent," with which the volume closes, in which "the theme is much too big / to cover all o'er, a decorative frieze / out of earthly proportion to the page." Even so, the "margins of the page flare forth," and "There is only / the one continent, the one sea– / moving in rifts, churning, enjambing. . . ." Like the earlier Pindar poem, "Apprehensions" begins with a quotation from a text, an essay on Renaissance cosmologies:

> *"If the Earth were animate*
> *it should not experience pleasure when grottoes and caves are dug*
> *out of its back"*

> From which argument my mind fell away
> or disclosed a falling-away,
> and I saw an excavation–but a cave-in of the ground,
> hiding in showing, or showing in hiding,
> a glass or stone, most valuable.

The mind slips into its state of obedience or negative capability, awaiting its instruction. The poet has actively solicited a "dream or vision" in order to "open Night's eye," and as the title suggests, the outcome is not fully known. But surely the title is equally a pun; there is to be some apprehending, understanding. The method for this is given in the second section, in the familiar terms of the architecture of the poem:

> The architecture of the sentence
>   allows
> personal details,   portals
> reverent and enchanting,
> constructions from what lies at hand
>   to stand
> for what rings true.

"What rings true" includes "Structure of Rime XIV," which is incorporated wholly into the poem as its fourth part, and in the fifth section, before the poem's "Close," readings from the Tarot deck. The "Close" itself begins with an enlightening prose account–exactly like the "editorial" passage at the end of the Pindar poem or the Woodstock memories of "The Dance"–followed by the statement, the assurance, "Wherever we watch, concordances appear" (concord dances), and the only question, "in what scale?" The poet lists ten of the "orders" of such a scale, concluding:

> There is no life that does not rise
> melodic from scales of the marvelous.

> To which our grief refers.

The strength of such a poem in maintaining an equilibrium of elements makes possible "the Passages Poems" to come. The first thirty of "the Passages Poems" are interspersed within *Bending the Bow* (1968), with a subsequent five appearing separately as *Tribunals: Passages 31–35* (1970). The poems from *Tribunals* collected along with other poems of the series in *Ground Work: Before the War* and *Ground Work II: In the Dark*. Begun in 1964, the series was conceived as the first truly "open" poem. There was to be no coda as in Williams's *Paterson* (1946–1958), no proposed or longed-for conclusion as in Pound's *Cantos,* and no final poem as in Olson's *Maximus*. Duncan sought to take Whiteheadian process at its literal value and to its inevitable consequence, go beyond Olson, and be more faithful to the advantage of "projective verse," the commitment to openness, than Olson himself. In this series, Duncan says in an interview, "theoretically, everything can coexist." It is to be a poem without boundaries (and thus steps beyond the "bounds" of those in *The Opening of the Field*). It is a process even before it is a system; composition is "total" throughout the poem. Consequently, it can include poems from other series such as "Structure of Rime" or occasionally share designations with them. Eventually Duncan drops the numbers. Boundless forms such as these can also appear within other forms–"Passages 36" appears as part of *A Seventeenth Century Suite* (1973), and "Structure of Rime XXVI" shares the designation "Passages 20." Eventually all ordination ceases for "the Passages Poems" numbered beyond 37 and titled "O!" (both for the exclamation and

Duncan in San Francisco, 1969 (photograph by Ann Charters)

for the initial of Olson, whose notes provided the impetus for the poem, but also a possible pun on zero or the cessation of numbering). "But," Duncan points out to Howard Mesch, "I leave the earlier numbers as possibly an incidental statistical happening within a posed field that doesn't have any boundaries at all," adding that such a "chronology" is simply an "ordination" that can go on, arbitrarily or not. If the series, constantly unfolding, appears uneven, it is because, in the words of the Roman emperor Julian the Apostate that serve as epigraph to it, "the uneven is without bounds and there is no way through or out of it." In that sense its form is a true infinite. The poem is, as Duncan writes in his introduction to *Bending the Bow,* a "living productive form in the evolution of forms." It is the life of the poetic mind itself, "the primal wave of it, writing itself out in evolution." Of "the Passages Poems" themselves he says, "I number the first to come *one,* but they belong to a series that extends in an area larger than my work in them. I enter the poem as I entered my own life, moving between an initiation and a terminus I cannot name." Duncan thought of the poems as belonging to the whole body of his work and specifically to the context of the books in which they appeared. Without

numbering, the poems were released from the causal relationships of a linear structure. It is a view consistent with his understanding of the universe, a poetics faithful to that universe as described at length in the essay "Towards an Open Universe." But no matter how exhaustive or capacious the concept, the proof still lies in the value of individual poems.

In the second "Passages Poem" (titled "At the Loom"), invoking Homer through Pound's *Cantos*—though this time not the striving Odysseus, not even the patient Penelope, but the craft of the witch Circe—the method for achieving such a form is declared:

> my mind a shuttle among
> set strings of the music
> lets a weft of dream grow in the day time,
> an increment of associations,
>
> luminous soft threads,
> the thrown glamour, crossing and recrossing,
> the twisted sinews underlying the work.

What is the subject of all this? Whatever impinges on the heightened and extended consciousness of the poet in his full mythopoeic readiness, often through his reading. Among the threads are interwoven quotations from the poet's wide reading (of Blake, Jakob Böhme, Charles Baudelaire, John Adams, Dante, Olson, Thomas Carlyle, Victor Hugo) and etymologies from the *Oxford English Dictionary* effectively juxtaposed with the "soft luminous threads" of his own imagining. The result is an imagined universe without bounds, as majestic as the poet's mind is capable of making it—his method, a "*grand collage.*" Included is one of the most rousing and effective denunciations of warmongering, along with Allen Ginsberg's "Wichita Vortex Sutra" of the same period. The ringing rage of rhetoric is seen, for example, in "Up Rising," beginning "Now Johnson would go up to join the great simulacra of men, / Hitler and Stalin, to work his fame / with planes roaring out from Guam over Asia." Duncan is careful, though, within his righteousness (Blake is his model) to offer an alternative, positive value to uphold: "There being no common good, no commune, / no communion, outside the freedom of / individual volition." Poem 35 of the series, "Before the Judgment," reaches new heights in prophetic rhetoric as it cries out for peace in the community of all peoples. Duncan published two long essays on Whitman's poetry, "Changing Perspectives in Reading Whitman" and "The Adventure of Whitman's Line." For the poems in *Bending the Bow* and then in *Ground Work: Before the War* and *Ground Work II: In the Dark,* Duncan assumes Whitman's voice of prophecy, his vision of democracy for the nation, his hope for the betterment, and his fear of the damaging drive of political power and corruption.

Bending the Bow also includes the major independent poem "My Mother Would Be a Falconress," beginning with the nimble rhymes:

> My mother would be a falconress,
> And I, her gay falcon treading her wrist,
> would fly to bring back
> from the blue of the sky to her, bleeding, a prize,
> where I dream in my little hood with many bells
> jangling when I'd turn my head.

With dexterous repetitions and echoings it is the most consistently musical of all Duncan's poems; with added endless psychological fascination, dramatic play, tensions of language and concept, it is Duncan's major poem about homosexual love. It, along with "The Torso: Passages 18," prepares the way for "Circulations of the Song," one of the finest love poems in postwar American poetry.

Between *Bending the Bow* and *Ground Work: Before the War,* Duncan continued to publish pamphlets and broadsides. *Achilles' Song* (1969), *Tribunals: Passages 31–35* (1970), *Bring It Up from the Dark* (1970), *In Memoriam Wallace Stevens, Structure of Rime XXVII* (1972), *Poems from the Margins of Thom Gunn's Moly* (1972), *A Seventeenth Century Suite* (1973), and *Dante* (1974) were collected along with poems from magazines in *Ground Work: Before the War.* In his introduction to *Bending the Bow,* Duncan placed that book in the context of the Vietnam War, a war of "foreign desperation." In the same introduction he used the phrase *grand collage* to define the poetics of an individual poem, the fabric of his whole body of work, and the larger historical context to which his poems belonged. Images and ideas, quotations and references come into the poem from a variety of sources in the same way that images and words in a collage come into a context in which they are defined in a new way. In like manner, all of Duncan's poems are part of a larger body of work; his poetry belongs to the one world poem, as Shelley called it, to which all poets contribute in their time. In this volume and the next, *Ground Work II: In the Dark,* "IT" refers to the "*grand collage,*" the process of the poems and the larger context in which they appear. In Duncan's imaginative time, which follows Pound's directions, "all ages are contemporaneous." "An aggregate of intentions," as Duncan phrases it in "Passages 33 Transmissions," comes into the poems.

If the tone of the early poems is elegiac, the tone of the later poems is pessimistic. In Duncan's view, the United States as a country has betrayed the democratic vision of Whitman, given up paying attention to the good of the people, driven itself into political corruption, and engaged in a war of mass destruction of people and the landscape. In his essay "Man's Fulfillment in Order and Strife" Duncan propounds that war is the contrary of peace, the necessary point of contention in a dualistic cosmos which provokes imaginative and social progress, but in this time the nation has betrayed the dualistic view and launched itself on a monistic drive of destruction. The poet stands before the darkness of war as before a mirror and reads out the lineaments of terror that total war will bring. He writes in "Bring It Up from the Dark":

> The great house of our humanity
> no longer stands. Men from our own country
> stamp out, burn back, flush up from their refuge
> with gasses, howling or silent, whatever
> human or animal remains living there.

He begins the presentation by assuming the voice of Achilles in "Achilles' Song":

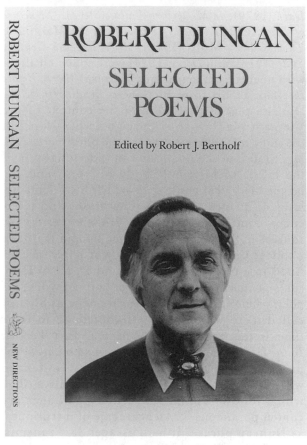

Dust jacket for a posthumously published collection of poems spanning Duncan's career

I do not know more that the Sea tells me,
told me long ago, or I'overheard Her
   telling distant roar upon the sands,
waves of meaning in the cradle of whose
   sounding and resounding power I
slept.

This is not Duncan's voice speaking, but Achilles'. Duncan as a poet posits that the poem takes place in a body of poetic lore and a massive accumulation of imaginative literature. Achilles, the Greek hero at Troy, emerges as a questor who comes forward in the following poems—"Despair in Being Tedious," for example, as "a circling man / in a seizure of talk that he hears too as he goes on," who moves through the contemporary world with the same ease as he moved through the ancient world. The questor appears in the poems that make up *Tribunals,* where a prayer for a spiritual community of humankind ends the poem "Before the Judgment." The book then moves through the contemplation of contemporary ritual murders in "Santa Cruz Propositions" and through the darkness of the human condition back to the ancient world in "Poems from the

Margins of Thom Gunn's *Moly,*" a set of poems which was actually written in Duncan's copy of Thom Gunn's book. The classical world is as close to the core of Duncan's poetics as the world of seventeenth-century poetry which he explores in the section titled "Seventeenth Century Suite." In all ages Duncan finds affiliations of the imagination, indications of the vision of the possible good of humankind being subverted by deceptions and faults of a few. This was Whitman's message, one of Duncan's foundations; and it was also Dante's, which is fully explored in the section titled *Dante Études,* a series of "études" in response to an "assignment" in a "Curriculum of the Soul" originally proposed by Olson. Here Duncan rehearses the themes of his poetics which involve the necessity of human freedom, the household as the basis of ideas of Eros as an aspect of the creative imagination, of an empire of poetry which can include the work of all poets "brought under the orders of the living." "I draw upon my 'own' thought in reading Dante as from a well-spring," he writes in the preface to establish his spiritual and poetic affinity with Dante and so to provide a foundation for the movement of the remaining poems in the volume. In close order the poems move through a discussion of the broken friendship with Denise Levertov, which was caused by different reactions to the Vietnam War—"The Torn Cloth"—to another view of the dark world in "An Interlude of Winter Light," and then to a re-engagement with Homer's world (which began the volume) in "'Eidolon of the Aion.'" The penultimate poem, "The Presence of the Dance/The Resolution of the Music," returns to the theme of the healing powers of the dance and the universal presence of music that were so much a part of the poems in *The Opening of the Field.* The final poem, "Circulations of the Song," gives a prophecy that the foundations of human life rest in love found in the household and extend out through the lines of imaginative thought to the whole empire of poetry. Based on Rumi's poetry and vision, the poem is a love poem which is both delicate and profound, personal and universal:

       And from this household ours
Heaven is range,   In the Grand Assemblage of Lives,
    the Great Assembly-House,
this Identity, this Ever-Presence, arranged
   rank for rank,   person for person, each from its own
sent out from what we were to another place
   now in the constant exchange

      renderd true.

The whole volume has spread out a vision based on the view that nations have subverted the community of all peoples, but the vision of the essentially human, based on love in the household, has persevered from Homer's antiquity to the present. That same vision persists throughout the final volume, *Ground Work II: In the Dark.*

Ground Work II: In the Dark, Duncan's final book, includes poems written between 1977 and 1985. The title has a double meaning. Beginning as early as *A Seventeenth Century Suite,* Duncan had expressed a death wish, and in this volume the darkness and blackness, the grimness seen in the human condition, take on the dimensions of reaching his own death, of even wishing for it so he could be released from the traumas of living in and after the war. As the beginning of the poem "To Master Baudelaire toward His Malaise" puts it:

> When I come to Death's customs,
> to the surrender of my nativities,
> that office of the dark too I picture
> as if there were a crossing over,
> a going thru a door,   in obliteration
> —at last, my destination Time will not undo—

But the darkness also has the meaning of a primordial time latent with all the possibilities for human good. In the vision of this book, the potentialities of the primordial world remain unrealized. Darkness prevails.

> We draw the black water, pure and cold.
> The light of day is not as bright
> as this crystal flowing

> Three thousand years we have recited its virtue
> out of Hesiod.

In contrast to the dark world, Duncan rehearses and celebrates the love in his household: "Love / that overtakes and pervades the falling of the light / touches upon a presence that is all," he writes at the end of "An Alternate Life." "In Waking" refers to the beginning of Duncan's relationship with Jess and to the early poem "The Song of the Border-guard": "I saw the borderguard," and "And who am I? the man sleeping at the border asks," while "From the fall of 1950/December 1980" celebrates the thirty years of living with Jess. The major collection of "the Passages Poems," "The Regulators," now an unnumbered series, celebrates the powers of love and the drive to create a poetic universe to live within as well as the awareness of the dark world of human despair and death. The volume has the effect of adding up, of reaching back to Olson's admonitions against "Wisdom as Such" in "The Dignities"—"Wisdom as such must wonder for sortilege is

all"—or the poem "Close," where Olson's "elements in trance" enter the moving river of artistic expression.

In the 1980s Duncan began to experience kidney failure because his kidneys were blocked with "light chains," protein chains produced by a disorder of the bone marrow. In 1984 he was hospitalized. The volume's final poem was written after that period and is titled "After a Long Illness":

> In the real I have always known myself
> in this realm where no Wind   stirs
> no Night
> turns in turn to Day, the Pool of the motionless water,
> the absolute Stillness. In the World, death after death.
> In this realm,   no last thrall of Life stirs.
> The imagination alone knows this condition.
> As if this were before the War,   before
> What Is,   in the dark this state
> that knows nor sleep nor waking, nor dream
> —an eternal arrest.

Duncan is surely preeminent. He has upheld the status, the stateliness, of poetry in an age of impatience. He has maintained the tradition of the poet as revolutionary seer, shaman, necromancer, and sage, at the same time advancing the art by his achievements of measure and commitment to a poetry of process. With full confidence in his own powers, he has stubbornly preserved Romanticism, interest in the old lore, the glamorization of the poetic ideal, and the tradition of total and lifelong commitment while actively pursuing postmodern immediacy. He has partaken so fully of the vast cultural inheritance that he can be, by his own terms, nothing less than grand. His poetry accomplishes exactly what he found to be poetry's own greatest accomplishment. Modifying his own words slightly, it might be said almost as an epitaph, even for a generation: his is the poetry "that most moved us to a need for poetry."

Letters:

A Great Admiration: H. D./Robert Duncan Correspondence 1950–1961, edited by Robert J. Bertholf (Venice, Cal.: Lapis Press, 1992).

Interviews:

Robert Duncan: An Interview by George Bowering & Robert Hogg (Toronto: Beaver Kosmos, 1971);

Howard Mesch, "Robert Duncan's Interview," *Unmuzzled Ox,* 4 (February 1977): 79–96;

Ekbert Faas, "Robert Duncan," in his *Towards a New American Poetics: Essays & Interviews*

(Santa Barbara, Cal.: Black Sparrow Press, 1978), pp. 55–85;

Aaron Shurin and Steve Abbott, "Robert Duncan: Interview," *Gay Sunshine,* nos. 40/41 (1979): 1–8;

Jack R. Cohen and Thomas J. O'Donnell, "An Interview with Robert Duncan," *Contemporary Literature,* 21 (Autumn 1980): 513–548;

Rodger Kamenetz, "Realms of Being: An Interview with Robert Duncan," *Southern Review,* 21 (January 1985): 5–25.

Bibliography:

Robert J. Bertholf, *Robert Duncan: A Descriptive Bibliography* (Santa Rosa, Cal.: Black Sparrow Press, 1986).

References:

Charles Altieri, *Enlarging the Temple: New Directions in American Poetry during the 1960s* (Lewisburg, Pa.: Bucknell University Press / London: Associated University Presses, 1979), pp. 128–169;

Audit/Poetry, special issue on Duncan, 4 (1967);

Robert J. Bertholf, "The Concert: Robert Duncan Writing out of Painting," in *Jess: A Grand Collage,* edited by Michael Auping (Buffalo, N.Y.: Albright-Knox Art Gallery, 1993), pp. 67–92;

Bertholf and Ian W. Reid, eds., *Robert Duncan: Scales of the Marvelous* (New York: New Directions, 1979);

George Bowering, "Robert Duncan in Canada," *Essays on Canadian Writing,* 4 (1976): 16–18;

Dolores Elise Brien, "Robert Duncan: A Poet in the Emerson-Whitman Tradition," *Centennial Review,* 19 (Fall 1975): 308–316;

Donald Byrd, *The Poetics of Common Knowledge* (Albany: State University of New York Press, 1994), pp. 82–103;

Joseph M. Conte, *Unending Design: The Forms of Postmodern Poetry* (Ithaca, N.Y.: Cornell University Press, 1991), pp. 47–69;

Dennis Cooley, "Keeping the Green: Robert Duncan's Pastoral Vision," *Capilano Review,* nos. 8/9 (Fall 1975/Spring 1976): 368–385;

Robert Creeley, "'A light, a glory, a fair luminous cloud,'" in *A Quick Graph: Collected Notes and Essays,* edited by Donald Allen (San Francisco: Four Seasons Foundation, 1970), pp. 195–197;

Maria Damon, *The Dark End of the Street: Margins in American Vanguard Poetry* (Minneapolis: University of Minnesota Press, 1993), pp. 142–201;

Michael Davidson, *The San Francisco Renaissance* (Cambridge: Cambridge University Press, 1989), pp. 125–149;

L. S. Dembo, *Conceptions of Reality in Modern American Poetry* (Berkeley: University of California Press, 1966), pp. 208–217;

Ekbert Faas, *Young Robert Duncan: Portrait of the Poet as Homosexual in Society* (Santa Barbara, Cal.: Black Sparrow Press, 1983);

Stephen Fredman, *The Grounding of American Poetry: Charles Olson and the Emersonian Tradition* (Cambridge: Cambridge University Press, 1993), pp. 96–130;

Thomas Gardner, *Discovering Ourselves in Whitman: The Contemporary American Long Poem* (Urbana & Chicago: University of Illinois Press, 1989), pp. 99–143;

Scott Hamilton, *Ezra Pound and the Symbolist Inheritance* (Princeton: Princeton University Press, 1992), pp. 194–210;

Ironwood, special Duncan issue, 11 (Fall 1983);

Wendy MacIntyre, "The Logos of Robert Duncan," *Maps,* no. 6 (1974): 81–98;

MacIntyre, "Robert Duncan: The Actuality of Myth," *Open Letter,* second series 4 (Spring 1973): 38–54;

Nathaniel Mackey, "From *Cassire's Lute:* Robert Duncan's Vietnam War Poems," *Talisman,* no. 5 (1990): 86–99; *Talisman,* no. 6 (Spring 1991): 141–164; *Talisman,* no. 7 (Fall 1991): 141–163; *Talisman,* no. 8 (Spring 1992): 189–221;

Maps, special issue on Duncan, no. 6 (1974);

James F. Mersmann, *Out of the Vietnam Vortex: A Study of Poets and Poetry against the War* (Lawrence: University of Kansas Press, 1974), pp. 159–204;

Cary Nelson, *Our Last First Poets: Vision and History in Contemporary American Poetry* (Urbana: University of Illinois Press, 1981), pp. 97–144;

Rudolph L. Nelson, "Edge of the Transcendent: The Poetry of Levertov and Duncan," *Southwest Review,* 54 (Spring 1969): 188–202;

Charles Olson, "Against Wisdom as Such," in *Human Universe and Other Essays,* edited by Donald Allen (New York: Grove, 1967), pp. 67–71;

Sherman Paul, *The Lost America of Love: Reading Robert Creeley, Edward Dorn, and Robert Duncan* (Baton Rouge: Louisiana State University Press, 1981), pp. 169–276;

Peter Quartermain, *Disjunctive Poetics: From Gertrude Stein and Louis Zukofsky to Susan Howe* (Cambridge: Cambridge University Press, 1992), pp. 161–165;

M. L. Rosenthal, *The New Poets: American and British Poetry Since World War II* (New York: Oxford University Press, 1967), pp. 174–184;

Michael Rumaker, "Robert Duncan in San Francisco," *Credences,* 5–6 (March 1978): 12–55;

Sagetrieb, special issue on Duncan, 4 (Fall/Winter 1985);

Marta Sienicka, *The Making of a New American Poem: Some Tendencies in Post-World War II American Poetry* (Poznan, Poland: Uniwersytet im Adama Mickiewicza w Poznaniu, 1972);

Southern Review, special section on Duncan, 21 (January 1985): 5–62;

Warren Tallman, "Robert Duncan's Devotion to Language," *Open Letter,* third series 6 (1976–1977): 70–74;

Charles Tomlinson, "Poetry and Possibility: The Work of Robert Duncan," *Agenda,* 8 (Autumn/ Winter 1970): 159–170;

A. K. Weatherhead, "Robert Duncan and the Lyric," *Contemporary Literature,* 16 (Spring 1975): 163–174;

Robert C. Weber, "Robert Duncan and the Poem Resonance," *Concerning Poetry,* 2 (Spring 1978): 67–73.

Papers:

The most extensive collection of Duncan's papers is housed in the Poetry/Rare Books Collection, University Libraries, State University of New York at Buffalo. Smaller but important collections are housed in the Bancroft Library, University of California at Berkeley; Archive for the New Poetry, University of California at San Diego, La Jolla; Special Collections, Washington University; Special Collections, University of Connecticut, Storrs; and Special Collections, Kent State University, Kent, Ohio.

Larry Eigner

(6 August 1926 – 3 February 1996)

Benjamin Friedlander
State University of New York, Buffalo

BOOKS: *From the Sustaining Air* (Palma de Mallorca: Divers Press, 1953; enlarged edition, Eugene, Oreg.: Toad Press, 1967; republished with original contents, Oakland, Cal.: Coincidence Press, 1988);

Look at the Park (Swampscott, Mass.: Privately printed, 1958);

On My Eyes: Poems, photographs by Harry Callahan, introduction by Denise Levertov (Highlands, N.C.: Jargon Press, 1960);

Six Poems (Portland, Oreg.: Wine Press, 1967);

Another Time in Fragments (London: Fulcrum Press, 1967);

The- / Towards Autumn (Los Angeles: Black Sparrow Press, 1967);

Air: The Trees, illustrated by Bobbie Creeley (Los Angeles: Black Sparrow Press, 1968);

The Breath of Once Live Things: In the Field with Poe (Los Angeles: Black Sparrow Press, 1968);

A Line That May Be Cut: Poems from 1965 (London: Circle Press, 1968);

Valleys, Branches (London: Big Venus, 1969);

Flat and Round (Brooklyn, N.Y.: Pierrepont Press, 1969);

Circuits: A Microbook (Quebec: Athanor Books, 1971);

Selected Poems, edited by Samuel Charters and Andrea Wyatt (Berkeley: Oyez, 1972);

Looks Like Nothing, The Shadow Through Air: Poems, relief blocks by Ronald King (Guildford, Surrey, U.K.: Circle Press, 1972);

Words Touching Ground Under (Belmont, Mass.: Hellric Publications, Pyramid Pamphlet no. 3, 1972);

What You Hear (London: Edible Magazine, 1972);

Shape, Shadow, Elements Move (Los Angeles: Black Sparrow Press, 1973);

Things Stirring Together or Far Away (Los Angeles: Black Sparrow Press, 1974);

Anything on Its Side (New Rochelle, N.Y.: Elizabeth Press, 1974); republished in *What Is Inside, What Is Outside?: O One / An Anthology,* edited by

Larry Eigner (photograph by Debra Heimerdinger)

Leslie Scalapino (Oakland, Cal.: O Books, 1988);

My God the Proverbial: 42 Poems & 2 Prose Pieces (Berkeley: L Publications, 1975);

Suddenly It Gets Light and Dark in the Street: Poems 1961–1974 (Winchester, U.K.: Green Horse Press, 1975);

The Music Variety (Newton, Mass.: Roxbury Poetry Enterprises, 1976);

The World and Its Streets, Places (Santa Barbara: Black
    Sparrow Press, 1977);
Watching How or Why (New Rochelle, N.Y.: Elizabeth
    Press, 1977);
Cloud, Invisible Air (Rhinebeck, N.Y.: Station Hill,
    1978);
Heat Simmers Cold & (Paris: Orange Export Ltd.,
    1978);
Flagpole Riding (Alverstoke, Hampshire, U.K.: B.
    Hemensley, 1978);
Country Harbor Quiet Act Around: Selected Prose, intro-
    duction by Douglas Woolf, edited by Barrett
    Watten (Berkeley: This Press, 1978);
Time, Details, Of a Tree (New Rochelle: Elizabeth
    Press, 1979);
Lined up Bulk Senses (Providence, R.I.: Burning
    Deck, 1979);
Now There's a Morning, Hulk of the Sky (New Rochelle,
    N.Y.: Elizabeth Press, 1981);
*Earth Birds: Forty-Six Poems Written Between May 1964
    and June 1972* (Guildford, Surrey, U.K.: Circle
    Press, 1981);
Waters/Places/A Time, edited by Robert Grenier
    (Santa Barbara: Black Sparrow Press, 1983);
Areas Lights Heights: Writings 1954–1989, edited by
    Benjamin Friedlander (New York: Roof
    Books, 1989);
Cloudy All Right, tel-let (Charleston, Ill.), no. 5 (1990);
A Count of Some Things (Oakland, Cal.: Score Publica-
    tions, 1991);
*Windows Walls Yard Ways (Lines Squares Paths Worlds
    Backwards Sight),* edited by Grenier (Santa
    Rosa, Cal.: Black Sparrow Press, 1994);
Readiness Enough Depends On, edited by Grenier (Los
    Angeles: Sun & Moon Press, 1998).

SELECTED PERIODICAL PUBLICATIONS–
UNCOLLECTED: "Murder Talk: The Reception"
    (a play), *Duende,* no. 6 (1964): n. pag.;
"[Letter to the Editors]," *El Corno Emplumado,* no. 13
    (January 1965): 183;
"Come to Some Thing?" (a play), *Acts,* no. 2 (June
    1983): n. pag.

Larry Eigner is associated with the Black
Mountain Poets of the 1950s, and his work was included under that heading in the landmark 1960 anthology *The New American Poetry,* edited by Donald
M. Allen. More recently Eigner served as an influence on the Language Poets, with whom he had
been in conversation since the early 1970s. Formally, Eigner's poetry marks an important development in the use of line and page introduced by E. E.
Cummings and other Modernists in the 1920s, carried forward in the later work of Ezra Pound and

William Carlos Williams. The *shape* of Eigner's poetry is one of the most distinctive features of his
work. His abandonment of the left margin and subsequent break from a phraseology determined by
normative habits of sentence construction led the
way to a similar development in the poetry of Charles Olson, Paul Blackburn, Robert Duncan, and
many others. These formal aspects of the poem are
always subordinate, however, to the particularity of
perception which quickens Eigner's language and
gives meaning to the form. The poem, for Eigner, is
above all a mode of apprehending reality, a means
of engaging with the world. As Cid Corman wrote
in "*Another Time in Fragments* (Eigner)":

> In a way what is *most* startling, at least to me, is the san-
> ity of his vision, the straightness of it, which *may* be
> straitness. As if the strictness in this poetry were in the
> engrossment of the poet and that engrossment existen-
> tial in the extreme.

Eigner's poetics, which emphasize the exploratory
possibilities of language, have inspired an equally
fruitful exchange with the experimental writers of a
subsequent generation. Poet and critic Ron Silliman
paid tribute to this exchange by dedicating his 1986
anthology *In the American Tree* to Eigner. Silliman's
introduction especially remarks on Eigner's "rigorous and honest practice." Eigner's response to this
anthology–offered in a letter to Carroll F. Terrell
and eventually published in a book of Eigner's criticism, *Areas Lights Heights: Writings 1954–1989* (1989)–sums
up the poet's interests nicely:

> Hm, maybe this "language" poetry is centered on think-
> ing–the descendant or else the parent of speech?–rather
> than speech itself. Putting it up my alley. Thinking that
> gets man from one thing to the next. And realization,
> recognition or real awareness of things, may not be a
> different kettle of fish, much.

Lawrence Joel Eigner was born 6 August 1926
in Lynn, Massachusetts, the eldest of three sons.
Shoe City (as Lynn was then known) lay one town
over from the family residence in Swampscott,
where Eigner was to live until the age of fifty-one,
moving west shortly after his father's death to settle
near a brother in Berkeley, California. A forceps injury sustained at birth developed into cerebral
palsy, marking the poet's life from the beginning as
what one poem calls "a solid wall to eternity."
Eigner describes this injury and its related difficulties in many fictional and autobiographical prose
pieces. An error in measurement led to complications; Eigner's head was too large for his mother to
deliver. The mistake was caught only after it was

Larry Eigner (seated) with his brothers, Joe and Richard, and his parents, Bessie and Israel Eigner, early 1950s

too late to perform a caesarian. Until cryosurgery froze Eigner's left side at age thirty-five, the poet was a spastic, a condition to which Eigner attributes his "exacerbated" curiosity. As he says in his short statement "Not Forever Serious," "in order to relax at all I *had* to keep my attention away from myself, *had* to seek a home, coziness in the world."

The particularity of Eigner's relation to language and to his environment plays a prominent role in his mature work. Both parents, for instance, came from immigrant families, and Yiddish (or "brochen English," as Eigner quotes his grandmother as saying), often spoken at the dinner table, led to a fascination with unusual or hybrid locutions. Because Eigner grew up in the 1930s, a necessary thrift became second nature, finding its ultimate poetic expression in a general disdain for wasted words. (Eigner's prophetic environmentalism—evident in many poems and in such essays as "Integration Interchange"—shares the same source.) Early memories include visits to the seashore and excursions to Boston in the family's Model T; the mangled remains left by a hurricane also left an im-

pression, as did the wide expanse of trees surrounding his neighborhood. Eigner writes of these trees, which hid the sea from view: "pretty remote in the understanding was how they weren't infinite in their number and indestructible."

Eigner recorded this detail in "What a Time Distance," a prose piece included with his *Selected Poems* (1972). Here Eigner also describes the rigors of physical therapy, which seem to have been the most difficult aspect of his childhood:

> exercise on mattressed tables with the therapist trying to work your fingers to touch their tips, open and close to a tune "this little piggy went to market," bend your knees separately and together, and ankles.... Then trying to walk, to let go, mother or a therapist in front holding him by his wrists, the other person closing just behind, lift to step forward, now curve to go back, but left knee and hop jumpy, and there was an edge, ankle his shoe hurt unlikely to go down, heel in the air, everybody helping out right except him. The head therapist really grim and determined, footwork, pushing at his shins with her soles, swift knocks when they could get in, stepping on his arch.

One gets a sense from these lines that the body is under attack and that in the confusion of its response, a foot is put down (but not all the way), an anxious muscle stretched. This description also provides a glimpse into the true nature of thinking and writing for Eigner, for he commonly compares these two activities to walking. As Eigner says in "Not Forever Serious," "If you're willing enough to stop anywhere, anytime, hindsight says, a poem can be like walking down the street and noticing things, extending itself without obscurity or too much effort." The disparity between Eigner's difficulty in walking and the ease with which he takes notice of the world in a poem alerts the reader to a profundity in ordinary experience—and to the grace of mind which redeems experience by transposing its difficulties into the pleasures of an *extra*ordinary writing.

The impact of Eigner's palsy on his work cannot be underestimated but must be weighed carefully against the similarity of his insights about body and poetry to those of his contemporaries. The abstract clarity of a statement such as Charles Olson's "Limits / are what any of us / are inside" in "Letter 5" of *The Maximus Poems* (1983) finds moving corroboration in such observations as "The self is some head you can't go around," Eigner's wry comment on his own birth, given in the essay "Rambling (in) Life." What distinguishes Eigner's career from those of his closest associates is not so much the character of his experience—his "handicap"—as the urgency this experience confers upon the act of writ-

Dust jacket for Eigner's 1967 book, with a note by Robert Duncan, who wrote that Eigner's "phrasings are not broken off in an abrupt juncture but hover . . . suspended in their own time within the time of the poem"

ing, upon the task of writing as Eigner came to understand it. In his apprehension of this task, in his "stance toward reality" (to borrow Olson's phrase from his 1950 essay "Projective Verse"), Eigner was the sure ally of his contemporaries. Robert Duncan, for example, wrote a concise note on Eigner for the dust jacket of *Another Time in Fragments* (1967):

> We wanted not fragments of consciousness or utterance but immediacies set into motion, comparable to the localities of color in which Cézanne built up his visual world, to the instances of impulse in which American action painters work, to the immediacies of the music in which Webern composed; and here, Larry Eigner, "*against the abyss*" which he knows as a spastic, has over the last fifteen years raised the very body of a world whose reality we sought in poetry.

More particularly, Duncan notes, describing the aspect of Eigner's verse from which he himself derived the technique of his later work (especially "Passages"), Eigner's "phrasings are not broken off in an abrupt juncture but hover, having a margin of their own—stanzaic phrases—suspended in their own time within the time of the poem."

If there was a turning point in Eigner's life, it was the evening he first heard Cid Corman on the radio in 1949, tuning in by accident to the opening installment of "This Is Poetry," a program that was to issue for the next three years from WMEX in Boston (a period of time encompassing the inauguration of Corman's influential magazine *Origin*). Eigner, taking issue with Corman's manner of reciting poetry, struck up a correspondence. Corman soon put Eigner in contact with Robert Creeley, and a second correspondence was begun. On his own, Eigner had discovered Hart Crane and Cummings. Under Corman's tutelage Williams and Wallace Stevens were soon added to the list along with Corman's own poetry and Creeley's, and Olson's "Projective Verse." (Creeley soon had Eigner reading D. H. Lawrence, Robert Graves, Fyodor Dostoyevsky, and Francis Parkman as well.) Paul Blackburn also became a correspondent of Eigner around this time.

In 1953 Creeley's Divers Press brought out Eigner's first book, *From the Sustaining Air*. In these early poems there is a characteristically halting delivery but not the syntactic fragmentation of the work that was written even two or three years later. The reign of the left margin is but tentatively broken, the poem not yet loosened from the mark of the line's habitual return. Eigner's work in this book is close to the poetry of the early 1950s by his closest associates—Creeley, Corman, and Blackburn. Rhetorical and earnest, it cloaks within a carefully studied vernacular a sharp response to the received value, the complacent. As in Creeley's "The Rites" or Blackburn's more comical "The Assistance," the ordinary is upheld, fitted to a language as efficient as Marianne Moore's, as authoritative as Pound's.

The development of Eigner's work is swift and sure, evidenced in *From the Sustaining Air* by a roughly chronological arrangement that highlights about three years of writing. At the end of the book he states:

from the sustaining air . . .

There is the clarity of a shore
And shadow, mostly, brilliance . . .

When, wandering, I look from my page

I say nothing

   when asked

I am, finally, an incompetent, after all[.]

The lineation of the poem is clear but broken—like the shadows of a venetian blind. Despite the poet's avowal of incompetence, there is a mastery of speech rhythms highlighted by the affecting redundancy of the final line and by a marvelous sense of timing. Only after the fact does the reader notice how the pivotal words "I say nothing" conclude one sentence and begin another; the grammatical overlapping, so artfully conceived, complicates but does not disturb the reading. Here the poem underscores its larger meaning, that the world-sustaining language is not sustained *by* it. For all the clarity of our experience, all the beckoning disclosures of light, the very thing we would with simple competence relate is likely to remain ungraspable, unspeakable.

Eigner spent the summers of 1953 and 1954 at Camp Jened, a resort in the Catskills for physically disabled children and young adults. A short, as yet unpublished novel, "Through, Plain," eventually came out of this experience. Before beginning this novel Eigner had already written and published two short stories—"Act" and "Quiet," now collected with the rest of Eigner's fiction in *Country Harbor Quiet Act Around: Selected Prose* (1978)—and had quite probably begun work on two lengthy book reviews commissioned by Creeley for *The Black Mountain Review,* one on Kenneth Rexroth's *The Dragon and the Unicorn*

(1952), the other on John Steinbeck's *East of Eden* (1952). Several more stories were to follow. Indeed, before shifting emphasis for good in 1956, Eigner wrote more fiction than poetry.

The response to Eigner's work, though favorable, was still limited to a coterie of readers. William Carlos Williams—having received *From the Sustaining Air* from Creeley—wrote an admiring response, and Olson, too, now held the poet in high esteem, initially because of Eigner's strong sense of individual responsibility. In 1954, while attending a reading by Olson in Gloucester, Eigner had interrupted by asking the older poet (referring to "Letter 5" of *Maximus*), "Why did you attack Vincent Ferrini in your poem?" The significance of the question—and Olson was quick to realize this—was the reminder that poetry is not merely a statement, but an act. The Black Mountain Poets—Blackburn, Corman, Creeley, Duncan, Denise Levertov, Olson—all shared this insistence. Cid Corman narrates the entire story in his introduction to *The Gist of Origin 1951–1971* (1975). Olson would eventually memorialize the moment in *Maximus* with a poem called "(Literary Result)":

as Larry Eigner the one day yet, so many years ago I

read in Gloucester—to half a dozen people still—

   asked me

why, meaning my poetry doesn't

help anybody[.]

Soon Robert Duncan was also taking an interest. In 1957 Duncan circulated an open letter analyzing three poems published in the first issue of John Wieners's magazine *Measure,* one of them Eigner's "Brink"—later published in *On My Eyes: Poems* (1960). Not long after, Duncan and Eigner established a more direct contact, with Duncan assisting Eigner in the preparation of typescripts. Duncan also hoped at this time to produce Eigner's play "Murder Talk: The Reception" in San Francisco. Though the play eventually appeared in a 1964 issue of the magazine *Duende* dedicated to Eigner's work, the staging itself never occurred.

In 1958 Eigner's parents financed the publication of a second poetry collection, *Look at the Park.* Visually and in other ways the work resembles Eigner's maturer verse. The left margin no longer rules omnisciently; the poem assembles itself across the entire page. Structurally, two competing techniques are at play. In some places Eigner uses enjambment to unite the disparate elements of a broken form. In others the isolation of the line allows

*Eigner (second from right) at Golden Gate Park, San Francisco, in 1968 with his brother Richard
(far right) and poet Robert Duncan (third from right)*

these elements to maintain their discreteness, an equilibrium of phrases that gives meaning to the gaps between lines, charging that space with the upkeep of meaning.

One of the most striking poems in *Look at the Park,* "Do It Yrself," begins with the following observations:

> Now they have two cars to clean
> the front and back lawns
> bloom in the drought[.]

The poet also takes care to record the language of this scene—his own or the others' (the reader cannot tell)—no longer drawing a clear distinction between words and experience as he did in *From the Sustaining Air.* The poem now records the experience *of* words:

> why not turn the radio on the
> pious hopes of the Red Sox
>
> yes, that's a real gangling kid coming down the street[.]

Three seemingly unrelated assertions end the poem:

> sponges with handles
>
> we got trinaural hearing
>
> —they are taller than their cars[.]

There is no irony in the use of vernacular speech, no tension between the poet's perception of the scene around him and the language with which the scene makes itself known (nor is there tension between the scientific word "trinaural" and the slurred usage of "we got"). In "Do It Yrself" the "pious hopes of the Red Sox" and "a real gangling kid" are natural effects, the vividness of a spoken language let into the poem with all the generosity of William Carlos Williams, whose "pure products of America" are the very forebears of Eigner's apish teenager, his baseball fan pining for a radio, his family with two cars wasting water in a drought.

The poet, as Eigner's work presents him, is a spectator, as astonished by his own strangeness as by the world's. He remains one of and yet aloof from his fellows. Eigner's "they"—as in "they are taller than their cars"—are not the same "they" as the squares derided by the Beats or "the people—ourselves!" of Denise Levertov's "Merritt Parkway"; nor are they the same citizens of Massachusetts addressed so avuncularly in Olson's *Maximus.* Eigner's "they"—like their cars—are peculiar, powerful machines.

"Whether man is mostly animal, vegetable or mineral is an open question," writes Eigner in a letter to Louis Dudek, published in 1960 in the magazine *Delta.* "I imagine anybody would agree that an animal has the most overflowing and abundant existence of the three." Eigner's unwillingness to privilege one kind of existence over another, or even to assume that such differences are knowable, shows itself in his acceptance of "man," not simply as "animal" but as "vegetable" and "mineral" too. Levertov remarks on this openness in her introduction to

Eigner's first large collection, *On My Eyes,* published by Jargon Press in 1960. Levertov writes,

> He gives to the humblest pebble the same attention—and so the same value, by implication—as to, let's say, a man. Instinctively, pride cries out against this—until perhaps pride breaks and we look again, and see there is no contempt for man in this attention given to a pebble, only the sense that both are strange, unknowable, unpredictable.

An early poem first published in *On My Eyes,* " . . . ance," provides an extreme example of this equanimity of attention. The title is a suffix generally denoting an action or process—the substantive of a verb. Existence, Eigner suggests, is just such an "-ance," the action or process of Being, which roars on incessantly, invisible sea in a seashell:

> I am a machine for walking . . .
>
> the fly is
>   complicated
>
> she sits and hears the wind
>   coming . . .
>
> The girl
> is no marble[.]

How to distinguish an insect's sentience from the bluster of the wind, the poet asks, the stillness of a girl from marble immobility? "They" (the fly, the wind, the girl—and then oneself, a machine, perhaps, for walking) are all functions in the calculus of creation.

The photograph on the cover of *On My Eyes*—black trees in snow, lit from behind—provides a startling image for the work. The white of the page—interrupted by a dense foliage of print, or by a stand of words bent against the reader's attention—is the snow. The poems—variously shaped, yet a single growth—are inhabited by birds and squirrels, wind and rain, as the trees of Eigner's Swampscott are, massed in black against a spacious day:

> the great matter at the end of my soul
>
> the dog deciding to bark up my feet
> and all the trees, with the wind
>   dragging its roots
>   blown to bits, eyes that are stopped[.]

Where the soul's horizons are the limits of the familiar, so Eigner seems to say, the adventure of writing will require no other courage than attention.

But nature is not Eigner's only interest, and Eigner's immediate surroundings do not provide the only clues to the meaning of his work. In its construction on the page, for instance, Eigner's poetry is also akin to architecture, an "evolvement of space" accomplished with words instead of glass and steel. Eigner writes during the late 1950s in an essay on Walter Gropius, "Man modifies, adds to, even creates space, temporarily, let's say, by 'framing' it, by performing various actions." The reader sees the effect of these "actions" and hears their "evolvement" in several of the poems in *On My Eyes:*

> Boulevards, terraces
>   touch
> THE CONCRETE GLASS . . .
>
> staring at the supermarket
>   close the eyes, it is still there
>
>   this is the invisible
>   added to what there was[.]

The wall of the left margin has been cut away, revealing the interior spaces of a poetry that, like modern architecture, is a "participation in space." (Eigner further explores these ideas in an essay on Gertrude Stein's *Three Lives,* "Walls Dispose a City," first published in 1963 in the magazine *Kulchur.*) As a product of the mind, a supermarket—*even* a supermarket—is essentially invisible. For what Eigner admires about buildings—and the same is true, metaphorically, of poems—is not the imposing presence of their materials or form but the way such architectural structures can excite the imagination.

In the late 1950s Eigner also wrote his one attempt at a long poem, *The Breath of Once Live Things: In the Field with Poe,* published in 1959 in the magazine *Foot* and brought out in book form by John Martin's Black Sparrow Press in 1968. (Black Sparrow then became Eigner's principal publisher, bringing out major collections of his poetry in the 1970s, 1980s, and 1990s.) The poem is an experiment in continuity, ungainly perhaps for the effort, resembling less the long poems of Eigner's contemporaries than the sorts of work first produced in the 1970s and 1980s by the Language Poets. In its discontinuities and free associations, in its powers of description, *The Breath of Once Live Things* calls to mind especially the work of such readers of Eigner as Clark Coolidge in his *American Ones* (1981) and Lyn Hejinian in her *Writing Is an Aid to Memory* (1996). As Coolidge declares in *L=A=N=G=U=A=G=E* magazine, giving articulation to the influence, "Eigner is an *on-going* register." Especially effective in *The Breath of Once Live*

Things is the description of a storm witnessed from inside a house:

> divided windows
>   bring in the shattering depths
>
> then clouds
>
> I think what passes over our heads
> are huge things
>
>   lightning, blind
> split
>   naked immensities of the whole[.]

In 1962 Eigner underwent a surgical procedure to freeze the brain cells responsible for his uncontrolled movements. From boyhood on, he had contended with the flailing of his spastic limbs, with the wildness of his left arm and the wound-up energy of an "ungovernable foot." Typing, of all activities, provided relief from the wildness, from the distraction of the flailing, and from the effort of holding the body still, or trying to. Reading–dependent upon the ability to concentrate–was more difficult. "I used to sit," Eigner writes in his story "Globe," "screwed up whole days, my left knee and ankle crossed around by right." The operation was a huge success. Writing Douglas Blazek three years later, Eigner sums up the procedure and its aftereffects as follows:

> Sept. 62 cryosurgery, frostbite in the thalamus (awakened to see if i was numbed, test whether they had right spot, felt much like killing of a tooth nerve!), tamed (and numbed some) my wild left side, since when I can sit still without effort, and have more capacity for anger etc. Before, I had to be extrovert, or anyway hold the self off on a side, in this very concrete, perpetual sense. A puzzlement of the will.

Fragmentation rather than coherence of the will, the care and commotion of a self held "off on a side," expresses itself in Eigner's work as an openness to what is outside the self–the breadth of the world, vision's wealth. The correlation of "I" and "eye," self and sight, is habitual. For Eigner, the self, like the glassed-in porch of his Swampscott home (the vantage point for much of Eigner's poetry), is but a focal point of attention, is not in and of itself important.

A poem published in *Air: The Trees* (1968) makes vivid this outward cast of Eigner's thought. Tracing a movement from his own room, filled with music, to a distant stillness of birds, he writes:

> I in the foreground
>   mirror of time huge as
> I may be small
>   face puffed short

> music comes
>
> we have a forest
>
> trees the leaves mass
>
> summer autumn too
>
> wind, sun and
>   stars move[.]

In 1964, traveling for the first time by airplane, Eigner visited his brother Joseph in St. Louis. Two years later the poet ventured further west to stay with a second brother, Richard, in San Francisco, stopping in Missouri again on the way back. The San Francisco trip included a first-time meeting with Robert Duncan (they would meet again in 1970 when Eigner again ventured west and then more frequently after Eigner relocated to California in the 1980s). The widening of reference in Eigner's poetry, partly traceable to his widening experience of the world beyond Swampscott, becomes especially noticeable in his work of the 1960s. A visit, for instance, to the site of the former St. Louis slave mart leads in one strange poem to a meditation on freedom and necessity. In this poem (published in *Air: The Trees*) Eigner wonders about the place of history in everyday experience. Can such reminders of the past as the cotton gin, for instance, tell something about the capacity or incapacity of the imagination? Eigner asks:

> why risk your shirt no
> hands to pick the cotton no
>   gin
>   in a man's thoughts[.]

The poet's increasing concern with such questions–"the drunk stagger of human affairs," as Eigner puts it in his *Stony Hills* interview–showed itself more and more frequently in poems that made mention of Vietnam, the Kennedy and King assassinations, the destruction of the environment, as well as in poems that made reference to more oblique facts of history or politics.

Eigner's work continued at this time to develop formally as well. Already in the mid 1950s, but with increasing insistence as the 1960s progressed, Eigner produced a poetry of seemingly spontaneous grammar, a language capable of sudden starts and stops. Freed from the constraints of conventional stanzaic form to take the breadth of the page, Eigner began more and more to explore the *syntactic* possibilities afforded by the new relation of the poem to space. Using line and stanza breaks and the staggered presentation of his words to determine the voicing of the poem–following the

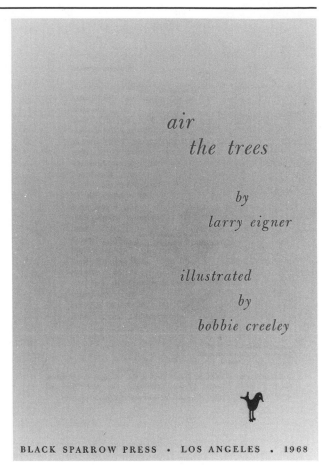

air
the trees

by
larry eigner

illustrated
by
bobbie creeley

BLACK SPARROW PRESS · LOS ANGELES · 1968

Frontispiece and title page for Eigner's 1968 book, which includes poems that demonstrate his widening experience in the world

lessons of Olson's "Projective Verse"—Eigner almost immediately began to abandon conventional sentence construction as well. This change first shows itself in a near-complete eschewal of punctuation and capitalization. The reader must instead intuit by the progression of ideas where one sentence ends and the next begins. In his most characteristic moments Eigner builds from sentence fragments a singular utterance parsed almost as if idiomatically by the visual presentation of the words. So widespread has this innovation become that it is difficult to credit any individual with its introduction. Given, however, the underground circulation of Eigner's work in the late 1950s—Charles Olson and Denise Levertov each reviewed the manuscript of *On My Eyes* and even had a hand in selecting poems, while Robert Duncan prepared the typescripts of Eigner's submissions to *The New American Poetry*—it is not far-fetched to assume a deeper and earlier impact than the publication record suggests. Eigner's role in the development of a phraseological poetics (for want of a better description) unfortunately has rarely been acknowledged. Indeed, the radicalism

of Eigner's syntax has largely gone unremarked—Barrett Watten's essay in *Total Syntax* (1985) being an important exception.

In Eigner's best-remembered poetry the arrangement of the poem on the page—despite disjunction—tends to maximize rather than minimize coherence, as in the following meditation on air travel first published in 1965 in the magazine *Wild Dog* and collected in 1969 in the short volume *Flat and Round:*

> Last day on earth
>   for a while at least . . .
>
> a plane goes over
>   my eyes
>
>   a shadow lost
> darkness space
>   not night, the day
>   24 hours[.]

Though there are complete sentences here and there, the poem largely consists of a staccato recitation of thematically related details—a fragmentariness that makes sense given the shifting viewpoints of the poem. In some places the poet imagines himself up in the sky; in others he places himself on the ground, looking up. Some lines evoke commercial air travel; others seem to describe the experience of an astronaut. Yet by cutting away all extraneous verbiage, Eigner arrives at a compactness of utterance that can evoke this wide array of thoughts without confusion. Indeed, like any mosaic, these bits of description achieve their greatest effect when incorporated by the eye—the mind's eye of the reader—into a single whole, something which concision alone makes possible. The lacuna inserted between "darkness" and "space" and the elision of verb between "day" and "24 hours" are thus essential to the effect of the poem. In these signature moments the layout of the poem on the page becomes something other than a mere score for oral performance—it becomes an integral part of the grammar of the poem.

Poems such as the above led Samuel Charters—in his introduction to Eigner's *Selected Poems*—to speak of Eigner's poetry as "a purifying fact":

> The poetry is strong—immediate, open, direct. . . . To read work as deliberately pure as Eigner's is to be forced . . . to be conscious of the point where other poets have been less rigorous with themselves.

Yet if Eigner's most admirable qualities as a poet are directness and openness—his openness to perception and his directness of expression—he has written obscurer verses on occasion also. Strangely, this obscurity shares the same source as the purity. Eigner's curiosity—his openness, not only to perception but also to the oddness of what perception allows the reader to think or say, the directness with which Eigner expresses even the *incomprehensibility* of existence—leads here and there to a writing as dense as any achieved by Gertrude Stein. The following lines from Eigner's second large collection, *Another Time in Fragments,* are an example:

> the bodies we have to name going
> through them, the air
> fires the dead falling away
>   every moon, the trees waving
>   rabbits, the cores of stars
>   and giants worming the world
>   the reasonable range
>   Uranus drinks on its axis[.]

The whorl of associations offered here—cadged, no doubt, at least in part, from astronomy texts and books of mythology—remains bewildering. For that reason they are attractive to poets more interested

in the materiality of language—the density of sound and sense language can afford—than in its purity. Yet *Another Time in Fragments* also includes many more straightforwardly evocative poems, including several written in the hospital:

> this time your water is golden
>   I smell like a bad wing
>
> about to die maybe   I
>   who could do nothing about it[.]

The widening of Eigner's experience shows itself also in an increased number of correspondents. Many of these correspondents were the small press publishers who brought out so much of Eigner's output in the 1960s, 1970s, and 1980s. Samples of these letters appear in well-known journals of the time such as *Yūgen* and *El Corno Emplumado* as well as in obscurer magazines such as *The Mile High Underground, La-Bas,* and *Tamarind.*

The year 1972 saw the publication of Eigner's *Selected Poems. Earth Ship,* no. 8 (a special issue devoted to Eigner), also appeared that year. Eigner's introduction to this special issue (a short statement now called "Arrowhead of Meaning") offered a summation of his past and present goals as a poet:

> I once wanted to do big things and to try of course is the only way to begin, and to quite an extent continuing depends on it too. . . . I wonder about purpose, what priorities if not principles are possible, how to balance things.
>
>   Enough it seems has been produced, enough writings, enough cars, enough music, enough of a lot else.

In the early 1970s an era of poetry—the period which gave historical definition to Eigner's generation of poets—was coming to an end. Both Olson and Blackburn were dead while Corman—disenchanted with life in America—had resettled in Japan.

In 1970 Eigner first met Robert Grenier, who was then an instructor at Tufts University. Grenier had been reading Eigner's poetry since 1960, after first discovering the work at the Grolier Bookshop in Cambridge and in the Poetry Room of the Lamont Library at Harvard University. In 1968 Grenier taught Eigner's poetry at the University of California at Berkeley to such students as Ron Silliman and Barrett Watten. After moving on from Tufts in 1971 to teach at Franconia College, he kept up both the personal and intellectual relationship, bringing Eigner from Swampscott three times to give readings in New Hampshire. Except for the occasional visit from a passing poet, all of Eigner's contacts with other writers had been conducted by mail—a circumstance that would not really change until the move to California. As a consequence Eigner's ongoing exchange with Grenier took on great importance. Asked in 1977 in his *Stony Hills* interview about giving poetry readings, Eigner remarked, "Starting up a conversational or reactive situation I can relax and go along in is something I've been more or less incapable of." "At Franconia," on the other hand, "back at the instructor's place (Bob Grenier's), there was quite a bit of dialogue, enough anyway so I learned a few things—at least the 2nd and 3rd times when I was there a few days and people came up now and then." Grenier also assisted Eigner in manuscript preparation, typing up the two major Black Sparrow collections of the 1970s, *Things Stirring Together or Far Away* (1974) and *The World and Its Streets, Places* (1977). Grenier at this time was also coeditor of *This* magazine with Barrett Watten. *This* published Eigner's work in each of its first five issues, and Watten himself eventually edited and published Eigner's collected fiction, *Country Harbor Quiet Act Around: Selected Prose*. These collaborations show the beginnings of what came to be known as Language Writing.

The year 1973 saw the release of *Getting It Together, a Film on Larry Eigner, Poet,* which featured Allen Ginsberg reading and discussing Eigner's work, as well as footage of Eigner himself. The film was made by Leonard Henny and Jan Boon, based on a text by Michael F. Podulke. In 1974, in addition to *Things Stirring Together or Far Away,* The Elizabeth Press brought out *Anything on Its Side* (the first of many Eigner books which this elegant press, directed by James Weil, would publish). In collections as large as these the reader begins to appreciate both the singularity of Eigner's work and the gradations of tone and difficulty that mark his poetry as the work of his *life.* Thus, alongside charming aphorisms and haiku-like description are more involved renderings of nature or evocations of meandering thoughts; there are poems that communicate their meaning idiomatically and poems that strive for a more poetic utterance.

The following example of Eigner's ear for the vernacular comes from *Things Stirring Together or Far Away:*

> a brand new car
>   is a brand new car
> I'll see it in the morning[.]

And the following example of Eigner's gift for aphorism comes from *Anything on Its Side:*

> Time the unflagging
>   bird . . .[.]

This example of Eigner's powers of description is from the same book:

> Music is human in the event . . .
>   the great sea is orchestrated with men
>
>   the wind and the waves[.]

And this quote shows Eigner at his most haiku-like, from the 1975 collection *My God the Proverbial: 42 Poems & 2 Prose Pieces:*

> a hole in the clouds moves
>   the hole in the sky[.]

In 1976 Charles Bernstein and Bruce Andrews inaugurated *L=A=N=G=U=A=G=E,* a magazine that gave focus to the growing "tendency" (as Ron Silliman has put it) called Language Writing. The opening piece of this issue was Eigner's "Approaching Things Some Calculus How Figure It of Everyday Life Experience," which appeared alongside Clark Coolidge's "Larry Eigner Notes." In "Approaching Things" Eigner ponders the role of the poet in a world of happenstance:

> Well, how does (some of) the forest go together with the trees. How might it, maybe. Forest of possibilities (in language anyway)—ways in and ways out. . . . And I feel my way in fiddling a little, or then sometimes more, on the roof of the burning or rusting world.

A year later another collection appeared, *The World and Its Streets, Places,* Eigner's largest and richest to date. Among the noteworthy pieces in this book are several political poems ("the philosophy of risk / can breed indifference," "Madness!," "what a / uniform is," "peace / peace"), poems about time ("let / time / go on," "s e q u o i a," "time passes," "the jarring firecracker," "Time goes where"), and many other, less easily categorized works. Here, for instance, is one of Eigner's most hauntingly beautiful poems, "The Lights Go Out," which begins:

> Now we are alone with our thoughts
>   but where are they
>
>   tomorrow I can continue reading[.]

Here we also find "(t o r e c o g n i z e w o r l d w i d e a n i m a l s t a t e o f n a t u r e)," which concludes:

> no billboards
> in the sky, we may walk

the limits of jobs, not too much

listening, sing

somewhat, learn
what to do with ourselves[.]

In 1978 Eigner moved to California, living first in a group home (an experience partly narrated in the essay "Course Matter") and settling finally into a house in Berkeley provided by his brother Richard. Eigner's caretaker in this house for the next decade was Robert Grenier, who undertook the living arrangement as part of his "commitment to literature." During this time the two worked together to fashion a series of verified typescripts of Eigner's poems, accumulating some twelve hundred transcriptions of Eigner's often difficult-to-make-out originals. These verified typescripts represent about half of Eigner's output and will provide an invaluable guide for those who work in the future on Eigner's manuscripts without benefit of consultation with the poet. Grenier also edited Eigner's next large collections for Black Sparrow Press, *Waters/Places/A Time* (1983) and *Windows Walls Yard Ways (Lines Squares Paths Worlds Backwards Sight)* (1994). This latter collection includes a preface by Grenier, "How I Read Larry Eigner."

Another poet who worked with Eigner on his manuscripts was Robert Kocik, a student of Grenier and also of Duncan at the New College of California. Kocik with Joseph Simas edited a volume of Eigner's letters to the French poets Joseph Guglielmi (Eigner's translator) and Claude Royet-Journoud. This book was published in Paris in 1987. Especially noteworthy about this edition is the painstaking reproduction of Eigner's typescripts. The documentary value of these typescripts is enormous, for they reveal much about the effort Eigner put into writing, both physically and intellectually. As Eigner said in the *Stony Hills* interview, "letters get crowded just from my attempt to save time, i.e., cover less space, avoid putting another sheet in the typewriter for a few more words as I at least hope there will only be."

In 1983 Eigner read at the St. Mark's Poetry Project and with Grenier conducted a workshop. The statement written for this occasion, "How Much? What's Up? A Bit of the Questionable World," includes the following self-reflections:

I've been, am, more or less a nut about having things adequate to staying, keeping alive and taking my ease without much pain or discomfort—loafing as Whitman had it—while I've been goal-oriented more generally (speaking) too, as well as curious as to things beyond or partly beyond reach, out of sight and/or hearing; and boredom has never been a problem with me, likewise, for instance I al-

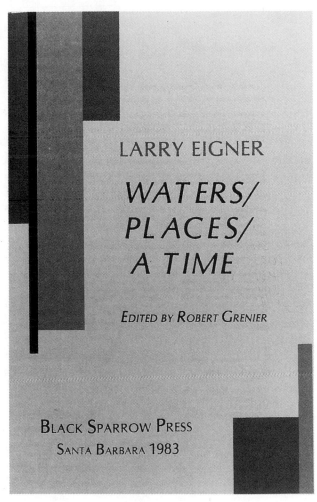

Title page for Eigner's 1983 book, which won the San Francisco State Poetry Center Award in 1984

ways believed in appreciating things and making them out to myself, making it and coming from behind getting knowledge and so on under my belt.

The following year Eigner's *Waters/Places/A Time* received the San Francisco State Poetry Center Award, judged by Beverly Dahlen. This volume again includes a substantial mixture of poems taking up favorite themes as well as new ones, offering meditative, sometimes difficult poems about time and history, nature, human affairs, and poetry itself. One poem begins:

There is no community

he goes to

Work   mornings[.]

And another—one of many that concern music in this collection:

piano and strings

the wind and rain

go together[.]

In 1989 Eigner's *Areas Lights Heights: Writings, 1954–1989* appeared. Long in the making, this annotated compilation of Eigner's essays and short statements of poetics includes also a few letters and topical poems.

In recent years Eigner principally gave himself to the writing of shorter poems, affirming his lifelong affinity for haiku. His "Quiet grass // still air // rocks // the locust // cries," written "*after Bashō*"—published in *Waters / Places / A Time*—captures what Robert Hass has called (in an essay on haiku) "some feeling in the arrest of the image that what perishes and what lasts forever have been brought into conjunction, and accompanying that sensation . . . a feeling of release from the self." Eigner echoed the latter portion of this statement in his "Blurb for Disabled Calligraphy": "Self-assertion (or the isolated I, like anything else enough by itself) is none too interesting, is unlike (self/) discovery a blind alley."

In Eigner's work, as Barrett Watten has written, "the imagination is thought through to a real demonstration of its power." Eigner, in a poem from *Windows Walls Yard Ways,* describes his project this way:

here I go again

what to make of
the slightly exotic

or the whole world for that matter[.]

Letters:

"Obscenity, Civilization, Literature & Forests" (a letter to Louis Dudek), *Delta,* no. 10 (January–March 1960): 19;

"[Letter to LeRoi Jones]," *Yūgen,* no. 7 (1961): 44–48;

"Dear J . . . , L . . . , . . . , . . . ," *Mile High Underground,* 1 (Summer 1967): 2;

"[Letter to the Editor]," *La-Bas,* no. 6 (March 1977): n. pag.;

"[Letter to Marcia Lawther]," *Tamarind* (August 1982): n. pag.;

Larry Eigner Letters (to Joseph Guglielmi and Claude Royet-Journoud), edited by Robert Kocik and Joseph Simas (Paris: Moving Letters Press, 1987);

"Letters [to Douglas Blazek] (Selected by Benjamin Friedlander)," *Revista Canaria de Estudios Ingleses,* no. 18 (April 1989): 11–18.

Interviews:

Peter Bates, "Interview with Larry Eigner," *Stony Hills,* nos. 3, 4, 5, and 6 (1978–1980); republished in revised form as "Qs & As (?) Large and Small / Parts of a Collaborate," in Eigner's *Areas Lights Heights: Writings, 1954–1989*;

Marian Kindel, "Larry Eigner," *Kaleidoscope,* no. 5 (Spring 1982): 10–14;

Benjamin Friedlander, "Larry Eigner Talking," *Chumolungma Globe,* no. 1 (1987): 50–53.

Bibliographies:

Andrea Wyatt, *A Bibliography of Works by Larry Eigner 1937–1969* (Berkeley: Oyez, 1970);

Irving P. Leif, *Larry Eigner: A Bibliography of His Work,* with a preface by Larry Eigner (Metuchen, N.J.: Scarecrow Press, 1989).

References:

Clark Coolidge, "Larry Eigner Notes," in *The L=A=N=G=U=A=G=E Book,* edited by Bruce Andrews and Charles Bernstein (Carbondale: Southern Illinois University Press, 1984), pp. 224–227;

Cid Corman, "*Another Time in Fragments* (Eigner)," in his *At Their Word: Essays on the Art of Language,* volume 2 (Santa Barbara: Black Sparrow Press, 1978), pp. 145–150;

Corman, "Introduction," in his *The Gist of Origin 1951–1971* (New York: Grossman, 1975), pp. xv–xxxvii;

Robert Hass, "Images," in his *Twentieth Century Pleasures: Prose on Poetry* (New York: Ecco Press, 1984), pp. 269–308;

Ron Silliman, "Language, Poetry, Realism," introduction to *In the American Tree,* edited by Silliman (Orono, Maine: National Poetry Foundation, 1986), pp. xv–xxiii;

Barrett Watten, "Missing 'X': Formal Meaning in Crane & Eigner," in his *Total Syntax* (Carbondale: Southern Illinois University Press, 1985), pp. 168–190.

Papers:

Eigner's papers are housed in the Department of Special Collections, Kenneth Spencer Research Library, at the University of Kansas Libraries, Lawrence, Kansas.

Carolyn Forché

(28 April 1950 –)

Constance Coiner
State University of New York at Binghamton

BOOKS: *Gathering the Tribes* (New Haven & London: Yale University Press, 1976);

The Country Between Us (limited edition, Port Townsend, Wash.: Copper Canyon Press, 1981; trade edition, New York & Cambridge, Mass.: Harper & Row, 1982; London: Cape, 1983);

The Angel of History (New York: HarperCollins / Newcastle upon Tyne: Bloodaxe, 1994);

Colors Come from God—Just like Me, illustrated by Charles Cox (Nashville, Tenn.: Abingdon Press, 1995);

Lani Maestro: Essays, by Forché, Rina Carvajal, and Stephen Horne (New York: Art in General, 1996).

OTHER: *Women in American Labor History, 1825–1935: An Annotated Bibliography,* by Forché, Martha Jane Soltow, and Murray Massre (East Lansing: School of Labor and Industrial Relations, Michigan State University, 1972);

Claribel Alegría, *Flowers from the Volcano,* translated by Forché (Pittsburgh: University of Pittsburgh Press, 1982);

El Salvador: Work of Thirty Photographers, text by Forché, edited by Harry Mattison and others (New York: Writers and Readers Publishing Cooperative, 1983);

"Sensibility and Responsibility," in *The Writer and Human Rights,* edited by the Toronto Arts Group for Human Rights (Garden City, N.Y.: Anchor Press/Doubleday, 1983);

"A Fantasy of Birches," in *Singular Voices: American Poetry Today,* edited by Stephen Berg (New York: Avon, 1985), pp. 55–60;

"A Lesson in Commitment," in *The Writer in Our World: A Triquarterly Symposium,* edited by Reginald Gibbons (Boston: Atlantic Monthly Press, 1986), pp. 30–38;

Robert Desnos, *The Selected Poems of Robert Desnos,* translated by Forché and William Kulik (New York: Ecco Press, 1991);

Carolyn Forché

Shooting Back: Photography by and about the Homeless, text by Forché, catalogue to accompany a Smithsonian Institution traveling exhibition (Washington, D.C.: Washington Project for the Arts, 1991);

"The Province of Radical Solitude," in *The Writer on Her Work,* volume 2, edited by Janet Sternburg (New York: Norton, 1991);

Against Forgetting: Twentieth-Century Poetry of Witness, edited by Forché (New York: Norton, 1993).

RECORDINGS: Audiocassette of Forché reading from *The Country Between Us* (Washington, D.C.: Watershed Foundation, 1982);

Audiocassette of Forché reading selected poems (New York: Academy of American Poets, 1994).

SELECTED PERIODICAL PUBLICATIONS-
UNCOLLECTED: "Six Blocks from Velco's," as
    Carolyn Sidlosky, *Seventeen* (January 1969):
    85, 110;
"Upheaval in El Salvador–Stories of Three
    Women," *Ms.* (January 1980): 91–96;
"Anatomy of Counterrevolution: The Road to Re-
    action in El Salvador," *Nation* (14 June 1980):
    712–716;
"El Salvador: The Next Vietnam?," *Progressive* (Feb-
    ruary 1981): 27–29;
"El Salvador: An Aide Memoire," *American Poetry Re-
    view,* 10 (July/August 1981): 3–7;
"Letters to an Open City," *American Poetry Review,* 16
    (November/December 1987): 9–13.

Carolyn Forché's poetry of witness, which engenders human empathy, subverts the dominant
American poetic since World War II, which generally cultivates individuation. From early in her career Forché has been preoccupied with kinship, including cross-cultural kinship. Forché's work has renewed controversy about the relation of art to politics, about "suitable" subjects for poetry. Although
the poet rightly argues (in "El Salvador: An Aide
Memoire" and elsewhere) that all language is political, that "vision is always ideologically charged,"
she has nevertheless been categorized as a leading
"political" poet. Her work has been compared to
that of Denise Levertov, Adrienne Rich, Muriel
Rukeyser, Pablo Neruda, and Anna Akhmatova–all
anti-imperialist, politically engaged writers who pro-
mote global as well as personal kinship. The private
anguish of Sylvia Plath's, Anne Sexton's, and Robert Lowell's confessional poetry provides a provocative contrast to the public issues of human rights
violations, foreign policy, war, and poverty addressed in Forché's work.

Carolyn Louise Forché, the eldest of seven
children, was born in Detroit on 28 April 1950 to
working-class parents, Michael Joseph and Louise
Nada Blackford Sidlosky. Forché's mother encouraged her daughter's voracious reading as well as her
poetry-writing, which she first undertook at age
nine. Her father labored as a tool and dye maker ten
or twelve hours a day, six or sometimes seven days
a week. Forché's spirited paternal grandmother,
Anna Bassar Sidlosky, an immigrant from Czecho-
slovakia who lived for extended periods in the Sidlosky household until Forché was eighteen, profoundly influenced the poet's life. Forché first
learned to invent language from her grandmother,
who spoke little English and created her own color-
ful, if limited, version of the language, partly to display her resistance to American culture. In "A Fan-

tasy of Birches," for example, Forché tells us that
Anna called a colander a "macaroni-stop-water-go-
head." In exchange for modeling such inventiveness, the poet continues, "Anna has in the years
since her death determined to be included in any
book of poems I might complete. *I want to be in the
book,* she says, standing behind me in a room late at
night, leaning on her old potato shovel." This formidable woman "never assimilated," Forché has written in "The Province of Radical Solitude," "and although she was 'naturalized,' never became more
than a refugee from a country erased by war." Another element of Anna's legacy, then, "was an insistence that the world as I knew it was not the only
world, and American life not the only possible life."

Forché attended Our Lady of Sorrows School
for twelve years. In an interview with Constance
Coiner, Forché observed that one of the lasting effects of her Catholic upbringing has been that she is
"a person in moral dialogue with the world." She
was deeply affected by the poverty she saw in Detroit, by the civil rights movement, and by the Vietnam War, which she actively opposed. On 14
March 1969 she married Bruce Charles Forché;
they divorced in 1970. Forché received a B.A. from
Michigan State University in 1972 and an M.F.A.
from Bowling Green State University in 1975. In
1981 Forché married James Grantham Turner; the
couple divorced in 1983. A professor at George Mason University in Fairfax, Virginia, the poet lives
with her husband–Harry Mattison, a documentary
photographer, whom she married in 1984–and their
son, Sean Christophe, born in 1986.

Forché's first book of poems, *Gathering the Tribes*
(1976), received the coveted Yale Series of Younger Poets Award in 1975. These poems derived partly from
Forché's alternately living among Pueblo Indians near
Taos, New Mexico, and backpacking in the desert re-
gions of Utah, on the Pacific Crest Trail, along the
Olympic Peninsula, and in the Okanogan region of
British Columbia. As its title suggests, this volume is
characterized not by the self-absorption predominant in
twentieth-century American verse but by a desire for
community, incorporating, among other voices, those
of Pueblo Indians and her own Slovak ancestors, especially her paternal grandmother, Anna.

"Burning the Tomato Worms"–the central
and longest poem in the volume, divided into thirteen sections–establishes the grandmother's significance in the poet's life and work. "Before I was
born," the poet writes, "my body as snowfat / Crept
over Wakhan," a mountainous region in northern
Afghanistan to which the poet has traced her ancestors. (They later migrated north into the Russian-
Czech borderlands.) Uzbek, to which section 3 re-

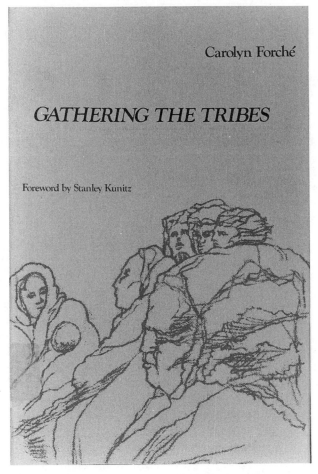

Carolyn Forché

GATHERING THE TRIBES

Foreword by Stanley Kunitz

*Dust jacket for Forché's first book, published in 1976 as part of
the Yale Series of Younger Poets*

fers, was a language spoken by the people of Wakhan. Anna passes on to her granddaughter a homily, perhaps an Uzbek proverb: "Eat Bread and Salt and Speak the Truth."

The following lines recall Anna's escaping from her Slovak village during World War II:

> *When time come*
> *We go quick*
> *I think*
> *What to take*
>
> On her back ground wheat and straw dolls
> In the sack white cheese, duck blood[.]

History has uprooted Anna, who in escaping the pogrom to the United States had to raise her children in "a foreign country," and she transmitted this sense of dislocation to her granddaughter. Acknowledging a deep ambivalence about her native United States, Forché has traveled widely, is fluent in Spanish and French, and has studied other languages, including Tewa (Pueblo Indian). Forché's

poetry probes the validity of Anna's angry declaration about the United States, "*You have nothing,*" a charge first appearing in "Burning the Tomato Worms." This poem also introduces the preposition "between" ("Nothing of her [Anna's] old age or my childhood / Came between us"), which in Forché's work refers to that which joins as well as to that which separates individuals, communities, and countries. Employing images that recur in Forché's poetry—blood, fire, whiteness, snow, bread, flesh—"Burning the Tomato Worms" includes rituals and rites of passage, such as the ceremonial breadmaking and the girl's sexual initiation. More importantly, the poem includes the challenge Anna makes to her granddaughter—and the poet in turn implicitly extends to her readers: "She [Anna] was asking me to go with her / To the confrontation of something."

"Burning the Tomato Worms" and "Kalaloch" are probably the most frequently anthologized of the poems included in *Gathering the Tribes*. Like "Tomato Worms," "Kalaloch" is ritualistic and deploys imagery characteristic of Forché's poetry—wood, bleached whiteness, stone, bone, fire, flesh. "Kalaloch" refers to a remote wilderness spot on the Olympic Peninsula's Pacific coast where the poet and her companion, Jacynthe, sensuously, silently commune with nature and with one another. Like Native American poets, Forché has a regard for all living things, and the poet and Jacynthe make love while simultaneously coupling with the earth and sea:

> I stripped and spread
> on the sea lip, stretched
> to the slap of the foam
> and the vast red dulce.
> Jacynthe gripped the earth
> in her fists, opened—
> the boil of the tide
> shuffled into her.

As if removed from history and suspended in time, "Kalaloch," as described by Kenneth Rexroth in 1976 in *American Poetry Review*, "is a little drama of peace found out of the world" or "in the world as it used to be." "Kalaloch," however, is not merely nostalgic for a simpler, preindustrial world. Like *Gathering the Tribes* as a whole, the poem implicitly opposes the dominant cultural values of acquisitive individualism that deify profit while denigrating humanity and the natural world.

In *Gathering the Tribes* Forché is preoccupied with kinship; extending that work, *The Country Between Us* (1981) resonates with a sense of international kinship. From January 1978 to March 1980 Forché made extended trips to El Salvador, each lasting several months. During this period she documented human-rights violations for Amnesty International, to which she has belonged since 1975. While living in El Salvador, she also wrote eight of the twenty-two poems included in *The Country Between Us,* her second volume of poetry and the Academy of American Poets' 1981 Lamont Poetry Selection. The collection has three sections, In Salvador, 1978–80; Reunion; and Ourselves or Nothing. (The longest poem in the volume, "Ourselves or Nothing," stands alone, a section in itself.)

In 1980 Forché worked closely with Monsignor Oscar Romero—the beloved archbishop of San Salvador who was assassinated that year by a rightwing death squad while saying mass at a hospital for the terminally ill—and later dedicated a portion of *The Country Between Us* to his memory. In "El Salvador: An Aide Memoire" Forché relates that in March 1980, after several attempts had been made on her life, Monsignor Romero asked that she return to the United States to "tell the American peo-

ple what is happening." In the same essay she says that her El Salvador experience transformed her life and work: it prevented "me from ever viewing myself or my country again through precisely the same fog of unwitting connivance." After returning to the United States, the poet visited nearly all fifty states, reading from *The Country Between Us* and carrying out Romero's last request of her.

As previously noted, *The Country Between Us* has renewed controversy about the relation of art to politics. This peculiarly North American debate assumes that only certain poems are political, stigmatizing "political" poems and failing to acknowledge the ideological constitution of all literary texts. The opposition to "political" poetry, as Forché observed in "A Lesson in Commitment," extends beyond explicitly polemical work to any "impassioned voices of witness," to any who leave "the safety of self-contemplation to imagine and address the larger world." Forché is disturbed that issues she considers essentially moral and ethical are treated as political in the narrowest sense: imprisonment for matters of conscience, torture, the slaughter of civilian noncombatants in time of war, the expenditure of the world for arms exceeding the total income of the poorer half of humanity.

Readers need to understand something of the situation in El Salvador in order to understand more fully the eight "Salvador" poems in *The Country Between Us.* They also need to be aware of the role the United States played in El Salvador's twelve-year civil war that ended 1 January 1992 in a United Nations–brokered peace accord. In "A Lesson in Commitment" Forché recounts the events that led to her going to El Salvador—an interesting, even amusing, story. Forché's "El Salvador: An Aide Memoire"—which introduces, theoretically frames, and explains some of the references in the "Salvador" poems—comprises useful preparatory reading. The film *Romero* (1989), directed by John Duigan and featuring the late Raul Julia as Monsignor Oscar Romero, also provides background for understanding *The Country Between Us.*

One of the "Salvador" poems, "The Colonel," for which Forché invented the term "documentary poem," is perhaps the most frequently anthologized of all the poems included in *The Country Between Us.* This alternative form works partly because Forché sparingly employs traditional poetic forms as touchstones within it and partly because its seeming artlessness elicits belief from her readers. In the journalistic way that she sets the scene in "The Colonel," Forché takes little poetic license, inviting readers to trust that the poem is not a caricature of the truth. Its simple, declarative sentences do not resemble poetic lines. Even visually, with its justified right-hand margin, the piece resembles a newspaper report more than a poem.

Forché first draws the readers into "The Colonel" by conversing with them about the rumors that have crept north of brutal Latin American military dictatorships: "WHAT YOU HAVE HEARD is true." Forché extends that sense of familiarity for her reader by creating in the first lines a scene that, except for the pistol on the cushion, could occur in any North American home: the wife serves coffee; the daughter files her nails; and the son goes out for the evening; there are daily papers, pet dogs, a TV turned on even at mealtime. The minutiae of ordinary domestic life draw the readers into the scene as if they are entering the room with Forché, as if *they* are having dinner with the colonel.

"The moon swung bare on its black cord over the house" is one of two tropes foregrounded in the poem, and Forché deliberately draws attention to its artfulness. Although the image is ominous, suggestive generally of the gothic and particularly of a swinging interrogation lamp or of someone's hanging naked from a rope, it is too decorative for its place between a pistol and a cop show; thus it announces itself as art.

The following lines portray the colonel's house as a fortress: "Broken bottles were embedded in the walls around the house to scoop the kneecaps from a man's legs or cut his hands to lace. On the windows there were gratings like those in liquor stores." The outside of this fortress, constructed to mutilate anyone who tries to get inside, stands in stark contrast to the several images of "civilization" and affluence inside: "dinner, rack of lamb, good wine, a gold bell [that] was on the table for calling the maid."

Until the parrot says hello from the terrace, triggering the colonel's anger and the action of the poem—that is, his spilling human ears on the table—the poem is a string of "to be" verbs. As passive as her verbs, the poet can only catalogue nouns, unable to exercise control or take action. In fact, the friend who has accompanied her warns her with his eyes: "say nothing." And so many readers identify with the poet rather than feel manipulated by her; like the readers, she is frightened, wary. (Forché did not invent the colonel's displaying severed ears as a startling, violent metaphor. The incident actually occurred, she has reported.)

The contrast between the single stylized line—"the moon swung bare on its black cord over the house"—and the weak-verb sentences suggests the range of possible responses to situations such as dinner with the colonel as well as the range of possible responses for *reading* about dinner with the colonel:

Will the poet run away from this experience by lyricizing it? Will the poet remain impotent, unable to invent strong verbs—in other words, be unable to take action? Forché thus puts her readers in her place, in that room with the colonel, in a state of nascent political and moral awareness. The form itself suggests that the reader must make choices, take positions.

With the poem's second foregrounded trope, a simile describing the ears as "dried peach halves," the poet is at once manipulating the mundane and confined by it. She knows her readers have all seen dried fruit and so she cannot more vividly describe those severed ears, but she apologizes for the limits of her inherited poetic and of language itself, acknowledging simply: "There is no other way to say this." However, she simultaneously defends poetic language. Because "there is no other way to say this," she must rely on a poetic device, a simile, to communicate with us.

The colonel shakes one of the ears in the faces of his guests. A human ear is an unusual metonymy, representing, in this case, the Salvadoran people—those who have been mutilated and murdered as well as those who continue to resist the military dictatorship. The colonel, as if performing a perverse magic show, is able to make a severed ear come "alive" by dropping it into a glass of water, just as the death squads are able to make Salvadorans disappear. The sweeping gesture ("He swept the ears to the floor with his arm and held the last of his wine in the air") is theatrical, sending the ears down to the floor while the colonel elevates his glass of wine. The glass of wine recalls the "good wine" at dinner and the other markers of the affluent life maintained within the colonel's fortress at the expense of those in extreme poverty outside. The glass of wine, then, is a metonymy for all the trappings of "civilization" seen in the colonel's fortress and for the power of the military over ordinary Salvadorans. And as the ears of ordinary Salvadorans go down to the floor, that wine glass—that metonymy for the affluence of the few—is hoisted triumphantly above them.

With this theatrical action come the colonel's climactic words: "Something for your poetry, no?" Most immediately, "Something" refers to the grand show the colonel has put on for his guests' "entertainment." But the colonel's ironic sneer also mocks Forché's position as a North American poet, drawing attention to the belief held by many North Americans that poetry has certain "proper" subjects, and that mutilation—and by extension politics—is not among them.

In the poem's concluding lines—"Some of the ears on the floor caught this scrap of his voice.

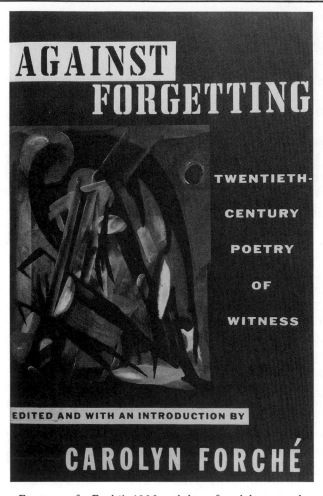

*Front cover for Forché's 1993 anthology of work by poets who
"endured conditions of historical and social extremity during the
twentieth century"*

Some of the ears on the floor were pressed to the ground"–some of the ears seem to be alive, listening and feeling for vibrations, for sounds and motions of resistance outside the colonel's fortress. This poem, especially these final lines, implicitly questions the reader: Is *your* ear pressed to the ground? Are *you* listening? Have *you* "HEARD" (to return to the poem's opening words, written for emphasis in uppercase)?

"Because One Is Always Forgotten," another "Salvador" poem, comprises an excellent companion piece to "The Colonel." Again, Forché writes in calculated relation to traditional poetic forms, calling attention to their limitations and yet insisting that poetry can be used for political as well as aesthetic purposes. The obverse of "The Colonel," which appears artless, this elegy is the most highly structured piece in *The Country Between Us*.

Forché wrote "Because One Is Always Forgotten" in memory of José Rudolfo Viera, who was El Salvador's deputy of agrarian reform under President José Napoleon Duarte. Viera discovered that

money designated for agrarian reform (that is, dividing some of the largest landholdings so that the country's wealth would no longer belong disproportionately to a few families) was being pocketed by members of Duarte's administration and men at a high level in the military. Some of that money was coming from the Carter administration–that is, from United States taxpayers–and going not toward agrarian reform but to support the lavish consumption of a few. The reader recalls details from "The Colonel"–rack of lamb, good wine, a gold bell for calling the maid–as in "El Salvador: An Aide Memoire." Forché describes the affluence of the colonel's cohort: "I was taken to the homes of landowners, with their pools set like aquamarines in the clipped grass, to the afternoon games of canasta over quaint local *pupusas* and tea, where parrots hung by their feet among the bougainvillia and nearly everything was imported, if only from Miami or New Orleans." When Viera reported the corruption on a televised news program in San Salvador, he was murdered by "the White Glove," a right-wing death squad. He was shot along with two North Americans, Michael Hammer and Mark Pearlman, who were in El Salvador as consultants for agrarian reform. Some North American newspapers reported the deaths of Hammer and Pearlman, but because Viera's death was not included in those accounts, Forché felt the need to memorialize him.

"Because One Is Always Forgotten" tightly compresses rhythm and images, suggesting that traditional forms necessarily strain or snap under the weight of political imprisonment, murder, and mutilation. After the second line Forché starts dropping beats from the lines, as if atrocities in El Salvador defy even one more word or beat. Forché undercuts the stylization that would comfort us, that would offer the consolation and closure that elegies have traditionally provided.

She also uses "heart," a word common in poetry, in a startling way:

> I could take my heart, he said, and give it to a *campesino*
> and he would cut it up and give it back:
>
> you can't eat heart in those four dark
> chambers where a man can be kept years.

"You can't eat heart" is a spondee—all unaccented syllables have been removed. Because English is more naturally a combination of accented and unaccented syllables, a spondee represents language at its most compressed, its most structured. "You can't eat heart" also announces the limitations of poetic language. It cannot, literally, sustain human life. In other words, an elegy, however necessary, is not a sufficient response to events such as those in El Salvador.

"Those four dark chambers" refers to the left and right ventricles and auricles of the heart. The term "dark chambers" also refers to prisons and, more particularly, to *la oscura* (the dark place), a prison within a prison that inspired "The Visitor," another "Salvador" poem. (In her introduction to "The Visitor" on the Watershed audio recording and in "El Salvador: An Aide Memoire," Forché describes her visit to *la oscura,* where men were kept in boxes too small for them to stretch out, with one barred opening the size of a book.)

In the fourth stanza of "Because One Is Always Forgotten"—"A boy soldier in the bone-hot sun works his knife / to peel the face from a dead man"—the second line stops abruptly. Again, it is as if the atrocities in El Salvador defy even one more word or beat. The poem's jarring, monosyllabic accents, as staccato as gunfire from automatic weapons, suggest the nature of Salvadoran life under a brutal military dictatorship. (The three references to "heart," as well as the poem's arrhythmic accents, also suggest the condition of arrhythmia—an irregular, deformed heartbeat.) Thus the poem's form (as well as its content) is intended to startle the reader. "To peel the face from a dead man" is no more an invented metaphor than are the severed ears in "The Colonel"; in El Salvador Forché actually saw human faces hanging from tree branches. "Flowering with such faces," in stanza 5, uses conventional poetic language in a striking way.

The last, paradoxical stanza—"The heart is the toughest part of the body / Tenderness is in the hands"—asks readers to examine something they have long accepted, the cliché of the tender heart. Forché implies that the readers should probe some of their other assumptions as well. Hands can *do* something; hands can take action. *The Country Between Us* includes many other references to hands, suggesting a wide range of possibilities for their use. Rather than provide consolation and closure, as would a traditional elegy, "Because One Is Always Forgotten," like "The Colonel" and other poems in *The Country Between Us,* asks readers to consider choices about their hands, their actions, their lives.

"As Children Together" appears in the section of *The Country Between Us* titled "Reunion." Addressed to Forché's girlhood friend Victoria, this poem gives the readers a sense of the poet's working-class roots. Victoria, ashamed of the "tins of surplus flour," the "relief checks," and other trappings of poverty, longs to escape: "I am going to have it," Victoria asserts, while believing that granting sexual favors to men is her only conduit to upward mobility.

The first stanza represents the girls' lives and futures as boxed in, closed off: the snow is "pinned"; the lights are "cubed"; the girls wait for Victoria's father to "whittle his soap cakes away, finish the whisky," and for Victoria's mother to turn off the lights. Confined by "tight black dresses"—which in this context arguably represent a class marker—they nevertheless attempt to move away from the limitations of class, "holding each other's coat sleeves" for support. They slide "down the roads . . . past / crystal swamps and the death / face of each dark house, / over the golden ice / of tobacco spit." They try to move away from their diminished options—the "quiet of ponds," "the blind white hills," "a scant snow." But, sliding on ice, their movement is literally as well as metaphorically precarious.

Victoria does not escape the cycle of poverty and battered men. In the second-to-last stanza the

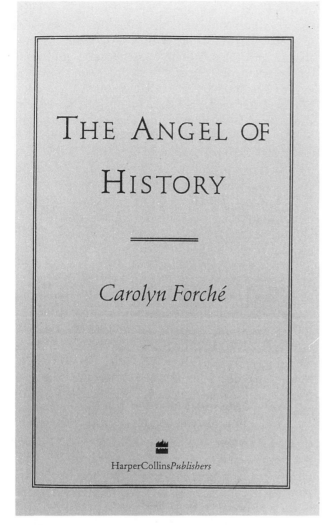

THE ANGEL OF
HISTORY

Carolyn Forché

HarperCollins*Publishers*

*Title page for Forché's 1994 book, poems chiefly about the
Holocaust and Hiroshima*

have imagined it possible. None of my friends, no one I grew up with and knew well, went to a university." In "A Lesson in Commitment" Forché reports that her interest in Vietnam was fueled partly by her first husband's fighting in Vietnam and his suffering "from what they now call 'Post-Vietnam Syndrome.'" The Vietnam War, as well as her opposition to it, schooled Forché for "another Vietnam" in El Salvador.

"As Children Together" provides a good starting point for a discussion of the deliberately ambiguous title, *The Country Between Us.* "Between" can mean something that separates and distances people, but "between" can also mean that which the readers share, that which connects them. The "country" is El Salvador, but it is also the United States. "Us" can be people on opposing sides of a civil war, people polarized by their opinions about political issues, or people sharing a common opposition to oppression. "Us" can be people inhabiting two nations (El Salvador and the United States). "Us" can also refer to two individuals, such as the poet and Victoria, who may be separated by geography and recent experience but also connected by common roots and class origin. The poet's saying to Victoria "write to me" suggests a desire for "between" as separation to become the "between" of reunion and connection.

Forché has adopted strategies throughout *The Country Between Us* that invite readers into the poems. One of those strategies is to acknowledge her own ignorance rather than to point didactically to the reader's; another, related strategy is to place herself or someone else in the poem as an object of ridicule or admonition rather than the reader. Forché deploys both strategies, for example, in "The Colonel" and in "Return," where Josephine Crum, an older woman who had lived in Latin America for many years, admonishes the poet for her previous naiveté about conditions there.

One of Forché's most recent volume of poetry, *The Angel of History* (1994), is an extension of the global awareness of *The Country Between Us* and *Against Forgetting* (1993), an anthology of work by poets, as Forché explains in its introduction, "who endured conditions of historical and social extremity during the twentieth century—through exile, state censorship, political persecution, house arrest, torture, imprisonment, military occupation, warfare, and assassination." One primary subject of *The Angel of History* is the devastation of war in the twentieth century. The collection, which won the 1994 Los Angeles Times Book Prize for poetry, focuses chiefly on the Holocaust and Hiroshima but also refers to the Soviet Union's 1968 invasion of Czecho-

poet reports a rumor that Victoria lives in a trailer near Detroit with her children and with her husband, who "returned from the Far East broken / cursing holy blood at the table" and whose whittling of soap cakes associates him with Victoria's whiskey-drinking father.

At first glance, "As Children Together" seems far removed from El Salvador's civil war. In the context of *The Country Between Us,* however, "As Children Together" links "the Far East" (Vietnam) to El Salvador. Young men from Forché's working-class neighborhood were drafted by or enlisted in the military when many of the more privileged of their generation managed student deferments or, after the draft lottery was established, other alternatives to military service. "Had it not been for President Johnson's 'Great Society' programs," Forché remarked in an interview with David Montenegro, "I would never have gone to a university. I wouldn't

slovakia, the Chernobyl nuclear disaster, and genocide in El Salvador. A second key subject of *The Angel of History* has to do with the (in)capacity of language to record such events.

The title and epigraph of *The Angel of History* derive from Walter Benjamin's "Theses on the Philosophy of History." The epigraph is central to an understanding of the book:

> This is how one pictures the angel of history. His face is turned toward the past. Where the readers perceive a chain of events, he sees one single catastrophe which keeps piling wreckage and hurls it in front of his feet. The angel would like to stay, awaken the dead, and make whole what has been smashed. But a storm is blowing in from Paradise; it has got caught in his wings with such a violence that the angel can no longer close them. The storm irresistibly propels him into the future to which his back is turned, while the pile of debris before him grows skyward.

The Angel of History is one sustained, experimental poem without closure, rendered in five sequences, each beginning in medias res and composed of fragmented elegiac meditations. The narrator floats through the volume like an angel or a ghost, and yet the readers feel the anchoring, heavy, vigilant presence of those who have suffered this century's catastrophic events, "as if someone not alive were watching" (the phrase is repeated as a refrain). Three long sequences—"The Angel of History," "The Notebook of Uprising," and "The Recording Angel"—form parts 1, 2, and 3 and, as their titles suggest, are somewhat interwoven.

In a note appended to *The Angel of History* Forché explains that the "first-person, free-verse, lyric-narrative poem" of her earlier work has given way to "a work which has desired its own bodying forth: polyphonic, broken, haunted, and in ruins, with no possibility of restoration." Along with Walter Benjamin, *The Angel of History* cites René Char, Elie Weisel, Robert Desnos, Elias Canetti, Georg Trakl, Günter Eich, Paul Valéry, Ludwig Wittgenstein, and others. The poet has said to David Montenegro that she is herself uncertain of some of the voices and that "one seems to be the voice of the poetry itself and not a human being." The multivocal, citational form is reminiscent of T. S. Eliot's *The Waste Land* (1922), which depicts the fragmentation of modern Western culture following World War I and also alludes to many other writers.

At a videotaped reading in Los Angeles, as Nora Mitchell and Emily Skoler report, Forché "described the conditions" of the genesis of *The Angel of History*. When the poet "sat down to write, what filled the page were various voices that inhabited her consciousness. 'I felt like a courtroom stenographer. . . . Voices arguing with each other, questions, stories, cutting each other off, interrogation . . . like writing subtitles for a film, but you don't get to see the film.'" Forché explained to Montenegro one of the prominent voices in the title sequence, "The Angel of History" (part 1):

> I recognized [the voice] as [that of] a woman who had shared a hospital room with me in the Hôtel Dieu in Paris two years ago. We were together for a week. She was a German Jew who had spent the war years hiding in barns in Europe, making her way farm to farm. The first night when I was brought into the hospital, I was very depressed, particularly at having to leave my husband and newborn son. I was given a room with Elie [spelled "Ellie" in the poem]. She was awake in the middle of the night, sitting at the edge of her bed, peeling her skin from her body. She had acute eczema. She turned to me and asked, "And *what* are you?" She didn't say: Who are you? or What is your name? So I answered, "I am a poet." And she responded, "I am also a poet." We talked all night and all the next day and next. Her voice later entered this work.

Ellie and the poet-speaker are in a sense interchangeable or transindividual, recalling the kinship between Forché and writer Claribel Alegría in "The Island" (in *The Country Between Us*) and suggesting the shared humanity and vulnerablity of the victims of atrocities in this century.

At different points in the title sequence, both the poet-speaker and Ellie seem to be on a boat leaving Beirut: "Years later, on the boat from Beirut, or before the boat, an hour before, helicopters lifting / a white veil of sea. / A woman broken into many women." Throughout her work Forché belies the myth of robust, autonomous individualism as well as the myth of poet/poetry as residing in some rarefied realm of art, transcending history's horrors. Both Ellie and the poet-speaker, like other people, are fragmented and interdependent; indeed, in "The Province of Radical Solitude," Forché explains the "many voiced" form of *The Angel of History* as affected by her "own brokenness."

"The Notebook of Uprising" (part 2) loosely resembles a journal, as the title suggests. The twenty-eight numbered sections obliquely record a trip to Eastern Europe with the Czech-born American poet Svetozár Daniel Simko. In the Czech Republic, Forché finds the niece of her grandmother Anna and accompanies Simko to an attic where he had left his belongings twenty-two years before when he was fleeing the Soviet invasion. In the attic they find the "word on the empty box: *Important* (all boxes empty)" and "a diary open to the words *cannot remain here.*" Anna herself appears in "The

Forché at a poetry reading (photograph © Lynn Saville)

Notebook of Uprising," commanding her grand-daughter to "carry this" and "follow behind me," echoing the request she made of Forché in *Gathering the Tribes* "to go with her / To the confrontation of something" ("Burning the Tomato Worms"). Section 20 of part 2 suggests what *The Angel of History* as a whole represents, "a reliquary in a wall of silence."

"The Recording Angel" (part 3) is the most difficult to follow of the three long sequences, perhaps because the surreal and spectral images are accompanied by fewer recognizable historical events than appear elsewhere in the volume. The ethereal narrator wings her way through "the worst of centuries," from a "comic wedding in which corpses exchange vows"; to Hiroshima, where they "lost every alternate route"; to a "pall of exhaust over Paris"; to a "no-name village," where everyone is "chômeur" (unemployed); to El Salvador, where hundreds "of small clay heads" are discovered by workers "while planting coffee." Part 4 is composed of three elegiac commemorations—the first to the late Terrence Des Pres; the second to a restored ornamental garden in Hiroshima, in which an elderly female survivor of the atomic bomb states matter-of-factly, "I don't like this particular red flower because / it reminds me of a woman's brain

crushed under a roof"; and the third to Hiroshima itself.

Part 5, the final section of the volume, is divided into Book Codes I, II, and III. In three short, largely unpunctuated poems Forché questions the power of language to render historical events even though she acknowledges that the reader has "nothing except what can be said." Book Codes II (about the Holocaust) and Book Codes III (about Hiroshima) are rendered in parallel forms of equal-length stanzas, with "closure" on a haunting, typographically separated line. It is useful to consider the "closing" lines of these two poems as a pair. In the separated concluding line in Book Codes II, Forché urges her readers to become collaborators: "whoever can cry should come here." In the separated last line of Book Codes III, the poet appropriates the surreal—yet oddly familiar—cinematic image of the atomic mushroom cloud and yokes it, strangely, to the act of writing this collection of poems. The line of "closure" ("at the moment of the birth of this cloud"), then, refers to her writing—and our reading—this volume of poems. The concluding words of the book, following Book Codes III, are those of Paul Valéry, who opposes a sense of art as separable from history: "the book melted, until it could no longer be distinguished from this world that is about us."

The Country Between Us and The Angel of History have raised questions among some critics about the hazards involved in portraying oppressive conditions through poetry. How does a poet such as Forché avoid voyeurism, "revolutionary tourism," or a witness's unconscious egotism? How does she avoid appropriating, for literary gain, the lives of people she is trying to save from historical erasure? Does the witnessing of atrocity, at some point, move beyond poetic and political necessity to an exploitation of the horror for sensational effect? There are no simple answers to these questions, ones that Forché herself has addressed, explicitly and implicitly, in essays, in interviews, and in the poetry itself. A few critics argue that the risks of a poetry of witness are too great, whereas many critics see considerable courage in Forché's extraordinary engagement with history, with life beyond "the self."

"What depends on my life?" Forché asks in Book Codes I, using a formulation that turns on its head the familiar version of that question (What does my life depend on?). Supplanting individualism with transindividualism, Forché poses the question with "the other" rather than "the self" as the starting point, moving her readers with a forceful sense of "the other" rare in contemporary American verse. In "Elegy," from The Angel of History, the poet poses another crucial question to herself and to her readers: "To what and to whom does one say yes?" Forché's words imply that one does say "yes," after learning "to what and to whom" one should respond.

Such questions frame the whole of Forché's work, recalling the poet's debt—and kinship—to Anna Akhmatova. In "Ourselves or Nothing" (in The Country Between Us) and elsewhere Forché acknowledges Akhmatova's inspiration, especially in "Requiem," an elegy for all victims of Stalinist oppression (although the particular occasion for the poem was the imprisonment of the Russian poet's own son). In a prefatory note to "Requiem" Akhmatova explains that she spent seventeen months standing in line in front of several Leningrad prisons trying to learn her son's fate. The catalyst for "Requiem" was a question from an or-

dinary Russian woman standing next to Akhmatova in the prison queue, her lips blue from the cold. She did not know that she was speaking to a poet—indeed, had never heard Akhmatova's name—and yet whispered in her ear, "Can you describe this?" With Akhmatova, Forché has responded, resoundingly: "I can."

Interviews:

Jonathan Cott, *Visions and Voices* (Garden City, N.Y.: Doubleday, 1987), pp. 115–136;

Paul W. Rea, "An Interview with Carolyn Forché," *High Plains Literary Review,* 2 (Fall 1987): 150–164;

Constance Coiner, *Jacaranda Review,* 3 (Winter 1988): 47–68;

David Montenegro, *American Poetry Review,* 17 (November/December 1988): 35–40;

"Jill Taft-Kaufman Talks with Carolyn Forché," *Text and Performance Quarterly,* 10 (1990): 61–70.

References:

Terrence Diggory, "Witnesses and Seers," *Salmagundi,* 61 (Fall 1983): 112–124;

Michael Greer, "Politicizing the Modern: Carolyn Forché in El Salvador and America," *Centennial Review,* 30 (Spring 1986): 160–180;

Anita Helle, "Elegy as History: Three Women Poets 'By the Century's Deathbed,'" *South Atlantic Review,* 61 (Spring 1996): 51–68;

John Mann, "Carolyn Forché: Poetry and Survival," *American Poetry,* 3 (Spring 1986): 51–69;

Nora Mitchell and Emily Skoler, "History, Death, Politics, Despair" (review essay including *The Angel of History*), *New England Review,* 17 (Spring 1995): 67–81;

Paul Rea, "The Poet as Witness: Carolyn Forché's Powerful Pleas from El Salvador," *Confluencia-Revista Hispanica de Cultura y Literatura,* 2 (Spring 1987): 93–99;

Kenneth Rexroth, Review of Forché's *Gathering the Tribes, American Poetry Review,* 5 (November/December 1976): 44;

Leonora Smith, "Carolyn Forché: Poet of Witness," in *Still the Frame Holds: Essays on Women Poets and Writers,* edited by Yvonne Pacheco Tevis (San Bernadino, Cal.: Borgo, 1993), pp. 15–28.

Alice Fulton
(25 January 1952 -)

Sergei Lobanov-Rostovsky
Kenyon College

BOOKS: *Anchors of Light* (Oneonta, N.Y.: Swamp Press, 1979);

Dance Script with Electric Ballerina (Philadelphia: University of Pennsylvania Press, 1983);

Palladium (Urbana & Chicago: University of Illinois Press, 1986);

Powers of Congress (Boston: David R. Godine, 1990);

Sensual Math (New York: Norton, 1995).

OTHER: "Of Formal, Free, and Fractal Verse: Singing the Body Eclectic," in *Conversant Essays: Contemporary Poets on Poetry,* edited by James McCorkle (Detroit: Wayne State University Press, 1990), 185–193.

SELECTED PERIODICAL PUBLICATIONS– UNCOLLECTED: "To Organize a Waterfall," *Parnassus,* 16, no. 2 (1991): 301–326;

"Outlandish Powers: Dickinson's Capsizals of Genre and Tone," *Emily Dickinson Journal,* 2, no. 2 (1993), 97–103.

Alice Fulton, 1994 (photograph by Hank De Leo)

In her essay "To Organize a Waterfall" Alice Fulton describes the central concern of her poetry as "an exploration of mind." The phrase hints at the paradox of Fulton's work: her poems are at once deeply personal and defiantly abstract. Her implicit subject is the workings of the poetic imagination, the way poetry emerges from the mind's web of associations, stimulated by memory, experience, and the seductions of popular culture. She notes the central role of random associations in her compositional method: "The quirk, the oddity, the extreme, the line where the language tilts, can be the most valuable facet of a poem. They are the linguistic equivalents of genetic 'point mutations': variants produced by small changes in an organism's chromosomes." As the poem emerges from the imagination, it resembles a waterfall in which each idea incites the next and the form of the poem "is based on the continuous chain of a cascade." This metaphor, with its origin in the scientific theory of "cascade experi-

ments," reflects the complex relationship between content and form in Fulton's poems. Ideas are crucial to her poetry, yet she rarely writes about science or philosophy in any real sense. Instead Fulton's poems explore the way ideas are transformed by their inclusion in the poem and the power such ideas possess to reshape the more traditional lyric subjects of the poem: family history, landscape, erotic love. She celebrates the power of the poetic imagination to transform the most mundane experience into a beauty defined by abstraction; as she said in a 1988 interview with Karen Clark: "My poetry asks people to think, to become more conscious. It asks the same of me. The greatest thing about writing poetry has been the way it's made the world more interesting: every facet of the world. I can sit in a fast food restaurant and become interested in a grove of streetlights across the road, the way they cast veils through the trash and hard horizontals."

In a similar manner Fulton's poetry regards the objects of memory as the substructure on which metaphor can be shaped. She was born in Troy, New York, 25 January 1952 into a Catholic family. Her early poems, such as "Another Troy" in *Palladium* (1986), reimagine the battered industrial city of her childhood as the material for parodic myth:

> In the seismic hiss of the Volcano
>
> Restaurant I invented Armageddons
> guaranteed to free us: fires coasting down from heaven,
> spumes of air pollutants hurled into the stratosphere
> and we, the *damnificados*, fleeing.
> An erupting Italian restaurant—
> that would put us on the map!

Yet this urge to see her native city's "rough edges / . . . buffed by the crumbled palladium / of ash" gives way to Fulton's perception of how memory—and poetry itself—transforms by the simple act of description:

> Oh, if I sing of icicles
> dangling like syringes from friezes
> "neo-grec" or French,
> of roses battened down with sackcloth, trees
> lumbagoed under lumpen winters,
> I'm minting an insignia. Take this, "Troy—
> the City without Glibness,"
> for your spartan tribute.

Such gestures of memory evoke the traditions of mainstream American poetry only to defy them: the insistent play of language and parodic tone of Fulton's memory poems suggest her darker purpose. When she writes memory poems, as in "On the Charms of Absentee Gardens," also from *Palladium,* they are about the ambiguous process of memory rather than its banal products:

> Leaving meant commencement.
> Legend says an angel banished us
> with a sword of flame, though rumor
> claims the owners torched
> our hangouts for insurance.
> In any case, we preened with self-
> congratulations as though our origins were ruinous
> accidents from which we'd walked away.
>
> Fire fixes the magnetic alignment
> of clay, and wooden beams remember
> weather in their rings. But what Cortez will come
> in search of tambourines and beads? We'd like a past
> that won't decay with distance or yield
> to interference. Failing that,

> we want what we've abandoned
> to wear: that is to crumble
> and to last. We want a ruin: uselessness
> permitted the luxury of existence.

Her poems devoted to family history are in many respects her most accessible, yet Fulton is insistent in regarding the autobiographical detail as only the raw material for the mind's habit of metaphor. As she noted, with some irritation, in her interview with Clark two years after the publication of *Palladium,* "I've written as many, if not more, poems on the ontological struggle between engagement and estrangement as I have on 'family,' but only one critic has commented on the former topic. It's a more subtle topic than 'family,' and like most subtleties it can be completely overlooked." Indeed, the memory work of Fulton's poetry affirms the relationship of these two themes: engagement with a past that retains its power to shape the poet's consciousness becomes a process of estrangement. Family history, while the subject of many of her early poems, is only visible through the distorting lens of the imagination. What memory excavates from her own life proves to be the influence of this same quicksilver substance, "imagination, kicking like a worm in a jumping bean." Fulton adopts voices in many of her poems, or she regards her own experience from the distance of an analytical third-person ("From Our Mary to Me"), deploying it as evidence of a profound mistrust for the ideology that memory carries with it ("Cherry Bombs," "All Night Shivering").

Fulton graduated from Empire State College in Albany, New York, with a B.A. in creative writing in 1978. She completed her M.F.A. at Cornell in 1982, where she studied with A. R. Ammons. Since 1983 she has taught at the University of Michigan, where she is currently a professor of English. She was Visiting Professor of Creative Writing at Vermont College in 1987 and at the University of California, Los Angeles, in 1991. She is currently a fellow of the MacArthur Foundation and has received many fellowships and awards, including MacDowell Colony fellowships in 1978 and 1979; a Millay Colony fellowship, 1980; the Emily Dickinson Award, 1980; the Academy of American Poets prize, 1982; the Rainer Maria Rilke Award, 1984; Michigan Council for the Arts grants, 1986 and 1991; Yaddo Colony fellowship, 1987; Guggenheim fellowship, 1986–1987; the Bess Hokin prize from *Poetry,* 1989; and an Ingram Merrill Foundation award, 1990. In 1980 she married the painter Hank De Leo, with whom she lives in Ypsilanti, Michigan.

Cover for Fulton's 1986 book, which includes some of her memory poems

In her interview with Clark, Fulton credits Ammons with helping her "regard a poem less as a product, a neatly packaged, finished thing, and more as a reflection of mind." In Ammons's work Fulton found a model of poetry presenting "the course of the mind as continual high points, continually interesting travel, though part of his method is to allow the mundane to accompany the complex." This variation of tones is crucial to her own poetics as well. Fulton delights in allowing her language "to have a will of its own . . . wily, duplicitous," refusing "to be subdued into an orderly, simple form." W. D. Snodgrass began his introduction to Fulton's first book, *Dance Script with Electric Ballerina* (1983), by christening her "the veritable Lady of Logopoeia," celebrating the "constant delight and dazzle in language textures,

the ever-shifting shock and jolt of an electric surface." Her poems draw the language of science, advertising, and pop culture into an uneasy juxtaposition. In doing so, her poems celebrate the protean nature of such language. Scientific terms acquire multiple meanings through the shifting contexts of the poem, as in the "slant truths" of the word *palladium* that organize her second major volume or the "lexicon of recurring words and images" that give shape to *Powers of Congress* (1990). Yet, as she notes in "To Organize a Waterfall," the inclusion of scientific language has a deeper metaphoric significance for Fulton; wrenched out of its traditional context, scientific language illuminates "the poem's real investments: the way our present beliefs affect or distort our future knowledge; the unreliability of human perception; the old-fashioned question of whether consciousness might in any way continue after death." The implicit subject of Fulton's poems, then, is faith, which she defines as "the suppositions and convictions that allow us to live in the world." Science proves a crucial source for Fulton's poetry because it represents a mode of discourse which "strains our capacity to imagine, let alone believe."

This conflict between the role of science as metaphor and its power to expose the limits of metaphoric consciousness lies at the heart of Fulton's work. In *Powers of Congress* Fulton reflects on the fragility of this impulse to reason in several poems. "Behavioral Geography" considers the desire "to make the world / look one way to us all" by invoking reason free of "ecstasy":

> I cling to wishful visions
> like someone clinging to a tree, complaining
> that the tree won't leave.
> Hope springs up in me.
> Lost, found, bewildered,
> when will I learn
> to like unsettling transits,
>
> to use the universal
> corrective of the sky,
> a continental drift
> with nothing fixed about it?
> Once a woman dressed in wood
> lunged down the falls,
> as if her flesh were not
>
> irreparable, and lived.
> The beauty's the impossibility. Proving?
> All views are seasoned
> subjectivities, beds
> carved by freshets,
> warps of the heart.
> Ecstasy has its reasons.

In the final poem of the book, "Art Thou The Thing I Wanted," Fulton rejects the seductions of reason, preferring instead "problems / more interesting than solutions, / solutions being perfect. . . ." The poem offers a meditation on its own metaphoric consciousness, how the mind naturalizes the unfamiliar into a landscape that fits its assumptions:

> Like others,
> I mistake whatever is
> for what is natural.
>
> You know the commonplaces. How people think
> women are good
> at detail work when that's the only work
> they're given. Or how

> the city's invisible
>
> engines jiggled our coffee
> till we believed quivering a constant
> property of liquid.

Reason, in these terms, is simply one more metaphor by which the mind describes for itself a world it nervously takes on faith. Viewed in this context, Fulton's taste for oxymoron and dramatic variations in tone reflects the mind's struggle to imagine itself as distinct from what it perceives:

> Everything happens to me, I think,
> as anything reminds me of you: the real estate
>
> most local, most removed.
> As on the remains of prairie
> the curving earth becomes a plinth—
> from which we rise, towers
> of blood and ignorance.

The self is an oxymoron, a work in progress, as the mind struggles to assemble itself from conflicting shards of memory, perception, and popular culture. The poetic imagination embodies this dissonance, drawing upon multiple discourses—pop culture, advertising, science—juxtaposed in a style that celebrates oxymoron, tonal variation, and the tension between lyric tradition and the chaotic movements of mind.

Fulton foregrounds this conflict within her poetry by such "perverse" strategies as acrostic lines (constructing the phrase "BOWLING DEVELOPS THE RIGHT ARM" along the left margin of "The Fractal Lanes") and her insistence upon the interplay of structure and chaos in her compositional method. In her essay titled "Of Formal, Free, and Fractal Verse: Singing the Body Eclectic" in *Conversant Essays: Contemporary Poets on Poetry* (1990), she argues for an understanding of the implicit structure within apparently chaotic forms. Drawing upon the mathematician Benoit Mandelbrot's theories of "self-similar fractal form," in which "each part of a fractal form replicates the form of the entire structure," Fulton offers the following precepts for "fractal" verse:

> Any line when examined closely (or magnified) will reveal itself to be as richly detailed as was the larger poem from which it was taken: the poem will contain an infinite regression of details, a nesting of pattern within pattern (an endless imbedding of the shape into itself, recalling Tennyson's idea of the inner infinity); digression, interruption, fragmentation, and lack of continuity will be regarded as formal functions rather than lapses into formlessness; all directions of

Dust jacket for Fulton's 1990 book, in which she considers the desire "to make the world / look one way to us all"

motion and rhythm will be equally probable (isotropy); the past positions of motion, or the preceding metrical pattern, will not necessarily affect the poem's future evolution (independence).

While the mathematical origin of this central thesis of Fulton's poetics reflects her interest in such "nonpoetic" discourses as the language of science, it also suggests the range of her poetic resources. With her delight in juxtapositions of tone and voice, Fulton challenges the privileged language of emotional experience that is the legacy of lyric tradition. Her style is dialogic, contrasting multiple voices and perspectives, including all that poetry traditionally excludes; as she says in her interview with Clark:

> Most broadly, my poems try to question assumptions. I like to juggle cultural notions of centrality and sneak in what we consign to the periphery. I try to bring hidden relationships to the fore, disrupt assumptions surrounding gender, muddle in the fuzziness of ethics. The poems' language, including syntax and grammar, can provide a means of unhinging complacency and cliche. . . . I like my

poetry to be insidious, rather than didactic; multiplistic, rather than singular in meaning.

What poetry traditionally excludes is not the prospect of multiple meanings, but the unheroic voice: the everyday, the commonplace, the feminine. Fulton's "inclusions" subvert this dominant tradition, creating a style that she describes as "more disjunctive than contiguous, more discursive than linear."

In her earliest work Fulton's feminism appeared to take second place to her interest in creating a poetic style that could accommodate her sense of the poetic imagination as a cascade of associations. Yet this concern with the exclusion of female voices, as she notes in "To Organize a Waterfall," this concern was always implicit in her poetry:

> The feminist strategies of my work are embedded because I believe linguistic structures are most powerful when least evident. . . . Whereas concealed meanings usually enforce the status quo, I use recondite structures to say subversive things. Few readers have noticed the preoccupation with gender in my work because it's eclipsed by the poems' starring subjects. The unnoticed female lizards [in "Cascade Experiment"] suggest that many "facts" about females are obscured or influenced by our existing notions.

In "Cherry Bombs" (*Powers of Congress*) Fulton associates the culture's gendering of childhood expectation with a game of false choices: "Would you rather be liquidated / or boiled in oil?" The binarisms that define gender in the poem–"Out/in. Girl/boy. Truth/lies."–are the *opposite* of the oxymoron by which Fulton imagines consciousness: instead, the culture demands that the speaker give in, choose between each pair of terms, become complicit in her own reduction to the "compulsory unsung heroics" that define a woman's life.

In her fourth book, *Sensual Math* (1995), Fulton articulates more explicitly the feminist implications of her poetics . In almost every poem she reflects on the urge to comprehend–to define, to contain–as a metaphorical violence, an act of repression that poetry must contest. Yet the book is impressive for its coherence, less a traditional book of poems than variations on a single theme: the conflict between this urge to comprehend and a style of response that she calls "immersion." In Fulton's vocabulary these are opposite terms; she rejects the mode of reading enacted daily by the checkout scanner in favor of the "treason" of immersion, which demands real presence, the dissolution of self into the poem's dark matter. As she says in "Fuzzy Feelings":

> Metaphor is pure immersion. Pure sinking
> one into another and the more

difference that's dissolved the more = =

often I'll sink
into a book that swimless way.

In return for this immersion Fulton offers her readers wonder. If the poems resist her readers at times—and they do—that only serves to draw the readers in, to demand that they dissolve their difference in the poem's fluid meanings, to be—at once— both "rapt" and "wrapped."

Fulton anchors the book with two set pieces. In "My Last TV Campaign: A Sequence" an advertising man comes out of retirement to sell one final product—"the beauty of dissolving / boundaries." "Give: A Sequence Reimagining Daphne and Apollo" envisions Apollo as Frank Sinatra, in "snap-brim hats, // alligator shoes and sharkskin / suits from Sy Devore's Hollywood men's store"; Cupid as the young Elvis, "gyrating / primitive / and part of nature"; and Daphne as the poem's "dark matter," the vinyl on which the Voice is pressed. In "A New Release," from that sequence, she describes:

Easing the new release from its sleeve, I saw myself
bent
out of shape in its reflections: a night whirlpool or a
geisha's
sleek chignon, an obsidian never reached by skin
since skin
always has a warmth of blood beneath. It was a synthetic
Goodyear black,
like all records, pressed with a tread the needle traced,
threading
sound through ear and nerves and marrow. I touched its
subtle
grain sometimes wondering how music lurked in negative
space
that looked so unassuming. The marvel was—the missing
had volition.

If "the missing had volition," it has voice in Fulton's poem. Both sequences use the language of pop culture not only to articulate Fulton's ideal of immersion but also to enact it. In "The Profit in the Sell" the adman's Madison Avenue sales pitch echoes the postmodern aesthetic that makes such language the vehicle for poetry:

I'd rather be emerging than retiring. I came out

to sell a big account
that needs to keep its identity
hidden. They're deep
into everything it seems.
A job so sweet you'd do it
for free. Career candy.
I couldn't wish away the rush I felt
once I grasped what they were after:

A campaign that demonstrated the beauty of dissolving
boundaries between yourself and the Martian
at the heart of every war.
An ad that pushed viewers to incorporate-embrace
rather than debase-slash-erase the other
gal-slash-guy. A commercial saying blend,
bend, and blur, folks. It works!

Fulton's taste for paradox becomes, in "Fuzzy Feelings," a metaphor in its own right—the binding of contradictory terms and tones to produce a visible seam in her text, a flaw that perfects:

Simulants

tend to be flawless, while natural
emeralds have defects
known as inclusions, imperfections
with a value all their own.

Like Daphne, she refuses Apollo, but she pays homage to Elvis Presley. Indeed, it is Elvis who serves as the book's patron spirit in the poem "About Face," embodying both its poetics ("the mixed metaphor of his jumpsuit that flared to wedding / bells white / as a pitcher plant's") and its vision of a self betrayed by its own defenses:

I do not suffer
from the excess of taste
that spells embarrassment:
mothers who find their kids unseemly
in their condom earrings,
girls cringing to think
they could be frumpish as their mothers.
Though the late nonerotic Elvis
in his studded gut of jumpsuit
made everybody squeamish, I admit.
Rule one: the King must not elicit pity.
Was the audience afraid of being tainted
—this might rub off on me—
or were they—surrendering—
what a femme word—feeling
solicitous—glimpsing their fragility
in his reversible purples
and unwholesome goldish chains?

Such embarrassment, for Fulton, is desire's reverse image, "intimacy for beginners, the orgasm no one cares to fake." In the late Elvis she finds an image of strange authenticity, an image with the power to negate the daily repressions ("Elvis from the waist up") by which the self struggles to affirm its separateness.

To this same end Fulton creates her own punctuation ("= ="), a sign that she calls "a bride / after the recessive threads in lace." She deploys this symbol in the poem titled simply "= =" to compel the readers' attention to "the unconsidered / mortar between the silo's bricks":

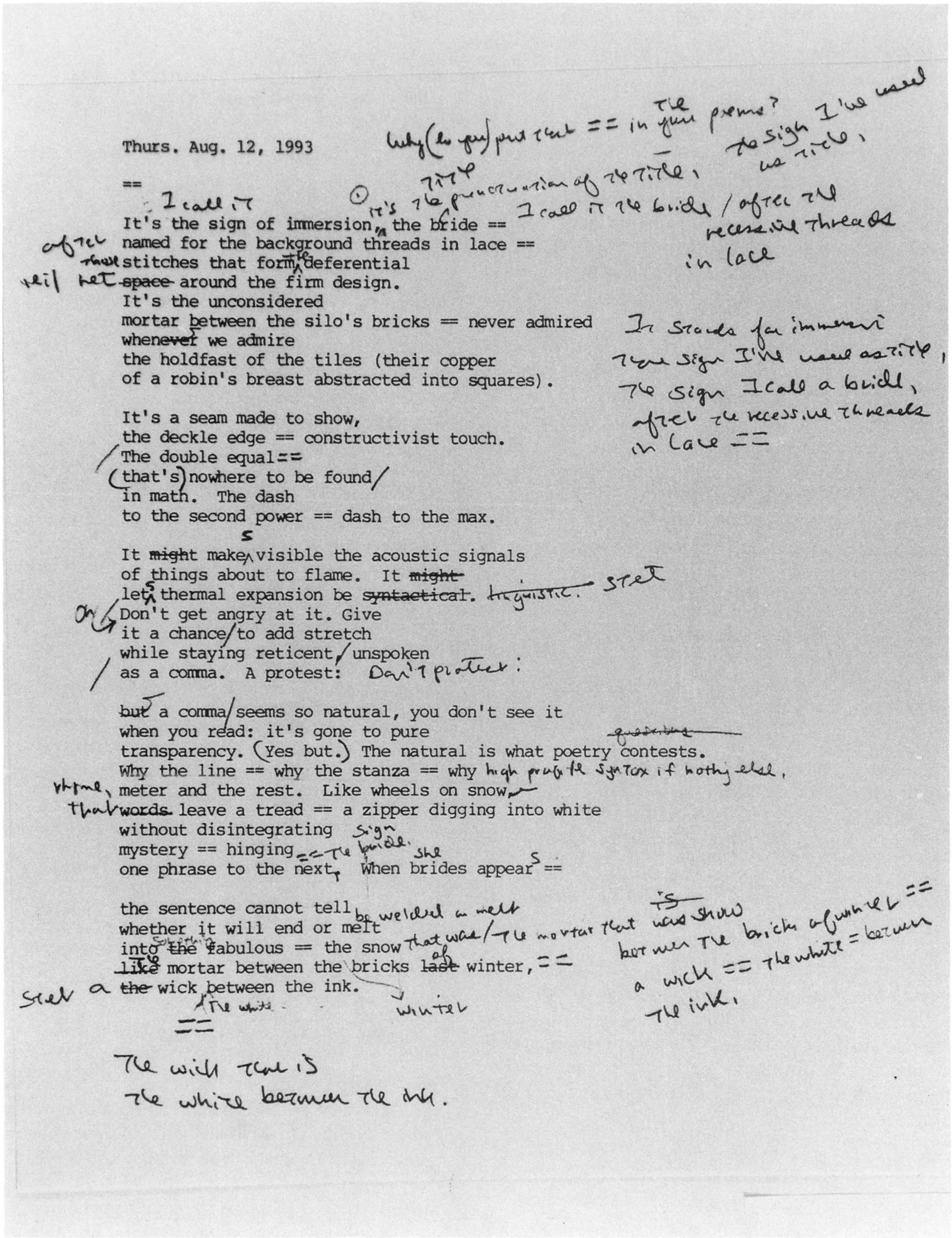

Thurs. Aug. 12, 1993

==

It's the sign of immersion, the bride ==
named for the background threads in lace ==
stitches that form deferential
space around the firm design.
It's the unconsidered
mortar between the silo's bricks == never admired
whenever we admire
the holdfast of the tiles (their copper
of a robin's breast abstracted into squares).

It's a seam made to show,
the deckle edge == constructivist touch.
The double equal ==
that's nowhere to be found
in math. The dash
to the second power == dash to the max.

It might make visible the acoustic signals
of things about to flame. It might
let thermal expansion be syntactical.
Don't get angry at it. Give
it a chance to add stretch
while staying reticent unspoken
as a comma. A protest:

but a comma seems so natural, you don't see it
when you read: it's gone to pure
transparency. (Yes but.) The natural is what poetry contests.
Why the line == why the stanza == why high
meter and the rest. Like wheels on snow
words leave a tread == a zipper digging into white
without disintegrating
mystery == hinging
one phrase to the next, When brides appear ==

the sentence cannot tell
whether it will end or melt
into the fabulous == the snow
like mortar between the bricks last winter, ==
a the wick between the ink.

The wick that is
the white between the ink.

Draft for "= =," collected in Fulton's 1995 book, Sensual Math *(Collection of Alice Fulton)*

144

It might make visible the acoustic signals
of things about to flame. It might

             let thermal expansion be syntactical. Let it
add stretch

             while staying reticent, unspoken
as a comma. Don't get angry = = protest = = but a
comma seems so natural, you don't see it
when you read: it's gone to pure
transparency. Yet but.
             The natural is what

poetry contests. Why else the line = = why stanza = = why
       meter and the rest. Like wheels on snow

Fulton offers this improvised sign as a symbol for immersion, "a seam made to show," which compels our attention to what our reading ignores, "the white between the ink." Yet this symbol also serves as a summary device that draws together Fulton's complex themes. It embodies, at once, horizon, immersion, lace, and suture, Fulton's images for what the mind embraces—and represses—as it contends with the world. She explains in "Immersion":

Let it be horizon levitating on horizon
with sunrise at the center = =
the double equal that means more
than equal to = = within.

It's sensual math
and untied railroad tracks = =
the ladder of gaps and lace
unlatched. It's staples
in the page and the swimmer's liquid lane.
Those sutures that dissolve into the self.

These images are multiple in their meaning. Lace, in particular, appears most often as Fulton's image for the acts of repression by which a culture naturalizes its concealed violence, as in this meditation in the dentist's chair from "Fuzzy Feelings":

             Lace
is a form of filth I hate.
As for the dying moan and gush

of the deer killed by hunters down the road–
I'd find it more tasteful
done in plastic or an acrylic
venison Christmas sweater.
I'd rather wear vinyl than hide.

I didn't mean what I said about lace.
Lace in a vacuum would be okay.
Even beige would have its place. It's context,

culture makes them = = wait, I'll take the novocaine.

In "The Lines are Wound on Wooden Bobbins, Formerly Bones," the third poem in Fulton's Daphne and Apollo sequence, this image of lace evolves into a metaphor for the woman's role as sexual prey:

A daughter like the openwork of lace = = between
             the raised motif

             the field, formed by lines
of thread called brides, shies back

in order to let shine.

The image hints at the complexity of Fulton's metaphor, its doubleness: the bride "shies back," but in this act of receding, she shines. Fulton summons the repressed into the foreground, displays what the culture habitually conceals:

             = = the dense
omissions crystallize the lack

that's lace. She is to be that
       yin of linen

       that dissolves
under vision's dominion = = be the ground

of silk that's burned away with lye = =
       the bride.

Daphne, in "Splice: A Grotesque," embodies all that male desire negates, "the lack / that's lace," a fabric that both entices the male gaze and demands to be torn. The object of Apollo's desire, she is "neither-nor," "nevergreen"–the antimatter that is destroyed by contact with Apollo's maleness:

      Given the heavens, he's the stellar,
not the black bridle between stars. He's the type
      on white, he's text. He's monarch, please,
he's god. The impressive = = living end.
Though luminous matter is less than one percent
           of the whole
required for closure, though foreground
was an afterthought, he's the great attractor the field falls
      on its knees before. Go figure.

Yet Fulton's imagery subverts this easy opposition, even as she constructs it: Daphne, by implication, is the page that makes the type visible, the unseen matter "required for closure." She is the desire that defines him, the repressed that Fulton's poem brings into view.

Cover for Fulton's 1995 book, which includes her most explicitly feminist poems

Daphne's transformation into the laurel in "Turn: A Version" becomes for Fulton an image of immersion, an "engagement" with nature that offers refuge from Apollo's predatory desire:

> People get a kick
> out of ambivalent
> betrothals and collisions full of give. Flowers that
> remodel
> themselves to look like bees are nice, but the scientist whose
> atoms get commingled
> with a fly's might be my favorite. "Help me! Help me!"
> I can identify.

Fulton reclaims the laurel ("Tree of completion– presence–and immersion") from Apollo and transforms it into an image of poetry that demands engagement. Where poets have traditionally taken the laurel, Fulton's imagery makes it a figure for the dissolution of self that poetry demands of us ("collisions full of give"). Daphne escapes into the laurel's embrace, as if heeding the admonition in Fulton's earlier sequence to "blend, / bend, and blur, folks. It works!"

One implication of this revision of the iconography of Apollo's laurel wreath is Fulton's more pro- found "re-imagining" of the poet's craft. She identifies Daphne closely with her own poetic method, "the deep / meanders of her / mind" through the culture's multiple languages, navigated in "Mail" by the associative pattern she calls "echolocation":

>   she'd bounce
> sound
> off distant objects to predict their motion, shape, and place.
> Echolocation
> is what she used to navigate, traveling up to one hundred
>   miles
> a day.
> Her sonar let her see right through opacities: read
> the entrails
> coiled inside the trees. . . .
>   But her gift for visualizing the inner
>
> chambers
> of words was most impressive. She'd tell of *wedlock's* wall
> that was a shroud
> of pink, its wall that was a picket fence, the one of chainlink
> and one
> that was all strings.
> . . . .

This idea of echolocation–the ability to navigate, like a bat, by reflected sound–is central to Fulton's method: her poems strike the reader like the echo bouncing off the visible objects of culture. Yet what those echoes reveal most clearly is all that remains hidden. In "Some Cool" Fulton associates the pig ornaments she hangs on her tree with the memory of pigs hauled to slaughter; she describes this movement of mind as a form of "cultural incorrectness," the insistent presence in her poetry of thoughts that the culture tries to repress:

> Now when people ask what kind of poetry I write
> I say the poetry of cultural incorrectness–
> out of step and–does that help?
>
> I use my head
> voice and my chest voice.
> I forget voice
> and think syntax, trying to add
> so many tones to words that words
> become a world all by themselves.
> I forget syntax
> and put some street in it. I write
>
> for the born-again infidels
> whose skepticism begins at the soles
> of the feet and climbs the body,
> nerve by nerve.

Fulton offers her readers a handy critical phrase here–"the poetry of cultural incorrectness"–but the more revealing moment of this brief *ars poetica* is the inclusive compositional method she confesses to in the second stanza. The inspired tonal variations that characterize her best work reflect a kind of immersion in her own writing process ("trying to add / so many tones to words that words / become a world all by themselves"). In these terms her claim on our skepticism extends to our own process of reading. Like the students in the summer immersion course in "Drills," who "must speak the language they're learning / in brittle artificial dialogues," readers are prompted to confront the limits of their comprehension:

> . . . the teacher plucked me from the chorus
> with a question out of sync with all our drills:
>   "Does suffering help one understand
> the suffering of others? What do you think, *Alice?*"
> I wanted to describe an essay I'd received—
>   I also was a teacher—
> from a former Marine
> who wrote of the wounds, humiliation,
>   he'd endured in the war
>   and how he'd held up well
> until a medic touched him gently.
> I wanted to build complex sentences,
>   quivering with clauses that reveal
>   the meaning sheath by sheath
>   and lead to, or perhaps enact, the fact
> that understanding is itself unbearable.
>   Sentences beyond the depth
> of my thin French. So I just said yes.

This is not agreement, but surrender. The poem emerges as an elegy for her niece ("Laura: Latin feminine of *laurus,* bay laurel"), linking the abstractions that govern Fulton's poetics to the most personal of griefs. No language can express—or allow readers to comprehend—such suffering. At best, as in Fulton's intricate riffs, it can dare readers to wonder. That's no small thing, but as Fulton notes: "What causes less comfort / than wonder?"

Fulton's self-awareness in these poems tempts her readers to the conclusion that such meditations on her own poetic imagination must be read as statements of aesthetic intent—an ongoing ars poetica that commences in the aspirations to a dangerous grace in "Dance Script with Electric Ballerina" and reappears in such poems as "The Wreckage Entrepreneur," with its description of a woman who rescues beauty from what the culture casts aside. Yet Fulton's poetics resist such attempts to impose coherence on the movements of the poetic imagination. Her poems demand from her readers nothing less than immersion, a process in which they share the creation of meaning by allowing the poem to shape—but not dictate—their own consciousness. Her meanings are multiple, fluid, and provisional; reading her work reveals our minds to be the same. As she celebrates the transformative power of poetic language, it becomes clear that it is her *reader* that is transformed, made aware by these "explorations of mind" that the poet simply sketches a horizon, displaying for her readers—as she notes in *Palladium*—"this reliable frame / that lets color be // color and light light." The rest she leaves to imagination.

Interview:

Karen Clark, "Alice Fulton Talks with Karen Clark," *Poetry Society of America Newsletter,* 28 (Fall 1988): 4–11.

Allen Grossman
(7 January 1932 -)

Gary Roberts
Brandeis University

BOOKS: *A Harlot's Hire* (Cambridge, Mass.: Walker-de Berry, 1961);

The Recluse and Other Poems (Cambridge, Mass.: Pym-Randall Press, 1965);

Poetic Knowledge in the Early Yeats: A Study of The Winds among the Reeds (Charlottesville, Va.: University Press of Virginia, 1969);

And The Dew Lay All Night Upon My Branch: Poems (Lexington, Mass.: Aleph Press, 1973);

The Woman on the Bridge over the Chicago River (New York: New Directions, 1979);

Against Our Vanishing: Winter Conversations with Allen Grossman on the Theory and Practice of Poetry, edited by Mark Halliday (Boston: Rowan Tree Press, 1982); revised and expanded as part 1 of *The Sighted Singer: Two Works on Poetry for Readers and Writers* (Baltimore, Md.: Johns Hopkins University Press, 1992);

Of the Great House: A Book of Poems (New York: New Directions, 1982);

The Bright Nails Scattered on the Ground: Love Poems (New York: New Directions, 1986);

The Ether Dome and Other Poems: New and Selected (1979-1991) (New York: New Directions, 1991);

The Sighted Singer: Two Works on Poetry for Readers and Writers (Baltimore, Md.: Johns Hopkins University Press, 1992);

The Philosopher's Window and Other Poems (New York: New Directions, 1995);

The Long Schoolroom: Lessons in the Bitter Logic of the Poetic Principle (Ann Arbor: University of Michigan Press, 1997).

RECORDING: *The Song of the Lord,* Watershed Tapes, 1991.

OTHER: "Criticism, Consciousness, and the Sources of Life: Some Tasks for English Studies," in *Uses of Literature,* edited by Monroe Engel (Cambridge, Mass.: Harvard University Press, 1973), pp. 19–48;

Allen Grossman

"Contributor's Notes to 'The Piano Player Explains Himself,'" in *The Best American Poetry: 1988,* edited by John Ashbery and David Lehman (New York: Collier Books, 1988), p. 219;

"Contributor's Notes to 'The Ether Dome (An Entertainment),'" in *The Best American Poetry: 1991,* edited by Mark Strand and Lehman (New York: Collier Books, 1991), pp. 284–285;

"Contributor's Notes to 'Poland of Death (IV),'" in *The Best American Poetry: 1992,* edited by Charles Simic and Lehman (New York: Collier Books, 1992);

"Contributor's Notes to 'The Great Work Farm Elegy,'" in *The Best American Poetry: 1993,* edited by Louise Glück and Lehman (New York: Collier Books, 1993), p. 236;

"Whitman's 'Whoever You Are Holding Me Now in Hand': Remarks on the Endlessly Repeated Rediscovery of the Incommensurability of the Person," in *Breaking Bounds: Whitman and American Cultural Studies,* edited by Betsy Erkkila and Jay Grossman (New York: Oxford University Press, 1996), pp. 112–122.

SELECTED PERIODICAL PUBLICATIONS–
UNCOLLECTED: "Teaching Literature in a Discredited Civilization," *Massachusetts Review,* 10 (Summer 1969): 419–432;

"Lyric Reformation: Two Books on Stevens," *Virginia Quarterly Review,* 51 (Winter 1975): 152–160;

"Why is Death in Arcadia? Poetic Process, Literary Humanism, and the Example of the Pastoral," *Western Humanities Review,* 41 (Summer 1987): 152–188;

"The Calling of Poetry: The Constitution of Poetic Vocation, the Recognition of the Maker in the Twentieth Century, and the Work of the Poet in Our Time," *TriQuarterly,* 79 (Fall 1990): 220–238;

"Inquiry into the Vocation of Sir William Topas McGonagall, Poet and Tragedian: The Poetics of Derision and the Epistemic Nobility of Doggerel," *TriQuarterly,* 79 (Fall 1990): 238–258.

To describe the poetry of Allen Grossman as "eccentric" seems inevitable: it is relatively unimitated; it is independent of the predominant schools and movements of contemporary poetry; and it is difficult in ways that other difficult poetry of its time is not. In other words, it is not representative of a given kind of postmodern American poetry, nor does it conform to common notions of exemplary originality. Like most poets of his generation, Grossman was greatly influenced by the work of the modernists–in his case, especially by William Butler Yeats, Wallace Stevens, and Hart Crane; but unlike his contemporaries, he has not mitigated these modernists' claims about the high office of the poet. Instead Grossman has consistently attempted to regain their poetics, and especially their practice of an elevated style, at the risk of the obscurity that follows from his disinterest in the rhetorics of contemporaneity pioneered by other more famous poets maturing in the 1950s and 1960s.

The importance of poetic communities to the poetry of this time cannot be underestimated, but Grossman has not participated in or aligned himself with any. Except for a few important poems (three of which are elegies), his poetry does not refer to friends, peers, colleagues, or fellow living poets by name, and the textual apparatus of nominal affiliation–dedications, acknowledgments, and quotations–employed by many different postmodern poets to allude to their social networks and personal allegiances is conspicuously absent from his work. In his criticism Grossman speaks feelingly about some of the poetry of his contemporaries which matters to him, notably that of Robert Lowell, Sylvia Plath, Allen Ginsberg, and John Ashbery. He does not, however, use his prose to relate himself personally to them, nor does his poetry much resemble theirs. Because Grossman does not chronicle his participation in a quasi-official group endeavor sponsored by his intimates, literary historians have not enhanced his reputation by retrospectively placing him in a literary movement or group. A passage from his early poem "The Recluse" (the title alludes to William Wordsworth's unfinished epic project of the same name) captures his sense of isolation as he tries to imagine his companion muse:

> And who will tell me that I do not pray
> (Being unfashionable) with the profoundest right
> Of a deserted man to that vague thing
> Which has usurped my empty hearth and altar
> And is a common bird, and yet unknown
> To me except by cries, and by the breath of wings.

Few poets trying to establish a career in the early 1960s could hear a viable sound in this kind of writing, and none except Grossman has followed it to its source in the hope of making it known and new.

Despite its apparent autonomy, readers should be careful in labeling Grossman's work as "exceptional" or even "eccentric" because they thereby presuppose both a center and a periphery that American poetry since 1945 seems to deny. In a time of poetic heterogeneity characterized by a great range of diverging and perhaps mutually exclusive intentions, procedures, and outcomes, readers are likely to find it difficult to determine which contemporary poets and poetics are central and which peripheral, or even which are typical and which uncommon. This difficulty is complicated by the deliberately ambiguous ambitions of poets such as Ashbery and A. R. Ammons, who are typically designated "central," "important," or "major" but who are themselves skeptical of this status and proclaim within their poems, at times ironically, their "willed disavowal of majority," as Grossman has described it. In such a context his own avowed ambitions for

Grossman in 1993

poetry are especially problematic for him, his contemporaries, and their critics.

Readers may dispel this problem by embracing eclecticism, thereby accepting as a happy feature of the times what Ashbery has called the "amazing accidental abundance" of poetry, which in turn becomes the inevitable ratification of Walt Whitman's famous defense of American self-contradiction: "I am large, I contain multitudes." Such an encompassing embrace, however, would be untrue to the equally inevitable need of most contemporary poets and critics for distinctions, usually founded on arguments for a specific relationship between stylistics and cultural politics, in order to justify some poetry and to delegitimize other poetry. From these distinctions come the most compelling generalizations about the center of recent poetic history and the most useful descriptive categories of it (as well as the most hackneyed and simplistic ones). But for the most part these critical ways of sorting and evaluating this

poetic abundance, whatever their convenience, do not easily account for Grossman's poetry or accurately describe it. Given this situation, his poetry becomes "eccentric" in the same way as the pronounced elliptical orbit of a heavenly body such as a comet around a greater gravitational source: such an orbit passes close to the center in its apogee but presses toward the outer limit of the center's influence in its perigee, and it is both of these relationships to the center which define its course.

The most apparent evidence of Grossman's eccentricity relative to the center of postmodern poetry is his use of a high tone and sublime style. Perhaps the only contemporaries whom Grossman resembles in practicing the high style are the American poet Robert Duncan and the British poet Geoffrey Hill. The histories of these three poets, however, cannot really be compared, and readers cannot posit any shared intentions for them though all three are singularly heterodox religious poets. An early example of Grossman's blank verse from

"A Poem for Statesmen" gives the sound of his poetic voice as it tries to explain its undertaking:

> My muse is a mourner, for these wars
> Have been unspeakable, and peace is the sense
> Of some incredible hurt still to be borne.

This style distinguishes his work from that of his contemporaries because it is not qualified by the most typical postmodern strategies of irony and deflation, nor is it routinely objectified with representations of local, naturalistic details or references to private social exchanges. Although Grossman's high style is not without its own mitigations, it eschews the conventions of pastiche, vulgarity, and realism that characterize the central postmodern response to certain kinds of modernist weightiness, impersonality, and abstraction. A vernacular poetics of psychologized everydayness, put forward with varying degrees of earnestness by some modernist poets, has shaped the principles of style for most postmodern American lyric poetry, whether meditative, confessional, or surrealist. But Grossman, who undeniably writes out of the Romantic tradition of lyric poetry, cannot be comfortably placed alongside these later demotic versions of it, having proclaimed poetry to be "fundamentally antipsychological" and having described his own poetry to be a matter of "ugly seriousness" unamenable to the requirements of conciliatory familiarity or amusing estrangement. Grossman's high style manifests itself not only on the page but also in his oral performances of his poems. Through these he seeks to convey the difference between social speech and poetic speech by a dramatic enactment of the "daemonic" character of the poem's language.

Grossman's eccentricity is certainly a function of his seemingly anachronistic high style, but it also can be ascribed to his understanding of what he calls the "bitter logic of the poetic principle." In an overwhelmingly agnostic age, Grossman has conducted through poetry and criticism a radical research into the hypotheses (the groundwork) of transcendental knowledge and its representation. Such literary research seeks to disclose the implications of its claims for the "keeping" (an important term in Grossman's work) of Western personhood in the present "discredited civilization," which has now attained the ability to erase all persons. But according to Grossman the implications of a postmodern transcendentalism are not inevitably in accord with the needs and desires of poetry, individuals, or the narrative and structural totalities created to encompass them (organic form, canonicity, self-actualization, love, family, gender, ethnicity, generation, community,

nation). He therefore insists on a dialectic of skepticism not only in which the "human forgetfulness" of Being, as Grossman defines it following the German philosopher Martin Heidegger, is repudiated but also in which the institutions of memory, continuity and hope, and their representational hierarchies are deconstructed in order to acquire the authentic speech of the poet in search of the transcendental sources of the laws of new song. This ancient, indeed original, dialectic, pressed anew upon the postmodern world by the barbarism of World War II and the Cold War, makes poetry a necessary but impossible "calling." In the face of an unresolvable situation, Grossman sees his own poetry as "a frightened poetry from beginning to end."

Grossman was born 7 January 1932 in Minneapolis, Minnesota, to Louis and Beatrice Berman Grossman. Louis was a Chevrolet dealer, and Beatrice seems to have been an aloof, exceptionally spiritual person, but the facts of their lives are not available. Grossman has chosen to reveal little of his biography except as it is set down in his poems, and, unlike central poets such as Lowell or Ginsberg, he does not harbor a postmodern need to investigate the poetics of autobiographical representation as a means to secure the possibility of individual and cultural renewal; according to his thinking, "all poems that are meritorious are inherently anonymous" because they proceed from without personal history. And yet, paradoxically for the contemporary reader, Grossman's relationships to his father and mother are of primary importance to his poetry. This belief is clear from many of his poems such as "The Book of Father Dust," "The Runner," "Lament Fragment," "Of the Great House," "Bow Spirit," and "Poland of Death." Indeed, for the poet, reference to father and mother are crucial both to the positing of a "lineage," or an account of origin in terms of the universe's intelligibility, and to the definition of the successful appropriation of the means of giving and receiving poetry.

Similarly, although the information about his youth is scant, Grossman's poetic recollection of his childhood is important and constant. Beginning at about the age of ten (about 1942), he witnessed and participated in rural life and work on farms near Gibbon, Minnesota, and these early experiences of domesticated nature have influenced much of his later "pastoral" poetry, as he has named it. The traditional imagery of the shepherd and the field is pervasive in Grossman's poetry and serves to locate his speculations on the labor and economy of representation itself and to enable his narrations of "the birth of death." (A thorough recapitulation of his understanding of the importance of pastoral poetry can be

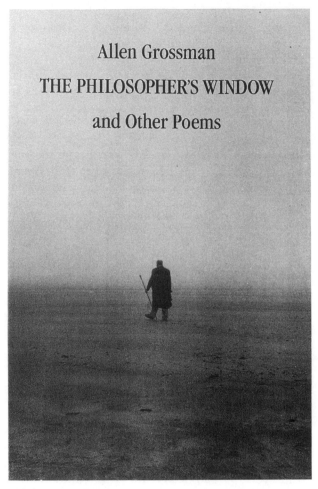

Allen Grossman
THE PHILOSOPHER'S WINDOW
and Other Poems

Cover for Grossman's 1995 book, a collection of five poems narrated by "an old man compelled by the insistent questioning of the children to explain *himself"*

has said, "thrown out" a few times, he graduated Phi Beta Kappa in 1955; during this time he became editor of the *Harvard Advocate*. His poems began to be published in 1952, and in 1955 he received two poetry awards, the Garrison Award for Poetry and an Academy of American Poets Award. He thereafter began graduate work at Harvard and completed an M.A. in English in 1957.

Grossman's long association with Brandeis University began in the same year, when he started his doctorate degree, completed in 1960. His dissertation was revised and published in 1969 as *Poetic Knowledge in the Early Yeats: A Study of The Winds among the Reeds*. This book examines how Yeats in the formative years of his poetic life (1892–1899) devised an "account of personal origins in terms of an imaginary culture dominated by the Wisdom figure which is both the source and identifying soul of personal existence." Grossman expounds a detailed account of how Yeats's style in *The Wind among the Reeds* (1899), a style crucial for twentieth-century poetry, emerges from his initiation into occult rites of renunciation and compensation as a way to find (remember) the Imagination and to forestall its secularization.

For more than thirty years Grossman taught at Brandeis, where in 1983 he became the Paul E. Prosswimmer Professor of Poetry and General Education. For more than twenty of these years he directed and taught in the school's now-defunct General Education Program. His reputation as a particularly dedicated teacher was officially confirmed twice in his career: in 1965 he received an Outstanding Teachers Award from Brandeis, and in 1987 he was named a "Professor of the Year" by the Council for Advancement and Support of Education. In 1991 Grossman left Brandeis to work at Johns Hopkins University, where he now holds the position of the Mellon Professor in the Humanities. He has been married to Judith Grossman, a novelist and teacher of fiction, for more than thirty years and has five children: Jonathan (a Union official), Adam (a musician), Bathsheba (a sculptor), Austin (a gamemaker), and Lev (a writer).

Many of the facts of Grossman's life can be misleading if taken to be reliable indicators of his poetic output or critical views; his career as a professor is no exception. It is a truism that, for better and worse, postmodern poetry was institutionalized in American universities during the postwar period. Avant-garde poets attacked this arrangement between poetry and the academy, and although they were unsuccessful in breaking it (ultimately they did not have to be in order to carry their poetics to fruition), they did succeed in leaving a tenuous but last-

found in the uncollected essay "Why is Death in Arcadia?," published in 1987.)

Recently Grossman has traced the start of his vocation as a poet to his first encounter with the origins of English poetry itself: "I first put myself to school, in 'the long schoolroom' [quoting Yeats] of the poetic principle, when I began reading with the intention of making poems–in 1951 (I was nineteen), on a hot August morning (in my memory, it is always 11 A.M.), in a rural public library in Colorado: bright, cleanly smelling of wax." It was then that he first read Caedmon's seventh-century dreamhymn about the origin of the world, from which he intuited that poetry was demanded of mortal voices by "an axiomatically nonhuman 'first' reality." All the rest of his schooling, writing, and teaching follow from this intuited demand for an etiological poetics.

In 1949 Grossman began an undergraduate degree at Harvard University, and after being, as he

ing characterization of the "academic" poet of Grossman's generation—one who complacently conserves the Anglo-American traditions of form and performance under the delusory auspices of an enlightened bourgeois gentility.

Although he is a successful teacher and literary critic, Grossman cannot readily be called an "academic" poet, especially not in the derogatory sense bequeathed to his generation by avant-gardists. Like Josephine Miles, John Hollander, and the British poet-critic Donald Davie, Grossman is an accomplished critic of English and American poetry whose own poetry builds on the examples of the past while insisting on its responsibility to the new needs of the present. To gather these different contemporaries together, merely because they are professors, under the banner of New Critical formalism, the dominant mode of poetic criticism during their early professional careers and the main target of midcentury avant-garde poets, is an egregious misrepresentation of their poetry and criticism.

The best gauge of Grossman's profession of academic literary criticism is of course his own writing. Contrary to many contemporary complaints, the act of criticism for him is neither disinterested nor parasitical but part of "our urgent, common work," as he explains in the essay "The Poetics of Union in Whitman and Lincoln: An Inquiry toward the Relationship of Art and Policy": "We do criticism because we are busy about something else. In this sense, we do not intend the poem; we intend the intention that brought the poet to poetry, which is not the poem but the reason for taking poetry in hand." The pronoun "we" is more than a rhetorical generalization of the critic's voice: it is a way to announce the constituency of teachers and students, writers and readers, formed by mutual interest in poetry. And for Grossman, the stakes in the social organization of this mutuality are the highest. An important uncollected essay on the structure and purpose of teaching provides an unambivalent self-portrait of Grossman as a teacher concerned to find an authentic pedagogy upon which to base the practice of criticism. "Teaching Literature in a Discredited Civilization," published in 1969, admonishes professors to undertake a "critique" of their "instruments" and shows that Grossman was capable of distinguished prose at a relatively early stage of his career:

> Language learning in the more advanced sense of "style" is the archetypal rite of passage by which the young enter history, a deed of blood exacted by the gods which acknowledges and seals the child's sharing of the guilt of social life. It is as legitimately resisted and as inevitably undertaken as Orestes' murder of his mother. The practice of social language is the threshold at which vital forces in the self, all labeled "Life and Meaning," are in dreadful conflict. Where in a discredited, and unforgivable, civilization is the goddess who votes the casting vote on behalf of the child? The literary *paideia* which does not understand these problems is falsely innocent.

"These problems," as Grossman sees them, are much graver than even this passage suggests, since they arise at a time when the teacher not only can but must ask, "To what extent does the substance of our civilization and not merely the circumstances of its transmission make it hostile to life?" Needless to say, the type of the tweedy poet-professor tagged as "academic" is not speaking here. Despite his anger at the academy's "criminal alliances with industry and government," and indeed because of it, Grossman's recommendation for a radical teaching that deserves its name does not flinch from invoking authority: "The teacher must seek authority as the member of an academic community to stop teaching, to teach this and not that, to teach this person and not that person, to protect students from destructive grids of requirements and moronic sanctions, to foster self-possession without preempting criticism, and above all to understand and say clearly what he is about, so that he does not commit the final pedagogic crime of conferring the problem unsolved upon those who have come for something else." These responsibilities are especially pressing for the teacher of poetry, since poetry is "an irreplaceable mode of the visibility of man to man."

In addition to his book-length study of Yeats, Grossman has published many articles—some recently collected in *The Long Schoolroom: Lessons in the Bitter Logic of the Poetic Principle* (1997); a series of dialogues in *Against Our Vanishing: Winter Conversations with Allen Grossman on the Theory and Practice of Poetry* (1982); and his critical masterwork, a handbook of aphorisms and commentary on the nature of lyric poetry in the West, *Summa Lyrica: A Primer of the Commonplaces in Speculative Poetics* (the last two published together in 1992 as *The Sighted Singer: Two Works on Poetry for Readers and Writers*). His readers should familiarize themselves with the three works listed above, both for the acuity of their understanding of canonical poets such as John Milton and Whitman and for their insights into his own poetry. The *Summa Lyrica* is especially important: no other postmodern poet has in one work of criticism put forward such an encompassing synthesis of the postulates, discoveries, and intentions of the lyric mode. Its unusual textual format, numbered paragraphs arranged under numbered rubrics, is derived from

Allen Grossman

several traditions of theoretical and pedagogical writing and features the same combination of discursive and recursive exposition found in the prose of Nietzsche, Ludwig Wittgenstein, and Wallace Stevens. The following sample is from section 36 concerning the relation of breathing to the "Line":

[The Greater Breath] is the breath taken in, during which there can be no speech. This breath comes to an end with the *limit of expansion,* when the body is full as can be of the nurturant air. This silent feeding on the world to the limit of the expansion . . . prepares for *the line opening* (or, in appropriate degree, the lesser medial caesura). The Lesser Breath is the breathing out, during which speech occurs as the reticulation of the dead breath . . . [and] explores the opposite limit . . . of contraction— . . . *the line ending.* The strong sense of the contradiction of speech and feeding lends weight to the preference of silence to speech, and adds a further bitterness to the paradox of storytelling.

The conflation of speech and writing here is characteristic, and readers should be wary of taking it only as a metaphor: the critic has deferred to the authority of the poet, whose performance enacts the conflation by giving "voice" to his words. This deeply em-

bodied conception of language belies the stereotypical notions of the professorial style caricatured as bloodless and pedantic. Readers should remember, however, that although the term "academic" is of no use for describing it, Grossman's account of poetic speech is antithetical to the most pervasive ideas of postmodern avant-gardism, especially those of the Language Poets.

As with his family life and his work as an academic critic, Grossman's Jewishness has a direct bearing on his poetry, but it does not give access to the poems if his reader expects from them a legible social identity. Although the Holocaust is a defining personal and poetic event for him, Grossman has resisted the most parochial claims of his ethnicity on his identity as a poet even at a time when such claims are widely accepted as authentically empowering. Instead of representing Jewish life as if it were intelligible to him through the poetics of imitative realism, Grossman investigates the transcendental grounds for representation itself and in particular the representation of textual presence as it is given to the West in biblical Scripture. Presence and its mortal corollary, Personhood, have been the subject of intense philosophical debate in the postmodern period, and Grossman's writing has been profoundly engaged in this debate. How are speaking, singing, and writing possible; how are they related to violence; and how are poems and books generated from these questions? From these questions are derived Grossman's poetics, which are Jewish only to the extent that he has chosen to direct himself to a point of departure at the limit of, and thus also at the unknowable origin of, Judeo-Christian representation and monotheism. Perhaps the closest analog to his approach to a Jewish poetry is the work of Egyptian-French poet Edmond Jabès (1912–1991).

Only his first book, *A Harlot's Hire* (1961), which he published at his own expense, is recognizably interested in Jewish topics, as can be seen by some of the titles to its poems: "The Sands of Paran," "Lilith," "Samson," "The Discourse of Shemaiah and Abtalion," "The Breaking of the Law." Grossman has stated that a principal impetus for his earliest published poetry was to define his place in a Jewish "cultural lineage" erased almost to extinction by the Nazi genocide. His poems attempted both to describe "the kind of evil" which he "felt abroad in the world" and "to repeat the language of affirmation by imitating the traditional cultural languages in which affirmation had last been heard." "The language of affirmation" used in this book, a tentative language at best, is heavily indebted to Hebrew scripture but also leans on the classical literature of the West's pagan culture, as in poems such as "En-

Cover for Grossmans's 1997 book, a collection of his critical essays

dymion," "Creusa," "From the Tomb of Galla Placidia," and "Pompeii." These dual traditions from which Grossman first draws his poems are definitive sources for the rest of his poetry, but in *A Harlot's Hire* they are not yet integrated successfully. Grossman has usefully described the limits of the book to be a consequence of its inability to find a "simultaneity of speaking and praxis" in its "inherently speculative and culturally divided language." Although he is always writing "speculative" poems about poetry, or as Stevens put it, poems "of the mind in the act of finding / What will suffice," Grossman's first such writing casts its passionate energies into rhetorical patterns which lack the conviction of a sustaining future for his high style.

Three brief passages from three poems sketch the lineaments of the problem of an authentic high style. The first line of the first poem in Grossman's first book asks a primary question that the entirety of his poetry thereafter attempts to confront, defer,

or rephrase: "Where are the objects of desire?" With this question Grossman initiates a quest for the place of his fulfillment within the provenance of poetry. The congruence of Romantic diction, Freudian vocabulary, and existentialist terminology indicates the crossing paths which the lyric poet will tread toward what he wants but is without, namely the words of the Beloved, the Mother, the Other. But these desired words cannot be heard by the postmodern poet who has been deafened by World War II, a predicament described in "A Poem for Statesmen": "We live in the silence after speech, / And the silence before speech begins." In "The Voiceless Star" Grossman links speech, for the first time in his poetry, to the representation of the human countenance, an act which he will later argue is crucial for the establishment of personhood; in this early poem he can only be a prophet of his power for this act because the transcendental precedence for it has been invalidated: "Having been born when everything was ended / Or almost over / . . . I now turn round and round declaring, 'My God / Is faceless, and I am made in His strange likeness.'"

In his second book, *The Recluse and Other Poems* (1965), Grossman moves closer to his distinct version of the Romantic lyric in the high style: it is, following Stevens, grounded in the conviction that "Death is the mother of beauty," and it desires to tend a specifically and definitively poetic fruit from this knowledge. The gigantic language of catastrophe in his first book ("What Helen walks these shattered battlements?") begins to be supplanted by the language of pastoral elegy; Grossman, in a sense, reverses the trajectory of Virgil's career (or Edmund Spenser's or Milton's) by moving from epic to eclogue and georgic. If in his first book the heroic poets William Blake and Percy Bysshe Shelley are apparent as predominant English influences, then in his next book the domestic poets Wordsworth and John Keats have taken their place. For example, in addition to the title poem, a second poem borrows one of Wordsworth's titles, "An Evening Walk" (the English poet's first important poem). In Grossman's much shorter poem, the poet departs into the autumnal "wreck" of nature, which is precisely *not* also imagined as history's ruins: "Weary of all the obscurer ways of death / I move beside the stream that moves beside me / Attended everywhere I turn by birds." The poet finds in this kinetic space (and the speech that defines it) an auspicious sign of his "proper company." In "Spring Song" Grossman elaborates an understanding of the meaning of his new lyric voice; it is "somewhat visionary" because it describes an apprehension of "something" beyond "the ghostly limit of the familiar." Thus Grossman finds a revised poetic project in looking for responses to the indifference of what Stevens memorably called "the necessary angel of earth" that is always "a figure half seen, or seen for a moment." The poet is now recognized as one who, faced with inevitable failure, perseveres to introduce what is unknown among the objects of desire without destroying them.

Personally published in 1973, *And The Dew Lay All Night Upon My Branch* shows Grossman consolidating the strengths of his first two collections but beginning to look for new ways of framing and presenting his style. He reprints several of his earlier poems among new poems written in a conspicuously greater variety of compositional forms. Until now, blank verse has been the main, if not exclusive, focus of the poet's attention; this book includes the results of many experiments with lines of two, three, and four beats as well as poems written with less discursive and even strictly repetitious patterns in mind. Thus readers find a villanelle ("The Ghost"), a poem with an antiphon ("The Clear Light"), another poem with a refrain ("Moving The Trees Around"), and poetic sequences structured around repeated words ("Waves" and "A Scarf of Glories"). The most extreme example the poet calls a "Benediction," and he uses its title phrase, "As For The Tower," 125 times in the 120 lines of the poem. Grossman tries to cast his voice into new acoustical spaces, not all of which in return promise to house his poetry. But one experiment, "A Curse," does introduce his discovery of a new relationship between sound and text that shapes his next three books:

> In my youth
>   I studied
>   the *impossibilia*
> Setting a tree of language
>   in void space
>   on fire

The formal model in this poem is the triadic step-pattern invented by William Carlos Williams in his poetry of the mid 1950s; although Grossman does not hereafter adhere to its numerical regularity, he does continue to explore extensively the placement of the poem on the page in such a way as to make rhythmical and semantic use of the "void space" surrounding it.

Grossman announces arrival at his incontrovertibly distinct authority in his fourth book, *The Woman on the Bridge over the Chicago River* (1979). The translator and poet Robert Fitzgerald in his forward to the book describes its "elemental" style as "falling as unlaboredly on the page as light falls through a framing window on a wall." This new prosodic ease, however, is not a sign that the difficult conceptions of the world and the place of poetry in it have relented. The mourning muse of Grossman's first poetry, written more than twenty years earlier, still interposes herself between the light and the page, upon which falls the shadow of her crying, as when in the title poem "A small woman wrapped in an old blue coat / Staggers to the rail weeping." The backdrop of this remembered scene on Michigan Avenue, where Grossman lived briefly during his late teens, is an extraordinary catalogue of universal lamentations, in which, for example, "Cormorants / Weep from the cliffs" and "Eternity and Time / Grieve incessantly in one another's arms." Thus the promised realism of the title of the book and the poem is belied by the impetus toward abstraction; or rather, the precondition for the weeping woman's appearance in the poem is the poet's rehearsal of the antinomic rules of art, whereby what is other than the actual woman and her circumstances must assume its place in language. In "After Repetition" Grossman defines the intention of poetic abstraction

as a way "To place a poem among these poems /
Without darkening the scene of / Placing the
poem—"; such care requires a distinction between
"the mere poet broken in the / Saltmill of the manifest" and,

The self-determined maker

> the *yogin*

> > whose walking

Lightly is a way—
Each good line a lineament—to make
More sure

> the slow overcoming of in-

Credulity

> the welcoming.

In this account of making and the reception of the
made, Grossman advocates a discipline of mind toward language, one that honors the goal of the ap-
prehensible and well-made poem without conceding
the need for difficulty; ponderousness has its limits,
as does blitheness. In recognition of his work thus
far, Grossman was given the 1980 Witter Bynner
Prize in poetry from the American Academy and Institute of Arts and Letters.

With his fifth book of poems, *Of the Great
House: A Book of Poems* (1982), Grossman has found
the "simultaneity of speaking and praxis" that
eluded his earliest poetry. Like *The Woman on the
Bridge over the Chicago River,* the book divides and organizes its contents using titled sections in order to
indicate that individual poems do not form a mere
collection of new work but partake of a larger conception, in this instance "an inventory of destruc-
tions," as the final poem names it. As part of this inventory, Grossman also reprints together in a separate section fourteen poems from *A Harlot's Hire*.
The title poem, "Of the Great House," itself broken
into sections, is Grossman's most comprehensive attempt up to this point to represent the workings of
the poet's mind as he tries to imagine "beautiful,
beautiful poems." Their existence is predicated on
the claims, expounded and illustrated as poetry,
that "Everyone must write a book of mother, and /
Father"; and that "There is / No singing without a
woman who wants / An answer sufficient to her injury— / Such is the Muse. . . . " These claims are obligations on the poet that must be understood and
worked through before he can "Establish rest profound," which is also the only way to truly inhabit

"the only thing that is— // the world / With winds
and rivers."

The book also includes Grossman's only poem
("Bow Spirit," subtitled "*stanzas on the pathos of our
generated life*") discussed in a literary critical history.
In *Introspection and Contemporary Poetry* (1984) Alan
Williamson honors Grossman by placing him as the
last poet in the argument, "for the sake of our sense
of possibility regarding the future of personal poetry." The poem is addressed to the mother of
Grossman's poetry, Beatrice, here figured as the
wounding front of a "death-ship" whose course
must be intercepted with a "poem in the likeness of a
countenance." The narrative of the poem seeks to
determine whether this encounter will fragment or
reintegrate the poetic voice, which itself is predicated on the knowledge that "Everyone has a face, a
blowing shroud, / A sheer wealth of furnishing, a
sailing / Gaze and lineage, like a torn net." Although
Williamson may overstate the extent to which the
selected poem is "confessional," he usefully discusses the mediation of impersonal language in the
creation of "a poem about a poem that never quite
gets written—and thus at once a painful account of
creative blockage and a rather lovely meditation on
those prior emotional resonances which are never
fully made visible," by which he means the psychological resonances of frustrated parental nurtur-
ance.

*The Bright Nails Scattered on the Ground: Love Po-
ems* (1986) repeats the format of titled sections but
presents a more unified display of intention, focus,
and revelation. The volume orchestrates the predominant imagery of Grossman's poetry—for example, the gate, the house, the stair, the tree, the sea,
night and day, lightning and thunder and rain—into
a grand sequence of limpid love poems for a man
(sometimes called "Allen") and a woman (sometimes called "Luce"). The familiar constituent parts
of Grossman's poetic domain are summoned to construct a world in which these lovers are knowable to
each other and at least capable of hope in a provisional safety. The epistemological, ethical, and representational difficulties of such construction, as
narrated throughout the book, cannot easily be
paraphrased but may be illustrated by the following
problematic: "To the bodies by which nature maintains / The world the eye of man is blind."

In 1991 Grossman published his next book
of poetry, *The Ether Dome and Other Poems: New and
Selected (1979–1991),* which also reprinted selections from his three previous books. The new poems, gathered under the subtitle "Pastorals of Our
Other Hours in the Millennium," again show a significant amount of thematic coherence. As the

subtitle indicates, Grossman has also continued to use his oldest imagery in the service of thinking about poetry. These "pastorals," however, settle into a meditational mode that for the most part abandons the open textual and syntactical spacing of the work published since the mid 1970s. Nonetheless, Grossman presents poetry as an indispensable discourse of access to what is unknown; for example, the poems are full of questions, as in "Phoenix": "What will the hours *mean* in the next world? / For the gods are not attracted to us." Although the theme of ending has been a constant in Grossman's career, its reiteration here takes on the urgency of a plighted responsibility to speak truly about "Eternity" and "Insectivorous Time" as the end of the century and the millennium approach. The magnitude of this responsibility for the millennial pastoralist is daunting because it requires his "dead" poetry to provide, through its patterning of didactic and prophetic language, the means to measure out a living, mortal, imperfect response to the irrevocable knowledge of the singularity of mankind within infinity. Poetry must do this in any case but now is provoked and inspired by the historical pressure for acknowledgment of the supreme fictions of apocalypse and rebirth.

Grossman's most recent book of poems, *The Philosopher's Window and Other Poems* (1995), perpetuates the impetus toward narrative and grand design evinced in all of his later work. As the short prose preface to the volume indicates, the five poems "tell one story with a beginning, a middle, and an end" and are voiced by "an old man compelled by the insistent questioning of the children to *explain* himself." The beginning, "The Great Work Farm Elegy," recounts among other things the poet's remembered participation in the salvation of "a thousand bales of timothy" from a storm and is his fullest poetic representation of his pastoral labor at discovering, acquiring, and distributing the terms of the manifestation of persons. It is "the poem of explanation" that is finally also "the poem of the myth of explanation—the blank page," as Grossman puts in his endnotes. The middle poem, "The Philosopher's Window," is his longest poem to date: 155 strophes of nine lines each, subdivided into a sequence of twenty-three titled sections. Its central conceit is the journey of the poet, figured in several ways but most touchingly as a speaking parrot, across "the gathered doggerel of ocean" to the Gate of Night; this allegory in turn is floated on the story of a famous mid-nineteenth-century steamer, the *Great Eastern*. The best qualities of Grossman's poetry, including his recent penchant for comedic elements and formal regularity, are synthesized into this account of the demand made of the poet for a prophetic imagining of the creation of the world and heaven, to be told in the time "between the calling out of thought [and] / The telling of the history of the heart // In the delay of the answering glance." The concluding three poems—"The Snowfall," "Whoever Builds," and "June, June"—negotiate the old poet's return from the limit of the cosmogonic mind to the mind waiting for conclusion according to "the laws of materials."

Grossman's poetry is dark and uncompromising, but it is also without dismay: it is resolute. The prefatory poem to *Of the Great House* harks to the reader with a bleak "picture" of life in hand: "The dream that wakes the sleeper does not end." And what is the poet's relentless dream? "—This is my dream: 'I am dragged toward an abyss by an animal.'" It looks like Whitman's hand extended in greeting, but it smells of mortality. And readers may take it because it gestures to them, not out of what Stevens called despair's "strange malice" but from the generosity of Grossman's conviction that "By poems we help one another to the world."

Reference:
Alan Williamson, *Introspection and Contemporary Poetry* (Cambridge, Mass.: Harvard University Press, 1984), pp. 183–191.

Barbara Guest

(6 September 1920 –   )

Sara Lundquist
University of Toledo

BOOKS: *The Location of Things* (New York: Tibor de Nagy, 1960);

Poems: The Location of Things, Archaics, The Open Skies (New York: Doubleday, 1962);

Robert Goodnough, Painter, by Guest and Bernard Harper Friedman (Paris: Musée de Poche, 1962);

The Blue Stairs: Poems (New York: Corinth, 1968);

I Ching: Poems and Lithographs, by Guest and Shelia Isham (Paris: Mourlot, 1969);

Moscow Mansions: Poems (New York: Viking, 1973);

The Countess from Minneapolis (Providence, R.I.: Burning Deck, 1976);

Seeking Air: A Novel (Santa Barbara, Cal.: Black Sparrow Press, 1978);

The Türler Losses (Montreal: Mansfield Book Mart, 1979);

Biography (Providence, R.I.: Burning Deck, 1980);

Quilts (New York: Vehicle Editions, 1980);

Herself Defined: The Poet H.D. and Her World (Garden City, N.Y.: Doubleday, 1984);

Musicality, illustrations by June Felter (Berkeley: Kelsey Street Press, 1988);

Fair Realism (Los Angeles: Sun & Moon Press, 1989);

The Altos, illustrations by Richard Tuttle (San Francisco: Hine Editions/Limestone Press, 1991);

Defensive Rapture (Los Angeles: Sun & Moon Press, 1993);

Selected Poems (Los Angeles: Sun & Moon Press, 1995; Manchester, U.K.: Carcanet, 1996);

Stripped Tales, by Guest and Anne Dunn (Berkeley: Kelsey St. Press, 1995);

Quill, Solitary Apparition (Sausalito, Cal.: Post-Apollo Press, 1996);

The Confetti Trees: Motion Picture Stories (Los Angeles: Sun & Moon Press, 1998);

If True, Tell Me: Short Poems (London: Reality St. Editions, forthcoming).

PLAY PRODUCTIONS: *The Ladies' Choice,* New York, Artists Theatre, 1953;

The Office, New York, Cafe Chino, 1961;

Port, New York, American Theatre for Poets, 1965.

RECORDINGS: *Barbara Guest Reading Her Poems with Comment in the Recording Laboratory, 2 June 1969,* Library of Congress;

Barbara Guest Reading Selections from Her Poetry, 1 April 1992, Buffalo, N.Y.: the Poetics Program;

Barbara Guest Reading Her Poems in the Mumford Room, December 5, 1996, Library of Congress;

Barbara Guest Reading Her Poems, 1996, Lannan Foundation.

OTHER: "Robert Goodnough," in *School of New York: Some Younger Artists,* edited by Bernard Harper Friedman (New York: Grove, 1959), pp. 18–23;

"Jeanne Reynal," *Craft Horizons,* 31 (June 1971): 40–43;

"Helen Frankenthaler: The Moment & The Distance," *Arts Magazine,* 49 (April 1975): 58–59;

"A Reason for Poetics," *Ironwood,* 24 (Fall 1984): 153–155;

"Leatrice Rose," *Arts Magazine,* 59 (Summer 1985): 13;

"June Felter at 871 Fine Arts," *Art in America,* 73 (October 1985): 145;

"Mysteriously Defining the Mysterious: Byzantine Proposals of Poetry," *How(ever),* 3 (October 1986): 12–13;

"The Vuillard of Us" [about James Schuyler], *Denver Quarterly,* 24 (Spring 1990): 13–16;

"Shifting Persona," *Poetics Journal,* 9 (June 1991): 85–88.

Selected Poems, a lavish volume published in 1995 by Sun and Moon Press, has served to draw much deserved attention to the demanding, versatile, and prolific contributions to American poetry of Barbara Guest, who has written more than a dozen books and chapbooks of poetry since 1960 as well as plays, art criticism, a novel (*Seeking Air,* 1978), and a much-admired biography of the Modernist poet, H.D. (*Herself Defined: The Poet H.D. and Her World,* 1984). Guest began writing in New York

Barbara Guest, 1990 (photograph © Star Black)

City during the 1950s as part of a closely knit group of poets including John Ashbery, Frank O'Hara, Kenneth Koch, and James Schuyler, informally known as the New York School of Poets (a half-joking homage to the New York School of painters, the Abstract Expressionists they so admired). Her work, like theirs, was buoyant and energetic, linked aesthetically to painting and music and to the traditions of Surrealism. Like them she extended the formal experiments of world modernism into the second half of the century. Her work appeared in both Donald Allen's important anthology of 1960, *The New American Poetry,* and in John Bernard Myers's 1969 *The Poets of the New York School.*

During the late 1960s and 1970s Guest's visibility as a poet was eclipsed somewhat by the rising fame of Ashbery and O'Hara and also by women poets whose work was more stridently political and feminist (Denise Levertov and Adrienne Rich can serve as examples) or displayed a greater taste for narrative self-expression (Sylvia Plath and Anne Sexton). In her review essay for the *Women's Review of Books,* Rachel Blau DuPlessis has pointed out that Guest suffered both from the tendency of avant-garde groups to marginalize their female participants and from the inattention accorded women whose poetry deviated from "personal-political naming." Guest's work is marked instead by indirection and a fine reticence. She remains continually wary of the traps of oversimplification or exaggeration into which language can fall; she wishes to trace

poetically what is mysterious, not in order to explain it away or contain it but instead to elaborate and perpetuate the richness of human consciousness. Both as a quintessential New York poet and in her own evolving manner she makes the most of the poem as a field of the allusive freedom of verbal collage and practices a "disjunctive" poetics, according to Robert Long, "moving from one level of comprehension to another. From the easily accessible to the obscure."

While publishing her major collections of poetry, she also produced chapbooks and collaborations with visual artists (June Felter, Shelia Isham, Warren Brandt, Anne Dunn), staying open to various kinds of experimental drifts and energies available in the interchange of artistic media. Her individual poems were solicited by numerous avant-garde publications and New American Poetry magazines (including *Sulfur, Blue Mesa, Hambone, O.blek,* and *Temblor*) and came to influence poets later called the Language Poets. During the 1980s her work was published and written about in the radical journal *How(ever)* (published in San Francisco and edited by Kathleen Fraser), providing sustenance and encouragement to women writing in experimental genres. She has since influenced a whole generation of writers, including Fraser, DuPlessis, Charles North, Mei-mei Berssenbrugge, Rosemarie Waldrop, Lyn Hejinian, and Susan Howe. The prejudices that have hitherto rendered Guest the least remarked of the New York School poets have begun to dissipate as these working poets discover her indispensable strain of linguistic possibility. Recent anthologies, both appearing in 1994–Douglas Messerli's *From the Other Side of the Century* and Paul Hoover's *Postmodern American Poetry*–with their generous selections from Guest's work, attest to her achievement, as does the addition of her poems to the latest (fourth) edition of the "canon-defining" *Norton Anthology of Poetry* (1996).

Guest was born Barbara Ann Pinson in Wilmington, North Carolina, in 1920 to James Harvey and Ann Hetzel Pinson. She was raised variously by her parents, her grandmother, and an aunt and uncle in Los Angeles, landscape which figures largely and resonantly in her work. She graduated from the University of California at Berkeley and then settled in New York at the age of twenty-three. In 1952 she sent a poem to *Partisan Review* which came to the attention of Frank O'Hara and the others who became known as the New York School poets. "I was writing like them without knowing anything about them," she claimed, but she soon became an integral member of a shifting and gregarious group of artists who congregated at the Cedar Bar: Schuyler there remarked of a poem she had written: "It was only about a pineapple, but what a pineapple!" O'Hara, Schuyler, the sculptor Tony Smith, and the painters Jane Freilicher, Helen Frankenthaler, Joan Mitchell, and Grace Hartigan became special friends who influenced and promoted her work. She read at the Artists' Club on Eighth Street and briefly became the poetry editor of *Partisan Review,* trying her best to publish French and Russian poetry as well as keeping an eye out for innovative American poetry. "We were interested in French poetry," she remembered in a 1992 interview with Mark Hillringhouse. "What we were writing was so totally alien to anything going on at that time in American poetry."

Guest's first volume of poetry, *The Location of Things* (1960), was published by an art gallery, Tibor de Nagy, under the aegis of John Bernard Myers (as were the first volumes of Ashbery, O'Hara, and Schuyler). In a groundbreaking early essay about these poets written to accompany his anthology, Myers identified the traits they held in common, their "unique tradition." Specifically, they turned to the plastic arts rather than to contemporary poetry for their inspiration and "cultural nourishment"; they were stimulated by the sense of "le mérveilleux" in Surrealism, particularly its capacity to restore "potency, resonance, magic" to a literary world which felt to them dry and flat; and they employed an animated technique of attention to surfaces, the tactile properties of language, the look and feel and effect of word assemblage. Like the paint-

Dust jacket for Guest's 1962 book, poems about the way the self occupies space and history, reacting to change within and without (jacket drawing by Robert Dash)

ers, Myers asserted, the New York School poets "understood the need to keep the literal surface lively. . . . The surface of a work of art *is* the work of art." Of Guest's poetry in particular he wrote: "The very rhythm of her lines implies a quicker breathing. . . . We are confronted with a newly found world that fills her and the reader with astonishment, with wonder."

Guest's second volume, *Poems: The Location of Things, Archaics, The Open Skies,* published by Doubleday in 1962, reprinted the early volume and added a considerable number of poems. All are already mature poems–accomplished, sophisticated, with a sure sense of voice and direction. Most of her major themes appear–new, fresh, and vivid in their presentation–in no sense embryonic. The self and the ways it occupies space and history, interacts with others, countenances change from within and from without: these are her early and late concerns. Yet the poems carry no "confessional" feel, despite their concern with self. The persona shifts from startlingly direct emotional statement to practice rich indirections, suspensions, and ambiguities as well as radiant and realistic looks at the natural and social worlds that surround the self. Her persona is a heroine, an aerialist, an acrobat, a parachutist, a deep-sea diver, a pioneer, an adventuress, a lover, a poet, and a traveler. She is likely to begin poems with questions about a prescient possibility, an imaginative flight, about transformations of current circumstances to other, stranger ones. "I wonder" is a recurrent phrase; she asks repeatedly "Do I dare?" "Why is this so?" and "What will happen if?" Indeed the word *if* dominates whole poems, holding the present in a suspension of what might or might not happen next, superbly sensitive to signs of imminent change, vagary, danger, possible sources of diversion, seduction, and ravishment. "Am I to find a lake under the table / or a mountain beside my chair," she asks in the opening poem, "and will I know the minute water produces lilies / or a family of mountaineers scales the peak?" She loves "the regard of dramatic afternoons"; she fears and delights in shifting sands, horizons at the shimmering edge of sight, the onset of storms, "precarious architecture," and "the gifted night, the billowing dark." In "Santa Fe Trail," frequently anthologized and featured in *Selected Poems,* the protagonist, a latter-day pioneer, follows, albeit "separately," a much-traveled, still-haunted route in the wake of lost trappers, Native Americans, gold seekers, Chinese workers, immigrants, and itinerant salesmen:

> I go separately
> The sweet knees of oxen have pressed a path for me
> ghosts with ingots have burned their bare hands
> it is the dungaree darkness with China stitched
> where the westerly winds
> and the traveler's checks
> the evensong of salesmen
> the glistening paraphernalia of twin suitcases
> where no one speaks English.
> . . . .
> . . . What forks these roads?
> Who clammers o'er the twain?
> . . . .
> We have reached the arithmetics, we are partially quenched
> while it growls and hints in the lost trapper's voice
> She is coming toward us like a session of pines
> in the wild wooden air where rabbits are frozen,
> O mother of lakes and glaciers, save us gamblers
> whose wagon is perilously rapt.

Guest's protagonist is often such a gambler, betting on an uncertain outcome, both in peril and rapturously present, spellbound and alert, simmering and tossing, and always cognizant of those who have gone before. Into the mix she casually and humorously throws an occasional poeticism (characteristi-

cally formed as a question): "What forks these roads? / Who clammers o'er the twain?" On her strange, postmodern Santa Fe trail, echoes abound, to be gathered and personally and imaginatively voiced.

Also characteristic of her New York School affiliation, and to become a career-long devotion, are poems about painting and painters. As a reviewer for *ArtNews* from 1951 to 1954 she spent many hours in museums and galleries, engaged in rapt observation of the "sister art," painting, and in working out the difficulties of representing the visual in writing. The poems to and about the abstract expressionist painters that she knew personally (Grace Hartigan, Mary Abbott, Robert Motherwell, and Helen Frankenthaler) are premised on reciprocal respect and sympathy, a fellowship of artisanry during a time of cultural tumult and redefinition of the artistic imagination. "The imagination's at its turning," writes Guest in "Piazzas," dedicated to Abbott, and she considers what it means to belong to a generation creating, risking, and glorying in that turning. We "met a confusion of weather and felt / the alphabet turning over when we landed," writes Guest of that heady sense of vertigo and possibility that both poets and painters experienced. In several poems to and about Hartigan, Hartigan figures as a knight, a hero, a quester, one of the painters "who have drawn those deep lines on the globes"–an exemplar for Guest herself, not least because both women were forging their careers in artistic marketplaces dominated by men. Throughout this early work Barbara Einzig's 1996 assessment of Guest's work as a whole already applies: "Painting is the poems' cosmology, and the world is read as a painting." She is a colorist acutely sensitive to black and white; she is attentive to line and its gestures; she is knowing about the psychological and emotional values of both literal and painterly space. "To make an Elegy of Spain," she writes in empathetic response to Robert Motherwell's mostly black-and-white abstractions on the theme of the Spanish Civil War, "is to make a song of the abyss. // It is to cut a gorge into one's soul / which is suddenly no longer private."

Privacies have been crucial to Guest's sense of herself as a poet. While her claim that "all poetry is confessional" unequivocally expresses the idea that all artistic representation functions as autobiographical projection and necessarily tells a story of self, her routes are subtle, abstract, and oblique rather than confrontational and conspicuous. In interviews she is evasive about her personal life, a long-standing choice and habit that deeply informs, rather than inhibits, her poetics. She has written that it is the poem, not the poet, whose autobiography

Cover for Guest's 1976 collection of alternating lineated and prose
poems that read like a novella (cover design by Keith Waldrop,
after Robert Koehler's painting Rainy Evening on
Hennepin Avenue)

matters; she solicits attention for the ways the poem goes about revealing and unveiling its intimate "self." "In whatever guise reality becomes visible," she wrote for a talk at St. Mark's Poetry Project in 1986, later published in part in How(ever) as "Mysteriously Defining the Mysterious: Byzantine Proposals of Poetry," "the poet withdraws from it into invisibility. In the cloak of Byzantine colors the poet spins a secret life." So facts and details particular to the life of this elusive poet almost never become the stuff of which her poetry is constructed.

What she *has* made known is very little: she was born Barbara Ann Pinson; graduated from the University of California at Berkeley; married Stephen Haden-Guest, son of Lord Haden—formerly a Fabian leader and prominent in forming the Labor Party—in 1949; and gave birth to a daughter, Hadley. She was divorced in 1954 and married Trumbull Higgins, a military historian and author known for his anti-Churchillian stand regarding World War II and for his opposition to the war in Vietnam and President John F. Kennedy's landing in Cuba. They had one son, Jonathan. Yet, perhaps this sketchy biography has left some traces in the work. Several of the poems in her early volume, including what is perhaps Guest's best-known poem, "Parachutes, My Love, Could Carry Us Higher," concern romantic love, attempting to locate the imaginative and thinking self amid the suspensions, ambiguities, and excruciations of love.

Guest lived with Higgins and the children in New York City; Southampton, New York; and Washington, D.C., with frequent trips to California to visit with family. She writes in her poetry of being possessed of a "vast / journeying sensibility," of constituting in her self "a compleat travel agency." She

traveled with her family extensively to Asia, the
Carribean, and to Europe (where Higgins gathered
material for his books), especially Paris and London, where she invariably gathered touring artist
friends around her—these are experiences, landscapes, and cityscapes her poetry abundantly ex-
ploits. Yet, she admitted in 1992, rather poignantly:
"It's very hard on me not having a definite place. It
has created a great deal of anxiety. . . . I never really
had a 'home' . . . so I am grateful for this house [in
Eastern Long Island] as long as I am permitted to
live here. When I say the word 'home' I almost
whisper it." With or without this biographical alert,
it is not difficult to find in Guest's work poems of exile and loss and homelessness, houses under the
threat of hurricane, lovingly realized rooms and studios, agonized leave-takings, and grateful returns.

The Blue Stairs, published by Corinth Books in
1968 with a cover painting by Frankenthaler, is also
dominated by questions of travel as searching as
those presented by Elizabeth Bishop in her *Questions
of Travel* (1965). Exotic place-names abound: the
Bosphorus, Siberia, Vladivostock, Yokohama, Yal-
ta, Morocco, Granada, the Sierra Nevada. The sensory richness and particularity of place sometimes
express themselves in gorgeous, almost abandoned
diction and rhythms: "Well wild wild whatever / in
wild more silent blue" she writes, and

> There's a ringing in my ears
> as if a poem were beating on stone
>
> The room fills now with feathers,
> the birds you have released, Muses,
>
> I want to stop whatever I'm doing,
> And listen to their marvellous hello.

Yet "Direction" seems to ask whether the inveterate travelers who are the protagonists have any
direction at all, whether there is any difference between staying home and pacing "to and fro" on trips
to foreign shores. The speaker feels deeply the need
to set out on metaphoric journeys, emotional voyag-
ings toward fearful intimacy, taking in whole landscapes of neglected domestic issues and urgencies.
Home, she claims, is not familiar or comforting; it is
"the Scandinavia of all Russias"; here at home:

> The light is not idle, it is full of rapid
> changes we can call voyages
> if we like, moving from room to room.
> . . . .
> Our eyes are viewing monuments
> constantly, the angry sculpture
> of the facade it is also a journey
> to the center where the rock is uncut.

> Climbing it tests our strength, our bruises
> are so many cities, the blood we shed
> is ours, so I say we can belong
> nowhere else, here is the counter
> of our wounds and our delicacies.
>
> On our own soil that is an excavation
> desolate as the place whose name
> we must never pronounce.

Again and again the poems in this volume conflate
the usually opposed terms of home and travel,
moving and standing still, house and world, alien
and familiar, embarkation and destination.

The collection ends with a poem—the wild
and surprising "Handbook of Surfing"—an anti-
Vietnam War poem unlike the austere and lovely
title poem, "The Blue Stairs," printed elsewhere
accompanied by a blue-and-white geometrical
painting by Robert Goodnough. The poem asserts
in its form and content that poetry must be at once
a thing of beauty and a thing of purpose, of in-
exorability. It must discover the "humility of
sound" yet employ the most extraordinary of techniques: "delicate / fixity," spatial selectivity, "radiant deepness," occasional "giving way / to the
emotions." Here as well Guest employs the tropes
of travel: "There is no fear / in taking the first step
/ or the second / or the third." She understands art
to be a pilgrimage of gradual ascent to a summit
which "can be reached / without disaster." Of
course, both the pilgrim's stated faith and her co-
vert fears inform the poem, revealing her awareness that in 1968 her abstract, experimental lyrics
were apt to fall into a critical climate ill equipped
to appreciate them. Indeed, James Atlas, reviewing *The Blue Stairs* for *Poetry* (March 1969) repeatedly stressed his sense that the poems were chaotic, lacking in narrative clarity, disconnected,
confused, and marked by "the uneasy quality of
her speech." It is exactly these characterizations
that have been purged over the years of their pejo-
rative sting by readers more sympathetic to the
modus operandi of the poems: DuPlessis, writing in
Women's Review of Books (October 1995), admires,
rather than excoriates, Guest's "evanescent, shifting subjectivity," her "elegant, sinewy, evocation"
of what is fragmentary, hesitant, edgy, and permeable. She is one of "Gertrude's granddaughters,"
according to Marianne DeKoven in *Women's Review of Books* (November 1986), working along
"Steinian lines of radical disruption of sense and
syntax . . . to render openness, multiplicity, indeterminacy, density." Einzig in *American Poetry Review* (January/February 1996) writes about the
ways in which Guest's formal irregularities evince

Guest in Southampton, New York, 1982

"less a harmony of the spheres than an orchestrated tension between them," which can express "the tension and violence of our time." Kathleen Fraser, writing in "Line, on the Line . . . " for *The Line in Postmodern Poetry* (1988), looks to Guest as a practitioner capable of disturbing "the learned prohibitions" that women poets have worked against in order to "uncover and catch partial knowledge, fragmentary perception that disappears as fast as it arrives." And Marjorie Welish values rather than derides Guest's "marked sensitivity to the sensible forms indefiniteness takes . . . her rare and exacting intelligence registering and ordering every phoneme."

Between 1973 and 1989 Guest published three major poetry collections: *Moscow Mansions* (1973), *The Countess from Minneapolis* (1976), and *Fair Realism* (1989), as well as smaller letterpress productions, some of these in collaboration with visual artists—*The Türler Losses* (1979), *Biography* (1980), *Quilts* (1980), *Musicality* (1988)—and the H. D. biography (which she has admitted required of her immense labor and discipline and five years of her writing life). *The Countess from Minneapolis* alternates lineated poems with prose poems and reads like a fragmented novella. Some of the poems are titled, but most are merely numbered; all are early experiments in the telling of "stripped tales" (the title of Guest's 1995 collaboration with Anne Dunn). Here the New York poet takes up Midwestern themes, themes of the heartland, as, skeptically and a trifle mockingly, she studies "Minneapolis and its posture on the Mississippi" and the incongruous presence there of a sensitive and artistic Easterner. In love with anachronism, the "story" evades both linear narrative and definitive setting in time—it variously suggests frontier times with its logging camps, sod huts, and immigrants, the early twentieth century still Victorian in its speech rhythms and manners, and a present moment in which Tony Smith bestows a sculpture titled *Amaryllis* on the Walker Art Museum in Minneapolis. There is a constant overwhelming awareness of nature: the storms, the wind, the prairie, the dust, the mud, the "low glaucous clouds," the "long unsettling, barren Minnesota winter." Into this Guest (or the Countess) continually interjects the (sometimes discordant, sometimes salvational) concerns of literature, love, and art.

Moscow Mansions and *Fair Realism,* spanning sixteen years, are similar in resplendently displaying Guest's lyric gifts. A deft allusiveness reveals the range and depth of her cultural knowledge: into her capacious and shimmering postmodern net she draws George Gordon, Lord Byron; August Strindberg; Joan Miró; John Coltrane; Duke Ellington; Paul Cézanne; Dora Maar (French photographer and painter, companion to Pablo Picasso); Eugène Delacroix; Giacomo Balla; Warren Brandt; Charles-Pierre Baudelaire; Georges Bizet; Arshile Gorky; James Joyce; Aleksandr Sergeyevich Pushkin; Gertrude Stein; "Frank and John" (O'Hara and Ashbery); John

Dust jacket for Guest's 1989 poetry collection, which reveals her interest in art

Donne; Wassily Kandinsky; Wolfgang Amadeus Mozart; Gustave Flaubert; John Keats; Samuel Taylor Coleridge; Murasaki Shikibu; Henri-Emile-Benoît Matisse; Ovid; and the mythical characters of antiquity. She seems on genial terms with all these personages, collaging them unaffectedly into the space of her poems. She exults in Miró's erotic and exuberant abstract portrait of a woman poet and borrows his healthy ignorance of the troublesome gender connotations of the word "poetess." She recognizes suddenly that she is in "a landscape inhabited by Baudelaire / his *îles,* his *fantômes,* his *sang.*" She is struck with the similarity between her window's melancholy view of Union Square in New York and the view from Kandinsky's window, his "last peek of Russia / an intimate one." She takes Stein up on the issue of whether or not there is air in paintings. She shares her thoughts about replacing an "abstract picture of light" with an illustration from *The Tale of Genji* on one of the walls in her home. Genji becomes "a prince whose principality I now share, / into whose confidence I have wandered." Guest's poems share, and invite the reader to share, multiple "principalities." They invite readers to understand that reading,

looking at art, and listening to music are intimate connections, confidences abundantly available. This shared intimacy counters a prevailing and serious misreading of Guest that has held her extensive acquaintance with art against her, characterizing her subject matter and tone as elitist. Reviewing *Moscow Mansions,* Alicia Ostriker claimed that "the values are essentially and purely esthetic. . . . " The poems "are a little like conversations in refined places among refined persons. They are, like Alice's biscuits, very dry." Similarly, Robert F. Kiernan in *American Writing Since 1945* (1983) claimed: "There is an inveterate chill to her poetry, a cosmopolitan refinement that supersedes anything truly personal." Instead poem after poem betrays passionate engagement with art and with artists. The tone of the "conversation" varies readily—a certain wryness can give way to hilarity or solemnity or awe. She can chide or tease or revere; she can speak boldly, tentatively, serenely, sarcastically, joyfully, ruefully. The notion that her poetry speaks only in the voice of the cool cultural "high talk" is belied by the almost tactile intimacy she establishes with the art she alludes to. Guest's insight into the work of her painter friend Felter is also true of her own. She wrote that the paintings were "tactile in a virtually possessive manner; 'I have so intimately touched this that it belongs to me.'" In the poems Guest makes a synthesis between herself as original working artist and the history of art in its various media.

One of Guest's characteristic styles in the poems from these collections is a dense compound of words, articulating in its luxurious surface interarticulations the plenitude of life, an almost Jamesian consciousness of layered experience ("pleated moments," Guest calls them). In "Rosy Ensconcements" (from *Moscow Mansions*) she runs three immensely complex sentences through four stanzas and thirty-eight lines (with the help of nine commas), repeating words and phrases with a sestina-like lavish regularity, to delineate the charged erotic aura surrounding a "Spanish bed" over which a painting of a Chinese courtesan is hung and in which an amorous couple are glowingly and privily ensconced. The very meaning and essence of *ensconcement* are the subject of this poem—the secure privilege of the close and erotic fit between persons and place that the word connotes. This poem is so intricately woven that it is difficult to extricate a passage for quotation, but any part will reveal the stamp of Guest's strangeness and her mystery, her inability to adhere to conventions which falsely or prematurely order experience. Similarly solid in construction and true to rich complexities and wayward detours of emotion, sensation, and thought arc "The Interruptions," "Museum," "Illyria" (another measured defense of Guest's poetics), "Nebraska," "Even Ovid" (dedicated in typescript to Ashbery), and the long, seriocomic bravura piece "Knight of the Swan" (all from *Moscow Mansions*); and "The Rose Marble Table," "Words," "Twilight Polka Dots," and a long meditation on time and loss, "The Türler Losses" (all from *Fair Realism*). Several other poems in *Fair Realism* dramatize Guest's intense and shifting assessment of male painters who use women as subjects and models for their work; the poems manifest her sophisticated, profound feminist sensibility. Reading "The Nude" and "Dora Maar" in the context of Guest's essay on poetics, "Mysteriously Defining the Mysterious" (1986), DuPlessis invented the category of "polygynous poetries" to describe Guest's "plural attitudes towards femaleness, maleness, gender, femininity, and sexuality"; her unwary embrace of the beautiful and the sensuous; and her subtle, insistent creation of sites "in which the gender materials of culture can be examined in their mystery and impact."

Cover for Guest's 1993 book, which, she says, moves away from density toward "space, sparseness and openness"

Also in *Fair Realism* Guest began to experiment with a new style that would come to prevail in her most recent writing. One of her own favorite poems, "The Farewell Stairway" (another colloquy with a male painter, Giacomo Balla), employs white space as much as it does type and gives the impression of leaving out rather than putting in, of erasure rather than inscribing. Divided into eleven unnumbered sections separated only by asterisks, the poem meanders loosely and lavishly over six full pages of *Selected Poems,* reading the Persephone myth into Balla's precisely rendered drawing of three women descending a staircase. A masterpiece of shifting perspective, the poem has an "I" who speaks variously in the painting and outside of it, both viewer and viewed, both character and tale-teller. The "tale," however, is stripped of its forward movement as Guest borrows the stasis of the painting in order to focus and refocus, with a wonderful plasticity, on the opening line—"The women without hesitancy began to descend." The notion of descending, of yielding to the erotic, "whirling, urgent"

Dore Maar

A woman weeping about an imaginary fall foom a
bicycle, a woman who claimed her bicycle had been
stolen when he knew it waited outside her door,
asleep   with a piece of tailleur on the brake,
like the spy .

"Her hair was all disheveled and her clothes were torn"
Enemies overturned the wheel, they upset her and threw
her to the ground she had a knob on her forehead from
the fall, she said, but when he placed his hand there
he found nothing, only the shift of veins he once
had painted.

This girlishness should feed on mirrors, if there had been
a fairy tale influence her noise about damnation and
enemies, "she moved about the room so nervously" her
mania was beginning to catch up with him. He did not
like her mystical exhortations, she told him to repent
while there was still time. "As an artist you may be a
extraordinary, but morally you are worthless."

Her character was pasted with dramatic scenes, heavy
lines indicated traps. rough boulders, and a few
connective objects feverish as collage.

He could avoid her distress and go to a cafe, have
coffeee, drink from a carafe of water, talk to an
attractive woman without tears.

Working draft for a prose poem (Beinecke Library, Yale University; by permission of Barbara Guest)

Dust jacket for the 1995 collection that has drawn critical attention to
Guest's poetry

pull of the future gradually reveals its promise and potency, clear and effective among the surrounding hush of all that white paper. Also in this poem, identifying with Persephone as a sister traveler setting out for the underworld, Guest dramatizes one of her convictions about the art of poetry: "The poem is the unburdening of the ghosts, after the trip to the labyrinth."

In *Defensive Rapture* (1993) Guest worked almost exclusively in this more austere style, moving away from density and toward "space, sparseness, and openness." "One of the ways to break this density is to move the lines out and around. I would like very much just to take out indiscriminately—just remove ten words. And in 'Chalk' I did." She spoke of wanting her work to resemble the paintings of Agnes Martin, plainly and minimally presented but somehow also suggestively rich and mysterious. She abandoned even the shards of character and allusion that loosely anchor a poem such as "The Farewell Stairway."

The poems are bewildering, difficult, unrelenting abstractions packed with concrete particulars, often reminiscent, in a free and broken way, of themes she has made her own over the years: travel, nature, art, perception, love. The titles provide ambiguous stays, fugitive focusings: "Paulownia," "Geese Blood," "Borderlands," "Otranto," "Winter Horses," "The Glass Mountain" (written in memory of Schuyler). But statement and subject matter, never the crux of a Guest poem, are particularly beside the point in these oblique and elusive poems. The dash, as a disconnective connector, is the preferred mode of punctuation in those few poems that employ any punctuation at all. Syntax is erased; phrases can be ordered and therefore understood in multiple, sometimes contradictory ways. In a videotaped poetry reading released by the Lannan Foundation, Guest spoke of "Dissonance Royal Traveler" as the first of several pervaded by the spirit of the composer Arnold Schoenberg. The poem, which seemingly pays tribute to another traveler, royally courting dissonance, is generously open in its spacing:

sound opens sound

shank of globe   strings floating out

something like images are here

opening up avenues to view a dome

a distant clang reaches the edifice

"I keep writing about him and not reaching him," she said, claiming to admire the "stringency that Schoenberg wanted in his music. I'd like to get a little of that stringency. And I'd like to go as far as I can in poetry, which is what Schoenberg did in music. And not everybody liked it." Laughing, she added, "But I don't really care." This comment evinces a continuing serene confidence in her calling (noted by Anthony Manousos in 1980 as he assessed her work). She appears willing to go her own way as far as it takes her without feeling overly defensive about the raptures that result.

Now in her late seventies, her husband having died in 1990, Guest has settled in Berkeley, California, a return to the landscape of her childhood and a move that seems to have been elicited from her poignant poems of memory, like the pellucid "She Considers With Awe." Books appear from her more regularly than ever: after *Defensive Rapture* have come *Stripped Tales* in 1995 and *Quill, Solitary Apparition* in 1996. A tantalizing series of funny, piquant, and profound prose poems about movies called *The Confetti Trees: Motion Picture Stories* (with a memoir of herself in Los Angeles hidden in it) was published in 1998 (a few of them were published in *American Poetry Review* in 1994), as Guest takes on, in her inimitable fashion, a poetic connection with yet one more of the arts. One of these poems reads " . . . and no one denies Petaluma is a sister of the Muses . . . virile her camera work . . . intuitive in its grasp of loca-

tion . . . goddess-like her notion of spatial situations with physical bodies in space cutting into each other . . . areas blocked in adding objects no one else notices . . . reflection on distance . . . the fluidity." In this short quotation the language and the themes of Guest's earliest work in *The Location of Things* reverberate. She has abandoned nothing but transformed all during her long and distinguished career.

Interview:

Mark Hillringhouse, "Barbara Guest: An Interview," *American Poetry Review* (July/August 1992): 23–30.

References:

Rachel Blau DuPlessis, "'All My Vast / Journeying Sensibility': Barbara Guest's Recent Work," *Sulfur,* 39 (Fall 1996): 39–48;

DuPlessis, "The Flavor of Eyes: *Selected Poems* by Barbara Guest," *Women's Review of Books,* 13 (October 1995): 23–24;

Barbara Einzig, "The Surface as Object: Barbara Guest's Selected Poems," *American Poetry Review,* 25 (January/February 1996): 7–10;

Kathleen Fraser, "Line, on the Line . . . ," in *The Line in Postmodern Poetry,* edited by Robert Frank and Henry Sayre (Urbana: University of Illinois Press, 1988);

Fraser, "One Hundred and Three Chapters of Little Times: Collapsed and Transfigured Moments in the Fiction of Barbara Guest," in *Breaking the Sequence: Women's Experimental Fiction,* edited by Ellen G. Friedman and Miriam Fuchs (Princeton: Princeton University Press, 1989), pp. 240–249;

Brenda Hillman, "The Artful Dare: Barbara Guest's *Selected Poems,*" *Talisman: A Journal of Contemporary Poetry and Poetics,* 16 (Fall 1996): 207–220;

Sara Lundquist, "Reverence and Resistance: Barbara Guest, Ekphrasis, and the Female Gaze," *Contemporary Literature,* 38 (Summer 1997): 260–286.

Papers:

The major collection of Guest's papers (including correspondence, writings, printed materials, audiotapes, daybooks, and photographs), covering the years 1949 to 1992, is held in the Beinecke Rare Book and Manuscript Library at Yale University in New Haven, Connecticut.

Carla Harryman

(11 January 1952 –)

Chris Stroffolino
Rutgers University

BOOKS: *Percentage* (Berkeley: Tuumba Press, 1979);
Under the Bridge (Oakland, Cal.: This Press, 1980);
Property (Berkeley: Tuumba Press, 1982);
The Middle (San Francisco: Gaz Press, 1983);
Vice (Elmwood, Conn.: Potes & Poets Press, 1986);
Animal Instincts: Prose, Plays, Essays (Berkeley: This Press, 1989);
In the Mode of (Canary Islands, Spain: Zasterle Press, 1991);
Memory Play (Oakland, Cal.: O Books, 1994);
There Never Was a Rose without a Thorn (San Francisco: City Lights Books, 1995);
The Words (Los Angeles: Sun & Moon Press, 1998).

Eighteen years after the publication of her first book, Carla Harryman remains a difficult writer to place. One of the many challenges her writing presents is the question of genre. Of the ten books she has published, no two have been characterized under the same genre heading, and the range of her work includes plays, poetry, essays, experimental fiction, and serial prose poems. If there is a common thread connecting these works, it is an idea of poetry. In fact, one of Harryman's central achievements is to place the conventions of poetry (especially experimental poetry) in dialogue with the conventions of prose narrative, fiction, essays, and plays. In this dialogue, in which not only poetry but also narrative "might be thought to be a character," as she says in "Toy Boats" from *Animal Instincts: Prose, Plays, Essays* (1989), no genre is allowed a final triumph. Such a dialogue may be precisely what is needed in the present moment to dislodge poetry from its relatively recent marginalized status as a mere aesthetic object.

Carla Harryman was born in Orange County, California, 11 January 1952. She received a B.A. in literature from the University of California in 1975 and an M.A. from the Creative Arts Interdisciplinary Program of San Francisco State University in 1978 after teaching literature at Marymount High School in Los Angeles during the school year 1975–1976. After receiving her M.A., Harryman di-

Carla Harryman (photograph © 1995 Barrett Watten)

rected the American Poetry Archives in San Francisco (1978–1982), directed and served as a writer/consultant for the University Art Museum (1982–1987), and served as a writer/consultant for Bedford Arts Publishers (1988–1991). In addition to these and other administrative positions Harryman also taught secondary and elementary creative writing workshops in Berkeley and Oakland public schools from 1986 to 1993. More recently she has taught a variety of college-level courses at the University of California, San Diego; the Naropa Institute in Boulder, Colorado; Wayne State University; and the Detroit Institute of the Arts. In 1994 Harryman; her husband, social critic and poet Barrett Watten; and their son, Asa, moved to Detroit, where she currently resides.

Percentage (1979), Harryman's first chapbook, has long been out of print. Some of the pieces in it, however, have appeared in more-recent collections. Aside from the title piece, a play for two voices, it includes three other "mixed genre investigations": "Cult Music," the minimalist lyric "Obstacle," and "Heavy Curtains," a collaboration with Watten. The look of these pieces is characteristically discursive prose, yet the disjunctions between the sentences read more like the sentence-based, philosophical poetry of John Ashbery. While other Language Poets such as Bruce Andrews have modeled their work more on the earlier Ashbery of *The Tennis Court Oath* (1962), Harryman's early work has far more affinities with the Ashbery of *Three Poems* (1972) and *The Double Dream of Spring* (1970). These similarities can be seen most clearly in "Cult Music":

> Got worn out screaming in the theatre as if words could be a substitute for hard work; furthermore, the soft line of the jaw by pampering leans into the steaming table, mutton, greens and potatoes. Fed period music in a boxcar. Something infantilism–roams around, captures monsters, wants alot. A great mind to waste.

Although meaning is not discarded, the reader is practically forced to piece together how the relationship between words and hard work connects with the relationship of jaw to potatoes. The "theatre" is not a defined place that is fleshed out in the course of the poem as in most conventional poetry. The traditional expectations that poetry have a locatable "speaker" and "situation" are discarded. Instead the acts of writing, thinking, and selecting are foregrounded. This writing places Harryman firmly in the tradition of the twentieth-century "avant-garde," whether one sees such a tradition in terms of Gertrude Stein's "continuous present," James Joyce and Virginia Woolf's "stream of consciousness," or the French Surrealists' practice of "automatic writing." The political and cultural themes of this piece–which resonate more strongly to a reader familiar with her later work–are less foregrounded than the style of the writing. The "meaning" of this piece is the liberation from conventional forms that its stylistic disjunction allows. Harryman's line "A great mind to waste" may be read as less of a lament for the loss of coherence than as a celebration of the power of such stylistic freedoms.

In the centerpiece of *Percentage* Harryman marks out a literary territory that is more distinctively her own. Although "Percentage" has been performed as a play, it can be read just as effectively as a dialogue poem. In an interview with Manuel Brito, Harryman warns against reading it as a conventional play or as a poem such as Yeats's "Dialogue of Self and Soul." None "of the speeches are contextualized, so it does mimic perhaps the movement of one's silent speech that could be called a manifestation of the self; however, it is not interested in identity. There is no dilemma of the self being proposed. . . . I wanted to hear the voice liberated from narrative determinants but to allow it speech-like gestures." "Percentage" may not be interested in identity, but it *is* interested in relationship. The two characters, *D* and *E,* are carefully differentiated, although they may not seem to be on first reading. Because the conversation is presented by means of highly dense metaphorical associations that may require a well-read mind to catch, it almost seems as if the characters don't listen to each other at the beginning of the play:

> D: The staggering kind of . . .
> E: I want to talk about the gloves.
> D: THE?
> E: In town yesterday several kids found a hidden orchestra pit.
> D: I want you to tell me what's on *your* mind.
> E: I want to go to the store. You know what I know and then you don't anymore so what happened?

As this dialogue continues, that their idioms and points of view are presented as opposites becomes clearer. It becomes a stichomythia in which *E* listens to *D* more than *D* listens to *E. E* is more demanding, playfully judgmental, and interested in the improvisatory making of a relationship ("I like presents"), while *D* is more prone to memory, flights of fancy, narrative (s/he tells two stories), and deterministic self-dramatization. Although Steve Benson has written that "the two personae share a virtually equal status in perpetual imbalances, destabilizing their own and each other's modus operandi in an effort to realize equality," there is also a decided asymmetry in which *D* virtually becomes *E*'s straight man.

When the play was performed in 1978, both *D* and *E* were played by women: Harryman and Eileen Corder. And, just as narrative is absent from this piece, so are blatant gender markers. Nonetheless, part of the point of this piece, as in Harryman's contemporaneous play *Third Man* (whose eponymous character bears more than a little resemblance to *D*), is to question what has historically been called male and female and how to reallocate these roles both within a person and within society. Regardless of whether the relationship between *D* and *E* is homosexual or heterosexual, the erotic tension between these two voices is undeniable. *E* plays the role of the seducer, wants to be disturbed, loves imitating, and reacts to *D*'s self-absorption. After a while *E* becomes aware of the futility of ridiculing *D* and says, "I'm going to make up my own cardgame so I don't have to look at yours." *E*'s last speech is a complaint about *D*'s being absent even while present. *D* seems to be more to blame for the failure to connect, yet *D*'s last line ("Water seeps in.") shows that *E*'s victory is not unqualified.

Harryman has characterized her second book, *Under the Bridge* (1980), as a book of experimental fiction and poetry. As is usually the case with Harryman, specifying exactly which pieces fit under what category is difficult. At fifty-eight pages, this book offers a more substantial collection of early Harryman than *Percentage* does. Although its nineteen pieces, ranging from less than a page to the nine-page prose poem "Third Rail," are built around paragraphs rather than stanzas, *Under the Bridge* remains Harryman's most purely lyrical book to date. The prose poems that characterize it contrast with the poems in her later works since the emphasis here is on the tension between thought and play of language. Questions of narrative structures, such as characters and plot, though not entirely absent from this book, are less central than questions that stem from the spatial conceit the title raises. Tom Mandel has written in *Jimmy and Lucy's House of K* that under the surface of the writing in this book "there is a strong logic of connected thoughts and literary forms, syllogistic, brilliant, and even learned. But then such knowledge and certainty is held at arm's length, even mocked. The writing toys with, plays upon, improvises against, and just generally swoops all around this underground structure with a tremendous permission and inner illumination that comes from the knowledge of structure." One way Harryman makes a structure visible is through using the titular word *bridge* as a dividing line between two orders of existence. The structural conceit is of a bridge seen as a boundary. This boundary, however, is not static but ever shifting and hard to locate: "Boundaries mark the time spent looking for boundaries." In the foreword to the book Harryman writes: "Abstractions, fundamental photographic representations of unembellished objects, swarm onto the bridge." On the other side of the bridge are "too human humans . . . who behaved as if thought was a curse on matter." Harryman alternates between celebration of the times when she's "engaged in the moment the mind collapses under pressure into full detail" and times when she sides against fear of these "fright-

ening packages of detail." She is not content to accept the traditional poetic stance of the "fortunate fall" from thought into immanence. Neither is she content to remain an abstraction. The moments of anti-Cartesian synthesis occur most successfully not when "bridges above water follow the construction of the water" but when "a bridge collapses water into wave" as well as when

> the conscious woman on the boat in the harbor,
> the one who drives everyday back and forth across
> the water to the island returning with her catch,
> jeers at the animals who bark under the docks,
> meaning that she has no patience with anyone who
> wishes to please her.

Although most of the pieces in *Under the Bridge* subordinate linear narrative to a looser, more lyric mapping of the subjective, even in this book such clear narrative passages are not absent. Perhaps the best example of a straightforward narrative occurs in "Au Nom":

> It was after midnight. There wasn't any moonlight
> that I could see but lots of light inside. I was there.
> You were permanent. It seemed like there was about
> to be a dance. It was all very agitated. The street seemed
> loaded down. We couldn't hold each other up. No pre-
> planned program. It wasn't exactly like that. It was
> more like a space we didn't notice. "Do you like this?"
> "I don't know, I like everything about you." What's
> enough. We were oversensitized. I tried to hit you in
> the stomach. You tried to block me. Neither one of us
> missed, although neither one of us was precise.

This piece, reprinted and put into a new context in *The Middle* (1983), puts the lyric musings on abstract dualisms central to many other pieces in the book in dialogue with narrative conventions. The speaker may be addressing another person, but it is equally likely that "you" refers to the *writing* itself. This piece foreshadows such later work as "Sublimation," in which the relationship between form and content becomes part of the content. Another piece constructed around a tight narrative, "Architecture and Landscape of All Countries," begins "Sometimes it seems that people are children living in caves" and presents a comic picture of a matriarchal family in the cave in which the speaker casts herself as a child. Aside from presenting playful feminism, this piece also raises a riddle about representation, for if people are children living in caves, then the mother and the father presented here are not, strictly speaking, people. By calling attention to the fictiveness of the family romance painted here, Harryman opens up a space for alternative representations of the family.

The dominant pleasures of *Under the Bridge*, however, remain more the abstract ones of experimental lyric poetry than those of narrative. In "Sex Story," for instance, Harryman writes "I've been trying to get to the sex story but it's hard not to be crowded out." The long poem, "Third Rail," is probably the best example of the difficult joy to be had in such crowding out. Although Harryman is not usually celebrated for purely aesthetic pleasures, Mandel finds them in "the movement of the vowels through this work" and shows how Harryman is "more devoted to that variety and enjoyed for that variety than any writer I can think of," as in lines such as "broom in hand, mama's nose, pudgy in baby's eyes."

According to Mandel, between *Under the Bridge* and *The Middle*, "Balzac, Colette and Stendahl entered Carla's writing (or emerged from it), and *Property* is like some incredible historical novel about kin who move about on vehicles of instant apprehension: it used to take 500 pages to get to the west; now it can be done in 22." But although *Property* (1982) certainly constitutes a radical departure for Harryman, it is not a novel. In fact, it is more genreless than any of her previous books, partially because, provisionally at least, it accepts a wider range of genre conventions. Divided into seven sections, this writing, though mainly prose, is, in the words of Jean Day in "Two Books by Carla Harryman," "likely at any moment to jump straight into dialogue or snatches of verse skimmed off the flux of daily life. Its behavior is polymorphous. Its impulse isn't formal experimentation per se, but a push accurately to be as well as represent an hectic, ordering and partial language." It combines the emphasis on dialogue in "Percentage" and "Third Man" with the avant-garde lyricism of *Under the Bridge* with startling results. More explicitly than in *Under the Bridge*, the idea of private sentiment and the inflation of the individual voice is completely undermined here. Yet, unlike other Language writers, Harryman does not reject subjectivity or the person. Rather she reminds the reader that the root meaning of "person" is mask and, as such, is always and already social. Day's useful review of (essay on) this book gives many examples of how verbal forms become "characters and as such engage in power relationships. . . . Intentionality," for instance, "is obstinate." Harryman herself has written that "*Property* imitates characters as if they were words or syntax."

The Middle shares with *Property* a wide stylistic range, yet its emphasis is more didactic and polemical. If *Property* seems to work against the backdrop of a traditional novel, *The Middle* works against the backdrop of a traditional essay, and the seemingly autobiographical and narrative elements woven into the polemic may recall Virginia Woolf's rejection of the strictures of the conventional essay in her *A Room Of One's Own* (1929). Harryman, however, goes further than Woolf. Like Woolf's "essay," *The Middle* was originally given as a talk. Because of the digressive leaps and mixed genres here, critics have claimed that Harryman has no point to make. David Sheidlower has argued in "The Dawning of an Aspect (Unlineated)" that *The Middle* is "not a polemic; it's a book about a certain kind of experience. . . . Aspects of issues are raised but conclusions are not drawn." Yet in her interview with Brito, Harryman herself makes quite clear that *The Middle* has a didactic element that should not be overlooked. In *The Middle* she writes:

> *Freud* was used as a household word or as a location—or as an excuse to localize an examinaton. The place Freud is related to the place tragedy—"an interior cosmogeny of fate." Tragedy, when viewed from the perspective of being central to culture, is not an extreme. Same with Freud. When seen from the point of view of an improviser, one who works off the idea that if there is a "center" it is everywhere and where one might choose to move to, or make, or be in . . . , Freud might represent an extreme of cultural identity and place—interior.

In addition to critiquing Freud's tragic deterministic view of life, *The Middle* also challenges Freud from a feminist perspective:

> an outsider like me, i.e. a female, one who provides the "background" or subcentricity to the male—the central figure in Freud—might feel free to create an outsider's vocabulary. And I do not have access to tragedy in the same way because of, for instance, social uses of languages. In one scenario, *Man* is a tragic figure and *women* and *children* are merely victims. In another scenario man is a tragic figure and women and children are demonic. All of this is a kind of frozen and all-too-powerful ideological hysteria.

The Middle, however, cannot be reduced to a critique of Freud. It may be read as a transitional work in which Harryman sets up a wider range of idioms in which to work out a problematic similar to the central one of *Under the Bridge*. Whereas the reader is still invited to see the moments of synthesis in the earlier work as strictly subjective or linguistic, here Harryman's characterizations of "the middle where what's enlarged (subjective) and what's reduced (external) by speaking gather" is more dramatically dynamic.

In part one Harryman quotes and comments on writings she has published elsewhere. But the dialogue made possible by putting these pieces in a new context foregrounds and subverts the institutional nature of the distinction between "text" and "commentary." The writings she sets off as "primary texts," whether her own or others, respond equally to the commentary on them. A particularly insightful example for readers of contemporary poetry is the contrast she makes between Bernadette Mayer and Robert Creeley:

for Creeley, the daily proliferation arouses an argument to simplify. . . . Where "one" lives produces a series of conceits: house, body, mind. So no matter how reduced the aspect there is a potential for clutter. Conceits might be what's given to us, with pressure. Pressure to accept what's unacceptable. "Must be literal fact of so-called objects is unacceptable," says Creeley.

Creeley: inside the mind.

Mayer: inside the family. I.e. Bernadette Mayer's MIDWINTER DAY.

Even though we live neither in a tribe nor a community nor near a grandfather but in these rude, private and ignorant separate houses where love is like fame and fame is more like sin and for love to be so tricky for a family is just asking for it. . . .

This poem about daily life is an expression of the acceptance of that life. The challenge of the poem and the life is time, to rush through a day in a day. The world of objects is tackled by the mother; it is almost celebratory of there being no conflict from outside the family and friend world of the poem.

Cover for Harryman's 1995 collection of reprinted and new verse

The tension between these juxtaposed points of view is similar to the tension in *Under the Bridge*. Here, however, Harryman's appropriation of other texts more fully allows her the illusion of exteriorization. Later sections of *The Middle* include Harryman's most blatantly sustained quasi-autobiographical narrative to date; her social critique becomes more effective as she becomes more willing to argue as a character rather than as a disembodied spokeswoman for indeterminacy.

Animal Instincts is essentially Harryman's first "Selected Works." Although published three years after *Vice* (1986), all the work in this collection was written earlier (spanning the late 1970s to the mid 1980s). It republishes the entire chapbook *Property* and the title play of *Percentage* in addition to reworking previously published material. Most of the work, however, appears for the first time in book form. *Animal Instincts* is certainly her most difficult book. It may strike some readers as ironic that a book titled *Animal Instincts* should begin with a piece titled "Sublimation." Yet one of Harryman's points in this piece is that sublimation, contrary to popular belief, is an animal instinct. Sublimation is seen in both its erotic and writerly contexts, and it becomes hard to tell whether the erotic drama is a metaphor for the relationship between a writer and a reader or vice versa. In "My Story," one of the shorter pieces, Harryman interrogates "realistic" representations of a singular originating birth in a way that complements sixteenth-century writer Michel Eyquem de Montaigne's similar critique of "death" in his essay "On Training." Throughout *Animal Instincts* (especially in "The Male," "Beginning To End," "Typical Domains," "Counterplan," and the title piece) Harryman weaves a dense polyvocal and polygenre web that no summary can do justice. She shows readers the kind of structures that have to exist in order for them to begin identifying with the dilemma of a protagonist; she gives him enough of narrative to want more; and then she pulls the rug out from under him. Harryman displays a more acute awareness of the limits of narrative than either those who unreflectively churn out stories like machines or those who work in strictly essayistic or strictly poetic forms.

Harryman's next book, *Vice,* is as expansive as the work collected in *Animal Instincts,* but it lacks the tightly woven structural complexities found there. In an interview with Manuel Brito published in *A Suite of Poetic Voices* (1994) Harryman appears, for this reason, to be somewhat apologetic about its place in her works:

> *Vice* was written in between my child's naps when he was an infant and to a smaller degree at the museum where I worked during ten to fifteen minute breaks. At that time in my life, I either had to learn to write under literally fragmented conditions or forget it. . . . The work is constructed from the experience of having to make do with what I had easy access to, because I had very little time to contemplate otherwise. . . . The technical constraints on the work itself are semiautobiographical but the work itself is not autobiography. It is a method of playing with the conditions of one's life . . . rather than of experiencing some kind of defeat because the conditions are all wrong for what one wants to do.

Yet such a disclaimer is also a defense, not only of *Vice* itself but also of a freeing of writing from standards of coherence and consistency. The looser and longer sentences in many of the passages are more like "automatic" writing than anything else in Harryman's work while at other times (as in "Warhol and De Chirico") a more lyric use of page space prevails. The critiques of Noam Chomsky and a catalogue for a Max Beckmann art exhibition lend *Vice* the tone of a Renaissance "commonplace book." Despite, or perhaps because of, the admittedly "all over the place" quality of *Vice,* it may be read as a quest both for subject matter and for a form that suffices as "an adequate vice to limit the liquid of this voice." The search for such containers leads Harryman to expound on the virtues of "Biscuit tins," "the stabilizing you," and other forms that "invite spatial resistance." But the intellectual, emotional, and political restlessness that often characterizes Harryman's writing is so attenuated here that such "vices" never last long. The ending of the book is telling on this point:

> Once the reader has come to the conclusion that a monster lurks behind every habitual expression, the jig is up and one's own quotidian problems reassert themselves. . . . No longer under "its" spell, one's experience of having read the book seems about as spectacular as having eaten a candy bar. But, once starved, then satiated, and now dissatisfied, one goes out for another.

That there is never a single adequate vice found is not so much a failure as the recognition of authorial identity as a function on particular, albeit undefinable, situational contexts. Some passages, however, sustain more of a structure than others. Two of these were reprinted in *There Never Was a Rose without a Thorn* (1995) under the titles "The Rock" and "Vice."

Harryman also strategically adopts a kind of Neoplatonic stance when she writes "I believe in an order that does not exist, that will never exist and that one must seek in order to preclude its existence." It would be a mistake, however, to read Harryman as a Neoplatonist. Rather one should apply her characterization of Jane Austen's "transformed earthly social Platonism," as she states in Bob Perelman's *Writing/Talks,* to her own work as well; for Harryman's notion of identity as a mask, a role, distinguishes her from both imitative "realism" as well as a "pure poetry" of abstract, and finally merely aesthetic, idealizations and allows her art a more proactive, intersubjective stance. As she says in *The Middle,*

> When entering the room where the others had already settled, I had the sensation of becoming a person. I do not recall having thought about being a person before that moment, as if until then my own existence had never caused the slightest uneasiness within. Each person in the room was an extension of my own desire to burst out of my skin and dissolve into light.

Although *In the Mode of* (1991) includes two aleatory poetic ruminations—"Dimblue" and "Why Yell"—that bear a closer resemblance to the work in *Under the Bridge* and certain passages in *Vice,* this collection's most celebrated pieces—"Of" and "In the Mode of"—return to the philosophical and poetic uses Harryman made of conventional narrative structures in *Animal Instincts.* Here, however, the pact Harryman makes with both fairy-tale and pornographic narrational conventions is even more sustained and thereby accessible to a wider readership. Harryman calls attention to the power of fiction to embarrassingly contextualize a poetic/philosophic for the audience who would rather, presumably, be "condemned to an irrelevent and private zone" in which neither the author nor they can "identify their own smells, colors, textures and lives with the story."

The story in "Of," in between the theoretical and philosophical framing one comes to expect from Harryman, is a deliberately conventional tragicomic fairy tale about a girl who lives in Iraq during the Gulf War. The story heats up when the protagonist is visited by a cloud (that bears a stronger resemblance to the ghost in *Hamlet* than it does to the sun in Frank O'Hara's "A True Account of Talking to the Sun at Fire Island") that tells the girl to be on the lookout for those "mendacious ones" who will destroy her city. Harryman never explicitly identifies these "mendacious ones" with either the United States or Hussein's government; the suggestion that they can be read as *both* governments is part of Harryman's point. According to the cloud, these people "will tell you they are dividing the good from the bad . . . but no one knows whether or not they can really tell . . . or if they are just making it up." The cloud's message puts the girl on a doomed quest for conceptual clarity. By the end of the story the girl's refusal to even *think* about good and bad (though the cloud told her only not to *say* the words) can be seen as a kind of self-censorship that avoids ethical responsibility. On the other hand, the fairy tale ends with a tender vision of a somewhat realistic domestic reunion.

It is the *story,* however, and not the piece itself that ends on the tender note of domestic reunion between mother and child. The "happy ending" does not smooth over the darker elements of those who Harryman referred to in *Third Man* as "warring ignoramuses." A large part of the controversial value of "Of" is the way it humanizes Iraqis and provides insight into a more complex situation than the one put forth by the anti-Arab propaganda that has dominated the American media since the breakup of the Soviet Union. In this light it becomes highly significant that the Iraqi girl's mother is an engineer—for such a characterization challenges even the so-called liberal American intellectuals' justification of anti-Arab sentiments on the grounds that women are allegedly more dehumanized there than they are here. Yet Harryman goes beyond mere topicality to emphasize, among other things, the centrality of the mother-child bond that gets left out of most official historical accounts.

"In the Mode of" begins by parodying the "unobtrusive" narrator of many novels:

> I will conclude now that "I" am no more than the story. The "I" identifies with the story in a neutral light; therefore, "I" do not know my own sex.

Such an attempt to find a synthesis that does not require gendered immanence, though futile, still holds tremendous satiric possibilities. The author places her genderless self in an art gallery viewing a female nude. The situation is almost nothing more than a pretext for intellectual exercises on the issue of gender. When Harryman writes " a woman can almost experience a nude in the mode of a man," it becomes clear that putting one sex in the other sex's shoes, as it were, allows more drama than the urge to find a spot that is neither male nor female. Yet because these intellectual exercises exist in a highly elaborated dramatic context, one cannot simply sum up "In the Mode of" as an essay on gender construction. Among other things, Harryman also manages to take to task the marriage of censorship and capitalism:

> The collector is making a large contribution to some fanatics who want to censor art. The removal of nudes from public art spaces will give them the glamour, forbidden pleasure of a black market item and drive the prices up.

Even this passage, however, ties back to the central theme of the value placed on the nude bodies of actual women. Though this piece can be read as feminist, it avoids the pitfalls of an ahistorical essentialism as well as those of a purely constructivist view of gender. Although Harryman severely satirizes the need of male "collectors" to commodify the female nude in order to be attracted to it, she does not deny its sex appeal. By the end of the piece the narrator is willing to let herself imitate the nude while at the same time taking on the role of the observer as she observes the nude as well as the men who look at it.

Memory Play (1994) is Harryman's only book-length play to date. Compared to the four plays collected in *Animal Instincts,* it most clearly resembles "Third Man" in its length, its number of characters, and the complexities of the relationships between them. Like Harryman's other plays, it works at least as well as a closet drama as it does in theater performance. According to Barbara Henning, "the dramatic events are not central to this play. It is the proliferation of meaning that is the most remarkable here." The themes of this play cannot finally be separated from character differentiation, which is more central than plot. The three main characters are carefully delineated in their attitudes toward memory in the self-characterizations that make up the prologue. Reptile is initially presented as sincerely earnest, if a bit naive:

> If I provide you with several of my most esteemed memories, you will probably believe there are more where those came from, and I will have earned your respect. This will make theatre a little more like real conversation.

Pelican's attitude is a polar opposite to Reptile's and can be seen as either worldly or mercantile, depending on one's viewpoint:

I have a job and it is virtually all I can think about; however, I think this: memory is nothing but words stored up in an inefficient computer. What you will remember of this conversation will be nothing like what went into its construction. Such understanding promotes success in business. I know that people want to see the tip of the iceberg only. Business is like a successful cabaret.

In contrast, Fish's attitude can be seen as a kind of synthesis. Fish is clearly the protagonist; and insofar as there is drama, it revolves around Fish's attempt to position herself in relation to these other two attitudes toward memory and sincerity:

I had suffered for a long time from the illusion that remembering inhibited one's experience. Now that illusion is almost my only memory—and that I am cold and have been cold for a long time and that this coldness was brought on gradually by an illusion. Yet, it is likely that I will not be cold later. Then I will remember something else and not this. I will have forgotten the story to which I currently refer.

It would be unnecessarily reductive to read Fish as torn between the viewpoints of Pelican and Reptile. The other characters in the play complicate and decentralize its morality-play psychomachy. The Miltonic Humiliator is a bully to Reptile but is easily deflated by the others. A Child (whose mother is Fish) and a character named Instruction round out the dramatis personae.

According to Henning, *Memory Play* "refuses to present memory as a simple interiorization of experiences or the art of theatre as a re-presentation of an interiorized experience." It also qualifies Pelican's more mercenary view of theater and memory. The dialogic tension between Fish and Pelican (who, in the natural world, eats fish) is especially interesting. For most of the play Fish is somewhat willing to heed Pelican's advice that she needs "a little more theatre" and "a few more characters." Yet Fish is also prone to soliloquies that disrupt the ideas of "a successful cabaret" Pelican so resolutely adheres to. Pelican's view is victorious insofar as *Memory Play* accepts such narrative conventions. Yet Fish does not in the end join Pelican's "toy movie set." Pelican bullies Fish as the Miltonic Humiliator bullies Reptile. He is, however, unable to bully her child successfully in one of the play's most effective stichomythias (act 2, scene 2), and in the dramatic climax of the play Fish turns the tables on Pelican by utilizing silence as a deflationary strategy. In their final encounter Pelican exclaims with approval: "Now you've got it! You're starting to act like a professional," to which Fish replies, "You are starting to let down your guarantees." It is her last word in the play proper. A stage direction reminds the audience

that when Fish exits, "identity becomes fluid as memory." In an epilogue, however, Fish returns with Child to remind the audience of a world outside of the play, a world that, in short, is nothing but a creative potential. This brief synopsis, though reductive and distorted, illustrates that the works Harryman has published in the 1990s so far tend to be less self-protective about their tendency toward myth and allegory than earlier works. On a mythic level *Memory Play* shares similarities with both "Of" and many of the new works in Harryman's selected *There Never Was a Rose without a Thorn*.

Among the previously uncollected pieces in *There Never Was a Rose without a Thorn* are the lengthy title piece, which among other things favorably contrasts the writing of the Marquis de Sade to the writing of Jean-Jacques Rousseau, as well as selections from *The Words* (1998) and the forthcoming "Games." Although all these works deserve attention, the eight pieces from "Games" mark a new stylistic direction in Harryman's work. The concision and clarity of expression make these pieces among her most accessible without sacrificing any of the abrasive, playful, skeptical intelligence that marked her earlier work. It is these pieces that make especially plausible Jewell Gomez's assertion in the cover blurb that "her newest work is an alchemical gem that sparkles" and that "each new image settles irrevocably inside us." And there does seem to be a reliance on an authority outside the relationship(s) presented in these poems that Harryman does not second-guess, even if it is unrepresentable. The centrifugal vertigo one comes to expect from Harryman is still there, but each piece is structured and ordered around a kind of metaphysical conceit that both utilizes and explodes binary logic (mind versus body, self versus society, margin versus center, male versus female). These prose poems, however, are also meant to be literal games. In "Mud" Harryman asks, only half-mockingly, "If this were a board game would it be better than Monopoly? Would it be able to compete in the marketplace of games?"

Some of these "games" ("Mothering," "Murdering," and "Mud") foreground Harryman's project of rewriting patriarchal myths while others ("Margin," "Membership," and "Magic") foreground the tensions between the individual and society. These two central themes overlap in complex ways. The central relationship in "Matter," for instance, can be read as between a male and a female, as well as the speaker's relationship with an abstraction, figured alternately as "love" and as "my body," or even with the poem itself. "Mud" rewrites patriarchal myths by deconstructing the traditional connotational associations of women with "cabbages" and men with "skyscrapers." For Harryman "the amazonian mud woman's original condition" remains something "we can't quite picture." But rather than lamenting the lost original, Harryman celebrates the freedom of representational maneuvering such a loss allows. In recognizing the limits of language, games, self-characterizations, and acts of identification Harryman is able to assert her own myths *as myths* here in ways that celebrate women, and even men, as fiction-making animals.

"Membership" is constructed around a distinction between an "us" and a "them" and is one of Harryman's most powerful social critiques to date. It begins with a characterization of those who:

> placed their demented musings outside themselves, and called the displacement society and public space. Therefore, society and public space were the projected fantasies of individuals onto the ground we once occupied.

One of the many ways this statement can be read is in terms of the contemporary debate between the Language writers and the "humanist" values of authenticity and private interiority that dominate mainstream contemporary American poetry. It almost seems as if Harryman is retracting the very values that elsewhere ground her work. Yet this is only the case insofar as Harryman identifies more with the "we" than she does with the "they" here. As the piece progresses, it becomes clearer that such an assumption about where the speaker stands is not at all a safe one. The narrator may be more like these "lunatics" than the "rest-of-us" whose perspective she ostensibly speaks from. The "rest-of-us" may be those who, in their proud, victimized, complacent sense of self refuse public responsibility for their actions and writings. Harryman, however, rejects easy binaries and reveals the inadequacies of, but necessity for dialogue between, both stances:

> Those who had been all made institutionalized and those who had shirked imprisonment, all made up a reciprocating form of knowledge.

Harryman here, as elsewhere, gestures to a place both "within and without the institutional walls." Her relentless examination of the inescapable roles institutions play here should not be read as a dehumanizing or a depersonalizing but rather as a refiguration of what it means to be human. "Games" may be able to bring this central message of Harryman's to a wider audience, even if Milton-Bradley refuses to take her offer seriously.

In addition to "Games" Harryman is also currently at work on her first full-length novel, tentatively titled "Gardener of Stars." She has also published in magazines selections from "The Wide Road," a long collaboration with Lyn Hejinian. Harryman already has a significant body of work behind her, and though her work remains difficult to characterize, any consideration of the contemporary poetry of her generation cannot afford to ignore the work of this major voice.

Interviews:
Bob Perelman, "The Middle," in his *Writing/Talks* (Carbondale: University of Southern Illinois Press, 1985), pp. 135–156;

Manuel Brito, "Carla Harryman," in his *A Suite Of Poetic Voices* (Santa Brigada, Spain: Kadle Books, 1994), pp. 46–63.

References:
Steve Benson, "Hooks and Conceits in La Quotidienne," *Jimmy and Lucy's House of K,* no. 2 (August 1984): 21–24;

Jean Day, "Two Books by Carla Harryman," *Jimmy and Lucy's House of K,* no. 6 (May 1986): 118–123;

Barbara Henning, "Carla Harryman's Memory Play," *St. Mark's Poetry Project Newsletter,* no. 157 (April/May 1995): 21;

Tom Mandel, "Carla Harryman," *Jimmy and Lucy's House of K,* no. 2 (August 1984): 24–27;

Stephen Paul Martin, "Carla Harryman: Mixing Genres," *Open Form and the Feminine Imagination* (New York: St. Martin's Press, 1989);

Laura Moriarty, "On Carla Harryman's 'Sublimation,'" *Jimmy and Lucy's House of K,* no. 2 (August 1984): 30–33;

Bob Perelman, *The Marginalization of Poetry* (Princeton: Princeton University Press, 1996), pp. 30–36, 129–130;

David Sheidlower, "The Dawning of an Aspect (Unlineated)," *Jimmy and Lucy's House of K,* no. 2 (August 1984): 27–30.

Ann Lauterbach
(28 September 1942 –)

James McCorkle

BOOKS: *Vertical, Horizontal* (Dublin: Seafront Press, 1971);

Book One (New York: Spring Street Press, 1975);

Many Times, But Then (Austin & London: University of Texas Press, 1979);

Later That Evening (Brooklyn, N.Y.: Jordan Davies, 1981);

Closing Hours (Madison, Wis.: Red Ozier Press, 1983);

Sacred Weather, with a drawing by Louisa Chase (New York: Grenfell Press, 1984);

Greeks, with text by Lauterbach and Bruce Boice and photographs by Jan Groover (Baltimore: Hollow Press, 1985);

Before Recollection (Princeton, N.J. & Guildford, U.K.: Princeton University Press, 1987);

How Things Bear Their Telling, with drawings by Lucio Pozzi (Colombes, France: Collectif Gènèration, 1990);

Clamor (New York: Viking/Penguin, 1991);

And For Example (New York: Viking/Penguin, 1994);

A Clown, Some Colors, A Doll, Her Stories, A Song, A Moonlit Cove, with photogravures by Ellen Phelan (New York: Whitney Museum, 1996);

On A Stair (New York: Penguin Poets, 1997).

OTHER: "Light Repositories: On David Rohn's Watercolors," in *David Rohn's Watercolors: 1969–1984* (Springfield: Museum of Fine Arts, 1984), pp. 21–23;

"Nocturnes for the Nineties" (on Chris Martin), in John Goode Gallery catalogue (New York: John Goode Gallery, 1990), pp. 29–30;

"On Memory," in *Conversant Essays: Contemporary Poets on Poetry,* edited by James McCorkle (Detroit: Wayne State University Press, 1990), pp. 519–524;

"Louisa Chase: Figure in a Landscape," in Brooke Alexander catalogue (New York: Brooke Alexander, 1991);

"Brian Wood: Perverse Science," in Lieberman Saul Gallery catalogue (New York: Lieberman Saul Gallery, 1992);

Ann Lauterbach (photograph by Diana Michener)

"First Words" and "The Free-Lance Muse," in *The Practice of Poetry,* edited by Chase Twitchell (New York: HarperCollins, 1992), pp. 3–4;

"Genesis (Eden)," in *Communion: Contemporary Writers Reveal the Bible in Their Lives,* edited by David Rosenberg (New York: Anchor Books, 1995), pp. 451–465.

SELECTED PERIODICAL PUBLICATIONS—UNCOLLECTED: "Poets and Art," *Artforum,* 23 (November 1984): 87–88;

"Is I Another? A Talk in 7 Beginnings," *American Letters and Commentary,* no. 2 (1989): 81–96;

"James Schuyler's Fifth Season," *Denver Quarterly,* 24 (Spring 1990): 69–76;

"Links Without Links: The Voice of the Turtle," *American Poetry Review,* 21 (January/February 1992): 37–38;

"What Is the Grass? Notes Leading up to and away from Walt Whitman," *American Letters and Commentary,* 5 (1993): 46–59;

"Unpicturing (Fair) Realism: Notes on Barbara Guest's Poetics of (Defensive) Rapture," *American Letters and Commentary,* 7 (1995): 1–13;

"The Night Sky," *American Poetry Review,* 25 (May/June 1996): 9–17;

"The Night Sky, II," *American Poetry Review,* 25 (November/December 1996): 9–15;

"Misquotations from Reality," *Diacritics,* 26 (Fall/Winter 1996): 143–157;

"The Night Sky, III," *American Poetry Review,* 26 (March/April 1997): 19–25;

"The Night Sky, IV," *American Poetry Review,* 26 (July/August 1997): 35–42;

"The Night Sky, V," *American Poetry Review,* 26 (November/December 1997): 33–39.

Ann Lauterbach's poetry is of ravishing presence pressured and fired by memory, desire, myth, and dream. To read Lauterbach's poetry is to immerse oneself in the rich textures of language as well as to participate in the re-visioning of the modernist lyric. Hers is not a didactic, discursive, or instructional poetry; rather it is a poetry moved by intuition, juxtaposed fragments, oblique narratives, and stunning images. This is not to say Lauterbach's poetry is sensational—that is, demanding of the senses while implying a diminishment of the intellect. Rather, in their evocation of the senses her poems explore the most central of lyric and human conditions—eros, mortality, the coil of time, and the material of language.

Ann Lauterbach was born in Manhattan on 28 September 1942 to Richard Edward and Elisabeth Stuart Wardwell Lauterbach. Richard Lauterbach was a writer and correspondent. During Ann Lauterbach's childhood he served as a war correspondent for *Life* and *Time* magazines in Moscow and was head of the Moscow Bureau of *Time.* After World War II he wrote three books on Russia and the Far East and worked for *PM* magazine and others with a leftist bent and as a lecturer on Russian politics until his death in 1950. The process of writing has early associations for Lauterbach with her father. In her essay "On Memory" she writes, "My father, a foreign correspondent during World War Two, was often away, and my sense of vulnerability was greatly enhanced by his absence. He seemed to have taken the

present away with him, leaving a gap, a void in which *was* and *will be* collided. When he returned from his trips, he brought with him *presents,* perhaps my first misheard misreading, the initial pun, the rhyme that healed broken time. When he left again, he carried with him a small Hermes typewriter, which I must have thought of as a magic tool, the agent of his adherence, his attachment to the world he traveled."

Lauterbach graduated from the High School of Music and Art in New York City in 1960, with an emphasis in painting. It was there, she states in a 1992 interview with Molly Bendall, that she became "enamored of the Abstract Expressionists for the combination of sensuousness and mystery; they seemed to answer something in me, to substantiate the encounter with the unknown." After graduating from the University of Wisconsin at Madison (B.A. in English, 1964) and attending Columbia University for a year of graduate study on a Woodrow Wilson Graduate Fellowship (1966–1967), she lived until 1974 in London, where she worked as an editor at Thames and Hudson Publishers, taught at Saint Martin's School of Art, and served as the director of the Literature Program at the Institute of Contemporary Art.

After returning to the United States, Lauterbach worked at the Max Protetch Gallery, the Art Latitude Gallery, the Fabric Workshop, as a consultant for the Rosa Esman Gallery, and again with Protetch as assistant director of the Washburn Gallery before teaching in the Master of Fine Arts Program at Brooklyn College in 1985. Since 1989 she has been the Theodore Goodman Professor of Creative Writing at City College, City University of New York. In 1994 she became a member of the English faculty at the Graduate Center of the City University of New York. Her teaching responsibilities also include teaching in the summer MFA program at Bard College, where she has been codirector of the writing faculty since 1991. She has also taught in the writing programs at Columbia, Princeton, and the University of Iowa. She received grants from the Creative Arts Public Service (1978), the Guggenheim Foundation (1986), the New York State Council for the Arts (1988), and the Ingram Merrill Foundation (1988). She received the Jerome J. Shestack Prize from *The American Poetry Review* in 1990. In 1993 she was a recipient of a fellowship from the prestigious John D. and Catherine T. MacArthur Foundation.

Ann Lauterbach's poetry has been associated most often with the New York School of poetry, notably the poets John Ashbery, Barbara Guest, and James Schuyler. Although a diverse and loosely defined group, the New York School poets share an interest in contemporary visual arts; their poetics also proposes that the general attribute of language is its artifice and that language structures our lives rather than serving as

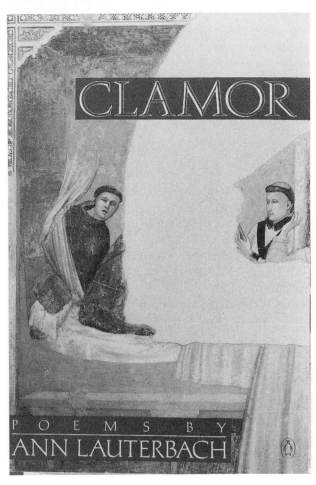

Cover for Lauterbach's 1991 collection, poems that capture the same sense of emptiness and distance as the cover illustration, a detail from Giotto's Vision of the Ascension of St. Francis

(1975) and *Later That Evening* (1981). In her interview with Bendall, Lauterbach comments that the poems of this volume "seem both to have a quirkier surface and to be more constricted than those in the second book [*Before Recollection,* 1987], and they seem not to have fully questioned the centrality of the self." While there is often a disjunctive narrative, the poems of *Many Times, But Then* tend to have a shared voice or authorial sensibility. The title of the collection illustrates this sensibility: it is concerned with the rhetorical surface and locates within grammar the moments of shift, hesitation, conjunction, and qualification. The title suggests the movement of the mind through the world, structuring that world through linguistic frames yet never finalizing or completing that structure. There is no absolute statement, narrative, or truth: exceptions to the rule abound and become manifest as the mind explores both the world and the process of thinking that world into being. The title also is temporally framed: it expresses two modes of time: general ("many times") and the momentary, present, or interruptive ("but then"). Language moves by time (and timing); stories unfold in time (and often never are completed in time). The title also creates a threshold, which humans cross at the moment of the conjunctive comma, where they move from a general condition to a qualifying condition.

The title poem of the collection amplifies these elements suggested by the title. Lauterbach uses the two component phrases of the title to anchor and generate the poem. At several places the poem turns upon or depends upon the phrase "many times" or "but then." The way humans think and apprehend the world is, Lauterbach suggests through the poem's rhetorical structure, linguistically motivated. The precise though almost abstracted imagery complicates the surface of the poem and the implicit narrative: the autumnal setting seems to be a resort and frames the moment of leave-taking. The grounding of the moment shifts—the literal and the potential are conflated, as are the conditions of eros and mortality: "What days have come have gone / and today is the anniversary of someone's death / but then I am familiar with things that pass." Here Lauterbach interjects a stunning image which shifts the scope of the poem from the pathetic fallacy to an ideological analysis of a European-centered culture: "even as the sun flares descending, an image / for which cathedrals have been made, glass cut / to let it in." What is let in is the sense of passing, transience, or mortality: this culture's moral and aesthetic values seem dependent upon and celebratory of loss. The cut glass of the cathedral magnifies the fleeting light; the fleetingness, not the light, is the object of devotion.

an ornament to our experiences. Lauterbach's poetry has its roots as well in the materiality of language found in Gertrude Stein's work, the conjoining of lyric imagism and the ironic in Ezra Pound's early poetry, and the lush precision in Wallace Stevens's poems. It is probably Ashbery's work, however, that serves as both mentor and challenge for Lauterbach. While Ashbery's poetry often traces the indeterminacy of the quotidian and always resists lyric expressionism, Lauterbach's poetry is often the inverse of Ashbery's poetics: lyric expressionism is the base of her work, rather than a moment that intrudes, interrupts, or serves only as one of many discursive modalities. Yet like Ashbery's poetry, Lauterbach's seeks to map the provisionality of thought as well as to reveal, especially in her later poems, the potential capaciousness of poetry.

Many Times, But Then (1979) was the first book by Lauterbach published by either a trade or university press. Lauterbach included in *Many Times, But Then* poems published in two chapbooks, *Book One*

The poem closes with a secularized depiction of devotion. The narrator of the poem kneels before a window, straining to see:

> From time to time I lose you in the glare
> of a blue robe in summer but then the window has me
> kneeling to see. The birds masquerade as song;
> the leaves, futile and passionate, abstract gold from green.

There is a lushness to the language and imagery here that Lauterbach maintains throughout her poetry. The intensity of the narrator's gaze can be likened to that found in gazes of Renaissance paintings, of Giotto or Masaccio, in which the gaze annunciates desire. The movement across the threshold of desire is an abstracting of emotion, which Lauterbach reimages with the autumnal changes of leaves that "abstract gold from green."

The motif of the threshold assumes many forms throughout Lauterbach's poetry. The poem "Window" illustrates this liminality:

> The distance between heat and cold
> a window's width, glass light
> held by an incursion
> the way love is always shadowed.

The distance between differing states is narrow and easily crossed. Using the metaphoric conceit of the window, Lauterbach creates one of her most imagistically unified poems. With the binary play of heat and cold, interior and exterior, proximity and distance, the poem in fact becomes static: the window contains the dynamics of eros and serves as a site to which our gaze can always return. Lauterbach's poetry is the site of a controversy between an image-laden poetics and a rhetorically driven one. "Window," while illuminating the conditions of eros, reveals the potential drawback of the image—its static iconicity.

In *Many Times, But Then* many of the poems maintain a lyric centeredness; that is, the "I" assumes a speaking authority and unity associated with a traditional lyric voice. The "you" is anonymous but most often denotes a lover and does not intend to place the reader in its position. In "The Green Scarf" the narrator maintains a reflective voice. The "I" seems much more a dramatic character than a rhetorical counter or part of a fragmented narrative: the narrator admits, "I am not good at guesswork" and "Last year I knew more than this; / yesterday I was better at today than now." The poem maintains its explicit unity or centeredness through the authorial "I" and the use of the scarf as a sustained metaphor. The scarf serves as a metaphor of time, connections, and mortality: "today is a scarf / made of silk and silk, as you know, perishes." The scarf, which is the narrator's focus, is given a history: "The one my mother had I now have: it is emerald. / Just above the hem it frays, becomes less and less / until it is not." Although there is an autobiographical resonance, the metaphor of time, kinship, and life fraying or disintegrating is the central concern of the poem; hence, the poem resists a strictly autobiographical interpretation. Humans are left with artifacts, each weighted with history and sentiment, but even these artifacts fade. Nothing can be sustained; nothing is immutable—not memory, eros, or any object. Yet rather than ending with despair at this condition of loss, Lauterbach closes by asserting, "I know that absence is a form of holding, as love is." How secure that knowledge is, however, has been put in question earlier in the poem, for the narrator also suggests that as humans move further into life, they move further into unknowing.

Many Times, But Then includes three sequences of poems: "The White Sequence," "Chalk," and "The Yellow Linen Dress." The latter is an elliptical meditation and elegy on Lauterbach's mother and grandparents composed in nine compact, ten-line sections. The more ambitious and complex sequence, however, is "Chalk." Composed of five sections and a prelude, "Chalk" is a meditation on writing and erasure. The metaphor of chalk is evoked throughout the poem: the prelude defines chalk as the "Moon marked sky; sky writings. / Trace of birds" or "The moist residue of sex / dries chalk" or "The extension of fingers; / an intensity of veils" or "Transparencies of love" and "The thing recalled." Each of these analogies provides the metaphoric and thematic grounds for the poem. The poem performs, rather than narrates, the shifting grounds of perception, writing, and relationships. As do many of the poems of *Many Times, But Then,* "Chalk" explores the overlay of dream and waking life insofar as that distinction always entails liminality and thus is a metaphor for other conditions, including the erotic and aesthetic.

> You tie
> my arms behind my back
> with the red velvet belt
> from my robe.
> I love feeling helpless;
> I am not.
> I am tired, I sleep.
> You go away, an image.

Here eros is formed as dreamed desire: this moment of reverie arises from "reading as snow flurries / Monday, in February, in a / hot dry room." This reverie also demarcates the complex conditions of gender: "I love feeling helpless; / I am not." The assertion "I am not" indicates that the narrator, presumably a woman, is not helpless; however, the assertion also has the implication of denial—that she is simply "not."

The choice of the term *chalk* suggests the materiality of writing since, of all writing media, it is perhaps the most tactile and is always leaving its residue. Conversely, chalk is always associated with erasure, when past writing becomes a mere trace before vanishing. This association recalls Freud's analogy equating the unconscious with the child's novelty item, the Mystic Writing Pad, where there is always a trace, or as Lauterbach suggests, "A residue of seeing / frame within frame within us." And as Freud argues, one's consciousness and one's dream and memory states are linguistically anchored. Thus, for Lauterbach, the performance of language in the poem can remap the linguistic structuring of the mind.

Lauterbach's second collection, *Before Recollection,* published in 1987 in the Princeton Series of Contemporary Poetry, continues her investigation of the erotic, linguistic, and liminal within the intensity of lyric expression. The collection is divided into four sections: "Naming the House," "As Far as the Eye can See," "Psyche's Dream," and "A Simple Service." The collection thus moves from a sense of place, to a consideration of outward, expansive vision, and then, in "Psyche's Dream," to the mythic and interior worlds, and in the final section, especially the six-part poem "Sacred Weather," back to the elemental world of landscape, season, and weather. The relationship of memory, presence, and writing is central to these poems. In her essay "On Memory" Lauterbach suggests that writing is a process similar to dreaming, for each is "a reconstruction or revision of the real, if the real is what is already known or understood. . . . I like to say I write 'into the unknown,' which is, I suppose, another way of saying 'I write into the future.' But of course it is not possible to write into the unknown, the future, without the known, the past. The past is always there, the setting, the stance: it constitutes us, and we are its constituents."

The cover photograph, made especially for this collection by the noted photographer Jan Groover, indicates the tonal and compositional sensibility of the poems. Groover had earlier collaborated with Lauterbach and Bruce Boice to produce the limited-edition artists' book *Greeks* (1985). Groover contributed thirty platinum palladium photographs of the Cypriot votives found in the Metropolitan Museum of Art in New York, and Lauterbach and Boice contributed texts: a poem ("Where Was Is") set in many voices and an apocryphal speech of a Greek soldier fighting for Achilles, respectively. In this overlay of myth, aesthetics, and history is a plea against war and inhumanity. Like the earlier long poem that made up the chapbook *Vertical, Horizontal* (1971), "Where Was Is" has not been collected in any subsequent book.

For the cover of *Before Recollection,* Lauterbach gave Groover different objects (a postcard, a dragon, talismans from her life chosen for the idea between object and recollection). From these Groover made a collage of photographs to represent recollections. Groover's art suggests themes found in the poetry: annunciation, revelation, eros, self-reflection, and ritual as well as a sense of compositional juxtaposing of narratives, a lushness of image, and a disquieting clarity or precision. The photograph conveys a stillness also found in the poems. This stillness is not the quietude of completion but the illusion of movement stilled in which time is sliced to the quick. There is always a resistance to conclusion; as the literary critic Charles Altieri wrote in 1995, "Lauterbach invites us to dwell in the moment when everything is in an unstable transition." This is a moment of stillness when language becomes dispossessed of self and thereby reveals its own incompleteness and the pain implicit in this revelation signifying our condition. This effect is explicitly commented upon in Lauterbach's "Still Life with Apricots," which is in part a response to Groover's photographs:

> Each topic is a surface
> Ingrained and potential, a reverie emptied,
> A breach drawn easily, singularly. Tones
> Shift across a slab like the boundaries of grief.

Art or any process of composition may be, as Lauterbach continues in this poem, "A field abounding in new orders of discrepancy" where "Beauty is a way of meriting surprise."

Just as the title of her first collection did, the title *Before Recollection* denotes a temporal condition: the immediacy of the present, which ironically eludes definition, naming, or description. Thus, to be "before recollection" is to be in the sheer moment of life and of unknowing. The title also suggests a moment of threshold or the line between the lived moment and memory. Memory becomes a house or a place of collecting again what has passed. Groover's photograph emphasizes this gathering again of details, especially as the arrangement suggests a desk cluttered with favored objects collected over one's life. The word *before* anchors this liminality in a linguistic structure. How humans perceive time is conditioned by language; similarly, they cannot apprehend the moment except through the tracery of recollection. Lauterbach, however, implies through this title that the lyric should be a linguistic phenomenon that exists in the sheer present and that the presence of the lyric reveals the paradox that language is, otherwise, recollection.

The metaphor of a house is developed in the first section of *Before Recollection*. Within it the reader finds, as in an Emily Dickinson poem, "The sleeping urgencies are perhaps ruined now / In the soul's haphazard sanctuary, / Ignored like a household." In the poem "Still," which opens the collection, Lauterbach suggests that there is a latent energy which transforms the household from the place of "nocturnal waste" and constriction to "potentially, a revelation." For Lauterbach, writes Susan Schultz, "to be at home is both a blessing and a curse, for it metaphorically represents a feminine line of creation at the same time as it closes her out of Whitman's open road. She attempts to get past this impasse by opening her house to infinitude, as Dickinson did."

The challenge women poets face is that of "naming the house" or knowing, as Lauterbach writes in "Naming the House," that "the metaphor of the house is ours to keep / And the dark exterior only another room / Waiting for its literature." What must be retrieved is the power to name and to hold, rather than to be named and to be held, or as Lauterbach writes in the concluding lines of "Naming the House": "The joy of naming it this, and this is mine." Yet Lauterbach is always aware that language is also a house or, to apply the title of one of her poems to this condition, a "walled palace": "At best things are untidy, latent, fugitive. / Words fail where no present is / And we age in our own narration." Often the narrators of the poems refer to an unnamed "she" who is given no context but who seems to be the genius of the place or the inhabiting spirit. She has given the place its life and serves as an informing imagination, as in "In the Garden":

> I have in my mind's eye an ancestral place
> Thick with iris, lily, tulip,
> Whose high grass, parted by a path, I
> Never saw but which she painted, sitting out
> On the lawn, in late spring, everything seen.

This unknown woman, who seems to show forbearance, provides order as well as imagination: the house can be stable but not constricting if the terms of the imagination are met.

"Where I Am" conveys the power of the imagination when confronted with conscripting social forces that penetrate the consciousness and seek to control the imagination. Against a scene that seems almost taken from one's dreamwork, or the Freudian processes of displacement, condensation, and symbolic revision, the narrator empowers herself:

> I wear a wardrobe of birds, heirloom wings, talons.
> Now the heron tempts me to believe

Cover for Lauterbach's 1994 collection, in which the lines have the quality of a whirlwind, like the figures from the Pergamon Altar pictured on the cover

> All things named are immanent. These leaves
> Swirl upward from the simple task of water;
> The river is fastened by the radiance of a shield.

The narrator invests herself and her words with the power both of ravishment and of rapture. The image of birds in sudden flight becomes a marker of the imagination and the suddenness of presence in these poems. Thus, at the end of the Stevensian poem "Carousel," the unknown "she" literally assumes the guise of the bird and "makes her descent, plucks it, rises into the blue." Here Lauterbach witnesses the power of the imagination to seize what may or may not be there and make it her own.

Lauterbach has been able to fuse lyric intensity with an abstract language, often laden with a social critique that is a rarity in contemporary poetry. *Before Recollection* does not turn away from experiments in discontinuous or depersonalized narratives. Though the language and themes are singular, bespeaking an identifiable poetic voice, the idea of a single, unified, knowing self is always under question. Lauterbach's

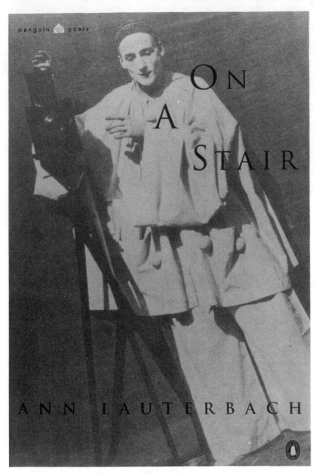

Cover for Lauterbach's 1997 collection, which includes poems about disrupted movement as in climbing or descending a staircase

poetics, as Altieri wrote in 1988, "is based on a return to the ideal of eloquence." Altieri argues that "Lauterbach equates identity with the constant pressure on one's language to take responsibility for the mode and degree of physical investment that it can maintain in its objects. And then poetry becomes intensely personal simply in its displaying an ear constantly elaborating a sense for who and where one becomes in one's expressive acts." The accuracy of his analysis is illustrated, for example, in how the poems reappraise eros. Lauterbach uses a generative structure in "Psyche's Dream" to conclude that "If dreams could dream" then "within each dream is another, remote / And mocking and a version of his mouth on her mouth." Dreams are sites of displaced representations; as such, they arguably mirror language's own displacements of signification as well as the always shifting versions of the self. While this Poststructuralist philosophy of language and self informs Lauterbach's poetry, there is also an implicit resistance in which the woman writing or the

woman as subject must maintain an identity or risk disappearance:

> But here is a twig in the form of a wishbone.
> Aroused, I take it, and leave its outline
> scarred in snow which the sun will later heal:
> form of the real melts back into the ideal
> and I have a twig.

Here, in the poem "Platonic Subject," waking, eros, and the authority of writing all are conjoined. Though the writing may heal, the writer will not disappear but asserts her power or desire to write.

The cover of *Clamor* (1991), Lauterbach's third collection of poems, is a reproduction of a detail of Giotto's *Vision of the Ascension of St. Francis* (circa 1396) found in the Bardi Chapel. A fragment of this detail was one of the reproductions found in Groover's photographic assemblage for the cover of *Before Recollection*. This choice of cover is significant because it suggests a continuity with the earlier poems as well as a focus on a particular aspect of those poems. However, instead of our attention being drawn to the portrait (that is the condition of the self in the poems of *Before Recollection*), the emptiness, distance, lacunae, or effacement captures our gaze in both the cover of *Clamor* and the poems. Whatever ecstatic moment of revelation is depicted by Giotto is forever lost: what we have is the record, here worn by time, of the witnesses' expressions, their clamor, and as stated in the title poem, "ruptured attention."

Clamor is divided into three sections—"Remorse of the Depicted," "Tribe (Stamina of the Unseen)," and "The Elaborate Absence." As these section titles suggest, Lauterbach is concerned with vision—both the way one sees and hence navigates the world of phenomena and desire as well as the ecstatic or revelatory state. While critics such as Altieri and Schultz found *Before Recollection* a significant departure and reinvigoration of the poetics of Stevens and Ashbery, *Clamor* with its publication by Viking/Penguin brought Lauterbach's work to a wider audience. Hence its reception ranged from the caustic pronouncements of the poet Mark Jarman to the highly commendatory reviews of such poets as Donald Revell and Rachel Blau Duplessis. There are moments in *Clamor* in which the disjunctive poetics seem too facile or strained either in the impulse to move from an abstract statement to naming prosaic objects or in the unfounded urgency of the assertion. Yet, more often these discontinuities are revelatory—the poems demand readers to ask how they see and what they see. Furthermore, the sudden and surprising insertion of the mundane occurs perhaps less for the sake of making the world less familiar than for invoking the sustenance humans derive implicitly from the perishable world. The discontinuous narratives, images, memories, conversational fragments, and assertions may form a latticework of interludes. They are overlays of temporal states: to be reading and remembering as well as desiring involves a multiplicity of states of being, none of which is coterminous with the others.

The poems of *Clamor* tend to be longer and far more layered than those of Lauterbach's previous collections. Such poems as "Mountain Roads," "Lakeview Diner," and "Forgetting the Lake," for example, move through a variety of spaces and temporal modes. The poems begin abruptly, almost in midconversation, as in "Forgetting the Lake": "Look, this leaving may last indefinitely / Branching into the cool siphons / Of this first last afternoon which is filling / Or spilling an atmosphere of sensuality." The reader becomes the one addressed in this colloquial but dramatic imperative: "Look." Dependent or modifying clauses provide a means of extending or generating the poem as do internal rhyme and wordplay.

Grammar allows choices: the conjunction *and* can move the poem in different directions rather than serving only as a device for accumulating detail. In "Mountain Roads" the use of *and* shifts the perspective from that of the narrator's experience to that of the unknown woman found earlier in the poems of *Before Recollection*:

> And we were cosmetic; briefly, we were in the grips
> Of awe, like the mild tourists pointing
> And the girl smiling down into the pond.
> She has not yet seen her face, she has seen
> Only the Greek poet searching a soul for his soul.
> But she has been riding the shaped water in a small boat,
> Scanning for admissible events. It is twilight and,
> From the edge of the wood, a hermit thrush
> Begins to memorize the tentative
> And to seduce us directly.

Here the poem moves closest to an allegorical center: the girl bending over the mirrored water sees only a figuration of Narcissus, or one "searching a soul for his soul." This image defines the poet's self-reflective process. But the gaze returns to the girl who is "Scanning for admissible events": punning on the term *scan,* with its application to prosody, the girl is the imagination that seeks the "admissible events" or the informing music. The poem then turns on the liminal moment of twilight: the girl is refigured as the thrush, who seduces us by its music. But Lauterbach resists a Keatsian release; instead, she concludes the passage with the vernacular, "Pretty soon we'll start remembering / All over again, but there were no weddings."

Perhaps the most powerful poem of *Clamor* is "Tuscan Visit (Simone Martini)," which is centered on the scene of the Annunciation. Lauterbach describes her interest as the moment Mary is interrupted while reading—hence, "the painting as a depiction of a narration," as Lauterbach states in her interview with Bendall. Thus the moment represents the interruption of the lives of all women to bear children and to take care of the life. Although *Before Recollection* had several poems responding to the work of visual artists—such as "Portrait" (Pablo Picasso), "Still Life with Apricots" (Jan Groover), or "The Vanquished" (Bill Jensen)— "Tuscan Visit (Simone Martini)" is one of Lauterbach's most accomplished poems drawn directly from the visual arts. Here Lauterbach queries the condition of seeing when at the threshold of a revelation: "What did she see? / The hills as a journey, / The sky as a sign, / Cypress beards–." The Annunciation is, however, also an interruption which is a form of violation: "Her thumb holding a book open, / Her body recoiled from the offered lilies."

Perception and permanence are among Lauterbach's persisting themes. In "Boy Sleeping," a title again suggesting liminality, the poet wonders, "is the solid figure of the night / Only a wish to survive the last word said." This poem advances through a continual questioning of the poet's vision; questioning becomes a method and form of remembering; thus, memory depends upon the particulars of the world. Lauterbach questions how one can insert or exert the authority of a poem into or onto a multitudinous world—that is, how to begin in a world that is continually becoming. In "How Things Bear Their Telling" and "Prom in Toledo Night" Lauterbach creates poems formed from a collage of fragments from various sources of discourse. Yet such a process leaves the choices too wide and many and omits the poet's movement into the world with her informing intelligence.

Such self-scrutinizing intelligence is found in "Blue Iris," which, like "Boy Sleeping," illustrates Lauterbach's self-reflective questioning:

> But is it ever enough to submerge
> One question under another
> And then to scramble for a vow
> Bringing something–anything–to light?

Bringing to light something–anything–is one of the writer's difficult tasks. For Lauterbach it is illumination in the fullest sense: she asks, "Why not see the sun hit glass?" The poem is a continual opening: the iris fuses the eye and the flower, the seer and the seen. The blue iris becomes an emblem of the visionary that exists "Briefly beyond what we can imagine / And so capture." Lauterbach celebrates the lushness of the world: "Everything now ample and wet / And the tall blue iris / Is the result of water / Unhurt where the sky could never be." In these lines there remains the poet's desire—ample and generative—to find and celebrate.

In her fourth collection, *And For Example* (1994), a more demanding, even urgent and compressed, tone emerges as in the opening poem, "Eclipse with Object":

> Do you know the name of this thing?
> It is a rubbing from an image.
> The subject of the image is that which trespasses.
>
> You are invited to watch. The body asleep
> in complete dark casting nothing back.
> The thing turns and flicks and opens.

Lauterbach's poems form rubbings from images in which the poems overlay something other and, through the physical act of rubbing, form a shadow of it. The reader is "invited to watch" as Lauterbach draws together into provisional relationship utterances and objects. The space in which we live—and the space of the poem that readers read and in so reading also live—is resistant to our gaze, even though the poet has invited us to become witnesses. But the underlying ethos is the necessity for us to be witnesses to the inchoate and painful.

The title of the collection also points to the effects of supplementary and multiple reproductions. The poem becomes a rubbing or example of some part of the world. Each example is displaced by another, just as one can produce endless rubbings of an image from the original. As in previous collections, the title also indicates the poetics of the volume: "and for example" is the grammatical moment of transition or threshold between the assertion and the example. Like language itself, such a grammatical structure is neither thing nor pure idea. Indeed, it suggests that knowing is only achieved through supplementing or substituting uncertainty with something previously known; thus, the aporia remains, though veiled.

Broken into three parts, the collection's subtitles—"The Untelling"; "For Example," which is a series of seven poems; and "Ashes, Ashes"—point to many of Lauterbach's recurring themes: the difficulty of constructing an inclusive narrative and supplemental language; transience; and mortality. The poem "The Untelling" has as its premise the tension between the demand to know and the multiplicity of narratives one might respond with. Untelling is threefold: it may be resistance to telling or the revelation of knowledge to others or oneself; the unraveling of narratives; or that which is not self-evident or obvious. This conditionality is not simply a philosophical concern: in an earlier version of "Rapture of the Spoken" appearing in *The Denver Quarterly* (Summer 1993), Lau-

terbach poses the potential extremes of language in a phrase later omitted—"Redundancy or song." Lauterbach questions the revelatory potential of art thus in the final version of "Rapture of the Spoken":

> Years later, the brush leaves its mark
> overtly, like a kiss.
> But the picture does not respond.
> The picture goes on staring at the morning.

These concluding lines suggest both the sensuality of art and its resistance to our presence. "Like the written utterances of oracles," writes Garrett Kalleberg in 1995 on *And For Example,* "removed from their context of question and answer, Lauterbach's poems read as if they were extracted from an original dialogic context and interpreted through the act of writing until they come to us in their mixed and strangely enigmatic form."

The play of light against dark, in the painterly form of illumination through the juxtaposition of color and brush stroke, density and transparency of paint, as well as figural gestures, informs Lauterbach's poetry, especially the seven-poem sequence "For Example."

"The world," Lauterbach writes in "Stepping Out," the first poem of the sequence,

> loosed like a hem, is
> what we step out on
> and are pulled along away from our doors
> not so much appeased as grafted
> onto the long dark pause.
> Pointing, not seeing anything, not knowing
> the name for what isn't there.

One is always moving across thresholds toward the unknown, where

> . . . the body takes its dreams with it
> like a city buried under the rubble of ages
> never to be found. Strange, too,
> how what is and what is not
> make a quixotic braid
> which, like weather, has no end
> other than those we invent
> to measure change. Rain again today.

Because "We are not located in the world but in its / particulars," humans are finite and defined by what they are not or by the presence of others.

Throughout the sequence "For Example" there is the pressure of destruction and dissolution at work. Like the figures of the Pergamon Altar reproduced on the cover of *And For Example,* the lines have the quality of a whirlwind, each rushing at the other, conveying in this dynamism an emotional violence. Lauterbach has loosened her lines from a lyric grounding much as the bas-relief figures of the Pergamon Altar have nearly removed themselves from the anchoring background. As in the Pergamon Altar, the architectural order of the poems seems overwhelmed by the gestural sweep and emotional energy, as in the concluding passage of the final poem of the sequence, "And the Fire Spread":

> What is unfinished is not by choice,
> gathering inconvenient slang
> to ride the large dark over the dark city.
> I can see this thing opening onto another thing
> but I cannot pronounce it,
> neither the one with the frieze of antlers
> nor the one with the clocks. Taking off gloves
> is a theatrical event, like tossing a pail of water
> at an immense flame
> or following a script in which a boy
> impales himself on a mast as the crowd watches.
> The crowd always watches.

> On the walls/in the starkest/in the wrong
> with our physical/of fire/on fire
> to the Hebrews/of plans/of sins
> without the/in this century
> in a revelation/on the other hand/ in this century/to a
> perception/at least/for a moment/for us
> in which/of the relation/from the great/between
> surfaces/of experience/in every/of their
> to their diction/to each/between surfaces
> in a forward/from which/by myself/into my innermost
> by my soul's/with love/in a region
> with my eye/above my mind/before the light
> with love/into an awareness/with love
> from you/in time/out of which features
> for forces/of something/by mismanagement/from his face
> of information/on the soundtrack.

These lines draw images and phrases from the previous poems of the sequence into their own consuming energy. Rather than finding stylistic or thematic parallels with a poet such as John Ashbery, Lauterbach is here much closer in spirit to Hart Crane's "Atlantis" section of his poem *The Bridge* (1930), in which language is pushed to an extreme condition that combines eros with the violence of history and the difficulty of love with the nihilism of the spectacle.

The collection closes with three homages: "Ashes, Ashes (Robert Ryman, Susan Crile)," "When Color Disappoints (Joseph Beuys)," and "In the Museum of the Word (Henri Matisse)." These poems reflect Lauterbach's ongoing interest in the visual arts and her ekphrastic poetics. These poems do not transcribe or describe the works of these artists; rather they are accumulations of responses; or as Lauterbach stated in her 1992 interview, she attempts to "construct, around the terms of the work, a new site of response. Paintings are real events; an extension of na-

ture." The relation of the aesthetic to the pressure of the real is part of the shared thematic concern of these poems, as suggested in these lines from "In the Museum of the Word (Henri Matisse)":

> They are scooping out the blood in jars
> the real has a stench /it is not
> the tableaux we elicit.

The violence of this imagery, which is threaded throughout the poem, is doubled with Lauterbach's use of the slash as a form of urgent assertion and rupture. Matisse utilized such formal devices as the caesura, aporia, and ellipsis, which have a certain correspondence to Lauterbach's poetics. Lauterbach provides lines which draw us to specific Matisse paintings, not so much in order to provide description or commentary but to be anchoring moments for her own history of gazing:

> I was shown two rivers, their vistas

> snailfooted /waterskinned abyss
> wheelwinged staring at muck
> weedy, indifferent, purplepronged
> up
> in avid rays/their comprehensive is
> bearing emblems smaller than time[.]

The visual analogue seems to be Matisse's *Bathers by a River* (1909–1910), which is divided into discrete panels, the divisions or caesuras subverting the logic of the scene, as John Elderfield has written in his *Henri Matisse: A Retrospective* (1992). Like Lauterbach's poem, these breaks suspend time and create the stillness of uncertainty or aporia. Matisse's blocks of color, never pure but always somehow worked or seemingly insufficient in depth, imply the absence of something expected; this ellipsis, as Elderfield terms it, in Matisse's work parallels Lauterbach's paratactic movements. By reinvestigating Matisse, Lauterbach's poetry re-engages modernist rhetoric: if Matisse suggests a privacy to painting and the gaze of the viewer, Lauterbach has re-visioned that underpinning rhetoric so as to insist on the dark urgency of those rhetorical structures. Not only is the displacement of the pressure of the real in Matisse's painting under scrutiny, but also the viewer's capacities to hold onto the revelations of the painting, especially in our period's commodification of the aesthetic: "*Is it possible to memorize this blue?*"

Following *And For Example,* Lauterbach collaborated with the artist Ellen Phelan, whose work with the figure of a doll initiated the collaboration. Phelan contributed thirteen hand-colored photogravures to Lauterbach's twelve-part poem, "A Clown, Some Colors, A Doll, Her Stories, A Song, A Moonlit Cove," which also serves as the title to this collaborative work published in 1996. Like the earlier chapbooks—*Sacred Weather* (1984), with its drawing by Louisa Chase; *Greeks;* or *How Things Bear Their Telling* (1990), with its drawings by Lucio Pozzi—*A Clown, Some Colors, A Doll, Her Stories, A Song, A Moonlit Cove* demonstrates Lauterbach's continued interaction with the visual arts and complements her writings with contemporary artists.

In "A Clown, Some Colors, A Doll, Her Stories, A Song, A Moonlit Cove" the clown and doll are figures representing human states of being: "the child sees herself / as an oval tracing // disguise after disguise, her / picture and merit." The doll both projects and receives human fears and violence: it is mute and still, much the way humans in their moments of fear are silent:

> Am I poor or wise?
> Am I awake?
> Am I bride or nun?
> What is fun?
> I know I am strange and fake.

By transforming an object into a doll, nonbeing is made real. Lauterbach negotiates with the unknown through language as humans might negotiate their fears through the intercession of a doll, puppet, scapegoat, straw man, or double. The doll or clown becomes an example or supplement to the human figure: "It wants to sit up, make it sit up! / It wants to sleep, sing it to sleep."

In "A Clown, Some Colors, A Doll, Her Stories, A Song, A Moonlit Cove," as in many of her previous poems, and particularly those from *And For Example,* parataxis is perhaps the most demanding rhetorical structure. Any interiority of the self as a private, unified being is constantly resisted by parataxis, which operates at the linguistic level where connectives between phrases are absent as well as at the level of ethos where voice, identity, and narrative become discontinuous. The formal demand of parataxis informs a cultural and social vision: where culture demands a formal partition into structural groupings so as to order, contain, and discipline, parataxis disrupts this enforced and amnesiac continuity. Parataxis also implies that any connection must be made dialogically and outside "decorum's permanent cage." This is not to say that Lauterbach has ceded the poem to the reader; instead, the poem enacts the possibility of an ongoing transmission of our—the poet and the reader held in the embrace of reading—negotiation of eros and grief. Parataxis becomes a way of knowing: it insists on the *about-ness* rather than the absolute *is-ness* of the difficult condition of being-in-the-world, as signaled in the closing passage of the poem:

> . . . Will you close my eyes?
> Will you shave my pelt? In this auditorium
> we are an offering, a crust, a pitter and patter
> you cannot mimic.

> *The cliff is*
> *Greek where I go*
> *with large hands, my embrace*
> *(pray that the road is long,*
> *full of adventure, full of knowledge)*
> *tidal in effigy/tallow ebbed from the heart/cut at the heel.*
> *Biographical incision, I will see the very garden*
> *you intended to plant.*
> *Angel of Time, are you so absent*
> *I must trade this shelter for that?*

> Nest in a rock slit, unfledged creature
> cast upon sand.

> Witness no Voice.

Reprinted in her 1997 collection *On A Stair,* which features the photograph "Pierrot the Photographer," the poem "A Clown, Some Colors, A Doll, Her Stories, A Song, A Moonlit Cove" falls in the center of the collection and signals a self-interrogation, or a crisis of self-representation, by the poet/artist/pierrot-figure. "*Ur* " is the beginning word, and the *Beginning* migrates into "*ur ur,*" sounding like a warning growl or perhaps a purring, but then shifts into "*ur our urn,*" as if to circle completely a cycle of life and death. Language, like identity and the phenomenal world at large, is never stable.

As the title of the collection signals, the poems of *On A Stair* are often about movement, particularly that cantilevered, disrupted movement of climbing or descending a set of stairs, in which movement is simultaneously horizontal and vertical, thus echoing the sense of language being both a synchronic and diachronic event. The image of the stair has as its allusions the Italian poet Dante and the French painter Marcel Duchamp with their movements toward vision. The title also invokes Ralph Waldo Emerson's essay "Experience" with its opening question and response: "Where do we find ourselves? In a series, of which we do not know the extremes, and believe that it has none. We wake and find ourselves on a stair: there are stairs below us, which we seem to have ascended; there are stairs above us, many a one, which go upward and out of sight." Emerson continues, "Our life is not so much threatened as our perception." It is this statement that Lauterbach's work focuses upon: how to rescue our abilities to perceive or to become intellectually mobile within the field of language. In these poems, meaning is always in transit and necessitating the engagement of the reader. On this point, Lauterbach's own reading habit is telling: "Every frame is danger and security. Poems that interest me are poems that show me how to proceed, not where to go or what to look at. . . . The poem attests to the mobility of the frame, not to the totality of the picture," writes Lauterbach in "Misquotations from Reality." Poems, argues Lauterbach in this essay, exhibit "points of attachment between a poet and her world. This place of attachment is a crucial determining value. The poem demonstrates attachment. The poet's primary attachment to the world is to the world as language." Lauterbach's concern is the rescuing of language from a commodity-driven culture that constricts the inherent generative movement within language.

The title of the opening poem of *On A Stair,* "A Valentine for Tomorrow," suggests a moment of sentimentality, but throughout its three parts the poet traces meaning, though meaning is never captured or commodified, through disjunction, imagistic juxtaposition, and rhythmic variation. The first section is a continual opening, for the lines are cantilevered: likewise, parentheses are left incomplete as though there could not be center or closure. In contrast to the first section's proposition that commodification and cultural forgetfulness or the lapsing into cliché-bounded thinking are intrinsically linked, the second section creates a logic of music, in which the momentum of the disjunctive but imagistically charged lines rises to a visionary end: "in a glittering parade / and the mobile digressive figments collide / legacy of heavens where darkly dressed figures scavenge for stars." The final section meditates upon the discrepancy between the sentimental and the world: within sentimentality we are "acquiescent" and "adrift"—oblivious to the world's "incendiary fuel / tearing roof from house, rats from dream."

Lauterbach's poetry in *On A Stair* considers a "figure musically witnessed" around which "the tangles rivet sound into fan shapes," as in her poem "Blake's Lagoon." Yet the experiment with sonic arrangements in space is not reduced to a formula, for as this poem exemplifies, the poet meditates upon the processes of representation, gaze, and eros within the field of the visionary. The human form is divine, yet it is also the agent of predation as well as the object of a deathly, predatory gaze. Humans cannot locate themselves as purely one or the other of Blake's contraries but instead must find themselves in the embrace of those contraries.

On A Stair concludes with poems that are far more direct and, in some instances, more autobiographical than earlier ones. Perhaps most startling of these is "N/est," which is a meditation on childhood, childless-

Lauterbach, circa 1997

ness, and the making of poems. Shifting from prose to linear arrangements that appear to be like passages from poems, to quotations from other texts, Lauterbach creates a field of ruptures and parallel events. In the title "N/est" the slash's violent cut demonstrates the field of choices one has: the title's construction includes *nest* or home, and the breaking apart of the word into the French *est* (the verb for "state of being") and its negative. *Nest,* that constructed habitation, is both affirmed and negated. The poet's practice is an indwelling—or inscaping, to borrow from Gerard Manley Hopkins—of words; however, it is also a banishment from habitation, from the familiar, from the safety of nests, family, and social controls that limit imagination.

Near the end of the poem, Lauterbach writes,

> one word instead of another
> they call to each other sometimes/constructing a place
>
> in which to live a life
>
> words are acts of the world they are prior to us
>   issued forth
>   they become facts in the world
>   an address[.]

It is to words both the reader and writer come. Each must sift and choose and in that choice comes responsibility or an ethics of freedom. Lauterbach's unit of composition is the page and, as she writes in her essay "The Night Sky, III," a shifting of "the reader's attention away from temporality and narrativity toward a metonymic mapping, an embodiment."

"N/est" is a reconstruction of a past and explains how one was and is in the world. But most important, it explains how memory is formed by words; how humans remember is structured by the language available to them. The memories of her father and his absences and then death (thus her fatherlessness, with that replete symbolism) as well as the decision to forestall maternity, and then its displacement into the social role not of mother but of poet, are examined through the social impingements or pressures upon language. The pressures against language parallel the pressures placed upon a woman's body: it is she who must bear the consequences of abortions; it is she whose body is sexually transgressed; it is she for whom certain normative positions are expected. At times the poem is flatly understated: "I have been pregnant three times // two abortions while in college, one in Milwaukee / without anesthetic after which I bled // in the Emergency Room I was afraid they would send me to jail." In so doing, Lauterbach expressly moves the poem into the public sphere and allows the act of writing to become a register of injustice and violence. The poem moves toward a visionary didactic: "Each choice / measures the relation between freedom and fate." If "words are acts of the world," then freedom and fate are what Lauterbach considers in "N/est": the poet tests these conditions.

"Knowledge is form," Lauterbach writes in "Missing Ages" from *And For Example*. This is the challenge that Lauterbach puts before us, as the best of experimental artists do. The lyric is reappraised rather than abandoned; the self as a controlling voice has become unanchored. Instead, the lyric voice, as Lauterbach has developed it, is the accumulation of figures, much like those of the Pergamon Altar, in a rush toward revelation even while they seem to move toward conflagration. In her interview with Bendall, Lauterbach stated, "I think of myself as a scanner. I also think the poem has a way it wants to be, and I'm its servant or expediter. As a result of this method, most of the poems are the result of revision. The whole thing is dialectical, a balancing between *listening* and *willing for*." Lauterbach's poems refuse with ever greater urgency containment or constriction. Her poems have been moving toward the balancing of the difficult extremes of showing the poet listening to the world and yet willing a poem into being. As she notes, this is a dialectical process, one which comes to encompass the reader: the poem becomes a site for response and engagement where knowledge is given new form and new form creates knowledge.

Interviews:

Molly Bendall, "Ann Lauterbach: An Interview," *American Poetry Review*, 21 (May/June 1992): 19–25;

Jonathan Monroe, "Poetry, Community, Movement, A Conversation: Charles Bernstein, Ann Lauterbach, Jonathan Monroe, and Bob Perelman," *Diacritics*, 26 (Fall/Winter 1996): 196–210.

References:

Charles Altieri, "Ann Lauterbach's 'Still' and Why Stevens Still Matters," *Wallace Stevens Review*, 19 (Fall 1995): 219–233;

Altieri, "Jorie Graham and Ann Lauterbach: Towards a Contemporary Poetics of Eloquence," *Cream City Review*, 12 (Summer 1988): 45–72;

Thomas Fink, "The Poetry of David Shapiro and Ann Lauterbach," *American Poetry Review*, 17 (January/February 1988): 27–32;

Mark Jarman, "The Curse of Discursiveness," *Hudson Review*, 45 (Spring 1992): 156–158;

Garrett Kalleberg, "A Form of Duration: On Ann Lauterbach's *And For Example*," *Denver Quarterly*, 29 (Spring 1995): 98–109;

James McCorkle, "*Nimbus of Sensations*: Eros and Reverie in the Poetry of John Ashbery and Ann Lauterbach," in *The Tribe of John: Ashbery and Contemporary Poetry*, edited by Susan Schultz (Tuscaloosa: University of Alabama Press, 1995), pp. 101–125;

Donald Revell, "The Plural of Vision Remains Vision," *Ohio Review*, 48 (1990): 101–118;

Revell, "Rose as Decoy, Beauty as Use," *Ohio Review*, 53 (1995): 150–163;

Susan Schultz, "Houses of Poetry after Ashbery: The Poetry of Ann Lauterbach and Donald Revell," *Virginia Quarterly Review*, 67 (Spring 1991): 295–309;

Schultz, "Visions of Silence in Poems of Ann Lauterbach and Charles Bernstein," *Talisman*, 13 (Fall 1994/Winter 1995): 163–177;

Stephen Yenser, "Wild Plots," *Partisan Review*, 61 (Spring 1994): 350–355.

Jackson Mac Low
(12 September 1922 –)

Bruce Campbell
University of California, Riverside

BOOKS: *The Twin Plays: Port-au-Prince & Adams County Illinois* (New York: Mac Low & Bloedow, 1963, 30 mimeographed copies; second edition, New York: Something Else Press, 1966);

The Pronouns—A Collection of 40 Dances—For the Dancers (New York: Mac Low & Judson Dance Workshop, 1964; revised edition, London: Tetrad Press, 1971; revised again, Barrytown, N.Y.: Station Hill Press, 1979);

August Light Poems (New York: Caterpillar Books, 1967);

Verdurous Sanguinaria (Baton Rouge, La.: Southern University Press, 1967);

22 Light Poems (Los Angeles: Black Sparrow Press, 1968);

23rd Light Poem: For Larry Eigner (London: Tetrad Press, 1969);

Stanzas for Iris Lezak (Barton, Vt.: Something Else Press, 1972);

Four Trains (Providence, R.I.: Burning Deck, 1974);

36th Light Poem: In Memoriam Buster Keaton (London: Permanent Press, 1975);

21 Matched Asymmetries: The 10 Bluebird Asymmetries, the 6 Asymmetries for Dr. Howard Levy, & the 5 Young Turtle Asymmetries (London: Aloes Books, 1978);

54th Light Poem: For Ian Tyson (Milwaukee, Wis.: Membrane Press, 1978);

A Dozen Douzains for Eve Rosenthal (Toronto: Gronk Books, 1978);

Phone: A Poem & 10 Variations (New York: Printed Editions / Amsterdam: Kontexts, 1979);

Antic Quatrains (Minneapolis: Bookslinger, 1980);

Asymmetries 1–260: The First Section of a Series of 501 Performance Poems (New York: Printed Editions, 1980);

"Is That Wool Hat My Hat?" (Milwaukee, Wis.: Membrane Press, 1982);

From Pearl Harbor Day to FDR's Birthday (7 December 1981–30 January 1982) (College Park, Md.: Sun & Moon Press, 1982; corrected edition, Los Angeles: Sun & Moon Press, 1995);

Bloomsday (Barrytown, N.Y.: Station Hill Press, 1984);

French Sonnets (Tucson, Ariz.: Black Mesa Press, 1984; revised edition, Milwaukee, Wis.: Membrane Press, 1989);

Eight Drawing-Asymmetries [boxed serigraphs] (Verona: Francesco Conz, 1985);

The Virginia Woolf Poems (Providence, R.I.: Burning Deck, 1985);

Representative Works: 1938–1985 (New York: Roof Books, 1986);

Words nd Ends from Ez (Bolinas, Cal.: Avenue B, 1989);

Twenties: 100 Poems: 24 February 1989–3 June 1990 (New York: Roof Books, 1991);

Pieces o' Six: 33 Poems in Prose (Los Angeles: Sun & Moon Press, 1992);

42 Merzgedichte In Memoriam Kurt Schwitters (Barrytown, N.Y.: Station Hill, 1994);

Barnesbook: Four Poems Derived from Sentences by Djuna Barnes (Los Angeles: Sun & Moon Press, 1995).

PLAY PRODUCTIONS: *The Marrying Maiden: a play of changes,* New York, The Living Theater, 1960–1961;

Verdurous Sanguinaria, New York, Yoko Ono's Studio, 1961; New York, Ag Gallery, 1961; Baton Rouge, Southern University, 1967;

The Twin Plays: Port-au-Prince & Adams County Illinois, New York, Hardware Poets Theatre, 1963; University of Exeter, England, 1968;

Questions & Answers . . . A Topical Play, New York, Hardware Poets Theatre, 1963.

OTHER: "Statement" and "Some Remarks to the Dancers," in *The Poetics of the New American Poetry,* edited by Donald Allen and Warren Tallman (New York: Grove, 1973), pp. 384–385, 385–391;

"Short Statement in 'Elitism' after Reading Kathy's Piece on Me," *Vort 8* (1975): 51;

"The Poetics of Chance & the Politics of Simultaneous Spontaneity, or the Sacred Heart of Jesus (Revised & Abridged)," in *Talking Poetics from the Naropa Institute: Annals of the Jack Kerouac School of Disembodied Poetics,* volume 1, edited by Anne

Jackson Mac Low on the roof of his New York apartment building, 1997 (photograph by Anne Tardos)

Waldman and Marilyn Webb (Boulder, Colo. & London: Shambala, 1978);

"Something about the Writings of John Cage," in *Writings about John Cage,* edited by Richard Kostelanetz (Ann Arbor: University of Michigan Press, 1993), pp. 283–296; revised and expanded as "The Writings of John Cage up to the Late 1980s," in *Here Comes Everybody,* edited by David Bernstein (Chicago: University of Chicago Press, forthcoming, 1999).

No American poet of this time has been more exemplary in extending the range of the forms of poetry than Jackson Mac Low. He has done this partly through the use of "nonintentional procedures," that is, systematic chance operations and three types of deterministic procedures: "translation" of musical notations into words and vice versa (from 1955 on), "acrostic read-through text-selection" (mostly 1960–1963), and "diastic reading-through text-selection" (from 1963 on—seldom in the 1990s). Nothing stands as a greater rebuke to ego-hugging poetry than the quiet work of Mac Low. However, this fact not only has but continues to make Mac Low a limited case for a certain kind of literary sensibility. As Jerome Rothenberg has pointed out, the resistance many poets feel toward Mac Low's work is itself a sign that something important is happening there. Mac Low has been extraordinarily productive. His activities have extended far beyond poetry: he is a composer,

visual artist, and multimedia performance artist; he has written essays, radio works, and plays. The volume and variety of his poetry alone is staggering—all the more so if the wealth of unpublished material is included.

Born in Chicago 12 September 1922, Jackson Mac Low studied music from the age of four and began composing music and poetry at the age of fifteen. From 1939 to 1943 Mac Low studied philosophy, poetics, and literature at the University of Chicago. Though he had been doing graduate-level work in philosophy and structural criticism at the university, he left with only the Associate of Arts degree awarded to students who completed the "Two-Year College," which did not help him get jobs. In 1943 he moved to New York, where he has continued to reside ever since. In 1954 Mac Low wrote the music for the Living Theatre's production of W. H. Auden's *Age of Anxiety* (1947). He worked "intermittently as a factory or office worker, tutor, parents' helper, music teacher, or messenger—all for minuscule pay," as he says in the introduction to *Representative Works: 1938–1985* (1986). He also coedited a pacifist anarchist newspaper and a pacifist magazine. At thirty-three he found the conditions of his life unsatisfying. Changes were in store, both for his writing and for his life.

In 1955 Mac Low went back to college to get a useful degree, studying classical languages at Brooklyn College and emerging in 1958 with an A.B. degree, cum laude, in Greek. Receiving his degree led to a series of reference-book editorial jobs in publishing. Later he taught at New York University for seven years. In February 1962 Mac Low married the painter Iris Lezak (dedicatee of his 1972 *Stanzas for Iris Lezak*). In March 1963 a son, Mordecai-Mark, was born; and in February 1966 a daughter, Clarinda. Mac Low and Lezak were divorced in 1978, and in 1990 he married the visual artist, poet, composer, and multimedia performance artist Anne Tardos. In 1963 Mac Low was copublisher with La Monte Young (Young was the sole editor) of *An Anthology of Chance Operations* (1963), designed by George Maciunas. *An Anthology* was a major force in the development of the art movement Fluxus. Through his involvement with Fluxus, Mac Low was able to have his work performed for the first time in Europe in 1962–1963.

Beginning with "5 biblical poems" (written December 1954 to January 1955) Mac Low has employed chance operations and deterministic nonintentional procedures. Most of the poems he wrote before 1954 bear little resemblance to the poems he wrote after 1954. Although *Representative Works* covers forty-seven years according to its title, as "a consequence of the book's bulk," Mac Low said in a note in June 1995, only twelve pages are taken up with work from the first sixteen years, and only one was written in Illinois. As a consequence Mac Low is at some pains in his introduction to support his early work: "I can imagine a fairly substantial *Selected Earlier Works*." But more than a decade after he published these words, there is still no such book. Indeed, nothing in Mac Low's body of works is rarer than early work. While Mac Low has been able to publish rather prolifically over the last decade or so, that work, with few exceptions, has been recent. This means that there are still significant gaps in his published work. Consequently, a rather skewed picture of Mac Low may emerge (although Joel Kuszaí has begun an investigation of Mac Low's early works with a view to their book publication).

Given the change in his poetry, which Mac Low himself draws attention to, and the difficulty of acquiring his early work, a reader might assume Mac Low is a more conventional poet than he has been. The earliest poem in *Representative Works,* "H U N G E R ST r i kE wh A t d o e S lifemean," rings changes on the sounds of words; "water," for example, becomes "whater" (as in "whater you thinking about?"). The visual element of the poem cannot be ignored, but sound drives the poem. "H U N G E R ST r i kE" is doubly "sui generis," as Mac Low categorizes it. Not only is it unique or atypical—this is Mac Low's meaning—but, given the typewriterly nature of the transcript, it is also a nonrepeatable work. As such, "H U N G E R ST r i kE" looks forward to Mac Low's later work, both as a work of sound environ-

ment and as an event, which, by definition, is unique. Still, space limitations enforce choices, and the choices made affect the reader's understanding of Mac Low. It is the Mac Low after 1954 who must interest the reader, if for no other reason than that is the Mac Low he has.

Mac Low himself seems a little curious about the changes. He reports himself to have been skeptical about "chance methods" when he first learned of their use in musical composition by John Cage, Earle Brown, and Christian Wolff—rather ironically so, given Jerome Rothenberg's assessment in the preface to *Representative Works* that "Mac Low stands with John Cage as one of the two major artists bringing systematic chance operations into poetic & musical practice since the Second World War." There were influences, Mac Low notes—Zen Buddhism and the "post 1950 chance-operational and indeterminate" music of John Cage, to cite but two of the more important. Yet these influences quickly give way in Mac Low's accounting of the role of performance. "Why did I begin to view *performance* as central and texts as primarily notations for performance (if only by a silent reader)?" Mac Low does not offer an answer, but this central role of performance is a key difficulty in trying to consider Mac Low only as a writer. For example, it is questionable whether the poems in *21 Matched Asymmetries: The 10 Bluebird Asymmetries, the 6 Asymmetries for Dr. Howard Levy, & the 5 Young Turtle Asymmetries* (1978) are nearly as effective in print as in performance. (In this they may be similar to Rothenberg's "Navaho Songs," which seem dry and prickly on the page but are mesmerizing in performance.) For the most part Mac Low's activities do not seem directed toward the book (at least as understood and codified by Western traditions). In this respect, at least, he is a post-Mallarméan writer, though the French poet Stéphane Mallarmé "has been a continuing influence and inspiration!"

The book, conceived as score (even if just for the silent reader), cannot be considered a final product. Perhaps this attitude is responsible for Mac Low's reader-oriented view of writing. And this perception may account, more than any other, for the generosity with which he has received the Language writers and they him. Indeed, by date of birth Mac Low belongs to that company of poets associated with the New American Poetry, although many of that company have actually been hostile to the Language writers. In Ron Silliman's judgment Mac Low is "the first American poet to throw over the so-called Problem of the Subject, showing it to be a mere sum of the writing."

Two points may be drawn from the pivotal "5 biblical poems." First, Mac Low uses the "event" as a unit of measure; "event" refers here to "single words or silences." Still, "event" is a reminder that Mac Low

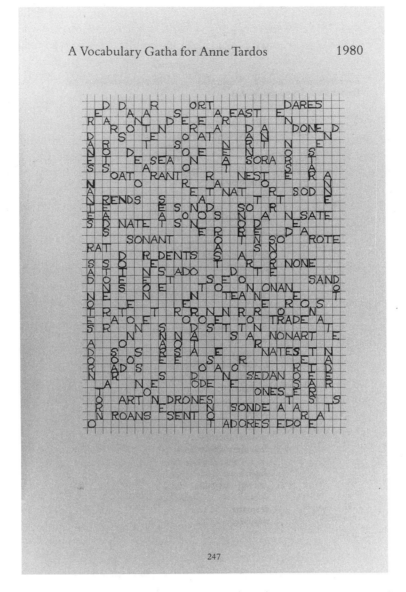

A Vocabulary Gatha for Anne Tardos — 1980

247

A performance poem in Representative Works: 1938-1985 *(1986) Each of one or more perfomers moves freely from any square to any other square, saying or singing letter names, phonemes, syllables, words and/or work groups, or playing their "letter-to-pitch-class" musical equivalents: A=any A natural, D=any D natural, E= any E natural, N= any C natural, O=any G flat or F sharp, R=any A flat or G sharp, S=any E flat or D sharp, and T= any B natural. (copyright © 1984 by Jackson Mac Low; by permission of the author)*

is a poet who received his first significant acclaim in the 1960s. Second, the systematic chance poem comes into the world defended by its own protocols (that is, prefatory material describing the methods employed in composition and the methods to be employed in reading/performing). This is one index that the poem is not written "directly" (as Mac Low later phrases it). Instead the poem is constructed through operations performed upon a source text—in this case, the Hebrew Scriptures. The effect may resemble that of the avant-garde freeing of words, but with a reservation. The protocols bind the procedure to a discipline. As the poet accepts a discipline, so must the reader. At the same time, there is often room in Mac Low for personal variation. Thus, in "And/___/ /___/ / /___/ / /___/statutes, | you: unto /___/ /___/with/___/ /___/ | /___/twenty sanctified ox," each box represents a silence "equal in duration to any word the reader chooses." Variable or not, the silence involves the questions, which most of Mac Low's work makes explicit, of attention and the means to which attention is put. Mac Low, then, creates a work in which the reader must exercise his attention—"attention delight" as he puts it in "Night Walk." To this extent Mac Low cannot be dealt with by reading into the language he employs. The reader must always be concerned as well with the poet's stance—his attitude toward the work as well as toward reality. One might even say that to this extent Mac Low is the John Milton of his generation. He shows that one cannot read the poetry without being mindful of the poet's beliefs, for his stance toward language is his stance toward the world.

Perhaps it is not by accident then that Mac Low's first successes occurred within the field of performance (through performance poetry or through plays). *The Marrying Maiden: a play of changes* (text composed in the summer of 1958; delivery regulations completed, summer 1959) was performed by the Living Theatre in 1960–1961, with music by John Cage. (Though not listed in the poet's bibliographies, a photocopy of the play, as well as a list of the accompanying action pack, "originally comprising about 1400 playing cards" with a series of commands, is available from the poet, thus making it a kind of unofficial publication). The typescript bears a dedication omitted in *Representative Works,* "For Alexandra Hontchar." "The Marrying Maiden" was composed strictly by chance operations involving the *I Ching* (or *Book of Changes,* an ancient Chinese text of Confucianism) and a random digit table. Indeed, "the marrying maiden" is the name of one of the hexagrams. In terms of measure it follows the "eventative verse" of the "5 biblical poems." There are many lines in the text that are either arresting or informative, though their grammar and syntax is hardly conventional. The "image The Taming Power of The Small" may be read as criticism of the then-current valorization of the image. However, this should not be taken to mean that Mac Low (or chance) eschews images for a "narrow street thru a whole day." But chance does unsettle any notion of gesture intrinsic in the action. "The actions in the Living Theatre production were determined by the director's (Judith Malina's) scenario interrupted by 'action cards' given to actors at random intervals."

On 29 February 1960 Mac Low (in the midst of writing "Night Walk") began the "Friendship Poems" (both works "for VBW"). In these he reached a directness hitherto absent in *Representative Works.* The poet knew how unusual these were: "I have started to write poems that say things to people." But the greater surprise is the revitalization the poet felt, for chance "has opened my life now again / Again again again beautiful life opening up and blossoming when it seems to have died to the roots." The secret, if you will, is in the opening up, or being open to the possibilities; chance is finally "a simple turning toward."

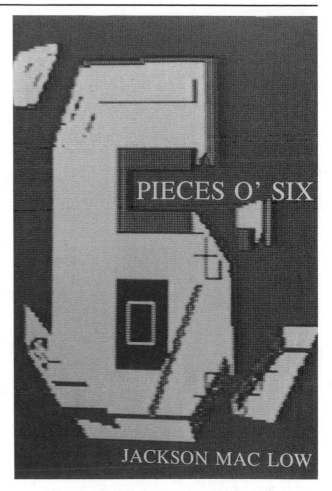

Cover for Mac Low's 1992 collection, including poems he calls "spontaneous" or "intuitive"

From the middle of May to early October 1960 Mac Low composed a work that extends to nearly four hundred published pages (more than four hundred with the afterword), *Stanzas for Iris Lezak* (1972). Published eleven years later by Something Else Press (as one of their last titles), the work has gained a notoriety, not to say infamy, among certain readers—not only on account of its size but also because of its resistance to casual reading, perhaps even to readings of intent. The poet Michael Palmer in the audience-response portion after a talk by Lyn Hejinian once called it "claustrophobic." More positively conceived, the stanzas seem designed to thwart the reader's ego to reach "the is of non-ego."

Mac Low uses a variety of source texts and methods, religious texts, scientific texts, and newspapers—in short, whatever he is reading. Indeed, he has said that the most "personal" element of the work (aside from its dedications) is the choice of material. The religious—or meditative—texts render words and phrases which help provide a rationale for the procedure; the newspapers channel information concerning life led in New York in 1960 and elsewhere. Yet, despite the variety, the effect on most readers is one of sameness. Doubtless this results, at least in part, from the foregrounding structure of the work (and backgrounding content) and the reader's training, which equates meaning with content. "Principle sense is conjugation hearsay." To foreground structure in the way that Mac Low's works (particularly those of the 1960s) do is to nudge the reader into attending to aspects of a work he generally ignores. Still, this sameness is but the frequency employed to tune in to the various spectra of word life. (Charles Bernstein, after all, in *Content's Dream* has termed Mac Low a "natural historian of language.") Yet there *is* content in Mac Low's work. The words keep their normal reference, although placed in new contexts, the references at times shoulder each other. Attention is strained, for some of the passages make sense and some do not. Those reading for content are constantly filtering out what does not fit. There is an irony here. While systematic nonintentional procedures do not prevent readings of content, they do align content-reading with the reading of a Ouija board. The irony is doubled, for nonintentional text generation is also aligned with divinatory readings (which is one of the uses of the *I Ching*). This point is perhaps where the fetish of chance becomes most suspect, as Steve McCaffery has noted in an interview with Andrew Payne printed in *North of Intention: Critical Writings 1973–1986* (1986). Still, messages do get through. "Effects Crude state the and Crude is effects state"—the reflexivity proffers a kind of "what you see is what you get" economy, although the condensation of the line allows for multiple readings. Still, the state (and statement) of "effects" is "crude" because, in the interest of being definitive (that is, "the"), the principle of cause and effect rarely considers the reifying cycle in which the statement affects the state, and so on. *Stanzas for Iris Lezak,* then, aims at something "Pure as transferences: half-syllable / Open form."

Directly after *Stanzas for Iris Lezak,* Mac Low composed a group of performance poems, *Asymmetries 1–501,* in 1960–1961. Thus, in a little less than a year Mac Low produced something like nine hundred pages. (However, although the first 160 were published in 1980 as *Asymmetries 1–260: The First Section of a Series of 501 Performance Poems,* the last half have never been published as a single book, although 121–127 appear in *Representative Works* and in *An Anthology* (1963), edited by La Monte Young. Without Dick Higgins, founder of Something Else Press and Printed Editions, perhaps neither *Stanzas for Iris Lezak* nor part of the asymmetries would have been published.) In formal terms the asymmetries are directly opposed to the preceding work, since they are asymmetrical while the stanzas were symmetrical. They are also more insistently performing texts—hence the use of "performance poems" in the subtitle. The asymmetries are a form of "lip-Zen" in which "absence became sensible." It is easy to forget how long it has been since they were composed; "nerve Eisenhower" was no historical reference. The asymmetries are a kind of "reason event" in which "need employ enclosure direction." But the reason of the asymmetries is hardly that of logic or science. They are instead a kind of readjustment necessitated by "educational dislocation" (as "Asymmetry #354" expresses it). They provide examples of "melted / presence; Thru sense / transmigration realization / . . . . / regard existence glad accidentally / read   discover." Reading is important in this passage, even if the reading is a form of divination.

Written January through February 1961 by means of chance operations involving twenty-six dictionaries, *Verdurous Sanguinaria* (1967) was premiered that same year at Mac Low's first concert of poetry, plays, and music in Yoko Ono's loft in a series organized by La Monte Young. It later became Mac Low's fourth book and the first published by a university press (to date, the only one). Although there are six acts in the play (by mistake only five were printed in the Southern University Press edition; a correct edition will appear in 1999 published by Sun and Moon Press), it is based on only twenty-six words, names, and two-word phrases. The limited vocabulary introduces severe restrictions. In January 1961 Mac Low composed a plan, titled "Tree* Movie," in which a stationary camera was to film a tree for an extensive period of time. (The "*" in the title serves as a reminder that other things can be the subject of the film in place of the "tree.") The plan (included in *Representative Works*) shows a different aspect of the Mac Low corpus; it serves to remind readers how limited, in the case of Mac Low, the focus on poetry is. "Tree* Movie" led directly to Andy Warhol's static movies, though "Warhol never acknowledged this," according to Mac Low and several movie critics.

In 1966 Mac Low's first printed book (excluding mimeo productions) appeared: *The Twin Plays: Port-au-Prince & Adams County Illinois* from Something Else Press in their Great Bear pamphlet series. Many of the Great Bear pamphlets concern "happenings"; the seventh is, in fact, a selection of scenarios by Allan Kaprow, the inventor of the Happening concept. Begun 21 March 1962 and completed shortly thereafter, the two plays are identical in structure. However, the language differs. In "Port-au-Prince" Mac Low has drawn words by chance operations from a list he made of partial anagrams of the title; in "Adams County Illinois" he has drawn by chance operations folk sayings from *Folk-Lore from Adams County Illinois* written by Harry Middleton Hyatt and published in 1935, a book given to Mac Low by writer Spencer Holst. Identical structure can, in such circumstances, lead to rather different results.

On 4 November 1961 Mac Low composed his "Word Event for George Brecht." In this scenario someone says a word and then analyzes it into successive phonemes and then into phonemes representable by its successive individual letters. Then "he orders phonemes from both series in random orders." "A later version, 'Word Event(s) for Bici Forbes,' frees the performer greatly and is based on actual performance practices." It is, Mac Low writes in a footnote added seven years after the composition, the third step that is the heart of the event. The "Word Event," therefore, is about permutations and "performers making spontaneous choices" as much as it is about an event. Mac Low's early interest in the use of computers for generating poetry is, therefore, not surprising. (In 1969 he participated in the Art and Technology Program of the Los Angeles County Museum of Art: with the aid of a programmable film reader he composed the "PFR-3 Poems." This interest has only strengthened in the last decade.) Indeed, *42 Merzgedichte In Memoriam Kurt Schwitters* (1994) is a series of poems comprising words, phrases, and sentences by and about Schwitters. The first Merzegedicht—originally no. 32 of *Pieces o' Six: 33 Poems in Prose* (1992)—includes materials drawn by "impulse-chance" from source texts, together with some statements by the poet. The second through thirtieth comprise materials drawn by computer-aided chance operations from the first poem as well as other words and phrases from the sources. In the last twelve, materials from some of the earlier ones were recombined and transformed by computer programs.

Mac Low's interest in event undergoes a new expression in *The Pronouns—A Collection of 40 Dances—For the Dancers*. Its initial appearance is as a self-produced mimeograph in 1964. It has been republished twice, each time with revisions, once in Great Britain in 1971 and again by Station Hill Press in 1979. *The Pronouns* can be seen as a development of the "action pack" for *The Marrying Maiden* by way of a performance card pack, "Nuclei for Simone Forti" (the dedicatee is a very innovative and influential dancer, choreographer, and improviser). Typed on each card are single words drawn by chance operations from the BASIC English Word List and action phrases from a separate pack made up of words similarly drawn from the BASIC list. After Forti had improvised around some of the "Nuclei" cards in 1961, the dancer-choreographer Trisha Brown did so in 1963 and borrowed the pack for teaching purposes in California. The dancer Fred Herko, who had seen Brown's performances, asked to

Cover for Mac Low's 1996 book, four poems derived from four sentences by Djuna Barnes

use the pack before Brown returned it to Mac Low, so the poet wrote a "He" poem for Herko by a deterministic (non-chance) procedure applied to the pack of action phrases that had "fed into" "Nuclei." Then he wrote a "She" poem for Forti, Brown, and other women dancers and subsequently thirty-eight other poems, each centered on another pronoun or pronounlike noun. Written February–March 1964, the forty dance-instruction poems have frequently been performed and published in magazines and in anthologies as well as in their three editions. Lanny Harrison and other performers have improvised around "Nuclei" cards in the 1980s and 1990s.

The Pronouns is a book of poems that are also scores for actions. Alliances of poetry and painting are more familiar than those of poetry and dance. Still, Michael Palmer has had an association with the Martha Jenkins Dance Company of San Francisco, and the poet and critic Bruce Andrews has collaborated on scores for movement with dancer-choreographer Sally Silvers. And yet there are differences between a score for action and a score for speech. Consequently, the words read might not be precisely what is seen, even though one method allows a dancer or another person to read the words while a dance is performed. *The Pronouns* is an inaugural text, for here word is made event. There is, thus, a ritual element which corresponds well to the poetic milieu created by the tribal anthologies of Rothenberg, in particular his *Technicians of the Sacred* (1968) and *Shaking the Pumpkin* (1972), although, as with Rothenberg, this is ritual fed through the filters of an historical avant-garde. In other words, even here Mac Low employs nonintentional methods: "I let the title letters 'select' the successive actions from the sets of one to five actions as they showed up. For example, in the '37th Dance–Banding,' the 'B' selected 'being flies,' the 'A,' 'having examples, the 'N,' 'doing something consciously," the 'D,' 'saying things about making gardens,' &c." The effect of using pronouns is to "take hold of those old workhorses of our language and, in a play with living nouns and verbs, make them come alive and enter a triumphant dance for all dancers," as Rothenberg explains. *The Pronouns* is still perhaps Mac Low's most widely appreciated work, parts of which often have been anthologized.

Beginning in June 1962 Mac Low began a series of poems he has continued over the years. Named Light Poems, the first twenty-two were published in 1968 by Black Sparrow Press, well-known for their publications of the works of New American Poets. *22 Light Poems* (1968) employs a variety of methods, usually incorporating chance elements with moments of extreme directness. That each poem is written for someone (as recipient) indicates the communal nature of Mac Low's work. Those who do not share this community often castigate such gestures as being intended simply for friends. Rather than being seen as exclusive, however, these gestures should be seen as a part of the sustaining dialogue of any artistic community. For the Light Poems, as with other works by Mac Low–particularly the performance scores he calls "Vocabularies"–the name of the recipient affects the choice of language. "The light names were drawn from a chart; materials between them were freely written." Using a chart of the light names, Mac Low often selects light names based on the letters of the recipient's name. The name is thereby encoded in the poem.

It may well be that Mac Low's most personal work, the "Odes for Iris," written during the breakup of his first marriage, from July 1970 to November 1971, is one of his least-known works. The lack of availability is a simple reason for this. The poems have never appeared in book form. Six odes appear in *Representative Works,* and several have been published in magazines. These are likely to be the most that readers have seen of them. (Rothenberg writes that, in odes not included in *Representative Works,* Mac Low "out-confesses the 'confessionals.'") The formal nature of the odes (strict syllabic verse) is likely to be overlooked in view of the rather naked emotions. This work presents, then, the same reading lesson as the *Stanzas for Iris Lezak* (written ten years earlier), though from the opposite spectrum. Here the content may well overshadow the reader's response to the structure. Even if the lesson is the same, the experience is not. To take the two Iris books together is to glimpse the range Mac Low has achieved.

Mac Low then is a formal poet: his emphasis is on form. One effect of his formalism can be measured by his *Representative Works:* his poems unallied to the larger projects tend to get overshadowed. Given the emphasis outside *Representative Works* on the larger projects, Mac Low's more occasional works tend to be rather fugitive. *Representative Works* represents most of the forms he has engaged in. The use of "representative" in the title allows him to accomplish two things: it avoids the deleterious connotations of a "selected poems," and it foregrounds the formal nature of his writing. Both are accomplished because the examples represent forms or genres rather than types or content. Some examples represent two or more forms or genres at once: for example, the fifth of "5 biblical poems" is also both "the 1st biblical play" and Mac Low's first "simultaneity" (in this case, three voices speak three poems simultaneously), and *The 54th Light Poem for Ian Tyson* is at once both a Light Poem and a Gatha. The Gathas are a series of performance poems written on graph paper. Each square is either blank (and that may be interpreted as silence) or filled with a letter. The letters spell words. At the beginning of the series (1961) the words are mantras. In 1973, however, Mac Low began to use nonmantric English words, beginning with The Black Tarantula Crossword Gathas, drawn from an extensive series of Kathy Acker's *The Childlike Life of the Black Tarantula* (1975).

A separate series (produced as single sheets) of Vocabularies, beginning in 1968 with *A Vocabulary for Carl Fernbach-Flarsheim* (a conceptual painter and sculptor), has a more insistently visual quality, most of them beginning as drawings. These too are performance texts. Each performer chooses and speaks or sings any of the words in any desired order and/or "translates" his letters into musical tones on an instrument (some Vocabularies include musical staves). As with the Gathas, there is no predetermined starting point or direction. The *Vocabulary for Peter Innisfree Moore* (February 1974–July 1975) is an excellent example of how one can become "thrown" into the work. This drawing/score pulses on the page, a labyrinth of language; varying sizes of lettering tip in various directions. (The fact that it is hand-lettered is important, as well.) But perhaps the most seminal of the Vocabularies is the *Vocabulary for Annie Brigitte Gilles Tardos,* a project commissioned by the Institute for Art and Urban Resources, Inc., "for exhibition as the 'Poetry Room' of 'Sound at P.S. 1,'" in Long Island from September 30 to November 1979.

Each Vocabulary is an array of as many partial anagrams as Mac Low could find and fit onto a single sheet of drawing paper or typing paper. Other poems may be made from words in each Vocabulary. (For instance, "Antic Quatrains" is generated by chance operations from the *Vocabulary for Annie Tardos.*) The poem exists in a larger context, the result of which is to encourage the reader to open his or her eyes and ears. Indeed, the most general discipline advocated by Mac Low has always been to "listen & relate." First formulated in relation to the poet's simultaneities (performance works in which two or more people speak, sing, and/or play instruments simultaneously), "listen & relate" has important ethical connotations for a poet who has no wish to be a dictator. But Mac Low doesn't wish simply to discipline the reader (or performer), nor should the discipline be seen as the goal. Instead Mac Low wants to "empower" the reader, as he phrases it in the preface to *Twenties: 100 Poems: 24 February 1989–3 June 1990* (1991). The reader is not someone who simply gazes upon the work or arrives at a prefabricated meaning; the reader helps to make the meaning. But this also means there can be no definitive reading (or performance) of a Mac Low work.

That the *Vocabulary for Annie Tardos*—the subject of which is a filmmaker, poet, composer, performance artist, and visual artist—should be so generative is hardly surprising. Its dedicatee (whose name yields all the letters in it) is Mac Low's present wife and most frequent collaborator in making and realizing performance works. She is also the dedicatee of the "58th Light Poem," written in 1979, eleven years before their marriage, and published in *Representative Works*), which begins "I know when I've fallen in love I start to write love songs / Love's actinism turns nineteens to words & thoughts in love songs / as your 'A' & the date made 'actinism' enter this love song." In his introduction to *Representative Works* Mac Low expresses sympathy for his 1950s self. If he had undergone changes in the mid 1950s (which, poetically, led him into systematic nonintentional procedures), by 1981 he was undergoing changes once again. One of the first indications of such a change in his writing is his first publication with Douglas Messerli's Sun and Moon Press (at that point still located in College Park, Maryland, but soon to move to the West Coast): *From Pearl Harbor Day to FDR's Birthday (7 December 1981–30 January 1982),* published in 1982. In this work the writing is usually "direct," although his "directness" is not the directness of the *Odes for Iris* nor that of most other poets. It connotes, instead, a text written without the mediation of source texts or systematic procedures—as opposed to, for example, the *Words nd Ends from Ez* (1989), a diastic reading through Ezra Pound's *Cantos* that yields a flux of letters, words, and syllables. Mac Low calls most of the works in *Bloomsday* (1984) and *Pieces o' Six, Twenties,* and *154 Forties*—Mac Low's latest project—"intuitive" or "spontaneous," but a few in *Bloomsday* and *Pieces o' Six* were composed by nonintentional procedures.

There are three facts, finally, to note about Mac Low. Few poets have been as varied and prolific throughout their careers. The lacunae in his body of works interfere with the reader's attempt to get an adequate sense of his achievement. And Mac Low may well be the first systems poet. Ron Silliman has observed, "Mac Low was more or less alone in the 1950s in his explorations of poetic form as system (to my mind a far more important implication of his work than his use of chance operations, which are merely one type of system)." In the face of immense difficulties, Mac Low has persevered to create a resource in American poetry. He will not be a guiding light for all, of course, but many writers will find that they quite simply could not do the work they do without the example set by Jackson Mac Low.

Interviews:

Manuchehr Sassoonian and Layle Silbert, "Craft Interview with Jackson Mac Low," *The Craft of Poetry,* edited by William Packard (Garden City, N.Y.: Doubleday, 1974), pp. 224–263;

Barry Alpert, "Jackson Mac Low, An Interview conducted by Barry Alpert, The Bronx, New York, April 6, 1974 (revised January–February 1975 by JML)," *Vort* 8 (1975): 3–33;

Gil Ott, "Dialog (with Gil Ott)," *Paper Air,* 2, no. 1 (1980): 18–29;

Kim Rosenfield, "Kim Rosenfield Interviews Jackson Mac Low," *Shiny,* nos. 7/8 (1992): 5–25;

Kevin Bezner, "Jackson Mac Low, Interviewed by Kevin Bezner," *New American Writing,* no. 11 (Summer/Fall 1993): 109–124;

Barrett Watten, "Poetic Vocabularies: A Conversation between Barrett Watten and Jackson Mac Low KPFA, Berkeley, CA 24 October 1985; edited and revised by Watten and Mac Low in 1992," *Aerial,* 8 (1995): 107–120;

Nicholas Zurbrugg, "Jackson Mac Low," in *Positively Postmodern: The Multi-Media Muse in America*

(Washington, D.C.: Maisonneuve Press, forthcoming).

References:

Charles Bernstein, "Jackson at Home," in his *Content's Dream: Essays 1975–1984* (Los Angeles: Sun & Moon Press, 1986);

John Cage, "Music and Particularly Silence in the Work of Jackson Mac Low," *Paper Air,* 2, no. 1 (1980): 36–39;

George Hartley, "'Listen' and 'Relate': Jackson Mac Low's Chance-Operational Poetry," *Sulfur,* no. 23 (Fall 1988): 189–203;

Charles O[ssian] Hartman, "Essay Ending with Six Reasons to Read Jackson Mac Low: *Representative Works: 1938–1985* and *The Virginia Woolf Poems,* [by] Jackson Mac Low" in *Prairie Schooner,* 62 (Spring 1988): 115–120;

Andrew Levy, "Introduction: Festschrift for Jackson Mac Low's 75th Birthday," in *Festschrift for Jackson Mac Low's 75th Birthday, Crayon* ([Fall] 1997);

Steve McCaffery, "Jackson Mac Low: Samsara in Lagado" in *North Dakota Quarterly,* 55 (Fall 1987): 185–201;

George Quasha, "A Concrete Dialog with Myself on, and for, Jackson Mac Low," *Paper Air,* 2, no. 1 (1980): 55–63;

Jerome Rothenberg, *Representative Works: 1938–1985* (New York: Roof Books, 1986);

Ron Silliman, "While Some Are Being Flies, Others Are Having Examples," *Paper Air,* 2, no. 1 (1980): 39–41;

Henry Taylor, "Jackson Mac Low: Gristlier Translations, Arcane Pronouns" in his *Compulsory Figures* (Baton Rouge, London: Louisiana State UP, 1992), pp. 245–266.

Papers:
The library of the University of California, San Diego, has archives of Mac Low's papers.

Eileen Myles
(9 December 1949 –)

Patrick F. Durgin
University of Iowa

BOOKS: *The Irony of the Leash* (New York: Jim Brodey
Books, 1978);

Polar Ode, by Myles and Anne Waldman (New York:
Dead Duke Books, 1979);

A Fresh Young Voice from the Plains (New York: Power
Mad Press, 1981);

Sappho's Boat (Los Angeles: Little Caesar Press, 1982);

Bread and Water (New York: Hanuman Books, 1987);

1969 (New York: Hanuman Books, 1989);

Not Me (New York: Semiotext(e), 1991);

Chelsea Girls (Santa Rosa, Cal.: Black Sparrow Press,
1994);

Maxfield Parrish: Early & New Poems (Santa Rosa, Cal.:
Black Sparrow Press, 1995);

School of Fish (Santa Rosa, Cal.: Black Sparrow Press,
1997).

PLAY PRODUCTIONS: *Joan of Arc, a Spiritual Entertainment,* by Myles, Barbara McKay, and Elinor
Naven, St. Marks Church, New York, 1979;

Patriarchy, a Play, by Myles, Naven, and Ann Rower,
St. Marks Church, 1980;

Our Town, Parts 1 & 2, by Myles and Tom Carey, New
York, Charas Studios, June 1982;

Feeling Blue, Parts 1, 2, & 3, New York, P.S. 122, June
1988;

Modern Art, New York, P.S. 122, May 1990;

Our Sor Juana, New York, Dixon Place, December
1994.

OTHER: *Ladies Museum: An Anthology of New Downtown
Women Poets,* edited by Myles with Susie Tim-
mons and Rochelle Kraut (New York, 1977);

Yuki Hartman & Michael Slater, eds., *Fresh Paint: An
Anthology of Younger New York Poets,* includes poems by Myles (New York: Ailanthus Press,
1977);

Dennis Cooper, ed., *Coming Attractions: An Anthology of
Poets in Their 20s,* includes poems by Myles (Los
Angeles: Little Caesar, 1981);

*Eileen Myles at Bard College, 1993 (photograph by
Dan Larkin)*

Andrei Codrescu, ed., *American Poetry since 1970: Up
Late,* includes poems by Myles (New York: Four
Walls, Eight Windows, 1987);

John Ashbery, ed., *The Best American Poetry, 1988,* includes poems by Myles (New York: Macmil-
lan/Collier, 1988);

Joan Larkin and Carl Morse, eds., *Gay and Lesbian Poetry in Our Time,* includes poems by Myles (New
York: St. Martin's Press, 1988);

Instant Classics: The Prose & Poetry Postcard Project, includes work by Myles (New York: Instant Classics, 1989);

Michael Klein, ed., *Poets for Life: Seventy-Six Poets Respond to AIDS,* includes poems by Myles (New York: Crown, 1989);

Anne Waldman, ed., *Out of This World: An Anthology of the St. Mark's Poetry Project, 1966–1991,* includes poems by Myles (New York: Crown Publishers, 1991);

Dennis Cooper, ed., *Discontents,* includes poems by Myles (New York: Amethyst, 1992);

Leslie Scalapino, ed., *Subliminal Time 0/4,* includes poems by Myles (Oakland: O Books, 1993);

Joan Nestle, ed., *Women on Women 2,* includes poetry by Myles (New York: Dutton, 1993);

Paul Hoover, ed., *Postmodern American Poetry,* includes poems by Myles (New York: Norton, 1994);

Miguel Algarin, Bob Holman, eds., *Aloud / Voices from the Nuyorican Poets Cafe,* includes poems by Myles (New York: Henry Holt, 1994);

Gerry Pearlberg, ed., *Classic Lesbian Love Poems,* includes poems by Myles (New York: St. Martin's Press, 1995);

The New Fuck You: Adventures in Lesbian Reading, edited by Myles with Liz Kotz (New York: Semiotext(e), 1995);

Clare Coss, ed., *The Arc of Love: An Anthology of Lesbian Love Poems,* includes poems by Myles (New York: Scribners, 1996);

Codrescu and Laura Rosenthal, eds., *American Poets Say Goodbye to the Twentieth Century,* includes poems by Myles (New York: Four Walls, Eight Windows, 1996).

SELECTED PERIODICAL PUBLICATIONS– UNCOLLECTED:

POETRY

"Sunshine," *American Poetry Review,* 25 (July 1996): 15;

"Infinity Mini," *Talisman: A Journal of Contemporary Poetry and Poetics,* no. 17 (Summer 1997): 57–59;

"April," *World,* no. 53 (Fall 1997): 6.

NONFICTION

"Mimeo Opus," *Poetry Project Newsletter,* 89 (March 1982);

"Nun's Tale / The Selling of Sor Juana," review of Octavio Paz's Sor Juana, *Village Voice Literary Supplement* (June 1989): 30–31;

"Eileen Myles for President," issue on Myles, includes facsimiles of campaign letters and poetry, *New Censorship,* 3 (September 1992);

"Jack Pierson at Tom Cugliana," *Art in America,* 80 (October 1992): 155;

"Perpetual Motion: What Makes Bob Perelman Run?," *Village Voice Literary Supplement* (November 1993): 31;

"Nicole Eisenman at Trial Baloon," *Art in America* (December 1993): 108–109;

"Giving Birth to Poetry," review of Debra Weinstein's *Rodent Angel, Nation,* 263 (28 October 1996): 56–58;

"Fear of Poetry," review of Muriel Rukeyser's *The Life of Poetry, Nation,* 264 (14 April 1997): 30–32.

Eileen Myles is one of the few openly lesbian American poets of her time to attract the interest of aestheticians as well as a general readership. Part of this rare accessibility is surely due to her having worked so successfully in multiple genres while always evincing a consistency of voice and clarity of purpose. Foremost of her achievements, however, is the stature of her work in poetry. Nurtured by the avant-garde and a firm grounding in diverse American traditions as exemplified by Walt Whitman, Wallace Stevens, Sylvia Plath, Allen Ginsberg, Frank O'Hara, and Language poetry, Myles has brought lesbian content and political activism to the so-called New York School poem and a thoroughly postmodern, if not somewhat confrontational, view to the problem of identity in twentieth-century American poetry. Such a varied poetic genealogy makes it difficult, or perhaps unnecessary, to place Myles's poetry into any one category; at the same time it serves as a testament to her important presence on the scene. Unflinchingly self-disclosing in an era marked by social alienation and information fetishism, Myles has managed to capture what is lost in the tally of raw data. She has played an integral role in the postindustrial and postmodern redefinition of public space in society and its arts by striving, and in many ways succeeding, by such means to bring a female persona into a predominately male public. She also has evinced an almost alchemical technical skill in blending the popular and the obscure, fusing progressive formal virtuosity with informal narrative strategies, and upholding moral responsiveness amid the treacherous contours of self-re-creation. In a review of Muriel Rukeyser's *The Life of Poetry* for *The Nation* (14 April 1997), Myles finds an analogue for what she sees as the poet's role in society: "Poetry's so tiny it's universal: A famous painter might be invited by *The New York Times* to give us a tour of the Met, to show us what he knows, but for poets there's no such building, or even bookstore. It's simply the world."

Myles in a performance at Ward-Nasse Gallery in New York City, 1976

Often but not exclusively underlining a female and/or lesbian presence, Myles's poetics interrogates the problematic authorial identity en masse. Thus to read even scarcely of her work in other genres inevitably will lead to a vision of her core concern, poetry. And there are many such inlets; Myles has written on literature and culture for the *Village Voice* and *The Nation* as well as on art criticism for *Art in America*. She has also written and produced dramatic productions, three books of fiction, and a column for *Paper* magazine. The scope of the periodicals in which Myles's work has appeared is vast: *A Gathering of the Tribes, Ploughshares, The New England Review, The Kenyon Review, The World, Nedge, The American Poetry Review, Out, BOMB, East Village Eye, Aerial, Lambda Book Report, Talisman, Avenue E, The Village Literary Supplement, Out There, New Directions, The Partisan Review, Koja,* and many others. Her poetry alone has been reviewed in such varied publications as *Ms., The New York Times, The Nation, Small Press Traffic, San Francisco Bay Guardian, Kenyon Review, Artforum, L.A. Weekly, Interview, Index, Out, The Village Voice, Harvard Gay & Lesbian Review,* and the *Los Angeles Times Book Review*. Myles also edited a poetry magazine, *dodgems,* from 1977 to 1979 and a book

with Liz Kotz, *The New Fuck You: Adventures in Lesbian Reading* (1995), which went on to win a Lambda Book Award. Since 1982 Myles has taught at the New School for Social Research, New York University, the California Institute of the Arts, Memphis College of Art, the Naropa Institute, Ossining Correctional Facility, the Rochester Institute of Technology, and others, in addition to conducting independent workshops. She has given performances and readings in Germany, Russia, and Iceland, as well as appearing across the United States, at the DIA Center for the Arts, the Museum of Modern Art, Rutgers University, the Detroit Institute of the Arts, Lesbapalooza, the Bearded Lady Cafe in San Francisco, Bard College, the Outwrite Conference, the Drawing Legion, Walker Art Center, Wesleyan University, Brown University, and elsewhere. She has received many grants, among them a CEC Arts Link grant, a Djerassi Foundation fellowship, and an NEA Inter-Arts grant. Over the last two decades Myles has been extremely active on the scene at the Poetry Project of St. Mark's Church, one of the main pressure points of the New York School of poetry of the 1960s to 1970s, eventually serving as artistic director from 1984 to 1986.

Myles and Andrei Voznesensk at the National Arts Club in 1978

Born to working-class parents—Terrence Myles, a mail carrier, and Genevieve Preston Myles Hannibal, a secretary—in Cambridge, Massachusetts, and educated in Catholic schools, Myles went on to take her bachelor's degree in 1971 from the University of Massachusetts (Boston). In 1974 she moved to New York and briefly attended graduate school at Queens College. But Myles finally left academia, not to return until her stature as a writer created a demand for her teaching, a demand she generously fulfilled. Giving her first reading at the seminal rock music club CBGB's on the lower east side of Manhattan, she then plunged into active participation with the Poetry Project of St. Mark's Church, where poets such as Ted Berrigan and Alice Notley made a great impact on her work and her notion of the contemporary poet's role in society. Myles sought immediate influences and contextualized the tenets of such avant-garde traditions with the influence of the first generation of the New York School resonating from decades past. Whether one conceives of the New York School as does John Bernard Myers in his *The Poets of the New York School* (1969), linking it to avant-garde, interdisciplinary traditions dating to pre-Surrealist-era Paris, or as Greg Masters does in his essay on the mid-1970s St. Marks scene, "Eileen Myles: An Intro" (*Talisman,* 17, Summer 1997)—"Its aesthetic was decidedly antiacademic with a focus on the daily personal response to ordinary events and an activist's call for engagement"—Myles soon brought a face to these conceptions.

In 1975 Myles attended a workshop conducted by Paul Violi where she was encouraged to curb any tendency toward a baldly confessional voice in her work, to foster instead a concern for and valorization of more formally innovative techniques. Through these, however, Myles maintained a focus on identity—not an abstract identity that would somehow arise through form but a poetic of identity as confrontation, or as stated in a letter, "proprioceptive": metabolism, sexuality, needs, and desires in tandem to the stuff of the world. Even the early poetry was not the unified, lording sort of voice, perhaps typical of much confessional-style poetry of its time. But Myles certainly gave form to the page as much as the woman coursing through the work, identified with and by real, gritty, or mundane contingencies.

In 1977 Myles wrote the poem that was to serve as the title of her first collection, *The Irony of the Leash* (1978), which she has stated was the first piece to incorporate disparate notions of formal aesthetics and identity poetics in a fashion that she deemed her own. "I am prey to the materials / of me," she writes, "combinations / create me into something / else, civilization's inventions . . . carry me around." Herein appears a sort of resignation to the self, yet presented (or represented) among the things of the world, poems included. What separates Myles's self-reflection from that in the confessional vein is that the reader inevitably senses that the denuding process is a foregone conclusion. A confession, strictly speaking, insinuates that readers are made privy to something which, in Myles's aesthetic, was always in the fore, assuming the nature of traditional wisdom. Her type of disclosure precludes the tension inherent in coming clean. "So," as Alice Notley writes in her essay for *Talisman*, "Eileen Myles in Performance" (Summer 1997), "there's always the possibility of the reader's reacting to this work as if it were a person to be loved or liked or disagreed with or found obnoxious."

One doesn't stop to question the tenancy of the author's identity, and Myles doesn't feel the need to posture for the sake of credibility. Instead, the audacity of her approach serves to reinforce the traits that bind the self by continually crossing those boundaries, basically inhabiting the public by means of poetic gestures. In "The Irony of the Leash" there emerges a virtual intergender or interspecies metamorphosis of the subject into the author, a technique that recurs in subsequent works by Myles in several genres. The dog in the poem comes to display loyalty, obstinance, masculinity, and life force, but it is first a reference point for identity. So Myles identifies with the animal without attaining to its every quality, qualities presumably easier to recognize, categorize, and enumerate than the human animal, stating that she must perpetrate something "as artificial and snide / and self-perpetuating" as writing or she "would be less than a dog." The proof of the narrator's tenancy is that she doubts it: "Intrinsically they have a grip / on things."

Between the publication of her first volume of poetry and the second, *A Fresh Young Voice from the Plains* (1981), Myles worked closely with other aspiring poets associated with the Poetry Project on, as Myles described in a letter to the author, "epic one-shot dramatic productions"; edited a poetry magazine, *dodgems;* and served as a personal assistant to New York School poet James Schuyler at the end of his life. These activities created a personal and artistic oasis from the raucous life—late nights, alcoholism, and drug use—of these years documented in her volume of autobiographical fiction, *Chelsea Girls* (1994). Some formal characteristics of her work at the time can be seen as arising from such valuable interaction with Schuyler, a poet whose own self-reflexive voice and anecdotal focus were influential on Myles, as was his intimate understanding of the work of his close friend the poet John Ashbery, from whom Myles has noted that she learned her line breaks. "They flicker," she wrote in a letter. She further summarizes his influence in her prose essay "The Lesbian Poet" in *School of Fish* (1997): "a style" evolved "that took his wavering into account." But Myles's particular wavering is from "I" to "I," combining conversational qualities, surprising shifts in rhetorical timbre, and mock-exalted personae as standard features of her work, indicative of postmodern avant-gardism as opposed to the typical confessional or identity poetics of that era. And as much as her lines are chopped into scrawny columns, the bits of sentences and, ostensibly, utterances which they represent function as a more typical Ashbery-esque line would. The streamlined text emphasizes the mimetic, conversational aspect as much as the abstract disjunctiveness of her later work.

In "Medium Poem" from *A Fresh Young Voice from the Plains* Myles's mastery of such elements allows her to trace a momentary conception of the rhetorical "I" from womb to afterlife, both of which she finds "dubious." Concluding that while such transcendental conceits may frame experience, she offers as an aside, "I'll tell you when I get there."

> I smoke a cigarette for Wednesdays
> when I am comfortable. And it is always
> Wednesday. And I am never
> sure. And I am always here.

Provocative as isolated units of perception, the lines are set off in such a way as to suggest a wavering in the significance of the sentences as well as an alchemical skewing of the personae. As Myles's lines became thinner in subsequent works, this same sort

Myles in 1984, when she was director of the St. Mark's Poetry Project in New York City

of ideational tension is exploited in even more masterly fashion.

In readings of this 1977 period Myles came out as a lesbian, in a performance context that has been seen, perhaps too simplistically, as the defining purpose behind her poetics. Usurping the claim of literary avant-gardism on the female body as "the battle ground of its freedom," she stated in a letter, "I'm just being myself, a very American tradition." In the interest of her poetics Myles discounts those codes which would require the omission of fundamental truths. But it was not until the 1982 collection, *Sappho's Boat,* that patently lesbian content entered into a collection. In "Romantic Pain" Myles narrates a night in New York from lesbian bar to lesbian bar, to the New York Ferry, to a scene in a women's restroom where she suddenly hovers for a moment over the scene: "I can see us from overhead / and call the configuration 'Feminism.'" She claims her masculine predecessor and iterates the book's theme: "I feel / like Hart Crane. The wind smacks

my / hair, washes it over my cheeks & / I wish I could cry. / The boat feels right this time."

The period from 1980 to 1985 was one in which Myles practiced her craft while accustoming herself to the multifarious tasks inherent to the poet of "the world." Writing, publishing, performing, and recording her poetry in many magazines and through various venues across the nation, she collected the material for her next volume of poetry, *Not Me* (1991). In 1983 she underwent more true-to-life metamorphoses, beginning her recovery from alcoholism and in 1984 beginning a two-year position as the artistic director of the Poetry Project. Reading around the country and meeting the literary artists and performers from all over the world that populated the East Village area of New York, she found even wider considerations of alterity informing her poetics.

Traveling to Mexico in 1985, Myles wrote most of the stories that comprise her first collection of fiction, *Bread and Water* (1987). This volume and the 1989 collection, *1969,* later figured into *Chelsea Girls,* about which she remarked in an interview with Liz Galst for the *Boston Phoenix* of July 1994: "This is a lesbian book, and it's a poet's book. . . . If anything, my work is about being inside your body and taking your time and taking your space and telling it your way. . . . And that's . . . important in terms of being a female and a lesbian—that you can take that time." The significance of this prose work lies to some extent in the way she utilizes an autobiographical strategy to inform her poetics. Although for a time Myles was less interested in verse, this period of her career nonetheless opened further angles for her development as a poet.

In 1990 Myles took to the stage with "Leaving New York," a touring performance billed as "a retrospective in stories and poems." Myles had been memorizing her work for readings throughout the 1980s, and the scope of this performance also called upon her to utilize notions gained in prior theater performances. In "Leaving New York" Myles fused multiple literary genres with the disciplines of theater work; the performance was the foremost example yet of her facility for interdisciplinary work, a fusion which met with critical acclaim.

But when *Not Me* appeared, Myles's imbuing of her work with the American traditions to which she was heir and with her long and concentrated work teaching, performing, and "telling it" her "way" produced a poetic presence which was visceral, dynamic, uniquely defined, and, in her estimation, "proprioceptive." With consistent formal concerns and autobiographical angles as hallmarks, her poems were always somewhat serial, but *Not Me* delineated this tendency by comprising two long serial sequences, "The Real Drive" and "Not Me." The latter sequence opens with "American Poem," in which she takes on the persona of the Kennedy family. But this virtual metamorphosis is again rooted in the author's identity, her sexuality, and her increasingly adamant facility for showing up the inequities of the American societal power play. "Are you normal tonight?" she jests, "... It is not normal for / me to be a Kennedy." But what Myles could no longer ignore were the political implications of her role as a lesbian, a woman, a writer: "we are all Kennedys. / And I am your president." Taking Whitman and Ginsberg's cue of expansive, purportedly objective reportage and adding lesbian evaluation to American narrative poetry, she is forced to confront the notion that lesbianism and being a woman who claims her own place in society are somehow construed as transgressions against that society which bore her. As the title "American Poem" implies, the very name Kennedy is a societal institution, public space.

Myles's writing as a whole and all that becomes the process of writing circle in on the notion of self-disclosure, an idea at the heart of her poetics. With "Leaving New York" and *Not Me* Myles came to be seen as an exemplar of the so-called new narrative movement of the time. With a sort of new-traditionalist stance ironically coupled with a focus on recognizing the grime of the commonplace, Myles excelled far beyond these terms in her work, mainly in her further recognition of the dubious nature of her role as a writer once contextualized amid the so-called me decade of the 1980s and early 1990s. Myles's is a poetic that never attains to perfect virtues such as absolute truth, a specter lurking beneath the authorial authenticity of perhaps most typical new narrative work. In this light one could take as an aphorism, "And I am never / sure. And I am always here."

With the same sort of concision she upended certain expectations of narrative traditions aimed at drawing attention to the inequitable representation of herself and those with whom she identified in *Not Me* and "Leaving New York." Thus she became politicized in her work and embarked on her 1992 campaign for the presidency. Writing many campaign letters (which included original poems), drawing up policies on taxation and foreign relations that were remarkably well-informed, eventually getting on the write-in ballot in twenty-eight states, and attracting coverage from popular media such as MTV and *Interview* magazine, Myles ran on a platform described in these letters as "total disclosure.... Don't you get

weird when nobody's looking? I do." Later, in her 1994 *Boston Phoenix* interview, Myles drew the correlation with her poetics: "I was simply being a writer, a poet, in public. And there was no other way to do that other than to say you're a presidential candidate."

Of the poems written during this time, "The Windsor Trail" best illustrates the larger sense in which Myles considered her political activism as synonymous with the life and wares of the poet "out there," participating as well as lending vital criticism, as the campaign letters explain, "an opportunity for me to vote." "The Windsor Trail," which was included in her next collection, *Maxfield Parrish: Early & New Poems* (1995), finds the narrator, "Lady Eileen," considering the spurious beauty of a sunny meadow from the shaded enclosure of a neighboring forest, on the path leading to a distant mountain. The poem is at once a pastoral and an allegory: "Lady Eileen / wants to rest / in your / decision / trees & money // ... Lady Eileen / wants to / rest in / your shade." But she notices that to surmise the role, the very being, of what she sees in the light is dubious business from such a vantage point. Some of the trees, she suddenly notices, are dead ("the dead / lean gently / on life"); some are twisted; but all are varied in their demeanor or appearance, having metamorphosed into the perpetrators and victims of an analogous society: "this whole area / is a catastrophe / of fallen / trees."

if it
doesn't
come in
words

the big blue
mountain

leave room

it doesn't
mean it
didn't
happen.

This stupefying illustration of the representational fallibility of language and furthermore what it is to be a woman, an American, and a lesbian poet marks a departure from the cool, though not uncritical, self-assuredness of Myles's earlier work. She remains critically devoted to her edens but allows nature to enter in, to contextualize and deepen the problem of identity. Another piece, "Waterfall," which appeared in *The New England Review* (Fall

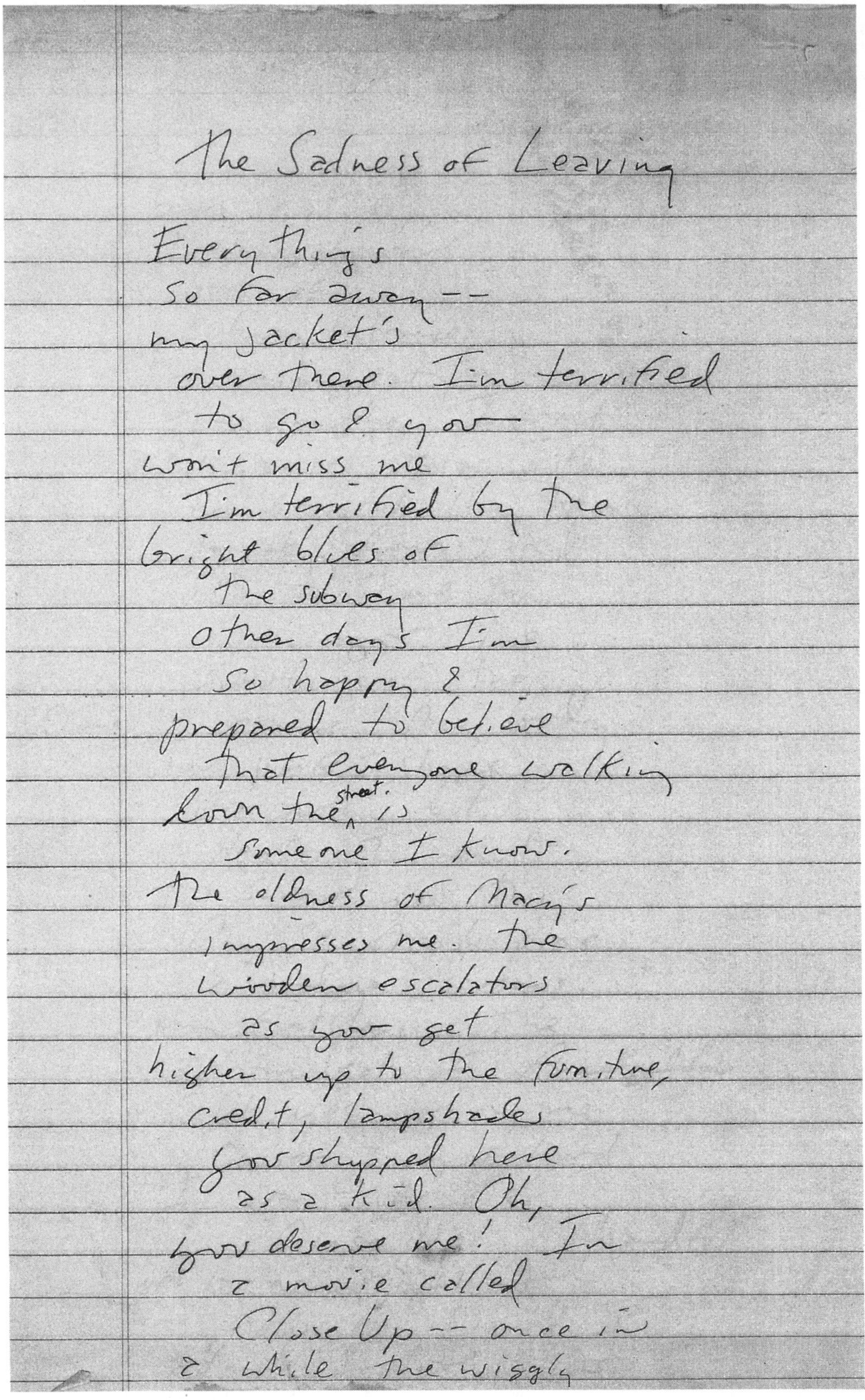

The Sadness of Leaving

Everything's
so far away --
my jacket's
over there. I'm terrified
to go & you
won't miss me
I'm terrified by the
bright blues of
the subway
other days I'm
so happy &
prepared to believe
that everyone walking
down the street, is
someone I know.
The oldness of Macy's
impresses me. The
wooden escalators
as you get
higher up to the furniture,
credit, lampshades,
you shopped here
as a kid. Oh,
you deserve me! I'm
a movie called
Close Up -- once in
a while the wiggly

Page from the manuscript for Myles's "The Sadness of Leaving," collected in her 1991 book, Not Me
(collection of Eileen Myles)

Myles in New York City, 1995

1992), plainly exemplifies this conceit: "I'm a poet. / I must find a way / to say that in human."

Continuing to search for this human language, Myles recorded and toured with the San Francisco, lesbian, spoken-word group Sister Spit and taught and wrote in New York through 1997, when her most recent collection of poems, *School of Fish,* was published. The collection, which also includes the deeply enlightening prose essay "The Lesbian Poet," was met with generous praise for Myles's continuing mastery of maintaining the vitality of the problem of identity. One reviewer, Jonathan Taylor, titled his piece on the book for *The Nation,* "The Female in Poetry," perhaps overstating the focus of the material although grasping its essential quality. Taylor points out Myles's continuing interest in metamorphosis as a view to delineating the rhetorical "I" as well as in turning to nature and the human element within it. The book also shows Myles taking her place among the largely masculine forebears of American poetry, with her thin lines like William Carlos Williams's in "In the Rain": "chickens spilling / over a wall, chickens / jumping like there's / a war." There is no shade to rest in for the contempo-

rary poet, surely not the shade of the American grain.

More than ever, Myles confronts the traditions of the western canon at large. In "The Troubador" she projects her own impressions of the great Verdi opera *Il Trovatore:* "suppose /, you know / I've taken / poison. Know / the Spring we / had last / year. That / was my / last // These lights are / nice // let me warble / like a nice / sad bird." Leanora is observed and spoken through in turns; Myles's discursive syntax and lines that "flicker" reinforce the narrator's irreverent interjections. In the troubadour tradition of courtly serenade Myles embodies not only the troubadour's object of desire but also "My male side"–the fallen, duped, and decapitated hero–in an intergender metamorphosis of great effect: "Turning she / sees me on the stair / *lesbian* / her hands / cut the air / we point two / ways. Perfect / design." Concluding with a skewed elegiac, Myles traces the libretto as faithfully as its implicit contempt for the female body will allow: "*don't leave / me.* Dawn / & you are meant / to die. The / fire is / lit / & so is / the sky." Myles assumes the postmodernist stance prompted by Marcel Duchamp's axiom that the observer finishes the piece, possessing the characters in order that they might represent her experiences. Although not irreverent, Myles's poetics is far from resignation to the omnipotence of the western, masculine, and heterosexual canon.

Myles states in "The Lesbian Poet": "More men ought to start unwriting themselves." By "unwriting" Myles attempts to shake off the authorial proclivities of a male creativity and performs this task by means of metamorphoses, rewriting men as herself. She explains further that the debris that accrues in the process is "the poem. I own her." Acutely aware of her femininity being suspect in her chosen field with its predominantly male traditions, her purpose might therefore be simply to disinter herself from beneath the writing so that a woman such as she "in such an endangered place could be free." But what is notable is that this essay is in a collection of poems, apparently an explication of the work which it accompanies. The implications of such a move aren't necessarily vaster than Myles denotes. As she writes in the poem "Sullivan's Brain" that follows: "then we move / towards living in art / interfacing in awe."

Eileen Myles has derived and yet furthered the tone, interdisciplinary tendencies, and reclamation of the mundane as a context for the ecstatic (carrying on an American tradition going back to Whitman) and daring formal contours of the New York School that largely preceded her mature work and coupled this derivation with social, sexual, and identity politics at a necessarily guttural pitch. Developing a poetics based on the proprioceptive approach has made her work uniquely vibrant and important to both mainstream and so-called fringe readerships. And more generally, Myles's engagement with the redefinition of public space in a time that has seen visceral personal outcry favored over collective activism has established her importance to end-of-the-millennium American poetics.

"Today," writes Rosalyn Deutsche in *Evictions: Art and Spatial Politics* (1996), "totalizing impulses are routinely manifested in indifference to feminism—to feminism's difference from other social analyses, its internal differences, and its theories of difference." History writes itself, perhaps, but writers (poets often foremost among them) take that dictation. One can only welcome the irrepressible tenacity of Eileen Myles into such discourse as people continue to appraise and valorize their own identities in greater social matrices. At present Myles is working on "Cool for You," a novel that comprises a female human history.

Interviews:
Sarah Schulman, "It Could Be Verse," *Interview,* 20 (December 1990): 48;
Lisa Liebmann, "Eileen Myles for President," *Interview,* 22 (March 1992): 56;
Liz Galst, "Local Hero," *Boston Phoenix* (July 1994): 18;
Edward Foster, "An Interview with Eileen Myles," *Talisman,* 17 (Summer 1997): 44–56.

References:
Noah De Lissovoy, "Backyard History: Searching for the Social Whole in the Poetry of Eileen Myles," *Talisman,* 17 (Summer 1997): 77–83;
Lori Lubeski, "On Eileen Myles," *Talisman,* 17 (Summer 1997): 72–76;
Greg Masters, "Eileen Myles: An Intro," *Talisman,* 17 (Summer 1997): 68–71;
Alice Notley, "Eileen Myles in Performance," *Talisman,* 17 (Summer 1997): 67.

Papers:
The Poetry Project of St. Mark's Church holds a major collection of Myles's performances, symposiums, and workshops on audio- and videotape, documenting appearances there from 1976 to 1997.

Frank O'Hara
(27 June 1926 – 25 July 1966)

George F. Butterick
University of Connecticut

and

Robert J. Bertholf
State University of New York at Buffalo

See also the O'Hara entries in *DLB 5: American Poets Since World War II* and *DLB 16: The Beats: Literary Bohemians in Postwar America.*

BOOKS: *A City Winter and Other Poems* (New York: Tibor de Nagy Gallery, 1952);
Oranges (New York: Tibor de Nagy Gallery, 1953);
Meditations in an Emergency (New York: Grove, 1957);
Jackson Pollock (New York: Braziller, 1959);
Second Avenue (New York: Totem/Corinth, 1960; London: Centaur, 1960);
New Spanish Painting and Sculpture (New York: Museum of Modern Art, 1960);
Odes (New York: Tiber Press, 1960);
Lunch Poems (San Francisco: City Lights Books, 1965);
Love Poems (Tentative Title) (New York: Tibor de Nagy Editions, 1965);
Robert Motherwell (New York: Museum of Modern Art, 1965);
Nakian (New York: Museum of Modern Art, 1966);
In Memory of My Feelings: A Selection of Poems, edited by Bill Berkson (New York: Museum of Modern Art, 1967);
Two Pieces (London: Long Hair Books, 1969);
The Collected Poems of Frank O'Hara, edited by Donald Allen (New York: Knopf, 1971);
Belgrade, November 19, 1963 (New York: Adventures in Poetry, 1973);
The Selected Poems of Frank O'Hara, edited by Allen (New York: Knopf, 1974);
Hymns of St. Bridget, by O'Hara and Berkson (New York: Adventures in Poetry, 1974);
The End of the Far West (Wivenhoe, U.K.: Ted Berrigan, 1974);
Art Chronicles 1954–1966 (New York: Venture/Braziller, 1975);

Frank O'Hara

Standing Still and Walking in New York, edited by Allen (Bolinas, Cal.: Grey Fox, 1975);
Early Writing, edited by Allen (Bolinas, Cal.: Grey Fox, 1977);
Poems Retrieved, edited by Allen (Bolinas, Cal.: Grey Fox, 1977);
Selected Plays (New York: Full Court Press, 1978);

Amorous Nightmares of Delay: Selected Plays (Baltimore, Md.: Johns Hopkins University Press, 1997).

Frank O'Hara was a dynamic leader of the "New York School" of poets, a group that included John Ashbery, Barbara Guest, Kenneth Koch, and James Schuyler. The Abstract Expressionist painters in New York City during the 1950s and 1960s used the title, but the poets borrowed it. From the beginning O'Hara's poetry was engaged with the worlds of music, dance, and painting. In that complex of associations he devised an idea of poetic form that allowed the inclusion of many kinds of events, including everyday conversations and notes about New York advertising signs. Since his death in 1966 at age forty, the depth and richness of his achievements as a poet and art critic have been recognized by an international audience. As the painter Alex Katz remarked, "Frank's business was being an active intellectual." He was that. His articulate intelligence made new proposals for poetic form possible in American poetry.

He was born Francis Russell O'Hara in Baltimore, Maryland, to Russell J. and Katherine Broderick O'Hara but moved at an early age to Grafton, a suburb of Worcester, in central Massachusetts. While growing up, he was a serious music student and wished above all to be a concert pianist. He took courses at the New England Conservatory. O'Hara writes: "It was a very funny life. I lived in Grafton, took a ride on a bus into Worcester every day to high school, and on Saturdays took a bus and a train to Boston to study piano. On Sundays, I stayed in my room and listened to the Sunday symphony programs." After service aboard the destroyer USS *Nicholas* in the South Pacific during World War II, he entered Harvard (Edward Gorey was his roommate), first majoring in music but changing to English and deciding to be a writer. His first published work was some poems and stories in the *Harvard Advocate*. While living in Cambridge, O'Hara met poets Ashbery, who was on the editorial board of the *Advocate,* and V. R. "Bunny" Lang. In 1956 O'Hara was one of the original founders of the Poets Theater in Cambridge. On occasional visits to New York, he met Koch and Schuyler, as well as the painters who were likewise to be so much a part of his life, notably Larry Rivers, Jane Freilicher, Fairfield Porter, Grace Hartigan, Joan Mitchell, Michael Goldberg, Willem de Kooning, Franz Kline, and Jackson Pollock. He was the first of the young New York Poets to write regular art criticism, serving as editorial associate for *Art News,* contributing reviews and occasional articles from 1953 to 1955. He had a long association with the Museum of

Modern Art in New York, beginning as a clerk at the information and sales desk in the front lobby, later becoming an assistant curator at the museum and an associate curator of painting and sculpture in 1965, despite his lack of formal training. He was an assistant for the important exhibition, "The New American Painting," which toured eight European cities in 1958–1959. This exhibition introduced the painters of the Abstract Expressionist movement to European audiences. The title of the exhibition was changed when Donald Allen used it as the title of his anthology *The New American Poetry*. While employed by the Museum of Modern Art, O'Hara was the curator or cocurator of nineteen exhibitions. He was an active and articulate spokesman for the new painting inside the major collecting museum in New York. He performed his administrative and curatorial duties surrounded by ceaseless conversation about art, poetry, music, and dance.

O'Hara's work was first brought to the attention of the wider public, like that of so many others of his generation, by Allen's timely and historic anthology, *The New American Poetry* (1960). It was not until O'Hara's *Lunch Poems* was published in 1965 that his reputation gained ground and not until after his sudden death that his recognition increased. Now his reputation is secure as an important and even popular poet in the great upsurge of American poetry following World War II. His influence on the next generation of poets–including Bill Berkson, Alice Notley, and Ted Berrigan–was immense. He did not cultivate academic alliances or solicit editors and publishers. Painter John Button remarks: "When asked by a publisher-friend for a book, Frank might have trouble even finding the poems stuffed into kitchen drawers or packed in boxes that had not been unpacked since his last move. Frank's fame came to him unlooked-for." His recognition came in part because of his early death, the somewhat absurd and meaningless occasion of that death (he was run down by a beach taxi on Fire Island), the prominence and loyalty of his friends, the renown of his own personality, and above all, the exuberant writings themselves. His casual attitude toward his poetic career is reminiscent of the casual composition of many of the poems themselves. One of his poems, "Poem (Lana Turner has collapsed!)," for example, was written on the Staten Island Ferry en route to a poetry reading, and his most important statement of poetics, "Personism," was written in less than an hour while Allen, who requested it, was on his way across town to pick it up. Koch touches upon this particular quality of O'Hara's genius–his naturalness: "Something Frank had that none of the other artists and writers I know had to the same de-

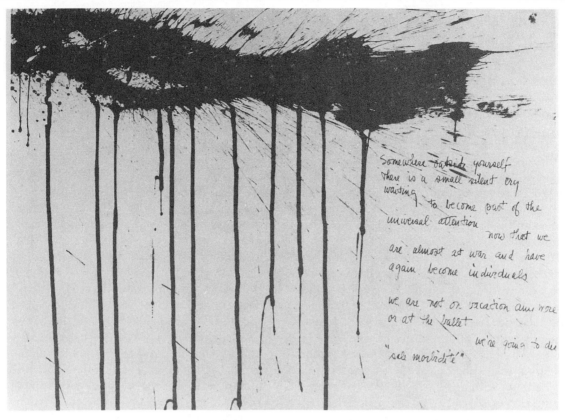

A poem-painting by O'Hara and Norman Bluhm, one of twenty-six such collaborations the two men completed in 1960 (from Bill Berkson and Joe LeSueur, eds., Homage to Frank O'Hara, *1980)*

gree was a way of feeling and acting as though being an artist were the most natural thing in the world. Compared to him everyone else seemed a little self-conscious, abashed, or megalomaniacal." When this quality entered his verse, his work was formally inventive and most compelling.

During his lifetime O'Hara was known as "a poet among painters," part of a group of such poets who seemed to find their inspiration and support from the painters they chose to associate with, writing more art reviews and commentary than literary opinion. O'Hara published only two book reviews: one of poetry collections by friends Chester Kallman, Ashbery, and Edwin Denby; the other of John Rechy's *City of Night,* 1963. His own art criticism, the major portion of which has been collected as *Art Chronicles 1954–1966* (1975), helped to encourage the painters he liked best and maintain the public awareness of them, although in itself it is nowhere as brilliant as, for example, Rainer Maria Rilke's writings on Auguste Rodin or Charles Baudelaire's on the Salon of 1846. Professional critics found O'Hara's criticism too subjective and lacking in the disciplines of critical analysis. Hilton Kramer was particularly critical

of O'Hara's book *Jackson Pollock* (1959), claiming that the excessive praise and poetic writing spoiled the discussion of the paintings. O'Hara's poetry itself is most painterly, making the best judgment of painting while participating in the actual techniques of abstract art.

The extent, the sheer volume of his writings, came as a surprise to many of even his closest friends. Most wondered where he had found time to do it all. Ashbery writes in his introduction to the 586-page *The Collected Poems of Frank O'Hara* (1971), patiently gathered and carefully edited by Allen: "That *The Collected Poems of Frank O'Hara* should turn out to be a volume of the present dimension will surprise those who knew him, and would have surprised Frank even more. Dashing the poems off at odd moments—in his office at The Museum of Modern Art, in the street at lunch time or even in a room full of people—he would then put them away in drawers and cartons and half forget them. Once when a publisher asked him for a manuscript he spent weeks and months combing the apartment, enthusiastic and bored at the same time, trying to assemble the poems. Finally he let the project drop, not because he didn't wish his work to appear, but because his thoughts were elsewhere, in the urban world of fantasy where the poems came from." Although he published more than a hundred poems in scattered magazines and in a few limited editions, there was no sizable representative collection of poems published in his lifetime. And there were no serious critical studies of his writings such as Marjorie Perloff's, Alan Feldman's, or Alice's Parker's. Before the *Collected Poems,* and later *The Selected Poems of Frank O'Hara* (1974), there were only two slight volumes—*Second Avenue* (1960) and *Lunch Poems* (1965)—readily available; other books were printed in editions of less than five hundred copies, one in only ten copies, and thus were inaccessible to most serious readers.

O'Hara's poetry, as it developed, joined the post-Symbolist French tradition with the American idiom to produce some of the liveliest and most personable poetry written in the 1950s and early 1960s. O'Hara incorporated Surrealistic and Dadaistic techniques within a colloquial speech and the flexible syntax of an engaging and democratic postmodernism. His special subject was the encounter of the active sensibility with the world about it through extravagant fantasy, a ready wit, and a detailed realism of feelings. The result, a unique blend of elements, has earned him a memorable place in American poetry. He hastened the development of an art form hitherto little practiced in English (*The Waste Land* [1922], for example, is seldom designated as authored by both Ezra Pound and T. S. Eliot) that was to become popular in the later 1960s and 1970s among younger poets—the collaboration: O'Hara wrote poems with Ashbery, Koch, and Berkson; created "translations" from the French; produced a series of lithographs with Rivers, collages with Goldberg, comic strips with Joe Brainard, "Dialogues for Two Voices and Two Pianos" with composer Ned Rorem, and a movie with painter Alfred Leslie. He was the subject of portraits by many of his artist friends—an indication not only of his association with painters but also of the esteem in which the artists held him. His early death only contributed to his legend and kept alive his memory until the publication of his collected writings confirmed for many what a few, mostly his friends and fellow poets, already knew—that he was an immensely gifted poet.

The collection of his poems by Allen and the arrangement of them in chronological order make it possible to discuss O'Hara's work in the order of its development; however, the contents of the first edition published during his lifetime are not preserved. Two subsequent volumes prepared by Allen, one including O'Hara's earliest poems, mostly from notebooks and unpublished manuscripts among his papers and the other poems overlooked or unavailable at the time of his compilation of the complete poems, supplement the *Collected Poems.*

O'Hara's earliest poems exhibit much of the promise and brilliance later fulfilled. Despite the somewhat casual method of composition he later became celebrated for and the colloquial air or ease of those poems themselves, O'Hara was from the start a skilled and knowledgeable poet, well aware, if not always respectful, of the long tradition of the craft. Brad Gooch's biography, *City Poet: The Life and Times of Frank O'Hara* (1993), makes it possible to trace the biographical, cultural, and literary information in the poems. The poems at times can be correctly read as intense personal statements, not just sleight-of-hand performances. A survey of his *Early Writing* (1977), written between 1946 and 1950 while O'Hara was still a student at Harvard, reveals a striking diversity of forms that includes ballads, songs, a blues (so-called), a madrigal, musical exercises such as a gavotte, a dirge (complete with strophe, antistrophe, and epode), and even more exotic forms such as the French triolet. There are also an imitation of Wallace Stevens (with a touch of Marianne Moore) titled "A Procession for Peacocks"; a strict sonnet; a litany; poems in quatrains; couplets, and heroic couplets; poems with faithful rhyme patterns; and various prose poems. O'Hara's most persistent interest, however, was the image, in all its suddenness, juxtaposed with an equally unlikely image, following techniques not of Imagism but those perfected by the French Surrealists. This period of experimentation and learning (although the imitations and parodies continued) advanced into an interest in post-Symbolist French poetry, especially that of Guillaume Apollinaire and later Pierre Reverdy, along with the big-voiced, roaring surrealism of Vladimir Mayakovski. At the same time O'Hara's innate Americanness was encouraged by writers such as William Carlos Williams and Marianne Moore, together with the colloquial W. H. Auden, whom he felt to be an "American" poet in "his use of the vernacular." O'Hara was alert to all developments in his chosen art. Between 1952 and 1958 he either attended or participated in discussions of the new poetry and the new painting at the Abstract-Expressionist meeting place in New York called The Club. His essay, "Nature and New Painting," indicating a surprisingly early familiarity with Charles Olson's "Projective Verse" essay (1950) before it became widely known later in the decade, was the subject of three panel discussions in January and February of 1955.

Among the poems of this early period, "Oranges" stands out. A series of twelve prose poems (originally nineteen) written while he was home from Harvard during the summer of 1949, they are less the "pastorals" of their subtitle than a decidedly anti-Arcadian surrealistic parody beginning: "Black crows in the burnt mauve grass, as intimate as rotting rice, snot on a white linen field." About twenty copies of the poems, with a painting by Hartigan on the cover, were later published on the occasion of an exhibit of Hartigan's *Oranges* paintings. As Terence Diggory has demonstrated, Hartigan did twelve paintings for twelve O'Hara poems in the fall of 1952, and by so doing redefined her relationship to Abstract Expressionism and proposed a mode of "collaboration as a dialogue of multiple selves" between poets and painters that influenced poets and painters alike. The poems themselves do not even mention the word of the title, a cleverness the poet was well aware of. O'Hara gives an account of the series in his more justly famous "Why I Am Not a Painter," written in 1956:

> One day I am thinking of
> a color: orange. I write a line
> about orange. Pretty soon it is a
> whole page of words, not lines.
> Then another page. There should be
> so much more, not of orange, of
> words, of how terrible orange is
> and life. Days go by. It is even in
> prose, I am a real poet. My poem
> is finished and I haven't mentioned
> orange yet. It's twelve poems, I call
> it ORANGES. And one day in a gallery
> I see Mike's painting, called SARDINES.

Goldberg did in fact make an abstract painting with the word *Sardines* written on it as the title. Two other poems written at Harvard—the "Poems," beginning "At night Chinamen jump" and "The eager note on my door"—although among his earliest and having the same daring imagery as the surrealist poems, are exceptional as well for their narrative and dramatic poise. They remain among his finest, and he readily included them in later collections. Following his four years in Cambridge, O'Hara went to the University of Michigan on the advice of John Ciardi, his creative-writing teacher at Harvard, to compete in the Hopwood Awards, winning an award in writing for his manuscript "A Byzantine Place" and his verse play *Try! Try!* (later produced by the Poets' Theatre in Cambridge, Massachusetts, which he helped found). He missed the activity of New York and returned in 1951, working briefly as private secretary to photographer Cecil Beaton and then at the Museum of Modern Art. During this period the New York School took its distinct shape,

O'Hara in his kitchen at 791 Broadway, New York City, 1963 (photograph by Mario Schifano)

the name parodying, according to poet Edwin Denby who was there, the School of Paris, "which also originated as a joke in opposition to the School of Florence and the School of Venice." O'Hara himself describes the milieu in a memoir of the painter Rivers: "We were all in our early twenties. John Ashbery, Barbara Guest, Kenneth Koch and I, being poets, divided our time between the literary bar, the San Remo, and the artists' bar, the Cedar Tavern. In the San Remo we argued and gossiped: in the Cedar we often wrote poems while listening to the painters argue and gossip. . . . An interesting sidelight to these social activities was that for most of us non-academic and indeed non-literary poets in the sense of the American scene at the time, the painters were the only generous audience for our poetry, and most of us read first publicly in art galleries or at The Club. The literary establishment cared about as much for our work as the Frick cared for Pollock and de Kooning."

O'Hara's poems at this time were still heavily surrealistic, as exemplified by "Memorial Day 1950," "Chez Jane," and "Easter," which prefigured the more ambitious *Second Avenue* (1960) with its catalogue of random juxtapositions. In "Easter" the images are fully nonreferential, or referential to their own reality alone: "The razzle dazzle maggots are summary / tattooing my simplicity on the pitiable." Only the accustomed syntactic structures prevail—subjects, predicates, clauses—supporting the progression that becomes a tramp of alien, autonomous images over an otherwise familiar bridge. When the images expand out, however, and a narrative occurs, as in "A Terrestrial Cuckoo" from this same time, the results are delightfully comic:

> What a hot day it is! for
> Jane and me above the scorch
> of sun on jungle waters to be
> paddling up and down the Essequibo
> in our canoe of war-surplus gondola parts[.]

This is O'Hara at his best, combining his voice and personality with the most far-flung word montages.

Among the early poems, *Second Avenue,* in eleven parts, is easily the most ambitious. It was written in the spring of 1953 but not published in book form until 1960. The artist Rivers recalls how this "long marvelous poem" was written in his "plaster garden studio overlooking" the avenue of the title, with the poet finishing it between poses for a sculpture Rivers was making of him. Koch, who also had some role in the poem's composition, finds it "among the wonders of contemporary poetry," and Albert Cook, the first of the academics to recognize O'Hara, finds it "too perfect of its kind, which it has invented, to induce anyone's strictures." Most readers, however, have found difficulty with it. Perloff calls it O'Hara's "most Byzantine and difficult poem," while even Ashbery in his introduction to the *Collected Poems* speaks of "the obfuscation that makes reading 'Second Avenue' such a difficult pleasure." O'Hara sensed some of the difficulties and later offered a few thoughts concerning the poem in a letter to a reader or editor who had apparently found it obscure. In his letter he identifies some of the components, including a derisive portrait of "a poetry critic and teacher," a description of painter Hartigan at work, and "a true description of not being able to continue this poem and meeting Kenneth Koch for a sandwich while waiting for the poem to start again." He also insists: "actually everything in it either happened to me or I felt happening (saw, imagined) on Second Avenue"—even though the landscape is neither recognizable nor significant on its own terms. Koch writes elsewhere that the poem "is evidence that the avant-garde style of French poetry from Baudelaire to Reverdy has now infiltrated American consciousness to such an extent that it is possible for an American poet to write lyrically in it with perfect ease," although when he states that the language of the poem resembles William Carlos Williams's in being "convincing and natural," nothing could be further from accuracy. Koch also suggests the chief persona of the poem is "a sort of Whitmanian I," though this is hardly discoverable. Rivers's painting *Second Avenue* (1958) needs to be mentioned as well.

Second Avenue is a poem of brilliant excess and breakneck inventiveness, beginning: "Quips and players, seeming to vend astringency off-hours, / celebrate diced excesses and sardonics, mixing pleasures, / as if proximity were staring at the margin of the plea. . . ." This is language in love with itself. The poem is dedicated to Mayakovsky, one of O'Hara's great heroes (though an early draft is inscribed to de Kooning), and certainly the images throughout are as wide-ranging and as startling as Mayakovsky's, but they arrive more rapidly and with less continuity, jostling for attention, a bewildering mixture. Moreover, they do not have Mayakovsky's large, carrying, unifying voice. O'Hara himself explained: "where Mayakovsky and de Kooning come in, is that they both have done works as big as cities where the life in the work is autonomous (not about actual city life) and yet similar." Here the result is a highly mosaic-like, patterned surface. "The verbal elements," by the poet's own insistence, "are extended consciously to keep the surface of the poem high and dry, not wet, reflective and self-conscious." But it is perhaps the most difficult of all accomplishments in art, the texture of surface appearance. "Perhaps," O'Hara continues, "the obscurity comes in here, in the relationship between the surface and the meaning, but I like it that way since the one is the other (you have to use words) and I hope the poem to *be* the subject, not just about it." At this point O'Hara began adapting the processes of surrealism to the conception of poetic form founded on the idea that the poem is an enactment of the actuality of perception and the realization of thinking. The achievement of a form, then, which was also the imperative of Abstract Expressionism, brought O'Hara into the creative ambience of the painters.

This last statement is, in effect, a succinct definition of nonrepresentational art—and in that sense, *Second Avenue* is an embodiment of the techniques of Abstract Expressionism, the series of strokes that in their totality alone completes a form. There is a cinematic "sleet" of images, colored vaguely by the city's lights and shapes glimpsed from the window on Second Avenue, falling with such rapidity that the dissolves occur before the gestalt-making powers of the mind can focus them. These images are, in the words of the poem, "diced essences"—sharply cut and full of chance. "Butter. Lotions. Cries. A glass of ice. Aldebaran and Mizar, / a guitar of toothpaste tubes and fingernails, trembling spear"—they are hardly full-bodied; rather they are subliminal phantoms, too fleeting even for associations. The poem projects intense energy as it enacts the process of motion, of the eye and the mind moving on and around the urban scene. The area described, the canvas of the poem, is huge, and without a guiding narrator; the poem attempts to allow chance events, the random thought and image, to enter the design. This is a large poem to maintain without a narrator; but, on the other hand, the situation removes the ego of the poem from the process of the poem and then allows a multitude of gestures to run in at all points. It could be called an "action poem." Like Pollock, who created a procedure of entering the field of action of the painting, O'Hara creates the illusion that he has entered the process of writing to such an extent that the surface details in all their seeming discontinuity actually constitute the form of the poem itself. The generation of an idea of form in the poem, then, becomes much more important than a doctrine of composition or a sermon about city life. When the Surrealists left Europe for America just before and during World War II, they injected Surrealism into American poetry and painting. O'Hara's poem of 1953 is the leading example of an attempt to install the European model in contemporary writing, but as Koch writes in his review of *The Collected Poems* in the *New Republic:* "For all their use of chance and unconsciousness, Frank O'Hara's poems are unlike Surrealist poetry in that they do not programmatically favor these forces (along with dreams and violence) over the intellectual and conscious. He must have felt the beauty and power of unconscious phenomena in surrealist poems, but what he does is to use this power and beauty to ennoble, complicate, and simplify waking actions." The poem might be said to be, in light of the manner of composition and success of the later poems, overworked, trying too hard to assert the mode of composition. One need only compare the "Poem" beginning "Now the violets are all gone, the rhinoceroses, the cymbals"—the same catalogue of disparate objects—to see how, when the personality takes over, a true, more shareable lyricism flowers. Perloff wisely points out that when the two strands are merged—the surrealistic, with its endless variety and high-spirited inventiveness, and the personal, the spoken American, the colloquial narrative with its charming persona—O'Hara attains his triumph.

As long as the succession of rapid-fire discontinuous images does not extend beyond tolerance,

Title page for O'Hara's 1965 collection of poems, one of only two books readily available until after his death

and, further, when there is some attempt to relate those images to an order of reality beyond themselves, O'Hara's surrealism works. In "On Rachmaninoff's Birthday," beginning "Quick! a last poem before I go / off my rocker," the final line—"You'll never be mentally sober"—comments on the previous assortment of images and relates to the initial "I," rounding out the poem while adding a dimension of self-reflection and conscious control to an otherwise indulgent randomness. (This is just one of seven poems O'Hara wrote for the Russian composer's birthday over the years.) Or where the images are consistent, added to with like elements, as in "Romanze, or the Music Students," beginning:

> The rain, its tiny pressure
> on your scalp, like ants
> passing the door of a tobacconist.
> "Hello!" they cry, their
> noses glistening . . .

—almost like an animated cartoon—this is the cleverness that makes O'Hara most appealing.

The lyrical/narrative "I," the "I" with verve and personality, the distinctive O'Hara persona, the "I" of what he himself called his "I do this I do that" poems, makes its appearance as early as "Music," written in 1954. There too the persona is set upon a representational landscape of midtown Manhattan, where landmarks are called by name, as they exist in public reality (the Equestrian statue, the Mayflower Donut Shoppe, Bergdorf Goodman's, Park Avenue itself). Just how personal and lyrical this "I" is can be seen in "To the Harbormaster," a love poem written for Rivers that sustains the metaphor of a ship. Other poems from this period concern images of a different order, including movie stars such as James Dean, both a symbol and a victim of popular culture, to whom no less than four poems are dedicated. There is also the mock-heroic "To the Film Industry in Crisis," addressed "to you, / glorious Silver Screen, tragic Technicolor, amorous Cinemascope, / stretching Vistavision and startling Stereophonic Sound, with all / your heavenly dimensions and reverberations and iconoclasms!" The mock epic continues later with the equally amusing "Ave Maria," beginning: "Mothers of America / let your kids go to the movies!"

A meditative poem such as "Sleeping on the Wing" from 1955 is a further advance and indication the poet's personality has fully emerged; specifically, that he is aware of the precious advantage, indeed the great comfort, of undisguised human "singularity," which he knows to be "all that you have made your own." Interestingly, despite all the appearances of a prolonged, considered meditation, the poem was actually composed with great rapidity, increasingly typical for O'Hara, a sign perhaps of the confidence, embodied by Li Po, of the poet come into his own. Schuyler remembers: "The day this was written I was having breakfast (i.e. coffee) with Frank and Joe [O'Hara's roommate Joe LeSueur] at 326 East 49th Street, and the talk turned to Frank's unquenchable inspiration, in a teasing way on my part and Joe's. The cigarette smoke began jetting from Frank's nostrils and he went into the next room and wrote SLEEPING ON THE WING in a great clatter of keys." "In Memory of My Feelings" (1956) can be thought of as a transitional poem from "Second Avenue" to the "Odes." In the poem O'Hara demonstrates the process of assuming and then rejecting many possibilities of self-definition. The self, in the process of conceiving and reconnecting its emotional nature—the heart is the counter to the evil of life in the serpent—finally recognizes that "the scene of my selves" is constantly moving within the process of endless change. Art cannot grant fixity; it can produce no statues; it can, however, demonstrate the very processes of generating artistic form.

"A Step Away From Them" from 1956 has come to be known as the first of his so-called lunch poems, beginning:

It's my lunch hour, so I go
for a walk among the hum-colored
cabs.

. . . .

                              A
Negro stands in a doorway with a
toothpick, languorously agitating.
A blonde chorus girl clicks: he
smiles and rubs his chin. Everything
suddenly honks: it is 12:40 of
a Thursday.

The poet is immersed in his mode, his *monde*. The perceptions and information follow along with the acts of seeing and thinking. The same is true of his poem of determined optimism dedicated to painter Mitchell ("Poem Read at Joan Mitchell's"), where happiness is "the least and best of human attainments," or the cohesiveness of "Platinum, Watching TV, Etc.," preserved in *Poems Retrieved* (1977), or the equally expansive poem to another painter friend titled "John Button Birthday." These are all poems written when O'Hara was most at home in his world and at the full strength of his style. They are followed by a series of *Odes* (1960) and continue into his most productive years, 1959 and 1960. When he wrote them, it was another dawning in American poetry and he one of the chief instigators, as he knew himself in his "Poem Read at Joan Mitchell's," when he wrote: "tonight I feel energetic because I'm sort of the bugle, / like waking people up. . . ."

One of the highlights of O'Hara's collected works is *Odes,* all written in 1957–1958 and originally published in a highly priced limited edition (in a boxed set with similar collections by the other principal New York School poets—Ashbery, Koch, and Schuyler). There are nine odes in the book, along with three prints by Michael Goldberg. Goldberg made the prints after the poems were written, but the large format of the book provided the opportunity for the typography of the poems to emulate the spatial forms of the prints and introduced another basis for understanding a collaboration between a poet and a painter. It is one situation for a poem to refer to a painting, but it is a different act when the processes of making forms are the same in the poem and the painting, or as here, in the prints. "Ode on Causality," the first poem in the book and the poem in memory of Pollock, begins with the line, "There is the sense of neurotic coherence." A young girl in the poem indicates that Pollock is not in his grave but in the woods, that he and his art are part of the process of death and rebirth, conceiving and reconceiving artistic forms. The sense of movement is here, of the flight and motion that were parts of "Second Avenue" and became parts of "Ode to Michael Goldberg ('s Birth and Other Births)," the final poem in the volume. The long ode to Goldberg is more like the Romantic– specifically Wordsworthian–ode than any of the others. It concerns the growth of both the poet's mind and of his role (as poet), autobiographically moving through memories of childhood toward a confrontation with mortality. The poem is neither celebratory nor congratulatory (it is not, despite the title, a birthday poem for the painter but was written during the three months after his birthday). The poem includes details about O'Hara's life in Baltimore, his trip to the "first movie," observations about "trysts," adventures in the South Seas during World War II, a statement about his first homosexual experience in a hay barn, and his life in New York at the "Five Spot" and around the city. The poem is also dedicated to "Other Births," so it is about the stages of O'Hara's life moving from one birth of consciousness to another as his poetic sensibilty renews itself in experience. Images of movement, transportation, and the journey of life appear and reappear to establish a coherence in the collection of information about history and contemporary living in the poem. The daily activities of motion, of moving from one version of a self to another, integrate the poet's life into the artist's life. It begins with memories first of Baltimore (O'Hara writes of his affinity for the magnolias and tulip trees mentioned in the poem in autobiographical fragments published in *Standing Still and Walking in New York,* 1975), then of Grafton, where aesthetic as well as sexual awakening occurred:

> Up on the mountainous hill
> behind the confusing house
> where I lived. . . .
>   there,
> the wind sounded exactly like
> Stravinsky
>   I first recognized art
> as wildness, and it seemed right,
>   I mean rite, to me. . . .

The allusion to *The Rite of Spring* is obvious enough. The poem proceeds through recollections of O'Hara's personal life, including wartime days in the South Pacific and psychosexual hints, to the present that must be faced, where "too much end-

lessness" is "stored up, and in store," awaiting. It is not his alone, but the human and historical condition. There are repeated reminders of the "darkness" at the center of life, but even as that darkness occurs it appears "a glistening / blackness in the center / if you seek it . . . capable of bursting / into flame or merely / gleaming profoundly." Amidst all, the poet has been selected to bear like Prometheus "the gift of fire" to a "foreign land," a "temporary place of light, the land of air." It is this land toward which the poem moves, concluding with almost a historical imperative:

> for flowing
>   as it must throughout the miserable, clear and willful
> life we love beneath the blue,
>   a fleece of pure intention sailing like
> a pinto in a barque of slaves
>   who soon will turn upon their captors
> lower anchor, found a city riding there
>   of poverty and sweetness paralleled
>   among the races without time,
>   and one alone will speak of being
> born in pain
>   and he will be the wings of an extraordinary liberty[.]

O'Hara advances this poem by the spatial relationships of blocks of information and by using different internal voices, which are indicated by indentations and internal margins. He has learned lessons from Rivers, who in a painting like *The Wall* (1957) or *The Accident* (1957) spreads derivative images–like O'Hara drawing up blocks of memories from his life–over the field of the canvas and attempts a narrative guided by spatial relationships of the images and not a linear, causal argument. Ashbery is often recognized as the master of telling parables in poems, but here O'Hara demonstrates that he also has mastered the form. From out of the process of death and rebirth "beneath the blue," or living the life of the imagination as Stevens imagined it, a poet will emerge who understands that life is lived within contrary forces–"poverty and sweetness," "pain" and "an extraordinary liberty." Still, he resists oversimplification and insists on discontinuities. Toward the end he offers this quotation and potential hope:

> "the exquisite prayer
> to be new each day
> brings to the artist
> only a certain kneeness"

–not *newness,* not *keenness,* but an absurd *kneeness.* The use of the word might even be a Platonic joke. The artist is brought down to his knees, not just by

O'Hara at a benefit reading for the magazine Yūgen *at the Living Theater (2 November 1959) in New York City with Ray Bremser, LeRoi Jones, and Allen Ginsberg*

the prayer for creative novelty, one of the values necessary for his art, but by being reduced to a certain futility and awkwardness. Ironies and apparent contradictions abound: "you pull a pretty ring out of the pineapple [a grenade] / and blow yourself up"; everything is simultaneously "all right" and "difficult"; "wit" and "austerity" are shared; we fall sobbing to the floor with both "joy" and "freezing." Even at the end, in the city of the future, almost a new world, "poverty" and "sweetness" persist as parallels.

The "Ode to Michael Goldberg" should answer any charges that O'Hara cannot sustain a long poem. Drawn from the full flood of childhood memory, it courses up through "A couple of specifically anguished days" of the present which "make me now distrust sorrow, simple sorrow / especially, like sorrow over death." It is perhaps his most encompassing poem, most ruminative, introspective; it includes the darkness at the very quick of his soul that obviously haunted him and that he lived with so cheerfully and so well. And like the configuration of the lines on the page in "Ode on Lust," this poem demonstrates O'Hara's process of writing like a

painter with an awareness of the spatial dimensions of language. He lived caught between sweetness and poverty, between longing for love and being rejected in love, but also attempting to keep "the poem 'open'" in the "extraordinary liberty" of the daily enterprise.

Resonance of Whitman and great rolling tones are evident in the opening lines of "Ode: Salute to the French Negro Poets":

From near the sea, like Whitman my great predecessor,

I call

to the spirits of other lands to make fecund my

. . . .

It is a voice of majesty, announcing a large theme.

The diction is self-consciously exalted, proper to an ode, compared to the breezy familiarity ordinarily expected of O'Hara: Love is "traduced" by shame; "reticence" is paid for by a poet in his blood; "fortuity" is in "the love we bear." O'Hara even forgoes his tendency to wisecrack before the seriousness of his intended theme: "here where to love at all's to be a politician," he writes, threatening sarcasm, and continues with a mocking rhyme, "as to love a poem / is pretentious, this may sound tendentious but it's lyrical." The drift into smartness ("it's lyrical") is checked, however, and the poem is restored to seriousness, even gravity, by what follows—"which shows what lyricism has been brought to by our fabled times"—and elevated diction such as "cowards are shibboleths" and "one specific love's traduced." This ode is actually one of O'Hara's most directly political poems, mounting almost to a rhetoric of defiance: "blood! blood that we have mountains in our veins to stand off jackals / in the pillaging of our desires and allegiances. . . ." The poem is formal even in its line arrangement—a series of long waves of couplets. There is not one drop of silliness or playful avoidance, as he continues: "for if there is fortuity it's in the love we bear each other's differences / in race." It is almost a somber poem, certainly stately, as it moves in assured and measured cadences to its end: "the only truth is face to face, the poem whose words become your mouth / and dying in black and white we fight for what we love, not are." It is a comment on racial relations in his own America at the beginning of the Civil Rights era, an important political and social statement; he is turning his back on the "terrible western world" to invoke such anticolonialist poets as Aimé Césaire. It may even be a noble poem, like "Ode to Joy," in pleading for "no more dying," and in the hurry and demands of the city, to live with love. Mitchell chose *Ode to Joy* as the title of her triptych in homage to Frank O'Hara, as if she knew that the poet's incessant effort to find love and a bit of peace within the pressure of daily living caught the core of O'Hara's life and art.

The year 1959 was probably O'Hara's best, when one of his most famous poems, "The Day Lady Died," was written. Like Joel Oppenheimer's "Billie's Blues," this poem is a tribute to the jazz singer Billie Holiday. Told in terms of the unconnected events of normal living, with nothing revealed ahead of time, the powerful realization of an ending is suspended until events mount up and force the realization of great loss. The poem demonstrates the process of the poet finding in the noncausal relationships of events that a singular coherence precipitates strong emotions. It begins with a (possibly) feigned and protracted preoccupation with cultural paraphernalia and distractions of the quotidian but moves with suddenness to testify to the sanctity of human life and talent, and the eternality of art that is literally, mimetically, breathtaking. It moves through a series of choices until there are none, until the poet arrives face to face with the

unchosen, the uninvited but inevitable, irreversible wonder of loss. Names abound—"Bastille," "Easthampton," "an ugly NEW WORLD WRITING to see what the poets / of Ghana are doing these days," "Miss Stillwagon," "Verlaine"—but "hers" never is (only hinted at in the title, with her own title, Lady Day, reversed). Time likewise is held up or too freely given at the beginning—

> It is 12:20 in New York a Friday
> three days after Bastille day, yes
> it is 1959 and . . . I will get off the 4:19 in Easthampton
> at 7:15 . . .

—but then held suspended, as up a sleeve, until the end, and released when most appropriate, in the natural order of events:

> then I go back where I came from to 6th Avenue
> and the tobacconist in the Ziegfeld Theatre and
> casually ask for a carton of Gauloises and a carton
> of Picayunes, and a NEW YORK POST with her face on it
>
> and I am sweating a lot by now and thinking of
> leaning on the john door in the 5 SPOT
> while she whispered a song along the keyboard
> to Mal Waldron and everyone and I stopped breathing[.]

Death silences the trivia. The last line merges object into subject (at precisely "everyone") in the flux of events in the continuous postmodernist universe. Writing in the simultaneous present, the poet seeks control over both time and timing—the arrival (or denial) of images, the coming (or postponing) of a conclusion, but the conclusion of the value of life and art comes because of the mounting of a series of transactions in the daily enterprise.

O'Hara's level of accomplishment remained at its peak through 1961, through a series of love poems—later published as *Love Poems (Tentative Title)* (1965). Poem after poem is of a high order of achievement—"Rhapsody," "Adieu to Norman, Bon Jour to Joan and Jean-Paul," "Joe's Jacket," "You Are Gorgeous and I'm Coming," and "Personal Poem." These are all poems with the identifying characteristics of an O'Hara poem, all the same quick-stepping, name-dropping, vivacious, uninhibited narrator (name-dropping because he is utterly at home in his surroundings and in the poem). Artists and their creations continue to decorate the poems as comfortably as they do a sunken living room. John Bernard Myers, the publisher of Tibor de Nagy Editions, remembered: "I waited for these poems for three or four years; Frank could never get himself to type them up. When he did give them to me I couldn't induce him to arrange them in their proper sequence nor give me a title. I wrote 'Love

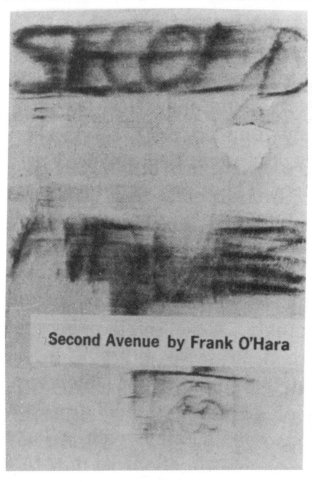

Front cover for O'Hara's eleven-part poem, which was written in 1953 but not published until 1960

poems of frontal immediacy, heartfelt, with feeling no longer hidden behind a bravado of brilliant images and discordant segments. O'Hara moves out of the modernist mode of dada, surrealism, and cubism and into the postmodern advantage: a variety of techniques, which actually incorporate the salient gains of modernism while losing nothing of the flexibility and possibility of openness, the "going on your nerve" of "Personism." At its worst or most excessive, his style lapses into giddiness, or what Stuart Byron calls "Queertalk." While surely not limited to sexual ambiguity, the language of the poems is ripe with in-talk of the 1960s; these qualities are indeed dominant in O'Hara's poems from the start. They also happen to be the reason for their great success.

His last major effort was a long poem titled "Biotherm" (after a brand of skin lotion which Berkson's mother left around and O'Hara found). Perloff praises it as a "great" poem, while other critics understand it as a demonstration of writing as the physical activity of speech—writing and language as part of the physiological response that Olson had advocated. Multu Konuk Blasing uses models from Sigmund Freud, Jacques Lacan, and Jacques Derrida in an attempt to unlock the poem. However complicated it is, the poem also had a strong influence on younger poets such as Berkson, to whom it is dedicated, Berrigan, and Ron Padgett (specifically, their collaborative *Bean Spasms*, 1967). It was composed over an extended period of time, from August 1961 to January 1962. O'Hara wrote to Allen: "I've been going on with a thing I started to be a little birthday poem for B[ill] B[erkson] and then it went along a little and then I remembered that was how Mike's Ode ["Ode to Michael Goldberg"] got done so I kept on and I am still going day by day (middle of 8th page this morning). I don't know anything about what it is or will be but am enjoying trying to keep going and seem to have been able to keep it 'open' and so there are lots of possibilities, air and such." The structure is complex: images and reference build up on the surface of the poem and are not given order by generalization or summaries. The poem joins eating with the making of language, as a "MENU" for Berkson suggests, but there is also the connection between eating and talking:

oh god what joy
you're here
sob and at the
most recent summit
conference they
are eating string
beans butter

Poems (Tentative Title)' on the first page, then arranged them so that the sequence would show the beginning of a new love, its middle period of floundering, the collapse of the affair with its attendant sadness and regret. Frank liked the arrangement and my 'tentative' title. And that was that." Homosexual love is the subject of the poems. While the poems were written at about the same time, the narrative sense of the book was provided by the publisher. Surrealism is at easy reach but not overshadowing; there is care for what Olson called the "dailynesses," varied rhythms, syncopation gained by restricting punctuation, an organic syntax, the trust to natural speech (although still very much the speech of a dashing sophisticate), the informed chatter, the management of time in a poem such as "Fantasy," the recurrent optimism of "Poem (Khrushchev's coming)." The series of love poems to dancer Vincent Warren—including "Les Luths," "Poem (Light clarity avocado salad)," "Having a Coke With You," and "Steps"—are all affirmative, delicate, precise,

smootch slurp
pass me the filth
and a coke pal
oh thank you[.]

The frame of reference is immense, and there are puns and playful connections on and with French and English. As in the early "Ode to Michael Goldberg," this poems stresses movement, quick passages through the details of life and thought, and in its spread it too engages the spatial dimensions of language. The process of language achieving articulation through the body and then collecting itself in a web of multiple associations finally becomes the subject of the poem. It also engages the process of the painters in that, like the "Odes," it relates information spatially, not always linearly; it uses indentations and internal margins to specify different voices inside the poem. The poem sets out the history of O'Hara's relationship with Berkson, but it also presents around that history remarks or observations on "the music of the fears," of "September 15 (supine, unshaven, hungover, passive, softspoken)," of routines of eating, lists of fantastic favorites, "a long history of populations," and comparisons to the poetry of Wallace Stevens and William Carlos Williams, "pretty rose preserved in biotherm." Like Stevens, in "An Ordinary Evening in New Haven," O'Hara is a poet of the city who concentrates on enacting the processes of the mind as it contacts reality. Perceiving reality and attempting to remodel it in poetic form, he is perceiving and thinking spatially in blocks of information, both personal and referential, as a way to demonstrate that the acts of poetry are fully engaged in the activities of loving people, interacting with historical as well as contemporary events.

on Altair 4, I love you that way, it was on Altair 4 "a happy day"
I knew it would be
yes to everything
                              I think you will find the pot in the corner
where the Krells left it
                              rub it a little and music comes out
the music of the fears
                              I reformed we reformed each other
being available
                              it is something our friends don't understand
if you loosen your tie
                              my heart will leap out
like a Tanagra sculpture
                              from the crater of the Corsican "lip"
and flying through the heavens
                              I am reminded of Kit Carson
and all those smiles which were exactly like yours
but we hadn't met yet
                              when are you going away on "our" trip
why are you melancholy

if I make you angry you are not longer doubtful
if I make you happy you are not longer doubtful
                              what's wrong with doubt

. . . .

favorites: going to parties with you, being in corners at parties
    with you,
    being in gloomy pubs with you smiling, poking you at parties when
    you're "down," coming on like South Pacific with you at them
    shrimping with you into the Russian dressing, leaving parties with
    you alone to go and eat a piece of cloud[.]

In some of the poems following "Biotherm," O'Hara continued using the spatial relationships of language in such poems as "Legend," "The Old Machinist," "Poem" ("At the top of the ring"), for example. Williams's tripartite line and his sense of measure also come into poems like "Walking," "Poem" ("I to you are you to me"), and "Trirème." From "Second Avenue" to "Biotherm" and then to these final poems, O'Hara moved away from the direct influences of Surrealism and projected a process of perceiving and writing grounded in the need to generate poetic forms.

It is not possible to say what direction O'Hara's work would have taken if he had lived—perhaps more social satire or a mock epic like Edward Dorn's *Gunslinger,* tighter and with more theater in it than "Biotherm." Given the nature of subsequent political and social events, he might have become the Juvenal of his day. It is as unlikely that he would have abandoned the world of art as it is unlikely he would have abandoned poetry, despite the slowdown in production during the last years (he wrote only three poems the last year and a half of his life). He had always said poetry was his life. More likely, his growing recognition among young poets would have spurred him further. The "original decorations" of thirty poems collected by Berkson under the title *In Memory of My Feelings: A Selection of Poems* (1967) testify to O'Hara's attunement with the vision and process of the new movements in the arts, and *Homage to Frank O'Hara* (1978) collects many additional drawings, paintings, memories, and testimonies to O'Hara as a poet and advocate for the arts. He left a record of an active intelligence as well as a body of poetry that challenged the norms of poetic form and reengaged the activity of creating with the normal events of the daily enterprise.

Bibliographies:
Alexander Smith Jr., *Frank O'Hara: A Comprehensive Bibliography* (New York: Garland, 1979);

Vincent Prestianni, "Frank O'Hara: An Analytic Bibliography of Bibliographies," *Sagetrieb,* 12 (Spring 1993): 129–130.

Biography:

Brad Gooch, *City Poet: The Life and Times of Frank O'Hara* (New York: Knopf, 1993).

References:

Charles Altieri, *Enlarging the Temple: New Directions in American Poetry during the 1960s* (Lewisburg, Pa.: Bucknell University Press / London: Associated University Presses, 1979), pp. 108–122;

Bill Berkson and Joe LeSueur, eds., "Homage to Frank O'Hara," *Big Sky,* nos. 11–12 (1978); revised as *Homage to Frank O'Hara* (Berkeley: Creative Arts, 1980);

Mutlu Konuk Blasing, "Frank O'Hara's Poetics of Speech: The Example of 'Biotherm,'" *Contemporary Literature,* 23 (Winter 1982): 52–64;

Blasing, *Politics and Form in Postmodern Poetry: O'Hara, Bishop, Ashbery, and Merrill* (New York: Cambridge University Press, 1995);

Gregory W. Bredbeck, "B/O–Barthes's Text / O'Hara's Trick," *PMLA,* 108 (March 1993): 268–288;

James E. B. Breslin, "Frank O'Hara," in his *From Modern to Contemporary: American Poetry 1945–1965* (Chicago: University of Chicago Press, 1984), pp. 210–249;

Paul Carroll, *The Poem in Its Skin* (Chicago: Big Table, 1968), pp. 157–168;

Terence Diggory, "Questions of Identity in Oranges by Frank O'Hara and Grace Hartigan," *Art Journal,* 52 (Winter 1993): 41–50;

Jim Elledge, ed., *Frank O'Hara: To Be True to a City* (Ann Arbor: University of Michigan Press, 1990);

Alan Feldman, *Frank O'Hara* (Boston: Twayne, 1979);

Roger Gilbert, "Frank O'Hara and Gary Snyder: The Walk as Sample," in his *Walks in the World: Representation and Experience in Modern American Poetry* (Princeton: Princeton University Press, 1991), pp. 173–208;

Susan Holahan, "Frank O'Hara's Poetry," in *American Poetry Since 1960, Some Critical Perspectives,* edited by Robert B. Shaw (Cheadle Hulme, U.K.: Carcanet, 1973), pp. 109–122;

Richard Howard, *Alone with America: Essays on the Art of Poetry in the United States Since 1950* (New York: Atheneum, 1969), pp. 396–412;

Kenneth Koch, "Frank O'Hara and His Poetry: An Interview," in *American Writing Today,* edited by Richard Kostelanetz (Troy, N.Y.: Whitston, 1991), pp. 201–211;

Anthony Libby, "O'Hara on the Silver Range," *Contemporary Literature,* 17 (Spring 1976): 240–262;

John Lowney, "The 'post-anti-esthetic' Poetics of Frank O'Hara," *Contemporary Literature,* 32 (Summer 1991): 144–264;

Thomas Meyer, "Glistening Torsos, Sandwiches, Coca-Cola," *Parnassus,* 6 (Fall/Winter 1977): 241–257;

Charles Molesworth, "'The Clear Architecture of the Nerves': The Poetry of Frank O'Hara," *Iowa Review,* 6 (Summer/Fall 1975): 61–74;

Panjandrum, O'Hara supplement, nos. 2 & 3 (1973);

Alice Parker, *The Exploration of the Secret Smile: The Language of Art and of Homosexuality in Frank O'Hara's Poetry* (New York: Peter Lang, 1989);

Marjorie Perloff, *Frank O'Hara: Poet Among Painters* (New York: Braziller, 1977);

William Weaver, "Remembering Frank O'Hara," *Southwest Review,* 79 (Winter 1994): 139–146.

Papers:

Manuscripts and letters in the Bill Berkson papers, as well as O'Hara's letters and manuscripts to Donald Allen, are in the Literary Archives, University of Connecticut Library, Storrs; small collections are at the Museum of Modern Art and Special Collections, Syracuse University. The largest collection of O'Hara's papers is at Harvard University.

Mary Oliver
(10 September 1935 –)

Woodstock Academy

See also the entry on Oliver in *DLB 5: American Poets Since World War II.*

BOOKS: *No Voyage and Other Poems* (London: Dent, 1963; Boston: Houghton Mifflin, 1965);

The River Styx, Ohio, and Other Poems (New York: Harcourt Brace Jovanovich, 1972);

The Night Traveler (Cleveland: Bits Press, 1978);

Sleeping in the Forest (Athens: Ohio Review Chapbook, 1979);

Twelve Moons (Boston: Little, Brown, 1979);

American Primitive: Poems (Boston: Atlantic, Little, Brown, 1983);

Dream Work (New York: Atlantic Monthly Press, 1986);

Provincetown, with engravings by Bernard Taylor (Lewisburg, Pa.: Appletree Alley, 1987);

House of Light (Boston: Beacon Press, 1990);

New and Selected Poems (Boston: Beacon Press, 1992);

White Pine: Poems and Prose Poems (New York: Harcourt Brace, 1994);

A Poetry Handbook (San Diego: Harcourt Brace, 1994);

Blue Pastures (New York: Harcourt Brace, 1995);

West Wind: Poems and Prose Poems (Boston: Houghton Mifflin, 1997);

Rules for the Dance, A Handbook for Writing and Reading Metrical Verse (Boston: Houghton Mifflin, 1998).

Mary Oliver (photograph by Barbara Savage Cheresh)

The writing career of poet Mary Oliver spans three decades. She has produced thirteen volumes of poetry and prose and two books on the craft of writing poetry. Oliver's poetry offers a transcendental view of the natural world in terms accessible to the twentieth-century reader. In particular she depicts the New England landscape with metaphors underscoring the lessons humans can derive from nature. Among Oliver's many honors are a National Endowment for the Arts Fellowship (1972), a Guggenheim Foundation Fellowship (1980), and an American Academy and Institute of Arts and Letters Achievement Award (1983). In 1984 Oliver was the recipient of a Pulitzer Prize for poetry following the publication of *American Primitive* (1983). *House of Light* (1990) won both the Christopher Award and the L. L. Winship Award in 1991, and *New and Selected Poems* (1992) won the National Book Award in 1992. Douglas Burton-Christie explains the vast appeal of Oliver's poetry: "Oliver evokes a deeply integrated

227

Cover for Oliver's 1983 book, which won a Pulitzer Prize for poetry

spirituality of the ordinary, helping us to see and embrace what is, after all, one world, where nature, spirit and imagination rise together."

Mary Oliver was born in Cleveland, Ohio; her parents were a teacher, Edward William Oliver, and Helen M. Vlasak Oliver. In a 1994 interview with Renee Olander, Oliver describes herself as "a serious thirteen-year-old" who wanted to write. In 1950 when Oliver was fifteen, she wrote a letter to Norma Millay Ellis, the sister of the recently deceased Edna St. Vincent Millay, requesting permission to visit Steepletop, Millay's home in upstate New York. This initial visit was followed by more visits and eventually an extended stay during which Oliver assisted in the task of organizing Millay's papers.

In her 1995 prose volume, *Blue Pastures,* Oliver states that she was "young, and deeply moved by the intimacy of living in the poet's house, among her possessions." The lyrical influence of Millay upon Oliver's early work is apparent, and many parallels can be drawn between the lives of Millay and Oliver, as both embraced country life, studied at Vassar, and moved in the bohemian circles of Provincetown, Massachusetts.

Oliver also studied at Ohio State University. She has had a series of scholarly engagements at various academic institutions—including Case Western Reserve University, Sweet Briar College, and Duke University. Having been appointed to the Catharine Osgood Foster Chair for Distinguished Teaching at Bennington College, she is now a resident of Vermont.

Oliver has been compared to many poets and traditions, yet these comparisons invariably fall short of the mark, as she conveys a unique attitude in her treatment and perception of nature. Oliver's intense focus on the natural world has inspired many to compare her to Robert Frost. The influence of American Romantic poets such as Walt Whitman and the British Romantic poets—including William Blake, William Wordsworth, and John Keats—has been noted in Oliver's work. Yet Oliver strikes out into new territory as she humbly seeks to merge with and learn from nature, expressing both terror and love for that which she readily admits she does not and cannot understand. Thus Keats's concept of negative capability—which Douglas Bush defines as "a refusal to seek for clear-cut answers, a willingness to maintain a state of suspension, to let the mind and imagination be a thoroughfare for all kinds of ideas"—is clearly a guiding philosophy in Oliver's work.

No Voyage and Other Poems (1963), Oliver's first book, introduces the poet's interest in the relationship between interior and exterior landscapes. Although she titles this book *No Voyage,* it is actually about the type of psychological journey one makes when one deepens the psyche through commitment to staying still and facing oneself. The title poem expresses this resolve in the final stanza:

> O, I go to see the great ships ride from harbor,
> And my wounds leap with impatience; yet I turn back
> To sort the weeping ruins of my house:
> Here or nowhere I will make peace with the fact.

The title *No Voyage* is also somewhat paradoxical, since many of the narrative poems take place in various locations, including Ohio, New England, London, and the River Ayr in Robert Burns's Scotland. Wherever the poems are situated, they deliver spiritual insights largely derived from contact with nature. In "Hawks at Task," Oliver turns a steady eye to the work of predatory birds, expressing her pained admiration for and acceptance of what they must do:

> —He folds his wings from the golden noon:
> That grief will sweep against me soon
> That still must cleave me when I see

A creature dealt with painfully,—
But hunger drives the heated wing,
And hunger is a decent thing. . . .

This brutally clear perception of the hawks illustrates Oliver's honesty. Mark Doty observes that "Oliver's nature is never sentimentalized. The world she meets is gorgeous, but not pretty."

The conventional form of the poetry collection in *No Voyage* may suggest simplicity, but this impression is misleading. Among the many complex themes Oliver addresses in this first book is the theme of emotional distance arising out of an inability to grieve adequately for others and their losses. In "The Murderer's House" the poet describes a "house of dark and mumbled fame" where shame lives. She brings the reader's attention to the shame of those who heartlessly pass by this house:

This is our failure, that in all the world
Only the stricken have learned how to grieve.
Safe in our cars, we pause along the highway
As one by one the leveling seasons fall;
And one by one we drive away, rejoicing
In such a distance as could strike us all.

Oliver's exploration of the complicated landscape of human emotions is but one example of the keen focus she trains on matters ranging from mortality to the grace of the running fox. Douglas Burton-Christie notes that "this attention to the particular is for Oliver a discipline." Oliver's ability to render the normally invisible visible—whether the details of light on water or the unconscious neglect of neighbors—imbues her poetry with a luminous vision transcending everyday perception.

Oliver uses her mastery of the poetic form to develop deep and personal poems in her second volume, *The River Styx, Ohio, and Other Poems* (1972). Here she frequently calls on childhood memories such as the juggling game she once played with her father. Yet Oliver's disciplined delivery of memory balanced by insights prevents her work from lapsing into nostalgia. In "The Juggler" Oliver conveys the anxiety-driven subtext of the alleged game:

When my father threw saucers into the air
And caught them spinning, one by one,
So rapidly the wheel seemed never broken,
We thought it was only for fun.

But the glazed faces of the saucers, and my father's hands
Moving like clockwork, and the lines of strain

Showing under his big laughter have stayed like a strange design
Of almost everything. Again and again

In my childhood I wept among the broken crockery:
My failure. I could not master the trick[.]

As the reference to the mythic River Styx of the underworld in the title of the book suggests, the theme of death is pervasive in this volume. "The Burial Ground" recounts the story of a cherry tree under which the narrator buried animals killed by her cat; eventually the cat itself lay "where killed and killer rest as one." In "New England Houses" the point of the poem is that houses outlast the carpenters who "drove the nails in straight and deep / Pounding for love and a kind of salvation."

In *The River Styx, Ohio, and Other Poems* Oliver fearlessly evokes childhood memories, contemplates the inevitability of death, and challenges the meaning of everyday conventions. The poem "Going to Walden" questions being a tourist; the poet's unique perspective is best summed up by these lines:

Going to Walden is not so easy a thing
As a green visit. It is the slow and difficult
Trick of living, and finding it where you are.

The journeying motif continues in Oliver's next book, *The Night Traveler* (1978), which was published as a chapbook. The poet develops a dynamic tension between the human and personal world, and the impersonal and awesome natural world as Oliver's poems range from childhood memories of breeding horses to the dream of hibernating with "the drowsy she-bear" in "Winter Sleep."

In "Entering the Kingdom" the narrator expresses her desire to bridge the world of humankind and nature, yet she finds herself regarded with suspicion by the crows: "I am possibly dangerous, / I am entering the kingdom." According to Mark Doty, "What allows [Oliver] to see the world, to know and sing about it, is precisely the consciousness that sets her apart." Through the distinct collection of poems in *The Night Traveler*, Oliver speaks of humankind's exile from the natural world, as in these lines from "Entering the Kingdom":

The dream of my life
Is to lie down by a slow river
And stare at the light in the trees—
To learn something by being nothing
A little while but the rich

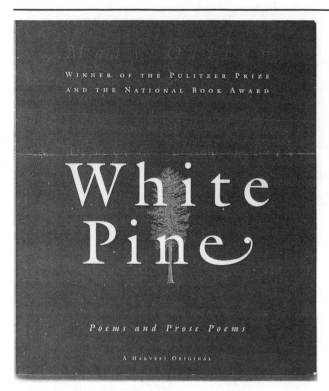

Dust jacket for Oliver's 1994 book that includes her first prose poems

Lens of attention.

But the crows puff their feathers and cry
Between me and the sun,
And I should go now.
They know me for what I am.

The elegiac nature of *The Night Traveler* collection explores the various levels of loss, from the loss of childhood to the ultimate loss of life. Death's presence is alluded to in the final lines of "The Lamps":

But of course the darkness keeps
Its appointment. Each evening,
An inscrutable presence, it has the final word
outside every door.

Loss is no stranger to Oliver. In *Blue Pastures* she writes about how she turned to books in her youth, since the voice of Whitman was one she could rely upon: "Whitman was the brother I did not have. I did have an uncle whom I loved, but he killed himself one rainy fall day; Whitman remained, perhaps more avuncular for the loss of the other." Oliver's next chapbook, *Sleeping in the Forest* (1979), consists of twelve poems excerpted from *The Ohio Review*. This brief edition illustrates the poet's skill at weaving together human narratives and the dramas of the forest. In "Storm" the narrator observes her own

distress at the approaching maelstrom and notes the contrasting resignation of the animals and birds. They are described as "patient":

As stones or leaves or clumps of clay,
What saves them is not knowing they are mortal—

What saves them is thinking that dying
Is only floating away into
The life of the snow.

The human narrator finds herself saying "Heaven help us," while the creatures of the forest are buoyed by their faith in and acceptance of nature's process. Yearning for the peace of animal consciousness is a recurring motif in Oliver's works.

Several of the poems in Oliver's next published volume, *Twelve Moons* (1979), were published previously in the chapbook *The Night Traveler*. This ambitious collection of fifty-one poems concentrates on nature imagery and cycles, including twelve poems dedicated to different lunar phases, such as "Pink Moon—The Pond," "Flower Moon—How She Travels," and "Wolf Moon." The symbolic equation between natural phenomena and what is most enduring and heartfelt in human experience is made manifest in these lines from "Harvest Moon—The Mockingbird Sings in the Night":

And the moon steps lower,
quietly changing
her luminous masks, brushing
everything as she passes
with her slow hands
and soft lips—
cluster of dark grapes
apples swinging like lost planets—
melons cool and heavy as bodies—
and the mockingbird wakes
in his hidden castle. . . .

This is a love story as the luminescent moon awakens the mockingbird into "spilling long / ribbons of music / over forest and river."

In the poetic landscape of Oliver's mythic worlds, stellar bodies, flora and fauna, and humanity are all interconnected. The poet invites the reader to become immersed in the natural world, to become engulfed. "Sunday Morning, High Tide" describes listening to the sea: "We listen / to the booming under the wharf, / the smashing of the water's gray fists / among the pilings, its desire / to eat us up, to carry us. . . ." Robin Fast writes that in "Sunday Morning, High Tide," "Oliver's evocation of the sea's desire might suggest a sense of relatedness, of affinity with nature that promises an openness to engagement with the other; on the other [hand], the pathetic fallacy belies the acknowledgment of otherness, of alien if wondrous power, that initially gives the poem its impact."

With the publication of *American Primitive* in 1983, Mary Oliver secured her place as an important American poet when she received the Pulitzer Prize for poetry in 1984. David Barber heralds the volume with these words: "The headlong breathlessness of *American Primitive,* its delirious immersion in wood and swamp and creaturehood, staked out an exclusive poetic territory for Oliver." This accomplished text reveals the range of skills Oliver had cultivated after twenty years of successfully publishing volume after volume of poetry.

Oliver deftly employs the primal and wild as a metaphor for human sexuality when she develops this theme in "The Snakes" and "Blossom." "The Snakes" narrates the vision of two snakes gliding through the woods: "they traveled / like a matched team / like a dance / like a love affair." In "Blossom" a series of images leads the reader through ponds reflecting moonlight: "the moon / swims in every one; / there's fire / everywhere: frogs shouting / their desire. . . ." Then the poem turns to the topic of the place of the human in nature's scheme and the ways humans must conform to the trajectory of desire:

> . . . we are more
>   than blood – we are more
>   than our hunger and yet
> we belong
>   to the moon and when the ponds
>   open, when the burning
>   begins the most
> thoughtful among us dreams
>   of hurrying down
>   into the black petals,
>   into the fire,
> into the night where time lies shattered,
> into the body of another.

The repetition of the four short phrases beginning with the words *into the* in the last four lines of the poem creates a sensation of inexorably being hurled by desire into an "other." These lines are thus representative of what Fast determined to be Oliver's interest in "a dissolution of boundaries between self and other, self and nature."

Oliver also turns her attention to the history of the Midwest as she writes about human subjects whose narratives are intertwined with the forces of nature. "John Chapman" yields insights into the Johnny Appleseed story, as he walked "barefoot on feet crooked as roots. . . . / And everywhere he went / the apple trees sprang up behind him lovely / as

young girls." The legendary figure's secret sorrow is revealed in the third stanza:

> Mrs. Price, late of Richland County,
> at whose parents' house he sometimes lingered,
> recalled: he spoke
> only once of women and his gray eyes
> brittled into ice. "Some
> are deceivers," he whispered, and she felt
> the pain of it, remembered it
> into her old age.

The human narrative arising out of the Ohio landscape also develops in "The Lost Children," Oliver's poem about white children abducted by Native Americans. This narrative poem attests to Oliver's relentless exploration of possibility as she recounts the stories of two lost children, Lydia Osborn, age eleven, and Isaac Zane, age nine:

> I'm sorry for grief, I said that.
>
> But I think the girl
> knelt down somewhere in the woods
> and drank the cold water of some
> wild stream, and wanted
> to live. I think
>
> Isaac caught
> dancing feet. I think
>
> death has no country.
> Love has no name.

Oliver's interest in the human world is apparent in her next published volume, *Dream Work* (1986). Portraits of respected persons ("Stanley Kunitz" and "Robert Schumann") are included, as well as a poem titled "Members of the Tribe," which examines the way other artists—including Vincent van Gogh, Keats, and Whitman—struggled to live. Here Oliver espouses a life-affirming attitude with the following stanzas:

> I forgive them
> their unhappiness,
> I forgive them
> for walking out of the world.
>
> But I don't forgive them
> for turning their faces away,
> for taking off their veils
> and dancing for death—

Many of the poems in the aptly titled volume *Dream Work* are thematically unified by Oliver's decree that humans' work is to master their unconscious fears and learn to love the world. In "Starfish" through the narrated tale of a person fearfully

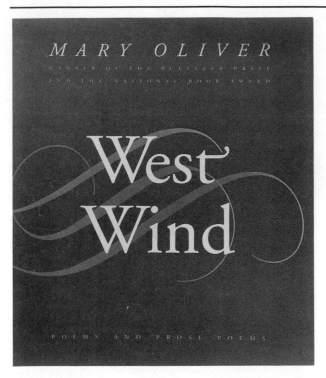

Dust jacket for Oliver's 1997 book, in which she explores the craft of poetry and its potential "to agitate our hearts"

examining starfish and with determination overcoming that fear, the author takes the opportunity to pose this question: "What good does it do / to lie all day in the sun / loving what is easy?" The poem "Dreams" develops the theme of bringing unconscious material into the light. Through an extended metaphor likening a dreaming human to a budding tree, Oliver clearly demonstrates the haunting power of dreams:

> All night
> the dark buds of dreams
> open
> richly.
>
> In the center
> of every petal
> is a letter,
> and you imagine
>
> if you could only remember
> and string them all together
> they would spell the answer.

Richard Tillinghast describes Oliver's style as one that conveys "the flux of her emotional life with an almost mythic but still light-fingered touch." Tantalizing promises of absolute answers ("if you could only remember") derived from the land of dreams suggest that there is a "kingdom" to be entered if one is willing to believe in the validity of the imagination.

Transcending the commonplace is an enduring theme evident in Oliver's 1990 book of poetry, *House of Light,* which pulsates with metaphysical thoughts and questions. The first poem in this collection, titled "Some Questions You Might Ask," launches into the incorporeal realm inquiring, "Is the soul solid, like iron? / Or is it tender and breakable, like / the wings of a moth in the beak of the owl?" Oliver continues her metaphysical questioning when she imagines death in "White Owl Flies Into and Out of the Field": "maybe death / isn't darkness, after all, / but so much light / wrapping itself around us−." This inversion of the concept linking darkness to death is indicative of the pervasive optimism in *House of Light,* its belief in the world as expressed in "The Ponds" with the lines "I want to believe I am looking / into the white fire of a great mystery." The poet herself speaks of this ebullient tone during a 1994 interview with Renee Olander: "I think *House of Light* worked well. I'm happy when I get to reading from that book."

Nevertheless, *House of Light* holds true to Oliver's pattern of delivering serious messages about the world through her acute powers of observation. The influence of traveling to exotic places and the insights gained during these experiences is relayed through "Indonesia" and "Singapore." The latter poem is merciless in its portrayal of a difficult moment when the narrator of the poem walks into an airport restroom to find a woman kneeling at a toilet washing ashtrays:

> Yes, a person wants to stand in a happy place, in a poem.
> But first we must watch her as she stares down at her labor,
>   which is dull enough.
> She is washing the tops of the airport ashtrays, as big as
>   hubcaps, with a blue rag.
> Her small hands turn the metal, scrubbing and rinsing.
> She does not work slowly, nor quickly, but like a river.
> Her dark hair is like the wing of a bird.

The poem succeeds in transmuting this image, which is at first perceived as humiliating, into one that accords beauty and dignity to the kneeling woman working at a steady pace "like the river."

White Pine: Poems and Prose Poems (1994) represents Oliver's first published venture into the realm of prose poems. In his review of this volume Tillinghast alludes to the Whitmanesque tenor of the poet's work: "Oliver's poetry, pure as the cottony seeds of the dandelion, floats above and around the schools and controversies of contemporary American poetry. Her familiarity with the natural world has an uncomplicated, nineteenth-century feeling."

In addition to celebrating nature and astutely developing metaphors between the human world and the animal kingdom, some of the poems in this collection explore what it means to be a writer. The narrator in "Work" describes herself working all day creating poetry from a verbal "fabric": "with the linen of words / and the pins of punctuation. . . ." The narrator's work, writing, is inspired by the daily pilgrimage to Pasture Pond, "How beautiful / this morning / was Pasture Pond," while the pond's "work" is the simple fact of existence: "It had lain in the dark, all night / catching the rain. . . ." Oliver's "Work" reveals how the solitary, nonverbal world of the writer draws breath from the landscape.

Inspiration frequently leads to transformation in *White Pine*. The long prose poem titled "In Blackwater Woods" is divided into fourteen sections that detail insights and turning points in the narrator's life, including a time in Ohio when she was witness to hundreds of swans coming "out of the sky / like an orchard / getting married / to the dark lake. . . ." Mark Doty's observation that "Oliver's poems remain fresh and alive because nature is viewed in the light of a spiritual crisis" rings true in the section of the poem that concludes with these lines:

> then they flew away
> my life in Ohio
> went on
> everything was changed
> do you know what I'm saying
> everything
> everything was changed.

Mary Oliver's poetic immersion in the world of nature is captured by the following comment she made during an interview with Renee Olander: "Once I was in the woods and I had no pen, so later I went around and hid pencils in some of the trees." Oliver advises her own writing students to keep a schedule, and in her *A Poetry Handbook* (1994) she provides what she calls "a more or less orderly discussion of things, which, over the years I have found to be useful, and interesting."

Blue Pastures, Oliver's 1995 prose collection, includes fifteen essays that offer autobiographical glimpses of the writer's life. In this text she reveals her understanding that the source of poems is not the mundane trivia of daily life: "Such activities . . . are surface activities—the curl up and breakage of waves. And poems do not come from that part of the ocean; they come from the dark and heavy and portentous and almost impenetrable depths."

The poet's capacity to delve into those impenetrable depths resounds in her latest collection, *West Wind: Poems and Prose Poems* (1997). This volume includes forty works, of which nineteen poems were previously unpublished. Oliver again addresses the question of what it means to work in the medium of language as she writes in her prose piece "Three Songs"

that if language were necessary, "it would have stayed simple; it would not agitate our hearts with ever-present loveliness and ever-cresting ambiguity; it would not dream, on its long white bones, of turning into song." The craft of poetry and its potential to "agitate our hearts" by creating a world is illustrated in the poem "Fox" as the narrator describes watching a fox and writing about it:

> . . . So I stood
> on the pale, peach-colored sand, watching the fox
> as it opened like a flower, and I began
> softly, to pick among the vast assortment of words
> that it should run again and again across the page
> that you again and again should shiver with praise.

Oliver is calling poetry an act of creation as well as an act of preservation. Her writing is purposeful and deliberate, and it invites the reader to be transformed through the sounds and images of the poet's craft.

In 1996 Oliver joined the faculty of Bennington College in Vermont. The poet has completed a second handbook, *Rules for the Dance,* which is on metrical poetry and was published in 1998. Oliver is also writing another volume of essays titled "Winter Hours," which she expects to publish in 1999. Oliver's writings have had a significant impact on twentieth-century American poetry. Through Oliver's work her readers may find that they too can explore the depths of the psyche through "entering the kingdom."

Interviews:

Eleanor Swanson, "The Language of Dreams: An Interview with Mary Oliver," *Bloomsbury Review,* 10 (May/June 1990): 1, 6–7;

Renee Olander, "An Interview with Poet Mary Oliver," *AWP Chronicle,* 27 (September 1994): 1–6, 8.

References:

David Barber, Review of *New and Selected Poems, Poetry,* 162 (July 1993): 233–237;

Douglas Burton-Christie, "Nature, Spirit, and Imagination in the Poetry of Mary Oliver," *Cross Currents,* 46 (Spring 1996): 77–88;

Mark Doty, "Natural Science: In Praise of Mary Oliver," *Provincetown Arts,* 11 (1995): 26–27, 29;

Robin Fast, "Moore, Bishop, and Oliver: Thinking Back, Re-seeing the Sea," *Twentieth Century Literature,* 39 (Fall 1993): 364–379;

Johanna Keller, "Review of Blue Pastures," *Antioch Review,* 54 (Summer 1996): 369;

Richard Tillinghast, "Stars and Departures, H̶ mingbirds and Statues," *Poetry,* 166 (A̶ 1995): 289–290.

Charles Olson

(27 December 1910 – 10 January 1970)

George F. Butterick
University of Connecticut

and

Robert J. Bertholf
State University of New York at Buffalo

See also the Olson entries in *DLB 5: American Poets Since World War II* and *DLB 16: The Beats: Literary Bohemians in Postwar America.*

BOOKS: *Call Me Ishmael* (New York: Reynal & Hitchcock, 1947);
Y & X (Washington, D.C.: Black Sun Press, 1948);
In Cold Hell, In Thicket (Dorchester, Mass.: Origin, 1953; San Francisco: Four Seasons, 1967);
The Maximus Poems / 1–10 (Stuttgart: Jonathan Williams, 1953);
Mayan Letters, edited by Robert Creeley (Palma de Mallorca: Divers Press, 1953; London: Cape, 1968);
The Maximus Poems / 11–22 (Stuttgart: Jonathan Williams, 1956);
O'Ryan 2 4 6 8 10 (San Francisco: White Rabbit, 1958); enlarged edition, *O'Ryan 12345678910* (San Francisco: White Rabbit, 1965);
Projective Verse (New York: Totem Press, 1959);
The Maximus Poems (New York: Jargon/Corinth, 1960; London: Cape Goliard, 1970);
The Distances (New York: Grove / London: Evergreen, 1960);
A Bibliography on America for Edward Dorn (San Francisco: Four Seasons, 1964);
Proprioception (San Francisco: Four Seasons, 1965);
Human Universe and Other Essays, edited by Donald Allen (San Francisco: Auerhahn Society, 1965; New York: Grove, 1967);
[...] by Creeley (New York: New [...];
[...] Goliard, 1966);
[...] *VI* (London: Cape Goliard / [...]sman, 1968);
[...]*rom Charles Olson to John Clarke* [...]65 (Buffalo: Institute of Fur-[...]8);

Charles Olson, 1957 (photograph by Harry Redl)

Letters for Origin 1950–1956, edited by Albert Glover (London: Cape Goliard, 1969; New York: Paragon House, 1989);
The Special View of History, edited by Ann Charters (Berkeley: Oyez, 1970);
Archaeologist of Morning (London: Cape Goliard, 1970; New York: Grossman, 1973);
Additional Prose, edited by George F. Butterick (Bolinas, Cal.: Four Seasons, 1974);

234

The Post Office (Bolinas, Cal.: Grey Fox Press, 1975);

The Maximus Poems: Volume Three, edited by Charles Boer and Butterick (New York: Grossman, 1975);

In Adullam's Lair (Provincetown, Mass.: To the Lighthouse Press, 1975);

Spearmint & Rosemary (Berkeley: Turtle Island, 1975);

Charles Olson and Ezra Pound: An Encounter at St. Elizabeths, edited by Catherine Seelye (New York: Grossman, 1975);

The Horses of the Sea (Santa Barbara, Cal.: Black Sparrow Press, 1976);

The Fiery Hunt and Other Plays (Bolinas, Cal.: Four Seasons, 1977);

Some Early Poems (Iowa City: Windhover Press, 1978);

Muthologos: The Collected Lectures and Interviews, 2 volumes, edited by Butterick (Bolinas, Cal.: Four Seasons, 1978–1979);

The Maximus Poems, edited by Butterick (Berkeley: University of California Press, 1983);

The Collected Poems of Charles Olson: Excluding the Maximus Poems, edited by Butterick (Berkeley: University of California Press, 1987);

A Nation of Nothing but Poetry: Supplementary Poems, edited by Butterick (Santa Rosa: Black Sparrow Press, 1989);

Maximus to Gloucester: The Letters and Poems of Charles Olson to the Editor of the Gloucester Daily Times 1962-1969, edited by Peter Anastas (Gloucester, Mass.: Ten Pound Island Book Company, 1992);

Selected Poems, edited by Creeley (Berkeley: University of California Press, 1993);

Collected Prose, edited by Donald Allen and Benjamin Freelander (Berkeley: University of California Press, 1997).

Charles Olson shaped postmodern American writing through his poetry and his essays. As the successor to Ezra Pound and William Carlos Williams and the inheritor of Herman Melville's prophetic voice, he was the leading voice of the Black Mountain Poets—which included Robert Creeley, Robert Duncan, Edward Dorn, and Joel Oppenheimer. He has claimed a dominant place in literary history with his epic series, *The Maximus Poems* (1953–1975); the theoretical manifesto "Projective Verse" (1950); essays such as "Human Universe" (1951); the lecture/essays published after his death as *The Special View of History* (1970); his study of Melville, myth, and America, *Call Me Ishmael* (1947); and his acknowledged influence on an entire generation of poets. He caused the reconsideration of poetic structures and reengaged contemporary poetry with its American traditions after the flirtation with European sources in the high modernist movement of the first part of the century. Warren Tallman in his preface to *The Poetics of the New American Poetry* (1973) speaks of "Olson's generation" the way Hugh Kenner has referred to "the Pound Era."

Olson's background reflects diverse interests and experience and somewhat explains why he did not publish his first poem until his mid thirties. He was born in Worcester, Massachusetts, on 27 December 1910 to Karl Joseph and Mary Hines Olson. Although raised in the central Massachusetts industrial city of Worcester, where his father was a mailman, Olson spent summers in Gloucester on the coast, which became the focus of his most important work, *The Maximus Poems.* He was a champion orator in high school, winning a tour of Europe as a prize. He chose Wesleyan over Harvard on the advice of his high-school debating coach and received his B.A. in 1932, continuing there for an M.A. (1933). He wrote a thesis on Melville, tracked down Melville's personal library as part of his research, and produced the first bibliography of Melville's writing. Olson eventually went to Harvard for further study in a newly begun American Studies program, completing all course work for a Ph.D. (1936–1938); but he left without the degree after receiving a Guggenheim Fellowship in 1939 for a book on Melville (the four-hundred-page draft was abandoned but emerged after World War II in remarkably different form as *Call Me Ishmael*). During the war Olson was assistant chief of the Foreign Language Division of the Office of War Information, until he resigned in protest against bureaucratic meddling and inefficiency. He served as adviser to the National Committee of the Democratic Party and as strategist (for which service he was offered significant governmental posts), but he withdrew abruptly from partisan politics to become exclusively a writer, as he chronicles in his poem "The K." It was the second time he turned his back on promising careers—that of a traditional scholar-academic and that of participant in national politics—valuing more his independence. In 1948, the same year he was awarded a second Guggenheim Fellowship, he was convinced to take a temporary teaching position vacated by his friend Edward Dahlberg at Black Mountain College, returning there to teach as a regular instructor in 1951 and to serve as rector of the school until its closing in 1956. Thereafter he returned to Gloucester and preoccupation with the *Maximus* series, remaining by choice in relative isolation and poverty until he accepted a teaching post at the State University of New York at Buffalo, where he was as effective as a teacher as he had been at Black Mountain. In 1961 he received an award from Longview Foundations for *The Maximus Poems,* and in

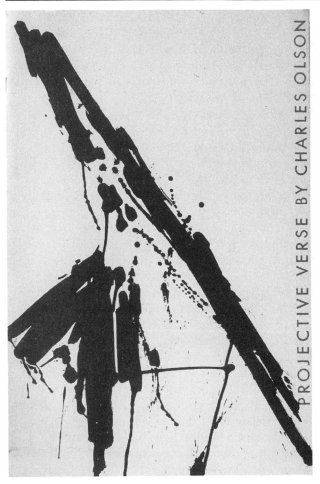

PROJECTIVE VERSE BY CHARLES OLSON

Dust jacket for Olson's 1959 book, the manifesto for "open field" poetry that was first published in a 1950 issue of Poetry New York

man born in America, from Folsom cave to now. I spell it large because it comes large here. Large, and without mercy." There are also striking images, such as "a sun like a tomahawk . . . a river north and south in the middle of the land running out the blood," and other forms of compression, including the incorporation of live facts whole into the narrative, the condensing of information (for a book with fewer than one hundred printed pages Olson investigated every book in the Library of Congress on the American whaling industry), and the technique of montage or juxtaposition. And thematically, there is the preoccupation with America ("we are the last 'first' people"), the delving into myth, and not least, the final chapter on the new, "prospective," post-Ahabian hero, directly anticipating Maximus.

Among his earliest poems, "The K" and "La Préface" most notably hint at the scope and concerns to come, while others of such balanced delicacy as "Pacific Lament" and "Lower Field—Enniscorthy" already strain against tidiness and, although quite formal, take advantage of rhythm and rhyme to move freely against the "closed" universe Olson rejects in "Projective Verse." In "Pacific Lament," an elegy for an acquaintance drowned in wartime submarine service, within the strictness of narrow lines the syntax follows the spirals of the boy's descent, mimetic of the fall of a body lost at sea. (It was, in fact, later danced by one of the students at Black Mountain College.) The effect is enhanced by careful curtailment of line, omission of punctuation, and occasional rhyme. Above all, the sense is of free invention within control. "Lower Field—Enniscorthy," part of a larger "Enniscorthy Suite" written while Olson was on vacation at a friend's estate in Virginia, is similarly composed in free lines but with advantageous placement of words for their ultimate effect:

A convocation of crows overhead
mucks
in their own mud and squawk
makes of the sky
a sty[.]

Somewhat stiffly formal and not yet the "open field" of "Projective Verse," it nevertheless tests the structures of formal metrics. The landscape is sharp-edged and nonromantic. Prevalent monosyllabic words contrast with occasional polysyllables, and attention is paid to sounds (in the subsequent line, "A bee is deceived"). It is a picture only, having no narrator, sharing Williams's nominalism and trust in the phenomenal world. It is a careful presentation of a natural world free from human presence and interference, a "peaceable kingdom," although with lurking dangers or unpleasantness: the sheep are like soldiers; an "am-

1965 he won the Oscar Blumenthal Prize from *Poetry* magazine. He taught again, briefly, at the University of Connecticut until he was overtaken by cancer. He died two weeks past his fifty-ninth birthday, having completed *The Maximus Poems* a month before. Writing autobiographically, he described himself not so much as a poet or writer as "an archeologist of morning," and the phrase has stuck to him and his vision.

Olson's first book was not poetry but a remarkable study of Melville and the writing of *Moby-Dick* (1851), *Call Me Ishmael,* for which he has been much praised. First published in 1947, it has been republished four times by different publishers. It has been seen as a continuation of the line of writings on American literature begun with D. H. Lawrence's *Studies in Classic American Literature* (1923) and including Williams's *In the American Grain* (1925) and Dahlberg's *Do These Bones Live* (1941). Among the qualities *Call Me Ishmael* shares with Olson's poems, however, is the brisk, confident, efficient style seen in its famous opening paragraph: "I take SPACE to be the central fact to

*Olson writing a Maximus poem at Black Mountain College, 1951 (photograph by
Jonathan Williams)*

bush" is possible; the crows "muck" and make of the
sky a "sty"; a bee mistakes a rotten stump for honey-
comb; the path is "undisciplined." There is a trust in
language to represent reality, even in the deliberate
flatness of the end—

> Report: over all
> the sun

—the staring eye of the camera, the photorealism,
tough-minded and unsentimental, the documentary
impulse characteristic of the later poems. "The K," appearing in *Y & X* (1948), a book of coordinates, is
among Olson's first poems, written in early 1945
when he was nearly thirty-five. It includes the same
mixture of personal and cultural reference that characterizes almost all his poems. An early version, written
while Olson was on a working vacation with the
Democratic National Committee at its winter head-
quarters in Key West, is significantly titled "Tele-
gram." The poem was written in response to offers to

keep him engaged in national politics through a position in the coming administration. The poem begins
with his rejection of the offers by quoting another
statesman in the words of another poet (Brutus in William Shakespeare's *Julius Caesar*) in order to reclaim
his personal freedom:

> Take, then, my answer:
> there is a tide in a man
>
> moves him to his moon and,
> though it drop him back
> he works through ebb to mount
> the run again and swell
> to be tumescent I[.]

And although this "tumescent I" is not yet a "Maximus," the poet suggests that finally the artist's concerns are more elemental than a Caesar's:

> Our attention is simpler
> The salts and minerals of the earth return

The night has a love for throwing its shadows around a man
a bridge, a horse, the gun, a grave[.]

Such language is as symbolic as Olson's was ever to get.

The other poems in *Y & X* are considerably more energetic and Yeatsian in their imagery than this one, though not sufficiently distinct to have gained the poet special regard. But "La Préface," written in the spring of 1946, is of unusual power. Again, it is both specifically autobiographical and of the widest cultural import. It can be read just as its title proposes, as preliminary to the work and new life ahead. It marks the poet's—as well as man-kind's—entry into the postwar, post-Holocaust, in-deed, postmodern age. Reminders of earlier voyag-ers are given, with Odysseus heard in the concentra-tion camps ("My name is NO RACE") and Dante ("in vita nuova") superimposed on present horrors in that most dead of times following the worst war and cruelty experienced by man. Man now is led ahead by the survivors of Adolph Hitler's death camps, Pleistocene survivors, who represent both the end of modern man and a new beginning for the future. The theme of rebirth and openness (and the mode of same) begins following references to the Tarot and other traditional symbols for birth:

Draw it thus: ( ) 1910 (
It is not obscure. We are the new born, and there are no flow-
　　ers.
Document means there are no flowers
　　　　　　　　　　and no parenthesis.

The year is the poet's first or actual birth, the open parenthesis the possibility to come. There is a point-ing ahead to the end of that time of global war and genocide, and a newborn hope in the courage and persistence of those who survived:

Mark that arm. It is no longer gun
We are born not of the buried but these unburied dead
crossed stick, wire-led, Blake Underground
The Babe
the Howling Babe[.]

The poem is as allusive and deeply private in its ref-erence as any of the later poems, with the same de-sire to represent an age, to speak on behalf of man-at-large (Maximus) as well as the poet himself. It may be the first—in theme and style—postmodernist poem.

Olson's first grand poem was "The Kingfish-ers," written in early 1949. It is a richly complex poem in which the historically conscious mind faces the upheavals of history and displacement of cul-tural values. It was originally part of an even longer poem, titled at one stage "The First Proteid," indica-tive of the ambitiousness of the effort. (Another por-tion was extracted and similarly published sepa-rately as "The Praises.") "The Kingfishers" prefig-ures the *Maximus* series in scope and concerns, and it might well be read as an introduction to Olson's ma-jor work. When it was first published, both Creeley and Williams responded with enthusiasm. Critics have since acknowledged it to be one of Olson's most significant poems, indeed one of the most im-portant of the entire postwar period. It certainly was conceived on an impressive scale—balancing the West against the East, weighing the present with the past. The principle of its composition is juxtaposi-tion, not of images as in Surrealism, but of whole continents of fact, metaphysics, and cultural evoca-tion. There are a series of separate movements, with little narrative intervention or overt causal relation-ships, in which the assembled blocks of information are permitted to speak for themselves and, in their dialectic, build a base from which the narrator can speak personally, in the final section, as a response to the terms of the proposition with which the poem opens.

There are three sections in all (and four parts within the first section), with the Roman numeral omitted to encourage direct entrance into the poem. It begins with the rallying proposition—

What does not change / is the will to change

—a modification of the Heraclitean doctrine of flux (which is continued in the body of the poem using Heracleitus's own words as presented by Plutarch) by the injection of human will (and responsibility), which some readers have given a Hegelian or Marx-ist interpretation. It is, in any case, a heroic call, enough so that Adrienne Rich titled one of her col-lections with reference to it, *The Will to Change* (1971). The emphasis, due to the fulcrum of the soli-dus or slash, falls ultimately on the "will"—a func-tion not allowed by Heracleitus, who also said, "a man's character is his fate." The will is the human element in the successive ebb and flow of history that makes up the poem, the intention that holds the poem together in tension. The structure of the open-ing line, divided as it is, is paradigmatic for the poem as a whole. The will holds the blocks of thought and historical example in balance, allowing the associations from which the argument emerges to flow freely.

The opening section continues as if to illus-trate or further the initial proposition, with a story (of birds put back in their cages after a night of ne-glect) told from personal experience. It is the start of a train of associations, leading to a recollection of the previous night and a party the poet had attended in Washington, in which the care of birds again figured, only on a wider cultural scale. One of the guests, an artist, bemoans the loss of value from the past: "The kingfishers! / who cares / for their feathers / now?" It is not clear at that point whether the "blue" and "green" birds previously mentioned are to be taken as symbolic or even as varieties of the kingfishers of the title of the poem, or just what symbolic properties the birds of the title do have, other than as emblems of cultural loss. Anyone with a tendency to treat the kingfishers themselves exclusively as symbols, however, is disabused in the next section of the poem with a description of the bird in the most ornithological terms straight from the *Encyclopaedia Britannica,* while a brief account of their legendary qualities is followed by the statements: "The legends are / legends. Dead, hung up indoors, the kingfisher / will not indicate a favoring wind, / or avert the thunderbolt." Symbols, nonetheless, are introduced in what follows—a mysterious, cultic *E* that has been "rudely" cut on "the oldest stone." This appears side by side, spliced, with a passage concerning Mao Tse-tung, whose revolution has just triumphed in China and whose victorious words are quoted in French (the way, in fact, they were reported to Olson).

The entire poem is rich with allusions and documentary borrowings, but because the allusions are unfamiliar or distant from their sources (Mao's words quoted in French), they appear to be more symbolic and less referential than in fact they actually are. The documentary nature of the juxtapositions is given a narrative life of its own. The *E*—it can be known, though hardly from the little evidence the poem has to offer—is a primitive form of the Greek epsilon as it appears carved on the stone *omphalos* at the temple of Apollo at Delphi—a symbol, in other words, of the source and navel of the Western world. It is perhaps enough for the reader that a sense of ancient mystery and elemental value is present in the *E,* but it does help to know that the stone is also representative of the essential West in the contrast with the East. The revolutionary present and perhaps (in 1949) future, located in the East, are contrasted with the past of the West. The contrasts continue throughout the poem—East and West, past and present, light and darkness, the "primitive" and the "civilized." There are not only the treasured kingfisher feathers of the ancient Khmers but also the European destruction of the indigenous American civilization, the newest West (summarized in the catalogue of Montezuma's treasure as reported at the Spanish court); the control of

data flow according to modern cybernetics; the metaphysics of change as discussed by Neoplatonists; reference to Dante among other representatives of the West; and borrowings from Pound and Arthur Rimbaud, Olson's modernist predecessors who brought the poet to the brink of his own position—that of "archeologist of morning," hunting among the ruins of the past (and, sadly, the present), which might include correctives for the present and directives for a future, though not necessarily a future of improvement or progress.

The dialectics of the serially opposed sections continue up to the concluding portion, in which the poet at last steps forth fully, the "I" for the first time dominating the facts in curiously formal quatrains:

> I am no Greek, hath not th'advantage.
> And of course, no Roman:
> he can take no risk that matters,
> the risk of beauty least of all.

"But I have my kin," he continues, "if for no other reason than . . . I commit myself, and"—now echoing Pound in *Guide to Kulchur* (1938)—"given my freedom, I'd be a cad / if I didn't." He then moves to invoke Rimbaud, whose "taste for the earth and stones" he shares, concluding, not negatively as T. S. Eliot had, but as the "archeologist of morning" who would himself in less than two years go to the Yucatán to dig among the Mayan ruins:

> I pose you your question:
>
> shall you uncover honey / where maggots are?
>
> I hunt among stones[.]

Given the fact of change—and there is enough evidence amassed throughout the poem of the movements of civilizations, their decline and rising like young kingfishers, or phoenixes, out of old "dripping, fetid" nests—the poet can do nothing better than embrace change, though not passively, mindlessly. He commits his will to the search, to the act of history, the activism of "finding out for oneself," which is central to his philosophy. The final line is not to be taken as despair or a futile scrabbling among the rubble of an Eliotic wasteland. It is the highest-willed engagement, a commitment to change itself, if that is what is necessary.

The poem moves with the methods, although not yet the full, spoken immediacy of a Maximus. Guy Davenport has called it "the most modern of American poems" and again "the essential poem in the Projectivist School of poets." Although rooted in

I, MAXIMUS, OF GLOUCESTER, TO YOU

Off-shore, by islands, hidden, in the blood
jewels and miracles, I, Maximus,
a metal hot from boiling water, tell you
what is a lance, who obeys the figures of the present
dance

1

the thing/may lie
around the bond/of the nest
(second, time slain, the bird! the bird!
there! (strong) thrust, the mast! flight

(o the bird, the kylix, O

D Antiony

of Padua, sweep low, o bless
the roofs, the old ones, the gentle steep ones/on whose ridge-poles
the gulls sit, from which they depart,
                                    and the flake racks

my city!

2

love is form, and cannot be without
important substance,(the weight
say, 58 carats, each one of us, perforce,
our goldsmith's scale:
            feather to feather added
            (and what is mineral, what
            is curling hair, the string
            you carry in your nervous beak, these
            make bulk, these,)
            in the end,
            are the sum

                        o my lady

                        (o my lady of)

                        good voyage,

                        in whose arm,

                        in whose left arm

no boy, but a carefully carved wood, a painted face and schooner,
a delicate mast, a bow-sprit for

                        forwarding

"I, Maximus, of Gloucester, To You," revised typescript

121

Revised typescript for the first Maximus poem (Estate of Charles Olson)

its attack on *The Waste Land,* which it seeks to challenge and surpass, it begins to put into practice the techniques and attitudes of postmodernism and projective verse. The technique is still basically that of Eliot's juxtaposition, Pound's ideogrammatic method, and Sergei Eisenstein's montage. The difference is that Olson, while conscious of inheritance from his predecessors, seeks to advance beyond them, beyond history as accumulation and symbol, and into the fact of change, the instant by instant engagement, the openness where all things are possible.

"The Kingfishers" is followed in time and significance by "In Cold Hell, In Thicket," the title poem of Olson's first important collection of verse (after *Y & X*) and the first poem fully to put into practice the kinetics and the "breathing of the man who writes" as outlined in "Projective Verse," which he had been working on throughout that period. Written in May 1950, "In Cold Hell, In Thicket" is a long meditative poem of a civil war raging within the poet, a hell of indecision. Olson had been reading Dante at the time, but the *Inferno* supplies only the lightest touches—besides the title and perhaps the separated, celestial "beloved," only one reference deep within to "selva oscura," the dark woods Dante must emerge from to begin his quest. Rather, it is a secular hell:

> hell now
> is not exterior, is not to be gotten out of, is
> the coat of your own self, the beasts
> emblazoned on you[.]

The lines are tormented by commas and parenthetical interjections, echoing the speaker's doubts and anxieties. There is a battlefield within that must be crossed, just as the field of the poem is to be traversed. The poem moves through a series of questions, probings of the deepest sort, culminating in the basic one: "Who / am I?" Man is at war to find his identity, as the poet continues: "Who am I but by a fix, and another, / a particle, and the congery of particles carefully picked one by another"—the realization, as in "Projective Verse," that man is an "object" (rather than egoistic "subject") in a "larger field of objects." The poem, in fact, in many ways is illustrative of or a commentary on the "objectism" presented in "Projective Verse." Whereas in the essay Olson offers "objectism" as "a word to be taken to stand for the kind of relation of man to experience which a poet might state as the necessity of a line or a work to be as wood is, to be as clean as wood is as it issues from the hand of nature, to be shaped as wood can be when a man has had his hand to it," and he again writes, "It comes to this: the use of a

man, by himself and thus by others, lies in how he conceives his relation to nature, that force to which he owes his somewhat small existence"; in the poem he writes:

> that a man, men, are now their own wood
> and thus their own hell and paradise
> that they are, in hell or in happiness, merely
> something to be wrought, to be shaped, to be carved,
>   for use, for
> others
>
> does not in the least lessen his, this unhappy man's
> obscurities, his
> confrontations[.]

Salvation lies only in the precise use of oneself: "By fixes only (not even any more by shamans) / can the traceries / be brought out." Life, by the fact of birth, is a field to be entered:

> this at least
> is a certainty, this
> is a law, is not one of the questions, this
> is what was talked of as —
> what was it called, demand?

Life is to be faced without heroics or histrionics. By the end the poet is resolved that he will live "without wavering," even though "forever wavers" and he too "will forever waver." This struggle is a final acceptance, the only certainty possible, to be as "precise as hell is, precise / as any words, or wagon, / can be made."

Olson had begun his celebrated *Maximus* series in 1950, shortly before "In Cold Hell" was written, but that *Maximus* was to be a major work, the vehicle into which he would pour his greatest effort, did not become apparent to him until 1953. Meanwhile, following his instincts, he visited the Yucatán to dig among Mayan ruins (until his money ran out) and there wrote his indispensable essay "Human Universe" while continuing to develop the fundamentals set forth in "Projective Verse." His letters to Robert Creeley from Mexico were published as *Mayan Letters* (1953). In them Olson reveals his project of poetry as the historical conflict between European civilization and the civilization of the new world. Like "The Kingfishers," these letters and then the following *Maximus Poems* seek and then uncover the origins of the persistent myths of the Americas. He stretched them out in an assortment of long, often long-lined poems over the next ten years, many of which had as much influence as the *Maximus Poems* themselves. There was the proud declaration, written with "the power of American vocables," to the young German poet and editor Rainer

Olson with his first common-law wife, Constance Wilcox Bunker, and their daughter, Katherine, early 1950s

M. Gerhardt titled "To Gerhardt, There, among Europe's Things" (followed in 1954 by a majestic elegy to Gerhardt, "The Death of Europe," upon learning of Gerhardt's suicide). There was also the wrathful "Letter for Melville 1951," sounding like the crack of doom. Most of the important poems of this period are included in *The Distances* (1960), a volume of selected poems that Donald Allen helped the poet put together. These include "A Newly Discovered 'Homeric' Hymn," "As the Dead Prey Upon Us," "The Lordly and Isolate Satyrs," " Variations Done for Gerald Van De Wiele," and "The Librarian"–all written while the *Maximus Poems* were in abeyance. All move in the poet's familiar discursive patterns and with far-ranging associations, yet always propelled and directed by the unusual force of his intensity. The chief theme continues to be man's life on the largest terms–including psychological and mythological–seen even in the exquisitely formed "Variations Done for Gerald Van De Wiele," a series of spring poems composed for a student at Black Mountain. These precisely lyrical variations based on a passage in Rimbaud's A *Season in Hell* (1873)

show a refined rhythmic structure and movement while working within, instead of pushing, the limits of language. In the 1960s Olson's notable poems include the deftly controlled mobile "The Red Fish of Bones," the sweeping "Across Space and Time," and the '*West*' (1966) sequence. The rest of the poet's energies went into the *Maximus Poems* and the private struggles of living.

Among the poems written at Black Mountain in the mid 1950s, "A Newly Discovered 'Homeric' Hymn," dedicated to the historian of Greek religion Jane Harrison and drawing upon her account of the Athenian ritual of the *Chrythoi* or "pots," begins engagingly:

> Hail and beware the dead who will talk life until you are blue
> in the face. And you will not understand what is wrong,
> they will not be blue, they will have tears in their eyes,
> they will seem to you so much more full of life
> than the rest of us. . . .

The poem continues in haunting but stately long lines, concluding–typical of the seriousness of Olson's regard for the archaic–

> Fall off! The drink is not yours,
> it is not yours! You do not come
> from the same place, you do not suffer as the dead do . . .
>
>   Beware the dead. And hail them. They teach you
> drunkenness.
> You have your own place to drink. Hail and beware them,
>   when they come.

—rounding out the hymn, so that it, too, is a vessel of instruction. It is a poem of utmost credibility, not mere decorative imitation. The discrepancies and near contradictions readers are warned against, present throughout the poem, protect an ancient mysteriousness.

"As the Dead Prey Upon Us" is the first of several poems whose sources were literal dreams. A visitation occurs, an appearance by the poet's deceased mother, almost like the ghosts in "A Newly Discovered 'Homeric' Hymn." (The same haunting by the deceased mother, four and six years after her death, occurs in "Moonset, Gloucester, December 1, 1957" and "O'Ryan 6": "What a man has to do, he has to / meet his mother in hell.") "As the Dead Prey Upon Us" seems to confirm all the primitive senses of the restlessness of departed souls. The poet's mother returns in the life of his sleep, and the poem is filled with unsought images and the elasticity of dream. Strands of dream matter are interwoven like the automobile tires presented in the dream, "masses of rubber and thread variously clinging together." One of the functions of the poem—and the creative imagination—is to sort the strands. There are memories of his mother in her Gloucester cottage and of her neighbor, the "Indian woman" (in reality, of Indian ancestry), who with the poet enables a "blue deer" to walk and talk:

> and we helped walk it around the room
> because it was seeking socks
> or shoes for its hooves
> now that it was acquiring
> human possibilities[.]

And although the poem begins with all the abruptness characteristic of a dream (the poet's car "had been sitting so long unused. / I thought the tires looked as though they only needed air. / But suddenly the huge underbody was above me . . ."), in the poem, as opposed to the dream, the poet has a certain control. His imagination fuses a narrative; his intensity burns through with such extraordinary lines as:

> The vent! You must have the vent,
> or you shall die. Which means

> never to die, the ghastliness
>
> of going, and forever
> coming back, returning
> to the instants which were not lived
>
> O mother, this I could not have done,
> I could not have lived what you didn't,
> I am myself netted in my own being
>
> I want to die. I want to make that instant, too, perfect
>
> O my soul, slip
> the cog[.]

It is one of Olson's most dynamic and unshakable statements.

>   the nets of being
> are only eternal if you sleep as your hands
> ought to be busy. Method, method
>
> I too call on you to come
> to the aid of all men, to women most
> who know most, to woman to tell
> men to awake. Awake, men,
> awake[.]

The strands, the entangling nets of dream, which at first had seemed so extraneous to the main burden of the poem, are actually quite useful in resolving it at the end when the poet flatly announces that the automobile—source of much trouble and uncertainty (dreamed strangeness)—"has been hauled away." Despite the occasionally confusing dream time, the force of the poet comes through. Accepting the raw offerings of the unconscious mind, at the same time infusing dream with enormous lyrical capability, Olson created one of his most powerful separate poems. Another dream poem written at Black Mountain, "The Lordly and Isolate Satyrs" from 1956, offers an expansive mythopoeic experience, a choreography of archetypes, in which modern-day motorcyclists suddenly appearing on a beach are transformed into symbols of completeness: "the Androgynes, / the Fathers behind the father, the Great Halves," dimensionally larger than we are. And the result is such that

> the boy-town the scene was, is now pierced with angels and
> with fire. And winter's ice shall be as brilliant in its time as
> life truly is, as Nature is only the offerer, and it is we
> who look to see what the beauty is.

Then there are the final lines of that near *Maximus,* "The Librarian":

> Where
> is Bristow? when does 1-A

243

The apartment in Gloucester, Massachusetts, where Olson lived
after Black Mountain College closed in 1956 (photograph
by Ann Charters)

get me home? I am caught

in Gloucester. (What's buried
behind Lufkin's
Diner? Who is

Frank Moore?

—which Edward Dorn has called "my reunion with
the nouns and questionings" of his own life—had
visitors wandering the streets of Gloucester searching for Lufkin's and digging, reports had it, behind
the building at night by the beams of flashlights, unaware that the diner had long since been moved
from its original location. "The Librarian" is the
most Maximus-like of the out-of-series poems, even
beginning with an echo of the opening lines of the
first Maximus letter, and it ostensibly might have
been included in the series. But undoubtedly because of the personal and confusing nature of its
messages, coming especially at a time when the poet
realized the focus of the poem must be on the facts
of the place Gloucester, it was withheld and pub-

lished apart. It, too, was originally a dream (which
accounts for some of the discrepancies in the actual
landscape). Olson focused on Gloucester as the fac-
tual as well as imaginary place of his poems at about
the same time that he was recasting Alfred North
Whitehead's philosophy from *Process and Reality*
(1929) in his perspective on history. He delivered a
series of lectures at Black Mountain College titled
"The Special View of History" and then at the invitation of Robert Duncan delivered them again in
San Francisco in February 1957.

Finally, moving into the 1960s, called by some
the Age of Aquarius, "Across Space and Time" is a
poem from the midst of Olson's most productive
Maximus period and similar in scope to others in
the sequence, although completely without the figure of Maximus and, again, not focused on Gloucester. It is another long poem of cultural expanse reminiscent of "The Kingfishers," but more concentrated and systematized, again on the widest scale,
here not only historical, with the sweep of invading
peoples, the great Indo-European creation of the
West, but cosmological and zodiacal:

> horsemen from the Caucasus
> came in with Aries to shake the dead temple world
> and awake self and reason, the soft Aries people who ride
> horses backward, brilliant riders who only know the back
> is an engine of will to be sacrificed if the sons
> will have wives, they ride on into battle until all
> is divided between flesh and soul and Greece
> is the measure of what they were worth. . . .

When he chose the poems for *The Distances,* Olson
left many poems unpublished and uncollected. He
continued to write poems outside the *Maximus Poems.*
"Stone and Flower Series," "Being Altogether Literal, & Specific . . . ," "Buffalo Ode," "West," "The
Drum World," "The Grandfather-Father Poem,"
and many shorter poems all indicate Olson's persistence in working the form of a poem from the inside
out. He conceived human beings to be engaged in
the flow, the process of history, but affected by specific events. The measure of the rhythms of the
poem and the form the poem took on the page became indications of the individual's interaction with
that process. Many of the poems seek to answer the
question, raised in "In Cold Hell" on a personal
level: Who are we as a species? This is Olson's
mightiest contribution.

Olson would be a formidable poet from these
poems alone, but his most important work is *The
Maximus Poems,* that long series of epic intent in the
tradition of Pound's *Cantos* (1917–1969) and Williams's *Paterson* (1963). The poem, in three volumes,
is focused on the city of Gloucester, Massachusetts,

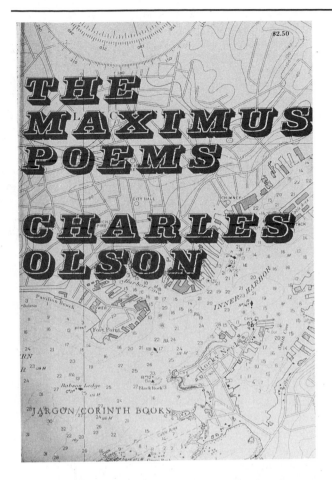

Cover for the 1960 volume in Olson's series of poems about an epic hero living in Gloucester, Massachusetts

which serves as microcosm to the larger America. Its theme is the development of a hero through the celebration of a place. It is a series of more than three hundred separate but interrelated poems, begun in the spring of 1950 and continued—with greater intensity at some times than at others—over the almost twenty years Olson was most active as a poet. Although it had roots in previous proposals for a long poem on the development of Western man, the series began spontaneously, almost casually (in light of the extent of its commitment), as a letter to Olson's friend and surrogate in Gloucester, poet Vincent Ferrini (the designation "letters" appears throughout the first volume, as an ordering device, but only occasionally thereafter). Too vast in scope to be at all times carefully orchestrated, it remains one of the most complex poems in the English language. The poet chooses for his hero the name (or title) Maximus, meaning "Greatest," derived in part from a little-known eclectic philosopher of the second century A.D., Maximus of Tyre, whose associations with his city make possible analogues between the modern world and the ancient,

and in part, undoubtedly, from the unlimited possibilities such a name offers in itself.

Following the close of Black Mountain College, Olson returned to live in Gloucester among the fishermen of Fort Square in a second-story cold-water flat overlooking the harbor. Thirty miles northeast of Boston, Gloucester was in the nineteenth century one of the leading fishing ports in the world. The city, which was founded in 1623 by settlers—mostly fishermen—from Dorchester, England, is on Cape Ann, an area of great natural beauty and variety, home of the intrepid fishermen Olson grew up among and admired, daily pitting their lives against the full North Atlantic. What made Gloucester a model or source of possibility for Olson was that he conceived of it as actually an island in the Atlantic, separated from the mainland (and mainland culture) by the Annisquam River, a tidal estuary that connects Gloucester Harbor with Ipswich Bay in the north. Until the mid 1960s its regular population (not counting the summer influx) had remained the same for nearly seventy years. It enabled Olson to offer an image of a city, a polis, in his words, a "redeemable flower that will be a monstrance forever, of not a city but City." For instance, he writes among his notes: "The interest is not in the local at all as such—any local; and the choice of Gloucester is particular—that is the point of the interest, particularism itself: to reveal it, in all possible ways and force, against the 'loss' of value of the universal." For the poet, through Maximus of Tyre, namesake of his hero, Gloucester is the twentieth-century analogue to the Phoenician city of Tyre, which was the last holdout against Alexander the Great's conquest of the known world. Tyre was captured only after Alexander laid siege to the city and constructed a causeway or mole, comparable to the present highway Route 128 (completed in 1959 during the course of the poems), which encircles Boston and ends in Gloucester, bringing with it mainland values or the corruption of true value. That is why the first volume, published in 1960, concludes: "as the mainland hinge / of the 128 bridge / now brings in / what, / to Main Street?"

Olson explores Gloucester as a historian and archaeologist rather than as a sociologist. He knew every corner and rock pool, talked himself into each cranny, as his neighbor Mrs. Tarantino well knew: "You have a long nose, meaning / you stick it into every other person's / business, do you not?" Most often the tone is stalwart, upholding, defiant:

> Holes
> in my shoes, that's all right, my fly
> gaping, me out

at the elbows, the blessing
            that difficulties are once more

—although when the "difficulties" are the continuously unrectified excesses of a people, the tone can be darker, especially toward the end:

    Hunched up
on granite steps in the part dark Gloucester
and ghettoes gone cities and an infantile people
set loose to recreate what was ground
and is now
holes.

Olson sought redemption through knowing. He sought to restore to America its "city on a hill," built out of sound like Amphion's Thebes by the power of poetry alone.

The theme of the poem in all its variety may be conveniently summarized from the maps on each of the covers of the three volumes. The first, a U.S. Coast and Geodetic Survey of Gloucester and its harbor, suggests the particular attentions of the poems, the streets and beaches delineated, the real-life topography of buoys in the harbor, the city-hall tower, the twin cupolas of Our Lady of Good Voyage Church, chimneys (like that of Le Page's glue factory), the salt marshes and mud flats, all as present-day and quotidian as "April Today Main Street." The second map shows Earth when it was most nearly one—mythologically, geologically, perhaps even culturally—a rendition of the archaic Earth according to current theories of continental drift; here, the mythological names of the supercontinents and seas before the landmasses separated reflecting the mythological dimensions of the volume. And finally, on the last volume, edited from among Olson's papers after his death, is a map purported to have been drawn from the deck of the flagship *Arbella* by John Winthrop, a hero of the poems, on his 1630 voyage to found the polis of Boston, a "city upon a hill"—in Winthrop's own words from the deck of the same ship—a model city, shining or "glowing" for all to see, like Glow*ceastre,* Gloucester in its earliest form. It is also a personal chart, just as so much of the volume is deeply personal, and an example of history as *'istorin,* finding out for one's self, drawn (a drawing) from one man's "eye-view" like that of Gloucester artist Fitz Hugh Lane, whose presence also continues to be felt in this volume. The complexities are inexhaustible, the relationships endlessly rewarding.

The poem itself begins with Maximus (in absentia, projected) addressing his city:

Off-shore, by islands hidden in the blood
jewels & miracles, I, Maximus
a metal hot from boiling water, tell you
what is a lance, who obeys the figures of
the present dance

—a mythical, even alchemical, hero with special knowledge and powers; clearly no mere man alone. He addresses his city to correct abuses and restore value, in all urgency and righteousness:

    that which matters, that which insists, that which will last,
that! o my people, where shall you find it, how, where, where
    shall you listen
when all is become billboards, when, all, even silence, is
    spray-gunned?

That is one goal of the poem, to awaken Gloucester to itself; but equally, to awaken Maximus to all his own possibilities. As the poem progresses, the persona becomes more a person, until Maximus and Olson are all but indistinguishable. The poet moves simultaneously to create a model (a "monstrance") city together with a hero who must be "an image / of man." Gloucester must be possessed by single-minded investigation. Maximus's governing principle is 'istorin, the Herodotean historian's "finding out for oneself." The poem explores the chosen territory to its deepest, most archaic roots, during which time the identity—and personality—of Maximus is developed. The focus on Gloucester is ever narrowing, down to local records from the city-hall vault, spreading out the city's concerns and passions. Maximus's consciousness and the personality of the city become interchangeable. Olson's concerns were specific, as his letters to the editor of the *Gloucester Daily Times* indicate. The history of his city was engaged in its houses, the record of human struggle and living. He fought to preserve them with as much energy as he fought to drive the city into his poems. The early poems are mostly concerned with the heroic fishermen and the early settlement at Gloucester Harbor, where the poet himself would take up residence two-thirds through the volume. The archaic makes its first appearance toward the end of volume one with the urging, "start all over" (Maximus has just said "the present is worse," meaning *pejorocracy,* a term derived from Pound, rules). "Step off the / Orontes" (the river north of Tyre), he continues, "onto land no Typhon [the "blue monster" that eventually becomes the Gloucester sea serpent] / no understanding of a cave [such as that ancient one of Trophonius, center of mysteries, or the Corcyrian, home of Zeus] a mystery Cashes [a fusing pun: both the fishing bank in the North Atlantic over which the *Rattler* of a later poem plunges, and Mount Casius overlooking the Orontes, where Zeus and Typhon fought]." As patience reveals, it all ties in, coiled, interlocking, "entwined / throughout / the system." The *Maximus Poems* welcome and reward such close readings. The lines are thick with allusions. In a poem of this size and scope it takes a while for the recurrent patterns to emerge. Olson's vision was massive and the spread of his interests wide.

The second volume turns its "Back on / the Sea," away from the harbor settlement, and moves inland to Dogtown, an area of wilderness at the heart of Cape Ann. Formerly the site of a settlement (the eighteenth-century cellar holes are still much in evidence) but abandoned to widows, witches, and their dogs, it is part moor, strewn with boulders left by the retreating ice, which puts Maximus in touch with the most primordial elements of creation. A crucial poem is the third of four long ones addressed to Dogtown. It is untitled except for a line from the *Theogony* by the Greek poet Hesiod (who lived around 800 B.C.) but known from its setting and its opening lines as "Gravelly Hill." Within it the poet seeks to identify the boundaries or divisions of the world into Earth, Heaven, and Hell, during the course of which Maximus *becomes* the hill. The poet is high up, "sitting there like / the Memphite lord of all Creation," and with the sense of the "bowl" of light at the top of Dogtown carried over from the previous "Cow of Dogtown." The same voice that earlier said, "I have had lunch / in this 'pasture'" and "It is not bad / to be pissed off / where / there is *any* condition imposed" now continues to speak as the hill itself, "leave me be, I am contingent, the end of the World / is the borders / of my being," as the poet and his place merge to one.

It is immediately apparent in this volume how the range of the poem opens up. Passages from Hesiod and the Norse Eddas stand side by side with Algonquian tales of the wife who lusted after a serpent in a pond or the witch who each Sunday has a liaison with a mountain. Whitehead, with his grand cosmology and philosophy of process, and Carl Jung, with his archetypism and theory of libidinal energies, more evidently offer guidance to the poems. Parallels and relationships are exposed and explored. Olson often objected that Pound had not gone back far enough in the *Cantos*—that the Renaissance had "boxed" him in. On the other hand, Olson seeks the very sources of civilization. The poems in this volume reach back to the continents before they drifted apart, back to Cape Ann depressed by the weight of the ice upon her mass, back beyond the Homeric and Hesiodic Greeks and the Phoenicians of Tyre and into the ancient Indo-European

homeland, to the migrations of the Western hero, the archetype in which Maximus participates (summarized in the poems "ALL MY LIFE I'VE HEARD ABOUT MANY" and "Peloria"), various predecessors of Maximus such as Manes and Odysseus and Herakles-Melkaart, and monsters such as the legendary Gloucester sea serpent or bulls both archetypal and real enough to gore a six-foot-seven Gloucester sailor (exactly Olson's height) to death. Amid poems of such clear and extricable individual power as "Maximus to Gloucester, Letter 27," "Maximus, at the Harbor," "A Later Note on Letter #15," "The Gulf of Maine," "I Am the Gold Machine," and "Civic Disaster" are studded briefer "tesserae," the poet called them, some only a line or two long. In their compression they must serve to summarize an entire area of thought or layer of history, no matter how it challenges the reader. Through all, Maximus continues to be the voice of responsibility, of authority, of self-possession. Only in the third volume is the true extent of his vulnerability revealed.

With the third volume, with Gloucester in transition all around him ("fake gasoline station / and A & P supermarket / construction") and with the loss of his own personal center (his wife suddenly killed in an automobile accident in 1964, a sense of isolation in Gloucester, intermittent moves from Buffalo to London to Connecticut), the poems become increasingly personal. Redemption is sought as much for the man as for the city. The spiritual quest is highlighted by the poem whose title is, literally, an almanac entry: "A 3rd morning it's beautiful February 5th," a meditation upon the landscape of Gloucester and specifically one "floating" island in the harbor outside the poet's windows, with a lighthouse on its snowy banks "looking / humpy and sorely bedraggled like America / since after the Civil War." The poem is full of digression and details that slow the reader while supplying a sufficient dimension to the focus of the meditation—too sudden, actually, to be a meditation, more a vision. While gazing at the island ablaze in the winter sun, the poet is struck with a realization summarized by an alchemical test he had been reading in Jung: simply, the "mystery / of creation" that in matter alone lies perfection, that matter can transform the spirit, and that neither matter, Ten Pound Island, Gloucester, nor the earth itself is "prison" for the soul of man. The poem is a great liberating one, itself a spiritual exercise, which the reader must follow in all its peregrinations to attain its value.

There are other poems of similar beauty and magnitude in the volume, specifically "West Gloucester," "Enyalion," "Cole's Island," "The Festival Aspect," "Maximus of Gloucester," "The win-

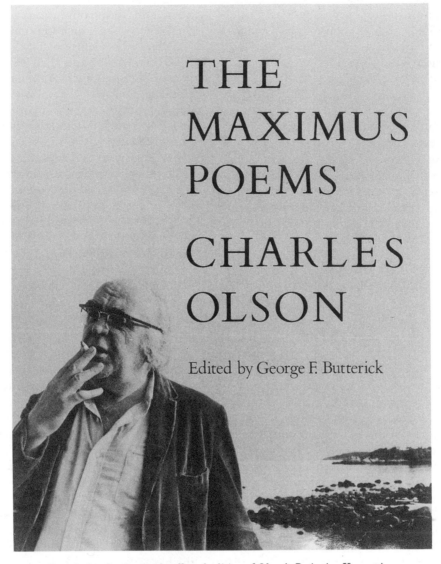

Dust jacket for the 1983 collected edition of Olson's Projective Verse epic

ter the *Gen Starks* was stuck," "When do poppies bloom," "Hotel Steinplatz," and "Celestial Evening," which are among the finest in the series and ought not be overlooked. Among many possible readings of the poems, one might speak of a "Maximusizing" of Olson, together with an "Olsonizing" of Maximus (similar to the overall structural pattern of *Don Quixote)*. If in the "Gravelly Hill" poem the Maximusizing of Olson is complete, in the final poems there is the Olsonizing of Maximus. As it becomes apparent that the vulnerabilities (already referred to in "Maximus to Himself" in volume one) are not going to diminish or be overcome, the voice of Olson speaks more from the heart than the mind and even wavers (wavers as "forever wavers" in "In Cold Hell"), his throat "tight from madness of isolation & / inactivity," hungry "for every thing." And

although with the next to last poem there is accomplished "the initiation / of another kind of nation," the final poem of the series reads, with no ease of resolution: "my wife my car my color and myself." Nothing more. It is as if once again he has learned "the simplest things / last." Olson chose the final, concluding poem himself, so the series does in fact end. In this sense, Olson rejects the endless process of meditation that pushed Williams's *Paterson* from book to book.

All the volumes include poems of immediate accessibility, their power undiminished even when removed from context; but the majority gain from one another incrementally. Randomness is only temporary; there is solidity beyond. Call it belief—in man, in the species—it is irrepressible, unwarranted, genetic, and always welcome. Names accumulate values and dimension as they recur, and eventually patterns emerge. It is not a poetry to be possessed easily, but there are enough rewards in startling images and direct wisdom to sustain Olson's vision of cosmology, history, and his great hope for humankind's endless spiritual journey of discovery.

Olson's initial reputation was confounded by warring impressions—the overstated claims of his enthusiasts and bemusement on the part of the doubtful or aloof. Although Olson designated the final *Maximus Poem,* at the time of his death in 1970 from liver cancer he left hundreds of pages of unpublished poems. In that sense, he died before he had defined the full scope of his major poem. He was described by early critics who had lost sight of the American tradition from Ralph Waldo Emerson, Melville, and Walt Whitman as an "aging beatnik" and a Poundian imitator. His roots as a poet and a poetic thinker were in Melville and the greater Romantic movement, which was not an agreeable position in post–World War II academic criticism. So the antagonism was strongest from that part of the academic and literary establishment that felt itself most exposed, rejected, or ignored. His work now stands in direct opposition to the institutionalization of poetry in the workshop. Yet his reputation held firm among a small body of fellow poets, including Robert Creeley and Robert Duncan, in the 1950s and extended to a widespread, if young and enthusiastic, audience in the 1960s in the United States and in England. Following his death, academic recognition accrued; his work became the subject of books, many articles, and dissertations, as well as being included in textbooks and the major anthologies. He is one of the most difficult of recent poets because of both the scope of his proposals and his own eccentricities—his refusal to simplify, the demand he makes on the reader no less than on himself (including "the secret of secrecy . . . that the work get done"). He was also one of the most provocative poets of his time, one who extended the domain and responsibility of poetry—or returned it to the Homeric and Hesiodic sense—to include cosmology, geography, history in the sense of finding out for oneself, spiritual transformation, as well as the self-generating exuberance language has in and for itself.

Olson is of interest not for his poetry alone but for his thought about poetry, about the function of the mind, the limits of the Western "universe of discourse," the uses of the past, the value of the local, and the glory of the unreconstructed individual. His essay "Projective Verse" rallied and focused the energies of the new poetry while forwarding the line of Pound and Williams. He was among the first to see the larger intellectual consequences of the new poetry and the first to use the term *postmodern* in its current significance. His writings have a pedagogical cast, simultaneously exploratory and insistent, often daring, at times angry or didactic, like a fist brought down upon a table. His writing has become a rich foundation, a point of reference for avant-garde movements in art and literature. He troubled himself with the larger issues of the universe, often moving ahead rather than waiting for the language to follow. His writing by its very nature can never be popular, save perhaps for the small memoir of his father titled *The Post Office* (1975) and, to a lesser degree, *Call Me Ishmael,* which is considered a minor classic. But his poetry and essays attract a steadfast core of readers who seek a poetry that extends thought and language beyond aestheticism and beyond self-expression.

Letters:

Charles Olson & Robert Creeley: The Complete Correspondence, volumes 1–8, edited by George F. Butterick; volumes 9–10, edited by Richard Blevins (Santa Barbara & Santa Rosa: Black Sparrow Press, 1980–1994);

Charles Olson and Cid Corman: Complete Correspondence 1950–1964, 2 volumes, edited by George Evans (Orono: National Poetry Foundation, University of Maine, 1987, 1991);

In Love, in Sorrow: The Complete Correspondence of Charles Olson and Edward Dahlberg, edited by Paul Christensen (New York: Paragon Books, 1990).

Bibliographies:

George F. Butterick and Albert Glover, *A Bibliography of Works by Charles Olson* (New York: Phoenix Bookshop, 1967);

William McPheron, *Charles Olson, The Critical Reception, 1941–1983: A Bibliographic Guide* (New York: Garland, 1986).

Biographies:

Tom Clark, *Charles Olson: The Allegory of a Poet's Life* (New York: Norton, 1991);

Ralph Maud, *Charles Olson's Reading: A Biography* (Carbondale & Edwardsville: Southern Illinois University Press, 1996).

References:

Christopher Beach, "Olson as Menicus and His Master, Pound: A Study in Poetic Tradition," in his *ABC of Influence: Ezra Pound and the Remaking of American Poetic Tradition* (Berkeley: University of California Press, 1992), pp. 110–135;

Robert Bertholf, "On Olson, His Melville," in *An Olson-Melville Sourcebook, Volume 1: The New Found Land, North America,* edited by Richard Grossinger, *IO,* 23 (Plainfield, Vt.: North Atlantic Books, 1976), pp. 5–36;

Charles Boer, *Charles Olson in Connecticut* (Chicago: Swallow Press, 1975);

Eniko Bollabas, *Charles Olson* (New York: Twayne, 1992);

Boundary 2, special Olson issue, 2 (Fall 1973/Winter 1974);

George F. Butterick, "Charles Olson's 'The Kingfishers' and the Poetics of Change," *American Poetry,* 6 (Winter 1989): 28–59;

Butterick, *A Guide to the Maximus Poems of Charles Olson* (Berkeley: University of California Press, 1978);

Donald J. Byrd, *Charles Olson's Maximus* (Urbana: University of Illinois Press, 1980);

John Cech, *Charles Olson and Edward Dahlberg: A Portrait of a Friendship* (Victoria, B.C.: University of Victoria, 1982);

Cech, Oliver Ford, and Peter Rittner, *Charles Olson in Connecticut: Last Lectures as Heard by John Cech, Oliver Ford, Peter Rittner* (Boston: Northeastern University Press, 1977);

Ann Charters, *Olson/Melville: A Study in Affinity* (Berkeley: Oyez, 1968);

Paul Christensen, *Charles Olson: Call Him Ishmael* (Austin: University of Texas Press, 1978);

Robert Creeley, *A Quick Graph: Collected Notes & Essays,* edited by Donald Allen (San Francisco: Four Seasons, 1970), pp. 151–194;

Guy Davenport, "Scholia and Conjectures for Olson's 'The Kingfishers,'" *Boundary 2,* no. 2 (Fall 1973/Winter 1974): 250–262;

Donald Davie, "The Black Mountain Poets: Charles Olson and Edward Dorn," in *The Poet in the Imaginary Museum,* edited by Barry Alpert (New York: Persea Books, 1977), pp. 177–190;

L. S. Dembo, "Charles Olson and the Moral History of Cape Ann," *Criticism,* 14 (Spring 1972): 165–174;

Edward Dorn, *What I See in the Maximus Poems* (Ventura, Cal.: Migrant Press, 1960); reprinted in *Kulchur,* 4 (1961): 31–44;

Martin Duberman, *Black Mountain: An Exploration in Community* (New York: Dutton, 1972);

Robert Duncan, "Notes on Poetics Regarding Olson's 'Maximus,'" in his *Fictive Certainties* (New York: New Directions, 1985), pp. 68–75

Vincent Ferrini, "A Frame," *Maps,* 4 (1971): 47–60;

John Finch, "Dancer and Clerk," *Massachusetts Review,* 12 (Winter 1971): 34–40;

Edward Halsey Foster, *Understanding the Black Mountain Poets* (Columbia: University of South Carolina Press, 1995);

Stephen Fredman, *The Grounding of American Poetry: Charles Olson and the Emersonian Tradition* (New York: Cambridge University Press, 1993);

Richard Grossinger, ed., *An Olson-Melville Sourcebook* (Plainfield, Vt.: North Atlantic Books, 1976);

Judith Halden-Sullivan, *The Topology of Being: The Poetics of Charles Olson* (New York: Peter Lang, 1991);

Robert von Hallberg, *Charles Olson: The Scholar's Art* (Cambridge: Harvard University Press, 1978);

Walter B. Kalaidjian, "Mapping Historical Breaches: *The Maximus Poems* of Charles Olson," in his *Languages of Liberation: The Social Text in Contemporary American Poetry* (New York: Columbia University Press, 1989), pp. 67–92;

Karl Malkoff, *Escape from the Self: A Study in Contemporary American Poetry and Poetics* (New York: Columbia University Press, 1977);

Maps, special Olson issue, 4 (1971);

Ralph Maud, "Charles Olson: Posthumous Editions and Studies," *West Coast Review,* 14 (January 1980): 27–33;

Thomas F. Merrill, *The Poetry of Charles Olson: A Primer* (Newark: University of Delaware Press, 1982);

Paul Metcalf, "Big Charles: A Gesture towards Reconstitution," *Prose,* 8 (Spring 1974): 163–77;

Minutes of the Charles Olson Society (Vancouver, B.C.), no. 1– (1993–);

Charles Molesworth, "Charles Olson and His Forces," *Georgia Review,* 30 (Summer 1979): 438–443;

OLSON: The Journal of the Charles Olson Archives (Storrs, Conn.), nos. 1–10 (1974–1978);

Sherman Paul, *Olson's Push: Origin, Black Mountain, and Recent American Poetry* (Baton Rouge: Louisiana State University Press, 1978);

Marjorie Perloff, "Charles Olson and the 'Inferior Predecessors': 'Projective Verse' Revisited," *ELH,* 40 (Summer 1973): 285–306;

J. B. Philip, "Charles Olson Reconsidered," *Journal of American Studies,* 5 (December 1971): 293–305;

Martin L. Pops, "Melville: To Him, Olson," in *Contemporary Poetry in America,* edited by Robert Boyers (New York: Schocken Books, 1974), pp. 189–220;

Jeremy Prynne, "On Maximus IV, V, VI," *Iron,* 12 (1971), n. pag.;

M. L. Rosenthal, *The New Poets: American and British Poetry since World War II* (New York: Oxford University Press, 1967), pp. 160–173;

Rosenthal, "Olson / His Poetry," *Massachusetts Review,* 12 (Winter 1971): 45–57;

Gavin Selerie, *To Let Words Swim into the Soul: An Anniversary Tribute to the Art of Charles Olson* (London: Binnacle Press, 1980);

Charles F. Stein, *The Secret of the Black Chrysanthemum: The Poetic Cosmology of Charles Olson and His Use of the Writings of C. G. Jung* (Barrytown, N.Y.: Station Hill Press, 1987);

Lynn Swigart, *Olson's Gloucester: Photographs* (Baton Rouge: Louisiana State University Press, 1980);

John Taggart, "Call, Me Ishmael, Call Me Pierre: Charles Olson's Misreading of Melville," *Boundary 2,* 16 (Winter/Spring 1989): 255–275;

Rosmarie Waldrop, "Charles Olson: Process and Relationship," *Twentieth Century Literature,* 23 (December 1977): 467–486;

Jonathan Williams, "AM-O," *Parnassus,* 4 (Spring/Summer 1976): 243–250.

Papers:

Olson's extensive papers, including his personal library, are in the Special Collections, University of Connecticut Library, Storrs. A smaller collection is in the Poetry/Rare Books Collection, University Libraries, the State University of New York at Buffalo.

Joel Oppenheimer
(18 February 1930 – 11 October 1988)

George F. Butterick
University of Connecticut

and

Robert J. Bertholf
State University of New York at Buffalo

See also the entry on Oppenheimer in *DLB 5: American Poets Since World War II*.

BOOKS: *Four Poems to Spring* (Black Mountain, N.C.: Privately printed, 1951);

The Dancer (Highlands, N.C.: Jonathan Williams, 1951);

The Dutiful Son (Highlands, N.C.: Jonathan Williams, 1956);

The Love Bit and Other Poems (New York: Totem/Corinth, 1962);

The Great American Desert (New York: Grove, 1966);

Sirventes on a Sad Occurrence (Madison, Wis.: Perishable Press, 1967);

In Time: Poems 1962–1968 (Indianapolis & New York: Bobbs-Merrill, 1969);

On Occasion: Some Births, Deaths, Weddings, Birthdays, Holidays, and Other Events (Indianapolis & New York: Bobbs-Merrill, 1973);

The Wrong Season (Indianapolis & New York: Bobbs-Merrill, 1973);

Pan's Eyes (Amherst, Mass.: Mulch Press, 1974);

The Woman Poems (Indianapolis & New York: Bobbs-Merrill, 1975);

Acts (Driftless, Wis.: Perishable Press, 1976);

names, dates, & places (Laurinburg, N.C.: Saint Andrews Press, 1978);

Just Friends / Friends and Lovers: Poems, 1959–1962 (Highlands, N.C.: Jargon Society, 1980);

The Only Anarchist General (Rocky Mount, N.C.: Arthur Mann Kaye, 1980);

Marilyn Lives! (New York: Delilah Books, 1981);

Houses (Buffalo, N.Y.: White Pine Press, 1981);

The Progression Begins, published as "special unnumbered issue of # *Magazine*" (New York: # Magazine, 1981);

Joel Oppenheimer

At Fifty: A Poem (Laurinburg, N.C.: Saint Andrews Press, 1982);

2 at Fifty (Rocky Mount, N.C.: Arthur Mann Kaye, 1982);

Del Quien Lo Tomó: A Suite (Minor Confluence, Wis.: Perishable Press, 1982);

Poetry, the Ecology of the Soul: Talks and Selected Poems, edited by David Landrey and Dennis Maloney (Buffalo, N.Y.: White Pine Press, 1983);

The Ghost Lover (Rocky Mount, N.C.: Arthur Mann Kaye, 1983);

Notes Toward a Definition of David (Minor Confluence, Wis.: Perishable Press, 1984);

Why Not (Rochester, N.Y.: Press of the Good Mountain, 1985; trade edition, Buffalo, N.Y.: White Pine Press, 1987);

New Spaces: Poems 1975–1983 (Santa Barbara, Cal.: Black Sparrow Press, 1985);

The Teacher (Rocky Mount, N.C.: Arthur Mann Kaye, 1986);

The Uses of Adversity (Vandergrift, Pa.: Zealot Press, 1987);

The Debt (Annandale-on-Hudson, N.Y.: Bard College, 1987);

Names & Local Habitations (Selected Earlier Poems 1951–1972) (Winston-Salem, N.C.: Jargon Society, 1988);

New Hampshire Journal (Perry Township, Wis.: Perishable Press, 1994);

Collected Later Poems of Joel Oppenheimer, edited by Robert J. Bertholf (Buffalo, N.Y.: The Poetry/Rare Books Collection, University at Buffalo, 1997).

Joel Lester Oppenheimer was born in Yonkers, New York, 18 February 1930 to Leopold Oppenheimer, a retailer, and Kate Rosenwasser Oppenheimer; he was raised there, in an "old-time" neighborhood. Young Joel became a New Yorker, a teenage fan of the Yankees, and an incipient poet. The themes of his origins followed him through all the periods of his writing. He attended Cornell University and the University of Chicago before finding himself at Black Mountain College, where he studied writing with M. C. Richards, Paul Goodman, and especially Charles Olson. He began lifelong associations with fellow Black Mountain writers Edward Dorn, Robert Creeley, Jonathan Williams, Michael Rumaker, and Fielding Dawson. (Later associates included Paul Blackburn, Allen Ginsberg, LeRoi Jones, Frank O'Hara, and Gilbert Sorrentino.) Having actually been a student at Black Mountain from 1950 to 1953, taking courses with Olson and having his work published in the *Black Mountain Review,* edited by Creeley, Oppenheimer is one of those writers most legitimately a part of the group known in recent literary history as the Black Mountain Poets. He is included as such in Donald Allen's famous anthology, *The New American Poetry* (1960). Oppenheimer's writing is hardly restricted to representing a literary movement, however, and his subsequent reputation as a poet is as much a result of his life and literary activities in New York as it is of his Black Mountain connections.

Oppenheimer married Rena Furlong on 5 June 1952 and lived in New York City beginning in 1953,

working for fifteen years in print shops—as printer, typographer, and production manager. Oppenheimer and his wife had two children, Nicholas Patrick and Daniel Eben, but divorced in 1960. Oppenheimer married Helen Bukberg in 1966; they had two children, Nathaniel Ezra and Lemuel Shandy Davin. In 1966 Oppenheimer became director of the St. Mark's Poetry Project, one of the liveliest series of readings and workshops on the East Coast, and remained as director until 1968. He was also the director of New York's Teachers and Writers Collaborative (1969). During these years he organized and began a program that grew into the famous "Writers in the Schools" project. During the years 1969–1984 he wrote a regular column in the *Village Voice*—on sports (baseball), politics, the seasons, occasional literary-cultural matters, over-coffee musings—a domestic Joseph Addison or Richard Steele. He was poet-in-residence (Distinguished Visiting Professor of Poetry) at the City College of New York. For almost ten years he lived in Westbeth, a federally sponsored artists' and writers' community rehabilitated from the old experimental laboratories of the Bell Telephone Company in Greenwich Village. The ambience of his poems is even more typically New York than that of the self-consciously named New York School poets such as O'Hara. By the mid 1980s Oppenheimer began looking outside of New York for employment and so spent time at the State University College at Oneonta, State University College at Buffalo, and the Rochester Institute of Technology. He then found a comfortable and rewarding position at New England College in Henniker, New Hampshire, in 1982. He and his second wife had divorced in 1976, and he married Theresa Marie Maier on 10 November 1985. In his poetry Oppenheimer's preoccupation has not been the evoking of a particular geographic place but the exploration of interpersonal relationships in his made-up space, his place. The recurring themes of his poems are erotic dreams and experiences, marital situations, family, daily activities, friends, and the interaction of the personal and psychological worlds of people.

An early influence was E. E. Cummings, the first poet whom Oppenheimer read and to whom he paid tribute by his use of lowercase letters in his own poetry. Also influential—at least for his early poems, those of the 1950s—was Robert Creeley, who shared Oppenheimer's sense of the personal. The most pervasive and persistent influence, however, was William Carlos Williams, to whom he was introduced at Black Mountain, at least the Williams of the *Collected Earlier Poems* (1951) and *Pictures from Breughel* (1962) rather than of *Paterson* (1946–1958),

Oppenheimer, circa 1935

to get in the way of the poem." He argues, "a cap on a proper noun . . . implies there are improper nouns," and he adds, "I also like the visual look of it. On my typescripts, I'll type the title in spaced capitals—single space between each of the letters and a triple space between the words because I like that appearance. So I'm not against capitals as letter forms. I guess I'm against miscegenation between capitals and lower case letters." Finally, he offers still another reason: "having made that determination that I liked the way it worked in the poem, in about 1955 when I was just beginning to get published a little bit consistently, the shift key on my typewriter broke, so the decision was made by God."

Oppenheimer wrote poems with short lines, using enjambment but little syncopation or other complicated metrical designs. The poems are gently rhythmic, unfolding from the live flow of speech. He trusts a simple vocabulary and the everyday commerce between people and—especially in the later work—a consistent, undistorted, unambiguous syntax. He is concerned with direct communication. He is certainly not unaware of the complexities of life (and art), however, and some of the best poems have faint brushes of irony or satire. Still, simplicity is his trust. The ear is not startled awake by the beat of an opening alliteration; no paradox is immediately issued to eventually be resolved; and images are not used to unwind a conceit. Repetition and sincerity, rather than a shock of image (or summarizing by image) or lyric exaltation, sustain the poems. There is an unhurried mildness, an unstudied repose— grace, it might be called—to the poems. That, and their inherent warmth, perception and defense of such human values as independence, fairness, tolerance, and frankness are the most admirable qualities of the poems.

Among Oppenheimer's first published poems, *The Dancer* (1951), fully in the manner of Williams and Olson—written in tribute to dancer Katherine Litz and published by Jonathan Williams with a drawing by Robert Rauschenberg—indicates the company it was possible to keep at Black Mountain. Oppenheimer himself found (in his interview with Whitney Jones) more care and craftsmanship in the lines in the earlier volumes, *The Dutiful Son* (1956) and *Just Friends / Friends and Lovers: Poems 1959–1962*. This book was not published until 1980, but the poems fill up the chronology from *The Dutiful Son* to *The Love Bit and Other Poems* (1962). The collections *In Time: Poems 1962–1968* (1969) and *On Occasion: Some Births, Deaths, Weddings, Birthdays, Holidays, and Other Events* (1973) are more discursive—not only in syntax but also in the range of material, the free slid-

which Oppenheimer thought was a magnificent and futile failure. And it was not Charles Olson's own poetry as much as Olson the teacher who significantly affected him, instructing him to discover his own voice and, specifically, to allow the full natural discursiveness of his speaking voice to enter the poems.

One of the most immediately noticeable characteristics of Oppenheimer's poetry is the absence of uppercase letters—a manner derived in part from Cummings but also consistent with his own poetics. This usage extends to his prose as well, whether his stories as collected in *Pan's Eyes* (1974), his fan's baseball book *The Wrong Season* (1973), or, until the publisher insisted otherwise, his *Village Voice* column. He responded to the issue in a 1974 discussion of poetics: "I don't think they [capital letters] serve any functional purpose. In general they seem to me to get in the way of a flat line, and I suppose if I had to talk that way I'd say that I don't want the words

ing between private feelings and public concerns, personal relationships and political issues–much like the 1960s themselves. He writes in "The Innocent Breasts":

> we are all, we know
> now, bone-pickers after
> darwin, rag-pickers after
> marx, brain-pickers
> after freud–we are
> trying to reconstruct
> our history.

The poems in *The Dutiful Son* and *Just Friends,* more so than the later poems of direct address, are obliquely evocative. Metaphors are sketched, not scored; they are seldom hardened into sharp visual images as in imagism. Ornament, when necessary, is worn lightly. Skill is evident in the effective parallels and repetitions of "The Bus Trip" and "The Bath." "The Tide" and "The Gardener," both first published in the *Black Mountain Review,* show the influence not only of Williams but also of Creeley, whose poems and stories Oppenheimer had immediately responded to when Olson read them in class. "The Tide" describes a woman braiding her hair at the sea's edge:

> she sits in the
> fringe of the
> waves, braiding
> her
> hair, and
> dark hair–and in
> the greenblue water coming
> in, seaweed
> afloat.

The lines create a rhythmic structure built on the hesitation to stop or not to stop at the end of the lines. This movement in the line is characteristic of Williams's poems, but it is a procedure Creeley also learned from Williams. These poems explore and celebrate the young poet's immediate world as it begins to form around him. There are poems to his new wife, to his wife as mother of their first child, poems for the second child, for the family of four, for himself as father. Gradually, the solid simplicity of pride in possession of "The Bath"–

> what he is most pleased about is
> her continuing bathing.
> in his tub. in his water. wife.

–gives way (as culturally, historically it would anyway) to much quicker-paced poems. The poem "The Fourth Ark Royal" represents a turning point in Oppenheimer's poetics. As he remembered: "Historically it's terribly inaccurate, but it's a nice poem.

It was the first long poem I'd ever written. And a lot of people got very upset by it. . . . Charles read it and said 'thank God you're finally getting some of the discursiveness in.'" An Oppenheimer poem can have several frames of reference going on at the same time, but the frames are sustained by the movement of a conversation, and so a repeated rhythmic structure, not the principles of a logical argument. In this poem the scene is the Cedar Bar. Sailors from the British ship *Ark Royal* are in the city and in the bar on leave, so the poem gives a history of the name of the ship, comments on the bar, the coming of spring, and the parts of the conversation going on at the bar:

> and even
> this has no bearing, until
> we give it one, whatever
> it deserves. my friend,
> i offer you a drink, my
> bare soul, and a half
> memory of when we last met.

This poem takes place in a social situation, as does "The Boys Whose Fathers," dedicated to Franz Kline. Kline taught Oppenheimer the lessons of living a private artistic life dedicated to the work at hand as well as a public, social life. The interaction of the private, with its lack of love and the dangers of isolation, and the public life, with its risks of rejection and perils of dissipating the strength of the commitment to poetry, is a theme that runs through all of Oppenheimer's work in poetry and in prose. Oppenheimer was fond of drawing houses and plans for rooms on graph paper (a result of his education at Cornell). In this early volume, and then later, the theme of the room or the houses is a persistent one that defines a world, public or private, actual or imagined, where the poet and the poem live. In another sense Oppenheimer moved from place to place, room to room, talking and imagining poems. He was not separated from the poems he wrote, in the same way that the poems were not separated from the life he lived. There was continuous interaction, which is the center of the poem "A Long Testament," in a prologue and nine numbered parts. The poem has the structure of a serial poem, which Olson worked so well in *The Maximus Poems,* Duncan in "The Passages Poems," and Oppenheimer would propound later in *The Woman Poems* (1975).

The attention to rhythmic structures and precise wording appears also in the title poem of *The Love Bit.* The snap of language, hip and alert, is evident not only in the end of the poem but also–in the catalogue of color images–in the ability to pull in images from different frames of reference:

the colors we depend on are
red for raspberry jam, white
of the inside thigh, purple as
in deep, the blue of moods, green
cucumbers (cars), yellow stripes down
the pants, orange suns on ill-omened days, and black as the
dirt in my fingernails.
also, brown, in the night,
appearing at its best when
the eyes turn inward, seeking
seeking, to dig everything but
our own. i.e. we make it crazy or
no, and sometimes in the afternoon.

It is a poem directly comparable, if not owing, to those in Creeley's 1962 volume, *For Love* (compare the structure of "The Invoice"). It wears its style appropriately, fully deserving to be the title poem of the volume. In "Blue Funk" the encouragement is jazz, as is evident by the title. Lines are deliberately "flattened," flatted like a blue note. There are careful repetitions and a keen delicacy but with muted sentimentality. Indeed, along with Williams and Creeley, trumpeter Miles Davis was an acknowledged influence: "You know those tiny little phrases that Miles was blowing," Oppenheimer reminds his audience in discussing the early poems at Kent State.

In his two larger collections, *On Occasion* and *In Time,* he proved himself master of the occasional poem, one of the most accessible and therefore popular poetic modes. He has written well of what he means by an "occasional poem" in his prefatory note to *On Occasion,* which, unlike *In Time,* stretches over the full extent of his poetic career from 1950 on:

> goethe says somewhere that occasional poetry is the highest form of art; when it succeeds i incline to agree with him—by success i mean when the poem moves past the personal impetus for writing it, but preserves the solid air of that impetus; in other words, that the poem, hopefully, may be meaningful far beyond the immediate situation.

> occasional poems also indicate, for me, a "usefulness" for poetry as a function of life and a benefit to society that belies popular rumor.

There are poems in both volumes addressed to Frank O'Hara, Ezra Pound, LeRoi Jones, Charles Reznikoff, Edward Dahlberg, Malcolm X, Marilyn Monroe, and to women he had known (including the delightful "Ladies of Westbeth"), two excellent elegies for Williams, and another for Olson. "The Polish Cavalry" is his tribute to Olson, written the day after Olson's death, in which images of various battles are mixed with a personal acknowledgment of a younger poet to his teacher, the "son" to his "father." It is a fitting memorial to a poet who appreciated the facts-as-events of history:

what i am trying to say is
that you brought two generations
to life, and you'll have to
live with that. you always did move
like a grampus and you still do.
the polish cavalry at least had lances.
what you've got only your sons and
your grandsons know

. . . .

                i'm sorry
i have to speak in different images,
but you told me a long time ago
to speak in my own, and i believed
that. . . .

There are also fine poems for his great-grandparents ("An Anniversary") and upon the marriage of young friends ("A Wedding"), and a particularly effective elegy for the son of Paul Goodman, killed in a mountain-climbing accident ("For Matthew, Dead"). Battles are waged ("The Only Anarchist General") and sometimes won ("Come On Baby"). As in a poem for his father's birthday ("For My Father, One Year Older"), "he remembers everything life / is, and shouldn't be—he knows / by now it is, in general, unfair—and / yet. . . ." There is always the "and yet" in Oppenheimer, the irrepressible. Sometimes he hurries the opportunity and creates his own occasion; the poem, thus begun, responds to itself, and this response resonates. Such a poem is as much a source for discursiveness as a superabundance of material pressing in, or the inability or reluctance to subordinate one experience to another.

"A Treatise" reflects the poet's other major concerns after human relationships—politics and history, which are actually the study of human relationships on the larger scale. Here the subject is the effect of the city on man, as it has persisted for more than seven thousand years. His is very much the anarchist's view: "what else the / concentration camp but / the perfection of the / city, what else the SS / but the perfection of / the state, what else / the factories and stores / but lesser gas chambers. . . ." Momentum is gained in the poem by progressive parallels, cohesion by strategic recapitulations. Also in *In Time* is a long, impassioned indictment of the United States, titled by its date of composition, "17–18 April, 1961." It is one of the first of the waves of poetic protests (along with those by Ginsberg, Olson, and Dorn) against American expansionism and "dreams of empire" that culminated in the Vietnam War and corporation rule at the expense of the nation's own dreams and premises:

i am just reminding you you did not
want to listen when allen yelled at you

like jeremiah, you did not listen when
charles patiently explained to you what
you had done to gloucester, you don/t
listen even now when ed tells you how
it is about charitable clothes. . . .

The poem that offers values that transcend politics—or
more precisely, values that are the essence of politics—is "A Poem for Children" from *On Occasion*. Written in 1970 during a time of confrontation—with his
own infant son in mind as well as the newborn children of two of his literary friends, poets Paul Blackburn and Tom McGrath—it challenges the threats to
individual liberty then evident in American society.
Images of police, their weapons and helicopters at
People's Park in Berkeley—site of just one notable
clash of the popular will with antidemocratic powers—intrude in the poem as they do in the world the
poet is seeking to make for the young:

> what we are saying is
> these children, born, are not going
> to eat shit; i have a better hope for
> it than ever—tom mcgrath is over
> fifty! paul blackburn is over forty! joel
> oppenheimer is over thirty! they are
> breeding children! those children
> will have children to learn from!
> they will be immune from teargas!
> they will come happily! even when
> young! they will be able to like
> tits without being hung up on them!
> they will recognize cops in one-fifth
> of a bartender's time! they will
> even know how to play in parks! they
> will even know how to shoot down
> helicopters over the parks!

It is a poem for the future of the young and one of the
few Oppenheimer poems in which exclamation points
appear, in which the voice or the line is raised from its
"flatness."

Perhaps "Sirventes on a Sad Occurrence," first
published separately in 1967, may be singled out for
discussion. It brings into play all his best qualities—heartfelt sympathy, the patient telling, a winsome
personality, accurate inflections of speech (in this case,
especially, a New York Jewish or Yiddish idiom), the
utter naturalism, a true democratic spirit. His authority comes from his deeply shared sense of humanity.
The poem begins with the poet, in all good cheer, setting out down his tenement stairs for work on a spring
day, when he inadvertently comes upon an old neighbor, a "great grandma," who has been incontinent, in-
voluntarily defecating on her way up the stairs to her
apartment. Her daughter, "older than / my mother,"
has gone back to the apartment to get something to
wipe up the mess: "don/t / tell, mrs. stern, the daugh-

ter screams, / i/ll be back, right away i/ll clean, /
don/t tell. . . ." The poet continues:

> what can she possibly
> tell, old woman, that you are old,
> that you have had your children, they
> have had theirs, they, theirs, and
> you are still here, your world
> still exists, where does she fit in?
> —as if there weren/t already
> shit in the world, and you invented
> it. what further indignities to
> allow besides inventing shit?

Conscious of the paradox of coming face-to-face with
old age and its weakness in the flush of spring vitality,
the poet has already announced his intention: "i will
write / against that which is in us to / make age an embarrassment in the / season of coming alive." He captures the simple drama of the moment of encounter:

> and on top of it, as you clung to
> the banister at the top step, almost
> around, fifteen feet from your
> door, to face me suddenly, coming
> down from one flight up, my hat no
> longer swinging but over my head,
> over my thin bearded face, my god
> the moan then, even your daughter
> scared by it, i thought you were
> dying /til i found out the truth. . . .

He goes on to uphold the woman's honor while effi-
ciently allowing the narrative to reveal the full circumstances:

> this is a
> natural act, why will you
> fear me for it, i see each day
> more shit than you could ever
> dream of making, screw your
> daughter, let mrs. stern watch
> out for her own steps, i am just
> standing here waiting for you
> to pass, too late now for me
> to go back up the stairs, i have
> just discovered what the fact is
> much too late, and will stand quietly.

This is the poet in his most necessary role—willing to
speak up for human dignity, to defend and extol
man's humanity amidst vast creation, to raise man
from his embarrassment to the acceptance of human
frailty and the celebration of an underlying common
nobility. He concludes by gently rebuking the old
woman:

> this is the east
> side, guns crack, people snort
> their noses full of life, and you

Joel and Helen Oppenheimer, 1966

are dying because you shat
upon these steps? and were faced
with me? old lady, act your age.

It is a voice of tender scolding, one that warms and chastens our own hearts.

During the period 1969–1984 Oppenheimer wrote articles and poems for *The Village Voice,* first occasionally, then as a regular columnist. The articles are topical. They are about raising children, shopping in the Village, eating at restaurants, reacting to social and political events and movements, baseball, the change of the seasons. They are always informed with precise information about what was going on in New York and the world. The political issues about the Vietnam War and governmental blunders were emotional and caused fragmented personalities, broken marriages, and physiological upheaval. Oppenheimer used this sort of writing to let his views be known; the forces that could tear the poems apart were dealt with in the prose and not the poems, and so the prose piece cleaned up the poems, took the social, domestic, and political pressure off them. In these articles Oppenheimer had a hopeful view of what humanity was capable of, and he championed fair play, the just cause, doing things for the good of the people; but above all he championed human freedom as one of the two necessities of living (love is the other). Pieces like "'72 olympics: switching back to real life" (21 September 1972), "The All Stars" (1 August 1974), "language & sexism in today's world: a code of honor" (26 September 1974), "How to lose a School System" (24 November 1975), "Truth and Destiny, Both Manifest" (17 February 1983), and "Phobophilia" (16–22 February 1983) all testify to Oppenheimer's intense engagement with daily living and his directives about honest government at all levels.

The poet's next book, *The Woman Poems,* a true serial poem, was written in 1973 and 1974. The book focuses his attentions to personal relationships, especially sexual relationships, but now they are perceived in all their mythological and psychological complexities. The book is a series of poems honoring and exploring the Great Mother in her various manifestations, specifically the four chief ones of Good Mother, Death Mother, Ecstasy or Dancing Mother, and Stone or Tooth Mother, which Oppenheimer had encountered in Robert Bly's *Sleepers Joining Hands* (1973), deriving ultimately from Erich Neumann's classic, *The Great Mother* (1955). Oppenheimer had not read Neumann's book before he wrote the poems. Later he commented during a reading of the poems in 1975: "I read the essay [by Bly] and got terribly excited and that's really what the book grew out of except that I was faced with a choice, which was either to write the poems or to do all the research. I chose to write the poems." In one sense he had been researching the subject all his life. The book opens with an unofficial prologue, consisting of the first four poems, and then moves to the new poems growing out of his attention to the Goddess: as he says in "Mother Poem," "ceaselessly in this / universe is the mother." The poems range from the obviously oedipal "Mother Poem" to those of explicit sexual fantasy such as "Dirty Picture Poem" or "Fantasy Poem." The lovely personal tribute to his wife's breasts in "The Innocent Breasts" in *In Time* becomes a celebration of the Feminine and her specific attributes in the more boldly titled "Your Tits Poem," which concludes with a celebration of the "goddess of nine breasts" whom he will continue to attend.

A paternal, at times patriarchal, quality comes into the poems–to the dismay, conceivably, of some women readers–but their sincerity is beyond question or reproach. In "Father Poem," which the poet begins by announcing, "i have fathered / four sons, they surround / me in an age of / women," and in which he describes himself as a victim of the wars of life and between the sexes, he also writes:

like always and always,
i will be defeated, they
will carry me ball-less and
regal into the house of
the dead where i will
pay for this sin, having
fathered only sons. . . .

"But," he continues,

this is in me rock
like, to do the wrong
thing, to pick the
wrong time. it is
obduracy, pride, a
need to go the wrong way.

Yet he surpasses self-pity with pride in his sons and the happily exaggerated prospect of being brought to his "golden throne" by them: "defeated, regal, honored. / when i get there i / will have a drink and / let them do the fighting." He concludes wryly: "the fathers of daughters / cannot say this." As with so many of his poems, this one is characterized by a generous good humor rather than dogmatism or a brittle and infernal cleverness. The book is full of the mystery of a spiritual presence that exists as a presence and also within the fleshly women he knows. The book advances the formal intricacies of the serial poem, which Oppenheimer had begun exploring in "A Long Testament." In a way *Marilyn Lives!* (1981) gives Oppenheimer another chance to explore his sexual fantasies in the person of Marilyn Monroe, while the focus of the poems begins to shift away from the discursive mode to a more lyric mode built of rhythmic ingenuity.

Occasional poems continue in his *names, dates, & places* (1978), a collection of poems written throughout the 1970s, its title alone evidence of its concerns. There is the vignette of a brief meeting on the street—the poet in red hat encountering a woman in red cape, making it a "red letter day"—its obligation to Williams given in the title, "Spring and Some" (a variation of Williams's *Spring and All,* 1923); an elegy for Pound, "E.P. 1885–1972"; and a poem about the end of the Vietnam War, "Celebrating the Peace, 9–15 May 1975." Also included is "The New Year," which was revised, its discursiveness somewhat compressed, from its first appearance as "Signs and Portents, Omens, Bodings, and Good and Bad Beginnings as Seen for the New Year" (1975)—mostly leaving out some of the topicality, such as "abe beame [then mayor of New York] asked / his wife which coat to / wear to his swearing-in, / whereas i chose mine with / firmness of purpose" or changing "nixon remains, but then, / so do i" to "the world remains but so do i." But the revisions point to a new direction in Oppenheimer's poetry. "The Birthright," for another example, begins:

there is a corollary
in astrology that tells us
it's not only the time

of our birth but place as well
that determines houses
we are born to[.]

In place of the discursive movement of the earlier poems, this poem has a sharper focus in which the lines maintain a rhythm that becomes a principle of the form of the poem.

In the introduction to *Names & Local Habitations: (Selected Earlier Poems 1951–1972)* (1988) William Corbett makes the point that "Oppenheimer's essential use" is the way he shows that "significant experience occurring in the ordinary run of things may be intensified through order and made memorable." Following Pound, Duncan and Olson created enormous frames of reference demanding from the reader knowledge of ancient and world history, the mysteries and occult religions, as well as Gloucester's history and the world of art history. Unlike his fellow Black Mountain Poets, Oppenheimer was not a scholarly man, or at least he did not import his learning into the poems. Only occasionally do references to military history and architecture come into the poems as a counter to the pervading perceptions of how to live one's life in an authentic way in the middle of the municipal complexities of New York City. He was informed, but the information at his command was like the information needed for a crossword puzzle in *The New York Times,* erudite perhaps, but immediate and useful. So, when he turned his attention to a new line and a different concentration on rhythmic form, the poems generated immediate complexity out of ordinary experiences. In *At Fifty: A Poem* (1982) he begins another serial poem, this one composed of four parts each with fifteen numbered poems. His theme is not the Great Mother or the Vietnam War but the ecology of lives and the necessity to make endless adjustments in order to get along with people. The agents of pollution he lists in poem "X" of the fourth part are as telling as the example of poem "XII" in part 3 in which he "stopped making love / to watch cleon jones / put the team ahead in a crucial game." Two of his made-up worlds, the erotic play and baseball, collide, but each demands his attention: "but that marriage is gone / and the team won the pennant," the poem concludes. He argues with the information of the day and with himself to find a place for his sensibility to live safely while risking interrelationships with other people. In one poem, referring to the "basques," he calls this a search for a "coercive apparatus" to get along:

at my age she said i
am tired of men who are
still working out their

Cover for the 1985 collection of Oppenheimer's poetry, which includes poems addressed to fellow poets Paul Blackburn, Louis Zukofsky, and Jonathan Williams

anger against mother

i said let it
serve notice[.]

Or:

surely in buffalo
there's one bar
where they want us
to come and sit
and talk all night
just a bar to talk[.]

New Spaces: Poems 1975–1983 (1985) brings together poems published in separate editions, poems from journals, and poems from manuscripts; the book is divided into two sections, "Drawing from Life" and "New Spaces." Oppenheimer continues writing poems about people close to him—"For Tom Blackburn"; "For Louis Zukofsky 1904–1978"; for Jonathan Williams, "The Way We Were"; "For Willie Sutton." The poem of the particular occasion or about a specific person was always one of Oppenheimer's strong points, such as "Nathaniel's Valentine" and "Meditations." The tone in poems of this kind, however, was changing. The book begins with "Statement to the Citizens":

we are here, working,
hungering for bread.

you are there living
hungering.

                 can there not
be commerce between us[.]

The poems line out territories of life experience, spaces where experiences exist and then interact with the spaces other people have generated. "There are / conversations / with real people / waiting for us," the poem "Talking" states as it moves away from the ghosts of the past to the events of the present days, like watching children in the park in "These Days." The space he creates does have a past. "The Answer Not Given" works a pun on Robert Frost's poem "The Road Not Taken" more subtly than "And miles to go before we sleep," the final line of "Waking in Bed by a Ringing Telephone," calling up Frost's poem "Stopping by Woods on a Snowy Evening." "Life Studies" in the same way calls up Robert Lowell's poem with the same name, but in Oppenheimer's version beautiful women riding bicycles replace the fins of cars in Lowell's poem; perceptions of an erotic life replace the dour obligations of history. Williams's poem "A Chinese Toy" appears in the middle of the poem "For Danielle," for another example. "A Village Poem" focuses the themes and attentions of "Drawing from Life." The poem is a monologue: Oppenheimer talks with himself about the literary histories of the White Horse Tavern and the Cedar Tavern, tells stories about Dylan Thomas, Edna St. Vincent Millay, Jackson Pollock, and Franz Kline. Then and now people seek out and create places for living and making art. These areas of creating become as much a part of Oppenheimer's space as his four sons and emptying the cat box ("Doing It"). "A Village Poem" maps out the territory:

it is our place where we are
and it is the place where
the work gets done
as even tonight it gets done

and tomorrow when we are alone

because we have this place
and we believe in it

and it is still bright
and perfectly formed
and it is where we are[.]

"New Spaces," the second section of the book, expands this process of creating spaces to live. As the first poem, "Time Out," says, Oppenheimer is as aware of his personal past as a present reality as he is of world events. "The process of death and rebirth," a consistent theme throughout the poems and the *Village Voice* articles, has been interfered with in the Everglades and the dams on the Nile. The interruptions are reported in *The New York Times* and immediately are reflected in his personal world: "we have forgotten how to be fathers." We have forgotten the obligations to raise children and care for the earth. The poems now deal with the forms or the patterns of events, so it is possible to relate and compare events from different contexts. "The Older Man Thinking of Kore" as a title specifies another and recurring attention of the poems: the death and rebirth of nature in the seasons told in the Greek myth has an active parallel in the imagination of his life. The two are alive in the same mix. The two poems "Lesson I" and "Lesson II" activate the principle. Both poems are based on the Homeric episode in which Menelaus gave up his revenge to kill Helen when he saw her naked breasts. In the second poem the episode is expanded to include a parable and a double story being told within the episode—of marriage, betrayal, and the changing of attractions:

yet we ask why
yet we dream why
yet we cry why
paris why him why
her
    where did i
go wrong[.]

Helen's flight with Paris, the Trojan War, and then the episode of Menelaus set out a pattern of action that comes in close to the poet's heart because his own marriage to another Helen is going wrong. He finds no redemption; he does not have the benefit of Menelaus's joy in taking Helen back home. The same use of telling a story, a parable, comes into the poem "Acts" (first published as a separate edition in 1976). Casually enough, the poem begins with a description of taking his son to school, meeting a woman on the way, then reading in *The New York*

Times the account of the death of Hugo Zacchini, "the first human cannonball." The poet has intersected with the world; the performance of Zacchini then becomes a lesson for him and for his son: "oh this act also / will be carried on / by my son," he writes. He concludes that he "learned my [his] methods / in some previous wars"—he is an experienced warrior in the battles of Kore and the woman on the street, and he knows that the strategies of these events are analogous to other events in military history. Oppenheimer is concerned with the way the rhythm of the lines forms into units of composition. Each stanza is a sentence that repeats rhythmic variations of the previous stanzas. Oppenheimer's poetry is completely within the tradition of Williams and what Oppenheimer himself calls a "flat" line, not the full Whitmanian majesty or bardic lengths of Duncan, Olson, or Ginsberg. The poem "The Progression" (published previously as *The Progression Begins* in the # *Magazine* of January 1981) works a similar procedure of starting off with a common enough activity of washing a child to the rhyme of "toe knee chest nut / is how i wash this body," and then gathers associations of visits to a psychiatrist, the poet's itching feet, a Japanese woman who gives massages by walking on people's backs with her toes, and a first lover who discovers that her toes are an erogenous zone. The poem has gathered to itself etymologies of words, and around the theme of the beginning lines, "all i know / the body / the poem," has moved out from the common to define a space in which the associations of feet and daily experience can abide one another:

the feet we walk by
as we walk by
as we keep
touching ground

as we keep moving[.]

The walker in this poem does not allow himself the flight to the abstract; he keeps his feet on the ground as he maps out the experience of the particular made alive by perceiving multiple associations in individual events.

Before the book comes to a close with two long poems, "Cacti" and "Houses," a section titled "The Man Observed through the Kitchen Window" explores a different point of view from the first-person narration. The first poem in the series, "Beginning the Portrait," begins "it is monday morning / he is washing / the breakfast dishes." While the poem takes place in Westbeth with a "realist painter" looking down from a floor above observing what the narrator does in the kitchen, the scene is fictive,

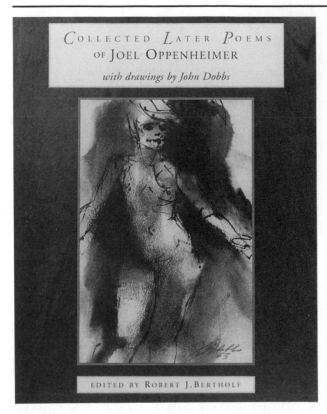

COLLECTED LATER POEMS
OF JOEL OPPENHEIMER

with drawings by John Dobbs

EDITED BY ROBERT J. BERTHOLF

Dust jacket for the 1997 collection of poems Oppenheimer wrote after 1974

imagined as a scene in which the process of transforming particulars in paintings and poems is as much the subject as the events the narrator describes. The "realist painter" watches the poet clean the kitchen after breakfast and watches attentively as the poet cleans his dentures. These scenes suggest fascinating complexities, such as the artist (any artist) as voyeur, the problem of the representation of reality, life beyond the framed moment, all the basic concerns of the imagistic arts. Yet the space of the poems is realistic: the realist painter is Oppenheimer's friend John Dobbs, who, as the first poem makes clear enough, "observed" a man "through a kitchen window" and painted a portrait that in fact was a portrait of Stefan Wolpe. In the final poem of the series, "Making the Holiday Breakfast," the painter does not appear at his window, so the poet makes up what he is doing; that is, he reverses the activity of the painter making up the poet's actions. The series remains incomplete. "My circumstances changed," Oppenheimer tells Whitney Jones, "I was no longer doing dishes and then going right into writing. Now I do the dishes and take the kid over to school and then stop and have coffee and then get back. So that kind of energy is hard to sustain over that hour in between."

The indirect narration returns to the direct narration of "Cacti," a long discursive poem—half

narrative, half lyric. The longest lines are only five words, and there are occasional repetitions, usually direct narrative addresses ("i told you / i am not complaining"), with occasional light sound arousals such as "at the rear / of all these plants / rearing proudly." The poem itself is actually an extended analogy—perhaps even imitating the spare, spiky, elongated varieties of cacti described—in which the plants stand for the poet himself, persistent when given a little water, or love, once a month. The plants define a space for themselves literally, and for the narrator figuratively. "Houses" continues the lyric meditation and honest, earned wisdom that he has consistently sought. The occasion of the poems is a visit to the home of his first wife for the marriage of their first son. Showering in preparation for dressing, he recalls her habit of long baths when they were first married, and he quotes from the poem "The Bath," written for her twenty-three years earlier. The present poem is a long pondering, more rumination than reminiscence ("don't misunderstand me / i am not speaking / of romance / or rekindled love / or even second chances"), a tender accounting of how over the years the poet has come to peace with the knowledge:

> the house i've fought
> my way through to get to
>
> this house which is
> not so clean and neat
> as yours
>
>   i am a man
> i need a woman's touch
> might be the pity of it[.]

Bitterness over a failed relationship is not part of the space, the house of the mind as well as the actual house, now being presented.

> but i've learned to build
> without it
>   but now can see
> how pleasant such things are
> and where they come from
> in me
>   that is what
> i did not know
>   and what
> i now do know
> and will remember.

It is a time of rest, of release from the high-wired tensions and energy thrusts of another order of poetry. It is not sublime or ecstatic but welcome and usable. The pleasure in all such poems is their sense of resolution, a fitting end. Oppenheimer has said in an interview:

"A friend of mine . . . says that every human life has a kind of logic: it consists of 'a beginning, a muddle, and an end.' I thought that was good enough to put in a poem. The 'muddle' is one of my favorite themes."

In the preface to *Why Not* (1985) Oppenheimer begins by rejecting the position that the meaning and value of a work of art rest in the readers' or viewers' response to it, not in what it says: "every poem we re member has to do with real things, no matter how far the poet's imagination or invention takes it from those real things. . . . every poem is an investigation of the world we live in, the way we live, and the way we treat ourselves and others." He continues: "i hope also that the poems allow you to play as they have allowed me to play—with language, with ideas, with juxtapositions, with life. . . . perceptions of the universe are play, must be play." *Why Not* is a small book, forty-two pages, first published as a limited edition and then republished as a trade edition (1987). Familiar themes appear in the poems, like the cycle of destruction and creation of nature in the cycle of the season related to the activity of the imagination perceiving the everyday world, or as "The Garden" explores with flowers in a vase:

> these are city-bred
> conclusions as i know
>
> but they are conclusions
> in a world made new
>
> where flowers never were[.]

The flowers are transformed into centers that generate order distinct from themselves for a short time and then fade along with the imaginative orders. But the process of making up orders emulates the destructive/creative process of nature itself. The process is at the center of the poem "Spring," which is a poem-letter to the season by a poet living in a city. The poem acknowledges "persephone" but makes clear the poem is not for her but "her lover dis / who as lawrence tells us / sends that spring / chasing at her heels." The poet acknowledges the coming of the snowdrops, crocuses, and daffodils in his neighborhood and also acknowledges that life in the city is as bound up in the mythic patterns as life in the country:

> others have pictured
> this place differently
> they feel sorry for us
> locked
>   but dis knows
> cities too
>   the flowers
> come snapping at her heels

even here

so i announce spring[.]

The poem generates multiple associations from the simple event of spring coming and does it with a sense of joy and fun. The complexity arises in relating change to other frames of reference that are as immediate as the first flowers of the season.

"Changes" talks of this same process in a third-person narration, like the "realist painter" series, in terms of a story about a man who changes from meeting women when he smells bad to meeting women shining "in a new body." The bath becomes "a sexual act itself." He could "begin to learn to pray," the narrator concludes, and there is a sense of fun in the turn of the poem. The activities of the poem are embedded in the simple activities of living—this might be the central theme of the book. In "The New Line" the theme takes the form of telling "an old joke" in a new context that then makes "a new line," while in "Billie's Blues" it takes the form of recasting lines from Billie Holiday's songs into rhythmic units, and in "–etic" of making a whole poem out of words ending in *etic*. The beginning poem, "The Teacher," sets out the rules for the volume directly:

> you all pay attention to
> my simple profundities
> and do not understand the
> simplest fact which is
> that despite its simplicity
> the poem is a difficult thing
> and we are prey to all
> its various vagaries and
> vagrancies and shifts of
> time and space and meaning[.]

In this formulation the simplicity of the poem turns back on itself to complexity "no matter / how simply i [he] conceive[s] it." "Plus Ça Change" offers another aspect of this process as it recasts words from older love poems in an attempt to make them new for a new occasion; the poem is "searching / for words" in the same way that he is searching to balance the "record player" with a book in the poem "The Word." Simple words engaged in the particular make it possible for the poem to demonstrate acts of the imagination as well as joy in the action that they enact. In previous poems this process led to parables emerging inside poems, as in "The Charm," for example, which takes off from a card in a board game to string out a story about a tower. "For a Painter Beyond Hazardville" develops from seeing a sign for "the cutoff to hazardville" after visiting a painter. Then the beautiful landscape "in the valley of risk" has streams and other geographical features that emerge as parts of the process of perceiving and then writing: the poem is a parable about the risks and dangers of composing, and it has a postscript about getting too old, "when poems and paintings stop." Acknowledging the aging process puts the human beings in the same position as the flowers in the vase, always subject to death and the possibility of rebirth. As the poem "Flowers" says,

> everything has green stems
> cut and dying or loosely planted
>
> all ages all ages
>
> yes my gray hair also tinted
> almost a bloom on them
> stems going down
>
> into the vase
> into water[.]

Death and rebirth control the creation of safe spaces to live in, but Oppenheimer is determined to discover the elements of order in the ordinary life of the city. That desire continues in a series of poems published after his death as *New Hampshire Journal* (1994). He has given up his urban landscape for a rural one—

> the field
> determines
> what feeds us
> while we wait
> to fall back
> to grow again [.]

—but his attentions are the same, the perception of the marvels of living in everyday experiences. In poems such as "spring," "summer his route 9," "autumn," and the title poems of the booklet, a persistent theme is the change to the life of the country where the processes of nature are more immediate. He is aware that birds and animals live near him, nearer perhaps than the news from Washington, D.C. In "discovery," for example, he hears birds singing while snow comes down:

> no wind and even
> the few cars pass
> muted by the snow
> to silent muttering
>
> well i did not know
> birds sang in winter
> in the falling snow
> chattering to
> each other
> and to me[.]

Small events become perceptions of the marvelous, hints of the mysterious engagement of human beings to the forces of the natural world.

In *Poetry, the Ecology of the Soul* (1983), a volume that prints transcriptions of three talks—"Poetry, the Ecology of the Soul," "Black Mountain Poets," and "The Woman Poems"—along with a selection of poems, published and uncollected, Oppenheimer says:

> I'm asking for a world where you can feel like you're a human being, where you can feel like there is human contact, whether it's angry contact or loving contact or friendly contact or holistic contact, but contact, where there's a possibility of learning something about the world you live in, the place you're at, what you yourself are, instead of continually running from any of those knowledges because they hurt or because it takes time or trouble.

In the earliest poems and columns in the *Village Voice* Oppenheimer always insisted on this kind of world. His sense of humanity was intense, and his desire for people to live into and enjoy a life that they generated themselves without the encroachments of political or physical violence of any kind is a theme that rings throughout his writing. He reveled in love and the erotic enjoyment of it as a means of engaging people. He liked what he was doing as a writer, even enjoyed it, and was able to laugh at himself and others with kindness. His poetic line came through the maze of historical and poetic modifications of the Black Mountain Poets directly from William Carlos Williams, and back of him from the romantic imagination. Cancer claimed Oppenheimer and his needed views of humanity. The poem he wrote about his chemotherapy, "The Uses of Adversity," went through two printings, was reprinted for the Oncology Service of Yonkers General Hospital, appeared in the *Village Voice* and then in *New Directions in Prose and Poetry* (1988). It remains Oppenheimer's most widely distributed poem in its witty and sanguine descriptions of the action of the chemicals on his body and his psychology. The mixture of chemicals had the abbreviation CHOP:

> i take CHOP
> every three weeks
> a time span
> called a course
>
> combining thus
> the words *curse*
> and *corse:* the body[.]

He will be remembered as a master of the occasional poem, but he will also be remembered as a poet who specified relationships between people and relationships between himself and the natural world with a radical simplicity that makes the complexity of his views accessible to all.

Interviews:

"Interview with Poet Joel Oppenheimer," *Noiseless Spider,* 1 (Spring 1972): 2–5;

William L. Owens, "Joel Oppenheimer at Storrs, Conn.," *Credences,* 2 (July 1975): 13–25;

"Three Versions of the Poetic Line," *Credences,* 4 (March 1977): 55–60;

F. Whitney Jones, "An Interview with Joel Oppenheimer," *St. Andrews Review,* 4 (Spring/Summer 1977): 45–54;

William Sylvester, "Joel Oppenheimer Talks about His Poetry," *Credences,* 3 (Fall 1985): 69–76;

Christopher Beach, "Interview with Joel Oppenheimer," *Sagetrieb,* 7 (Fall 1988): 90–130.

Bibliography:

George F. Butterick, *Joel Oppenheimer: A Checklist of His Writings* (Storrs: University of Connecticut Library, 1975).

References:

Sam Abrams, "the only anarchist general, joel oppenheimer, 1930–1988," *And,* 2 (Fall/Winter 1988): 8–10;

Robert Bertholf, "On The Great American Desert and The Woman Poems," *Credences,* 2 (July 1975): 26–35;

Maxine S. Combs, "A Study of the Black Mountain Poets," dissertation, University of Oregon, 1967, pp. 167–172;

Robert Creeley, "'An intensely singular art,'" in his *A Quick Graph: Collected Notes & Essays,* edited by Donald Allen (San Francisco: Four Seasons, 1970), pp. 202–206;

Karl Malkoff, *Crowell's Handbook of Contemporary American Poetry* (New York: Crowell, 1973), pp. 243–245;

Donald Phelps, "The Simple Ecology of the Soul," *For Now,* 11 (1970): 28–31;

David Thibodaux, *Joel Oppenheimer: An Introduction* (Columbia, S.C.: Camden House, 1986).

Papers:

Oppenheimer's papers are in the Special Collections, University of Connecticut Library, Storrs.

Bob Perelman
(2 December 1947 –)

Steve Evans
Brown University

BOOKS: *Braille* (Ithaca, N.Y.: Ithaca House, 1975);

11 Romantic Positions (N.p.: KS Press, 1976);

Cupid & Psyche and Vienna: A Correspondence (San Francisco: Miam, 1978);

7 Works (Berkeley, Cal.: The Figures, 1978);

a.k.a. (Berkeley, Cal.: Tuumba, 1979);

Primer (Berkeley, Cal.: This Press, 1981);

a.k.a. (Great Barrington, Mass.: The Figures, 1984);

To the Reader (Berkeley, Cal.: Tuumba, 1984);

The First World (Great Barrington, Mass.: The Figures, 1986);

Face Value (New York: Roof, 1988);

Captive Audience (Great Barrington, Mass.: The Figures, 1988);

Virtual Reality (New York: Roof, 1993);

Chaim Soutine (Buffalo: Editions Hérisson, 1994);

The Trouble with Genius (Berkeley: University of California Press, 1994);

Fake Dreams (Elmwood, Conn.: Potes & Poets, 1996);

The Marginalization of Poetry: Language Writing and Literary History (Princeton: Princeton University Press, 1996);

The Masque of Rhyme (Tucson, Ariz.: Chax P, 1997).

OTHER: *Hills,* nos. 1–9, edited by Perelman (1973–1980);

Russian Poetry: The Modern Period, edited by John Glad and Daniel Weissbort, with translations by Perelman (Iowa City: University of Iowa Press, 1978);

"The First Person," *Hills,* 6/7 (1980): 147–165;

"Plotless Prose," *Poetics Journal,* 1 (1982): 25–34;

"Words Detached from the Old Song and Dance (A Talk Delivered at 80 Langton Street)," in *Code of Signals,* edited by Michael Palmer (Berkeley, Cal.: North Atlantic, 1983), pp. 224–241;

"The Alps" [a play], *Hills,* 9 (1983): 5–27;

"Sense," in *Writing/Talks,* edited by Perelman (Carbondale & Edwardsville: Southern Illinois University Press, 1985), pp. 63–86;

Bob Perelman

Ron Silliman, ed., *In the American Tree,* includes contributions by Perelman (Orono, Maine: National Poetry Foundation, 1986);

"Criticism," *Ottotole,* 2 (Winter 1986/1987): 141–148;

"Poetry in Theory," *Diacritics,* 26 (Fall/Winter 1996): 158–175.

SELECTED PERIODICAL PUBLICATION– UNCOLLECTED: "Confessing to the Listserv," "To the Past," and "To the Future," *Harvard Review,* 12 (1997): 7–14.

In the three decades since his first magazine publication in 1969 Bob Perelman has played a significant role in defining a formally adventurous, politically explicit poetic practice in the United States. From the start his work has called into question key presuppositions of contemporary mainstream poetry: the belief that poems must reflect the private experience of isolated individuals, for instance, or that the literary artifact stands in regal autonomy, somehow above and apart from social life. Availing himself of a variety of forms, from the conventional essay to the dramatic monologue, from the carefully measured units of verse to the giddily hybrid pleasures of all manner of counterfeiture—including mimicry, hallucination, ventriloquism, and fabricated dreams—Perelman has pressed toward a poetry of radical deconcealment, searching for the deep structure of social experience beyond the epiphenomenal shell game of postmodernity. His work asks us to

> Imagine a poetry that is not necessarily *contra naturam* in some jejune transgressive sense, but one that does not take "nature" as an order to which poetry has privileged access. No special effects attributed to form; no organicism; no shamanism; no intuitive well of sonic richness. No impossibly present shibboleths preventing migration between the reader's presence at the page and the long dialectic tangles of history. Such poetry would be part of history taking place on the page, transforming the logos into a multicolored prosthesis and the prosthesis back into a word that has present legibility.

In "Oedipus Rex," the closing poem of Perelman's 1986 volume *The First World,* a contemporary Oedipus, double-parked and quarrelsome, answers his "ancient uncle" Kreon thus: "I never meant to soliloquize, but since the government's gotten so big and secret, any jerk with an open mouth turns out to be in the center of an infinitely expanding universe of gloom and doom, each sound that comes out, even if it's just asking where there's a bathroom downtown, contains lonely world-shattering forces, Magellanic clouds, hot winds to obliterate all human obstruction. / But keeping silent just subsidizes television." In recent years Perelman has increasingly turned the same critical gaze on the avant-garde tradition to which he unquestionably belongs, showing an admirable facility for "arguing" with some of his "closest friends and mentors" about the value and nature of their common enterprise. As he said with a certain wry satisfaction in a 1997 statement: "I keep finding myself in situations where I'm critiquing the branch I'm sitting on, so to speak." From one of the central contributors to the controversial language-poetry anthology *In the American Tree* (1986), this is more than idle metaphor.

A deft satirist with a strong background in the classics, Perelman has been likened to Alexander Pope, but other comparisons also come to mind. He shares with Stendhal an insistently quizzical and erotically charged relation to questions of personal identity and autobiography. With a poet such as Kenneth Fearing, Perelman shares a capacity for penetrating insight into the web of cultural institutions that synchronize and solidify political power in American modernity. From a formal standpoint Perelman's lightning-quick syntactical changes call to mind the radical prose experiments of William Carlos Williams, especially *Kora in Hell* (1920) and *Spring and All* (1923), but more direct antecedents can be found in the New York School, especially in those works by Frank O'Hara and John Ashbery that fit American idiom to the impulse of European surrealism and futurism. Early in his own career, Perelman had a hand in translating various Russian poets of the heroic futurist years as a member of the Iowa Translation Workshop. Working closely with another translator, Kathy Lewis, Perelman contributed to the 1978 *Russian Poetry: The Modern Period* "A Cloud in Trousers" (1915) by Vladimir Mayakovski and poems by Velemir Khlebnikov, Boris Pasternak, and Bella Akhmadulina. While the megaphonic oratory and blunt propagandizing of a Mayakovski are uncommon in the first decade of Perelman's career (1973–1983), a period more characterized by the procedural and collage works collected in *Braille* (1975), *7 Works* (1978), and *Primer* (1981), these gestures return transformed in the work for which he is best known, the sharply political and satirical poems of *To the Reader* (1984), *The First World*—thought by many to be his most accomplished work to date—and *Face Value* (1988).

Perelman prefers a page "scrawled over with social messages" to the pristinely conserved pages of canonical texts. The deliberate privileging of social utterance, speech acts originating less in an individual subject than in what Fredric Jameson—by far Perelman's most illustrious interpreter—has called "the political unconscious," sets his work apart from the keen-eyed objectivism of Ron Silliman or—on a different scale—Rae Armantrout, the rigorous abstractions of Barrett Watten (Perelman's elder classmate in the MFA program at Iowa), the skeptical sensuality of Carla Harryman, the intimacy and hyperliteracy of Lyn Hejinian, the quick-witted lyricism of Kit Robinson, or the ever-rebounding reflexivities of Steve Benson, to name just a handful of the West Coast writers with whom Perelman worked most closely in the years between 1976 and 1990.

The decisive role these contemporaries played in one another's development as writers has been amply acknowledged, not least by Perelman himself in his critical study *The Marginalization of Poetry: Language Writing and Literary History* (1996). First appearing together in print as early as 1974 in the pages of Robinson's one-shot little magazine *Streets and Roads,* these poets participated in publishing projects such as Watten's *This* magazine and press (twelve issues of the former between 1971 and 1982), Hejinian's Tuumba chapbook series (fifty titles between 1976 and 1984), Silliman's *Tottel's* (eighteen numbers between 1971 and 1981), and Perelman's own magazine, *Hills* (nine numbers between 1973 and 1980). Their collaborative performances ranged from the incredibly demanding score of music and text that Celia Zukofsky made of her husband Louis's works in *"A"–24* (1969) with Perelman taking the crucial, tempo-setting harpsichord role in several Bay Area performances in 1978 to many productions of the San Francisco Poets Theater, including Perelman's "The Alps," given in January/February 1982 and published along with several others in *Hills,* 9 (1983). Their penchant for discussion manifested itself in countless formal and informal discussions of poetry, many of which took place under the rubric of Perelman's Talk Series, initiated in the spring of 1977 and numbering more than forty talks in three different San Francisco Bay area venues over the following four years.

Robert Perelman was born in Youngstown, Ohio, on 2 December 1947, the second of Mark and Evelyn Perelman's two children, his sister Nancy having been born a year and a half earlier. Evelyn Perelman held a degree in sociology from the University of Chicago and had worked for a time as a social worker prior to her marriage. Mark Perelman was at the time of his son's birth a successful appliance wholesaler just entering his fortieth year. In an as yet uncollected 1997 poem, "Confessing to the Listserv," Perelman jokingly refers to his childhood in the lines: "That old stuff, the fork / in the head, first home run, // Dad falling out of the car– / I remember the words, but I / just can't get back there. I / think they must be screening my // sensations." The passage winks at the clichés of the American bildungsroman ("that old stuff"), to which Perelman casually, but effectively, joins popular conspiracy theories having to do with suppressed or altered memories ("they must be screening my // sensations")–a topic explored with relentless and hilarious thoroughness in Perelman's still uncollected long poem from the mid 1990s "The Manchurian Candidate" (which borrows and transforms the structure of John Frankenheim's 1962 movie).

Oedipal scenarios abound in Perelman's works, though the steady parade of state-power-wielding autocratic fathers and tenderly eroticized mothers is referred to general social, and often specifically literary, sources rather than naturalized as part of Perelman's own psychological experience. In "Youngstown," a poem from his first volume, *Braille,* Perelman depicts the maternal gaze as a "coat that weighed three thousand pounds with many darling glances to tell me how to ask not to know how to do it." In "An Autobiography," collected in his second full-length volume, *7 Works,* Perelman works extensively with

passages taken verbatim from Stendhal's great autobiographical text *The Life of Henry Brulard* (1890). Echoing the novelist's exuberant love for a mother lost in childbed when he was only seven, Perelman cites: "I abhorred my father. He brought with him memories of how it feels to be intensely, fiercely hungry. He came and interrupted our kisses." In "The Unruly Child," the opening poem of *To the Reader,* the 1984 chapbook that marks an important shift in Perelman's poetic stance, César Vallejo's famous line "Hay, madre, un sitio en el mundo, que se llama Paris. Un sitio grande y lejano y otra vez grande" is revised to read "There is a company called Marathon Oil, mother, / Very far away and very big and, again, very / Desirable." The cosmopolitan city becomes a capitalist conglomerate, but the son's gentle, albeit somewhat condescending, address to his mother is retained. In "To the Past," an uncollected lyric published in 1997, Perelman sounds a similar note by beginning "Take down my books, mother," though he then relocates the origin of the statement by writing "the song says and I see / rain streak the sacred tablets, / graffiti between music and speech."

One hears less of the echoes of Stendhal, Marcel Proust, and Vallejo in parallel statements addressed to paternal Figures, one witty instance of which in "The Family of Man," collected in *Face Value,* synopsizes the approach with great economy: "Why is there money, Daddy?" a child's voice is heard asking, and then with more than childlike insouciance comes the chiastic reversal: "And why is there daddy, Money?" Elsewhere in *Face Value* the United States attorney general under Ronald Reagan, Edwin Meese, joins actor Sylvester Stallone, Odysseus, Captain Kirk (of *Star Trek*), political commentator George Will, and "the nameless face on the dollar" as icons of masculine privilege on a par with the "phallocentric lawyers" and CIA operatives in *To the Reader,* while in poems from *The First World* such as "Anti-Oedipus" and "Oedipus Rex," Kreon is only one of the murderously harassing elders bent on seeing the plot lines through to their awful conclusions.

Whether this strong insistence upon the centrality of Oedipal relations in contemporary society has its genesis in Perelman's own upbringing or is the result of a dispassionate examination of objective social forces is a matter not to be decided here. What is known is that he left Youngstown to attend the Putney School, which his sister also attended, in Vermont at the age of twelve. There he encountered the poetry of T. S. Eliot and Walt Whitman, but his attention at this time and into his late teenage years was more seriously focused on music. His ambition to become a concert pianist led him to train at Inter-

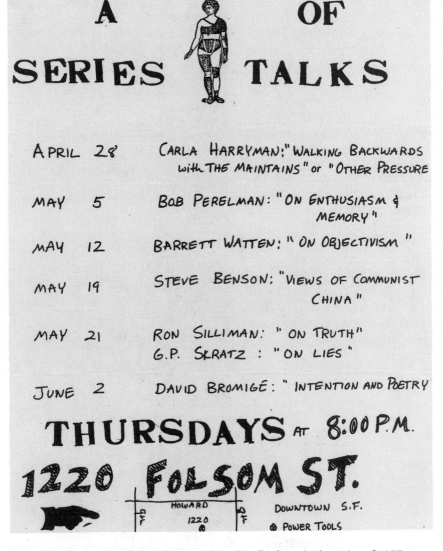

A SERIES OF TALKS

APRIL 28   CARLA HARRYMAN: "WALKING BACKWARDS WITH THE MAINTAINS" OR "OTHER PRESSURE

MAY 5   BOB PERELMAN: "ON ENTHUSIASM & MEMORY"

MAY 12   BARRETT WATTEN: "ON OBJECTIVISM"

MAY 19   STEVE BENSON: "VIEWS OF COMMUNIST CHINA"

MAY 21   RON SILLIMAN: "ON TRUTH" G.P. SKRATZ: "ON LIES"

JUNE 2   DAVID BROMIGE: "INTENTION AND POETRY

THURSDAYS AT 8:00 P.M.
1220 FOLSOM ST.
HOWARD 1220   DOWNTOWN S.F. @ POWER TOOLS

Flier for a series of poets' lectures initiated by Perelman in the spring of 1977

lochen the summer prior to his entering the University of Rochester as a music major in 1964. By his own retrospective account it was while performing Brahms's difficult Second Piano Concerto (opus 83)–which requires a specific trill with the left little fingers–that he admitted to himself the lack of athleticism and mastery required of the virtuoso pianist. Influenced by Ezra Pound's *ABC of Reading* (1960), Perelman changed his major from music to the classics, a course of study in which he continued to distinguish himself upon transferring to the University of Michigan's impressive classics department in 1966. Relatively late in his undergraduate career, in his junior or senior year, Perelman enrolled in an introductory lecture class on poetry offered by the well-known poet and anthologist Donald Hall. Perelman found himself almost surprised

by his own enthusiasm for the topic and through Hall came to meet Tom Clark–then in the process of taking over from Hall the position of poetry editor at the *Paris Review*–as well as two of the transplanted Tulsans of the second-generation New York School of poets, Ron Padgett and Ted Berrigan. As graduation from Michigan neared, Perelman faced a difficult decision: whether to undertake graduate work in the classics at the University of Texas or to pursue the MFA degree in poetry offered at the Iowa Writers' Workshop. He settled on poetry and–brushing aside departing faculty member Berrigan's admonition to move to New York and study with Kenneth Koch–made the move to Iowa City in 1969.

Perelman's first published poem dates back to his final year at Michigan. Bearing the suitably "classical" title "The Birth of Venus," the poem was one of five by Michigan undergraduates to appear in the second volume of *Intro,* an anthology of college writing edited by R. V. Cassill, director of the then new Associated Writing Program (AWP), and published in mass paperback format by Bantam. It is perhaps only fitting that Perelman's literary career should commence with a poem on birth, and that the first of many classical references should be audible in the very title, with a goddess of love and art governing the mood. Poignant and admirably understated, skillful in its manipulation of a topic thick with millennia of connotations, Perelman's contribution is a twenty-two-line free-verse poem composed of three juxtaposed frames, each a sprawling sentence long. The poem begins with a pastoral prevarication of eleven lines, starting with a "while" clause that suspends the main predicate until the eighth line and filling the space thus created with assorted scenes of consumption. First an insect, then an animal, then a bird are shown eating, an act likened from the start to interpretation or "making / foreign sense of " things:

> While the butterfly wanders
> in a wheat field, making
> foreign sense of it,
> and the leapord claws the belly
> of the running zebra open,
> and the hummingbird keeps thrusting
> into orange and red blossoms,
> she stands. . . .

In contrast to the hungry dynamism of the natural world—reflected in gerunds such as "making" and "running" and "thrusting" as well as the simple verbs "wander" and "claws"—the woman who appears in line 8 is placid:

> she stands in the shallow water, facing the shore,
> dallying with ambiguities,
> and feeling the small backs of the waves
> divide around her ankles.

Awash in sensation, poised at the threshold of land and sea, ambiguous in emergence, the woman dallies with ambiguities, as yet unmotivated by the need to make sense, to take a stance, to fulfill urgent needs. One thinks of another poem set similarly at the edge of the sea, Wallace Stevens's "Idea of Order at Key West," as well as of the many paintings depicting the goddess's birth.

The action of the diminutive, lapping waves is the ostensible subject of the second, five-line, sentence:

> Just in front of her feet, they flatten themselves
> and hiss into the damp sand, leaving
> sour foam at the edge of the ocean,
> then drain back, licking the sand
> from under her feet.

The action of the waves reads on one level as simple description; but there is a trace of prostration in the first of these lines ("they flatten themselves"), of a negative reaction—perhaps resentment—in the second and third (in the verb "hiss" and adjective "sour"), and of a subtle undermining of the goddess in the final two ("licking the sand / from under her feet"). In the third and final sentence, comprising a half-dozen lines, Perelman subtly shifts the scene. The transition is not "prepared" by the poem; it simply occurs:

> On the double bed, silent
> and sliding back
> toward the same dreams, we wait
> for her careless fingers to graze us
> and to hear her breathing
> soft songs to herself.

The action of the waves segues into the ebb and flow of consciousness as sleep deposits the subject on the shore of wakefulness. The double bed—stolid emblem of domesticity—is a physical analogue to the shared dreams of a couple manifest only in the plural pronouns (we/us). The goddess's self-involvement may be interpreted as a figure of art's autonomy as well as its liminality: if it "touches," it does so "carelessly"; the songs breathed softly forth take no account of a possible listener (again Stevens's poem comes to mind). The receptivity of the dreamer is such that the touch and sound are anticipated—and therefore may never even come.

"The Birth of Venus" is more than the isolated exercise of a twenty-two-year-old college student. Its emotional depth and maturity, its controlled and understated handling of free verse, and its allusive economy all mark it as the work of a talented young poet with a strong potential to excel in precisely the type of post-Confessional workshop verse for which the writing program at Iowa, proud inaugurator of an institutional model widely imitated at universities and colleges across the United States in the years following World War II, was best known. Perelman, however, was by inclination and influence drawn in a different direction. The political radicalism of the decade, in no small part a direct outcome of such University of Michigan–born organizations as the Students for a Democratic Society (SDS), found a cultural ally in the New American Poetry tradition forcefully articulated in Donald Allen's 1960 anthology of that name and disseminated since that time to a fairly large audience through various countercultural channels. The presence at Iowa of Anselm Hollo, whose aesthetic commitments placed him firmly in the company—if not the camp—of Robert Creeley, Ed Dorn, and Allen Ginsberg, and whose arrival in 1968 compensated for the departure of Berrigan, signaled a kind of acknowledgment within the department for this alternative tradition. Born in Helsinki, Finland, in 1934, Hollo lived as a radio producer in London from 1958 to 1966 before coming to the United States, teaching briefly at the State University of New York at Buffalo in 1967, and settling in Iowa in 1968. Reviewing *Sojourner Microcosms* (1977) for the *San Francisco Review of Books* in January 1978, Perelman paid homage to his irreverent mentor's eclectic erudition in these terms:

> *Sojourner Microcosms* collects 20 years of Anselm Hollo's poetry, but actually it collects more than 4,000 years of the world's poetic activity. The Odyssey, the Kalevala, Apache myths, the Minnesingers, the French Encyclopedists, Whitehead, Jung, vampire movies, etc., all turn up in these pages. And holding them together is Hollo's firm, Poundian commitment to literacy, clarity, and a lyrical concision.

Perelman worked closely with Hollo in Iowa, and he made several lasting friendships with fellow students there as well, including Michael Waltuch, Tomaz Salamun, and Barrett Watten. Waltuch, with whom Perelman would cofound *Hills* magazine in 1973 (assuming sole editorship after the first issue), introduced fellow Yale alumni Kit Robinson and Steve Benson to Perelman at this time, though their period of intense collaboration would not truly begin until 1976. Through classmate Watten, Perelman came to a close appreciation of Charles Olson's work as well as to an important friendship with the poet Robert Grenier. The fates of Salamun, Watten, and Perelman almost took a tragic turn in the winter of 1972 when an Iowa to Cambridge, Massachusetts, road trip—motivated in part by Perelman's budding relation with Francie Shaw—ended with the car carrying the three friends skidding into a snowbank after a truck suddenly swerved into it. Watten had a broken leg and Perelman sustained a back injury, but the three young men all escaped this serious accident with their lives. It may be a residue of the vivid sensation of peril accompanying the crash that finds its way into "The Works," a prose poem collected in *Braille,* where Perelman writes: "Against impact I thumb my cultured nose, I hear my noise, then I give myself over to the crash, breath knocked out, caught in the ability to talk."

The summer after his first year at Iowa, Perelman returned to Ann Arbor to take his master's degree in Greek and Latin at the University of Michigan, and one year later in 1971 he completed the M.F.A. in creative writing at Iowa. With a psychological deferment from military service in the Vietnam War, Perelman traveled some at this time, visiting California and Mexico and seriously considering an extended journey to India. He found himself instead back in Iowa for one more year, partaking in the collective translation project that would eventuate in the 1978 anthology *Russian Poetry: The Modern Period* and working on solo translations of Catullus's Latin and the Spanish of Vallejo's *Trilce* (1922). The first issue of *Hills* dates back to this final year in Iowa, as do the daily improvisations—inspired by and loosely modeled on the experimental prose works collected in Williams's *Imaginations* (1970)—that would eventually make up his first full-length book, *Braille.*

In 1974 Perelman moved to Cambridge to be with Francie Shaw, who was then completing a degree in art at The Museum School. Having met in 1971, the couple married in the summer of 1975, the weekend of the ceremony happening to coincide with the publication by Ithaca House of *Braille,* a book that like all of Perelman's subsequent works would be dedicated to Shaw and that, like a great many of them, bears cover art by her. A curious little pamphlet dating from roughly this time, *11 Romantic Positions* (1976), takes the form of a collaboration between husband and wife in which Perelman's Grenier-influenced texts are juxtaposed with Shaw's line drawings. In one of the longer pieces the site of the newlywed couple's honeymoon, Guatemala, provides a title as well as the unusual vowel combination ("ua") in the initial word:

> Quarrelled, half
> quarrelled slow hours
> with Francie, Indians send
> rockets up, it's
> religion, explosions re
> verberating in volcanic
> rock bowl of air I
> was alive It was the
> rainy season And
> here I was still saying
> was, was, that old
> unsatisfactory busride
> back home[.]

Sexual pleasure—defined in the booklet's first short poem as a position where "I neither are nor am you"—is apparently displaced in "Quatemala," the quarrel between the American tourists echoing uncannily in the rockets sent up by the Mayans, the

Front cover of Perelman's 1986 book, whose title refers to childhood and to the wealthy nations of the world

and now here I was
reading *The Island*
wiping my ass about
to get up and make
love with Francie[.]

Candor about the body and its functions is an attribute of all these poems, though it registers at least as much as the mimicry of a period style as it does as a daring raid on bourgeois delicacy. Some twenty years after the trip Perelman recalled his travels in Central America from a slightly different perspective, one foregrounding political, rather than personal or sensual, revelation:

When my wife and I went to Guatemala in 1975 for our honeymoon, our eyes were opened to novel states of affairs. Money, for instance, was not continuous, but was kept in place only sporadically and with the broadest hints of violence. In Guatemala City, sixteen year old Mayan kids in army camouflage with submachine guns were stationed on every street corner where there was a bank.

This display of the repressive violence underpinning the monetary system of a nation was jarring because it revealed something effectively concealed from most first-world eyes. The arbitrariness of the social sign, like that of its linguistic counterpart as analyzed by Ferdinand de Saussure, is masked by convention. But whereas Perelman's modernist precursors Pound and Williams had railed against the merely conventional value of coin and word, equating arbitrariness with sexual perversion and political misrule, Perelman— like so many of his contemporaries in the post-1968 intellectual world—interpreted the situation differently. Rather than cleanse the language of the tribe and return it to its essential common core, Perelman and his contemporaries sought to discredit the putative universals, to expose the violence at the root of pseudo-consensus, and to resist "the tyranny of elemental words" that had been used to sanction everything from racial segregation to American imperialism in Southeast Asia, from gender oppression to an acceptance of nuclear warheads as a daily fact of life. In an interesting reversal of a common trajectory that moves from youthful political radicalism to a maturity of neutral domesticity, Perelman credits his marriage, and especially the birth of his two children, Max in 1979 and Reuben in 1983, with engaging his political passions in his late twenties and developing them throughout his thirties and forties.

The newly married couple were soon to set off from Cambridge to make a life in San Francisco, but in the remainder of 1975 and through the first half of 1976 they stayed in New England, where Perel-

vivid perception of which leads the writer to exclaim "I / was alive"—while at the same time conceding that the memory of pleasure, whether brought on by explosions or sexual encounters, is by definition "unsatisfactory." Was the "busride / back home" unsatisfactory because of its destination (home again, after the exotic sojourn) or because of the quarrel between husband and wife? Shaw's drawings work with a basic vocabulary of the open and the closed, the linear and the circular. Her coils, swirls, and crossovers are comically suggestive in relation to Perelman's often sexually explicit themes. One way to read the pamphlet is as an exercise in interpersonal candor as that had been codified poetically by The Figures important to Perelman such as Creeley, Hollo, and Grenier. The closing poem, in fact, directly alludes to Creeley's *The Island* (1963), a novel begun in Guatemala in 1960. While unquestionably slight, as is most of the work in *11 Romantic Positions,* "The Way of the White Clouds" does show the lengths to which Perelman was willing to go at this time to sound casual and uninhibited:

man taught sporadically at Hobart College, Northeastern University, and through Cambridge Adult Education. He made at this time, through the offices of friend and mentor Grenier–who was living in Franconia, New Hampshire–the acquaintance of Creeley, and Perelman mingled on occasion with the small circle of Creeley's students at the time, including Alan Davies, editor of the small magazines *Oculist Witnesses* and *100 Posters* and eventual associate of New York Language poets Bruce Andrews and Charles Bernstein. Perelman even met the venerable Objectivist poet Louis Zukofsky, who regaled the somewhat surprised younger poet with stories of Williams's intimate habits. Perelman would probably have listened carefully at this time to any discussion of Williams, no matter how slight, as Perelman was working in a sustained and serious relation to the early, "difficult" masterpieces *Kora in Hell* and *Spring and All* in the improvisational poems he had been publishing for several years in little magazines such as *This, Streets and Roads,* and his own *Hills,* which included a half-dozen poems from the series in its inaugural issue. In 1975 Perelman edited and lightly revised (often simply retitling) sixty-one of these daily improvisations and published them under the title *Braille.*

In titling his first full-length volume *Braille,* Perelman announced an aspiration toward tactility in language, raised contours felt at the fingertips rather than inked ciphers consumed at a safe distance by the eyes. But there is an equally strong drive toward musicality in these poems, an unmistakable facility for hearing extraordinary rhythmic possibilities in ordinary language. The dialectic of virtuosity and improvisation characteristic not only of early Williams but also of Jack Kerouac and the O'Hara of long poems such as *Second Avenue* (1960)–not to mention the innovative jazz artists who inspired so many American writers in the postwar years–plays itself out in these works, where messy exuberance and a dazzlingly precise feel for syntactical variations keep the words always a step ahead of the reader's expectation. This unique set toward the syntax of a poem, no matter whether the primary compositional units are lines and stanzas or sentences and paragraphs, holds from one end of Perelman's body of works to the other. It lends urgency to the improvisations of *Braille,* animates the collage texts in *7 Works,* steers the precise stanzas of *Primer,* and gives the "new sentences" of *a.k.a.* (1984) their distinctive flair. It is the specifically poetic element that raises the deeply political body of work after 1984–*To the Reader, The First World,* and *Face Value*– above any accusation of mere propagandizing. And it continues to mature and complexify

in a long poem such as "The Manchurian Candidate," where the mimicry of cinematic shot-structure does not minimize the specifically linguistic nature of its compositional units.

Braille debuts this syntactic intelligence. It also brings several of Perelman's strongest thematic concerns to the foreground. Formally the book is nearly evenly divided between the thirty prose pieces of one, two, or three short paragraphs and the thirty-one poems in some kind of stanzaic or open-field form. While there is work of interest in both of these modes, the prose pieces such as "Youngstown," "India," "We See," and "Aesthetics" are the more distinctive and memorable contributions. The tendency to evoke and then evade codes of autobiographical utterance manifests itself in "Youngstown" and returns repeatedly in Perelman's work, from "An Autobiography" in *7 Works* to the long prose work in nine parts, *a.k.a,* to recent uncollected poems such as "To the Past" and "To the Future." Each of the three paragraphs of "Youngstown" begins with a similar phrase, starting with the word *when* and coordinating it through the first-person pronoun to a state or action. "When I was the world" is the grandly monomaniacal way the first sentence begins; "When I lived in youngstown" sounds a more plausible note in the second; and "When to the sound of mind I bring these words" is the consciously poetic third sentence, the cadence and syntactical inversion paying open homage to Shakespeare's thirtieth sonnet. In each case the "when" phrase initiates a somewhat madcap process of accumulation and acceleration that drives to the final period as many as eight lines of prose-set print later. Here, for example, is the entirety of the third paragraph:

> When to the sound of mind I bring these words scattering them ahead of me in exact statement bingo! then attitudes jar and what else do you have except an attitude to shine said the anthropocentric sun sing said the line of song say these things and see where they put me get me revealed the crooked cries of bingo the large task.

While a certain structural allusion to the sonnet form runs throughout this paragraph, the overall spirit owes more to Frank O'Hara than to the Bard. The absence of punctuation and conventional sentence structure prepares the stage for many duplicitous situations in which grammatical object tumbles into subject which in turn tumbles into predicate. The dash-it-off bravado of "scattering" words "ahead of me" is integrated by an act of mind into "exact statement bingo!"–at once deferring to and lightly deriding the ideal of a word order revelatory of a world order. The conversation with the sun, here comically portrayed as "anthropocentric," already made into something of a set piece of modernist poetry by first Mayakovsky and then O'Hara (see the final chapter in Perelman's *The Marginalization of Poetry*), yields some advice about shining, just as the song tautologically advises one to "sing." The exhuberant "bingo!" decays by paragraph's end into "the crooked cries of bingo" before an awkward end is brought to the whole exhalation by the words "the large task."

The interpenetration of domestic and global sites is the subtext of the clever single-paragraph prose piece called "India." In the course of this poem, narrated in the same kind of oddly neutral voice heard in John Ashbery's early poem "The Instruction Manual," the title word expands one character at a time, the connotations shifting perceptibly with each addition, until finally the reader unexpectedly deduces the American heartland:

> First, there is the i-n-d-i-a, which should cohere fairly stably by now, but adding the n makes for a whole set of erosions, indecencies, and unmistakable clues that the namers had imagined themselves in the wrong hemisphere. Then the a, which violates the inexact i-n-d-i-a-n by forming the inexact a-n-a, cousin to the even more tired r-a-m-a, as in f-o-o-d-o-r-a-m-a. The a-n-a implies a leveling of consciousness over a wide area.

By means of this clever conceit, which in its typography already looks ahead to the infamous equal signs in the journal $L=A=N=G=U=A=G=E$, Perelman is able to question deep geopolitical structures linking seemingly unrelated spaces. The final sentence works in a sharply critical jab at the bad universality of consumer America ("an all is one howard johnson orange glow"), increasingly a target of Perelman's caustic observation as his work progresses, as the dialectic of here and elsewhere takes another hermeneutical turn:

> So, you have the search for i-n-d-i-a totally incomplete, and before anything of substance was initiated in the mind, it spread itself out insistently and destructively in an all is one howard johnson orange glow that is called health here, steel mills and florida orange juice, but is understood elsewhere as violence, appetite disembodied, misspelled.

In the short poem "How It's Done" the first five lines dissect in neutral descriptive language the deceptive rhetorical strategies of the American Pentagon as it prosecuted the war against the Viet Cong while the two-line denouement of the poem abruptly introduces an image of vaguely sexualized violence, a kind of surrealist antidote to the rationalizations of power:

> Responding to reports that american bombs
> had hit POW camps the pentagon said that
> if true then north vietnam had violated
> the geneva convention accords

by placing such camps in dangerous areas
the usual thing is to think of a bunkhouse girl
tangled in the bedsprings[.]

Such graphic entanglements of state power and individual sexuality serve frequently as a theme for Perelman's mature reflections on libidinal and political economies. In "We See," a title that attracts notice in the context of the braille metaphor, the ubiquity of social messages ("everywhere society is spoken") is registered in a string of apposite clauses that finally drifts off in an ellipsis that bespeaks a deep skepticism as concerns the political vision of identity- and property-obsessed citizens who have effectively abdicated democratic agency in favor of delegated responsibility:

> In the universities, in the supermarkets, in the language, everywhere society is spoken, we see people unable to dress themselves in human proportion, we see them fooled into cannibalism by sweet talk, we see them drawling on the beach, looking each other over, looking for fingerprints, yet at the same time unable to identify their own assholes in a series of simple political mugshots, we see them irritated, searching . . . [.]

Perelman's own search next led to the West Coast. He and Shaw made the cross-country drive to San Francisco late in the summer of 1976 and within a day of their arrival were setting up house in a loft on Folsom Street found for them by Geoffrey Young, the energetic, talkative young poet and soon-to-be influential publisher who would bring out some of Perelman's most important texts in handsome editions over the years, starting with *7 Works* (1978) and continuing into the next decade with *The First World* (1986) and *Captive Audience* (1988). The arrival of the young couple coincided with the sparking of a literary scene built on affective ties dating back in some instances to high school (in the case of Barrett Watten and Ron Silliman), college (Steve Benson and Kit Robinson), and graduate school (Perelman and Watten), though novelty animated even the pre-established connections as life and literature coincided apart from the institutional buffers of school and people such as Hejinian, Harryman, David Bromige, Alan Bernheimer, Tom Mandel, and others brought their own backgrounds, idiosyncracies, and ambitions to the mix.

To this fertile conjunction of emergent talents Perelman brought an enthusiasm to learn what people were thinking. His pragmatically oriented pluralism proved a welcome attribute in the context of the often didactic, calculated tendencies of men such as Silliman and Watten, neither of whom needed excessive coaxing to speak their opinions on a variety of literary and political topics. The first flier for the Talk Series that

Perelman organized and hosted at his and Francie's Folsom Street loft lists both Watten and Silliman, along with Harryman, Benson, Bromige, G. P. Skratz, and Perelman himself, as scheduled speakers for the inaugural spring series. More than forty talks occupied the evenings and exercised the passions of these San Francisco Bay area poets and their out-of-town visitors through 1981, and excellent representations of the range of work can be found in the special "Talks" double issue of *Hills* (1980) and the follow-up volume from Southern Illinois University Press, *Writing/Talks* (1985), both edited by and including contributions from Perelman.

Redefining the role of the listener and, by extension, the reader stands as a motive not only for the Talk Series but also for the writing Perelman did in the years immediately following his arrival in San Francisco, a writing that at least in its initial stages was collaborative and receptive. Perelman recalls one such method of working, incorporated in several of the texts in *7 Works,* in this way:

> Kit Robinson, Steve Benson and I began a writing project almost as soon as we met in San Francisco in 1976. One of us would read from whatever books were handy and two of us would type. These roles would rotate; occasionally, there would be two readers reading simultaneously to one typist. The reader would switch books whenever he felt like it, and jump around within whatever book was open at the time. Truman Capote's slam at Kerouac's work–that this was typing, not writing–would have been even truer here, though none of us could type as fast as Kerouac, who apparently was a terrific typist, an ability which undoubtedly helped give his writing its enviable fluidity.

> This was not automatic writing; automatic listening would be more like it. There was no question of keeping up with the stream of spoken words; one could attempt to attend to them or not. If I felt no spark of imagination I would type at or toward the next batch of them I heard, though the rates of speed of spoken syllable versus typed letter were so disparate that by the time a phrase such as "For the purposes of this paper, I will assume a familiarity with Foucault's critique of the notion of the author as an individual" was read I might have managed to type "For the purposes of paper." At this point, I may have started to hear a tone in the typed phrase I wanted to pursue. I can have a sickened fond loathing for sentences that start with "For": they remind me of an ersatz biblical loftiness, however many degrees removed from that I remain. So I might continue on my own unmarked track and write, "For the purposes of paper are not the purposes of words alone." By this time, the reader-as-pronouncer might be in the midst of pronouncing "or take the shuttle bus from Gare du Nord with poets, novelists, editors, bookstore owners, Lacanian psychoanalysts, and spend the day." That would certainly come in handy, for instance in producing: "For the purposes of paper are not the purposes of words alone but of poets and novelists, Lacanian psychoanalysts, bookstore owners, and other The Figures of speech bartering their thought balloons for a bronzed handle on the deeper cellars of the city's statuesque psyche."

> We did this for a few months, generating many pages which we worked on, picked through, or mostly filed away. A few lines show up in a few pieces of Robinson's *Down and Back,* Benson's *As Is,* and my *7 Works.* "Instead of ant wort I saw brat guts" begins my book, although in fact Robinson heard/typed/wrote it. It's in "his voice."

Positing the role of the writer as a "swamped receiver" works to reverse the poles of modernist literary production, in which the writer is omni-competent and the reader forever consigned to playing catch-up. Like the reader whose birth Roland Barthes proclaimed in the closing sentences of his famous essay declaring the death of the author, the protagonist of Perelman's "brat guts literary regime" is "second in the chain of command, which becomes a chain of suggestion."

Perelman has commented that he consistently hears three or four "tracks" in his head while writing: the choice between compossibles is a defining moment of poetic practice for him. The collaborations with Benson and Robinson worked in important ways to externalize and materialize the fact of discursive compossibility, and the 1978 stagings of Celia and Louis Zukofsky's *"A"-24,* a text intricately scored for four voices accompanied by carefully chosen harpsichord pieces by Handel, must likewise have served to make manifest the simultaneity and collectivity of the literary text. Nine months of rehearsal preceded the three performances given by a group comprised of Kit Robinson (Thought), Steve Benson and Carla Harryman (dividing the gendered roles of Drama), Lyn Hejinian (Story), Barrett Watten (Poem), and Perelman (harpsichord/piano) at the Grand Piano (a local poetry venue), the San Francisco State Poetry Center, and the University of California at Davis. Writing about the performances in the pages of *L=A=N=G=U=A=G=E,* 8 (June 1979), Perelman stressed the enormous difficulties associated with the endeavor, difficulties partly arising from Zukofsky's misleading analogy between music and language. "Language doesn't occur in time the way music does," Perelman points out. "Music is strictly sequence, absolutely dependent on time. Language merely uses time to embody itself in a string of phonemes, the meaning occurring both during the sounds and after they have vanished." Faced with the barrage of voices and sounds, the auditor of *"A"-24* truly is a "swamped receiver." "What the ear tends to do on first hearing '*A*'-24," Perelman observes, "is switch rapidly from voice to voice," attending for a time to one role or "track," then permitting another to rise into attention. Such was not Zukofsky's somewhat utopian intention, however. According to Perelman, Zukofsky tried to "hook up the physical instantaneous unconscious undistortable act of hearing with the fullest possible range of thought (all of a life). Performing and hearing 'A'-24 presupposes a thorough knowledge of Z's work, an ecstatically dilated time sense in which every syllable continues sounding until they all have resolved each other, and an eternity in which the whole work is present in any of its sounds."

The Talk Series and the close engagement with Zukofsky culminating in the *"A"-24* performances are important contexts for reading Perelman's first book of the San Francisco period, *7 Works*. Published in a mid-sized, NEA-supported run of six hundred by Geoffrey Young's The Figures in 1978, with a handsome four-color cover by Francie Shaw, the book is comprised of three prose collages; the sustained, complex, forty-two-paragraph "Essay on Style" (dedicated to Kit Robinson and Steve Benson); "Vienna: A Correspondence"; and "An Autobiography." The other four works include a cut-up of a self-improvement text, "How to Improve" (dedicated to Barrett Watten), a suite of short poems called "Cupid & Psyche," a seven-page work in long disassociative stanzas ("Road Tones"), and the performance/installation text "Before Water." Reviewing the volume in *L=A=N=G=U=A=G=E* in October 1978, Carole Korzeniowsky praised Perelman's "facility with different forms, lengths, subject/object distances," and "found material." The works "think differently" separately in Korzeniowsky's view, but together they yield an "overall sense of a highly trained intellect at work." In March 1979, discussing "How to Improve" in the context of Russian Formalist theory, Watten called attention to the work's "permanent 'laying bare'" of the "device," praising its "busted formality" for making "the splendors of the language available."

7 Works represents Perelman's most concerted foray into a strictly literary form of collage though mimicry, citation, and other techniques for embedding source material in the poetic text are constants throughout his career. The "Essay on Style" cycles its basic paragraph-length units through a complicated round of progressions and repetitions that not only has a musical structure but also takes musical training—along with scientific experiment, exploratory travels, and other less classifiable *topoi*—as part of its kaleidoscopic content. Perelman's use of the *Life of Henri Brulard,* an unfinished document composed by Stendhal in the space of four months in 1835–1836, in the sixteen paragraphs of "An Autobiography" focuses on the maternal/pastoral passages from chapter 3 (often cited in connection with Sigmund Freud and Proust):

My mother, Mme Henriette Gagnon, was a charming woman and I was in love with my mother.

I must hurriedly add that I lost her when I was seven.

When I loved her at about the age of six, in 1789, I showed exactly the same characteristics as in 1828 when I was madly in love with Alberthe de Rubempré. My way of pursuing happiness was basically unchanged; there was just this difference: I was, as regards the physical side of love, just as Caesar would be, if he came back into the world, as regards the use of cannon and small arms. I would have learned very quickly, and my tactics would have remained basically the same.

I wanted to cover my mother with kisses, and without any clothes on. She loved me passionately and often kissed me; I returned her kisses with such fervour that she was often forced to go away. I abhorred my father when he came to interrupt our kisses. I always wanted to kiss her bosom. Please be kind enough to remember that I lost her in childbed when I was barely seven.

She was plump, with a faultlessly fresh complexion, she was very pretty, and I think just not quite tall enough. Her features expressed nobility and utter serenity; she was very lively, preferring to run about and do things for herself rather than give orders to her three maids, and she was fond of reading Dante's *Divine Comedy* in the original. Long afterwards, I found five or six copies of different editions in her room, which had remained shut up since her death.

. . . .

One evening, when for some reason I had been put to bed on the floor of her room on a mattress, she leaped over my mattress, lively and light-footed as a doe, to reach her own bed more quickly.

Many of these sentences appear unmodified and unmarked in "An Autobiography" (as a sentence from Jane Austen's *Mansfield Park* does in the "Play" section of Perelman's 1988 volume *Captive Audience*), and the reader unfamiliar with Stendhal's original certainly would be tempted, despite the literary tone, to take these events for occurrences in Perelman's own life. Stendhal is an interesting figure not only for his candid, proto-Freudian articulation of incestuous longings—"An Autobiography" emphasizes the young boy's erotic hunger as literalized in an actual physical hunger that lush banquets cannot satisfy—but also for his political predicament as a radical republican in a time of post-Napoleonic retrenchment in France. Perelman alludes to the political side of Stendhal in "Journal des Debats," collected in *To the Reader,* but his fascination with the novelist's nonfictional prose, not just the *Life* but also the *Memoirs of a Tourist* (1838), is on record as well. Writing in the inaugural issue of *Po-*

etics Journal in 1982, Perelman characterizes Stendhahl's prose in terms that could easily be applied to work in the "new sentence" then being developed by Hejinian, Silliman, Watten, and others.

> Paragraph by paragraph, the prose is disjunct. And within paragraphs, consecutive sentences will jump in focus and scale. There is a wide range of effect, bound up less with the content of each sentence (though there's an infinite range there, since they deal with physical and social particulars), than with motion between sentences. Stendahl's relationship, and hence the reader's as well, to the content of what he's saying is constantly shifting.

While it would be misleading simply to equate Perelman's project in his next book, *Primer,* to the 1917 turn on the part of Eliot and Pound against free verse and toward the "chiselled quatrains" of Theophile Gautier, there is a grain of truth to the analogy. Together the collage-based prose and nonstanzaic poetry of *7 Works* make a sharp contrast to the exclusive use of stanza forms in *Primer.* This book, published in an NEA-supported edition of five hundred copies by Watten's This Press, also marks the full-scale arrival of the discourse of linguistics among the San Francisco Bay area poets. Linguistic terms of art dot virtually every page of the thirty-five-poem volume, and Watten's cover design consists of Pierre Delattre's spectographic-pattern analyses of various consonantal phonemes.

Perelman's first title, also one word, gestured toward a palpable form of language: *Braille.* His second had the ring of the generic titles given to artists' exhibits: *7 Works.* His third perfectly bound volume also adopts a generic title, that of a work meant to provide the rudiments of a field or practice: *Primer.* Along with the obvious pedagogic connotations, the word conjures other meanings as well: the gray cover already seems a gesture in the direction of the homonym meaning a base coat of paint. Since explosives make up a large part of the political unconscious, the sense of primer as a compound used in the preparation of explosive devices may also be intended here. The choice of the word also sets in motion an ambiguity in the graphic representation of phonemes: while the phonetic symbols arrayed on the cover are precisely correlated to voicing, alphabetic characters are susceptible to varying manners of pronunciation. While some Americans may follow the rule that tends to make the vowel in words such as *primer* long, the correct or received pronunciation utilizes a short-/i/ sound rather than the dipthong /ay/. Already, then, a hesitation, a complication, in what purports to be a *primary* text, one stripped of the complexities that come later, after the basics have been fully grasped.

"My One Voice," "Trainee," "Room," "China," and "History" are among the important poems collected in *Primer.* Since the dominant mode in the collection is stanzaic, one may speculate that the form forced a head-to-head confrontation with "the poetic" as such, hence the references: "To Baudelaire," Percy Bysshe Shelley ("Hymn to Intellectual Beauty"), and Maria Rilke (the concluding poem, "Musik") as well as to contemporaries such as Hejinian ("Measure"), Harryman ("Birthday Present"), Andrews ("Socialist Realism"), and Bernheimer (to whom the title poem "Primer" is dedicated). The one formally exceptional piece is the ten-section poem "Outlines," which first appeared in *Hills* in 1978. In "My One Voice," a set of five four-line stanzas, Perelman writes in lines reminiscent of Creeley's "The System": "At the sound of my voice / I spoke and, egged on / by the discrepancy, wrote / the rest out as poetry." There are three poems in tercets–"Gears," "Self Portrait," and "Abstract"– each a recombination of lexical possibilities introduced but not exhausted in the other two.

In a work so conspicuously devoted to stanzaic forms, the appearance of the word that translates the Italian *stanze* namely *room* cannot be viewed as accidental. Comprised of five quatrains, the poem (rooms) *looks* the part of its genre in a way that many of Perelman's earlier works purposefully avoided. Self-uttering, self-confirming words are the protagonists of the first stanza, where time itself greets them:

> The words mention themselves.
> They are literally true.
> Every minute another circle
> Meets them halfway.

In the second stanza the movement of the second hand is contrasted to the stasis and containment of self-identity:

> The locker locks
> From the inside. I
> is an extensive pun
> Born of this confinement.

While *I* is of course a pun in a "literal" sense ("eye"), the shut-tight self of the locker model, lock fastened from the inside, is refuted by the "extensive" pun it gives birth to. The title word "room" occurs in the third stanza:

> The echoes crossing
> North America, the room.
> The ear hears in no time.
> On the street, machines . . . [.]

The leap in scale from "North America" to the unspecified but generally diminutive "the room" is quite

Cover for Perelman's 1996 book, an insider's account of an avant-garde poetic movement

drastic. The reach, or extension, may be further evidence of the pun's fanning out, perhaps with imperial intentions. The collapse of space due to telecommunications is one possible referent of the first two lines: a voice on the phone from California can be heard in New York as well as, if not better than (depending on traffic and sirens), someone across the room. But as to echoes? The "ear hears in no time" reads as instantly ("in no time"), though a state is also indicated, one of no-time. The contrast machine/non-machine, which moves throughout the poems of this book, reaches articulation here as:

On the street, machines

Reveal the thought
Of non-machines. These
Objects have the right
To remain silent.

The voluble and the silent; words and things; the things that permit the thinking of nonthings to be per-

ceived as things (typewriters, for instance)—the specificity of "these" objects reads somewhat ironically in light of the Miranda ruling language: "These / Objects have the right / To remain silent." Finally, in the fifth stanza:

The pen wrestles with
The hand by the light
Of an open door. Things
Are their real size.

Just as "words mention themselves" at the start of the work, at the end "Things / Are their real size." Immediate self-identity is the starting and ending point of the poem, whereas the pen/hand are an antagonistic couple just before ("The pen wrestles with / The hand . . . ").

Bob Gluck, a contemporary whose readings of Perelman's work have combined great insight with a healthy measure of criticism, situates *Primer* relative to Perelman's preceding and succeeding volumes in this useful statement:

Primer is a unified book; like much of *7 Works,* and in contrast to *a.k.a.,* this poetry has a silvery quality, a patina, beautiful and "rescued" turns of phrase, an economy rather than anything goes. Although the poems are made up of images, they are not charged with symbolism and they don't generate the force fields of the surreal. These images reject those stakes, that inevitability. They are diffused; meaning becomes a block to move around like the furniture of rhetoric.

Perelman returned to the prose format in January 1979 when the first two sections of *a.k.a.* appeared as the nineteenth in the Tuumba chapbook series edited by Hejinian. It was brought out in an edition of 450 with a cover—a wobbly blue rectangle colored yellow inside—and title page designed by Francie Shaw. The seventeen pages of text are divided into two main sections, the first consisting of thirty-five prose paragraphs and the second consisting of twenty-nine. The sentences are short, crisp, quasi-declarative, and they seemed at the time of their publication to illustrate a whole new way of approaching prose poetry, one that would build from while transforming the path broken by Gertrude Stein and Williams. Two early paragraphs from *a.k.a.* (the second and third paragraphs of section 1) served as Ron Silliman's principal exhibit in the September 1979 "New Sentence" talk that christened and defined what could be called the signature device of the language-centered movement. While not as decisive as Jameson's mention of "China" in his 1982 and 1984 articles on the postmodern, Silliman's critical remarks on Perelman's work have had wide influence indeed on the way his poems have subsequently been interpreted. Watten and Harryman are also cited by Silliman—Watten's work as the first in which Silliman "noticed" the innovation and Harryman's as a fresh example illustrating the eight characteristics Silliman has advanced—but it is Perelman's plotless prose on which Silliman focuses. In the essay/manifesto Silliman isolates eight characteristics of the new sentence. These have to do with the paragraph, the sentence, their relation, and syllogistic semantic movement:

1) The paragraph organizes the sentences;
2) The paragraph is a unit of quantity, not logic or argument;
3) Sentence length is a unit of measure;
4) Sentence structure is altered for torque, or increased polysemy/ambiguity;
5) Syllogistic movement is (a) limited (b) controlled;
6) Primary syllogistic movement is between the preceding and following sentences;
7) Secondary syllogistic movment is toward the paragraph as a whole, or the total work;
8) The limiting of syllogistic movement keeps the reader's attention at or very close to the level of language, that is, most often at the sentence level or below.

While Silliman's piece on the new sentence has a pedantic tone that has understandably led to criticism, he does present in concise terms some of the key features of the new prose poetry that was increasingly being practiced in his circle and that would begin impacting other writers in this country and abroad after 1982 or so. Silliman saw the new sentence as preserving crucial elements from poetic convention, but shifting them decisively: "Grammar has become . . . prosody," he says with a nod to Roland Barthes, which means that sentence length and punctuation have taken on rhythmic functions, for one, and that the semantically complicating work of line breaks has been brought inside the sentence. New sentences are "pressurized" or "torqued" by the "internal presence of once exteriorized poetic forms."

From *Braille*—with its even division between stanzaic and paragraph forms—forward Perelman has shown a penchant for alternating and combining his compositional forms. With *To the Reader,* begun in 1979 at roughly the time of his son Max's birth and published in an edition of 475 as the penultimate chapbook in the Tuumba series in June 1984, Perelman again utilizes stanza forms, though their tempo and organization move away from the condensation found in *Primer* and toward the run-on verse paragraphs used with increasing confidence and impact in *The First World* and *Face Value*. The critic Jed Rasula, writing in the pages of *Temblor,* admirably captures the spirit of *To the Reader* when he calls it some of "the most adroit, informed, yet innovative political poetry published lately in this country." Rasula is impressed with the way in which Perelman's work—which he compares favorably to

the work of the Peruvian poet Vallejo—incorporates all manner of reference, not restricting itself to "the usual stuff of verse":

> The poems continually feed on images of refugees, terrorists, illegal aliens, military operations, death squads, interrogations, hostages, Nazi eugenics, nuclear weapons and "strategic materials," the Pentagon . . . , Grenada, Southeast Asia, Central America, and such domestic sightings as Toys R Us, "sex manuals, Christmas decorations," and second mortgages.

Benjamin Friedlander, in an especially perceptive overview of the transition from *Primer* to *To the Reader,* summarizes the thesis of the latter work as being "that war, commerce, and patriarchy are the products of a furiously misspent sexuality." The marked influx of fighting words—those heavily freighted lexical and phrasal units Jameson called ideologemes and defined as "the smallest intelligible unit of the essentially antagonistic collective discourses of social classes"—gives Perelman's work, from this book forward, the unrivaled social urgency of a dissident broadcaster temporarily in control of the airwaves. This rhetorical turn, favoring direct address and overt position-taking, may have been hastened by Jameson's clumsily psychologizing misreading of the politically inexplicit poem "China," circulating since 1982 and published in its definitive form in "Postmodernism, or the Cultural Logic of Late Capitalism," a landmark article that appeared in the pages of the *New Left Review* just one month after the appearance of *To the Reader*. While *a.k.a.* raised issues of subjectivity, borrowing from the lexicon of the outlaws' forced evasion of stable identity ("also known as") while at the same time eliminating or complicating first-person expression in its nonaccumulating sentences, *To the Reader* shifts the primary locus of activity to the second person, that "swamped receiver" already given center stage in the collaborative works, and to what Roman Jakobson called the conative function of language.

In a single stanza from "A History Lesson" one finds the elements of scathing critique, theatrical asides, quoted but free-floating speech, literary allusiveness, frenzied self-references, and an overall commitment to giving social fact oratorical form that characterize the upwards of eighty poems in *To the Reader, The First World,* and *Face Value:*

> I use my whole doctrinaire
> Vocabulary, praxis twice as hard
> And rhetorical as a shotgun in a pickup.
> Today's date, sigh, a heavily feathered
> Paperweight crammed down the group esophagus

For pleasure. Your bored longings–
That's how money is manufactured.

Reviewing *The First World,* published in an edition of eight hundred copies by The Figures in April of 1986, scholar-poet Michael Davidson points out the dual references of the title *First World,* which refers at once to "the political economies of capitalist institutions" and to "our Edenic childhood," the world "before the body became a fetish object of drives and fixations." Indeed, the word "body" is one of the most densely overinscribed ciphers of this text. In addition to six unqualified uses and one verb phrase ("washing the body"), there are many adjectives applied: the body is "crudely physical" (52), unspeakable (49), and blood-soaked (47); it is humanized (11) and historicized (32), it is non-narrative (33), know-nothing (32) and twice simply preceded by the word *no* (34 and 38); it is private (43), single (21), and tan (45); it is spoken (29) and pictured (45); it is one-time (but no longer) (39). Perelman uses such lexical motifs to weave together the poems in the book, uniting them thematically into a complex whole. Many of these motifs and themes can be seen in the opening stanza to a poem late in the book, called simply "Person" (the title provides the subject of the verbs in the first line):

> Eats, drinks, sticks pipe in mouth and asks
> What society (books on varnished desk, vanished races,
>   where have I smelled that smell before I was born, a kind
>   of hard-headed pragmatism standing in the empty spaces
>   . . .
> What society has ever failed to fashion a human
> receptacle for its narrative wastes?
> C'est la guerre the garage the riding mower
> the obtrusive stories that don't stop when the sun goes down
>   all at one time like a physical short story
> low blood sugar lowering the rate of vocabulary utilization
> the world the universe the mind of god cushioning the fall of
>   the dead letter
> water coming into the river from an unknown source.
> Sometimes you just have to go lie down with the un-
>   named by-products.

After a middle stanza in which references to Proust and to Alfred Hitchcock's *The 39 Steps* (from which a character, Mr. Memory, plays an important role in "A Literal Translation of Virgil's Fourth Eclogue" in *Virtual Reality*) share room with maxims such as "capitalism makes nouns / and burns the connections" and–this time a literal rewrite from a famous remark of Wittgenstein's–statements such as "if a TV could talk we wouldn't understand it," Perelman concludes:

The intimate journal protects its secrets.
The intimate flesh projects its secrets.
In the bathroom: Kill a (Jew crossed out) Nazi.

Perelman is rewriting Fenellosa and Wittgenstein; the graffiti writers stage their stealthy battles for public utterance in urinals, a scenario encountered again in the 1996 sequence "Fake Dreams." A poem concerned with the disposal of "narrative wastes" not surprisingly ends in a public restroom, where who's expendable is hotly if anonymously debated.

If the first decade of Perelman's work and of language-centered writing in general sought to foreground the linguistic underpinnings of many human relations, the work from the mid 1980s forward reveals facets of a complex social totality that are by custom and by strategic intention left unexpressed/unsymbolized in other media (including other poems). From *defamiliarizing* automatized linguistic expression to *deconcealing* (*revealing* would not capture the exact dialectical shading of the procedure) effective but invisible social forces, this is the shift in Perelman's practice. But he retains the earlier strategy and places it in the service of the later, differently motivated practice. Even the title *The First World* marks–opens to resignification and resymbolization–a category that was still frequently left tacit in all poetry that did not explicitly announce itself relative to the category "Third World."

The two photographs that compose the cover design and frontispiece for *The First World,* though not chosen by Perelman, are of more than ornamental importance. On the cover a rustic man and boy between whom a mysterious round boulder standing nearly shoulder high to the adult sits seem curious–perhaps proud of their contiguity to the fantastic structure–but calm, laconic. The thinned orchard behind them and the mountain in the far background almost give the impression that this stone ball has rolled from atop the mountain to where it currently stands, occasioning a measured interest on the part of the locals. The object-world represented here does not look so much like the "first world"–it is too rural, unmediated, and–if not grim–stern (perhaps theocratic). In contrast to the cover photograph is the one opposite the title page. Again, a large circular form governs the composition, but this time it is a ring engulfed in flame through which hurls, skate-blades first, a man, teeth clenched in a consternated grin, apparently bare-legged but with his arms, torso, and head decked out in a shiny, striped, semimetallic fabric. There is a trace of servility mixed into the display of virtuosity. The man is, after all, quite literally "jumping through a hoop." Perilously kinetic, this image is a foretaste of the authorial function as it acrobatically attempts to survive in a three-ring circus of syntax. It is—like so many of Perelman's inadvertent, intermittent, and fabricated flirtations with autobiography—a self-portrait.

In the decade following the publication of *The First World,* Perelman has continued to innovate and provoke. While *Face Value* (1988) remains recognizably within the formal and thematic idiom of *The First World,* the thirty-five poems collected in its pages are more capacious and deliberate than their predecessors. Also published in 1988, *Captive Audience* is a brilliant and highly regarded book-length poem in five sections ("Novel," "Play," "Writing," "Clippings," and "Movie") that traverses genres and entire media with witty facility. In the ambitious concluding section of the poem "Movie," 122 sentences stretch over 750-plus lines yielding implausible pairings such as Cary Grant and Jacques Derrida, Richard Nixon and Frederic Jameson and unanticipated seriocomic segues. In a note accompanying the poem in *The Best of the Best American Poetry* (1998), Perelman comments on his methods:

> The continual shifting in "Movie," line by line, sentence by sentence, came from trying to get the entirety of the American world-hallucination that played so widely during the Reagan years onto the page. The Reagan hallucinations came from the movies; my continual sliding of reference was—metaphorically—movie-like: hence, I suppose, the poem's title. But while "Movie" continually refers to political matters, its tonal register is far from 'political,' populist or single. Ice cream, the Vietnam War, the literary, the bufferings of media—I wanted all of them and their interconnected workings revealed in lines and sentences.

In 1993 Roof Books published *Virtual Reality,* sixteen poems employing a variety of devices, most conspicuously strict word counts and visual shaping. The major poems of this well-known but somewhat aesthetically uneven volume are unquestionably the longer works: "The Marginalization of Poetry," "Money," and the exceptional "A Literal Translation of Virgil's Fourth Eclogue," a poem that looks back to Perelman's classical training and ahead to uncollected poems such as "The Manchurian Candidate," which mimes cinematic shot structure while incorporating multiple modes

of address (essayistic, autobiographical, ethnographic, hallucinatory). It joins other works as yet available only in restricted circulation: the chapbook *Chaim Soutine* (1994), a four-part poem employing couplets, word counts, and dramatic-monologue form to explore the painter's fascination with a spoiled or putrescent reality; a series of *Fake Dreams* (1996) that neutralize the authority of the unconscious (as viewed for instance by the Surrealists) by exposing it to conscious fabrication; and the mock-naive melodies of the beautifully produced chapbook *The Masque of Rime* (1997). These works and others are slated for collection in 1999, and a volume of selected poems, as yet untitled, has recently been announced from Wesleyan University Press.

Interviews:

Jonathan Monroe, "Poetry, Community, Movement: A Conversation," with Perelman, Charles Bernstein, and Ann Lauterbach, *Diacritics,* 26 (Fall/Winter 1996): 196–210;

Clint Burnham and Deeana Ferguson, "Interview with Bob Perelman," *Boo,* 6 (1996).

References:

Robert Gluck, "Bob Perelman," in *80 Langton Street Residence Program 1982* (San Francisco: 80 Langton Street, 1983), pp. 47–59;

George Hartley, "Jameson's Perelman: Reification and the Material Signifier," in *Textual Politics and the Language Poets* (Bloomington: Indiana University Press, 1989), pp. 42–52;

Henriette Herwig, "Postmoderne Literatur oder postmoderne Hermeneutik?: Zur Theorie und Praxis der Interpretation zeitgenösser Literatur am Beispiel von Peter Handke, Botho Straus, Bob Perelman, und Nicolas Born," *Kodikas / Code: Ars Semeiotica,* 13, nos. 3/4 (1990): 225–244;

Fredric Jameson, "Postmodernism, or the Cultural Logic of Late Capitalism," *New Left Review,* 146 (1984): 53–93;

Eileen Myles, "Perpetual Motion: What Makes Bob Perelman Run?," *Voice Literary Supplement* (November 1993);

Ron Silliman, "The New Sentence," *Hills,* 6/7 (1980): 190–217;

Silliman, Ann Lauterbach, Steve Evans, Juliana Spahr, and Perelman, "Readings and Responses to *The Marginalization of Poetry,* with a counter-response by Bob Perelman," *The Impercipient Lecture Series,* 4 (1997).

Stanley Plumly

(23 May 1939 –)

Ronald Baughman
University of South Carolina

See also the Plumly entry in *DLB 5: American Poets Since World War II.*

BOOKS: *In the Outer Dark* (Baton Rouge: Louisiana State University Press, 1970);
Giraffe (Baton Rouge: Louisiana State University Press, 1973); partially republished in *How the Plains Indians Got Horses* (Crete, Nebr.: Best Cellar Press, 1973);
Out-of-the-Body Travel (New York: Ecco Press, 1977);
Summer Celestial (New York: Ecco Press, 1983);
Boy on the Step (New York: Ecco Press, 1989);
The Marriage in the Trees (Hopewell, N.J.: Ecco Press, 1997).

OTHER: "On Stanley Plumly's Poems," by Plumly and Maura Stanton, in "A Symposium of Young Poets," edited by Michael Ryan, *Iowa Review,* 4 (Fall 1973): 54–126;
"The One Thing," in *American Poets in 1976,* edited by William Heyen (Indianapolis: Bobbs-Merrill, 1976), pp. 254–261;
"The Abrupt Edge," in *Conversant Essays: Contemporary Poets on Poetry,* edited by James McCorkle (Detroit: Wayne State University Press, 1990);
"Sleeps ('Nobody Sleeps')," in *Introspections: American Poets on One of Their Own Poems,* edited by Robert Pack and Jay Parini (Middlebury, Vt.: Middlebury College Press / Hanover, N.H.: University Press of New England, 1997), pp. 213–219.

SELECTED PERIODICAL PUBLICATIONS–
UNCOLLECTED: "Chapter and Verse," *American Poetry Review,* 7 (January/February 1978): 21–30;
"In Answer to a Theory," *New England Review and Bread Loaf Quarterly,* 6 (Autumn 1983): 48–53;
"Reading Williams," *Field: Contemporary Poetry and Poetics,* 29 (Fall 1983): 47–49;
"Dirty Silences," *Tendril,* 18 (1984): 178–193;

Stanley Plumly (photograph by Star Black)

"Pound's Garden," *Field: Contemporary Poetry and Poetics,* 33 (Fall 1985): 19–22;
"Absent Things," *Field: Contemporary Poetry and Poetics,* 37 (Fall 1987): 31–34;
"Words on Birdsong," *American Poetry Review,* 21 (May/June 1992): 11–16;
"Revery Is a Solitude in Which," *Wallace Stevens Journal,* 17 (Spring 1993): 35–37;
"Season of Mists," *Green Mountains Review,* tenth anniversary issue, edited by Neil Shepard (Winter–Spring 1997): 13–21.

In "Field," a key poem in his most recent collection, *The Marriage in the Trees* (1997), Stanley Plumly presents a defining statement about himself as a man and a poet: "A man of sense, coming to a clearing, a / great open space, will always wait among the trees, in the / doorway, until the coast is clear." This guarded stance results from Plumly's more than thirty years as a poet who has focused on psychological dramas involving people and events central to his life—an alcoholic father, a long-suffering mother, and a series of problematic, often failed, love relationships and marriages. Plumly's poetry embodies a quest to resolve these conflicts and to move to exposed, open spaces of the heart and mind after reconnoitering from the doorway of memory.

Increasingly, the poet's chief concern is the *how* and *why* of memory, how and why exercising memory and writing poetry are virtually synonymous. He declares in a 1989 interview for *The Post-Confessionals* that memory is "a way of identifying sources" that "are still very much alive. In a way the poet is the medium between the expression of the poem itself and the source. That's why I would like to think that my poems are preoccupied with the self and the I, and yet are not egocentric. I place myself at the center, but I also see myself as a kind of invisible presence in the poem. . . . Remembering is that present, progressive way of saying the past is coming through me." The past that comes "through" the poet involves the triangular relationship among himself and his parents. As the 1995 *American Poetry Review* interviewers observed, "It seems a lot of your poems are about . . . how to read one's experience, that you're showing us how to read the experience, discovering the way as you go, showing us how to discover it too . . . by working through the choices and the options."

Plumly's serious inquiries into his own poetic processes have made him an important commentator on and theoretician of contemporary poetry in general. In his two-part 1978 essay "Chapter and Verse" he discusses the distinguishing features of the Post-Confessional school—those poets whose careers began to flourish in the late 1960s and early 1970s. Central to this poetic school is the use of two different kinds of "rhetoric": the rhetoric of voice and the rhetoric of image. As Plumly states, "Rhetoric ought to be no more or less than the presence of the poet, made manifest, in his poem. . . . If there is a general difference among younger poets today it is a difference of rhetorical sources: those who write out of an emotional imperative and those who write from an emblematic commitment." In his *Style and Authenticity in Postmodern Poetry* Jonathan Holden

identifies Plumly's work as belonging to a form Holden calls the "conversation" poem: "The first type we might label 'narrative.' It is usually in free verse, and it comprises what might be labeled the free-verse, narrative, conversation poem of voice, or what Stanley Plumly has accurately labeled 'the prose lyric.' The second type of conversation poem we might label 'discursive' though the more fashionable term has come to be 'meditative.' In this type of poem the conversation, instead of being anecdotal, tends to be digressive and abstract and to include philosophical speculation." Yet, Holden continues, each type of "conversation poem" utilizes both rhetorical strategies—the "silent" rhetoric of image and the audible rhetoric of voice. Plumly's free-verse "prose lyrics" have the accessibility of conversation overheard; the reader "listens" to the voice of the speaker recounting past experiences and simultaneously participates in the process of emotional discovery embodied in these complex, multilayered poems.

The son of Herman and Esther Wellbaum Plumly, Stanley Ross Plumly was born in Barnesville, Ohio. Herman Plumly, who died at the age of fifty-six of a heart attack brought on by his chronic alcoholism, dominates the poet's work: "I can hardly think of a poem I've written that at some point in its history did not implicate, or figure, my father," Plumly declares in a 1973 *Iowa Review* interview. His mother, who died in 1994, appears in the poetry as the proud, silent witness of her husband's downfall. Following Plumly's birth the family moved from farmwork to carpentry jobs and back to farmwork in Virginia and Ohio. Plumly graduated from Wilmington College, a small Quaker work-study school in Ohio, in 1962. He received his M.A. from Ohio University in 1968 and did course work toward a Ph.D. at the same university. He has taught in many universities—including Louisiana State, Ohio, Iowa, Princeton, Columbia, Michigan, Houston, Washington, and (since 1985) Maryland, as well as at the Bread Loaf Writers' Conference from 1978 to 1980. Among his awards for poetry are Ohio University's Baker Fund Award (1972), the Delmore Schwartz Memorial Award for Poetry (1973), the William Carlos Williams Award (1979) for *Out-of-the-Body Travel* (1977), the National Endowment for the Arts Award in Poetry (1984–1985), and the Ingram-Merrill Foundation Award in Poetry (1986–1987). He has received multiple Pushcart Prizes: for "Wildflowers" (1979–1980), "Sonnet" (1983–1984), "The Foundry Garden" (1987), "Reading with the Poets" (1993), "Complaint Against the Arsonist" (1993), and "Will Work for Food" (1995). He was awarded a Guggenheim Fel-

Giraffe

New Poems by Stanley Plumly

Cover for Plumly's 1973 book, in which he employs the giraffe as a symbol for the poet

for facets of the self; he is the fisherman who dances in his long boat, which becomes in the poet's dreams a ceremonial vessel transporting the older man toward death; he is the violin player who gives sound to his song of inner agony; and he is the farmer who must stay drunk in order to endure slaughtering his cattle. The father is, in many respects, a version of the artist, moving toward ruin, the creative man who destroys himself a little bit at a time. Yet, as he recalls in a 1973 *Iowa Review* interview, the poet keeps his father alive through memories and dreams: "I remember my father used to get so drunk I thought he was going to fall off the planet. He was a bull in his body. He ran into, over things. Once set in motion, his momentum seemed a natural, terrible force. As a child I would lie awake in bed long into the early morning listening and waiting for him to come home. He was always late and always drunk, but he always came home. And as it was a dark house, he invariably seemed to break into it. My father's house. In those waiting, and wasted, hours I lost the secret of sleep."

In his troubled sleep the poet escapes from the body to return to his psychological origins, and as he sleeps, he moves as if underwater into the silence of dreams. In Plumly's cosmology water is often the medium for dramatizing events in the subconscious, the dreamworld in which people move in slow motion while re-creating pained moments of their lives. Sleep becomes a middle ground between the living and the dead. The sleeper assumes the posture and the loss of consciousness associated with the dead, and in so doing he recalls and resurrects the dead. "Now That My Father Lies Down Beside Me," for instance, depicts father and son together as they "lie in that other darkness, ourselves." The younger man cannot touch or see his father, but "I dream we lie under water, / caught in our own sure drift." The poet achieves a communion with his dead father in this spiritual drift of the two selves. Their proximity—one asleep, the other dead—causes a physical constriction within the writer so that he can "barely breathe" as, of course, his father cannot at all. Yet, instead of being fulfilled by such a meeting, the speaker feels much more keenly his own emptiness once he awakens. In his dreams and memories of the dead and dying, the poet seems more alive than when he is awake and oppressed by the sterile houses and rooms symbolizing his sense of personal isolation.

The poems of *In the Outer Dark* that treat the male-female love relationship are pervaded by this sense of isolation. "At Palmer House" envisions the lovers' meeting place as "rooms, / so well arranged, so sunlit, / so kept." Yet the speaker and his beloved

lowship in 1973 and was named Hawthorden Fellow in 1990 and a Robert Frost Fellow in 1991. He has served as poetry editor for major presses and journals, including *Ohio Review* (1970–1974), *Iowa Review* (1975, 1977–1978, 1984–1985), *American Poetry Review* (1975–), and the Wesleyan University Press Poetry Series (1982–).

Plumly's first collection, *In the Outer Dark* (1970), illustrates the poet's remarkably early realization of his aesthetic vision. The central figure of this work is the artistic self from which other subjects extend. The writer attempts to connect with the outer world but finds in that world only silence and emptiness. Since his movement outward results in isolation, the poet is eventually forced back into himself, into the world of inner dark.

In the Outer Dark introduces the poet's father, who assumes many roles in Plumly's works: he is the carpenter who builds houses and rooms that function, in Whitmanesque fashion, as metaphors

Dust jacket for Plumly's 1977 book, poems that examine his parents' marriage and his own troubled love relationships

feel ill-equipped to enter this inviting, orderly world: "As always, we have / wandered in from the outside / of ourselves, silent, empty- / handed, the shy way that deer / enter another part of the forest." In "Between Flesh and What Follows" the speaker attempts to overcome pervasive emptiness, silence, and darkness through touch, through love, as he seeks to share his personal isolation with another: "As when I put my hands / all over you, there is still / that darkness between the touch, / the blind breath still / between the teeth. / Even the talk / that love makes making love / is darker by the silence after." Touch serves as a possible means of connecting not only the outer and inner worlds of the speaker's self but also the worlds of the lovers. However, the emptiness that occurs after lovemaking creates a darkness and silence that love cannot diminish.

In the Outer Dark often employs painting as a metaphor for the poetic method. Plumly suggests that no matter how full of life and sound it may be, the painting or poem is finally static and silent; its vision is produced whole in the mind and then meticulously transferred onto the canvas or page. In

"For Seurat, 1859–1891" the poet marvels at the Pointillist painter endlessly and passionately plying his "science of dot / loving dot. Must have gone blind with seeing. Made the / touch of his paint / a braille of beauty, to coin a phrase." Immediately following his Seurat poem Plumly presents two works that attempt to duplicate the painter's method of creating precise images through externally accurate concrete details and then transforming these images, through the artist's personality, into impressionistic statements. "Inside the Drop of Rain" focuses upon the movement "inside the mind's rainfall" of a minute particle of dust trapped within a drop of water; the writer then imagines himself inside that raindrop with his "inverted feet already / turning to snow." "Study in Kore" presents another drama in miniature as the poet looks into the smallest unit of the eye to find his source of art: "I become the image / quick in that point of light, / the all-too-literal photography / of your eyes, twice-fixed / and clearly there / to float back into / the seeing mind, / transfixed in the imagination / to the sight I have become." This statement announces the

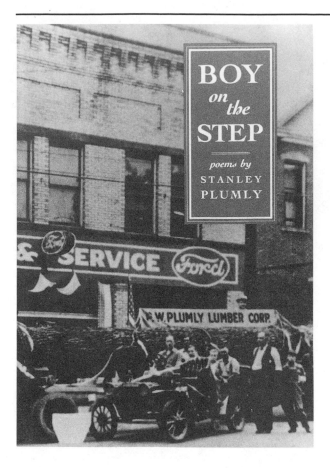

Dust jacket for Plumly's 1989 book, poems written from the perspective of an adolescent on the verge of experience and knowledge

poet's creative method: the detail is recorded and transformed through the imagination to create the image both of the poet and of the poem.

Giraffe (1973) demonstrates the writer's focusing of his poetic vision. Divided into three parts, each section of *Giraffe* centers on a major subject— the poet's creative method, his attempts at marriage, and his emotional connections with his doomed father. Each section employs an appropriate emblem from the outer world; the giraffe, the heron, and the horse become, respectively, symbols for the poet, the love relationship, and the father. The metaphor of water appears in almost every poem as well, functioning either as the medium by which the writer approaches life through the imagination or as the vehicle by which he is carried to death, for, as he declares in "Versions of Water," "to die / is to drown."

The first section, titled "Giraffe," concentrates on the poet's method of creation, which involves his escaping from the body, the physical self, and immersing himself in the imagination. In

"Walking Out," for example, the writer wishes to "undress utterly" and leave behind his body, to become pure imagination, while walking to the water's edge on his hands. Those who follow after him will "imagine flight": "I would be silence. . . . I would be totally absent from myself, / . . . / . . . I would forget / myself entirely. . . . / . . . But I would still be walking, if I could, / out of body, leaving behind, in a wake / of absence, clothes, fingerprints, words." As the self is drawn from the body, so is the poem from the poet. As the poet's page fills, his life metaphorically drains from his body, and he becomes, as Plumly declares in his tribute to a dead poet, "Jarrell, 1914–1965," "a man about to walk out of his shadow / into the speed of light; / . . . / A man saying out loud, I give you back this / gift, having already put it down."

In the second section, "Heron," the love poems chronicle the failures of connection, of meaning in the speaker's marriages. "Three Wives," for example, employs familiar domestic objects to suggest the arid nature of these relationships: "Table and chair. / This is no marriage / but an arrangement." In "Light" the wives again make brief appearances and perform "the laying-on of hands" according to their separate identities. The light is intended to help clarify the difficulties in each relationship; however, the physical act designed to heal the spirit succeeds only in bringing the speaker "back / from whatever dark to whatever body is." Here Plumly reiterates his idea that through touch the lovers hope to diminish personal darkness and emptiness, to dispel private agonies. And when the two selves meet in the middle ground of love, they are for a moment made fuller by this connection. But when the moment has passed, they return to their separate selves and become more keenly aware of their individual darkness, just as the poet is emotionally drained when he has completed the poem.

"Horse," the third section of *Giraffe,* employs this emblem of beauty, strength, and virility to suggest the sense of loss the poet feels when his father's death becomes an actuality rather than an inevitability. In "By Heart" the poet recalls his father in his dreams, but the poetic imagery assumes a painful realism: "In my dream I see you / dressed out on a table, / filled with the clinician's blue light– / . . . / This is always like a memory. / . . . / In every sleep I dream your death. / I lie down and you lie with me. / In every room this is still / your house, your history." Employing a technical, almost cold voice as if reporting the procedures in tending a corpse, the poet masks his mounting grief and increased sense of isolation. As "One of

Us" asserts, the poet thinks about the future and about "how the mind, all alone, / makes it up in order to deal / with what is coming."

Out-of-the-Body Travel, published in 1977, addresses the poet's self-warning about "what is coming," his mature recognition that the body is unreliable, that it fails and dies, leaving relationships unresolved. The poet thus pursues a quest to transcend the body and to examine the function of the mind—the vehicle of art—as it "makes it up in order to deal" with life's anguish. Plumly suggests that those who can articulate the inner life through art find a degree of release from pain, if only momentarily; those who cannot creatively express grief are doomed to suffering and isolation. The poet himself travels out of the body with all its limitations to prove, through dreams and memories, what he has witnessed and experienced in his parental and marital relationships.

In this collection the poet's mother is portrayed as a lonely figure trapped in the isolation of her marriage. While the father's body fails him, the mother's heart fails her, draining away all hope. She is often remembered as standing in the doorway of her ordered but imprisoning house and calling her son to her. In "Small Dark Streets" she is portrayed in ever darkening imagery as "the woman in the doorway / who used to call / my name in the summer, / . . . / the woman who loved / clean floors and rain / on the streets after dark— / who knelt at my ear, / night after night, / whose story / could break your heart / if you listened, the woman / with her forehead pinned to the wall." Trapped within the confines of her house, her family, her life, she has no means of spiritual-artistic release. In "The Iron Lung" she stands "in a doorway / telling my father to die or go away." Yet her responses toward her drunken husband are generally more passive and thus more destructive of her selfhood. In "Linoleum: Breaking Down" she complains of bodily aches and numbness and lies on the cold kitchen floor: "And we would lie down with her, my sister / and I, and she would tell us not to worry, / that it was all right, this is what happens, / like a bruise above the heart, we would / understand in time." Her despair and resignation ultimately render her mute: "She has nothing / to say. She looks at me as if she were / looking at something. I feel I am standing / on her grave." The scuff marks on her floor gradually cause the linoleum to crack and break. The bruises on the mother's heart cannot be washed away by the rain she loves, and the emotional cracks that run throughout her life cannot be healed.

Dust jacket for Plumly's 1997 book, which includes poems on the deaths of his parents

In the title poem of the collection the poet's dead father is portrayed as a man who has played the violin, "this finest / of furniture," not to relieve pain but to communicate it. A roomful of relatives have perceived that "this was / drawing of blood . . . / . . . They saw even in my father's / face how well he understood the pain / he put them to." The suffering the father has conveyed to others is, of course, his own. When he must, for instance, slaughter his cattle, as in part 2 of "Out-of-the-Body Travel," the horror of his act is communicated through reference both to his violin and to the French Surrealist painter Marc Chagall: "And in one stroke he brings the hammer / down, like mercy, so that the young bull's / legs suddenly fly out from under it . . . / . . . he is the good angel in Chagall. . . . The violin / sustains him." Moreover, in his imagination the poet finds himself the recipient of the "merciful" pain his father communicated and inflicted: " . . . I know if I wake up cold, / . . . / I will feel the wind coming down hard / like his hand, in fever, on my forehead." To deliver such blows, Plumly declares in

"Such Counsels," his father "had to drink a week in a day / to stay cold sober." Finally, in "After Grief," the poet assesses both his father's pain and his enduring legacy to his survivors:

I remember how even near the end
you would go out to your garden
just before dark, in the blue air,
and brood over the failures
of corn or cabbage
or the crooked row
but meaning the day had once more
failed for you.

. . . .

I watched you as any son watches his father,
like prophecy.

These lines clearly suggest that both the father's pain and his difficult artistry in communicating it are reborn in his son: "And you, my anonymous father, / be with me when I awake."

Poems treating the writer's own love relationships are few in number in *Out-of-the-Body Travel,* but they eloquently testify to the sense of emotional estrangement bequeathed him by his parents' troubled union. "Wrong Side of the River" portrays two figures, presumably lovers, separated by a river and therefore unable to communicate. "For Hope" questions the validity of the "word"–the expected form of communication–and fastens instead on "silence": "I gave my word. And I broke it. I gave / it again, broke it again, gave it a third time, / and broke it. So much for honor among wives." Here the promise implied by "word" expands into an image of "*word / made flesh, one flesh,*" and these "words," the poet repeats throughout "For Hope": "I give back to the dark, to nothing. . . ." In every sense "word" is "broken," is ineffectual, Plumly insists, and, in a final statement that ironically comments upon his own failed marital relationships and upon that of his parents, he declares, "Heart, / you say to her, my word, silence is golden."

Plumly envisions *Summer Celestial* (1983), *Boy on the Step* (1989), and *The Marriage in the Trees* (1997) as a trilogy, for each volume provides variations on a set of related themes. Also, collectively these volumes mark a discernible maturation in his poetry that he attributes in part to his study of John Keats. As he states in an interview published in the May/June 1995 *American Poetry Review:* "For about five years or so, Keats was an obsession. I read everything. And there's a lot to read. It came at the right time because I think I was at a bit of an impasse after *Out-of-the-Body Travel.* Where was I going to

go? . . . What am I going to do now? Keats . . . really changed that. . . . I realized, I think for the first time, what poetry is really about, what its richness is and what its possibilities, having to do with the density of the language, having to do with the sense of the purity of the experience, as well as its perishability." Although his thematic and technical affinity with Keats becomes more apparent in his later works, Plumly has found artistic correspondences with such painters as Georges Seurat and James Abbott McNeill Whistler and such poets as Walt Whitman and Ranier Maria Rilke. In "After Whistler," for example, Plumly's verbal portrait of his grandmother parallels Whistler's painted portrait of Thomas Carlyle. Whistler "builds" Carlyle's inner character "from the color out: he calls it an arrangement / in gray and black . . . / . . . Carlyle is tired, beyond anger, and beautiful." Similarly, Plumly concentrates on his grandmother's character by envisioning her kneeling in the garden, in a prayerful, almost angelic posture, outlined by the sun that is "gold / as qualified in pictures." She had saved the narrator's life by volunteering her blood for an emergency transfusion when it was discovered at his birth that the umbilical cord had rotted at his navel. Years after her death, the poet resurrects her memory as he envisions her facing the dying sun and resolutely accepting the approach of her own death. The poet's association of death and birth leads him to "think of the weight by which we are doubled or more / through the lives of others." Of his blood relatives, she is the one person who has given of herself, literally and symbolically, to save him and to offer a quiet kindness. He commemorates their close blood bond with a painter's feel for color and image: "In a room real / with walls the color of buckwheat she would sit out / the afternoon dressed up, rocking me to sleep. / It would be Sunday, slow, no one else at home. / And I would wake that way, small in her small arms, / hers, in the calendar dark, my head against her heart." As in "Out-of-the-Body Travel," the poet's head–the repository of his memory, his imagination–is significantly referred to, in this instance in relation to the grandmother's heart rather than the father's fevered hand, suggesting that the poet's inheritance from this woman is an unconditional comforting love, a response absent from his other familial relationships.

Plumly creates another pictorial portrait in "Posthumous Keats," a poem that visualizes the dying poet's final days while traveling toward Rome. In his biography of Keats, Walter Jackson Bate describes the dying poet riding in a slowly moving carriage as his companion, the painter Joseph Severn, who is walking alongside, picks wildflowers with which he fills the carriage. Bate provides a scholar's account of this event, which Plumly transforms into a moving elegy that dramatizes the dying poet's funeral cortege. "The biographer sees no glory in this, / how the living, by increments, are dead, / how they celebrate their passing half in love. / Keats, like his young companion, is alone / among color and a long memory. / . . . / In his head he is writing a letter / about failure and money and the ten- / thousand lines that could not save his brother. / . . . / . . . He has closed his eyes. / . . . By the time they reach the Campagna . . . / Severn will have climbed back in, finally a passenger, / with one more handful to add to what is already overwhelming."

Plumly's portrayals of his grandmother and of Keats illustrate his adeptness at capturing the moment when lonely, often hurt figures reveal their private anguish but also their transcendence. The title of the collection, *Summer Celestial*, seems to suggest that a similar hopefulness or even sense of triumph will prevail. But the title poem focuses upon Plumly's grieving mother, a woman "more afraid of loneliness than death," and each of the six stanzas centers on a series of connected childhood remembrances relating to difficulties in giving and receiving love, couched principally in terms of money, dreams, and longing. "Summer Celestial" begins with the poet's recollection of a man standing in a boat passing out dollar bills. (Later, in *The Marriage in the Trees*, this figure is revealed to be the drunken father on a fishing trip with his son.) Using the psychological equation of love to money, Plumly dramatizes the differences between parents in terms of how each invests, gives, or withholds love, ranging from the father's thoughtlessly inebriated lavishness to his mother's anxious parsimony. She "still wakes crying do I think she's made of money." In the speaker's dream emotional transactions are directly or obliquely associated with water as he recalls parents and lovers involved in the currencies of the heart. "And out on the great surfaces, water is paying / back water. I know, I know this is a day and the stars reiterate, / return each loss, each witness. And that always in the room / next door, / someone is coughing all night or a man and a woman make / love, / each body buoyed, even blessed, by what the other cannot have." Love, like money, becomes the heart's investment in or withholding from another. In *Summer Celestial* love is frequently a balance sheet of loss and regret about what one "cannot / have" from another.

As a continuation of the emotional balance sheet image developed in *Summer Celestial,* Plumly originally intended to title his 1989 collection "A Doctrine of Signatures," a phrase used in the poem

"Above Barnesville," in which he states: "In the doctrine of signatures / the body is divisible, the heart the leaf of a redbud / or the blue ash in a fire. . . ." Carefully balancing the positive and the negative, the living and the dead, the credits and the debits, the phrase also suggests the official signing of documents, particularly those related to marriage, divorce, and death—three major occurrences affecting the poet's life. But the title he finally selected, *Boy on the Step,* focuses instead on the writer's perspective as an adolescent on the edge of something—on the periphery of a room, or in a doorway leading in or out (recalling Whitman's use of rooms and houses as metaphors of the Self)—approaching experience and knowledge. The concept underlying his choice of the title *Boy on the Step* is perhaps most fully explicated in "Field," a poem appearing in Plumly's 1997 collection. In this poem the speaker states: "In ornithology there occurs the phrase *the abrupt edge,* / which, according to the birdbooks, is 'the edge between two / types of vegetation . . . where the advantages of both are most convenient' . . . / . . . / The edge is the concept of the doorway / . . . / . . . . That is where the / richness is, the thick, deep vegetable life—a wall of life."

Boy on the Step is dominated by the speaker's concern with transcending the difficult emotional complexities of his life, particularly those symbolized by his parents' relationship. He hopefully considers possible reincarnation as a tree or a bird. Plumly declares in the May/June issue of the 1995 *American Poetry Review:*

> One of the great things that *Boy on the Step* posits, over and over again, is that the trees—this is actually true—are immortal. And if we have a chance for immortality on this planet, in the sense that we are changed into something else from what we are, why not come back as part of that system, the flower system, the tree system. . . . I also posit, in another poem, the possibility that I could come back as a bird, that the birds are part of the afterlife. In this sense, all of these materials are about fallen angels from the sky, from the celestial to the terrestrial. In that sense, I suppose, human beings are the most fragile and beautiful presences on the planet because they end up, depending on your religion, turned into everything else, animals, vegetable, mineral, whatever, with a little left over.

The first poem of *Boy on a Step,* "Hedgerows," establishes this thematic framework. Walking away from "Some trouble / or other" and wanting "to die," the speaker travels onto a country lane bordered with thorny hedges. In one sense the thick brambles reflect his interior condition, but in another they offer the respite of the plant world's "whole dumb life gone to seed." As the notion of

In the Øplus morning we sober up

Be of good cheer, like the waxwings in the juniper

Be of good cheer,
like the waxwings in the juniper,
three, four, dozens at a time,
sometimes in pairs,
passing the berries back and forth--
at nightfall, wobbling, wounded with joy, back to the nests.

It's called wing-rowing,
the circular motion of the oars of the arms extending,
walking the white, invisible line
drawn just ahead in the air,
the first sign the slur,
the liquid notes too liquid,

the heart in the mouth too close to the phone,
which starts the singing,
the long lyric silences,
then sentences and paragraphs, convictions and seductions,
starts the song of our undoing,
crooning, evensong.

It's called side-hop, head-forward,
a kind of militant display,
though courtship is the object, affection the compulsion,
love the overspill.
the body nods, still standing,
(as if) falling off to sleep,

back against the wall--
it's called bill-tilt, wing-flash, topple-over;
wing-droop, bowing, jump-flight
and (soar); or back-ruffle, wing-spread, strutting and soar:
song of the breath blown over
the bottle,
                with the cattle
dark of the night/at the ꜜꜜꜜꜜꜜꜜ of the pasture.

the bottle, my father,

dark of the night, under the moon, (who'd) come home hungry,
ꜱꜱꜱꜱꜱꜱꜱꜱꜱꜱꜱꜱꜱꜱꜱꜱꜱꜱꜱꜱ
who'd stand in the kitchen,
like aman out of jail, frying a steak.
Dionysus wanted Orpheus killed,
so sent the he sent the ﬁeared Baccantes,
noted for their taste for meat

and the wine of meat,
to find the poet-king in the temple of the Muses
but found instead their husbands

Revised typescripts for two drafts of "Cheer" (Collection of Stanley Plumly)

Like the waxwings in the juniper, three,
four, dozens at a time, sometimes in pairs,
passing the berries back and forth, and at
nightfall, wobbling, wounded with joy, back to

Like the waxwings in the juniper, three,
four, dozens at a time, sometimes in pairs,
passing the berries back and forth, and by
nightfall, wobbling, calling, wounded with joy.

It's (called) wing-rowing, the circle motion
of the oars of the (long) arms extending,
walking the white, invisible line drawn
just ahead in the air, first sign the slur,

the liquid notes too liquid, the heart in
the mouth too close to the phone, which then starts
the singing, the long lyric silences,
crooning, and the song of our undoing.

It's called side-hop, head-forward, a kind of
militant display, though courtship is the
object, affection the compulsion, love
the overspill, the body nodding, still

standing, half-falling off to sleep against
a wall--it's called bill-tilt, wing-flash, topple-
over; wing-droop, bowing, jump-flight and drift;
or back-ruffle, wing-spread, (shuffling) and soar.

Song of the breath blown over the bottle.
Be of good cheer, my father'd say, lifting
his glass in the middle of the night in
the kitchen where he'd be standing frying

steak. Weekends especially this was his
ritual, so sometimes when I got home
late I'd join him, the way when I was eight
or nine I'd sit all Saturday at Bing's

while he and his three lost friends played cards. I'd
alternate between beer and ginger ale
and watch, as if this were a school, the hard
shuffling, betting, lying and dumb love.

(It's called) song-bow, crest-raise, lopsided pose,
wine of the wheat, the caustic fire and thorn.

transformation from troubled human to senseless hedge captures his interest, the poet's tone changes from personal gloom to near joy. As part of the hedge, he envisions himself being cut away by an artisan who would refashion him, "wood and mind," into a new life as a useful and beautiful wooden object for the table. He merges his future imagined self as a "bowl on the wild cherry of the table" with a past image of himself as "the boy / who sits there, having come from the field / with his family . . . / . . . / . . . lost in the thought / of the turning of the year and the dead father." This convergence of the past and future versions of himself brings the speaker back to the present, returning him psychologically to the quarrel he has walked away from, though he now achieves a vision of at least potential renewal.

The theme that reincarnation through nature offers a possible escape from human anguish reappears in "Cedar Waxwing on Scarlet Firethorn," a poem recalling the suicide of a former teacher. As the speaker observes a cedar waxwing holding in its beak a "berry / against the moment like a drop of blood," he visualizes a series of related oral images, including that of a suicide placing a gun in his mouth "like swallowing the sword or eating fire." When as a child he was told that "suicide / meant the soul stayed with the body locked in / the ground I knew it was wrong, that each bird / could be anyone in the afterlife, / alive, on wing." Those in torment—the suicide-to-be, the troubled family, the anguished poet—exist on a precarious emotional edge that causes them to consider death as an escape. And consistent with the soul's possible afterlife as a bird, Plumly grants the dead the birds' capacity for melody: "We are in a room with all the loved ones / who, when they answer, have the power of song."

Yet some negotiations in the emotional wars between the poet's parents cannot be fully transcended, they are so brutal. In "Infidelity" the youthful speaker infers the angry quarrel he cannot hear or see, and as the family car caroms out of the driveway, his mother either jumps or is pushed from the car onto the gravel. When she regains her feet, she is bleeding badly: "I know / my mother's face was covered black with blood / and that when she rose she too said nothing. / Language is a darkness pulled out of us." Both the fleeing father and the wounded mother remain silent, but the speaker does at last express his emotion: " . . . I screamed that day she was almost killed, / whether I wept or ran or threw a stone, / or stood stone-still, choosing at last between / parents, one of whom was driving away." Deciding in favor of one parent forces an emotional infidelity to the other, which in turn cre-

ates the feeling that "the one who's faithless has / nothing more to say and the silence is / terrifying since you must choose between / one or the other emptiness." The boy on the step of his parents' house looks into the emptiness and darkness of their world and feels an estrangement that carries over into his adult life and work.

In *The Marriage in the Trees,* the final volume of his trilogy, Plumly conveys an even darker tone than in the other two; it may result from his mother's death in 1994. The poet cannot fully come to terms with the actuality of his parents' deaths since those deaths permanently deny the possibility of communication and healing. As he declares in his 1995 *American Poetry Review* interview: "In my case, my life with father was profoundly unresolved. I missed everything, including the funeral. As usual I was wandering around anonymously, in another country. I couldn't be reached. And I must've chosen that, see. And that's a kind of haunting." He has, in effect, abandoned both father and mother, just as they have emotionally and literally abandoned him. And instead of employing reincarnation to try to transcend the "kind of haunting" that has resulted, the poet now casts himself as healer and savior though his attempts to fulfill these roles ultimately fail.

In "Reading with the Poets" Plumly dramatizes the effects of both Whitman and Keats to save those they love from dying: "Whitman among the wounded, at the bedside, / kissing the blood off boys' faces, . . . / . . . Whitman in Washington / failed"; "Keats all his wounded life wanted to be a healer, / which he was, once at his mother's bedside, failed, / once at his brother's, failed." Their failure to save loved ones from agony and death adds to their need to compensate through poetry that survives and records their compensation. As Plumly notes, Keats was a distracted medical student "Not from indifference, not from his elegance: / his interest couldn't bear the remarkable / screams of the demonstrations. He sat there, still / a boy, already broken, looking into the living / body, listening to the arias of the spirit / climbing." And thus as Keats converts screams to arias, so too does Whitman convert suffering to song: "So the boy at the graves of the Union / singing, saying his vision, seeing the bodies / broken into the ground. Now the poem for Lincoln. / . . . weaving with the audience that gossamer, / that thread of the thing we find in the voice again. / Now in the night our faces kissed by the healer." Like Whitman and Keats, Plumly confronts personal anguish through art. He acknowledges that neither poetry nor the poet can rescue others from dying or death but instead offers "only / words on paper to compensate," as he declares in "Keats in Burns Country." As he envisions Keats's pilgrimage to Burns's grave, Plumly examines the relationship between the living poet and the dead and finds that the artist may grasp eternal truths, but he will enjoy little satisfaction from these truths: "All is cold / Beauty, pain is never done."

The poet's conviction that his pain of loss is unending causes him to meditate on the death of his father in "For My Father, Dead at Fifty-Six, / On My Fifty-Sixth Birthday": "you the dire sentimentalist, / who wouldn't let the dead hands of the doctor / inside you, while all four chambers of your heart / filled with effluvium of both our lifetimes."

The same conception drives his treatment of his mother's death in "The Last Parent." Here he envisions her dying as a setting off on an ocean voyage, "the oceanliner's / melancholy size towering like Manhattan." The poem's tone of weary matter-of-factness is established in the opening phrases "Of course she'll wave goodbye. . . . / Of course she'll be obscure standing at the rail." The seemingly offhand tone intensifies the speaker's sense of loss as the voyage begins. "And later on of course / she'll stroll the high elliptic of the deck / while each immortal hour plows the colder, / deeper shades toward where the sun perpetually sets its billion bullion lode and lays a gold / path leading west, easy to follow, within / whose wake, against the dark, this sail." If this vision of death carries a sense of possible immortality for the victim, it is in sharp contrast to the more emotionally convincing representation of the mother's death in "Red Somersault": "The night my mother died / she held on to me to keep / her body upright over depths / above which lying down means / falling. . . . / . . . holding fast to the fear / that she was alone and without / death would end up one of those / women on the street who / in weather sleeps in cars." Her forbidding vision of continued life is all that makes death attractive to her.

Plumly examines traditional Christian beliefs about death as spiritual release but finds the promise embodied in such beliefs uncertain and thus uncomforting to him as a survivor. His sense of loss and emptiness, both actual and spiritual, is conveyed through poems treating Christian subjects, such as "The White Bible" and "Lazarus at Dawn."

In the second poem Plumly adopts the perspective of Lazarus waking from the dead to meet Christ, an image which is transformed into a meeting between the dead father and his poet son: "You see your dead face in the gray glass close, / and see that it is already too late, / . . . the father standing in the doorway white, / . . . . / Nothing is said, though he knows you love him. / Nothing is said, though you know he loves you. / Longing, as a sickness of the heart, is / invisible, incurable, endless." The "longing" that binds yet separates these two figures—father and son, the dead and the living—will be the "endless" connection between them.

Finally, the poet assumes the stance, as prescribed in "Field," of the man using personal courage and art to insure his emotional, spiritual, and creative survival. He has been, and continues to be, immersed in the turmoil of his childhood and adulthood and now stands on the edge—at times the abrupt edge—waiting for the coast to clear, but knowing that it probably will not. His poetry, his art, is the only device that keeps him from falling into the dark "depths / above which lying down means / falling."

Interviews:

Wayne Dodd, "Stanley Plumly: An Interview," *Ohio Review*, 25 (1980): 33–57;

"The Path of Saying," in *Acts of Mind: Conversations with Contemporary Poets,* edited by Richard Jackson (University: University of Alabama Press, 1983);

"'The Why of the World': A Conversation with Stanley Plumly," in *The Post-Confessionals: Conversations with American Poets of the Eighties,* edited by Stan Sanvel Rubin and Judith Kitchen (Rutherford, N.J.: Fairleigh Dickinson University Press, 1989);

David Biespiel and Rose Solari, "Stanley Plumly: An Interview," *American Poetry Review,* 24 (May/June 1995): 43–50.

References:

Peter Stitt, "On Stanley Plumly: That Enduring Essence," *American Poetry Review,* 9 (March/April 1980): 16–17;

David Young, "Out Beyond Rhetoric: Four Poets and One Critic," *Field: Contemporary Poetry and Poetics,* 30 (Spring 1984): 83–102.

Carl Rakosi
(6 November 1903 –)

Elizabeth Losh
University of California, Irvine

BOOKS: *Two Poems* (New York: Modern Editions Press, 1933);

Selected Poems (Norfolk, Conn.: New Directions, 1941);

Amulet (New York: New Directions, 1967);

Ere-Voice (New York: New Directions 1971);

Ex Cranium, Night (Los Angeles: Black Sparrow Press, 1975);

My Experiences in Parnassus (Santa Barbara, Cal.: Black Sparrow Press, 1977);

History (London: Oasis Books, 1981);

Droles de Journal (West Branch, Iowa: Toothpaste Press, 1981);

Spiritus, I (Durham, U.K.: Pig Press, 1983);

The Collected Prose of Carl Rakosi (Orono, Maine: National Poetry Foundation, 1983);

The Collected Poems of Carl Rakosi (Orono, Maine: National Poetry Foundation, 1986);

Poems 1923–1941, edited by Andrew Crozier (Los Angeles: Sun & Moon Press, 1995);

The Earth Suite (London: Etruscan Books, 1997).

Carl Rakosi is perhaps best known as a founding "Objectivist" poet, part of a literary movement marked by both the transitory nature of association by publication and the longevity of its poets' individual careers. The Objectivists were originally promoted by Ezra Pound in the 1930s as a new generation of poets capable of answering the excesses of imitative and overblown contemporary poetry with the correction of an unmediated focus on the objective world. The Objectivist directive was to treat the poetic object without superfluous metaphors or metaphysics and thereby bring new technological precision to the poet's acts of sight and insight. In his essay introducing the Objectivists to the world in the pages of *Poetry,* member Louis Zukofsky defines the terms of Objectivism narrowly, using as examples the "objective" of a microscope or the poem itself as a physical and formal "object." During the course of their lengthy careers, however, the other Objectivists (Rakosi, George Oppen, and Charles Reznikoff) not only broadened the concept of the object to include the artifacts of popular culture (objects as signs) but also brought to Objectivism a concern for the political or ethnic other and the historical experiences of immigrant America. Although in later years Rakosi, Oppen, and Reznikoff defined their "realism" differently (as psychological realism, philosophical realism, and sociolegal realism, respectively), in pursuing different formal strategies each one of the Objectivists can be seen as applying the imagist tradition to the banalities and horrors of twentieth-century culture.

Rakosi may be the poet who, of all the Objectivists, was initially most influenced by the dominant styles of canonical modernism. In his early poems Rakosi employed the idioms and formal devices of William Butler Yeats, Wallace Stevens, and William Carlos Williams, down to their particular metrical peculiarities. Rakosi is also the poet, however, who most explicitly lampooned the rhetorical pretensions of high modernism, often to the point of burlesque. Even the supposedly plain style of Williams, which Rakosi greatly admired, was not safe from his satire. Rakosi is the poet who remade and further atomized Williams's famous lines beginning "so much depends / upon // a red wheel / barrow . . . " into "So much / depends // upon the / instant // wrist / watch // on the / executive . . . ," a vision ending with the executive's "clean bowel" and an overall impression in radical opposition to Williams's pastoralism. It is for his own original style, however, that Rakosi is most admired, a style that has developed over the course of his career from his early poems of the urban carnivalesque rendered with extraordinary precision of image to his later poems, which can roughly be divided into metaphysical explorations and commentaries on popular culture or the icons of American nationalism.

Like fellow Objectivist Oppen, Rakosi stopped writing for more than two decades during the height of the Cold War. When he began writing poetry again, he brought a new social engagement and personal reflection to his work that seemed to grow out of his lifelong professional commitment to his career

Carl Rakosi

as a social worker. Largely because of this hiatus from writing, the chronological organization of Rakosi's poems presents an immediate problem to the scholar of his work. Many of his earlier poems were rewritten and republished in his later books, often in fragmentary or composite forms as he reworked themes and images.

Carl Rakosi was born 6 November 1903 in Berlin to Hungarian parents. His father, Leopold Rakosi, had been born Leopold Rozenberg but as a citizen of Budapest had changed the family name to a variant of Rakoczi, after the dynasty of Hungarian national heroes. His mother, Flora Steiner, was absent even in his early life, and in his autobiographical essay for *Contemporary Authors Autobiography Series* (1987) Rakosi claims to have no memories of her. Although he was never able to confirm his suspicions, Rakosi came to believe that she suffered from profound mental illness and that his parents separated in 1904 as a direct result of her deep melancholia. After their parents divorced, Carl and his older brother Lester were moved to the town of Baja, Hungary, to live with their maternal grandparents. In *The Collected Prose of Carl Rakosi* (1983) he describes his grandmother, Rosalia Steiner, as "my mother, but more gentle and kind than a mother." At the age of six Rakosi parted from his grandmother permanently and emigrated to America. His father had remarried and had moved to Chicago, where the senior Rakosi was already forced to adjust to a much less affluent lifestyle than he had known as a partner in a Berlin walking-stick factory.

After a brief residence in Gary, Indiana, the family ultimately settled in Kenosha, Wisconsin, where Leopold became the owner of a jewelry store and repaired watches. In his autobiography Rakosi describes learning English quickly, "as if one day I didn't know a word of it and the next day I was speaking it like everybody else." In the school system Rakosi was advanced two grades and was subsequently always self-conscious about being smaller than his peers. He became an American citizen in 1917 with his father and the rest of his immediate family. At sixteen Rakosi began classes at the University of Chicago but was unhappy because he found it difficult to make friends when students vanished into an unfamiliar city after classes. Rakosi decided to transfer to the University of Wisconsin, where he was active in campus literary circles. He received his B.A. from Wisconsin in 1924 and continued there in order to receive an M.A. in educational psychology in 1926. At the age of twenty-one, as his father had also done when he had come of age, Rakosi changed his legal name. He chose "Callman Rawley," ostensibly to better assimilate and avoid mispronunciation. Although he kept it as a pen name, he also feared that a professional name like "Carl Rakosi" would serve to bar him from university teaching in a field structured around fundamentally Anglophile, if not openly anti-Semitic, English departments.

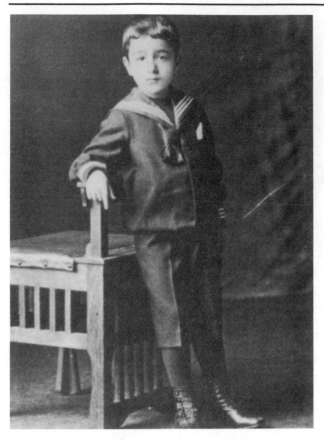

Rakosi at age seven

It was his friend and fellow Wisconsin writer Margery Latimer who encouraged Rakosi to approach Jane Heap, the editor of *The Little Review,* about his work. Rakosi had already been published in *The Nation* but was thrilled when *The Little Review* selected his work, because the magazine had become a forum for the major authors of what was later to be recognized as high modernism. *The Little Review* published poets such as Yeats, Ezra Pound, and T. S. Eliot, and even James Joyce's novel *Ulysses* in serial form.

Ironically, Rakosi first achieved fame as an Objectivist poet during a time of personal and professional crisis. He had been moving around the country, undertaking unsuccessful stints as an industrial psychologist, a mess boy on a freighter, a social worker, and a high-school English teacher; and he had begun programs for an English Ph.D., a law degree, and an M.D. degree, with only a year of each completed while he struggled with financial problems and changing academic interests. Although Rakosi felt far removed from the literary centers of the avant-garde, Zukofsky approached him about the 1931 special issue of *Poetry* that he was editing under the aegis of Pound. Rakosi had been deeply influenced by Pound's criticism and had al-

ready been published in Pound's magazine, *The Exile.* The Objectivist issue of *Poetry* ultimately developed into the groundbreaking *An "Objectivists" Anthology* (1932). From then on Rakosi's work was forever associated with the other Objectivists: Zukofsky, Oppen, Reznikoff, and, later, Lorine Niedecker. Although all four of the original definitive group of Objectivists (Zukofsky, Oppen, Reznikoff, and Rakosi) would later claim to share little in their poetic ideologies, they were all American "urban" Jewish poets who were attracted to Pound by a common interest in bringing greater "realism" (variously defined) to the poetic image and to a project that could establish their careers as distinctly apart from a dominant, less critical form of imagism. In the special issue on the Objectivists in *Poetry,* Rakosi's poems are notable for both their reserve (expressed in the language of detached, optical precision) and their candor (perhaps foreshadowing Rakosi's later lampooning of the classical ambitions of high modernism). For example, in "Fluteplayers from Finmarken" there is Objectivism in all its quintessential neutrality—"the mind directs a fine, white lens. . ."—while in "Before You" the speaker suggests that the gods "have broken wind / in a changing system."

The following year, 1932, Rakosi's "A Journey Away" appeared in *An "Objectivists" Anthology* along with "Parades." "A Journey Away" features the kind of erotic alienation of speaker and juxtaposition of scene that characterize the work of Eliot, but in many ways the poem is distinctly Objectivist in its use of metonymy and presentation of urban space. For example, "A Journey Away" includes striking dramatic monologues reminiscent of Eliot's work:

> On the esplanade at Cannes
> the awnings suddenly
> went black before me.
> I was carried to the belvedere
> of Villa Policastro.
> In the evening, dearly beloved,
> in the sight of blood and bandages
> I lay there like a dressed fowl.

In the middle of "A Journey Away," however, the reader is directed to see Rakosi's city in objective terms, as a place simultaneously public and private, a realm of high and low culture intermingled, which is exhibited in a sequence of successive images: "the men's shops with terrazzo floors, / the city desks, the shoe windows, / the Carlton waiters with a canape / of coral lobster, 666 for colds. . . ." The year the anthology appeared Rakosi had returned to social work and its urban problems and found his political commitments deepening as a result of the Great Depression.

Throughout the early 1930s Rakosi's work was published in periodicals such as *Poetry, Pagany,* and *Hound and Horn,* and his career is closely associated with Zukofsky. His first book of poetry, however, was not published until 1941, when *Selected Poems* appeared under a title suggesting several previous books. It is possible to argue, however, that in its ambitions Rakosi's *Two Poems* (1933) constitutes a book, despite its brevity. *Two Poems* is also the notable vehicle for Rakosi's much-anthologized poem "The Lobster," which is dedicated to William Carlos Williams. In "The Lobster" Rakosi pays additional homage to Williams by using a similar short metric line, although he employs detailed metonymic observations of sea life in a style reminiscent of the field-guide precision made famous by Marianne Moore. In the patterning of lines, the poem often tends toward a hypnotic trochaic rhythm:

Eastern Sea, 100 fathoms,
green sand, pebbles,
broken shells.
Off Suno Saki, 60 fathoms,
gray sand, pebbles,
bubbles rising.

"The Lobster," in many ways, can be seen as Rakosi's last poem to rely entirely on the imagistic presentation of an object separate from a social or personal context. By 1931 in his poem "The Athletes" Rakosi was already conscious of "something historical at the controls of North / America, heavyweight and metaphorical." "The Athletes" also introduces a new poetic figure: an "allotrope of vision," with the word *allotropic* defined in the Oxford English Dictionary as that which has "different physical properties though unchanged in substance." In other words, too simplistic a characterization of Rakosi's "objectivity" may be problematic, given what Rakosi recognizes as the dynamic properties of the "object" itself. Even the sea creatures of "The Lobster," for example, keep appearing to have different properties with each glimpse of animal the poet absorbs.

By 1935 Rakosi had, according to his autobiographical essay, "become convinced . . . that capitalism was incapable of providing jobs and justice to people and that the system had to be changed"; consequently, he joined the Communist Party. He found himself beginning to question the utility of the lyric poetry he had been writing while also facing the increasing hostility toward poetry among editors at *The New Masses,* a leftist press with which he identified. On 6 May 1939 he married Leah Jaffe,

Dust jacket for Rakosi's 1971 book, which includes poems about the Vietnam War

the daughter of immigrants from Russia. Although his wife provided support and companionship during the half-century of marriage that followed, Rakosi's literary production suffered while he established the stable career necessary to support a family which would eventually include two children, Barbara and George. Faced with the prohibitions of his political beliefs and the obligations of his family, Rakosi stopped writing poetry in 1940.

The following year *Selected Poems* appeared from James Laughlin's New Directions Press. *Selected Poems* showcased Rakosi's ability to use a montage technique to describe the urban experience with its multileveled spaces, cinematic details, and barrage of signs and advertisements meant for consumers of a "city wrapped in cellophane." Many poems in *Selected Poems* playfully draw from the forms and narratives of popular culture, everything from the rhymes and rhythms of popular songs to the iconography of the Western. *Selected Poems* also includes a longer poem which would be substantially revised as "The City (1925)" in *The Collected Poems of*

Robert Duncan, Charles Reznikoff, George Oppen, and Carl Rakosi at the National Poetry Festival, 1973

Carl Rakosi and even envisioned as part of the long poem "The City," which originally constituted much of "The Beasts" in *Poems 1923–1941* (1995). "The Beasts"/"The City (1925)" verges on encyclopedic description when Rakosi presents "illuminated on the operating table" a range of the city's prone inhabitants as though they too are displayed in a shop window: "naked glassblowers, / gunsmiths, barbers, clerks, importers, / old men from hotels, pink and tailored. / Napthasmelling Irish priests. / Cravat-and-boy face of the movie usher. / Frankel, Shmulik, Old Country watchmakers." Other parts of the poem dramatize the opposition between rich and poor by focusing on the material implements and ornaments of daily life as the signs that mark class distinctions. It is a world in which there are "Immigrants from Lodz / in a furnished room / close to the stores" with "Porcelain pitcher, / bath and hand towels / on the bed rails" who put a "new sign" in the window: "*Smocking / Hemstitching, Rhinestone Setting*." An "hour away" Rakosi presents a parallel universe with "a loggia / above the pepper trees, / a tiny cascade and vines / above the bath house, / men and women driving / on the fairway, laughing, / surrounded by Galloway pottery, garden furniture / and white daisies." Despite the beauty of these latter images, they are necessarily hollow as the signifiers of the oppression of the working class. In *Selected Poems* Rakosi is already writing the more directly political epistolary satire of "To the Non-

Political Citizen" ("Every man is entitled to his anger. / It's in the Constitution.") and "To the Anti-Semite" ("So you fought for the Jews / in the last war / and have become a patriot again!"), poems which, it could be argued, indicate the rhetorical direction that Rakosi would later take in the "Americana" poems after the end of his hiatus from writing.

In 1941 Rakosi received a master of social work degree from the University of Pennsylvania. The following year he applied unsuccessfully to the Guggenheim Foundation for a fellowship to write poetry, after having asked for letters of recommendation from Stevens, Williams, and Moore, all of whom effectively turned him down, although Stevens and Williams included encouragement for his poetic career with the rejection. Without funding and without what Rakosi considered to be the necessary political climate for the lyricism of his work, he stopped creative writing. During the years that followed, however, Rakosi was not completely silent. He published dozens of articles on a range of subjects related to social work under his legal name, Callman Rawley, and he also completed course work for a Ph.D. in social work at the University of Minnesota from 1952 to 1954. Much of his psychological expertise about therapeutic models for the treatment of manic depression was later channeled into his "Psychology of the Poet" lecture in the 1970s, and, as a longtime resident of the Midwest, Rakosi also began to analyze regional language and the origin of idioms that were based on the immigrant experience despite their consummately "American" character. During the quarter-century in which he developed the career of "Callman Rawley," however, Rakosi was known primarily as a successful administrator at Jewish Family and Children's Service in Minneapolis.

Unlike Williams, Rakosi was ultimately unable to combine his professional service to the public with life as a poet. It wasn't until 1965, when he was due to retire from social work and his position as executive director at Jewish Family and Children's Services, that Rakosi began to write poetry again. In his autobiography he credits his return to creative writing to a letter that came from a young English poet, Andrew Crozier, studying under Charles Olson; Crozier asked if Rakosi was still writing poetry. During the intervening years Rakosi had become something of a vanished legend in literary circles, and publisher James Laughlin had even heard that Rakosi had died behind the Iron Curtain.

In 1967 Rakosi reemerged definitively and published *Amulet,* which includes both new and early work. His subject matter had broadened, with meditations about the intimacies of family life (which now included grandchildren by his daughter Barbara) and more-mature poems about sexual union (such as "Brewing Night Herbs"). *Amulet* also includes the first of his Americana poems, which he claims began as a "lark" or "salt on a bird's tail" presented "for laughs at readings." In the Americana poems Rakosi makes observations about national character using materials drawn largely from newspapers, materials which he treats almost as found poems, although not to the degree of fellow Objectivist Reznikoff, who discovered darker ironies in his own choice of "found" texts (the annals of legal testimony). Rakosi came to consider the Americana poems just as essential to his poetic corpus as his more-"serious" poems, crediting E. E. Cummings's poem "Buffalo Bill" for the realization that poetry with critical self-consciousness could be done.

In 1969 Rakosi was made writer-in-residence at the University of Wisconsin, and he found himself offered a post teaching at the university, the profession that he had abandoned so many years earlier. He described his university position in analytic terms, not so much as teaching as helping students develop a skill in self-criticism. It was at Wisconsin that he met Jorge Luis Borges in 1970, an experience that he explored and treated ironically in his prose. Throughout the period from 1968 to 1975 Rakosi was also a resident writer at Yaddo in Saratoga Springs and enjoyed its informal atmosphere.

Rakosi's *Ere-Voice* (1971) continued the Americana series although the mood had changed "from comic to tragic" with poems about the Vietnam War. These Americana poems, which would later become part of one long poem in *Collected Poems,* were not without an Objectivist precision of vision as "XXI Americana" demonstrates in its portrayal of the U.S. Constitution "in a glass / and bronze / case / indecipherable / sealed / in helium." In other poems in *Ere-Voice* Rakosi explores the object of science (the "microscopic nebulae" of a fly chromosome stirred "into the figure of a Greek Orthodox cross") or the object of language (the "Nature of Yellow" affirmed in the case of "topaz," "dandelion," "crow's foot," and "quince" but questioned in the more Latinate "xanthite," "icterus," and "ecru"). *Ere-Voice* may furthermore be seen as part of Rakosi's profound exploration of the darker side of human nature; images of animal violence and the infirmities of age abound. In the same book, however, Rakosi is also explicitly reaching for uplifting universal values from other poetic traditions. For example, he writes a series of adaptations from Sephardic poets living in Spain in the twelfth century, distinctively apart from either the Greco-Roman or the Orientalist models of high modernism, including a free adaptation of Hebrew text, "Meditation: After Moses Ibn Ezra," which opens, "Men are children of this world / yet God has set eternity in my heart."

Rakosi took over the "American Character" seminar of the late poet John Berryman at the University of Minnesota in 1972 and found himself developing the thesis that the "American character" had actually ended in World War II. Throughout the 1970s Rakosi continued to garner long-delayed public acclaim: in 1972 and 1979 he received awards from the National Endowment for the Arts; in 1973 he served on the faculty for the National Poetry Festival; and in 1974 he became poet-in-residence at the University of Michigan. In 1975 Rakosi published his next book of both poetry and prose, *Ex Cranium, Night.* With this book Rakosi's poems become simultaneously more explicitly personal and more alienatingly analytical because, in content, *Ex Cranium, Night* includes poems of dream analysis and autobiographical narrative about his early life and its contradictions and vagaries. The poems are often written in what would come to be considered the signature formal style of Rakosi's later work: the split-line. In the opening of "The Open Casket" Rakosi writes movingly about his wife's two brothers, who were deeply bonded to each other, and uses the formal structure to accent the musicality of the phrasing:

Cover for Rakosi's 1983 collection of poetry, which includes meditations on the poet's dialogue with the divine

We had the same mother,
     the same father,
walked the same streets.
     Often we were waylaid
on our way to school
     and would scrap side by side.
Our underclothes
    with the fresh smell of soap
used to lie
   neatly folded
in the same drawer.

The volume ends with a series of poems about poetry—"The Poet"—that explicitly explores questions about form and figure. In "Nine Natures of Metaphor" Rakosi answers the claim that there is "a destiny in form / which led here" with his own observation that "the origin has been deleted / like the circle's / which entered geometry / and became a line."

When Rakosi resumed his poetic career, he candidly criticized fellow Objectivist Zukofsky's formal experiments for their elliptical opacity and willingness to sacrifice meaning for music (even drawing an analogy to the emptiness of the excesses of Johann Sebastian Bach in Zukofsky's work). In *Ex Cranium, Night* and his later *Collected Prose* (which includes the ironic spoof *My Experiences in Parnassus*) Rakosi begins to posit possible alternatives to a strictly formal project. Rakosi not only believed in the need to balance "feeling" and "objectivism" in poetry but also went so far as to celebrate the metaphysical union of the poet with his object in *Ex Cranium, Night:*

Matter,
    with this look
I wed thee
    and become
thy very
   attribute.

In this position as a "faithful spouse" Rakosi is writing his own epithalamion for a poetry of metaphysics in which "matter" and the "poet" can become united, not through the customary act of speech but through a more Objectivist "look."

In 1983 Rakosi published *Spiritus, I,* which developed his metaphysical rhetoric into the beginnings of a larger theory about poetic inspiration itself. In his previous book Rakosi had first described the voice of God to Moses and his personal understanding of this moment of original poetic inspiration. In *Spiritus, I* Rakosi develops his inspiration theory both in a poem about his earlier Moses revelation and in another in which he writes about the poet's dialogue with the divine in different terms: "If one could write / like St. Augustine, / not for an inner audience, / or readers, / but for God, / there would always be / an honest accounting. . . ." These "Meditation" poems in *Spiritus, I* could be said to demonstrate the profoundest distance of Rakosi from his early work: he uses the split-line refrain almost exclusively and explores the metaphysical realms forbidden by Pound and Zukofsky fifty years earlier. Yet *Spiritus, I* continues the Objectivist interplay of image and sign while bringing it into a realm of dreamlike juxtaposition. In "On the Way to the Law Courts" Rakosi writes mellifluously, "Antigone is fair and passed me / with a pair of soft gloves. . . ." This phrase is immediately followed by the presentation of an "inscription" on an "oil jug" that also reads "*Antigone is Fair.*" Because of this interplay with object as pure object and object as sign, in his *The Collected Poems of Carl Rakosi* he gives this poem an urban context and groups "On the Way to the Law Courts" with his much earlier "The City (1925)."

In his 1983 *Collected Prose* Rakosi explicitly analyzes the Objectivist movement and claims that the terms set for Objectivism, either initially in the first manifesto or later by scholarly criticism, may have failed as tools to characterize his own poetry and the others in the group of 1931 and 1932. Yet he finds Objectivism to be "a term . . . worth pursuing" and a concept which "would have had to" have been invented, if not by Zukofsky, then by "somebody else." For the reader's purposes Rakosi still makes his own affiliations and oppositions according to the Objectivist rubric: Rakosi sees his own style most closely analogous to the work of Reznikoff and furthest away from the radical externality of Zukofsky's formal experiments and Niedecker's clinically detached images. Part of Rakosi's increasing self-reflection about his identity as an Objectivist at this time may have been due to the friendship that he had developed with fellow Objectivist and Pulitzer Prize–winner Oppen after Rakosi moved to San Francisco. In the *Collected Prose* Rakosi describes himself as "friends for over sixty years" with Oppen despite never having met or corresponded with him before 1971. The *Collected Prose* is also notable for its aphoristic style that offers pointed critiques of both contemporary workshop poetry and canonical high modernism and highlights the fundamental egoism of both approaches to poetry. Nevertheless Rakosi's *Collected Prose* saves the sharpest barbs for critics of poetry. Rakosi attacks the English professor's practice of ranking poets as "major and minor" as "the bastard offspring of grading students," and he characterizes the literary critic as a "total stranger" who acts like a "master of ceremonies" after a book is published and who promptly asks the poet to "step aside," even on the "stage" of his own work.

Rakosi presented the first major retrospective of his work in 1986 with his *Collected Poems*. This book includes poems from both *History* and *Droles de Journal,* which were published in 1981 by small presses. *History* is a commentary on the bulk of the near-century Rakosi had already seen. Rakosi's observations are organized by decade and range from those of the social worker ("Hard-eyed daughter of Puritans, / mother of work, / on welfare now, / her youngest dead of leukemia, / in a condemned building . . ." in "The Fourth Decade") to the pundit ("the loyal center / will receive the medal of virtue" in "The Eighth Decade"). *Droles de Journal* is written out of Rakosi's complex sense of poetic comedy, oc-

casional poems seemingly without an occasion other than the regularity of the exercise of writing and observation, which, like "Americana," were continued as a series long after their first publication in 1981. In *Droles de Journal* Rakosi records the ironies of his personal frustrations with his own critical reception and even lampoons the literary pretensions of the Objectivists with the same irreverence that he directs at other lofty literary movements. In "Objectivist Lamp" he presents a "goddess, / ivory carved" that is humorous rather than inscrutable and comes fully equipped with "electric bulbs / and batik / lamp shade." The tone of irreverence and play is, in fact, set from the beginning of *Collected Poems* when Rakosi declares in his foreword:

> It seemed to me more creative and interesting to organize the poems as if I were making up a book for the first time, with the parts before me, the individual poems. And I followed the logic of that. A gamble, I know, because they are not, after all, a book in the sense of a composition. On the other hand, neither are they just an aggregation.

Rakosi would rather risk frustrating scholars than deny himself an opportunity for the pleasure of editing and ordering. By refusing chronological order Rakosi negates all the implied narratives on which reverent scholarship is based, subverting the use of his own work from the conventional purpose of charting the development of his career or his role in literary history.

As the Objectivists were recognized for their contributions to modernism and to twentieth-century poetry as a whole, fundamental differences were acknowledged between Rakosi's poetry and the work of others in the initial movement. Although other Objectivists abandoned the pose of rhetorical neutrality when treating the poetic object, in his letters Rakosi sees them as "tragic" poets who were working along "essentially a single mood" to achieve "great depth of feeling," while Rakosi sees himself as "sometimes tragic" but also "humorous, ironic, sarcastic, self-deprecatory. . . ."

Throughout the 1980s and 1990s Rakosi's work began to be included in the major poetry anthologies and taught in universities as the Objectivists as a group came to be recognized as an important part of the literary canon. Not only did the long careers of the Objectivists allow them to be important writers in both the modern and postmodern periods, but, in terms of influence studies, the Objectivists were quite literally deemed to be the inheritors of the legacy of Pound and Williams. It was a legacy that they would fundamentally call into question, even as they served as mentors themselves to many major contemporary poets. Although Rakosi

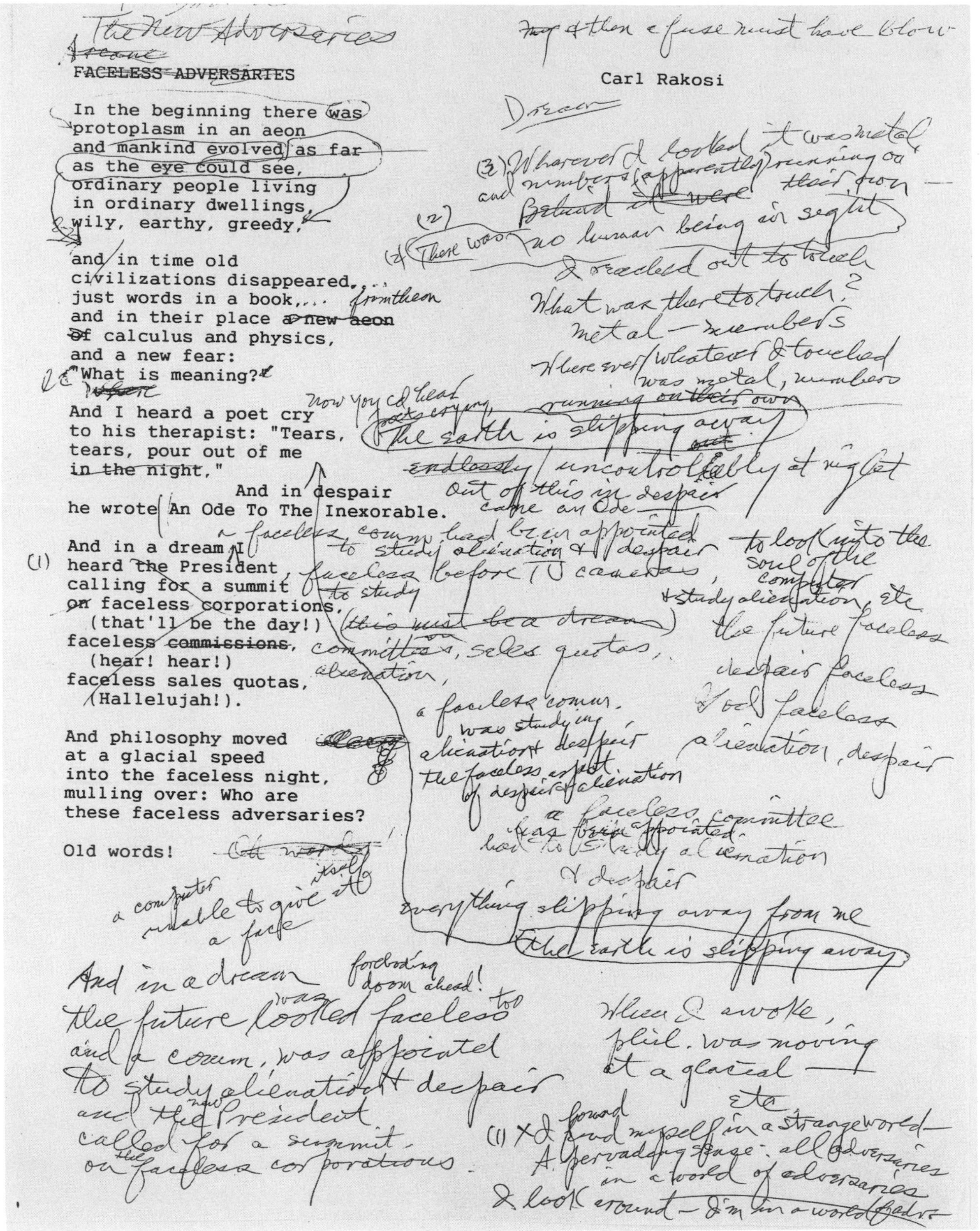

The New Adversaries

FACELESS ADVERSARIES

Carl Rakosi

In the beginning there was
protoplasm in an aeon
and mankind evolved as far
as the eye could see,
ordinary people living
in ordinary dwellings,
wily, earthy, greedy,

and in time old
civilizations disappeared,
just words in a book,
and in their place a new aeon
of calculus and physics,
and a new fear:
"What is meaning?"

And I heard a poet cry
to his therapist: "Tears,
tears, pour out of me
in the night,"
                And in despair
he wrote An Ode To The Inexorable.

And in a dream I
heard the President,
calling for a summit
on faceless corporations,
    (that'll be the day!)
faceless commissions,
    (hear! hear!)
faceless sales quotas,
    (Hallelujah!).

And philosophy moved
at a glacial speed
into the faceless night,
mulling over: Who are
these faceless adversaries?

Old words!

Revised typescripts for two poems by Rakosi (collection of Carl Rakosi)

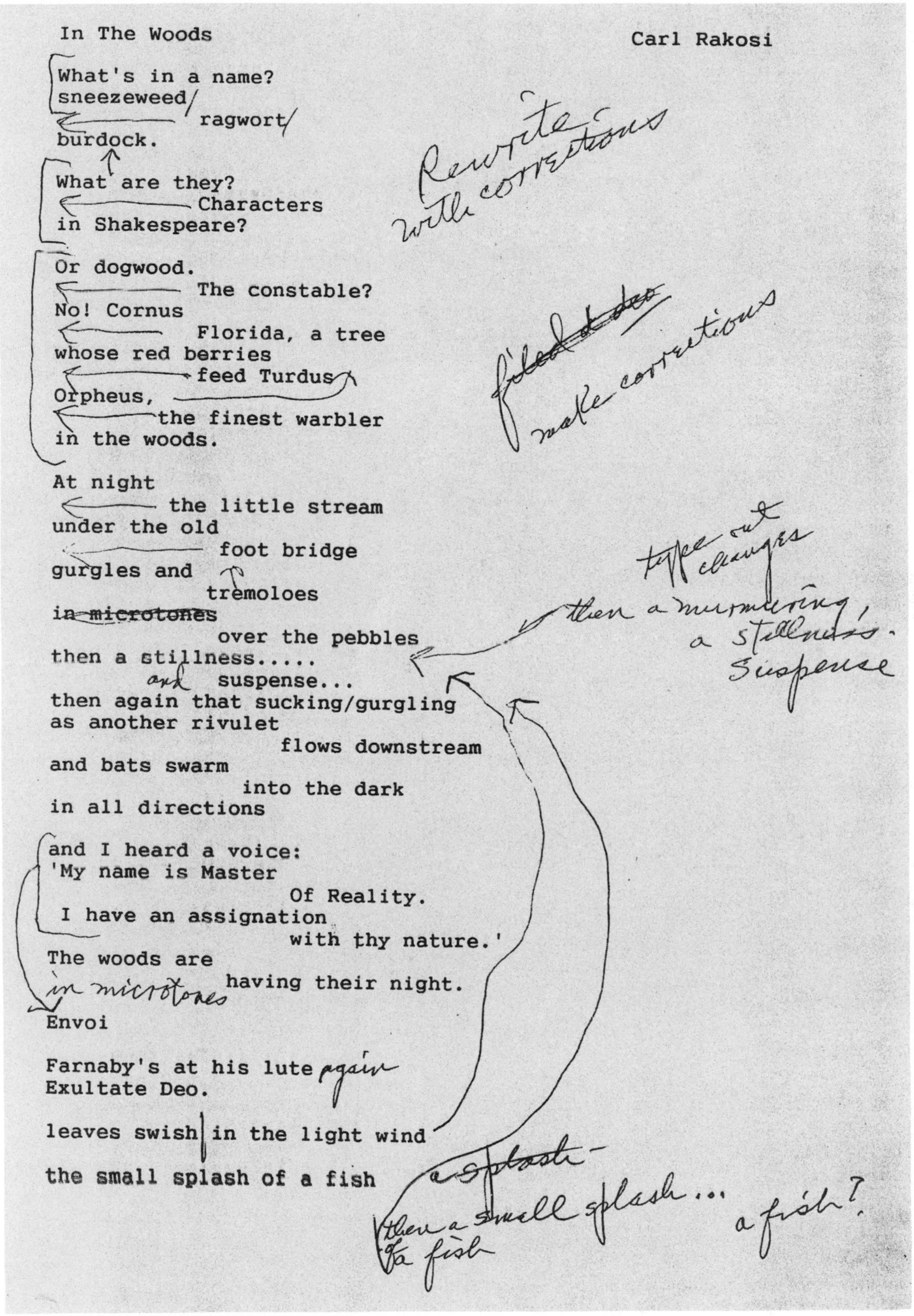

In The Woods Carl Rakosi

What's in a name?
sneezeweed/
ragwort/
burdock.

What are they?
Characters
in Shakespeare?

Or dogwood.
The constable?
No! Cornus
Florida, a tree
whose red berries
feed Turdus
Orpheus,
the finest warbler
in the woods.

At night
the little stream
under the old
foot bridge
gurgles and
tremoloes
~~in microtones~~
over the pebbles
then a stillness.....
and suspense...
then again that sucking/gurgling
as another rivulet
flows downstream
and bats swarm
into the dark
in all directions

and I heard a voice:
'My name is Master
Of Reality.
I have an assignation
with thy nature.'
The woods are
in microtones having their night.

Envoi

Farnaby's at his lute again
Exultate Deo.

leaves swish | in the light wind

the small splash of a fish

Rewrite with corrections

~~filed & dec~~ make corrections

type out changes

then a murmuring, a stillness. suspense

~~a splash~~

then a small splash... of a fish

a fish?

preferred the friendship of poets to acclaim by literary scholars, he eventually found himself serving as the last surviving Objectivist for posterity. He eulogized Oppen after his death in 1984. Rakosi's wife, Leah, died in 1989. Rakosi received a lifetime achievement award from the National Poetry Association and awards from the Fund for Poetry in 1988 and 1989.

Rakosi criticism was largely confined to book reviews and studies of the Objectivists as a whole until the appearance of *Carl Rakosi: Man and Poet* in 1993. Rakosi has continued to work closely with Andrew Crozier, the poet who initially encouraged him to return to writing poetry in 1965. Crozier introduced both the comprehensive 1995 collection of Rakosi's early published work, *Poems 1923–1941,* and Rakosi's most recent book of poems, *The Earth Suite* (1997). Rakosi lives in San Francisco and occasionally travels and gives readings.

Interviews:

L. S. Dembo, "Interview with Carl Rakosi," *Contemporary Literature,* 10 (Spring 1969): 155–159;

Burton Hatlen, "Interview with Carl Rakosi," *Sagetrieb,* 5 (Fall 1986): 95–123;

George Evans and August Kleinzahler, "An Interview with Carl Rakosi," *Conjunctions,* 11 (Fall 1988): 220–245;

Steve Shoemaker, "Carl Rakosi Interview," *Sagetrieb,* 11 (Winter 1992): 93–132.

Bibliography:

Robert Buckeye, "Materials towards a Study of Carl Rakosi," in *Carl Rakosi: Man and Poet,* edited by Michael Heller (Orono, Maine: National Poetry Foundation, 1993), pp. 451–488.

References:

L. S. Dembo, "The Poetry of Carl Rakosi," *Iowa Review,* 2, number 1 (1971): 72–80;

Michael Heller, ed., *Carl Rakosi: Man and Poet* (Orono, Maine: National Poetry Foundation, 1993);

Heller, "Carl Rakosi: Profoundly in Between," in his *Conviction's Net of Branches* (Carbondale: University of Southern Illinois Press, 1985), pp. 36–47;

Marjorie Perloff, "Looking for the Real Carl Rakosi: Collected and Selecteds," *Journal of American Studies,* 30 (August 1996): 271–283;

Carl Rakosi, *Contemporary Authors Autobiography Series,* volume 5 (Detroit: Gale Research, 1987), pp. 193–210.

Papers:

The major collections of Rakosi's papers are located at the University of Wisconsin, Madison; the University of California, San Diego; the University of Texas, Austin; and the Houghton Library, Harvard University.

Jerome Rothenberg
(11 December 1931 –)

Jed Rasula
Queen's University

See also the Rothenberg entry in *DLB 5: American Poets Since World War II.*

BOOKS: *White Sun, Black Sun* (New York: Hawk's Well Press, 1960);

The Seven Hells of the Jigoku Zoshi (New York: Trobar, 1962);

Sightings (New York: Hawk's Well Press, 1964);

The Gorky Poems (Mexico City: El Corno Emplumado, 1966);

Between: Poems 1960–1963 (London: Fulcrum Press, 1967);

Conversations (Los Angeles: Black Sparrow Press, 1968);

Poems 1964–1967 (Los Angeles: Black Sparrow Press, 1968);

Sightings I–IX & Red Easy, A Color (London: Circle Press, 1968);

Poland/1931 (Santa Barbara, Cal.: Unicorn, 1969);

Poems for the Game of Silence 1960–1970 (New York: Dial Press, 1971; revised edition, New York: New Directions, 1975);

A Book of Testimony (Bolinas, Cal.: Tree Books, 1971);

Poems for the Society of the Mystic Animals (London: Tetrad Press, 1972);

A Poem of Beavers: Seneca Journal I (Mt. Horeb, Wis.: Perishable Press, 1973);

Esther K. Comes to America, 1931 (Greensboro, N.C.: Unicorn Press, 1974);

The Cards (Los Angeles: Black Sparrow Press, 1974);

The Pirke & the Pearl (Berkeley, Cal.: Tree Books, 1975);

Seneca Journal: Midwinter (St. Louis, Mo.: Singing Bone Press, 1975);

The Notebooks (Milwaukee: Membrane Press, 1976);

Narratives and Realtheater Pieces (Lot: Braad, 1978);

Seneca Journal: The Serpent (St. Louis, Mo.: Singing Bone Press, 1978);

A Seneca Journal (New York: New Directions, 1978);

*B*R*M*T*z**V*H* (Mt. Horeb, Wis.: Perishable Press, 1979);

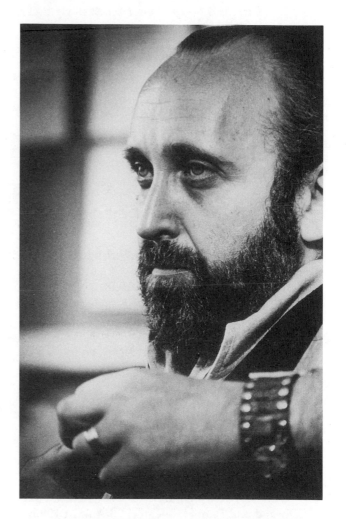

Jerome Rothenberg (photograph by John W. Alley)

Abulafia's Circles (Milwaukee: Membrane Press, 1979);

Numbers and Letters (Madison, Wis.: Salient Seedling Press, 1980);

Vienna Blood (New York: New Directions, 1980);

Pre-Faces and Other Writings (New York: New Directions, 1981);

Altar Pieces (Barrytown: Station Hill Press, 1982);

That Dada Strain (New York: New Directions, 1983);

15 Flower World Variations (Milwaukee: Membrane Press, 1984);

A Merz Sonata (Easthampton, Mass.: Emanon Press / Rosendale, N.Y.: Women's Studio Workshop, 1985);

New Selected Poems 1970–1985 (New York: New Directions, 1986);

Khurbn and Other Poems (New York: New Directions, 1989);

Further Sightings and Conversations (San Francisco: Pennywhistle Press, 1989);

The Lorca Variations (1–8) (Tenerife: Zasterle Press, 1990);

Improvisations (New York: Dieu Donné Press, 1991);

Six Gematria (London: Tetrad Press, 1992);

The Lorca Variations: I–XXXIII (New York: New Directions, 1993);

In a Time of War (Albuquerque: Salient Seedling Press, 1993);

Gematria (Los Angeles: Sun & Moon Press, 1994);

An Oracle for Delfi (Kenosha, Wis.: Membrane Press, 1994);

Pictures of the Crucifixion (New York: Granary Books, 1995);

Seedings and Other Poems (New York: New Directions, 1996);

Delight/Délices & Other Gematria, bilingual edition, with French translations by Nicole Peyrafitte (Nimes: Editions Ottezec, 1998);

At the Grave of Nakahara Chuya (Ellsworth, Maine: Backwoods Broadsides, Chaplet Series, 1998).

PLAY PRODUCTIONS: *The Deputy,* adapted from the German play by Rolf Hochhuth, New York, Brooks Atkinson Theater, 1964;

That Dada Strain, San Diego, Center for Theater Science and Research, 1985; Lexington, The Center for Theater Science and Research, 1987;

Poland/1931, New York, Living Theater, 1988;

Khurbn/Hiroshima, texts by Rothenberg and Makoto Oda, music by Charlie Morrow, New York, Bread and Puppet Theater, 26 August 1995.

RECORDINGS: *Origins and Meanings,* Folkways, 1968;

From a Shaman's Notebook, Folkways, 1968;

Horse Songs and Other Soundings, S-Press, 1975;

6 Horse Songs for 4 Voices, New Wilderness, 1978;

Jerome Rothenberg Reads Poland/1931, New Fire, 1979;

Rothenberg/Turetsky; Performing, Blues Economique, 1984;

The Birth of the War God, with Charlie Morrow and the Western Wind, Laurel, 1988;

"4 Settings from 'That Dada Strain,'" on Bertram Turetzky, *Compositions and Improvisations,* Winds Records, 1993;

"Chicago Dadagram," on George Lewis, *Changing With the Times,* New World Records, 1993.

OTHER: *New Young German Poets,* edited and translated by Rothenberg (San Francisco: City Lights, 1959);

Poems from the Floating World, edited by Rothenberg (New York, 1960–1964);

Some/thing, edited by Rothenberg and David Antin (New York, 1965–1968);

Rolf Hochhuth, *The Deputy,* translated by Rothenberg (New York: S. French, 1965);

Ritual: A Book of Primitive Rites and Events, edited by Rothenberg (New York: Something Else Press, 1966);

The Flight of Quetzalcoatl, translated by Rothenberg (Brighton: Unicorn, 1967);

Hans Magnus Enzensberger, *Poems for People Who Don't Read Poems,* translated by Rothenberg, Enzenberger, and Michael Hamburger (New York: Atheneum, 1968; London: Secker & Warburg, 1968);

Eugen Gomringer, *The Book of Hours and Constellations,* translated by Rothenberg (New York: Something Else Press, 1968);

Technicians of the Sacred: A Range of Poetries from Africa, America, Asia and Oceania, edited by Rothenberg (New York: Doubleday, 1968; revised and expanded edition, Berkeley: University of California Press, 1985);

The 17 Horse Songs of Frank Mitchell, Nos. X–XIII, translated by Rothenberg (London: Tetrad Press, 1969);

Alcheringa, edited by Rothenberg and Dennis Tedlock (New York, 1970–1974; Boston, 1975–1977);

Shaking the Pumpkin: Traditional Poetry of the Indian North Americas, edited by Rothenberg (New York: Doubleday, 1972; revised edition, New York: Alfred van der Mark, 1986; revised edition, Alburquerque: University of New Mexico Press, 1991);

America a Prophecy: A New Reading of American Poetry from Pre-Columbian Times to the Present, edited by Rothenberg and George Quasha (New York: Random House, 1973);

Three Friendly Warnings: Songs from the Society of Mystic Animals, translated from Seneca Indian by Rothenberg (London: Tetrad Press, 1973);

Revolution of the Word: A New Gathering of American Avant Garde Poetry 1914–1945, edited by Rothenberg (New York: Seabury Press, 1974);

Ethnopoetics: A First International Symposium, edited by Rothenberg and Michael Benamou (Boston: Alcheringa & Boston University, 1976);

New Wilderness Letter, edited by Rothenberg (New York, 1977–1982);

Gematria 27, translated by Rothenberg and Harris Lenowitz (Milwaukee: Membrane Press, 1977);

A Big Jewish Book: Poems and Other Visions of the Jews from Tribal Times to the Present, edited by Rothenberg, Lenowitz and Charles Doria (Garden City, N.Y.: Anchor Press, 1978); revised as *Exiled in the Word,* edited by Rothenberg and Lenowitz (Port Townsend, Wash.: Copper Canyon Press, 1989);

Symposium of the Whole: A Range of Discourse Towards an Ethnopoetics, edited by Jerome and Diane Rothenberg (Berkeley: University of California Press, 1983);

Wch Way / New Wilderness Letter, edited by Rothenberg, Jed Rasula, and Don Byrd (1984–1985);

Federico Garcia Lorca, *4 Lorca Suites,* translated by Rothenberg (Los Angeles: Sun & Moon Press, 1989);

"Ethnopoetics & Politics / The Politics of Ethnopoetics," in *The Politics of Poetic Form: Poetry and Public Policy,* edited by Charles Bernstein (New York: Roof, 1990), pp. 1–22;

"The Suites by Federico Garcia Lorca (complete)," translated by Rothenberg in *Collected Poems,* edited by Christopher Maurer (New York: Farrar Straus Giroux, 1991);

"Beyond Poetics," in *American Writing Today,* edited by Richard Kostelanetz (Troy: Whitston, 1991), pp. 510–516;

Note on St. Marks Church and the founding of the Poetry Project, in *Out of this World,* edited by Ann Waldman (New York: Crown Books, 1991), pp. 674–675;

"'We Explain Nothing, We Believe Nothing': American Indian Poetry and the Problematics of Translation," in *On the Translation of Native American Literature,* edited by Brian Swann (Washington, D.C.: Smithsonian, 1992), pp. 64–79;

"The Search for a Primal Poetics; Dialectical Anthropology: Essays in Honor of Stanley Diamond, II," in *Dialectical Anthropology: Essays in Honour of Stanley Diamond (Volume 2), The Politics of Culture and Creativity: A Critique of Civilization,* edited by Christine Gailey (Gainesville: University Press of Florida, 1992), pp. 229–237;

"New Models New Visions: Some Notes Towards a Poetics of Performance," in *Literally Speak-*

ing: Sound Poetry and Text-Sound Composition (Gotesburg County: Bo Ejeby, 1993), pp. 81–84;

PPPPPP: Poems Performance Pieces Proses Plays Poetics of Kurt Schwitters, translated by Rothenberg and Pierre Joris (Philadelphia: Temple University Press, 1993);

"From 'Je est un autre: Ethnopoetics and the Poet as Other,'" in *Anthology of North American Ideophonics,* edited by Marl Novak (Minneapolis: University of Minnesota Press, 1993);

"Ethnopoetics," in *New Princeton Encyclopaedia of Poetry and Poetics* (Princeton: Princeton University Press, 1993), pp. 388–389;

"Art at the Millennium: A Proposal for a New Configuration in the Arts," in *Worlds in Collision,* edited by Carlos Villa (San Francisco: San Francisco Art Institute, 1994), pp. 66–74;

"Corn Soup and Fry Bread," with Diane Rothenberg, in *The Sun and Moon Guide to Eating Through Literature,* edited by Douglas Messerli (Los Angeles: Sun & Moon Press, 1994), pp. 52–53;

Poems for the Millennium: The University of California Book of Modern & Postmodern Poetry, 2 volumes, edited by Rothenberg and Pierre Joris (Berkeley: University of California Press, 1995, 1998);

Kurt Schwitters, *A Flower Like a Raven,* translated by Rothenberg (New York: Granary Books, 1996);

The Book, Spiritual Instrument, edited by Rothenberg and David Guss (New York: Granary Books, 1996);

Introduction to *A Secret Location on the Lower East Side* (New York: New York Public Library / Granary Books, 1998).

SELECTED PERIODICAL PUBLICATIONS–
UNCOLLECTED: "On the Becks," *Third Rail* (1985–1986): 7, 33;

[{untitled} Statement on Poetry, Politics, and Vision], *Mississippi Review,* 3 (1991): 104–105;

"From American Indian Poetry and the Problematics of Translations," *Talisman,* 6 (1991): 108–109;

"The Poetics of the Sacred," *Five Fingers Review,* 10 (1991): 67–74;

[{untitled} Commentary on Traditional Ainu Poetry], *Kyoto Journal,* 22 (1993): 27;

"Statement on Translation from 'Tucson Poetry Festival Panel: What is Not Lost: Poetry and Translation,'" *Poetry Center Newsletter* (Tucson, Arizona), 17 (1993): 4–5.

Dust jacket for the collection of works about Jews that Rothenberg edited with Harris Lenowitz and Charles Doria in 1978

Rothenberg is a polymathic figure who is distinctly at odds with the career profile established by poets born a few years earlier. A. R. Ammons, John Ashbery, Galway Kinnell, James Merrill, and W. S. Merwin have practiced poetry—and thereby exemplified the role of the poet—as romantic outcast, dissent, and ironic standard-bearer of the life of imagination in a time of drought. Rothenberg, by contrast, has insisted on poetry as an art of reclamation, rekindling individual sensibility and communal ties in the same gesture. He stands apart from the dominant tendency in postwar American poetry in that he has steadfastly refused to acknowledge literary criteria as the sole frame for poetry, an activity he views as continuous with *duende, cante hondo* or deep song, the deep image of shamanic penetration into the starry sky of the body. "I've had a strong recoil from 'literature' & 'criticism' as a sufficient context for poetry," he says in *Pre-Faces and Other Writings* (1981). In an instructive exchange with William Spanos, Rothenberg displays considerable resistance to Spanos's

scholastic preoccupation with the periodizing distinction between modern and postmodern, as well as to his typological distinction between oral and literate. In his insistence on poetry as extraliterary resource, Rothenberg advances an exemplary model of poetry as liberation and commitment.

Jerome Rothenberg's multifaceted activities—as anthologist, performer, polemicist, and editor—have tended to obscure his own body of poetry. Characteristically, Allen Ginsberg honored Rothenberg on his sixtieth birthday by acknowledging Rothenberg's contributions to Jewish lore, Amerindian poetics, ethnopoetics, contemporary world poetics, international sacred poetics, his own poetry, and early twentieth-century Modernist breakthrough poetics: "He's certainly done me a favor in collecting specimens in above categories and putting them all in our hands, predigesting masses of reading for immediate inspirational or teaching use. What a lifetime job!" This remains the paradigmatic response. While Rothenberg's is an integrated project of writing, research, documentation, and performance, it would be a mistake to view the poetry itself as ancillary to the cardinal work of the anthologies—an error easy to succumb to, given the originality and copiousness of Rothenberg's achievements in this domain. His editorial prodigality will undoubtedly continue to overshadow his poetry; yet, with scrupulous attention, readers have noticed and will continue to recognize the emergence of a body of works unusual in its focal passion, rigorous and consistent, studious and joyful.

Rothenberg was born and raised in the Bronx—"a little behind the times," he says—with Yiddish as his first language, a legacy he proudly claims to share with Louis Zukofsky. Rothenberg's was not a particularly orthodox upbringing, however, and he credits the poet Robert Duncan with awakening his dormant sense of Jewish identity as the kernel of poetic selfhood, characterizing his own belated embrace of Jewish roots as akin to "coming out of the closet," as he said in *The Riverside Interviews 4: Jerome Rothenberg* (1984). The more formative of the poet's early influences derive from alliances forged at the City College of New York and, later, in the lower East Side poetry and interarts scene of the late 1950s and early 1960s, a matrix that included David Antin, Robert Kelly, Paul Blackburn, Jackson Mac Low, Armand Schwerner, George Economou, Rochelle Owens, Diane Wakoski, and Clayton Eshleman. While most of these poets had moved elsewhere by the mid 1960s, Rothenberg's enthusiasm for poetry as sacred ritual and his respect for art as process and event can be traced to this nexus. Uncharacteristically for poets of his generation, Rothenberg has also benefited from a secure family setting. Married in 1952, Jerome and Diane Rothenberg collaborated in editing *Symposium of the Whole* (1983), an important anthology cross-pollinating poetics with anthropology, and on several occasions his poetry performances have been augmented by the collaborative participation of son Matthew (born 1965).

There is an emotional dominant that may be taken as a guide to all of Rothenberg's activity, poetic and otherwise: celebration. His acclaimed anthologies, characteristically documentary in design, are motivated exercises in recovery and celebration of "ancestral" resources in an expanded sense. His own poems adhere to a sense of panegyric or praise poem, particularly as inflected by non-Western poetries. The liturgical feel of Rothenberg's work, from *White Sun, Black Sun* (1960) to *The Lorca Variations: I–XXXIII* (1993), is thus indebted to the ritual celebration of the traumas of life as well as its exultations. As a man of letters Rothenberg has been a facilitator, an agent of connections, a wizard of uncanny alliances. Somewhat unwittingly, as he has testified in an interview for *Riverside,* Rothenberg put into contact certain young West Coast poets with their eastern peers, who in concert ended up developing Language poetry. Rothenberg has been committed to a *provisional* and antimonumental sense of poetry. He favors serial forms and generic formats, emphasizing occasion and process, as indicated by such titles as *Sightings* (1964), *The Notebooks* (1976), *A Seneca Journal* (1978), *The Lorca Variations: I–XXXIII,* and *Gematria* (1994). His 1971 volume of selected poems was titled *Poems for the Game of Silence 1960–1970,* thereby casting his accumulated work to that point under the defining rubric of "game," a decidedly provisional template.

Rothenberg's poetic production has been steady after a late start. His first book–published by his own Hawk's Well Press–did not appear until he was nearly thirty. Despite the mature and purposive nature of his poetry in *White Sun, Black Sun,* in *The Seven Hells of the Jigoku Zoshi* (published by Kelly's Trobar Books in 1962), and in *Sightings,* he quickly came to regard this as, in some measure, apprentice work. As late as 1974 in an interview with Barry Alpert, in fact, he characterized "all of the early work–and hopefully all of the present work–as transitional." In his early forties at the time, this appears to be a disarmingly unambitious remark. It would be more accurate, however, to stress his use of the term "transitional," in that Rothenberg's work pointedly celebrates transit, particularly as honored by occasions of liminal thresholds ritually beheld *as* ceremonies of valuation.

Apart from the third of the "Poems for the Hell of Hungry Ghosts," the earliest work is not overtly pledged to ceremonial occasion. This was the period of Rothenberg's closest association with Robert Kelly, as the two men developed their thesis of "deep image." (Meanwhile Robert Bly, having been befriended by the Rothenbergs during his sojourn in New York, returned to Minnesota and began propagating a competing, if similar, doctrine of deep image.) In retrospect, deep image was more germane to Kelly's temperament than to Rothenberg's. Kelly's first book, *Armed Descent* (published in 1961 by Rothenberg as a Hawk's Well volume in format identical to his own *White Sun, Black Sun*), reveals a more nuanced, vigorous, and native accommodation to the quasi-mystical demands of deep image. What Rothenberg's *Seven Hells* reveals, by contrast, is a patience with sensory simplicity: "Pity their bones when the skin falls away / Pity the skin devoured by fire." Where Kelly's quest for imagistic depth would eventually result in the hermetic lore saturating *Songs I–XXX* (1968) and *Finding the Measure* (1968), Rothenberg would adhere to a more demonstrably international idiom in which the quality of depth appears less vertical than horizontal. That is, the image as node of translation requires a syntactic spareness, with a fairly rudimentary vocabulary; and these are features that Rothenberg began honing in the next (post "deep image") cycles of poems.

Gathered in *Poems for the Game of Silence* as Program Two, the cycles "Sightings," "A Steinbook," "Conversations," and "The Gorky Poems" share a simplification of idiom and address. In short order the wordiness of 1960, "And the thought of something I would not betray grows wild in my heart," has given way to a striking austerity: "He hides his heart." This was not a propitious period for such an apparently ascetic idiom. The discursive ramble of the Beats was in ascendancy, and stars of the metrics school of the 1950s were embracing a loquacious free-verse idiom that seemed suitable to the antiwar alliances poets were forming with political constituencies, as well as being more congenial to the expanding circuit of public readings. Unlike many of his peers, Rothenberg embraced orality as a semantic and morphemic minimalism. His affiliates in this enterprise were participants in Fluxus and other intermedia projects based in New York. The *performance* context of his mid 1960s poetry would, in turn, shortly be transformed into the *ceremonial* context of what he would call "ethnopoetics," a truly open-field poetics that would range from the "vocal-

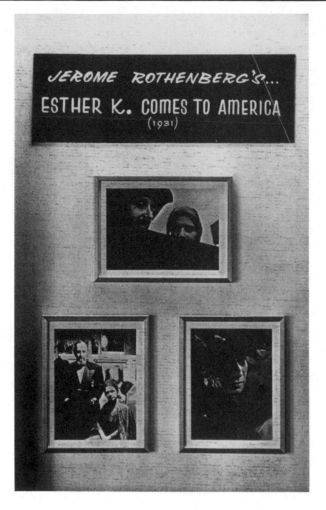

*Cover for Rothenberg's 1969 book, which he calls a "supreme
Yiddish surrealist vaudeville"*

ism" of Walt Whitman and tribal chant to chance-generated and other procedural operations, encompassing both literate and nonliterate (or in Rothenberg's preferred usage, "primitive") traditions—a global, multitemporal poetics.

The provisional, tentative, or "transitional" character of Rothenberg's poetry of the 1960s is emphasized by the collection *Between: Poems 1960–1963,* published in London by Fulcrum in 1967. This volume represents an important recognition of Rothenberg's emerging significance in the post–Black Mountain context. (Fulcrum published, during the same time, several volumes each by Robert Duncan, Edward Dorn, and Gary Snyder.) When John Martin prevailed upon the poet to submit a manuscript to the fledgling Black Sparrow Press, the equally transitional nature of the work occasioned the simple title *Poems 1964–1967* (1968). Together these two slim volumes (150 pages altogether) gather the bulk of the work of a decade. Rothenberg was

clearly earning respect, if not acclaim; nevertheless, a commercial publisher (The Dial Press) elected to republish a significant portion of this work yet again in 1971 as *Poems for the Game of Silence,* augmenting it with a survey of projects from the later 1960s–"A Shaman's Notebook," "Soundings," "Narratives & Realtheater Pieces," and the inaugural work of the next phase, "Poland/1931." At a time when his more productive, and more acclaimed, cohorts were confined to small press publications, Rothenberg landed a trade publishing contract. Clearly the poet was a beneficiary of a new career: the highly visible, successful, and arguably revolutionary role of anthologist.

Rothenberg's anthologizing inclination was, in fact, evident all along. Hawk's Well Press, in addition to its book publications, published the magazine *Poems from the Floating World* (1960–1964), "an ongoing anthology of the deep image," according to Rothenberg in his interview with Alpert. This editorial enterprise was succeeded by *Some/thing,* co-edited with David Antin from 1965 to 1968. Dick Higgins's Something Else Press published Rothenberg's first anthology, *Ritual,* in 1966. With the innovative *Technicians of the Sacred: A Range of Poetries from Africa, America, Asia & Oceania,* published by Doubleday in 1968, Rothenberg's singular talent for fielding idiosyncratic but accessible conceptual platforms was strikingly apparent. The editorial proclivity of *Technicians of the Sacred* was extended into the pragmatically open-ended framework of the journals *Alcheringa* (coedited with Dennis Tedlock) and *New Wilderness Letter. Technicians of the Sacred* initiated an enterprise that continues unchecked to the present, in which anthologies articulate the moving ground of Rothenberg's own poetry, while the poems rehearse the multifaceted and polyglot world of the anthologies in their own idiomatic register.

While not as prolific a theorist as Charles Olson or Robert Duncan, Rothenberg has been meticulous in mapping his theoretical proclivities at the convergent site of poetry/anthology. The three "programs" of *Poems for the Game of Silence* offer succinct indications: "The Poem is the record of a movement from perception to vision. . . . I will change your mind; . . . any means (=methods) to that end," Rothenberg writes, prefacing the work of 1960 to 1967, that auspicious date when he irrevocably proclaimed his tribe as nothing short of a global sect of shamans, seers, singers, *makars* (bards), rabbis, and messiahs. "I look for new forms & possibilities, but also for ways of presenting in my own language the oldest possibilities of poetry going back to the primitive & archaic cultures that have been opening up to us over the last hundred years." To work in such a continuum entailed a stance decisive for the development of Rothenberg's poetry, which is envisioned as fully interactive with its predecessors (and thus quite distinct from the agonistic evasions in Harold Bloom's "revisionary ratios" of poetic anxiety). These predecessors' poems constitute a poetic continuum in which the distinction between original and copy, source text and translation, is muted. What made *Technicians of the Sacred* so innovative was not its gathering of "primitive" poetries from Africa, Oceania, the Americas, and Asia— which had been attempted by none other than Tristan Tzara, as well as Blaise Cendrars in 1927, Roger Caillois and Jean Clarence Lambert in 1958, and Willard Trask's two-volume collection *The Unwritten Song* (1969)—but its incorporation of so many poet collaborators. The voluminous commentaries of *Technicians of the Sacred* (135 pages) incorporate a subordinate anthology of their own, as it were, citing entire poems by Rothenberg's associates (Antin, Mac Low, Schwerner, Ginsberg, Snyder, Wakoski, Duncan, Blackburn, Robert Cree-

ley, Amiri Baraka, Ed Sanders, George Oppen, and Denise Levertov among them). One section of the preface, "Primitive & Modern: Intersections and Analogies," instructively itemizes features of the anthology in terms that also catalogue Rothenberg's own poetry projects: (1) poem as score for performance; (2) noncausal poetic logic, as manifested in surrealism, deep image, and dream; (3) "a 'minimal' art of maximal involvement"—concrete and pictorial poetrics; (4) intermedia; (5) physicality as in sound poems, orientation to breath patterns, sexual energy; and finally (6) the visionary complex which, in Rothenberg's imagination, links the poet with the shaman. These practices constitute Rothenberg's vortex, through which his own poems are drawn into the skein woven by these ancestral technicians of the sacred. And, as he points out in *Symposium* and has never tired of pointing out, "primitive means complex."

Where his conservative counterparts work in specific forms of versification—a given volume flaunting examples of the villanelle, the sonnet, the terza rima—Rothenberg offers his own panoply of forms for expanded field poetics: dream work, kabbalah, gematria and numerological poems, ritual, ceremonies, performances or "events," in addition to his favored locution, the litany. His privileged guides in this work have been Jews, Indians, and Dadaists, as celebrated in the books *Poland/1931* (1969), *A Seneca Journal* (1978), and *That Dada Strain* (1983). Most recently, in *The Lorca Variations I– XXXIII* (1993) he has reclaimed his roots in the Spanish *duende* and *cante hondo* of Federico García Lorca. While Rothenberg's many translations have predominately been from the German (Hans Magnus Enzensberger, Eugen Gomringer, Roch Hochhuth, and others), his earliest work displays a clear sympathy for—as well as the influence of—Lorca's expansive lucidities and deep images. Lorca, alert to the syncretistic environment of the city in his *Poeta en Nueva York* (1940), had written a poem in commemoration of a Jewish cemetery. Rothenberg's avowal of his Jewish roots in Poland may be seen as, in part, instigated by Lorca's poem, and by the hybridizing intelligence of Lorca's poetry in general.

Poland/1931 is a carnivalesque book in much the sense that Mikhail M. Bakhtin intended—a saturnalia of the lower-body stratum, in fetchingly grotesque ribaldry, a "supreme Yiddish surrealist vaudeville" as the poet called it in *Pre-Faces. Poland/1931* is not without darkness, but all is suffused in a rich sensory glow. The trials of steerage for the immigrant are dedicated, fittingly, to Charlie Chaplin, and the immigrant tide Rothenberg beholds in visionary slapstick consecrates America to the Baal Shem, which has become a beaver. *Poland/1931* is the first fully integrated collection

Dust jacket for Rothenberg's 1971 collection, his first to appear under the imprint of a major trade publishing house

of Rothenberg's career, benefiting no doubt from the organizational experience of editing *Technicians of the Sacred* and *Shaking the Pumpkin: Traditional Poetry of the Indian North Americas* (1972). It also offers something rare in American poetry: an entire volume devoted specifically to the immigrant experience. Rothenberg claims for poetry aspects of Americana formerly associated with the novel—he holds Henry Roth's *Call it Sleep* (1934) in high esteem. In this collection there are always stories being told, as emphasized by section headings ("Galician Nights, or A Novel in Progress," "Esther K. Comes to America," "A Book of Histories," and "A Book of Testimony"), but the narrative function is finally subordinated to the register of detail, which is in turn absorbed into the rhythmic insistence of the panegyric. The immigrant experience, in its juxtaposition of stark contrasts, is inherently a collage. Rothenberg's early fascination with "deep image" matured into a recognition of subterranean logics of dream and vision that amalgamate surface oppositions into the phantasmagoria of continuity. The result is often grotesque—

gaily you put your lips to his then sneezed him
through the doorway   falling   saw his cruel life

snuffed under the feet of marchers
strikers you led down East Street & up into Heaven
became an Irish cop yourself but kept your earlocks
your gaberdines hidden you still ate radishes for lunch
scraps of chickenwings for dinner let the skin
slide down your throat & choke you
the contradictions were almost a relief

—and frequently humorous: "he had completely incarnated himself into a sacred lemon." In the end, *Poland/1931* is a text of convergent identities, culminating with "Moses in the Rockies" and the western desert where "grandfather's / ghost of Ishi was waiting on the crest / looked like a Jew / but silent."

Rothenberg's preoccupation with finding a Native American substratum in the Jewish experience is indicative of his hybridizing sensibility. It also reflects personal experience. Rothenberg has been adamant in repudiating any kind of essentialism; so part of his project in *Poland/1931* was to discover the Jew as radical migrant, which is to say, migrating or *metamorphosing* into non-Jewish conditions and apparitions. It was not a nostalgic embracing of "roots," or "sentimental reminiscences," he insisted in the *Riverside* interview. By working through a sense of exile as "cosmic principle" in *A Big Jewish Book: Poems and Other Visions of the Jews from Tribal Times to the Present* (1978), his third commercial anthology for Doubleday, Rothenberg embraced particulars of personal ancestry in order to rediscover himself *as poet* in the terms Marina Tsvetayeva suggested in her dictum that "all poets are Jews." Likewise, he was discovering a variant adage to the effect that all poets are Indians (or: natives, primitives, technicians of the sacred). Pragmatically, the Rothenbergs spent two years at the Allegany Seneca Reservation in Salamanca, New York (1972–1974), having made frequent prior visits beginning in 1967. The poet became an honorary beaver, and his wife and son became herons. It was a richly productive period during which Rothenberg developed his theory of "total translation" (essentially a means of admitting extrasemantic vocalized propensities into the translation process), completing *Poland/1931* at the beginning of the sojourn and inaugurating *A Big Jewish Book* at the end; compiling *Revolution of the Word: A New Gathering of American Avant Garde Poetry 1914–1945*, published in 1974 (his decisive recovery of early-twentieth-century English-language avant-garde poetry) while there; and writing *A Seneca Journal.*

Rothenberg has claimed the Salamanca experience as an immersion in *place*, rather on the model of Olson's Gloucester. The poems in *A Seneca Journal* are, however, altogether distinct from anything in Olson's *The Maximus Poems* (1953–1975) apart from the fact that both poets offer brief recitations of native tales. To some degree the book continues the theme of the wandering Jew from *Poland/1931*, and the Baal Shem is as overt a presence here as in that volume. Two sections, "Beavers" and "Serpent," gather poems preoccupied with these motifs. The other sections have a miscellaneous, yet programmatic, feel. "Midwinter" consists of rigorously minimalist poems:

EVENTS

fire a rifle

touch the sun[.]

Such poems clearly follow in the vein of *Sightings*. The final section, "Dreams," offers a more complex set, ranging from minimalist "event" poems to dream recitations, lyric reveries, and incipient narrative litanies, as in "A History of Surrealism in Cattaraugus County":

they look up at the sky they see
again the pink cloud move across the yellow cloud
again a pine cone bounce against the sun
again a diamond antler crack like sugar
again a new-born frog rise from the savage onions
again a flute melt to announce the light
again a blue eye peer from a headstone
again a dead bell speak without a tongue
again the animals shed their skins beside the furnace[.]

Rothenberg relies on structural devices as a way of focusing the disparate poems gathered in a single book. Where others present their work in chronological portfolios, the focus of which is entirely contingent on the dominant preoccupations (often deliberately kept from conscious consideration) of the poet at the time, Rothenberg has largely resisted this miscellany. The one exception is *Vienna Blood* (1980), uncharacteristically bulked out with occasional poems. Its value, however, is its explicit alignment of the ancestral Poland poems with an emergent claim of a different set of European roots in Dada, particularly in the culminating twenty-page reverie "Abulafia's Circles."

In a 1982 interview Rothenberg commented on the fecundity of the Seneca experience and clarified a key aspect of his poetry, indicating that "the books since *Poland* (or some major parts of them) make up a single larger work." As previously suggested, this "larger work" can be seen extending even to the material gathered in the anthologies, instances of Rothenberg's polyglot "ancestral" poetics. So *Poland/1931* may be read in the mirror of *A Big Jewish Book*, *A Seneca Journal* in the mirror of *Shaking the Pumpkin*, and, in a less precise synchrony, *That Dada Strain* in the mirror of *Revolution of the Word* and *Poems for the Millennium*. *Technicians of the Sacred* remains the sublime vision that subsumes all the others—to which there is no single correlative among the books of poetry. If anything, the "single larger work" Rothenberg speaks of the poems as inhabiting is nothing less than the expanded realm of *Technicians of the Sacred*. His poetic yin and yang have always been *method* and *inspiration* ("event" and "vision"). While the anthologies necessarily adhere to a more rigorous methodology, the volumes of poetry have been punctiliously organized as well. The organizational templates reinforce our awareness that Rothenberg's vision quests have rarely been indulged for their own sake. His is not an ego-centered stance but an avowedly and sedulously tribal one. The vision must be fed back to the community, just as the shaman's hallucinatory quests are nothing if not in service to communal ends. So when Rothenberg speculates on the coordinated

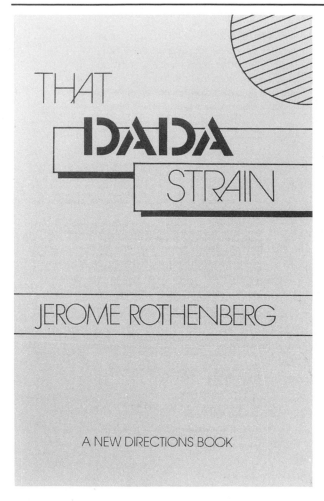

THAT DADA STRAIN

JEROME ROTHENBERG

A NEW DIRECTIONS BOOK

Title page for Rothenberg's 1983 collection of poems with roots in the European Dada movement of the early twentieth century

inherence of the post-*Poland* works around a dominant principle, he is indicating those conceptual paths along which readers may elect to travel from book to book.

The dream spectrum provides a rich source of continuities. The organizational cipher of "Dreams" in *A Seneca Journal* is revisited in the "Imaginal Geographies" section of *That Dada Strain,* and focused with uncanny fluency in the "Dreamwork" sequence in the "Ikons" of *Khurbn and Other Poems* (1989). Here the oneiric resources are indistinguishable from language itself: "to dream a language without syllables / to dream that he understands this language / to dream that all of language is a single word / to dream that he knows this word / to dream that he forgets it." Dreams are instances of a visionary threshold and provide a clue to Rothenberg's most ambitious poems. Dreams provide the clearest "natural" or involuntary directive, from within the organism, of the imaginal resources most insistently realized in po-

etry. In Rothenberg's case the proximity is so near as to verge on tautology, as in "Dream Poem, 24.ii.79" of *That Dada Strain:*

> riding the trolley line
> through streets of
> Salamanca
> past the new subway stop
> where crowds of Indians
> emerge   dark grains of maize
> still in my fist
> the dead of Salamanca
> rise   my mouth
> fills up
> with songs & tears[.]

The directive resources of his poetry are much in evidence even here in this abbreviated vignette. The Jewish lamentation of exile merges with the Indian trauma of dispossession, and both are subsumed in the mythopoetic cycle of generation. Such dreams are engaged in Rothenberg's poetry, not for their novelty nor for any conventional poetic touch, but because of the numinous call of their imaginal insistence. They are not anecdotes but road maps of emotional trial.

Another area the poet has insistently occupied is that of the "event," which ranges from sacred ceremony to secular "happening." Since such practices clearly court the extratextual, an "event" is difficult to comment on in a review of the published poetry. But the significance of this practice should not be underestimated, for it provides the pragmatic foundation on which Rothenberg has sought to develop, in his poetry as a whole, a depersonalized sphere of operations. As he said in the *Riverside* interview: "I think at some point I determined to direct the attention away from the self and to incorporate by various means that which is *not* the lyrical and subjective voice." A variety of "event" that has been enlarged in Rothenberg's practice through the years is *gematria,* or numerological poems, culminating in the large portfolio *Gematria,* published in 1994. This may strike many readers as procedural work with a vengeance; the poems offer no purchase on the readerly taste for personality, emotion, image pattern, symbolism, or narration. The consistency with which the frighteningly incisive gematria abstain from these pursuits is bracing indeed. In *Pre-Faces* Rothenberg defines the term: "*Gematria* is the general term for a variety of traditional coding practices used by the Jewish mystic-poets to establish correspondences between words or series of words based on the numerical equivalence of the sums of their letters or on the interchange of letters according to a set system." The procedural variety of these "coding practices" is striking and clearly provides a major incentive for a poet long captivated by the chance event and the chance metonymies of dream and Dada. So the relation of the letter code, given as the poem's title, and the numerological outcome, operate like an unveiled portent:

HE FLASHED LIGHT

with his finger.

The *Gematria* poems openly reveal a subliminal—and arguably *sublime*—assumption, namely, that all writing is collaboration, even where the collaborator is undetectable. This theory is patently integral to the poetic legacy of the Muse. Curiously, Rothenberg admits to having been led to explore "that Dada strain" because of a remark by Diane Wakoski to the effect that Tristan Tzara seemed to be his muse. His orientation to poetry as, in Robert Duncan's words, a "symposium of the whole," tacitly admits the ambient presence of others. Rothenberg has also been involved in more overtly collaborative forms. In keeping with the concern for the vision of design, evident in the organizations of the contents of his poetry collections, Rothenberg has participated in some innovative collaborative formats. The Unicorn Press edition of *Esther K. Comes to America, 1931* (1973) has an elaborate and atmospheric portfolio of photographs by Laurence Fink, most of which are not reproduced in *Poland/1931.* Rothenberg is himself one of the actors posing in the photographs, and this photo-vaudeville apparition of the man born in 1931 dressed in the garb of 1931 applies a phantom signature spanning two discrete times in the multitemporal "between" of the text. Another handsomely achieved publication is *Altar Pieces* (1982) with collages by Patricia Nedds in a foldout from the center into three tableaux, with collages suspended above the texts of "Hunger" and "The Little Saint of Huautla," and shorter poems on the verso panels. A notable success among Rothenberg's forays into a performance context is the collaboration with Bertram Turetzky, who amplifies the poems of *That Dada Strain,* chanted and crooned by the poet, with vocalizations coaxed from his string bass.

While these performative and event-oriented structures, like the gematria, rely on inspiration and chance to some degree, they are primarily instances of method. The sense of practical application and industriousness is foremost. The most *inspired* of Rothenberg's work, on the other hand (for which "preparation" would be beside the point), is the long title

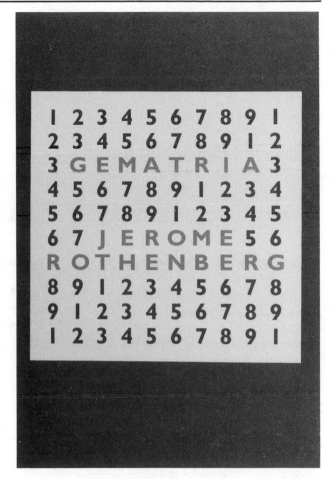

Cover for Rothenberg's 1994 book, a collection of numerological poems written according to "a variety of traditional coding practices used by the Jewish mystic-poets to establish correspondences between words or series of words"

sequence of *Khurbn.* (*Khurbn* is the Yiddish term Rothenberg prefers to holocaust, which he says in the book is "too Christian & too beautiful"). Yet here too there is collaboration of a sort—collaboration with the dead:

"practice your scream" I said
(why did I say it?)
because it was his scream & wasn't my own
it hovered between us

After *Poland/1931* Rothenberg was bound to come sooner or later to a reckoning with that open wound of the holocaust that Theodor Adorno suggested would invalidate poetry. Rothenberg's response is unflinching: "Our search since then has been for the origins of poetry, not only as a willful desire to wipe the slate clean but as a recognition of those other voices & the scraps of poems they left behind them in the mud." "Khurbn" is the paradoxical site of a renewal as it rehearses poetic origins, but at the same time it reasserts the motif of exile, particularly exile as corporeal displacement:

> Let a great pain come up into your legs (feel it moving like the earth moving beneath you)
> Let the earth drop away inside your belly falling falling until you're left in space
> Let his scream follow you across the millennia back to your table
> Let a worm the size of a small coin come out of the table where you're sitting
> Let it be covered with the red mucus falling from his nose (but only you will see it)
> Let the holes in his body drop open let his excretions pour out across the room

The grammar of "let" recalls Christopher Smart's "Jubilate Agno," along with the propositional formulae of logic and calculus. The result is a profound sense of brutality as uncannily familiar. By avoiding the customary resource of lamentation, which distances in its strategic familiarity, Rothenberg particularizes atrocity as a dismaying numbness. The recognition scenes enumerated in the poem are not repatriations or restorations but encounters with the *unheimlich* (the "unhomely," which is the German word for uncanny). Most striking about Rothenberg's poem of the death camps is his focus on place. Visiting his ancestral village in Poland, he was startled to discover that the site of a major concentration camp at Treblinka was only a few miles away. Rothenberg's preferred idiom, the panegyric, is here submitted to a necessary reversal. The accumulation of concrete details, rather than contributing to a coagulate of everydayness, leads instead to an emptying out, which is commensurate with the uncanny vacancy of the site where the concentration camp had been.

To adapt the masthead slogan of *Alcheringa* and *New Wilderness Letter,* Rothenberg affirms a mainstream of poetry borne along on a subterranean culture. This utopian model of an unproblematically healthy subculture lacked a vitalizing confrontation with the sacrificial violence at its roots—until "Khurbn," that is. "Khurbn" seems at this point to be the poem Rothenberg has been preparing for all along. Clayton Eshleman has called it "the great middle-length poem of our times." "Khurbn" also endows the poet's own earlier work with a premonitory character, drawing the threads of its emergent pattern more snugly together. It is a "major" poem, one that has the curiously beneficial effect of making Rothenberg's body of work look major as well; and because he is a poet who has insistently set his own criteria, the scale of his achievement is such that the entire enterprise of what poetry can be may have to be reconsidered in light of Rothenberg's precedent.

Interviews:

Mary Jane Fortunato, "Craft Interview with Jerome Rothenberg," in *The Craft of Poetry: Interviews from the New York Quarterly,* edited by William Packard (Garden City, N.Y.: Doubleday, 1974), pp. 37–51;

Barry Alpert, "Jerome Rothenberg—An Interview," *Vort,* 7 (1975): 93–117;

Kevin Power, "Conversation with Jerome Rothenberg," *Vort,* 7 (1975): 140–153;

The Riverside Interviews, 4: Jerome Rothenberg, edited by Gavin Selerie (London: Binnacle Press, 1984);

Frederick Garber, "Literacy and the Roots of Poetry: A Conversation with Jerome Rothenberg," *Forum* (Binghamton) (April 1987): 3, 6;

Manuel Brito, "An Interview with Jerome Rothenberg," *Revista Canaria de Estudios Ingleses,* 22–23 (1991): 235–246;

Karen Kaminker, "Questions of Meaning, Questions of Sound," *Subdream: The Vienna Journal of English Language Poetry,* 1 (November 1997).

Bibliography:

Harry Polkinhorn, *Jerome Rothenberg: A Descriptive Bibliography* (Jefferson, N.C., & London: McFarland, 1988).

References:

Paula Gunn Allen, "Uniting History in a 'Biological Fellowhood,'" *Contact II* (Fall 1978): 23;

Michael Castro, *Interpreting the Indian: Twentieth Century Poets and the Native American* (Albuquerque: University of New Mexico Press, 1983);

Paul Christensen, "Some Bearing on Ethnopoetics," *Parnassus,* 15 (1989): 125–162;

William Clements, "Faking the Pumpkin: On Jerome Rothenberg's Literary Offenses," *Western American Literature,* 16 (1981): 92–104;

Clements, *Native American Verbal Art: Texts and Contexts* (Tucson: University of Arizona Press, 1996);

Fedora Giordano, "Translating the Sacred: The Poet and the Shaman," in *American Indian Studies: European Contributions* (Gottigen: Herodot, 1981), pp. 109–121;

R. Barbara Gitenstein, *Apocalyptic Messianism and Contemporary Jewish-American Poetry* (Albany: State University of New York Press, 1986);

Gitenstein, "Coyote Cohen: Or, the Universal Trickster in Jerome Rothenberg's Evolving

Collection Poland/1931," *Studies in American-Jewish Literature,* 9 (Fall 1990): 176–185;

Judith Gleason, "Restorative Topographies: Notes on Ethnopoetics from a Province of the Mind," *Parnassus,* 11 (1984): 265–286;

Pierre Joris, ed., *Joy! Praise!: A Festschrift for Jerome Rothenberg on the Occasion of His Sixtieth Birthday* (San Diego: Ta'wil Books and Documents, 1991);

Hank Lazer, *Opposing Poetries* (Evanston, Ill.: Northwestern University Press, 1996);

Larry Levis, "Not Life so Proud to be Life: Snodgrass, Rothenberg, Bell, and the Counter-Revolution," *American Poetry Review,* 18 (1989): 9–20;

Eric Mottram, "Where the Real Song Begins: The Poetry of Jerome Rothenberg," *Dialectical Anthropology,* 11 (1986): 225–238;

Sherman Paul, *In Search of the Primitive: Rereading David Antin, Jerome Rothenberg and Gary Snyder* (Baton Rouge: Louisiana State University Press, 1986);

Marjorie Perloff, "The Contemporary of Our Grandchildren: Pound's Influence," *Ezra Pound Among the Poets,* edited by George Bornstein (Chicago: University of Chicago Press, 1985), pp. 195–229;

Perloff, "Soundings: Zaum, Seriality and the Discovery of the 'Sacred,'" *American Poetry* (February 1986): 37–46;

Roberts Peters, "Jerome Rothenberg: That Dada Strain," in *Great American Poetry Bakeoff,* third series (Methuen: Scarecrow Press, 1987): [XXX–XXX];

Jed Rasula, "On Rothenberg's Revised 'Technicians of the Sacred,'" *Poetics Journal,* 6 (1986): 135–140;

Henry Sayre, "David Antin and the Oral Poetics Movement," *Contemporary Literature,* 23 (1982): 428–450;

Sayre, *The Object of Performance: The American Avant-Garde Since 1970* (Chicago: University of Chicago Press, 1989);

Tadeusz Slawek, "Poland: Jerome Rothenberg's Readings of Emptiness," *Polish-Anglosaxon Studies,* 4 (1992): 207–218;

Vort, special issue on David Antin and Jerome Rothenberg, with essays and comments on Rothenberg by John Alley, Kenneth Rexroth, Robert Duncan, Armand Schwerner, Antin, Ian Tyson, Toronto Research Group, Gordon Brotherston, Donald Davie, Kevin Power, Eric Mottram, Harris Lenowitz, Charles Doria, John Bentley Mays, and Barry Alpert, 7 (1975): 118–191;

Diane Wakoski, "20th Century Music," *Parnassus,* 1 (Fall/Winter 1972); 142–147;

Eliot Weinberger, *Poetics, Politics Polemics* (New York: Marsilio, 1996);

John Zalenski, "Rothenberg's Continuing Revolution of the Word," *North Dakota Quarterly,* 55 (1987): 202–216.

Papers:

The major collection of Rothenberg's manuscripts is located in the Archive for New Poetry, University of California, San Diego.

Leslie Scalapino

(25 July 1947 –   )

Elisabeth A. Frost
Fordham University

BOOKS: *0 and Other Poems* (Berkeley, Cal.: Sand Dollar Press, 1976);

The Woman Who Could Read the Minds of Dogs (Berkeley, Cal.: Sand Dollar Press, 1976);

Instead of an Animal (Berkeley, Cal.: Cloud Marauder Press, 1978);

This eating and walking are associated all right (Bolinas, Cal.: Tombouctou, 1979);

Considering how exaggerated music is (San Francisco: North Point Press, 1982);

that they were at the beach—aeolotropic series (San Francisco: North Point Press, 1985);

way (San Francisco: North Point Press, 1988);

How Phenomena Appear to Unfold (Elmwood, Conn.: Potes & Poets, 1989);

The Return of Painting (New York: DIA Foundation, 1990);

The Return of Painting, The Pearl, and Orion: A Trilogy (San Francisco: North Point Press, 1991);

crowd and not evening or light (Oakland, Cal.: O Books/ Sun & Moon Press, 1992);

Defoe (Los Angeles: Sun & Moon Press, 1994);

Goya's L.A., a play (Elmwood, Conn.: Potes & Poets Press, 1994);

Objects in the Terrifying Tense / Longing from Taking Place (New York: Roof Books, 1994);

The Front Matter, Dead Souls (Hanover, N.H.: Wesleyan University Press, 1996);

Green and Black: Selected Writings (Jersey City, N.J.: Talisman, 1996);

Stone Marmalade, by Scalapino and Kevin Killian (Philadelphia: Singing Horse Press, 1996);

The Weatherman Turns Himself In (Canary Islands, Spain: Zasterle Press, 1996).

PLAY PRODUCTIONS: *leg,* San Francisco and Los Angeles, Poets Theater, 1985;

Or and *At Dawn,* New York, Eye and Ear Theater, 1989;

Fin de Siècle, San Francisco, ODC Dance Company, 1990;

The Present, San Francisco, New Langton Arts, 1993;

Leslie Scalapino, 1985 (photograph by Tom White)

The Weatherman Turns Himself In, San Francisco, The Lab, 1994;

Goya's L.A., San Francisco, New Langton Arts, 1995.

OTHER: *0/One in Anthology,* edited by Scalapino (Oakland, Cal.: O Books, 1988);

What Is Inside, What Is Outside?, edited by Scalapino (Oakland, Cal.: O Books, 1991);

Talking in Tranquility, edited by Scalapino and Stephen Ratcliffe (Bolinas, Cal.: Avenue B / Oakland, Cal.: O Books, 1991).

SELECTED PERIODICAL PUBLICATION–
UNCOLLECTED: "What / Person: From an Ex-
    change," by Scalapino and Ron Silliman, *Po-
    etics Journal,* 9 (June 1991): 51–60.

Among the most prominent of contemporary
avant-garde poets, Leslie Scalapino writes poetry,
prose, plays, and critical essays that challenge the
reader to reconceive literary form and its relation to
both personal experience and cultural politics. Her
book-length poems, fragmented and minimalist, reveal Scalapino's ties to practitioners of Language
writing–including Barrett Watten, Robert Grenier,
Carla Harryman, and Lyn Hejinian, all of whom
she has written about. Like other poets linked to the
Language group or, more broadly, to the Objectivist
tradition, Scalapino disputes the primacy granted to
the ego in much recent American poetry and initiates instead an innovative poetics of meticulous observation. In *Objects in the Terrifying Tense / Longing
from Taking Place* (1994) Scalapino explains her view
that "The current culture is produced in one as
one's inner self." That "inner self" is profoundly in
question in Scalapino's work: conventional subjectivity is replaced with what she whimsically calls the
"tiny self"–an ego diminished, though not necessarily denigrated–restored to its place in an infinitely
more vast social and phenomenological scheme.

Despite similarities to Language writing, however, Scalapino's work is far from typical of any particular movement. She herself traces much of her
thinking to quite a different source from poetic influences: her early immersion in Asian culture and
philosophy. Her formal innovations can be seen as
articulations of what she identifies in *Objects in the
Terrifying Tense* as an aspect of Zen: "In Zen practice
'appearances' which *are* the world are the same as
mind." Such questioning of the Western division between the conceptual and the experiential is fundamental to Scalapino's search for new poetic idioms.
Scalapino says in her spring 1996 interview in *Contemporary Literature* that she finds closure in poems
"completely stifling." In fact, Scalapino avoids both
fixed forms and the meditative short lyric, preferring instead what Joseph Conte in *Unending Design:
The Forms of Postmodern Poetry* (1991) calls "serial
form"–discrete units of text potentially infinite in
number, unconstrained by the basic linearity of a
beginning, middle, and end. Scalapino's repetitive
variations are anticipated in Gertrude Stein's 1914
prose poem *Tender Buttons,* as well as in the more recent work of Robert Duncan and Robert Creeley,
among others; the latter Scalapino discusses in
"'Thinking Serially' in *For Love, Words,* and *Pieces*" in
Objects in the Terrifying Tense. Scalapino's serial form

documents minute acts of observation: small blocks
of text, sometimes prose and sometimes the briefest
of lines, are set amid the impinging white space of
the page, unfolding intricate permutations that continually defy distinctions between external and internal "event." Scalapino summarizes her project in
How Phenomena Appear To Unfold (1989): "I am concerned in my own work with the sense that phenomena appear to unfold. (What is it or) how is it that
the viewer sees the impression of history created,
created by oneself though it's occurring outside?"
How individual perception creates historical narrative preoccupies Scalapino, along with what Gertrude Stein defined as the "continuous present," a
textual enactment of the immediate moment, which
Stein describes in "Composition as Explanation" as
"a constant recurring and beginning." Following
Stein's conception, Scalapino's writing concerns itself with processes unfolding. As she says in her *Contemporary Literature* interview, "I want the writing
simply to be finding out," so that, as she describes it
in her spring 1992 *Talisman* interview, "The form
creates what you're seeing."

Yet Scalapino's experiments are not solely
about what she calls in one essay "Pattern–and the
'Simulacral.'" On the contrary, she holds that social
convention is embedded in literary forms, especially
those involving gender and the body. Scalapino explains in her *Talisman* interview that her own writing
addresses social issues and that the erotic is a crucial
component: "If eroticism is eliminated, that leaves
only that social context, which has 'seen' it as sexist;
there is no area existing for apprehension or change.
We are split from ourselves." Indeed, seriality offers
a way to explore the nature of sexuality. Like other
modern and contemporary avant-garde women writers, Scalapino espouses a radically anti-essentialist
feminism that seeks to eliminate gender difference
and, through poetic innovation, imagine a state beyond fixed identities.

Leslie Scalapino was born 25 July 1947 in Santa
Barbara, California, to Dee Jessen Scalapino, a
singer, and Robert Anthony Scalapino, a political
scientist. Scalapino was raised in Berkeley, where
her father, who specialized in Asian politics, was a
professor at the University of California. Scalapino
states in the *Talisman* interview that she "grew up
with students or professors always living in the
house who were usually Chinese, Japanese, or Korean. . . . so we were always surrounded by these influences." On two different occasions–when Scalapino was seven and fourteen–the family traveled for
fifteen months in the Philippines, Taiwan, Japan,
Vietnam, India, Burma, Thailand, and Malaysia.
The second trip also involved car travel in the

Scalapino as a baby, with her mother and older sister, Diane

Congo, Kenya, Sudan, Egypt, and Jordan, as well as in Europe. Her early exposure to Asian history and philosophy sparked a lasting interest. She remarks in the *Talisman* interview, "On one of our fifteen-month trips to Asia, we took our books with us and did not go to school. . . ." Her father gave her "a book on Buddhism, which I read, and I was strongly affected by this." In recent years Scalapino has also traveled extensively—to India, Japan, Russia, Sudan, Egypt, and Yemen.

After earning a B.A. from Reed College in Portland, Oregon, Scalapino returned to Berkeley and received an M.A. in English from the University of California. Scalapino's anti-academic stance, apparent in her essays, may well have emerged during graduate school, which she describes in *How Phenomena Appear To Unfold* as "an experience so awful that it has not yet been erased from memory." At the same time as the bombing of Cambodia and the takeover of People's Park in Berkeley, Scalapino explains in the *Talisman* interview that she found herself in an "extremely conservative" academic department. In one course the professor "baited the women continually, telling the entire class, pacing up and down, screaming at us that women were not creative, could not be scholars, that they had inferior minds to men." In one particularly unpleasant incident she took an identification exam that the

professor later claimed showed that, by excelling at memorization, the women in the course had demonstrated their inferiority. Scalapino says this ordeal "was totally mixed in my mind with the sense of the war, and the tremendous contradictions of the kind of conventions we were asked to live in and my complete unwillingness or inability to do this. I understood this experience to be essentially ordinary, that such violence is always occurring." Scalapino's experiences in academia seem to have cemented her quarrel with both social and literary conventions, and she notes that she only started writing after she left graduate school. Nonetheless, Scalapino has gone on to teach at Bard College, Mills College, the San Francisco Art Institute, and the Naropa Institute. She married Wesley St. John in 1968 and divorced in 1973. Since 1986 she has been the editor and publisher of O Books, which she founded. Scalapino selects work by both seasoned and newer poets, with an emphasis on experimental and multi-genre works. The project, which she at first thought would be short-term, is a significant contribution to the publishing of alternative poetry. Scalapino lives in the San Francisco area with her husband, Tom White, whom she met in 1974 and married in 1987.

Scalapino's first major collection, *Considering how exaggerated music is* (1982), compiles three earlier small-press publications and several new serial poems. Unlike many poets, whose first publications tend to be derivative, even in her first book Scalapino develops highly original poetic forms. Particularly striking is the linking of formal considerations to sexuality and the body. In contrast to many Language writers, whose cerebral experiments shy away from musings about the body, Scalapino tackles the unease evoked by erotic subject matter. The opening series, *hmmmm,* consists of a series of surreal narratives that center on sexual fantasy, desire, and the sheer animality of the human body. (An epigraph reads, "This poem is dedicated to the Dog-Woman, who appeared to me in a series of dreams.") Unnamed characters appear in quoted dialogue and as speakers of self-contained accounts, each no more than a dozen or so lines, dotted with parenthetical statements, white space, and eccentric punctuation. Disrupting linear sequence, Scalapino's narratives are both flat in tone and provocative in subject, as in the following:

Haven't I said that part of having intercourse

Haven't I said that part of having intercourse
with anyone, is loving them when they are weak,
When they can't speak. When a woman, say, mews

(while being flipped over on her belly by a man) i.e.
if she utters some sound sort of like what a doll
makes, when *it's* flipped forward. What I mean by this
is: her eyelids, after flying open with her head
flipped back, will drop shut when her head is forward.
And in falsetto   (we might even say mawkishly),
the woman's mouth makes a sound like the word Mama.

Typical of much of *hmmmm* (and of *The Woman Who Could Read the Minds of Dogs*, 1976), this passage couples Scalapino's interest in extreme emotional states—especially those born from persistent desire—with her frequent depiction of human movement and speech as animalistic functions. As in all of Scalapino's work, this passage is the opposite of Confessional; this "I" is not identified with the poet. Scalapino defuses the potential feeling of intimate revelation by using a fictional frame. Rather than assuming a voice seemingly "overheard" solely by the reader (in the convention of lyric poetry), Scalapino fashions a scenario in which the speaker is addressing an unnamed listener. All the series in this volume evoke similar narrative contexts that consist not of plot events but of minute observations of a repeated act—in this case, the male speaker's account of a woman during intercourse. The act of speech is self-consciously referred to ("When they can't speak"), and the narrator himself seems utterly detached. His depiction of his partners resembles a voyeuristic revelation born from irrepressible curiosity—one that Scalapino's female speakers also share. Emptied of psychological depth, these voices are archetypes of desire: succumbing to a nonverbal, debilitating ecstasy, the woman reverts to infancy (making "a sound like the word Mama") and a still more primal sound: she "mews." As described by the speaker, the woman approaches the nonhuman, removed not just from the social world to which the erotic is frequently opposed, but also from her identity as a self-aware subject. Desire—or pleasure—has removed her from language, perhaps even from consciousness. As the mandates of the body claim her, language emerges as a secondary tool, an afterthought, the instrument of the observer.

Scalapino explores this liminal state throughout the volume. The many narrators in *Considering how exaggerated music is* describe animal sounds, from "kissing and barking" and "a bird's call" to a nagging desire to elicit a "yelp" from a passerby. In *The Woman Who Could Read the Minds of Dogs* a woman believes the movements she feels during labor come from "a foal / which was inside me and was kicking me with its four legs," while another speaker thinks "of a man / (someone whom I don't know) as being like a seal." In "*anemone*," the epilogue to *hmmmm,* the aroused body is described variously as "a plant,"

"the feelers of an anemone," and a fish, "as if it were about to swim up into the dark water above the bed." Defamiliarizing the female and male bodies, the bulk of *Instead of an Animal* (1978) is devoted to surreal imaginings of lactation and suckling, from "the as yet unweaned 12 or 15 year old" nursing to "the male opening his shirt in public, / and applying an infant to his chest as if he had breasts." This is writing that challenges the division between genders as well as between fantasy and reality; through its very detachment it requires the reader to consider the nature of our identity as human creatures.

These themes appear as well in *that they were at the beach—aeolotropic series* (1985), in which Scalapino develops with greater precision the use of repetition and permutation as a means to explore the moment-to-moment construction of experience. Key words and phrases recur in intricate patterns whereby new elements appear as others slowly diminish. Unlike the more autonomous sections of her first volume, the serial compositions in *that they were at the beach* are infinite forms that resemble the fluid, hypnotic repetitions of such "minimalist" composers as Steve Reich. The most ambitious section in this book is the title poem, which Scalapino identifies as an "aeolotropic series." Although Scalapino doesn't define this term, its characteristics are apparent. The clipped prose paragraphs, which are clustered in two's and three's on each page, include more abstract diction than the sequences in *Considering how exaggerated music is;* it becomes clear that these poems are about perception itself, troubling conventional representations of sequential events, especially causality. A fragmented syntax weaves together references that seem to suggest temporal and spatial clarity. Yet these recurring phrases ("in the foreground," "receded," "in the present," "contemporary in time," "retroactive," "in the past") never really situate the reader or the events. Instead, as Scalapino arranges them, they come to suggest that neither time nor place is truly fixed. Instead, Stein's "continuous present" is reiterated in a series of recurring events—girls playing ball, sailors entering a port, the driving and parking of a car. Each scene is poised on the edge of action as linear sequence is briefly asserted and then undermined. Apparently unrelated, these occurrences are woven together, presumably connected in a larger, unknowable scheme.

The first phrases in the poem, which introduce the first motifs, subvert linear thinking: "Playing ball—so it's like paradise, not because it's in the past." The reasoning implied by "so" and "because" never emerges, and even the language of simile ("like paradise") seems stretched to its logical limits,

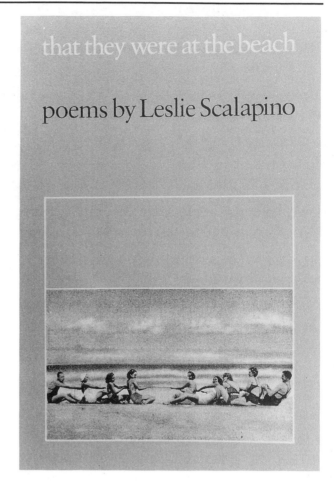

Front and back covers for Scalapino's 1985 book, poems that mock conventional notions of gender and sex

with little context for the comparison. Elsewhere as well analytical diction paradoxically leaves logic behind:

> Beginning to honk, because a man in a car behind me looked as if he were going to take my parking place, it's near shops, is crowded–I honked before seeing that he's old. And it appearing he hadn't wanted the parking place.
>
> (His being old not mattering because it's crowded–which is transparent, regardless of there being the one parking place–so it isn't sentient)

Here, as throughout the series, the terms "so" and "because" subvert the logical structures they posit, especially in conjunction with such elusive words as "transparent" and "sentient," with their uncertain referents. Causality is also subverted (why does crowding cause the man's age not to matter?). The title of one section suggests Scalapino's preoccupation with causal relationship: *"stemming from that–."*

Indeed, just what stems from what is at issue throughout *that they were at the beach*.

In his essay "Neither In Nor Out" (1992) Bruce Campbell reflects on the formal attributes that result from Scalapino's use of this shifting positionality. Scalapino's brief "frames" of text offer "perceptual" understanding. Although "what occurs within the frame is time-specific," "there is no meta-narrative" in these largely disconnected units: "while there is focus within the frame, there is no focus between frames." Campbell's observations are relevant to such series as *that they were at the beach,* in which Scalapino's form articulates the present moment from a variety of perspectives, each never fully available to another subject within the poem. Scalapino states in her *Talisman* interview, "My sense is of wanting to have the work and oneself be in present time, and not be anything else but that; the poem doesn't have any other existence except that form occurring."

As in *Considering how exaggerated music is,* Scalapino also explores the language of erotica. In Scalapino's mimicry of what she calls the erotica genre in "A sequence," an erotic scene between a couple is strangely defamiliarized, as "The parts of their bodies which had been covered by clothes were those of leopards." The bodies of the men and women, described in almost toneless prose, are deliberately objectified in moments of arousal by a speaker often recording the thoughts of an unnamed "she": "She compared the man to plants, to the plants having a nervous aspect and being motionless. The man coming when he had the sense of being delayed in leaving—as if being slowed down had made him come and was exciting, and it was during the afternoon with people walking around." The scenes replay, with episodes stressing both "feeling herself isolated" and "coming easily"; figures who seem "like herself" and those who are "different from" her. The breaking of sexual taboos underlines problematic relationships, as "sexual unions . . . between brother and sister" appear; similarly, an eroticized pregnant body dissolves the self/other distinction.

In the *Contemporary Literature* interview Scalapino describes her intention of using her characteristic repetitive form in "A sequence" to make the reader distinctly uncomfortable. Scalapino parodies easily consumable erotic writing to critique the linguistic and social conventions such generic constructs reflect: "It was making something be unromantic and essentially not palatable erotically. It's as though it were *just* erotica, with no point in it where you are describing any theory of what you're doing or any purpose—so that it would be completely identifiable with that genre. It would be revealing because of that." The tone is deliberately neutral: "The text is completely deadpan, flat. . . . It doesn't have depth, and because it doesn't have depth, you have a reaction to it." Her intention is to reveal the workings of domination in mass-consumed erotica. As in most of the compositions in *that they were at the beach*, "A sequence" develops the frequently abject depictions in *Considering how exaggerated music is*. Scalapino elaborates an intricate, highly controlled poetic grammar to explore explosive, nonrational forces.

way (1988), which won the American Book Award from the Before Columbus Foundation, raises again the issues of causality on the one hand and sexuality on the other as Scalapino's compositions become still more ambitious and more fragmented. The volume opens with a lengthy epigraph that provides a focus for the serial poems that follow. In an excerpt from *Causality and Chance in Modern Physics* (1957) physicist David Bohm asserts "the qualitative infinity of nature," according to which transformation is never-ending. Such a view of the universe leads to the radical conclusion that "because all of the infinity of factors determining what any given thing is are always changing with time, *no such a thing can even remain identical with itself as time passes.*" This notion of elemental flux is the point of departure of Scalapino's poems, which detail minute, ever-changing interactions.

The "way" of Scalapino's title implies Buddhist associations not dissimilar from the precepts of theoretical physics—in particular, the rejection of the Lockean concept of stable identity, supplanted by a belief in continual flux. But the title also suggests a more ironic reference to "way" as path, method, or means: as each series unfolds, emerging motifs center on the ills of the public sphere, a world in which the speaker observes hardship everywhere and seems powerless to effect change. In "Bum Series," "the men—when I'd / been out in the cold weather—were / found lying on the street, having / died—from the weather." And "no(h)—setting" tells of "the man crying out—whining—for / money from the people / walking by," "the people—whole / families—who'd gone to sleep on / the sidewalks," and "the thief—a boy / taking the grocery store / owner all the way into a / back room—having already / shot the guard—to shoot him." As though in response to the romanticized vision of the public park in William Carlos Williams's *Paterson* (1946–1958), *way* treats public places as sites of abjection. Yet the speaker of these abbreviated, deliberately awkward utterances rarely supplies commentary or even interacts with the figures described. Rendered analogous to the scenes she delineates, Scalapino's syntactic fragments contemplate the "way" that meaning is produced. Scalapino alternates between a prose line and extremely truncated verse lines, in which she breaks up syntax into particles of speech (suffixes, prefixes, articles), drawing attention to the neglected components of signification even as the poem explores the social ramifications of language-making.

Among the more self-contained of what Scalapino calls the "infinite series" that make up *way*, "The floating series" applies Scalapino's theoretical perspective to the division between sexuality and the public sphere. Alternating scenes of public and private exchanges in the poem require us to examine our investment in the separation of intimacy from the language of the marketplace. In Scalapino's playful allusions to the body, ordinary words take on sexual connotations, as in the motif of the "lily pad" and "bud": "the / women — not in / the immediate / setting / — putting the / lily pads or / bud of it / in / themselves // a man entering / after / having / come on her — that / and the memory of putting / in / the lily pad or the / bud of it first, / made her come."

How Phenomena Appear To Unfold

Leslie Scalapino

*Cover for Scalapino's 1989 book, which explores how
individual perception creates historical narratives*

The figures of the bud and lily pad recall Taoist icons of sexual organs. In Taoism, jadestalk, swelling mushroom, and dragon pillar represent the male, while jade gate, open peony, and golden lotus denote the female. Scalapino presents this iconography, which can be employed to praise God through a celebration of sexual parts, from the woman's point of view. In the notion of a "floating" form she also alludes to the amniotic experience linked to the female body. This detailing of what resides "in" or "on" the female body, often in the moment of climax, is also accompanied by attention to language as physical presence: the highlighting of prepositions and conjunctions on single lines permits us to pay heed to the connectives of language, to focus on words *as* words. Much like Stein, Scalapino makes language material, employs it for the pleasures of its textures and sounds, creating her own highly sensual grammar.

One of Scalapino's goals is clearly to provide an alternative to literary conventions used to portray sex, as she did in *that they were at the beach*. Yet, while the language in the earlier poem is deliberately flat, even "unpalatable" erotically, here Scalapino imagines a revitalized erotic language. In her *Contemporary Literature* interview Scalapino outlines an antiessentialist feminist stance that sheds light on this series:

> My articulation of feminism is in the gesture of trying to unravel how something is packaged or mirrored back to me—as part of the whole web of what's around us. . . . One's decisions about what one is as a formed being, as a woman for instance, are like placing the conclusion or the hypothesis on something before one has done it. It's a process of unraveling the hypothesis and the conclusion—there should *be* no hypothesis.

In service of this indeterminacy Scalapino destabilizes masculine and feminine positions in "The floating series": the lily bud, which initially suggests the penis, eventually suggests as well the clitoris—or, in more general terms, the sexual exchange itself. Her permutations enact a textual version of the "gender trouble" that theorist Judith Butler proposes as perhaps the most effective threat to an established heterosexual culture.

As "The floating series" continues, the poem moves beyond the couple to describe "people who're / there / already – though / the other / people aren't / aware of that." A political implication emerges, underlined in the next fragment: "not / being able to / see the / other people." Colonization and cultural invisibility are alluded to as the poem shifts from the conjoining of two—focused on the conventions of erotica—to a larger social context. Scalapino continues to juxtapose these sections—the woman and the man, using erotic language, and the anonymous "people" of the unnamed city. Eventually new words enter into the permutations, including "livelihood," "jobs," "high rents," "public figure," "small store," "race," "means," and "not enough." These terms alternate with motifs of the lily pad and bud as the man and woman engaged in their own *private* experience slowly become part of a larger, socio-economic picture. Like all of the series in *way*—including the theatrical "no(h)-setting"— "The floating series" reveals the extent to which, for Scalapino (unlike Modernists like Stein), the erotic is necessarily related to a larger social context.

In *crowd and not evening or light* (1992) Scalapino shifts from the longer poems of *way* to short series. The book reads as a single poem despite its nine sections (most only a few pages long), three of which are identified as plays. Scalapino's disjunctive style, in which dashes continually interrupt unfinished phrases, mimics the hesitancy and incoherence of thought: "can't imagine - what - someone's / protesting - or writhing - they - not with / change being relevant - or not - that kind of event - at / any time - and as grueling, deprivation / not existing - or that." Scalapino severs expected connections between words, keeping the reader guessing as to their referents. Similarly, such titles as "or" and "roll" suggest the experience of sound disassociated from conventional meaning, evoking many homophonic possibilities ("oar," and "role"). In this respect Scalapino focuses more fully than ever before on both the process of signification and the experience of "pure" sound.

And yet, as cerebral as the form appears, the motifs are just as frequently sensual as in Scalapino's earlier books. In particular, sexual and other adventures are alluded to in the first several series and plays of the volume. Among the motifs that enter Scalapino's permutations are bathers, a dog, a floating corpse, allusions to war, the radical youth group Weatherman, the avant-garde, nineteenth-century French poet Arthur Rimbaud, Japanese No(h) plays, and the motorcycle gang Hell's Angels. A "crowd" of social ramifications challenges the reader to evaluate the culture at large through ironic juxtapositions. In "as - leg" a portrait of a couple strolling down the street is followed by an account of the atrocities of war: "woman - in cart / but then killed for some / reason - by the men shouting / spitting - rubbed with shit - the women having been enslaved after / the war, the men dead - suffering, brutalizing / - humiliated, all of them - ." Although sections of *crowd and not evening or light* seem to be purely a linguistic experiment, the poem as a whole ultimately does confront the "suffering" and "brutalizing" that poetic language must engage—if not realistically "represent"—if it is to have an effect on readers' lives.

In addition to the erotic motifs that surface side by side with references to "rebellion" and social unrest (specifically Weatherman), Scalapino evokes differences between male and female opportunities for adventure in references to Rimbaud and stowaways. She also shows us women's strategies in the face of danger and degradation: "young / girl wanting to sell her / saxophone - which had been advertised - but her hitchhiking / home - a man had a peach can over his groin in his car / removing it - 'do you want to blow / me' - the girl - 'do you want to buy my saxophone' / the man had her get out of his car to go away." Scalapino emphasizes not just the speed of this encounter but also the disparity between the meaning of the same words—"blow" and "buy"—depending on the relative position of the speakers. Language may suggest power, but to speak does not guarantee that power; the humor of this exchange doesn't diminish the point that language involves the ability to set terms, according to hierarchical rules. Nonetheless, in this instance the girl succeeds in countering the man's sexual threat through language, making her the seller rather than the object of desire. Here, then, Scalapino implies that language can be reappropriated and turned toward alternative uses—much as in her poetry as a whole.

The most significant and provocative section in *crowd and not evening or light* is the final one, which occupies half the book's pages and supplies its title. A series of photographs (taken by Scalapino) is accompanied by handwritten phrases. The scrawled script (such as "drunks who are homeless wading in grass" and "people who've always been wealthy not knowing suffering") bears only an oblique relation to the photos, most of which are of groups of average-looking people at the beach. The everyday scenes suggest the "crowd" of the volume's title and, in their ordinariness, defy traditional standards for the art photograph. Neither posed nor produced in any way, the photos appear to be amateur snapshots—candid shots, awkward tourist pictures. Scalapino described the process of putting together this photographic series in her *Contemporary Literature* interview:

> I was using a cheap camera that focused automatically, and I'd not taken many pictures before. . . . I was trying to photograph people standing in the ocean—something that fascinated me was watching them as herds, a crowd of people, just standing and chatting with each other. I simply stood in one place and kept snapping the camera and didn't do anything to organize it. . . . The terrain is completely flat, and so are the photographs. They give the impression that everything's flat, that there's no inside to them. It was as if they give the inside of something else. I also wanted the photos to be a nonverbal surface that cannot be separated from the writing.

In exploring the dual surfaces of text and image, Scalapino once again blurs boundaries between the human and the animal, returning to a less erotic version of the motifs that comprise sections of *that they were at the beach*: the words "trunk" and "elephant" recur in conjunction with pictures of people, as though referring to the human body. The most surreal photographs show fields of cattle with words that suggest human privilege, as in "floating on those who have - nothing." The deliberate ambiguities of reference (are "we" the cattle? the innocuous bathers?) force readers to consider what it means to be human, or, more pointedly relevant to American culture, to "have - nothing."

The Front Matter, Dead Souls

A man vomits the blazing blue when he's black butterfly still flapping in it.

Leslie Scalapino

Dust jacket for Scalapino's 1996 book, which she calls a "political cartoon . . . in language"

Readers are also left uncertain as to how to "read" the images, often in dissonant relation to the text. On the one hand, this effect of disorientation suggests Scalapino's desire to defamiliarize the scenes of mass culture—the daily experience of being within a "crowd." On the other hand, Scalapino's images also subvert the notion of caption—of a line that summarizes a visual image—allowing for a more open-ended experience of both text and image. This rethinking of the visual implies as well that Scalapino's own text be considered not just discursively but for its imagistic qualities, particularly its disposition in scattered blocks on the page, mirroring the isolation of original acts of language in a culture saturated with information.

The social issues that have always preoccupied Scalapino take a more topical form in *The Front Matter, Dead Souls* (1996). Scalapino identifies this book as "a serial novel for publication in the newspaper" with "paragraph-length chapters" that "can also be published singly on billboards or outdoors as murals." This structure may seem more linear than

Scalapino's earlier work. But the epistemological language and elusive plot events—mixed with allusions to "real" figures, both political and artistic—lends *The Front Matter, Dead Souls* the quality of a work of theory more than of narrative. In her *Contemporary Literature* interview Scalapino brushes over generic distinctions, calling the book "a novel, really a poem," which "I began to write . . . as fast as I could at the beginning of the 1992 election campaign." She calls the project "a political cartoon . . . a cartoon in language, taking images as wild as possible, as extreme as possible, to be totally an expression of the actual event of the present time."

Scalapino acknowledges in her introduction that "Parts of it were submitted to various newspapers during the election campaign, though not accepted," and given Scalapino's elliptical style, the response may not seem unwarranted. Nonetheless, the topical motifs are easy to locate, from the Gulf War and the AIDS epidemic to the Rodney King trial, the confirmation of Justice Clarence Thomas, and the 1992 presidential campaign. The following, for example, is a pared-down version of the Gulf War: "While Bechtel is reconstructing the oil fields ours have bombed, in the oil fields their foreign workers who're treated like slaves are executed for sympathizing with their invaders. / Their foreign workers can't survive in their own countries. They will then work for Bechtel. / That's a poem." Scalapino's final sentence wryly indicates that her ambition includes both reflecting on political oppression and exposing the irrelevance and triviality of much contemporary poetry. Set in Los Angeles, Scalapino's surreal accounts involve a series of "characters," derived from a variety of sources, including stereotypical ones: there is a woman named Defoe, a Japanese woman named Dead Souls, a man called Akira (perhaps not coincidentally the name of a video game derived from a comic book), and a series of surreal images of a handsome sumo wrestler. This assemblage is situated in a culture of violent confrontation, corrupt policing, drug trafficking, and narcissistic self-absorption ("the bimbos that are men and women who are blond carrying boards floating with their legs in the air"). With its vacuous inhabitants and brutal street life, Los Angeles serves as a synecdoche for the United States as a world power out of control.

"I'm trying to write the modern world, which requires rewriting it," Scalapino asserts in the introduction, and in this rewriting she expands upon her opposition to predatory mass media, which package information for a passive audience of consumers: "The hyenas swarming for scraps are seen on the news, they're the anchormen." And, as in earlier collections, Scalapino juxtaposes scenes about physical violence with scenes impressionistically depicting heterosexual sex, noting in her introduction that "A dialogue about love is utterly crucial to the remaking of the modern world in writing." Yet despite its topical, political feel, *The Front Matter, Dead Souls* is also Scalapino's most self-referential book. Passages of artistic and philosophical commentary abound, including references to fellow artists ranging from H. D. and Jean Coctcau to contemporary poets Creeley, Grenier, Mei-mei Berssenbrugge, and others. Scalapino also comments frequently on the writing process: "Events are completely ephemeral. That's what I want. They're fabricated as such. Just keep going." Scalapino's compositional practice thus turns inward and outward at once—inward toward the act of writing and out toward the political world at large.

This combination of self-reflexive and highly topical passages seems to be a new preoccupation for Scalapino. In fact, *The Front Matter, Dead Souls* follows publication of Scalapino's play *Goya's L. A.* (1994), which presents virtually the same characters and motifs in a highly experimental, surreal montage of visual and verbal images. "This writing is scrutiny of our and 'one's' image-making," she notes in the introduction to *The Front Matter, Dead Souls* asserting once again, through the double meaning of "image," a fundamental connection between artistic forms and political realities. The real "event" in *The Front Matter, Dead Souls* is the reading experience itself—for if the writer can "isolate the shape or empty interior of some events real in time," then "To scrutinize their forms is to see the interior relation of experience." The text, then, flattens historical occurrences to provoke the reader into examining those external events (including political spectacle) as creations or reflections of consciousness itself. More than any other of Scalapino's texts, in *The Front Matter, Dead Souls* what *is* at the "front," or foreground, is in question: Scalapino's disjunctive style dislocates perspective and reorients the reader toward a potent internal reality. The political efficacy of such a gesture may be debatable. But Scalapino's intent is clearly to expose the emptiness of public spectacle and the near-extinction of our collective inner lives.

Recently Scalapino has published *Green and Black: Selected Writings* (1996), which includes several brief essays, excerpts from her novel "The Pearl," and selections from her long poems beginning with *that they were at the beach*. The book also includes two new works of poetry. There are excerpts from a poem called "New Time," soon to be published by Wesleyan University Press, and the poem "Green

and Black" appears in its entirety. The latter begins with what will become some of the poem's recurring motifs: "flowering gorges of black clear river meeting in wide separate green-clear-river." Such natural imagery is rare in Scalapino's work; its presence may in part represent homage to poet and novelist Philip Whalen, to whom part of the poem is dedicated. Yet there is also Scalapino's characteristic attention to the unfolding of the present moment, documented in the text itself: "there's no other to the / — horns begin — preceding apprehension // and perched there — as not apprehension 'only.'"

In "Note, 1996" from *Green and Black* Scalapino asserts a continuity in her writing by connecting her projects in "The Pearl" and the more recent *The Front Matter, Dead Souls*. Both are concerned with refuting, in poetic/novelistic form, what is essentially a Cartesian legacy—the pervasive belief that external and internal experience, "living" and "writing," are fundamentally divided. Scalapino's own perspective is closer to Zen philosophy. "One's physical motions," she writes, "are the same thing as their conception. Fictionalizing is the same as living"—or, as *New Time* affirms, "the mind is action literally, not departing from that—being events or movement outside, which is inside, so the mind is collapsing into and as action." Scalapino's claims for her work ring true, especially regarding the persistence of her theoretical concerns. From earliest to most recent, Scalapino's writings have focused on the collapse of generic distinctions as well as Western divisions between the conceptual and the experiential; equally prevalent is this poet's social engagement, especially with issues of sexuality, gender difference, and the unhealthy effects of consumer culture. Few recent poets combine these concerns, and certainly few create such consistently challenging and original forms. Compared to the many more traditional poets published by mainstream presses, Scalapino has a relatively small audience. One hopes that, if she continues to publish at her current swift pace, her audience will grow.

Interviews:

Ed Foster, "An Interview with Leslie Scalapino," *Talisman: A Journal of Contemporary Poetry and Poetics,* 8 (Spring 1992): 32–41;

Elisabeth A. Frost, "An Interview with Leslie Scalapino," *Contemporary Literature,* 37 (Spring 1996): 1–23;

Laura Hinton, "An Interview with Lyn Hejinian and Leslie Scalapino," *Private Arts,* 10 (Spring 1996): 47–77.

References:

Bruce Campbell, "Neither In Nor Out: The Poetry of Leslie Scalapino," *Talisman: A Journal of Contemporary Poetry and Poetics,* 8 (Spring 1992): 53–60;

Joseph M. Conte, "Seriality and the Contemporary Long Poem," *Sagetrieb,* 11 (Spring and Fall 1992): 35–45;

Stephen Ellis, "Lock-Step Chaos: Leslie Scalapino's Multiples of Time," *Talisman: A Journal of Contemporary Poetry and Poetics,* 8 (Spring 1992): 63–66;

Elisabeth A. Frost, "Signifyin(g) on Stein: The Revisionist Poetics of Harryette Mullen and Leslie Scalapino," *Postmodern Culture: An Electronic Journal of Interdisciplinary Criticism,* 5 (May 1995), n. pag.;

Edith Jarolim, "No Satisfaction: The Poetry of Leslie Scalapino," *North Dakota Quarterly,* 55 (Fall 1987): 268–275;

Susan Smith Nash, "Magic and Mystery in Poetic Language: A Response to the Writings of Leslie Scalapino," *Talisman: A Journal of Contemporary Poetry and Poetics,* 14 (Fall 1995): 90–100;

Marjorie Perloff, *Radical Artifice: Writing Poetry in the Age of Media* (Chicago: University of Chicago Press, 1991), pp. 49–51;

Stephen Ratcliffe, "Listening to Reading," *Talisman: A Journal of Contemporary Poetry and Poetics,* 8 (Spring 1992): 61–62;

Barrett Watten, "Political Economy and the Avant-Garde: A Note on Haim Steinbach and Leslie Scalapino," *Talisman: A Journal of Contemporary Poetry and Poetics,* 8 (Spring 1992): 49–52.

Jack Spicer
(30 January 1925 – 17 August 1965)

Edward Halsey Foster
Stevens Institute of Technology

See also the Spicer entries in *DLB 5: American Poets Since World War II* and *DLB 16: The Beats: Literary Bohemians in Postwar America.*

BOOKS: *After Lorca* (San Francisco: White Rabbit Press / London: Aloes Books, 1957);
Billy the Kid (Stinson Beach, Cal.: Enkidu Surrogate, 1959; Dublin: New Writers Press, 1969);
The Heads of the Town up to the Aether (San Francisco: Auerhahn Society, 1962);
Lament for the Makers (Oakland, Cal.: White Rabbit Press, 1962; London: Aloes Books, 1971);
The Holy Grail (San Francisco: White Rabbit Press, 1964);
Language (San Francisco: White Rabbit Press, 1965);
Book of Magazine Verse (San Francisco: White Rabbit Press, 1966);
The Red Wheelbarrow (Hove, Sussex: Peter Riley, 1968; Berkeley, Cal.: Arif Press, 1971);
A Book of Music (San Francisco: White Rabbit Press, 1969);
Admonitions (New York: Adventures in Poetry, 1974);
An Ode and Arcadia, by Spicer and Robert Duncan (Berkeley, Cal.: Ark Press, 1974);
Fifteen False Propositions Against God (South San Francisco: ManRoot Books, 1974);
The Tower of Babel (Hoboken, N.J.: Talisman House, 1994).

Collections: *The House that Jack Built: The Collected Lectures of Jack Spicer,* edited by Peter Gizzi (Hanover, N.H.: University Press of New England, 1998);
The Collected Books of Jack Spicer, edited by Robin Blaser (Santa Barbara, Cal.: Black Sparrow Press, 1975);
One Night Stand and Other Poems, edited by Donald Allen (San Francisco: Grey Fox Press, 1980).

Jack Spicer was born on 30 January 1925 in Los Angeles, where his father managed a hotel. The job provided a good income, and even during the Depression the family lived comfortably. Spi-

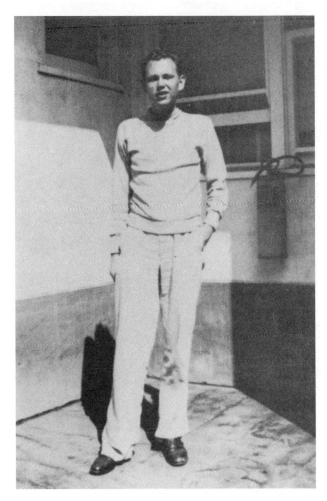

Jack Spicer

cer's only sibling was a brother, who became a college instructor and administrator in Missouri.

Spicer attended local schools and graduated from public high school. He was reared a Protestant and began his college career in a religiously affiliated college, the University of the Redlands. He claimed, however, that his life did not really begin until 1945, when he transferred to the University of California, Berkeley, and became acquainted first with Robin Blaser and then Robert

329

Duncan, poets who would remain among his closest associates.

Spicer is best known for *The Collected Books of Jack Spicer* (1975), which brings together all of his major work from 1957 until his death in 1965. A second collection, *One Night Stand and Other Poems* (1980), includes most of his shorter poems, but with the exception of his "Imaginary Elegies" (1950–1959) and short poems written in the last years of his life, he disowned all of these on the grounds that they were "filled (the best of them) with their own emotions, but pointing nowhere." He also wrote plays and a novel, *The Tower of Babel* (1994). He summarized his poetics in a series of four talks known as the "Vancouver Lectures," only the first of which has as yet been published.

Much of Spicer's poetry concerns problems in linguistic and poetic theory and as such has had great importance for ensuing generations of poets. He was also a mentor to many young writers with whom he met nightly at a workingman's bar, Gino's and Carlo's, in the North Beach section of San Francisco. Perhaps the most celebrated of those he encouraged was Richard Brautigan. Spicer died in the alcoholic ward of the San Francisco General Hospital 17 August 1965.

Spicer's poetry and poetics are largely concerned with questions of presence: the capacity or incapacity of words not merely to be labels, but in some fashion to *be* the things they name. Duncan told Spicer in 1951 that "to arrive at a great Poem we have to attack symbolism and insist upon the incarnation in the language." A poem, that is, should not merely represent or illustrate its subject but should also incarnate whatever it is that it speaks about.

In his book *The King's Two Bodies: A Study in Mediaeval Political Theology* (1957) the historian Ernst Kantorowicz, under whom Spicer and Duncan studied at the University of California, Berkeley, examined the medieval notion that a king was simultaneously both human, and therefore fallible, and God's vice regent: God's perfect law was made manifest through the person of the king. The phrase "the king's two bodies" in turn provides a useful metaphor for poetry of incarnation—the poem both as imperfect and infallible language and as expression of the poetically valid.

Spicer was well read in the literature of Calvinism, and its character, particularly its fatalism, entered his poetics. Above all Spicer believed that the poet did not act autonomously but "received" the poem much as an individual, according to Calvinist doctrine, received divine grace: neither the poem nor God's grace could be solicited or willed

into being but were bestowed for reasons, and from sources, that were ultimately mysterious and unknowable.

Spicer, Duncan, and Blaser formed the nucleus of a community of young poets in Berkeley in the late 1940s. All three sought a poetry of incarnation, but they pursued directions radically different from each other. For Duncan, the poem was part of a tradition, and it was the tradition itself, or the place of the poem in it, that was made manifest; "the poem," he wrote, "is thought of as a process of participating in a reality larger than my own, the reality of man's experience in terms of language and literature." Explaining Blaser's view, on the other hand, Duncan added, "the authority of [Blaser's] poetry must be first-hand"; the poet himself was in some manner manifest in the poem. (In fact, whatever Blaser owes to the Romantic view of poetry as self-expression, his poetics is also woven together with his Catholic background and his belief, like Spicer's, that poetry is a gift with inscrutable origins.)

Spicer at one point or another adopted both Duncan's poetics of tradition and a poetics of personal statement. Many of Spicer's early poems, such as "The Dancing Ape" and "When Your Body Brushed Against Me," are drawn directly from private or personal experience, and a poetics of tradition is evident, for example, in *After Lorca* (1957), which includes not only translations of poems by Federico García Lorca but also poems in which Spicer, for his own work, borrowed aspects of Lorca's sensibility. Spicer in much of his major work, however, sought roots and validation outside human experience and literary tradition: he desired poetry, as he said, "dictated" from "East Mars."

Spicer's poetry is complexly intertwined with his identity as a homosexual. Meeting Duncan for the first time, Spicer asked if Duncan knew anything about the homosexual circle, or "kreis," formed by the early-twentieth-century German poet Stefan George. The "Georgekreis" centered on memories of a young man, known in George's poetry as "Maximin," who had been his lover. Duncan had known a member of the kreis and was able to give Spicer an insider's account of its history and nature. In turn, as Ekbert Faas suggests in *Young Robert Duncan: Portrait of the Poet as Homosexual in Society* (1983), the kreis may have been the model for the circle of poets and intimate friends who surrounded Spicer, Blaser, and Duncan in the late 1940s.

The Georgekreis was in any case the inspiration for that circle of young poets, most of them male, who spent their evenings with Spicer at the bar Gino's and Carlo's. This community of writers provided its members with opportunities to pursue and discuss poetic objectives that might have seemed obscure or have been misunderstood in other quarters. Within the circle of friends, one had an audience that read the same books, shared interests, and had similar objectives in their writings.

Spicer also acquired from Duncan the notion of the serial poem–the concept, that is, of the long poem (or "book") as a series of interdependent short pieces. As Spicer wrote to Blaser in a letter defining the serial poem and included in *Admonitions,* written in 1958 and published in 1974: "Poems should echo and reecho against each other. They should create resonances." The first serial poem, as Spicer understood the term, was Duncan's *Medieval Scenes* (written in February 1948 and published in 1950); it is the prototype for works as various as Duncan's "Passages," Blaser's "Image-Nations" series, and all of the works in *The Collected Books of Jack Spicer.*

Duncan's *Medieval Scenes* also served Spicer as an early example of poetry of dictation. To write each of the poems in the series, Duncan took a line or passage from an essay or other work and used it as an epigraph for a poem that he then wrote spontaneously and fluidly as if it were dictated by some source outside himself. The notion of poetry determined by forces beyond the poet intrigued Spicer, who came to see the poet of dictation as a "radio" through whom the poem could pass into language.

Although *Medieval Scenes* was crucial to Spicer's development, his first interest in a poetics of dictation, according to Blaser in a note in the *Collected Poems,* can be traced to works by William Butler Yeats that draw on material seemingly dictated to his wife by unseen spirits while she was in a trance or asleep. Another important predecessor was Rainer Maria Rilke, whose "Duino Elegies" was a model for Spicer's "Imaginary Elegies."

Spicer's early poetry was encouraged by Josephine Miles, a professor in the English Department at Berkeley. Her own quite impersonal poems had great appeal for Spicer but were mocked or ignored by many poets in Berkeley and the rest of the San Francisco Bay area, particularly by those who, like Kenneth Rexroth, drew their poetics from Romantic models. (Rexroth thought Miles's poems were "small, very neat holes cut in the paper, a hole to a page.")

As individual and self-directed as both Miles and Spicer were, they followed poetic and scholarly paths that intersected at crucial points. Spi-

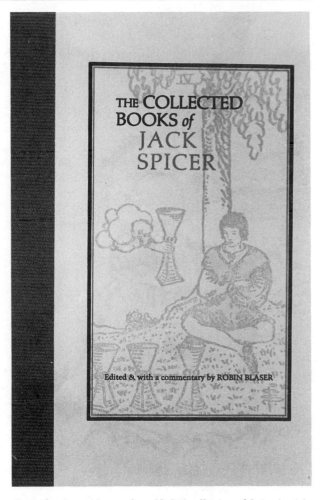

Cover for the posthumously published collection of Spicer's major writings between 1957 and his death in 1965

cer, who completed all but his dissertation in his work toward a Ph.D. in linguistics, was interested in regional and historical variations in the meanings and sounds of words. Perhaps this scholarly interest was at least in part stimulated by Miles's research into the poetic vocabularies of different eras. She was, she said, concerned with "the interrelationships of time and manner" and "the qualities and tempos of artistic change." As a graduate student, she had "deeply resented" the assumption "that each author wrote out of total power to choose what he wanted to say and how to say it, and that what was best said was most uniquely said." Like Spicer, she had no interest in the Romantic myth of the autonomous poet.

In the late 1940s the Romantic Emerson/Whitman poetic tradition had considerable appeal to Bay Area poets as otherwise dissimilar as Duncan and Rexroth. Spicer's poetry, on the other hand, was much closer to the work of French Symbolists such as Stéphane Mallarmé and writers whose work was in various ways indebted to his: George, Yeats, Rilke, Lorca, and T. S. Eliot, whose repeated insistence that poetry divorce itself from the poet's private self was deeply rooted in Mallarmé's concept of "La Poésie pure," or "pure poetry"–poetry that is its own justification. Spicer was not strictly a follower of Mallarmé's, but there are important temperamental affinities between Spicer's work and the work of those who were.

At first, however, Spicer saw his work in ways different from Mallarmé's. In 1949, for example, claiming that "pure poetry bores everybody," Spicer argued that there was "more of Orpheus in Sophie Tucker than in R. P. Blackmur." "Poetry," he said, "demands a human voice to sing it and demands an audience to hear it," a position fundamentally opposite from that of Mallarmé, for whom poetry was not something performed but intrinsic to the printed page. Spicer's view altered radically with time, however, so that in *Language* (1965), one of his last books, he declared, "No one listens to poetry"; poetry, he wrote in *After Lorca,* is "the pure word."

C. F. MacIntyre, the celebrated translator of Mallarmé, lived in Berkeley when Spicer was a student there. It is not known whether MacIntyre and Spicer met, but certainly they valued the French poet in different ways, and the differences are instructive. In the introduction to his Mallarmé translations, MacIntyre approvingly quotes Remy de Gourmont's statement "Mallarmé is the best pretext for reveries." Rexroth admired him for the same reason, but Spicer was deeply skeptical of reverie, in particular because of its capacity for presenting an agreeable, but false, image of the world.

Spicer's "An Arcadia for Dick Brown" is essentially a criticism of "L'Après-midi d'un Faune," Mallarmé's poetic revery in which he imagines a paradise of sexual pleasure. In Spicer's poem that paradise is surrounded by threatening, insidious creatures singing "oily hymns." In the protected (but also imprisoning) Arcadia, the speaker finds a faun whom he compares to Nijinsky (the dancer who took the part of the faun in a ballet based on the poem). He takes the faun in his arms and tries to fly out of the paradise/prison, but passing over the border, the faun slips out of his grasp and falls. Mallarmé's reveries, in other words, are always surrounded and threatened by the darker world around them, and the darker world ultimately wins.

"Pure poetry" is impersonal–not an expression of one's private feelings or sensibility. In *After Lorca,* Spicer criticized "the big lie of the personal," calling instead for a poetry of "real objects." By "real" he meant the collective identity that a word conveys rather than the singularity of a given thing in the world at large. "Things," he said, "do not connect; they correspond." Any lemon or boy in a bathing suit (to use his own examples) corresponds to a vast number of other lemons or boys in bathing suits, and the point at which all things of a certain type converge in a single word is where the poem has its seed. In arguing this, Spicer was merely following Mallarmé, who had pointed out that the flower in the poem was the perfect one that could not be found in nature.

In pursuing an impersonal poetry, Spicer also adopted Yeats's aesthetic of masks. Yeats often adopted a mask or identity counter to his own when writing a poem. The result is a merging of selves and, in this way, a poetry of greatly increased range. Spicer's "A Lecture in Practical Aesthetics," for example, borrows Wallace Stevens's vocabulary and cadences while simultaneously addressing and criticizing Stevens for his insularity, for existing in an imagined world "Out of sense and sight." The poem is both about Stevens and, insofar as it uses his cadences and diction, by him.

Translation inevitably requires the poet to adopt a mask, and early in his work Spicer began experimenting both with direct translations (as in his version of Rilke's "The Panther") and adaptations of other poets' works. "Orpheus After Eurydice," for example, is in part derived from Rilke, but it is not a direct translation. Spicer also wrote an adaptation of Euripides' fifth-century B.C. *Bacchae* and dramatic versions of Geoffrey Chaucer's *Troilus and Criseyde* (circa 1385) and the early-fourteenth-century romance *Sir Orfeo,* but his major, and most complex, work of translation is *After Lorca,* in which masks are utilized in radically different ways. In an introduction supposedly written by Lorca twenty years after his death, he says that Spicer, even in translations generally faithful to the original, added or changed a word or two, thereby altering the original moods and, often, the meanings. Other poems, says "Lorca," fuse material from his work with Spicer's own, "giving the effect of an unwilling centaur." "Lorca" also says that he wrote some of the other poems after his death. There are also poems that are completely Spicer's. The book, in short, includes a range of identities from "pure" Lorca to "pure" Spicer, but as these merge into one serial poem, the book in effect asks who the "true" author is. *After Lorca* is a complex exercise in masks; the various modes of translation provided means through which Spicer could abstract himself in various ways from a personal and subjective voice.

After Lorca marked the beginning of Spicer's major phase as a poet and an expanded effort to reach a poetry which could be "pure" and impersonal. Either it would incarnate an "other"–the voice from East Mars–or at the least would merge the other and the poet in Yeatsian fashion. Perhaps the most highly regarded of the works that resulted is *The Heads of the Town up to the Aether* (1962), which concludes, however, that a "pure," impersonal poetry is impossible. The poem strives for "logos" and settles for what Spicer calls a "Lowghost."

Given the concern with poetry that assimilates, or is assimilated by, an "other," it is not surprising that much of the later work is so deeply concerned with love or, more commonly, its absence. Spicer's "Three Marxist Essays" concludes that homosexuality is "essentially" solitude, but desire remains: "There is real pain in not having you just as there is real pain in not having poetry," he wrote in *Language*. Poetry and "the heart" are both trapped in conventions that prevent them from being expressed, made manifest, or made incarnate. As a result, both need a new language, one that is "ungrammatical," according to *Language*, one, in short, that can break the barriers that restrain them.

In Spicer's unfinished novel, *The Tower of Babel*, the protagonist discovers a new language through desire. A professor from an Eastern college and a thoroughly conventional poet, he realizes a new way of writing poetry when he falls in love with a young man during a visit to San Francisco. The irony is that the protagonist is not conscious of how deeply he is attracted to the other man, and their relationship is not consummated. During his early years as a poet, Spicer joined Duncan and Blaser in cultivating an erotics of "not touching"; sexual desire was directed away from its object and to the poem. In effect, *The Tower of Babel* proposes "not touching" as one way to achieve a new poetry, but the cost, of course, is tremendous.

Spicer himself maintained few intimate relationships during his life. Although he spent most of his time each day with younger poets, he generally returned home alone. But in that solitude he was comparatively free of convention and the "grammatical." Spicer's poetry correspondingly exists in an extreme reach of anarchism and independence. He worked within matrices–vocabularies, a kreis, or the serial poem–but the overriding

reality was solitude, within which he could reach toward a new language or poetry, turning of its own accord, and for its own unstated ends, in pure Mallarméan space.

Bibliography:

Gary M. Lepper, "Jack Spicer," *A Bibliographical Introduction to Seventy-Five Modern American Authors* (Berkeley, Cal.: Serendipity Books, 1976), pp. 379–382.

Biographies:

Robert Duncan, *As Testimony: The Poem & the Scene* (San Francisco: White Rabbit Press, 1964);

James Herndon, *Everything as Expected* (San Francisco: Privately published, 1973);

Joanne Kyger, *The Dharma Committee* (Bolinas, Cal.: Smithereens Press, 1986);

Lewis Ellingham and Kevin Killian, *Poet Be Like God: Jack Spicer and the San Francisco Renaissance* (Middletown, Conn.: Wesleyan University Press, 1998).

References:

Acts, special Spicer issue, 6 (1987);

Robin Blaser, "The Practice of Outside," in *The Collected Books of Jack Spicer* (Santa Barbara, Cal.: Black Sparrow Press, 1975), pp. 271–329;

Boundary 2, special Spicer issue, 6 (1977);

Bruce Campbell, "We Miss What We Hit: Jack Spicer's *Collected Books*," *Sagetrieb,* 8, nos. 1–2 (1989): 69–81;

Caterpillar, special Spicer issue, 12 (1970);

Lori Chamberlain, "Ghostwriting the Text: Translation and the Poetics of Jack Spicer," *Contemporary Literature,* 26 (1985): 426–442;

Samuel Charters, "Jack Spicer," in *Some Poems/Poets: Studies in American Underground Poetry Since 1945* (Berkeley, Cal.: Oyez, 1971), pp. 37–45;

Joseph Conte, "The Dark House: Jack Spicer's Book of *Language*," in *Unending Design: The Forms of Postmodern Poetry* (Ithaca, N.Y. & London: Cornell University Press, 1991), pp. 105–121;

Maria Damon, "Jack Spicer's Ghost Forms," *New Orleans Review,* 19, no. 1 (1992): 10–16;

Christopher Dewdney, "Some Statements on Whorf, Spicer, Morphemes, & 'A Palaeozoic Geology of London, Ontario,'" *Open Letter,* 7 (1974): 44–47;

Robert Duncan, preface to *One Night Stand and Other Poems,* by Spicer (San Francisco: Grey Fox Press, 1980);

Norman H. Finkelstein, "Jack Spicer's Ghosts and the Gnosis of History," *Boundary 2,* 9 (1981): 81–100;

Finkelstein, "'Princely Manipulations of the Real' or 'A Noise in the Head of the Prince': Duncan and Spicer on Poetic Composition," *Sagetrieb,* 4 (1985): 211–223;

Finkelstein, *The Utopian Moment in Contemporary American Poetry* (Lewisburg, Pa.: Bucknell University Press, 1988);

Edward Halsey Foster, *Jack Spicer* (Boise, Idaho: Boise State University, 1991);

Ironwood, special Spicer issue, 28 (1986);

Dawn Kolokithas, "On Jack Spicer," *Mirage,* "Santa Barbara" issue (unnumbered, undated): 46–55;

Manroot, special Spicer issue, 10 (1974/1975);

Paul Naylor, "Where Are We Now in Poetry?," *Sagetrieb,* 10, nos. 1–2 (1991): 29–44;

Miriam Nichols, "The Poetry of Hell: Jack Spicer, Robin Blaser, Robert Duncan," *Line,* 12 (1988): 14–41;

Frank Sadler, "The Frontier in Jack Spicer's 'Billy the Kid,'" *Concerning Poetry,* 9 (1976): 15–21;

Ron Silliman, "Spicer's Language," in *Writing/Talks,* edited by Bob Perelman (Carbondale & Edwardsville: Southern Illinois University Press, 1985), pp. 166–191;

Gilbert Sorrentino, "Jack Spicer," in *Something Said* (San Francisco: North Point Press, 1984), pp. 49–67.

Papers:
There are major collections of manuscript materials by and about Spicer at the Bancroft Library at the University of California, Berkeley; the Poetry/Rare Books collection at the State University of New York at Buffalo; and the University of California, San Diego.

John Taggart

(5 October 1942 –)

Mark Scroggins
Florida Atlantic University

BOOKS: *To Construct a Clock* (New Rochelle, N.Y.: Elizabeth Press, 1971);

Pyramid Canon (Providence, R.I.: Burning Deck Press, 1973);

The Pyramid Is a Pure Crystal (New Rochelle, N.Y.: Elizabeth Press, 1974);

Prism and the Pine Twig: An Interlude (New Rochelle, N.Y.: Elizabeth Press, 1977);

Dodeka, introduction by Robert Duncan (Milwaukee, Wis.: Membrane Press, 1979);

Peace on Earth (Berkeley, Cal.: Turtle Island Foundation, 1981);

Dehiscence (Milwaukee, Wis.: Membrane Press, 1983);

Le Poeme de la Chapelle Rothko (Châtillon-sous-Bagneux, France: Editions Royaumont, 1990);

Loop (Los Angeles: Sun & Moon Press, 1991);

Prompted (Kent, Ohio: Kent State University Libraries, 1991);

Aeschylus/Fragments (Tuscaloosa: Parallel Editions, 1992);

Remaining in Light: Ant Meditations on a Painting by Edward Hopper, foreword by Dore Ashton (Albany: State University of New York Press, 1993);

Standing Wave (Providence, R.I.: Lost Roads Publishers, 1993);

Tauler Sentences (Tuscaloosa: Lagniappe Press, 1993);

Songs of Degrees: Essays on Contemporary Poetry and Poetics, foreword by Marjorie Perloff (Tuscaloosa & London: University of Alabama Press, 1994);

Crosses (Los Angeles: Sun & Moon Press, 1998).

OTHER: *MAPS,* a literary magazine edited by Taggart, nos. 1–6 (1966–1974);

"Stone," in *Burning Deck Postcards: The Second Ten* (Providence, R.I.: Burning Deck Press, 1977);

Introduction to a special Theodore Enslin issue of *Truck,* edited by Taggart, no. 20 (1978);

"Were You: Notes and a Poem for Michael Palmer," in *Code of Signals: Recent Writings on Poetics,* edited by Michael Palmer (Berkeley, Cal.: North Atlantic, 1983), pp. 22–44;

"An Essay on the Sculpture," in *Sculpture of Bradford Graves* (Washington, D.C.: Georgetown University Intercultural Center, 1986);

"Of the Power of the Word," in *Conversant Essays: Contemporary Poets on Poetry,* edited by James McCorkle (Detroit: Wayne State University Press, 1990), pp. 59–64.

SELECTED PERIODICAL PUBLICATIONS–UNCOLLECTED:

POETRY

"Emily Dickinson in Goldenrod" and "Rupert Brooke Declaiming Poetry," *Crucible* (Winter 1965);

"Upon the Sweeping Flood," "An Egyptian Cat," and "Evening With Anna Akhmatova," *Crucible* (Spring 1965);

"A Marriage," *Poetry Handbill* (Summer 1965);

"Verses On An Ionian Analogy," "Ode on the Battle of Dannae," and "Ode on the Birds of Evil Omen," *Occidental Review,* 4 (1965);

"On the Death of Willis," *Phoenix* (1965);

"Passive Girl Reading," *Io* (1965);

"Georgia O'Keefe's Breasts which remember much forgetfulness," *Hyphen,* 3 (1967);

"One True Love," *Sumac* (1969);

"Winter, Radio Poem," "In My Father's House," "A Few Words for Stockhausen's Klavierstuck VI," "Augenblick," "Please forward if moved," "Replay," "There Was a Cat," "Shell," and "K Variations," *Origin,* 14 (July 1969);

"We Are Not Taken by Your Impeccable Manners, Corot," *North American Review* (Winter 1969);

"Dancing Lesson For Timid Or Tall Gentlemen," *North American Review* (Summer 1970);

"In Chicago," *Beloit Poetry Journal* (1970);

"Death-Bean Agent," *Origin* (1970);

John Taggart in his study, 1998

"Kore's Sleep Song," *Tuatara* (Summer 1970);

"Christopher Columbus and the Cigar Factory at Key West," *Quarterly Review of Literature*, 17 (1970);

"Waiting for Things to Become Clear," *Athanor* (Winter 1971);

"My Daughter Gives Me a Drawing," *Elizabeth* (1971);

"A Young White Man Steps Out of His Shower," *Massachusetts Review* (Spring 1971);

"Walking and Running," *Tottel's* (1971);

"According to Petrie's Survey," *Tottel's* (1971);

"Cube," *Curtains* (1973);

"Where I Live" and "A Disease Called Take-Off," *Occurence*, 1 (1974);

"The Weight," *Bartleby's Review*, 4 (1975);

"Rub Her Coke," *Painted Bride Quarterly*, 2 (1975);

"They and We," "Tsuzumi," and "After-Image," *Stations*, 3 & 4 (1976);

"Remote Flowers" and "The Young Poets," *Three Rivers Poetry Journal*, 7 & 8 (1976);

"Die Logik," *Poetry Review*, 67 (1977);

"Contrafact," *Earlhamite: Magazine of Earlham College Alumni*, 98 (Fall 1977);

"How to Find a Poem," *Poetry in Public Places* (1978);

Translation of Sappho's first fragment, *Hawk-Wind*, 2 (1979);

"On LZ," *Number Magazine* (1980);

"Not This, Not That," *Chicago Review* (1980);

"Sine Cura, Securum," *Multiples* (1983).

NONFICTION

Review of *Forms: Coda* by Theodore Enslin, *Back Door*, 7 & 8 (Spring 1975);

Review of *Primitive* by George Oppen, *Chicago Review* (Winter 1978);

"Two Possibilities, Neither of Which Offers What is Desired," *Montemora*, 5 (1979): 113–115;

Review of *A Still Life* by Thomas A. Clark, *L=A=N=G=U=A=G=E* (1980);

"An Environment is Any Space We Inhabit," *Difficulties* (1980);

"The Use of '*A*'" (review of Louis Zukofsky's "*A*"), *Boundary 2: A Journal of Postmodern Literature*, 9 (Winter 1981): 291–293;

"An Open Letter to Donald Davie," *Jimmy and Lucy's House of 'K'*, 5 (1985);

"George Oppen and the Anthologies," *Ironwood*, 13 (Fall 1985): 252–262;

Review of *Five Kwaidan* by Karl Young, *Archive Newsletter* (1987);

"Where All Beauty Resides: Surface/Texture in the Fiction of Toby Olson," *Review of Contemporary Fiction* (1991);

"The Poem as Instruction," *Anthology of North American Ideophonics* (1993);

"Ending in Ellipsis, the Sea in Our Ears: Robert Creeley's *The Island*," review in *Contemporary Fiction*, 15 (Fall 1995): 127–136;

"Approaching the Mountain," *Papers on Language & Literature*, 32 (Spring 1996): 213–216.

Taggart, Toby Olson, and another student at Aspen Writers Workshop, summer 1965

John Taggart is one of the most important figures of what one might call the third generation of twentieth-century American experimental poets. He grew up with the innovations of the High Modernists—Ezra Pound, T. S. Eliot, and Wallace Stevens—as a set of achievements almost too obvious to be acknowledged. Taggart turned for more immediate stimulus to the works of poets born in the first decade of this century, Louis Zukofsky and Charles Olson, and to an even younger group who followed them, including Robert Duncan and William Bronk. But Taggart's poetry is unusual among that of his contemporaries, for he has avoided both the talky, conversational poetics of the poetry workshop and the hypertheoretical technicalization of the art advocated by the proponents of Language poetry. Instead, he has with uncompromising single-mindedness pursued a poetics of both musicality and vision, exploring through his work aspects of the spiritual—even the religious—that have almost disappeared from contemporary verse. The critic Marjorie Perloff, in her introduction to Taggart's collected essays, describes his as "a vision based on invocation and incantation—an intricate incantation produced by permuting sounds and stillness in ways

that recall John Cage or Jackson Mac Low rather than the Eliot or Stevens who are Taggart's acknowledged mentors." The "incantation" of Taggart's work, its compelling marriage of repetition and variation, is indebted to specific musical models in both jazz and classical traditions, but there is nothing else like it in contemporary American poetry, and little that compares to it in intellectual density and emotional depth. His is a poetry that has questioned and sought to plumb the relationship of the human and the spiritual in ways that have analogues, not in twentieth-century poetry, but in the music of John Coltrane and Carlo Gesualdo, or the paintings of Edward Hopper, Mark Rothko, or Hans Memling.

Taggart was born in Perry, Iowa, on 5 October 1942 to Darrell F. and Pauline Farwell Taggart. His father was a Methodist clergyman who had served several churches in north and central Indiana. This religious connection must surely have had a lasting impact on Taggart, for the imagery and language of the Christian faith (especially the language of the classic Methodist hymns) are integral to his poetry, as is a sense of the possibility of attaining to the numinous through language and through concentration of sound. While he read widely as a child, Taggart did not consider himself a writer, much less a poet, until he entered high school, where he became involved as a high school newspaper and yearbook editor. He was encouraged by an English teacher he describes as "both imaginative and demanding," Joseph Casey. Perhaps as importantly, in high school Taggart became fascinated with rhythm and blues music, an interest that would eventually lead him to jazz—rhythm and blues' more intellectual cousin. Taggart's fascination with African American music has endured to this day and has developed in tandem with his growing knowledge of Western classical music. His knowledge of and relationship with music in large part dominates his poetry and his conception of how the word can operate upon the human soul.

Taggart entered Earlham College as a philosophy major but eventually changed his major to English. He was at this time writing fiction modeled after the French *nouveau roman* but eventually became impatient with what he describes as the "furniture-moving demands of prose narrative" and began writing poetry exclusively. Spurred on at Earlham by yet another "imaginative and demanding" English instructor, Kathleen Postle, Taggart published both fiction and poetry in *Crucible,* the campus literary magazine. After pursuing research during his junior year on Henry Miller and the "Whitman tradition" and writing a senior thesis on Stevens, Taggart graduated with honors in 1965. The summer between his junior and senior years at Earlham, Taggart had attended the Aspen Writers summer workshop, and the following year he returned as a staff member. At Aspen he studied with the poet Paul Blackburn and first made the acquaintance of fiction writer and poet Toby Olson, a long-standing friend. Perhaps more crucially, during his senior year at Earlham, Taggart started his own poetry magazine, *MAPS. MAPS* had only a brief life—six issues over a ten-year span—and a tiny print run, but it remains almost legendary for the quality of its editing. It metamorphosed early on from a poetry magazine into a journal which included criticism. Eventually Taggart edited special issues devoted to the work of David Smith, Robert Duncan, Charles Olson, Louis Zukofsky, and John Coltrane, some of which remain indispensable sources of commentary on their subjects.

Taggart went from Earlham to the University of Chicago as a Ford Foundation Fellow in an English/creative writing master's program. While he did not find much of interest happening there in terms of contemporary literature, he continued reading widely, making his first serious effort at reading Zukofsky. Zukofsky, a member of what one could call a second generation of modernist poets (born 1904), was an immensely complex and musical poet who had yet to receive *any* attention in the academy. Zukofsky's work proved crucial to Taggart's own poetics. At Chicago he also listened to a great deal of jazz, Ornette Coleman and Coltrane in particular, and made friends with classmate David Melnick—a philosopher, Zukofsky scholar, and quite extraordinary poet later associated with the San Francisco Bay-area Language poets.

Taggart received his M.A. in 1966 and—having happened to meet poet Donald Justice, who was leaving a position at the University of Iowa for Syracuse University—took Justice up on his invitation to study with him at Syracuse. Syracuse, however, did not offer a Ph.D. in creative writing, so Taggart changed to the Interdisciplinary Humanities Studies Program (which awarded him his degree in twentieth-century literature, fine arts, and creative writing). He initiated a correspondence with Cid Corman, editor of the important journal *Origin,* and Corman urged Taggart to write on Zukofsky, with whom Corman had a long-standing friendship and correspondence. (Corman would eventually publish Taggart in *Origin.*) At Syracuse, Taggart was also becoming acquainted with the work of Zukofsky's fellow Objectivist poets, in particular George Oppen, who was eventually to become a major influence on Taggart's writing. Taggart's interest in Oppen and particularly Zukofsky led eventually to a dissertation, "Intending a Solid Object: Objectivist Poetry and Poetics" (completed in 1974), which was the first dissertation to be devoted to Zukofsky's work. Pound/Williams scholar Walter Sutton was Taggart's dissertation director. Aside from his work with Sutton, Taggart did most of his course work with the musicologist and art historian Abraham Veinus.

When he had completed his graduate courses, Taggart accepted a teaching position at Shippensburg State College in Pennsylvania (now Shippensburg University) in 1969, where he has remained ever since. In 1966 Taggart married Jennifer Anne James; they have two daughters, Sarah Rose Taggart (born 1967, an artist and jewelry maker) and Holly Kathleen Taggart (born 1970, a museum curator). Taggart's teaching duties involve a combination of creative writing and literature courses; among the latter, he has most frequently taught the courses Shakespeare, Hawthorne/Melville/Poe, and Introduction to Graduate Studies. Taggart has been involved in revising the undergraduate and graduate curricula of his department and has designed and serves as director of an undergraduate interdisciplinary arts program. He and his wife live in a charming refurbished farmhouse, some miles outside town, among Taggart's extensive library, an impressive battery of pipes, an extraordinary collection of recorded music, and a succession of large, half-tamed retrievers.

Stevens, the poet whom Taggart claims (perhaps paradoxically) to be the "primary" twentieth-century American poet, writes that poetry is "the scholar's art," and all of Taggart's own poetry bears the stamp of his concurrent researches in music, art, and the poetics of earlier masters. The poems in his earliest collection, *To Construct a Clock* (1971), are clearly indebted to Zukofsky's shorter poems and to the statements of poetics that Zukofsky published in support of the short-lived Objectivist "movement" of the early 1930s. Zukofsky had prescribed two protocols for the poet: "sincerity," a scrupulous attention both to the subject matter with which the poem deals and to the language with which the poet constructs the poem itself; and "objectification," the concatenation of individual moments of sincerity into a tangible, objectlike whole. The poems of *To Construct a Clock* are correspondingly terse, specific, and taut. Zukofsky's influence is most apparent in the final poem, "Liveforever: Of Actual Things in Expansion," which draws upon Zukofsky's repeated image of "liveforever," a succulent plant of the *Sedum* genus, and is preceded by a lengthy epigraph from Zukofsky. Taggart's interest in the visual arts is also evident in such artwork-based poems as "Miro's 'The Kiss,'" "Corot's 'Woman With Child,'" and "Eroded Rock, 1942," based on an Edward Weston photograph. Taggart's long-standing involvement with jazz resulted in "The Drum Thing," a poem based on a performance from John Coltrane's album *Cresent*. In *To Construct a Clock,* however, Taggart had not yet achieved the relationship between poem and music he later sought: the music was more "an instigation, a prompting to begin, than a complete template." Nonetheless, Taggart said, "The Drum Thing" was "the first poem that truly pleased me," the first to have "an object existence of its own."

Taggart's 1977 volume, *Prism and the Pine Twig: An Interlude,* seems a return to the relatively straightforward presentational style of *To Construct a Clock,* in marked contrast to the works that precede and follow it, *The Pyramid Is a Pure Crystal* (1974) and *Dodeka* (1979). *Prism and the Pine Twig* includes such topographical poems as "The Black Puritan Trees of Pennsylvania," poems to Taggart's wife ("Jennifer's Poem") and daughter ("Sixth Birthday Poem for Holly, My Daughter"), whimsical moments such as "Square Order Shuffle"–"Watch me while you can. //

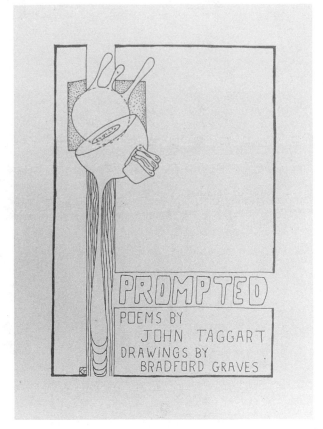

Cover for Taggart's 1991 collection of "jazz" poems

I'm the last / of the tap-dancing calvinists"–and in "Ars Poetica: The Palace of Crystal," self-deprecation of his most recent project: "I know what I have made / and I say // piss on it / piss on the palace of crystal."

Notwithstanding such half-serious reservations, Taggart was deadly serious about the complex procedural compositional methods that produced *The Pyramid Is a Pure Crystal* and *Dodeka*. In a 1979 interview in *Paper Air* magazine, Taggart noted how he was initially attracted to Zukofsky by the "infinite care that was evident in the poem," and by the possibilities, explored in such shorter works as "Songs of Degrees" and in Zukofsky's long poem *"A,"* for organizing a poem on musical principles. Particularly attractive to him was Zukofsky's notion of "fugal" form, in which the elements of the poem proceed out of a single "subject" and work variations thereon. In "A"-6, Zukofsky asks, *"Can / The design / Of the fugue / Be transferred / To poetry?"* and Taggart has eloquently analyzed both how the early movements of *"A"* seem quite self-consciously to adapt structures of the baroque fugue and how a fundamentally fugal principle underlies Zukofsky's later work. *The Pyramid Is a Pure Crystal,* which is

Dust jacket for Taggart's 1991 collection that includes "The Rothko Chapel Poem"

dedicated to Zukofsky, is a large-scale canon (in the musical sense) taking as its foundation, or cantus firmus, the single sentence "the pyramid is a pure crystal."

Heavily influenced by the compositional methods of Greek composer Iannis Xennakis, a close associate of French architect, painter, and sculptor Le Corbusier, Taggart was in this period fascinated by Pythagorean lore, mathematical systems, and the analogies between numerical and verbal languages. In the inscription of a copy of *The Pyramid* he sent Robert Duncan, Taggart quoted French chemist Antoine-Laurent Lavoisier: "Languages are not merely passive signs to express thought, they are also analytic systems by means of which we advance from the known to the unknown and to a certain extent in the manner of mathematics." In *The Pyramid* and *Dodeka* Taggart abandoned traditional compositional methods—sitting down, that is, and writing the words that come into one's head—for more-predetermined, systems-based approaches, approaches that bear a clear resemblance on the one hand to the chance-based procedures of Cage and Mac Low and on the other to the various systems evolved by such Language poets as Ron Silliman and P. Inman. The long (more than fifty pages) poem *Dodeka* is based on a vast array of Pythagorean lore, central among it the twelve-sided geometrical figure of the dodekahedron, held by the early Greeks to represent Earth. The poem begins with a "base line" of seven words, "dodekahedron, expands, ball, twelve, colors, maps, sky-sphere," which Taggart deploys as a cantus firmus upon which to work variations. There follows a series of short poems enclosed in squares, each of which "is made from the etymology (often pretty loose and 'distant') of the cantus firmus words." There are three "plaits" or "bracelets" to *Dodeka* as a whole, each of which consists of two of these seven-poem sequences, followed by a single longer poem that incorporates the words and phrases of the poems that have come before. The incredibly arcane procedure that produced this poem relies in large part upon a dodekahedron model Taggart constructed out of plaited strips of paper, using the number of squares in each strip to determine the number of poems in the series and using the conjunction of words in the model to derive actual lines in the poem. (This procedure rivals in its complexity Zukofsky's "A"-9 in which the older poet determines the distribution of n and r sounds through the mathematical formula for a conic section.)

But Taggart, unlike Cage or Mac Low, is more interested in the poem that results than in the procedure that produces it: while his procedure is important to him, he does not hesitate to alter the poems that result if he is not pleased with them. He arrived at his procedure, he claims, "out of a deep need to write poems that would provide me with information rather than their functioning as more or less well crafted reproductions of what I already know." Or, as he puts it rather movingly in a letter to Duncan, "It is a joke: I patch together a procedure that is so complicated I have no joy in thinking about it (call it a word calculus), only to end up face to face with *the* force." For Duncan, as he explains in the introduction he provided Taggart for *Dodeka,* that force is the primal, pre-Socratic knowledge that one also encounters in the writings of Charles Olson, postmodern poetry's primary "archaeologist of morning," who also dealt with Pythagorean themes in such works as "The Praises" and *The Maximus Poems* (1983). What Duncan finds extraordinary about *Dodeka* is the manner in which Taggart has been able to reconcile two seemingly opposite postmodern traditions, the procedural, musical poetics of Zukofsky and Olson's archaeological search for primordial, numinous origins: "Neither," Duncan comments, "certainly, could read each other at all. . . . Yet each alike appeared to push the art to certain limits of the mind to follow." In a 1978 review of Ronald Johnson's *Radi Os* (1977), Ron Silliman had criticized Taggart as one of a group of poets who read Zukofsky, not as "the compacted source of suggestion as to which directions poetry, if it is to stay vital, must move, but as the limit of possibility itself." The conjunction of Olsonian and Zukofskyan modes that Duncan notes in *Dodeka* clearly proves Silliman mistaken.

Dodeka can be seen as marking the end of Taggart's mid-period poetics, but the concern of the poem with music, color, and especially a single image, the laceration of the face followed by the *sparagmos*—"Face cut: seeds spill"—reappears throughout his later work. In a retrospective introduction to *Prompted* (1991), a collection of his "jazz" poems, Taggart writes of the "voice"—in particular the voice of the jazz saxophone—which "eats the face away," and this terrifying image recurs again and again in his writings as a figure for the rapt attention of the listener (or viewer) who finds his own identity being eroded in the presence of the numinous.

Peace on Earth, Taggart's 1981 collection of poems, marks his emergence into his fully developed mature style, a mode which openly acknowledges its reliance on the models of jazz. Taggart telegraphs this connection in his titles, in particular in such poems as "Inside Out" and "Giant Steps," titles taken directly from Coltrane tunes. This is a poetry that relies overwhelmingly on repetition. Each of the four poems of *Peace on Earth,* which range from the four-page "Giant Steps" to the thirty-eight-page title poem, is composed, not in the unit of the stanza, but in the unit of the page. There is considerable repetition from line to line, and each succeeding page is nearly identical to the one before it; changes are incremental, words and phrases substitute for earlier words and phrases, but by the end of "Peace on Earth," for example, the final page is considerably altered from the first. The poetics of *Peace on Earth* and Taggart's succeeding major collections—*Dehiscence* (1983), *Loop* (1991), *Standing Wave* (1993), and *Crosses* (1998)—are founded upon both the Zukofskyan notion of the poem as melody, as musical composition, and Olson's Projectivist emphasis on the poet's voice as active performer of the poem. These are poems explicitly designed for reading aloud, poems in which "if not enacted by the voice, the cadence makes no sense; its shifting motion only confuses and irritates the eye."

Such a shifting, incremental cadence owes much to the models, not only of jazz and rhythm and blues but also to the "minimalist" classical music of Terry Riley, Steve Reich, and Philip Glass. Disenchanted by the serial music promoted by the classical establishment in the 1950s and 1960s, these composers pioneered a new strain of composition that relied upon a harmonic language that the average listener would find familiar and upon a basis of steady, repeated rhythmic figures that owed much to Indian classical music, to the Balinese gamelan, and to American jazz and rock and roll. On a line-by-line basis the first few lines of "The Rothko Chapel Poem" from *Loop* serve as a germane-enough example of how Taggart has put a similar aesthetic of repetition to work in his poetry:

> Red deepened by black red made deep by black
> prolation of deep red like stairs of lava
> deep red like stairs of lava to gather us in
> gather us before the movements are to be made
> red stairs lead us lead us to three red rooms
> rooms of deep red light red deepened by black
> in this first room there is to be a wedding
> we are the guests the welcome wedding guests
> the groom welcomes us the bride welcomes us
> rooms full of deep red light room upon room . . . [.]

While the shifting and overlapping repetitions of these lines put one in mind of the minimalist composers, Taggart's work differs from their music in that he is at no point committed to the steady pulse that is at the heart of most of Reich's and Glass's works (in poetry, such a pulse would be a principle of *direct* repetition, either metrical or lexical). Taggart explains how the notion of *cadence* operates in his poetry: "The line is prevented from falling in on itself by a recurrent, but never exactly repeating cadence. This cadence undergoes a continuous motion (transformation). It is not quite accurate to say it shifts in and out of phase unless the phase of the cadence is understood to have no set identity. It is always identifiable in its overlapping *motion* of addition and decay."

In "A Preface" from his collected essays *Songs of Degrees* (1994) Taggart explains how the model of Steve Reich's music and Mark Rothko's paintings led him from the "nervously taut" short lines of *Dodeka* to the longer lines of *Peace on Earth,* in particular its "Slow Song for Mark Rothko." Two principles important to Taggart's sense of poetics are at play here. The first is the notion of *transformation,* as opposed to *translation:* that is, while the poet may take a previously existing work as his inspiration or model—a Rothko painting, or a series of Rothkos in "The Rothko Chapel Poem," or Marvin Gaye's album *What's Going On* in "Marvin Gaye Suite"—his aim must be not merely to *translate* that work into another medium but also to achieve the imaginative *transformation* that is the aim of the true artist. A true transformation of material makes it irrelevant whether the reader-listener is familiar with *What's Going On,* the circumstances of Gaye's death that figure so poignantly in the later sections of the "Suite," or the Aretha Franklin performance of "The Thrill is Gone" that underlies "Aria No. 17," both in *Loop.* And second, there is the notion of the poem as first and foremost a score for vocal performance, a situation in which poet and reader come together in "a liberation of participation, an ending of the silence and solitude." The poem is "the voice's enactment of language, one interior calling out to another, so there may be presence and community."

"Peace on Earth," which remains Taggart's longest published poem, is a crucial enactment of this principle and one that has occasioned a certain amount of controversy. It is a poem about the Vietnam War, a central experience for Americans of Taggart's generation, and in its incrementally shifting changes it aims metaphorically to lift into light the napalm-ravaged and slaughtered victims of America's last Asian adventure. Eliot Weinberger, editor of the magazine *Montemora* and a prominent translator of contemporary Latin American poetry, reviewed the poem with vituperative scorn in 1982, criticizing it as "a nostalgic vision of peace," "a flowering manured by dead peasants and by our dead contemporaries who were too poor or guileless to evade conscription." But Taggart's aim in "Peace on Earth" is not to register his own horror at the war: the poem "is meant to be more than one person's private response to the war in Vietnam." It is to stand as a "woven scarf" through which light can pass and through which the voices of others—phrases from *The Winter Soldier Investigation: An Inquiry into American War Crimes by the Vietnam Veterans Against the War* (1972), the words of a Tarahumara healing song, and the voices of whoever reads the poem aloud (as one is specifically directed to do)—might find expression and community. The poem is indeed, as Eliot Weinberger scornfully notes, the work of one of "those of us who stayed home," rather than of a Vietnamese poet or of a war veteran. But that fact does not diminish the power or majesty of the piece nor its very real, very serious aim of erecting a monument of both flowers and bones to those who died in the war.

"Peace on Earth" works on a principle of repetition from page to page. In more-recent poems Taggart has developed his poetic so that it is a remarkably subtle and compelling compositional principle, generating poems as brief as eight lines or as long as dozens of pages and holding even the silent reader's attention. Each of his successive collections—*Loop*

perhaps most impressive of them, if only because it is longest—has shown Taggart more and more comfortable with his style, able to adapt it to a wider range of subjects and emotions. Taggart's mature style, indeed, allows the poet to explore a broad palette of subjects: the musics of Coltrane, Thelonious Monk, Jerry Lee Lewis, Olivier Messiaen; the paintings of Rothko and Francis Bacon; the writings of Herman Melville, Thomas Traherne, and Thomas Bernhard; and much else. One of course might question this more-than-occasional reliance on previous artistic achievement, but Taggart has anticipated such cavils: "Now it might be asked whether this isn't terribly, maybe even incestuously, arty? My answer is that the work of Rothko and Reich [in "Slow Song for Mark Rothko"] exists for me as the ring of Blue Mountains surrounding this valley. They simply *are.* Their art exists in the same continuous reality, the same continuous *day* of those mountains. What is at stake is need. You find what you need, among the entire past and present universe, to get the job done."

In 1993 Taggart published *Remaining in Light: Ant Meditations on a Painting by Edward Hopper,* a 137-page monograph which focuses upon a single Hopper canvas, *A Woman in the Sun* (1961). In this volume Taggart demonstrates that his method, both as critic and as poet, is above all that of a *reader,* an almost obsessive contemplator of the verbal, visual, or musical artifact or experience before him. Beginning with a meticulous examination of the painting itself and of the various reproductions of it available to him, Taggart traces the implications and intimations of the painting—through a process of Derridean supplementarity—in the work of Emily Dickinson, Edmond Jabès, Søren Kierkegaard, Oppen, Taggart's contemporary Michael Palmer, and even the pop group Talking Heads, whose *Remain in Light* album furnishes his title. What Taggart finds is that reading—and by implication any sustained meditation—is a "push-pull relation of the spreading multiplication of supplementarity and its editing or suppression," a circling toward, back from, and around the subject at hand. Hopper's woman, who stares in the sunlight off the right of the painting as if she were about to be consumed by it (as the voice "eats away" the face in Taggart's poems), is herself a figure of the reader or poet who contemplates the numinous. Taggart pursues his meditation on the light as spirit, as an outside force assaulting or wounding the woman, who remains patient in the face of this assault, until his book itself becomes a meditation, not on Hopper or on his painting, but on the nature of reading or writing itself, of opening oneself to an outside that includes both "spirit" and the other.

The writer, as Taggart repeats in his prose, is "first a reader," and all of his mature work has developed out of this quest to encounter the numinous through a contemplation of what is outside, whether it be another's writings, paintings, music, or the natural world itself. In a generally disappointed 1977 review of Frank Samperi's poetry, Taggart contends, "The history of poetry in our century is only superficially the history of the struggle to make it new. More enduring is the struggle to regain the definition of poetry as spiritual ascesis." Samperi, though he aims to write an explicitly mystical poetry modeled in part after Dante's, fails because his work relies on "vague and nominal imagery," which can yield only "a vague and nominal Image, a blurred vision," and he fails because he has not engaged "the imagination at sufficient depth and duration in the complex, organized, and dynamic whole that is language." Samperi has not achieved true vision because he has not looked closely enough, has not been specific enough in his language—and more important, has not immersed himself deeply enough in his own medium, language itself. For his part, Taggart strives for this immersion through the cadences, the patterns of repetition and variation of his mature poetics. Just as Rothko strove to embody his own mystic insight in ostensibly monochromatic canvases that reveal their depths and complexities over long periods, or Lithuanian composer Arvo Pärt through extraordinarily minimal, slowly evolving musical works, Taggart attempts to yield himself to the "voice that eats the face away" by embodying the processes of standing still, of contemplation and meditation, through a poetics in which the voice repeats itself again and again, circling around its object as the reader circles around the text.

While Taggart's work is widely respected among poets and critics, he has only recently begun to receive the widespread formal recognition he deserves. He was omitted from the most-prominent, innovative anthologies of the 1980s, Silliman's 1986 *In the American Tree* and Douglas Messerli's 1987 *"Language" Poetries,* probably quite appropriately, since he has steered clear of the politicization of poetry favored by the Language school. In a 1979 review of Bruce Andrews and Clark Coolidge, Taggart comments acidly that their poetics "can force or encourage a more conscious experience of language; it can produce varieties of irony in the process. It is not clear that it can do anything else." Substantial selections from Taggart's work, however, have been included in Messerli's *From the Other Side of the Century* and Dennis Barone and Peter Ganick's *The Art of Practice: 45 Contemporary Poets* (both published in

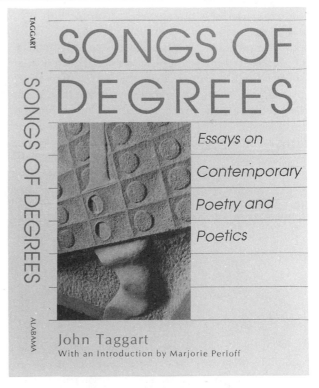

Cover for the 1994 collection of Taggart's essays and reviews

1994), as well as in several recent anthologies of "jazz" poetry. In 1994 the University of Alabama Press published *Songs of Degrees,* Taggart's collected essays and reviews, making available most of his critical writings and bestowing upon them an academic imprimatur.

Most recently, with the 1994 publication of Lew Daly's *Swallowing the Scroll: Late in a Prophetic Tradition with the Poetry of Susan Howe and John Taggart* and with Taggart's valorization in the journal *apex of the M* (edited by Daly and others), he has been somewhat forcefully conscripted as a precursor for a "new spiritualism" among a group of young innovative poets (among them Daly and Pam Rehm, a former student of Taggart's at Shippensburg). Daly's book, written in a thorny, hectoring style that aims to fold in both Martin Heidegger and Cotton Mather, makes some large claims for Taggart's work, casting him into a mystic, Levinasian frame in which one is uncertain he would be entirely comfortable. It is hard not to suspect that Daly is in large part using both Howe and Taggart as sticks to beat back what he feels as the weight of Language poetry orthodoxy. But Daly is correct in seeing Taggart as one of the few poets of the postwar period who has been committed both to exploring a spiritual vision and to pursuing an innovative poetics. These aspirations are rare indeed, and even rarer is the degree to which Taggart has succeeded. While his work has yet to prove itself a central influence on younger writers, it has solidly established itself as a body of achievement utterly unlike that of any of his contemporaries. Taggart has pursued a rigorously individual path in developing his thought and his poetics, and in consequence he has received little recognition either from the mainstream establishment of American poetry or the establishment of the avant-garde. But through that same individual vision, he has achieved a poetry of remarkable presence and power, a poetry that gives the lie to any conception of the experimental as arid, vapid, or ultimately without spirit.

Interview:

Gill Ott and Toby Olson, "Interview with John Taggart," *Paper Air,* 4 (Spring 1978): 46–50.

References:

Lew Daly, *Swallowing the Scroll: Late in a Prophetic Tradition with the Poetry of Susan Howe and John Taggart* (Buffalo, N.Y.: M Press, 1994);

Susan Howe, "Light in Darkness: John Taggart's Poetry," *Hambone,* 2 (Spring 1982): 135–138;

Ronald Johnson, "On Looking Up 'The Pyramid Is a Pure Crystal' in Webster," *Parnassus,* 3, no. 2 (1975): 147–152;

Paul Metcalf, Craig Watson, and Bruce Andrews, "Dodeka: 3 Views," *Paper Air,* 4 (Spring 1978): 67–71;

David Miller, "The Poetry of John Taggart," *Paper Air,* 4 (Spring 1978): 64–66;

Toby Olson, "Spirit Image, Kerry Clouds, Peace on Earth: A Few Old Memories and New Thoughts About John Taggart," *Paper Air,* 4 (Spring 1978): 3–4;

Rochelle Ratner, "The Poet as Composer: An Inquiry into the Work of John Taggart," *Paper Air,* 4 (Spring 1978): 59–62;

Craig Watson, "The Poetics of Community," *Northwest Review,* 29 (1981): 29–39;

Eliot Weinberger, "Peace on Earth," in *Works on Paper* (New York: New Directions, 1986), pp. 137–149;

Karl Young, "Towards *Peace on Earth,*" *Paper Air,* 4 (Spring 1978): 55–59.

Papers:

Taggart's papers are held at the Archive for New Poetry, the University of California, San Diego.

Mary TallMountain
(19 June 1918 – 4 August 1994)

Gabrielle Welford
University of Hawaii at Manoa

BOOKS: *Nine Poems* (San Francisco: Friars Press, 1977);

Good Grease (New York: Strawberry Press, 1978);

There Is No Word For Goodbye, Blue Cloud Quarterly (1980);

Green March Moons (Berkeley: New Seed Press, 1987);

Continuum: Poems by Mary TallMountain, Blue Cloud Quarterly (1988);

Matrilineal Cycle (Privately printed, 1988; reprinted, Oakland, Cal.: Red Star Black Rose Printing, 1990);

The Light on the Tent Wall: A Bridging (Los Angeles: American Indian Studies Center, University of California, Los Angeles, 1990);

A Quick Brush of Wings (San Francisco: Freedom Voices Publications, 1991);

Listen to the Night: Poems for the Animal Spirits of Mother Earth, edited by Ben Clarke (San Francisco, Freedom Voices, 1995).

PLAY PRODUCTION: *The Rain In Spain,* San Francisco, EXITheater, 30 July 1988; revised as *Sadie's Turn,* San Francisco, EXITheater, January 1990.

OTHER: "The Sinh of Niguudzagha" [excerpt from "Doyon"], in *Earth Power Coming: Short Fiction in Native American Literature,* edited by Simon Ortiz (T'saile, Ariz.: Navajo Community College Press, 1983), pp. 134–144;

"Voices in the Wind," in *Conspire: To Breathe Together,* edited by Merle Bachman, John Benson, Kate Brandt, and others (San Francisco: Fire in the Lake, 1985), pp. 38–39;

"You Can Go Home Again: A Sequence," in *I Tell You Now: Autobiographical Essays by Native American Writers,* edited by Brian Swann and Arnold Krupat (Lincoln: University of Nebraska Press, 1987), pp. 1–13;

"My Wild Birds Flying," in *A Gathering of Spirit: Writing and Art by North American Indian Women,* edited by Beth Brant (Ithaca, N.Y.: Firebrand Books, 1988);

"Haiku," in *Home of the Brave,* edited by Stephanie Salter (San Francisco: Bay Area Women's Resource Center, 1988);

"The Disposal of Mary Joe's Children" [excerpt from "Doyon"], in *Spider Woman's Granddaughters,* edited by Paula Gunn Allen (Boston: Beacon, 1989);

"Meditations on a Cat," in *With a Fly's Eye, Whale's Wit and Woman's Heart: Animals and Women,* edited by Theresa Corrigan and Stephanie Hoppe (San Francisco: Cleis Press, 1989);

"An Accident," in *Season of Dead Water,* edited by Helen Frost (Portland, Oreg.: Breitenbush Books, 1990);

"Untitled Poem for PGA (Paula Gunn Allen)," in *Dancing on the Rim of the World: An Anthology of Contemporary Northwest Native American Writing,* edited by Andrea Lerner (Tucson: Sun Tracks and the University of Arizona Press, 1990), pp. 201–202;

"Songs for Seven Lovers," "Old Motel," "Silver Trumpets," "Colloquy: World War II," "Reincarnation," "Counterpoint," "Marked Man," and "Lovers' Rubaiyat," in *Goddesses We Ain't: Tenderloin Women Writers,* edited by Lucy Jane Bledsoe (San Francisco: Freedom Voices Publications, 1992), pp. 47–56.

SELECTED PERIODICAL PUBLICATIONS–UNCOLLECTED:

POETRY

"Lament for Richard Oakes," *Hyperion,* 10 (1973);

"Canticle of the Body," *Way of St. Francis,* 30 (June 1974), pp. 20–21;

"Ishi, Man of Dawn," *Encore* (May 1976);

"In The Night Also: An Octet," *Way of St. Francis* (June 1977);

"Behind The Lights," *Women's Voices* (February 1992).

FICTION

"Clem's Journal," [excerpt from "Doyon"] *Shantih, Native American issue,* 4, no. 2 (1979);

Mary TallMountain (photograph by William Abranowicz)

"A Season Of Grace," *Way of St. Francis* (March 1981);

"The Man at Sum Ling's," *Way of St. Francis* (June 1982);

"Them Kinda Dogs," *Talking Leaf* (February 1983);

"The Night of Indin Bilijon," *Tender Leaves,* 3, no. 1 (1988);

"Street Scene," *Way of St. Francis* (May–June 1989);

"Them Pore Men," *Way of St. Francis* (May–June 1990).

NONFICTION

"Medicine Woman/Spirit Woman," review of *Medicine Woman* and *Spirit Woman,* by Lynn Andrews, in *Talking Leaf* (September 1982);

Review of "The One Who Skins Cats," by Paula Gunn Allen, in *Studies in American Indian Literature,* 7, no. 3 (1983);

Review of *The Woman Who Owned the Shadows,* by Allen, in *Calyx,* 9, no. 1 (1983);

"The Enabler," *Way of St. Francis* (March/April 1986);

"Meditations of a Wayfarer," column in *Way of St. Francis* (September 1987–May 1990).

When Mary TallMountain died in September 1994 at the age of seventy-six, she had been seriously writing and publishing for a little more than twenty-five years. Although her work never attracted the notice given to some Native American Renaissance women writers, her poetry and short stories have attracted a large and loyal following. Many of them are teachers who find that the spiritual quality of her work and her awareness of being a survivor (and more) often moves their students to tears. Her experience of being adopted out of her native Athabascan village at the age of six led TallMountain to write much about the pain of dislocation from one culture to another and of being displaced within American society. She has been a witness to the struggle for survival of the Athabascan people and of the poor and homeless who were her neighbors in the San Francisco Tenderloin for thirty years. Her stories and poetry delineate the experiences of a lifetime committed to bringing all her various worlds together in one body. These worlds were the Athabascan and the white cultures (Russian, Irish-American), pagan, Catholic, agnostic, tribal, middle-class Anglo, shamanic, and priestly– voices all clamoring to be heard.

Mary TallMountain was born Mary Demoski 19 June 1918 in the tiny Koyukon village of Nulato, Alaska, just below the Arctic Circle and west of Fairbanks. TallMountain's mother, Mary Joe Demoski, was Athabascan/Russian, and her father, Clem Stroupe, was an American soldier of Irish/Scottish descent who was stationed with the U.S. Army at Nulato. Like many native Athabascans at that time, TallMountain's mother was stricken with tuberculosis even before Mary TallMountain was born. When TallMountain was six and her brother Billy was four, Mary Joe Demoski, knowing that she would not live, made the decision to give up her two children for adoption to the Randles, the white government doctor and his wife. She hoped that in this way the children would receive the education and advantages she had longed for and, most important, that they would be saved from inevitably catching tuberculosis themselves.

TallMountain had been staying on and off with the Randles for several years as her mother grew weaker and less able to cope with the hard work necessary for staying alive in a northern Alaskan village and looking after the needs of her two growing children. The decision as to whether the two children should go permanently to be adopted by the doctor and his wife was left to the village council. The council decided to send six-year-old Mary "outside" and keep Billy in the village. If she had been a boy, TallMountain says, they would have kept her and she too would have died of tuberculosis, as her brother did at the age of seventeen. She tells parts of this story in "Naahulooyah" in *A Quick Brush of Wings* (1991) and in "The Disposal of Mary Joe's Children" in Paula Gunn Allen's anthology *Spider Woman's Granddaughters* (1989).

Although TallMountain was saved from dying of tuberculosis by being sent outside with the Randles, being taken from her mother and the environment that had formed her without the chance to say goodbye and brought into an alien and sometimes hostile world, she came close to losing her life anyway through the toll on her spirit and emotions. In Oregon she was exposed to the ridicule of white schoolchildren (she recounts the experience in her poem "Indian blood" in *The Light on the Tent Wall: A Bridging* (1990). Forbidden to speak her native tongue by the Randles and already being molested by her stepfather before they left Nulato, she can remember sitting in closets in dark hopelessness and biting her hands until they bled.

Although the molestation continued, the Randles did take the step of returning with their adopted child to a place where she would not be tormented for being Indian. They moved with her to the Aleutians in Alaska, where they lived until she was fourteen. In a 1989 interview TallMountain told Bill Moyers that a silent and self-destructive rage never left her until she began talking to the child inside her (a child she called Lidwynne), acknowledging the pain, reconnecting with her roots and her love for the people and land she had left behind. She also told Moyers that rage drove her to alcoholism and illnesses that nearly killed her before she realized that she had to choose whether to live or die. The two sides of this choice are well expressed in the poem "Schizophrenia" in *The Light on the Tent Wall*.

<pre>
            booming
           foghorns
              sad
behind my squandered heart
                        where has the sly moon hidden
                        trifling
                        with her lover stars
        so I burrow deeper
          into the gray
     maudlin buzzing caverns
                        poems wander gossamer
                        through
                        shadows in my mind
        out of the mazes
     I wake at evening asking
       why is morning so dim
                        dusk flows rich as canvas
                        painted in oil
                        by Rouault
              staring
          at a stranger's gun
           and into eternity
                        while somewhere monks
                        chant
                        gregorian masses
           knives flash
     blood drips in dust
       police sirens howl
                        and I hear the murmured
                        mantras
                        of life[.]
</pre>

On one side of a split that TallMountain portrays physically on the page speaks the voice of despair, the one who woke "at evening asking / why is morning so dim," who stared "at the stranger's gun / and into eternity." On the other speaks the voice of healing poetry and "the murmured / mantras / of life," which come through strong in stories such as "Indin Bilijohn" that would otherwise be totally despairing. TallMountain's commitment has been to giving space to all her conflicting voices. She says on the last page of *Continuum: Poems by Mary TallMountain* (1988): "From each level in this alien culture, I reaped something to put into my bag of laughs and tears."

Encouraged by her adoptive mother, Agnes Randle, who introduced her to the classics of British literature, TallMountain began to read and write at the age of four. As she says in "You Can Go Home Again 6" (1987):

Agnes was a teacher. My education lasted twelve hours a day. There was a lyric excellence in her that nurtured my early fascination with poems and stories. Literarily, I grew up with Shelley, Wordsworth, Keats; Dickens,

The Blue Cloud Quarterly
Final Issue

CONTINUUM

Poems by

Mary TallMountain

Cover for TallMountain's 1988 collection, about which she said, "From each level of this alien culture, I reaped something to put into my bag of laughs and tears."

Trollope, the Bronte sisters. A piercing memory returns. At Unalaska, Agnes and I walked along the narrow pebbled beach at night reciting poems to each other. Especially I loved Wordsworth.

TallMountain had her first story published in *Child Life* when she was ten, and she was writing a novel, "Tundra Country," between the ages of twelve and fourteen, only to abandon it when the Randles left Alaska the last time for central California in 1932.

Since TallMountain's adoptive father had spent all his savings on a chicken farm that folded in the Great Depression, the family was forced to become migrant farm laborers to survive, as TallMountain recalls in "The Summer Pond, A Short Story" in *The Light on the Tent Wall,* and they landed in Portland, Oregon. TallMountain's adoptive father died of heart failure just after she graduated from high school, and her husband, Dal Roberts, whom she married at the age of nineteen, died after only three years of marriage. TallMountain's adop-

tive mother committed suicide in 1945 because she was dying of Parkinson's disease and diabetes. Bereft again and alone in the world, TallMountain left Portland for Reno.

In Reno she learned the trade of legal secretary that would keep her employed the rest of her working life. She also met Reuel Lynch, a jazz musician who reintroduced her to the Catholic religion into which she had been born. She began an intense study of Catholicism that was to bring her in 1959 to professing to be a secular Franciscan. The intense mysticism of her Franciscan beliefs combines with the earth-rooted spiritual awareness of her Athabascan upbringing in her writing.

Paula Gunn Allen in *The Sacred Hoop: Recovering the Feminine in American Indian Traditions* (1992) sees all Native American writers, and especially the women, as having "as our first and most significant perceptual characteristic a solid, impregnable, and ineradicable orientation toward a spirit-informed view of the universe that provides an internal structure to both our consciousness and our art." She describes TallMountain's work as revealing "a deeply spiritualized sensibility" but is disturbed by the "difficult and uneasy alliance" that she perceives between her friend's "pagan awareness . . . and the less earthy, more judgmental view of medieval Christianity." The foreword Allen wrote for *Light on the Tent Wall* indicates she had come to understand by then that TallMountain was fully capable of embracing both beliefs and making her home within the transformation: "In telling her life and the life of her far away people, she tells all our stories; she tells our lives. And in so doing not only affirms life, but re-creates it." TallMountain's poem "Bright Shining" dwells within both her Franciscan mysticism and the sacredness of earthly things in Koyukon tradition, a joyful acknowledgment of the world. It is not coincidental that the Franciscan faith acknowledges spirit to be embedded in all things.

Companion to me in every place,
You stretch your hand: I see
Majesties of mountains
Crowned with living light.

Your arm flings wide: I see
Wild little islands wrapt in fog
Grey luminous; hidden folds
Of emerald and ermine earth.

I fly free clean through glowing
Cat's eye aquamarine
Filled with light air breath

Swaddled in this cocoon
This dense and lifeless mass

Yet weightless I
soaring with it shall be for you
Light bright shining[.]

From Reno, TallMountain moved to San Francisco, where she began working as a legal secretary, but the pain of her past drove her to secret drinking, and she continued to drink and live in what she describes as a "grey world" into her forties. Her work suffered, and she finally got up one morning wondering why it was so dark and found she had lost an entire day. "Disgusted," she says in her autobiographical essay, "You Can Go Home Again," "I went back to the apartment and took a good look at myself and my situation. It was then that I made up my mind to quit drinking, cold turkey. . . . The nights were the worst, but they gave me the blessed time of peace to think and to bolster up my firm intention to make a substantially useful life. And it worked." In her writing TallMountain's experiences of desolation and despair come through in her empathy for the homeless and abandoned.

Having quit drinking, TallMountain set up her own stenography business and, for a while, enjoyed a new feeling of "working free, for myself," as she says in "You Can Go Home Again." But she was floored by cancer in 1968. She fought and overcame it, but in the process she lost her business and her apartment and had to move to the Tenderloin, a poorer part of San Francisco to which many of the elderly poor, the homeless, prostitutes, and drug addicts gravitate. It was in the Tenderloin that she took up once more the journals that her adoptive mother Agnes had taught her to keep years before. TallMountain's illnesses eventually resulted in her inability to work and finally in her receiving a disability pension; the small income enabled her to spend her later years writing, teaching, giving readings, and getting published. Circumstances that might have thrown a less committed person into the street and destitution offered TallMountain the opportunity to dedicate herself to what she came to see as her life's work.

TallMountain had begun writing poetry in the mid 1960s, and Simon Scanlon, the editor of *The Way of St. Francis,* encouraged her. In an interview with Sheila Muto in 1990, TallMountain said Scanlon published something of hers in every issue after 1969. In 1977 Scanlon published *Nine Poems,* TallMountain's first chapbook through Friars Press in San Francisco. *Nine Poems* includes small, jewel-like verses that differ from TallMountain's later work partly in the sparse immediacy of their images and partly in not being related to her Indian heritage but to her current surroundings. In 1978 *Good Grease* was published by Strawberry Press in New York. This was a folded broadside consisting of just the title poem; it extols the winter virtues of good grease-dripping food, good especially when such food is not easily come by.

TallMountain's first encounter with Paula Gunn Allen, then teaching at San Francisco State College, had been in 1974. At this time TallMountain was looking for a teacher who could help her work on her writing, and a friend recommended that she take some of her poetry to Allen to read. Allen left the room to read TallMountain's poems and returned with tears in her eyes. Allen suggested that the two of them get together once a week to read over TallMountain's work. Every Tuesday evening for a year and a half they sat on the floor of Allen's apartment and read the poems aloud. TallMountain remembers little criticism, but she commented on how Allen's support shifted her subtly from writing without a vision to seeing herself as a writer with a purpose. Allen helped her return to her early identity and confirm in herself a sense of her own Indianness and of what that must mean in her writing. TallMountain says in "You Can Go Home Again: "In one of my quick clips of vision, Paula and I are caught changeless, sitting still and rapt, Indian women bound by the enduring thread of a common dream, a powerful purpose."

When TallMountain had fought through her first bout with cancer, Paula Gunn Allen persuaded her it was time to reconnect with her birthplace, Nulato. The journals TallMountain kept on that journey, during which she met relatives and tried to locate her mother's grave, are material that she uses extensively in the novel she was revising at the time of her death.

In the mid 1970s TallMountain was again struck down by cancer. Allen writes in her foreword to *The Light on the Tent Wall* that TallMountain embodies survival in her very being, having come back from death so many times.

Who is this woman, this survivor, this half-breed, this poet, this friend? If you know the land of her origins and the cadences of the People, if you recall the rhythm of Roman liturgy, the solemnity of the Mass, if you read this collection with care, hearing the eerie, powerful silences that surround the words, you will know who she is, what extinction is, and what survival engenders.

It was during her second hospitalization with cancer that TallMountain wrote the often-taught poem "The Last Wolf":

The last wolf hurried toward me
through the ruined city

and I heard his baying echoes
down the steep smashed warrens
of Montgomery Street and past
the few ruby-crowned highrises
left standing
their lighted elevators useless

Passing the flicking red and green
of traffic signals
baying his way eastward
in the mystery of his wild loping gait
closer the sounds in the deadly night
through clutter and rubble of quiet blocks

I heard his voice ascending the hill
and at last his low whine as he came
floor by empty floor to the room
where I sat
in my narrow bed looking west, waiting
I heard him snuffle at the door and
I watched

He trotted across the floor
he laid his long gray muzzle
on the spare white spread
and his eyes burned yellow
his small dotted eyebrows quivered

Yes, I said.
I know what they have done.

TallMountain's awareness of the horrors and destruction accompanying mainstream modern culture and her simultaneous compassion for those who struggle and suffer under it bring the shattered glass ruins, the wolf, and herself with cancer in the narrow bed together in a quiet ritual of healing. She knew indeed "what they have done," and she determined to fight it in her writing and in her teaching. The spirit of the wolf was TallMountain's poetic genius through which she saw the world with half-wild, knowing, and deeply caring eyes.

Shortly after the second cancer went into remission, TallMountain went to a Catholic charismatic retreat in Scottsdale, Arizona. Encouraged by Allen and remembering that the last rumor had placed her father Clem close by in Phoenix, TallMountain went to a phone booth and looked up his name. She found him immediately and phoned him. They had both thought each other dead. After a separation of fifty-two years, TallMountain spent the next two years living with and caring for him. He died of cancer in 1978. While she was living with him, her father told her tales she was to use later in her short stories and novel. She addresses her relationship with her father with deep compassion in the short story "Wild Birds" in *A Quick Brush of Wings*.

It was because Mary TallMountain had decided to face her past that she seized the chance to spend the last two years of her father's life caring for him and, incidentally, adding to her understanding of her background and her family history. She wrote of the experience in "My Wild Birds Flying":

When bayonet cactus thrusts its
Blossomy cap into desert sky,
A white cry announcing winter,
I remember my father.

Lost in my childhood, Clem
Perched forever, a wild bird
Fluttering in the cage of my head.
I could not set him free.

Years of search. I found him—
Old soldier, spiny as ocotillo.
A few years left for laughter.
Return to our Alaskan youth.

He thought I was Mary Joe
Stepping across the years,
Hair tossed in a scarlet band,
Dancing to his fiddle.

He was frail and ancient,
Flickered like fireflies of summer
In dreams he drove malamutes
Through the land with Mary Joe.

In a fleece-bright dawn
He cried out to her.
She came, bent into the light,
And took his hand.

Now in the silences of night
They come to me,

My wild birds flying.

In 1980 *There Is No Word For Goodbye* was published as an issue of *Blue Cloud Quarterly* in Marvin, South Dakota. It was reprinted in 1990 at Red Star Black Rose Printing, Oakland, California. All poems except "Old Whaling Station," "The Imprisoned Warriors," and "Jubilee" are also collected in TallMountain's volume *The Light on the Tent Wall*.

In *There Is No Word For Goodbye* TallMountain emerges clearly as a Native American poet. She chronicles, from her childhood in the early-twentieth-century Yukon, her memories of a world gone today from the village where she was born. The poems tremble with the depth of her feeling and have a clarity that brings that world close even to the most city-bound readers. The poem "Indian Blood" went through dramatic changes between its publication in Geary Hobson's *Remembered Earth* in

1979 and its appearance in the 1980 volume. The 1980 chapbook won a Pushcart Prize in 1981, and the poem "There Is No Word For Goodbye" was published in the volume *The Pushcart Prize, VII: Best of the Small Presses,* edited by Bill Henderson and published in 1982.

Discovered by Alaskan poet Geary Hobson and provided with a grant to travel and teach in local schools, TallMountain returned to Alaska after her father's death. In subsequent years she regularly traveled north to read poetry and teach in community centers, schools, and prisons. Teaching became an integral part of her existence as a writer. In an October 1992 telephone conversation Anna Poe at the Edgar Rasmuson Collection in Fairbanks, Alaska, said that Russell Williams Jr., an Indian inmate of Lemon Creek Correctional Center in Juno, Alaska, remembered TallMountain's telling him that his poetry could be part of his healing as it had been part of hers. Carol Heller in her 1990 dissertation for the University of California, Berkeley, "The Multiple Functions of the Tenderloin Women Writers Workshop: Community in the Making," wrote that TallMountain returned the "assistance offered her by Paula Gunn Allen . . . to members of the Tenderloin Women Writers Workshop."

The Tenderloin Women Writers Workshop, of which TallMountain was a founding member in 1987 (the same year *Green March Moons,* a short story about the kin rape of a young Athabascan woman, was published as a chapbook), was a support group where local women could share written expressions of their lives. Members were old and young, homeless and comfortably housed, former prostitutes, alcoholics, and drug users, middle and working class, nonwhite and white, who came seeking a forum in which to discuss their writing. The way in which this tremendously diverse group formed a community reflects the memory of her childhood community, Nulato, that TallMountain wrote of in "The Disposal of Mary Joe's Children."

The workshop became not just another writing support group but a living community with its own traditions, history, strengths, failures, and complex interwoven relationships. Ill and faced with disasters as she had been, TallMountain used them to form herself into a healer, a rememberer, a warrior. Her work there was one of the inspirations for Carol Heller in writing her dissertation. Heller described a red T-shirt TallMountain wore on which were the words "A Warrior is Geared to Struggle So Her People Will Continue." Heller wrote that " . . . Mary TallMountain and many members of the Tenderloin Women Writers Workshop, were, in fact, warriors" who "wrote so that their people would con-

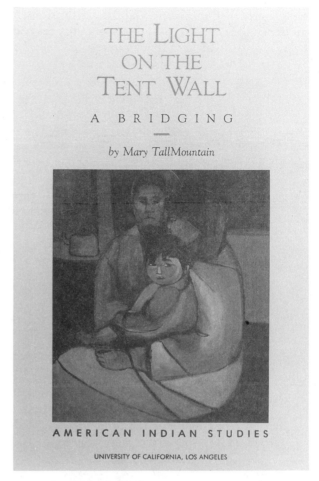

Cover for TallMountain's 1990 collection, which details her struggle for survival from child abuse, alcoholism, and cancer

tinue. Through her writing, Mary saw to it that her Athabaskan ancestors would continue. She also saw to it that her 'street brothers and sisters' would be offered stature and places of distinction in her stories." TallMountain became known as "Poet in Residence" of the Tenderloin Reflection and Education Center.

In 1988 *Continuum* was published as the final issue of *The Blue Cloud Quarterly* in Marvin, South Dakota. This collection strongly reflects TallMountain's Franciscan faith and at the same time expresses praise and a worshipful attitude that extends to all living things, a compassion for the world and an eye for sudden beauty in the midst of sorrow that are manifest in all her work.

Also in 1988 TallMountain published *Matrilineal Cycle* herself. (It was reprinted in 1990 by Red Star Black Rose Printing, Oakland, California.) All poems in this collection were later published in the volume *The Light on the Tent Wall*. With this collection TallMountain continued her exploration of and tribute to her matrilineal Indian roots, a path that has earned her the respect and loyalty of a wide audience of readers and poets alike. She uses Athabascan words which, in this volume as in *There Is No Word For Goodbye,* are not translated at the bottom of the page. In 1988 the poem "Matmiya" was chosen along with five other poems from *Harper's Anthology of 20th Century Native American Poetry* (1988) to be printed on a poster and displayed on buses in eleven cities across the country for three months.

By this time TallMountain had become so well known to anthologists that her work is present in a score or more anthologies (particularly of Native American writers, writings on aging, and women's writing), not to mention many appearances in literary journals. She was in constant demand to read around the country. In 1990 *The Light on the Tent Wall* was published by the American Indian Studies Center at the University of California, Los Angeles; it is the most complete volume of TallMountain's poetry and prose to date.

In *The Light on the Tent Wall* TallMountain treats earthy things—such as grease running down chins, hospital beds, ruined cities, and desert storms—with a personal sensibility and connection to the spiritual that ensures that the meditation on holiness and her delight in life come through. In this way the reader can enter that "sacred place of songs," as Joy Harjo commented on the back cover of the volume.

In 1991 Freedom Voices Publications, an associate of the Tenderloin Reflection and Meditation Center, published *A Quick Brush of Wings.* The poems in this volume are a continuation of the collage of spirit voices that appear and disappear, interwoven with daily events—shopping in Chinatown, peeling apples—in TallMountain's work. She shows how she remains connected to the Yukon even as she sits looking out of her window in the Tenderloin or lives in the New Mexico desert. The rootedness of home, family, and tradition, reclaimed by a woman torn away from her roots as a small child, is a gift to all American nomads of the spirit.

Only after a stroke left her with aphasia in 1992 did TallMountain begin to turn down the many requests to read that still flowed to her at her apartment in Petaluma, California, where she had moved that year. Keen, despite these setbacks, to start reading in public again, she appeared unexpectedly on 8 August 1992 at Laney College, Oakland. She had been scheduled to read with Joy Harjo, Creek poet and musician, and Wanda Coleman, African American performance poet from Los Angeles, but had canceled when she became ill. She was welcomed with delight and love, obvious signs

of the respect that the community of poets and poetry lovers had for her.

In Petaluma, where she had moved after almost thirty years in the Tenderloin, Mary TallMountain was surrounded by her writing. Her journals sat in boxes more than two feet high on her living room floor together with a myriad of poems, short stories, and six hundred pages of a novel. There were also spiritually incisive book reviews, essays, and letters. In a short introduction to her work in Geary Hobson's *The Remembered Earth: An Anthology of Contemporary Native American Literature* (1979), she said of the novel "Doyon": "It may help clear up a general ignorance about the Athabascans, who have been called 'strangers of the north.'"

Mary TallMountain was a small woman with a big presence. The dark eyes in her wide face brightened easily with humor. In fact, she had an ability to laugh at situations that would drive most people to rage and tears. She said in her commentary on *Continuum:*

> Going through changes might be the title of my life's story. Having sprung from a hugger-mugger meld of ancestors, I find I am unbelievably various and interesting, even to myself. I see myself a tot beside the mystical Yukon River, she who centered my mindset early, who colored the lives of all my Indian forebears, that river remote, stately, mischievous, illogical, and rowdy, whose beauty coils unforgettable in the seedbed of my mind.

Despite her presence in anthologies and journals, Mary TallMountain's work has attracted little in the way of critical reviews. Rayna Green in *That's What She Said: Contemporary Poetry and Fiction by Native American Women* comments on the critical status of Native American women writers in general:

> With the exception of Leslie Silko, whose extraordinary work receives some of the good critical attention it deserves, most writers in this volume are unfamiliar to the general reading public and even to readers of the most esoteric poetry and fiction. In spite of inclusion . . . in anthologies, prizes, awards, fellowships, and readings throughout the country, [they] find appreciation primarily among a specialized audience—Indian, feminist, politically attuned.

Very little academic criticism of TallMountain's writings is available except in Paula Gunn Allen's volume *The Sacred Hoop,* published in 1986, well before the appearance of *The Light on the Tent Wall.* Although TallMountain's work has received little formal criticism, she is recognized as one of its foremost poets and fiction writers by those who know the Native American Renaissance. Such public figures as Bill Moyers; scholars such as Allen, Geary Hobson at Oklahoma State University at Stillwater, Daniel Littlefield at the University of Arkansas, C. B. Clarke at Oklahoma City University, David Hales at the University of Alaska at Fairbanks; and such organizations as the Bay Area Poets Coalition readily rank TallMountain with writers of the caliber of Joy Harjo, Leslie Silko, Allen, Linda Hogan, Carol Lee Sanchez, and Wendy Rose–all of whom have received critical acclaim. However, the world of criticism is almost a blank where TallMountain is concerned.

Native Hawaiian writer Yvonne Yarber, who is working on a biography of Mary TallMountain, focused on some of the reasons for the neglect TallMountain's work has suffered. "TallMountain seeks out audiences that will connect with the spirit. Her meaning is not just an intellectual one. It is a deeply feeling one. She speaks of hard things in a vulnerable and personal way that makes you listen. TallMountain continues to touch in a deep way and always at a personal level on questions and facts that are familiar and painful to all of us–the death of a streetperson, the kin rape of a teenager, the mockery and xenophobia of school children."

Mary Hope Lee, an African American Community College teacher in Oakland, California, agreed that TallMountain does not share her experiences in ways that are easily romanticized. J. J. Wilson of Sonoma State University, California, suggests that among the poets who tend to remain obscure for no obvious reason are some who do so from "some basic eccentricity. If you go to visit such a person, she refuses to let you put her on a pedestal. She remains vulnerable, and by doing this forces you to see her as she is–perhaps ill, maybe having struggled with alcoholism or drug abuse, coping with pain in her life. You see her reality, vulnerability, and you get scared. It means that to do such a personal thing as write an essay on this person, you will have to face your own flaws."

Carter B. Clarke, president of Oklahoma City University, made it clear that the answer to the question of why TallMountain's work is not noticed academically depends on what means and measures one is using. On the one hand, TallMountain's work is "deeply esteemed" by Native Americans,

but "You have to bang your own drum academically." As a Native American himself, he could not help but be absorbed and affected by TallMountain's uncompetitive approach for recognition, but, as an academician, he realizes one has to be assertive in the academic community. Daniel Littlefield of the University of Arkansas and Yvonne Yarber had similar comments: people who review poetry review that of certain Indians in the lower forty-eight. TallMountain falls between more cracks than most. Allen comments in *The Sacred Hoop* that TallMountain's poetry is disconcerting in many ways, for she is not easily placed in one camp or another–politically, socially, or poetically. Among all these commentators there is agreement that Mary TallMountain's work deserves far greater critical coverage than it has received.

Interview:

Joseph W. Bruchac III, "We Are the Inbetweens: An Interview with Mary TallMountain," *Studies in American Indian Literatures,* 1 (Summer 1989): 13–21;

Bill Moyers, "Ancestral Voices," *The Power of the Word* [Videocassette] (New York: Public Affairs Television, 1989).

References:

Paula Gunn Allen, *The Sacred Hoop: Recovering the Feminine in American Indian Traditions* (Boston: Beacon, 1986);

Cornelia Jessey, review of *The Light on the Tent Wall, Way of St. Francis* (November/December 1991): 41–46;

Sheila Muto, "TL Poet, Alaskan Native, Spins Tales of Hope," *Tenderloin Times* (January 1990): 12–13;

Gabrielle Welford, "Mary TallMountain's Writing: Healing the Heart–Going Home," *Ariel,* 25 (January 1994): 136–154;

Welford, "Reflections on Mary TallMountain's Life and Writing: Facing Mirrors," *Studies in American Indian Literatures,* 9 (Summer 1997): 61–68.

Papers:

A collection of Mary TallMountain's works is at the Elmer E. Rasmuson Library, University of Alaska at Fairbanks.

Barrett Watten
(3 October 1948 –)

Jacques Debrot
Harvard University

BOOKS: *Opera–Works* (Bolinas, Cal.: Big Sky Books, 1975);
Decay (San Francisco: This Press, 1977);
Plasma/Paralleles/"X" (Berkeley, Cal.: Tuumba, 1979);
1–10 (Berkeley, Cal.: This Press, 1980);
Complete Thought (Berkeley, Cal.: Tuumba Press, 1982);
Total Syntax (Carbondale: Southern Illinois University Press, 1984);
Progress (New York: Roof Books, 1985);
Conduit (San Francisco: Gaz, 1988);
Leningrad: American Writers in the Soviet Union, by Watten, Michael Davidson, Lyn Hejinian, and Ron Silliman (San Francisco: Mercury House, 1991);
Under Erasure (Tenerife, Canary Islands, Spain: Zasterle Press, 1991);
Frame (1971–1990) (Los Angeles: Sun & Moon Press, 1997);
Bad History (Berkeley, Cal.: Atelos Press, 1998).

OTHER: *This,* edited by Watten and Robert Grenier, 1–3 (1971–1972); by Watten, 4–12 (1973–1982);
Poetics Journal (1982–), edited by Watten and Lyn Hejinian;
"Olson in Language: Part II," in *Writing/Talks,* edited by Bob Perelman (Carbondale: Southern Illinois University Press, 1985), pp. 157–165;
"Social Formalism: Zukofsky, Andrews, and Habitus in Contemporary Poetry," *North Dakota Quarterly,* 55 (Fall 1987): 365–382.
"Harry Mathews: An Experiment in Presence," *Review of Contemporary Fiction,* 7 (Fall 1987): 128–145;
"Political Economy and the Avant-Garde," *Talisman: A Journal of Contemporary Poetry and Poetics,* 8 (Spring 1992): 49–52;
"Radical Poetics," *Cultural Studies,* 6 (October 1992): 485–492;
"Making the Social Sublime: Doug Hall's Recent Work in the Public Sphere," in *Out of Place* [exhibition catalog], edited by Gary Dufour (Van-

Barrett Watten (photograph © 1997 Asa Watten)

couver, B.C.: Vancouver Art Gallery, 1993), pp. 88–100;
"Post-Soviet Subjectivity in Arkadii Dragomoshchenko and Ilya Kabakov," *Postmodern Culture* (January 1993), n. pag.; republished in *Essays in Postmodern Culture,* edited by Eyal Amiran and John Unsworth (Oxford: Oxford University Press, 1993), pp. 325–349;
"The Conduit of Communication in Everyday Life," *Aerial 8: Barrett Watten,* edited by Rod Smith (Washington D.C.: Edge Books, 1995), pp. 32–38;
"Nonnarrative and the Construction of History," in *The Ends of Theory,* edited by Jerry Herron and others (Detroit: Wayne State University Press, 1995), pp. 209–245; excerpted as "Nonnarrative History," in *Onward: Contemporary Poetry and Poetics,* edited by Peter Baker (New York: Peter Lang, 1996), pp. 209–245;

"New Meaning and Poetic Vocabulary," *Poetics Today*, 18 (Summer 1997): 147–186;

"The Bride of the Assembly Line: From Material Text to Cultural Poetics," *Impercipient Lecture Series*, no. 8 (1997);

"An Epic of Subjectivation: *The Making of Americans*," *Modernism/Modernity*, 5 (Spring 1998): 95–121.

"The idea," Barrett Watten says in his book-length poem *Progress* (1985), is not, as William Carlos Williams believed, "in things." Rather it "Is the thing"—as much materially, as psychologically, real. The significance of this linking of ideas with the materiality of language for contemporary poetry cannot be overestimated. In Watten's writing—as in much of the Language School, of which he is a leading figure—language itself, in its objective, material aspect, is the horizon of the work. By rigorously interrogating language's presumed transparency to meaning, Watten critiques the "system" of "discursive rules and operations" that, in Michael Davidson's words, underlie the "ideological interests of the dominant culture."

Watten's poetry is thus both a form of political engagement and a method of "calling existence into question"—a question which, without the slightest trace of idealist aesthetics, "becomes oneself," as he told Manuel Brito in 1991,

> Meaning in this sense becomes . . . practice by virtue of the interpretive distance necessitated by its objects. Its meaning is the questioning act.

Watten's poetry is often radically dissociative. Yet the work's disjunction is always articulated by means of a highly self-conscious structure. The intentionality Watten proposes as a possibility inherent in the formal dynamic of the work is intended to serve as a corrective to the "automatism" of everyday life. Watten's writing arrests closure as it eschews the structural hierarchy of a beginning, middle, and end. It solicits from the reader, instead, a constant questioning whose resolution is not guaranteed by plot or by character but is centered persistently (to borrow the emphatic title he and Robert Grenier gave to their seminal journal) on *this:* this page, these words, here and now.

The importance of Watten's writing has been widely acknowledged since the mid 1970s by experimentalist poets and more recently by a growing critical and academic readership. Within the past several years his work has been anthologized in many influential collections, including Ron Silliman's *In the American Tree* (1986); Douglas Messerli's books *"Language" Poetries: An Anthology* (1987)

and *From the Other Side of the Century: A New American Poetry, 1960–1990* (1994); Paul Hoover's *Postmodern American Poetry: A Norton Anthology* (1994); and volume 2 of Jerome Rothenberg and Pierre Joris's *Poems for the Millenium* (1998). In 1995 *Aerial* magazine devoted a special issue to a consideration of Watten's poetics, and in 1997 Sun and Moon Press brought out *Frame (1971–1990),* a major collection of much of his previously published poetry.

Barrett Watten was born in 1948 in Long Beach, California. His father was a research physician in the U.S. Navy, and the family moved frequently, living during the 1950s and 1960s on the West Coast, in Japan, and in Taiwan. Watten graduated from Skyline High School in Oakland, California, in 1965 and attended the Massachusetts Institute of Technology and the University of California, Berkeley, where he received an A.B. degree in biochemistry in 1969. Soon after receiving his degree, however, he decided against a career in science and enrolled in the Writers' Workshop at the University of Iowa. In 1972 he received his M.F.A. degree and returned to the West Coast. It was during this time that the Language Writing movement first began to organize itself in the San Francisco Bay Area (and a short time later, in New York City). In 1995 he earned a Ph.D. from Berkeley with a dissertation on the historical horizons of American modernism, focusing on Gertrude Stein and Laura Riding. He has taught at many universities—including the University of Iowa, San Francisco State University, the University of California, San Diego—and currently is teaching courses in modernism and cultural studies at Wayne State University.

Although they never constituted a formal group as such, the West Coast Language Poets (among whom, in addition to Watten and Grenier, were Steve Benson, Carla Harryman, Lyn Hejinian, Michael Palmer, Bob Perelman, Kit Robinson, Leslie Scalapino, and Silliman) shared similar aesthetic interests and political views, including a deep antagonism to the American military intervention in Vietnam, then in its closing stages. While attending Berkeley, Watten participated in the student resistance to the Vietnam War, and the recurrent references, such as those in *Progress* to "McNamara, / Johnson, Westmoreland, Rusk," reveal the extent to which, in Watten's words, Vietnam had "locked" his imagination "in place." Speaking to Andrew Ross about the formative role of the Vietnam War in the evolution of Language Poetry, Watten explains that "the central problem of reference" in the experimental writing of this period "may be seen in context as directly related to the administration of

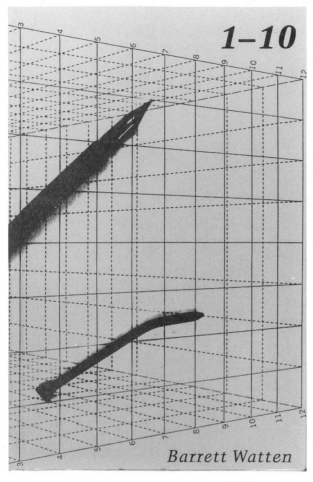

Cover for Watten's 1980 book, designed by the author

As Watten explains, "in the era of napalm, Agent Orange and the draft, the psychology of response to modernist terror that is found in earlier postmodern work—extending from Olson's corporeality to the 'body art' of Carolee Schneeman" needed to be "displaced onto . . . 'language' as ground of aesthetic distance and positive knowledge." Thus, language itself in its material substantiality became "the fantasy of objectification that replaced, discontinuously, the physicality of the earlier postmodernism."

This transference of aesthetic attention to language had, of course, been anticipated in the poststructuralist theory of Jacques Derrida, Paul de Man, and others whose work was coming into translation in the late 1970s at the same time that the Language Poets were developing their own approaches to poetry through a mostly literary genealogy. In the work of the French structuralists and poststructuralists (whose insights minimalist and conceptual artists would also subsequently explore) it is argued, as Hal Foster does in his crucial essay "The Expressivist Fallacy," that the "notion of self-expression, which governs the common idea of art in general, derives, according to de Man, 'from a binary polarity of classical banality in the history of metaphysics: the opposition of subject to object.'" Like de Man, Foster follows Friedrich Nietzsche in the recognition that

> "inner experience" enters our consciousness only after it has found a language that the individual understands—i.e., a translation of a situation into a familiar situation. . . .

information" about the purposes of American involvement in Indochina. In other words, "the formation of radical tendencies in the arts . . . was a response" to this "crisis of meaning."

It is this skepticism about the appropriation of truth by meaning that distinguishes the Language School from its avant-garde predecessors of a decade or so earlier, the so-called New American Poets. For although the New Americans' influence on the Language Writers was profound (there was, of course, the example of the San Francisco Renaissance close at hand, as well as that of the New York School poets, many of whom had recently migrated to nearby Bolinas, California), the Language Poets, responding to the "problem of reference" that Watten speaks of, shifted their attention away from the emphasis that so many of the New Americans had placed on the physical body in relation to the poetic line and toward a more self-reflexive preoccupation with the mediation of inner experience by language.

This "translation" precedes, indeed constitutes, any formed expression so that between it and the self a rhetorical figure intervenes (in linguistic terms, the subject of the *énoncé* and the subject of the *énonciation* are discontinuous). The adequation of self and expression is thus blocked—by the very sign of expression. Such is the pathos of the expressionist self: alienated, it would be made whole through expression, only to find there another sign of its alienation. For in this sign the subject confronts not its desire but its deferral, not its presence but the recognition that it can never be primary, transcendent, whole.

The claims for much poststructuralist theory of this period (particularly in the form associated with the Yale deconstructionists) were essentially apolitical. However, as an exception to this—and one with enormous importance for Language Writing—developments in poststructuralist theory took on a Marxist inflection in the work of Louis Althusser. Given the fact that ideology, in Althusser's view, is a *representation* of "the (imaginary) relationship of individuals to the relations of production," the constitution of social "reality" is seen by him to be materially and concretely connected to the reproduction of this system of relationships through language. In his essay on Ideological State Apparatuses, Althusser presents ideology as a process of textualization by which the individual is "written." As George Hartley explains:

> the conception of reading as the constitution of its object—in other words, the writing of that object—points to a conception of literary practice not just as the object of criticism but as a mode of intervention in ideological struggle. When that practice becomes conscious of itself as a practice *as such* (when it becomes "scientific practice" as Althusser would say), then that literary practice may serve as a mode of literary critique on a par with theoretical practice.

Althusser's close imbrication of ideology and representation made a decisive impression on nearly all the poets aligned with the Language movement. Though by no means strangers to institutional culture, they chose, nonetheless, to work for most of their careers at its margins and were anxious to investigate the possibilities of a counterinstitution as a site from which to advance progressive social values for the production, distribution, and reception of their work. Crucial to this effort was the Language Poets' involvement with many independent small presses, a front on which Watten was especially active. From 1971 to 1974 he collaborated on *This* magazine with Robert Grenier (whose first issue was, according to Bob Perelman, "as much of an originary moment as Language writing can be said to have") and continued as the sole editor until 1982. In addition to the magazine, This Press also published many books significant for the development of innovative poetry. The first of these, Clark Coolidge's *The Maintains,* appeared in 1974 and was followed by works of Silliman, Perelman, Robinson, Harryman, Alan Davies, Bruce Andrews, Ted Greenwald, Larry Eigner, and Watten himself. Almost equally significant for the formation of the Language Writing community were several reading series beginning in 1976, followed shortly afterward by Perelman's Talk Series and later by events organized at 80 Langton Street/New Langton Arts, for which Watten organized the writer in residence and literature programs from 1981 to 1994. During this period he also worked extensively in academic and arts publishing, with the New Historicist journal *Representations* (1984–1994) and as a contributor to the West Coast arts magazine *Artweek* (1989–1995).

In the important essay "Aesthetic Tendency and the Politics of Poetry" (1988) Watten—writing in collaboration with Silliman, Perelman, Hejinian, Harryman, and Benson—comments:

> If there has been one premise of our group that approaches the status of a first principle, it has been not the "self-sufficiency of language" or the "materiality of the sign" but *the reciprocity of practice implied by a community* of writers who read each other's work. In mainstream poetry such a community, rather than being a group of individuals, is a set of institutional norms. . . . Aesthetic tendency—the politics of *intention*—as opposed to aesthetic arbitration, offers an entirely different way of seeing the poem as produced and received. It explicitly proposes a different order of methods and values, unlike . . . the *excellence* that admits neither social affiliations nor theoretical claims.

The social practice that is promoted in Watten's poetry does not depend, therefore, on expressivist notions of the transcendental individual. Rather, aesthetic judgment is itself viewed as being contested and legitimized along a vertical organization of cultural power. It is the aim of Watten's work, as it is for Language Writing in general, to reveal the ideological structuring of language by laying bare the frames that organize perception. For Watten, "if the alienating processes of social atomization have been an unacknowledged basis of the institutional 'expressivist' aesthetics, they have likewise been a primary focus" of our "practice"—but only "to point out the process and its implications"—precisely what in mainstream poetry "is otherwise left out, elided, passed over in silence."

Commenting in a 1991 interview with Brito about the title of his first book, *Opera—Works* (1975), Watten identifies it "with two opposing possibilities: a writing that would theatrically display itself without need for persona . . . and a writing that would find a natural order in syntax by enacting its own processes." In an approximate sense, Watten says, "these two poles demonstrate the split between 'Opera' (theatrical display) and 'Works' (writing)."

Several features of *Opera—Works* (especially its dream narratives and autobiographical references) are downplayed in Watten's late work. Brought out by the New York poet Bill Berkson's Big Sky Press, the book includes, in fact, poems such as "Robert Smithson says . . . ," with a superficially New York Schoolish recourse to the visual arts as subject matter as well as allusions to friends such as "Rae" (Armantrout) of the kind that one would expect to find, say, in the works of Frank O'Hara or Ted Berrigan. But in this poem, as in the majority of others in the collection, there is also what Jerry Estrin called a re-

Cover for Watten's 1988 book, designed by the author

matic "aporias" in *Opera–Works* is already prescient of Watten's later and more developed concern with poetic scale in which "the various linguistic levels—word, line, phrase, sentence, paragraph—each" exist as "structural metonyms for language."

Decay (1977), Watten's second book, continues his critique of the poem as a communicative vehicle for expression. In this collection two works, "Chamber Music" and "Decay," have particular significance for Watten's developing aesthetic. "Decay" is divided into eight sections whose titles—"Call," "Insist," "Suicide," and so on—are seemingly both commonplace and strange. The first section, "Outside," begins with something of a paradox: "Outside the inner man's almost doubled back. / 'What a man is capable of letting alone / is his own.' . . . White waves high as / diagonals. The motives—I can't wait." Transitions between the sentences are far from clear, but in a move typical of the poem, it is evident the poet will not be located *in* the work; interiority itself has been displaced to the "outside." The "inner man . . . doubled back" is, it soon becomes apparent, the object "I" of his own reflection and simultaneously the language using subject ("The motives—I can't wait").

In "Chamber Music" Watten is credited by Silliman with the first use of the technique that Silliman calls the "New Sentence," a crucial innovation for much subsequent experimental work:

> Several of our famous relatives hid personal problems behind smiles.
> Maximum recognition of personal identity is found only at times of stress.
> Looking at the clock, flesh singed and blackened by the mysterious air.
> The circular motion endured by the inhabitants of the planet confused them.
> In order to more convincingly absent themselves, they placed great value on lies.

Extending for four and one-half pages, "Chamber Music" consists of a series of dissociated paragraphs, each a single sentence in length. While the line breaks occasionally appear to contribute to the internal disjunction of the sentence ("Looking at the clock, flesh singed and blackened by / the mysterious air"), the more decisive determination of their occurrence is clearly the length or measure of the sentence. In this passage the sentence lengths range from ten to thirteen words, the line breaks arriving always at the seventh or eighth word. The ambiguity of these sentence/paragraphs is produced, as Silliman observes of the New Sentence generally, by the absence of a sufficient referential context and/or the discontinuities of the syntax and not from any

lentless "return to a null point." In "Robert Smithson says . . . " this comes from the "writing's stress on its own centrifugal movement." ("You have to notice it without seeing it—itself comes across to hit you across—as if you'd never seen it before.")

Yet in the book considered in its entirety, the self-conflicting impression it makes arises, too, from the contradictory influences of the New York School—Louis Zukofsky, Robert Creeley, Allen Ginsberg, and so on—influences to which the title *Opera–Works* evidently alludes. However, the effect of entropy in the poems is a deliberate one; its motivation can be found in Watten's later theoretical and critical text, *Total Syntax* (1984). Writing about the sculptor Robert Smithson, Watten describes Smithson's work—and by extension his own—as taking the form "synthesis, thesis, antithesis," a dialectic which, though it consumes itself, will, "like a 'free radical' in chemistry," look around for some other "synthesis to prey on." But rather than being wholly negative, the expression of these sympto-

formal device (such as the line break) exterior to the sentence itself. Furthermore, the linguistic integration of the sentences in this passage into a level of meaning higher than that of the sentence/paragraph is closely restricted. (Taking a cue from the title, it is not inconceivable to suppose that the poem might perhaps be performed most effectively as a score for several different and discontinuous voices.)

This is not to say that the individual sentences have entirely no relationship to one another. On the contrary, many of the elements that appear in the passage above recur (images of identity, circularity, absence, and immolation), giving the poem itself an unusual coherence. Even locally it is possible to begin to frame small narratives. (For instance, the second sentence may or may not reflect a judgment about "famous relatives" who dissemble their anxiety "at times of stress.") But what is crucial for Watten's purposes is the poem's foregrounding of the material aspect of language (in which the emphasis falls on the signifier) at the expense of its referential dimension (emphasizing the signified). By disrupting, but not altogether canceling, the integration of the sentence into higher units, Watten makes visible the reader's own attempt to frame a referential context, an operation which, for Watten, is always related to—and revealing of—larger ideological formations.

In 1979 Watten received an NEA Fellowship in Creative Writing and published his third book, *Plasma/Paralleles/"X."* In this collection Watten says he was attempting to create as a theme the "dilemma" of the "simultaneous reinforcement and undermining of linguistic competence." The three long poems collected in this volume are composed of brief, disjunct paragraphs, many of which, as in "Chamber Music," extend for only a single line:

A paradox is eaten by the space around it.

I'll repeat what I said.

To make a city into a season is to wear sunglasses inside a volcano.

The "linguistic competence" that Watten speaks of is lost through the impossibility of reconciling the contradictory propositions that proliferate in the course of the reader's engagement with the poems—a competence that "would try to understand a meaning other than the present surface." "The competence gained," according to Watten, is "that which is oriented toward: 'A fact is what you can't get past,' and the name for that fact," in its intractability to transcendental significations, "is language."

During the 1980s Watten began co-editing *Poetics Journal* with Hejinian. Unlike *This,* the emphasis in *Poetics Journal,* as the title of the magazine suggests, falls on the side of theory rather than on poetry, its editorial format reflecting perhaps a shift in Language Writing away from, as Watten said to Brito, an "explanatory moment" toward a "synthesis of theory and practice."

During this time Watten's poetry became increasingly innovative and stylistically diverse as well. This tendency is immediately evident in the compositional format of *1–10* (1980), which, even more than his texts of the 1970s, is organized as a book rather than as a collection of poems. As such, it alternates between sections in verse forms that anticipate the measured stanzas of his subsequent work and sections of syntactically nonstandard prose, frequently interrupted by abruptly discontinuous phrases, either in parentheses or quotation marks. Watten opens the book with a kind of prologue, "Mode Z":

Prove to me now that you have finally undermined your heroes. In fits of distraction the walls cover themselves with portraits. Types are not men. Admit that your studies are over. Limit yourself to your memoirs. Identity is only natural. Now become the person in your life. Start writing autobiography.

Norman Fischer reads in these lines (the poem's concluding stanza) a statement of Watten's complete identification with the technique of his work. "This is autobiography to the limit," Fischer writes, "autobiography that falls off the edge of autobiography . . . canceling out at all points any tendency not only toward reference outside the work but also nonreference." Revealingly, the project Watten outlined in the above passage is already ironically qualified by the preceding stanza: "Could we have those trees cleared out of the way? / And the houses, volcanoes, empires?" Indeed in the same way that *1–10* begins at the letter *Z,* no direct statement in the book ever entirely escapes the possibility of its own inversion. Autobiographical reminiscence, to the extent that it exists in this work at all, is constantly decentered by language. For Watten "the main problem of language praxis," as Daniel Barbiero observes, is the division of "meaning and intention: the subjective control of language praxis" being inevitably "blocked or distorted on account of something prior to the expression of subjective intent in language." This is to say that language, as a social formation, carries its own prior meanings to which the individual must be "subjected," or which he or she must intentionally engage through a criti-

SUN & MOON
CLASSICS

FRAME
(1971–1990)

Barrett Watten

Cover for Watten's 1997 book, artwork by Allan McCollum

cally self-conscious practice such as that negotiated, for example, by a language-centered poetics.

Possibly the key breakthrough for Watten in the years between *Opera–Works* and *1–10* was his discovery of the various Russian/Soviet literary and linguistic theories advanced in the period extending roughly from 1915 to 1930 (in particular those of the Marxist philosopher Valentin Voloshinov and the Russian Formalists Roman Jakobson and Viktor Shklovsky). The device of using interrupting parentheses in the prose sections, for example, seems partly an attempt to work out the implications of what Voloshinov held to be the dialogical character of psychological phenomena:

> Each use (cement) of isolation (never turning) studies of same (clothesline) (laid-back posture) (against facts as such) was an inch-by-inch (in current use) thrash (divided into virus blocks) of language (inverted subject, moving away from accretion of names) (lights on lamps) features foreknowledge (without absolute) the point (to lack, or be without) disclosure separates (one makes two, in a voice)

brought down (deformities sinister) against itself (left to record) (no buildings left intact) fighting fire (separation of church and state) with fire (number).

Following Voloshinov's argument in *Marxism and the Philosophy of Language* (1929), Watten would likely approve of "a psychology based on *sociological,* not psychological or biological, principles." For Voloshinov, the psychic life of the individual is "just as social as ideology." But because it is individuals who "implement" ideology, that implementation, according to Watten, will also be as individual (as subjective) as inner experience. Moreover, the "personal" and the "social" share a linguistic basis—the structure of ideology being analogous to "the way dialogue is subordinated in recorded speech."

In the above passage from *1–10,* the parenthetical words—the poem's interior speech—act like a "virus," simultaneously penetrating and blocking the textual surface of the poem where "one . . . voice" now "makes two." Watten's use of various public discourses (legal: "separation of church and state"; scientific: "divided into virus blocks"; the dictionary: "to lack, or be without"; and others) in the "expressive" medium of the poem, in effect makes a problem of the opposition of public and private. The opposition between "inner" and "outer" is deconstructed on the physical space of the page as well, inasmuch as the parenthetical words, while figuratively interior, cannot be literally so, having been imposed onto the surface of the poem. The meaning of the poem is thus performative, the work itself being a homology for the complex intersection of linguistic and cultural transactions that construct subjectivity. "What," as Watten has asked in conversation, "are these blank spots for meaning 'saying'; what can I get them to say? How does the blank and incommensurate finally fit in as a kind of knowing, . . . as a process of learning?"

In *Complete Thought* (1982) Watten again attempts to deconstruct and reconstruct language through the processes of writing. He divides the book into four sections of approximately equal length, each of which, except for the final section, is broken down further into subsections with corresponding Roman numerals. The titles of the sections ("Complete Thought," "Universals," "Artifacts," and "Relays") seem to relate suggestively, both to the impossibility of complete consciousness and to its alienation by the distancing "artifact" of language. The first section, "Complete Thought," for example, is organized into fifty generally short, paired sentences ("complete thoughts"), each of which is discontinuous from the context into which it has been placed:

XIII

Connected pieces break into name.
Petrified trees are similar.

XIV

Everyday life retards potential.
Calculation governs speech.

The statements are "calculated" to convey an impression of incontrovertible truth. But "everyday life," which is fundamentally the reproduction of "petrified" experience, consists almost entirely of such completed (and, as here, isolated) thoughts. As Watten writes several lines later: "explanation effaces words"; that is, it "changes the scale of what is explained," as he argues in *Total Syntax,* "by means of 'improved' expression." However, in "Complete Thought" it is hardly possible for readers to map a new language onto the language of the poem itself. Rather, the work sets in motion a process that breaks off the dialectical movement toward an anticipated third term that would, for each of the paired lines, complete a syllogism. In this sense, the value of reading depends on recognition of the ineluctable presentness of the text in *time.* For it is through the temporal stasis of the poem that a more expansive syntax of *space* will become apparent. Put another way, the negative space which, in the intractable distance between each of the discrete assertions of "fact" in the poem returns it repeatedly to a zero degree writing–a kind of stylistic neutrality–lays stress, at the same time, on a more metaphorical "cultural" space. Commenting on the construction of such an expanded frame, Watten writes:

> We understand syntax as the relation of total sense to the order of elements in a language; that is, the way words make sense by means of sequence in time.
>
> However, interpretation demands context, and a statement also will be built of its possible contexts. Syntax has a spatial dimension, if space is taken in the broadest sense to be not only physical but cultural and linguistic. . . .
>
> Syntax taken in relation to art means how is the statement of the work made, both in time and space. . . .
>
> Statement causes a change of state. The objects and contexts of art are relative and continuous. A work of art can incorporate an exterior syntax within conventional or radical frames, and the interior syntax can likewise lead to a new context.

Watten's notion of poetic scale lies at the heart of the arguments made in *Total Syntax,* one of the crucial documents of the Language movement. Published in 1984 by Southern Illinois University Press, it was the first book-length critical work of the Language School, provoking attacks in the *New Criterion,*

Partisan Review, and other mainstream magazines. The essay "Total Syntax," from which the book takes its title (and which, like the other essays in the book, had originally been given as a "talk" within the Language Writing community), proposes, as George Hartley describes it, "an attention to both the internal, formal, temporal construction of a work and its external, contextual, spatial dimension." The two, according to Watten, are coextensive. Therefore, the external frames of the work ("aesthetic value systems, economic constraints, and ideological structures") mediate, but may also be affected by, its internal syntax. And it is the writer's exploitation of this "total syntax" that is, for Watten, key to the eventual political efficacy of the work: what in *Progress* is said to be "a form compelling events."

Published in 1985, a year after *Total Syntax, Progress* fully engages the possibilities of the extension of the work into "cultural and linguistic" space. Besides being ironic, the title, Watten notes in the Brito interview, calls to mind many shifting and provisional frames, "from Pilgrim's Progress (millennial horizons), the Progressive Era (standardized tests); the Progressive Labor Party (intellectual violence, breaking chairs over the heads of the SDS members); 'Work in Progress' (the unfinished project of modernism, Joyce)."

The form of *Progress,* a long poem of 120 pages, is essentially unvarying: each page includes five stanzas, all five lines long, each interrupted at some point by an ellipsis ending with a period. This last device works both to enclose the stanzas and, in a sense, to make any closure seem provisional:

A statement,
        an interpretation.
I visit Land's End to look
At wind readings, officials.
Together we look at the edge. . . .

Against broad fields of water,
   The end of the world is the
State,
       Republicans organize
Phone-in committees to agree. . . .

Several of the connotations of "progress" Watten alludes to occur here, even as the frames of reference are constantly shifting. Thus, the status of "statement" in the poem is that of "interpretation," only provisionally true. This status, as mentioned above, is made literal by the elliptical construction of the poem. But even the word "end" refuses to *end up* with a determinate meaning–the frame for "end" in the place name "Land's End" shifting in the seventh line to denote a "millennial horizon" in the phrase "The end of the world" then once again, in the next line, taking on a completely different meaning in the "intellectually violent" *ends* implied when "Republicans organize / Phone-in committees to agree. . . . "

It is through this unrelenting reflexivity that the poem serves as a critique of ideology. Yet with *Conduit* (1988), Watten's next work, there is for the first time—perhaps as a reaction to the extraordinary intellectual severity of *Progress*—"a loosening of control, an admission of the possibility," as Norman Fischer has observed, "of some sense of direction and spaciousness in the work, and an effort to clear a space within the work for communication." Still central to Watten's concerns is the reader's participation in the constitution of the meaning of the book. But now this is predicated, as Watten asserts in "The XYZ of Reading," the essay that opens the book, on the writer's "removal from the work." This absence, as Fischer describes it, paradoxically "takes the shape . . . of a person, the person of the reader, the unknown person whose unknowable mind receives the message in the work and decodes it in some unknowable way, thus making the work what it actually is."

In its format, *Conduit* also differs considerably from Watten's previous books. For while at least two of the poems that appear here ("Conduit" and "Direct Address") are not unlike the verse forms Watten had developed in *Progress* and *Complete Thought, Conduit* also includes, in addition to "The XYZ of Reading," several remarkably diverse works in prose. But perhaps the most striking element of the book is the heterogeneous poem "The Word," which, though difficult to describe, includes, among many other things, a page of numbers seemingly generated at random, an index to the introduction of *Total Syntax,* and a comic dialogue taking off from the quiz show *You Bet Your Life:*

> MAN: I'm from Long Beach.
> WOMAN: Oklahoma City. The trees are still green where I left them. Which is only partly true.
> GEORGE FENNEMAN: Distance breaks the distance record by being partly compressed, as in a dream.
> JUDGE: Disqualify that.
> GROUCHO: Well, let's get on with it. That reminds me of the time I left my necktie at the faculty association. I was looking for a psychology. I hope you remembered to tie your hands, not to mention bring your watch.

Here, in one sense, "distance"—the distance, for example, between Long Beach and Oklahoma City—has been "compressed as in a dream," making it impossible simply to "get on with it" because the speakers can only "run in place." Yet at the same time the writing, having been "structured on its own displacement," as Watten writes in "The XYZ of Reading," now increases the distance which, in a second sense, intervenes between the reader and the "very conditions of communication." Watten continues:

> This new medium is the resistance between writer and reader, speaker and hearer. . . . Any "statement" is blanked, negated, made into the form of an encompassing void—from the perspective of the reader, it indicates only the limits of the writer's form. . . . It is not by any means what he is "saying." Nothing can be compelled from the site of the speaker except the outlines of his form.

The effect, according to Fischer, is that "the sense of movement in these pieces is only that: a 'sense.' It is as if the movement were proposed not as a possibility of going anywhere, but rather as a counterforce to the assumed movement of the 'message' through the conduit of language. It is a movement meant to arrest movement, to open doors within language, not necessarily to go anywhere. In fact there isn't anywhere beyond this to get to."

In 1989, accompanied by the American poets Michael Davidson, Lyn Hejinian, and Ron Silliman, Watten traveled to what was then Leningrad to attend the first international conference of avant-garde writers permitted in the Soviet Union. The result was *Leningrad: American Writers in the Soviet Union* (1991), a collaborative work. Illustrated with many photographs of the trip and divided into four sections within which, in a different order in each section, the four poets alternately contributed a paragraph, the book is in equal parts travel narrative, prose experiment, and critical dialogue. Predicated as a way out of what Silliman calls the "pathology of the individual," the very act of collaboration (at least as it is practiced by the Language School) here is itself radical. By insisting on the value of writing as a reciprocal and transformative social process, collaboration gestures toward a redemption of alienated authorship. *Leningrad* confirms, as well, the growing international involvement of the Language movement with individual writers across national borders, French, British, Canadian, as well as post-Soviet writers have, from the late 1970s, collaborated with Watten and others on various literary projects, and these interactions have constituted a crucial contribution to *Poetics Journal.*

In *Under Erasure* (1991), Watten returns to a form of the long poem reminiscent in some ways of the simultaneously fractured and coherent stanzaic format achieved in *Progress.* Made up of alternating italicized and roman stanzas (the latter relatively unenjambed), *Under Erasure* posits excess itself as an "illustration of philosophical risk," unassimilable to totalizing interests that the narratives constituted by these interests inevitably attempt to "erase":

> Suddenly we all turn to make contact with language
> In solidarity with purposes efficiently understood
> As a speech continuous in transparent communication . . .
>
> It is that I have now achieved an age
> Of no caesurae,
>   and you are in this . . .
>
> Because of gravity,
>   they are falling
> To illustrate philosophical risk . . .

The two intersecting lines of presentation give the poem a double voice that defers its closure. In the reader's experience of the work, the meaning of each line and of each stanza will change constantly through its tentative and exploratory relationship with its neighbors. Thus, the sense of the word *falling* in the above passage resonates with all of its earlier occurrences in the concluding stanzas of the poem: the "*Fall of Saigon*," for instance, as well as the fall of the Berlin Wall. But these events cannot finally be reconciled here as they would be in a traditional narrative (this being, in a sense, the argument of the book) without, as Watten says elsewhere in the poem, "erasing"—or, to use its complementary word in the poem, *forgetting*—"to some degree." As Kit Robinson notices, the book is "in effect, a construction set, its parts laid out to suggest, on the one hand, likely assemblies (narrative or logical sequences), but also separated by means of the formal dynamics of the poem (line length, stanzas, italics, ellipsis) to highlight their functionality as shifting, variable instrumentalities."

Like *Under Erasure,* Watten's *Bad History* (1998) works with ideological discourse, but in different forms. The most immediately conspicuous feature of the poem—its striking disposition on the page—was suggested to Watten by his work in *Artweek,* where he wrote, in contravention of normative journalistic style, long subordinated paragraphs that were then published in columns of narrow width. In *Bad History,* this newspaper layout produces, in an aleatorical way, contingent rhythmic and syntactic effects. These seem entirely appropriate to the unusual interpolation of personal reminiscence and current events (such as the Branch Davidian massacre and the Gulf War) that are juxtaposed in the poem. Indeed, the historical and material dimensions of po-etry—suppressed in so much contemporary writing—are made forcefully visible here. More accessible, perhaps, than his earlier poetry, *Bad History* is nonetheless informed by "a practice of interpretation," to quote from the epigraph by Mark Cousins, "which prefers secondary sources and unreliable witnesses!" Yet it is by giving witness, finally, in a profoundly moral sense that Watten's work has, with almost painful self-consciousness, transgressed the staged realities of exploitive economies of meaning, not as theory, but in actual *fact,* in the participatory and multiple meanings of the poems themselves.

Interviews:

Michael Amnasan, "Barrett Watten Interviewed by Michael Amnasan," *Ottotole,* 2 (Winter 1986–1987): 28–60;

George Hartley, "Barrett Watten on Poetry and Politics," *Sulfur,* 8, no. 3 (Winter 1988): 196–207;

Manuel Brito, interview with Watten, in his *A Suite of Poetic Voices: Interviews with Contemporary American Poets* (Santa Brigida, Spain: Kadle Books, 1992), pp. 167–199;

Andrew Ross, "Reinventing Community: A Symposium on/with Language Poets," in *Aerial 8: Barrett Watten,* edited by Rod Smith (Washington, D.C.: Edge Books, 1995), pp. 188–199.

References:

Aerial 8: Barrett Watten, edited by Rod Smith (Washington, D.C.: Edge Books, 1995);

Bruce Andrews, *Paradise and Method: Poetics and Praxis* (Evanston, Ill. Northwestern University Press, 1996), pp. 235–245;

Ronald Day, "Beyond Epistemology's 'Thesis of the Precedence of Method': Language Writing as Postmodernism," Ph.D. dissertation, State University of New York, Binghamton, 1989;

George Hartley, *Textual Politics and the Language Poets* (Bloomington: Indiana University Press, 1989), pp. 85–86, 91–93, 96–98;

Jeffrey T. Nealon, *Double Reading: Postmodernism After Deconstruction* (Ithaca: Cornell University Press, 1993), pp. 138–141;

Bob Perelman, *The Marginalization of Poetry: Language Writing and Literary History* (Princeton, N.J.: Princeton University Press, 1996), pp. 33–36, 122–127, 177–179;

Sandra Kumamoto Stanley, *Louis Zukofsky and the Transformation of Modern American Poetics* (Berkeley: University of California Press, 1993), pp. 148, 164–171.

Harriet Zinnes
(18 April 1919 –)

Eric Miles Williamson
San Jose State University

and

Melissa Studdard Williamson
The City University of New York, Hunter College

BOOKS: *Waiting and Other Poems* (Lanham, Md.: Goosetree Press, 1964);

An Eye for an I (New York: Folder Editions, 1966);

I Wanted to See Something Flying (New York: Folder Editions, 1976);

Entropisms (Arlington, Va.: Gallimaufry, 1978);

Book of Ten (Binghampton, N.Y.: Bellevue Press, 1981);

Lover: Short Stories (Minneapolis, Minn.: Coffee House Press, 1988);

Book of Twenty (Wichita, Kans.: Ancient Mariners Press, 1992);

My, Haven't the Flowers Been? (Bozeman, Mont.: Magi Circle Press, 1995).

OTHER: *Ezra Pound and the Visual Arts,* edited, with an introduction, by Zinnes (New York: New Directions, 1980);

Blood and Feathers: Selected Poems of Jacques Prévert, translated, with a preface and an introduction, by Zinnes (Wakefield, R.I.: Asphodel Press, 1993).

SELECTED PERIODICAL PUBLICATIONS— UNCOLLECTED: "Anais Nin's Works Reissued," *Books Abroad,* 37 (1963): 283–286;

"Polar Night of America," *Parnassus 3,* no. 1 (1974): 204–209;

"John Cage: Writer," *Hollins Critic,* 17 (February 1981): 1–12;

"Nature and Design: 'Burying Euclid Deep in the Living Flesh,'" in *Ezra Pound: The Legacy of Kulchur,* edited by Marcel Smith (Tuscaloosa: University of Alabama Press, 1988), pp. 51–66;

"John Ashbery: The Way Time Feels As It Passes," *Hollins Critic,* 29 (June 1992): 1–13;

"We Are Like You, America," *Hollins Critic,* 30 (February 1993): 1–11;

"Paul Muldoon, 'Time-Switch Taped to the Trough,'" *Hollins Critic,* 33 (February 1996): 1–12.

Harriet Zinnes has made important contributions to the arts as a poet, a fiction writer, a translator, a teacher of literature and creative writing, an editor, and a critic of both literature and art. A contemporary of such poets as Charles Olson, Elizabeth Bishop, Karl Shapiro, Delmore Schwartz, John Berryman, Robert Lowell, Lawrence Ferlinghetti, Richard Wilbur, and Denise Levertov, Zinnes shares many aesthetic and social concerns with the major voices of her generation: strongly influenced by the age of high modernism, this generation of writers lived through the Great Depression, were young adults during World War II, and experienced the transition from the prenuclear age to the nuclear age—the transition from the modernist age of fragmentation to the postmodern age of existential angst. Their work ranges from the aesthetic and formal experimentations of Olson's Maximus poems, to the self-consciously populist works of Ferlinghetti and Shapiro, to the distant and socially removed works of Bishop and Lowell, to the breadth and span of poets such as Schwartz and Berryman. Zinnes's work can be categorized with the latter two poets, but this characterization is rather reductive, for what distinguishes Zinnes's poetry is that it has steadily developed, moving through the various inclinations and concerns of her generation while at the same time developing into a poetry that is beyond both the modern and the postmodern. As the Romanian critic Rodica Mihaila writes, "Harriet Zinnes is among those American poets whose talent

Harriet Zinnes

is cultivated in the modernist school, but who, though strongly influenced by the formalism of the New Critics, benefits equally from the avant-garde postmodernist explosion of American poetry of the 50's and 60's, from the liberating spirit of postmodernism." Zinnes says that her major early influences were Ezra Pound, T. S. Eliot, James Joyce (his poetry as well as his prose), Gertrude Stein, and the French poets Stéphane Mallarmé, Charles-Pierre Baudelaire, and Paul-Toussaint-Jules Valéry. But though she readily admits her influences, and though those influences are overtly acknowledged in her work, Zinnes has gone far beyond the mere assimilation of past writers: over the course of her career, she has become a leading voice in the ever-changing avant-garde. In effect, the development of twentieth-century American poetry can be traced through the work of Zinnes, and, in her fourth decade of publishing poetry and prose, Zinnes continues to serve as an astute indicator and index of the state of literary aesthetics.

Zinnes was born Victoria Harriet Fich in Hyde Park, Massachusetts, 18 April 1919. Her upbringing has played a significant role in the development of her aesthetics. Her father, Assir N. Fich, was a Russian immigrant from a long line of musicians, and though he went to law school, he worked as a relatively unsuccessful pharmacist for most of his life. At one point he sang in the New York Metropolitan Opera as a tenor. He read and wrote fourteen languages, kept books around the house, and talked about literature and philosophy with family and friends. He was a cynical and harsh man, restless and unhappy, and was not faithful to his wife (he would confide in young Harriet about his affairs). Zinnes says that her father's unhappiness figures largely in her work. Zinnes's mother, Sara Goldberg Fich, made Harriet, at the age of ten, write the following note to herself: "I must never make myself dependent on a man." After the death of Assir Fich, Zinnes discovered that he wrote poetry in his journals, and although she found that her father's poetry was not good, this discovery further solidified what she already knew to be the role her father played in her development as a writer. The family moved to New York City during the Great Depression, and Zinnes went to Washington Irving High School and then Hunter College, where she earned her B.A. degree in 1939 and studied literature and philosophy, becoming involved in the New York art scene. She preferred philosophy to literature as the literature courses of the time were not, as she says, "geared even to the New Criticism. The professors were still teaching literature as if it were merely a manifestation of history."

From 1942 to 1943 Zinnes was editor of Raritan Arsenal Publications Division, and in 1943 she married Irving Zinnes, a physicist. In 1944, the same year she earned an M.A. from Brooklyn College, she became associate editor of *Harper's Bazaar* in New York City, a post she held for three years. Her experience as an editor helped to shape her later aesthetics. Zinnes does not revise her work once it is on the page. Rather she prefers to convey

Cover for Zinnes's 1966 book, which includes poems that explore the relationship between emotion and pure aesthetics

retical chaos, the notion of order is problematic at best. Of Zinnes's work Joseph Parisi writes, "Harriet Zinnes' poetry invites analogies to modern painting and sculpture. Many of her poems are verbal collages, collections of 'found objects' (verse equivalents of Duchamp's 'ready-mades'), the significance of whose juxtaposition depends, at least in part, upon the ingenuity of the reader." Zinnes writes in her prose poem "Electrical Forces," included in *My, Haven't the Flowers Been?* (1995),

> There is no help but the disorder that bewilders the currents may come from peculiar small universes disrupting the ordinary, impelling the invisible currents to work their way into new orbital impulses, into new fractal geometries that bewilder the ordinary, tantalize the extraordinary, rework into odd new entanglements unusual installations of outrageous entropic environments, new diagrams of new disorders. . . .

In her work, rather than searching for order and rather than editing the phenomenological universe to suit her poetic needs, Zinnes prefers to let, as Emerson says, "the fact find the form." Consequently, in her books of poetry loosely formal poems are found alongside free verse, prose poems alongside verse poems; in her fiction the line between prose poetry and poetic narrative is often blurred beyond relevant distinction.

Zinnes's husband earned his Ph.D. from New York University, and together the Zinneses moved to Norman, Oklahoma, where Irving Zinnes took a teaching post at the University of Oklahoma. Harriet Zinnes opted for the life of a professor as well and has taught at Hunter College of the City University of New York (tutor, 1946–1949), Queens College of the City University of New York (tutor, 1949–1953), the University of Oklahoma (director, the Poetry and Fiction Workshop, 1959–1960), Rutgers University (lecturer, 1960–1962), the University of Geneva (visiting professor of American Literature, spring 1970), and finally as professor of English at Queens College, City University of New York (first as instructor in 1978, then as professor of creative writing and modern literature, now professor emerita). Their children, Alice and Clifford, have gone on to embody the poles of Zinnes's interests, Alice as a well-shown painter in New York City and Clifford as a professor of economics at Harvard University. Zinnes's husband's doctorate was in theoretical physics, and his involvement in physics during the shift from modernism to postmodernism helped to keep Zinnes abreast of the developments in theoretical science and philosophy, disciplines which, combined with her knowledge of literature and art, constitute the bulk of the points of depar-

the intensity of the creative act through the product of a single sitting: the act, for Zinnes, is as important as the product. Each of her poems, then, is in a way a "live" performance—a romantic, Wordsworthian practice shared by many of the writers of the Beat generation such as Allen Ginsberg, Jack Kerouac, and William Burroughs.

In 1953 Zinnes completed a Ph.D. from New York University, where she wrote her dissertation on Alexander Pope's *Dunciad* (1743). Pope's verse, highly structured and formal, had a profound influence on Zinnes's development. In a way her career as a poet has been a reaction to the formal limits historically placed on poetry. Whereas Pope's work is limited by the notion of form in the Neoclassical tradition, Zinnes's work is free of form and limited only by the imagination. The ramifications of this freedom (a freedom that both fosters the greatness of several contemporaries and the astonishing mediocrity of the current wave of solipsists) mirror the condition of postmodern thought in both the arts and the sciences: in an existential void and a theo-

ture of her poetry and prose. This fusion of fields outside of pure aesthetics and confessional autobiography enables Zinnes to transcend the more-common writers of each of the eras through which she has lived and written.

Her first two books of poetry, *Waiting and Other Poems* (1964) and *An Eye for an I* (1966)—the second book includes all the poems of the first, which was published in a limited edition—present an eclectic array of concerns ranging from works which are impressionistic and spare and read like verse versions of still-life paintings, to poems which overtly comment on the Vietnam war, to poems which deal with the possibilities of typographical and iconographic modes of generating and deconstructing meaning. Of her poetry Zinnes says, "I want my poems to declare the complexity of experience, its surprises, for to me a poem is the consequence of a deep realization that what is, is not; that what seems likely to arrive, will never; that what is least expected, will be." Fifty-six poems in all, *An Eye for an I* demonstrates the range of the poetic styles and concerns of a writer exploring the aesthetic limits of language. Zinnes says, "It is through language that I hope to achieve that tension, through its seductive music, its syntax and meanings, that can be chopped up, destroyed, denied, changed, or affirmed." This exploration yields a variety of results, and this collection includes the concerns that dominate Zinnes's subsequent work: the relationship of humanity to the construct of science; the possibilities and limitations of interdisciplinary artistic dialogues; the relationship of pure aesthetics to emotion; and the role of and hazy distinctions between love and lust, and sensual and sexual pleasure. The formal and artistic influences are modernist, but Zinnes's concern for postmodern issues pervades the formal experiments endemic to the poets of the 1960s: Zinnes comes at her subject matter like a passionate scientist, a lover of the unexplained and unexplainable. This is perhaps the most significant aspect of the book. Rather than using form for the sake of form, Zinnes uses form as a means to amplify her passions, as illustrated by her poem "Duchamp's Nude Again":

> The sinister
>   step
>   down
>   the
>   staircase
> Is
> Alone
> He
>   Alone
> Walking
>   down

> the
>   staircase.

> Holding back the smile that burrows
> (taut, beneath behind, lip concealed, teeth waiting)

> He   He
> is at the
>   bottom of the
>   stair

> and then
>   the floor
> and then
>   the door
> unbolted
> free him.

> Into the yard of air he goes.

> Air, grant him forgiveness
> Street, free him from frowning
> Stones, comfort him
> Him (who has been walking has been talking has been balking)
> where shoes and boots and rubbers
>   have been
>   have been

> where dogs have sniffed
> and horses have lain dead
> and trolley car tracks have
> and sports cars
>   into the
>   quiet sun[.]

> . . . .

> Twelve years ago he heard
>   the peacocks cry
> and looked upon the Indian pyramids.
> In his wallet is a small stone
> chiseled from a sun god
>   from Kerala
> twelve years ago.

> . . . .

> Air, grant him forgiveness[.]

Marcel Duchamp's famous futurist painting, *Nude Descending a Staircase #2* (1912), the starting point for this poem, is a painting that attempts, through a series of cubistlike stills, to give the impression of motion, much like the flickering images of a motion picture. However, the limitation of the plane of the canvas and the inertia of the paint itself make true motion impossible: hence, motion in stasis. What Zinnes does in "Duchamp's Nude Again" is present a scenario in which the nude is freed from the canvas, let loose into the world. Of course, doing this is impossible, and Zinnes knows it: the poem is as static

Cover for Zinnes's 1978 book, which publisher James Laughlin called "an important new direction in the evolution of the prose poem as a literary form"

erences and make use of juxtapositions: "Electronic Music IV" is based on William Accorsi's toy sculpture "The Clock," and "An Aged Man is But a Paltry Thing" is based on William Butler Yeats's poem "Sailing to Byzantium." The common theme of these two books is the poet's attempting to assimilate the phenomenological, the metaphysical, and the artistic worlds into an intelligible whole.

The success of Zinnes's *An Eye for an I* prompted Folder Editions to publish her next collection of poetry, *I Wanted to See Something Flying* (1976), a decade later. The development of Zinnes as a poet during the ten-year hiatus is remarkable. Whereas the first two books were largely responses to other artists, and whereas in the first two books readers can often pinpoint the specific writer or school of thought from which the works spring, in *I Wanted to See Something Flying* Zinnes finds a voice fully her own. No longer relying on tradition (or even anti-*tradition*) for her inspiration, in the thirty-five poems of her third volume Zinnes directly responds to her literary and artistic forbears only three times—in the poems "For Gertrude Stein From Gertrude Stein To Gertrude Stein," "The Sound and the Fury," and "John Cage Is Eating Mushrooms." And even in these responses the poet has manipulated the subject matter in order to convey her own ideas. "The Sound and the Fury" is a good example:

Novel   death   instrument

Flatiron sinks in water
instrument of death
in novel

Faulkner carefully constructed
        his Quentin chapter so that
        though dying – as Sartre said –
        Quentin was already dead

Already dead
while moving in novel

Novel   fixed form   dead

Character penalized by art to freeze in form
Quentin therefore anyhow dead

Outside art
formlessness
chaos   incipience
warmth   breath   being

Tea before drowning
Convulsiveness[.]

In this poem readers find Zinnes's characteristic concern with the relationship between art and life,

in reality as is the painting, and the words on the page supposedly generating meaning are nonetheless mere words, not truly generating meaning but merely attempting to do so. It is for the imagination to do the work of creating a reality through art. The nude has walked into reality and has found it an unpleasant place. The forgiveness Zinnes asks for on behalf of the nude is to be forgiven for leaving the realm of art in favor of the world of reality, a mistake Zinnes sees as a grave one indeed.

In many of the poems of the collection readers find similar juxtapositions of various works and forms of art with language: the poem "Electronic Music I: Sound Collage" takes as its subject both its title and Robert Rauschenberg's mixed-media work, *Oracle* (1965). About this poem and the series to which it belongs, Parisi writes, "In the four-part 'Electronic Music'" Zinnes "bows and points to Rauschenberg, splicing together the tapes and other electronic communications gear with the debris of a technological society." Other poems make their ref-

and although she has used Faulkner's novel *The Sound and the Fury* (1929) as a starting point, the movement of the poem is toward a personal philosophy of aesthetics: Zinnes believes that "Outside art" is "formlessness," "chaos," and "incipience," but although chaos awaits one who would venture outside art, nonetheless it is outside of art where one finds "warmth," "breath," and "being": "Tea before drowning." In order to be truly alive one must live outside of art. Art is that which imposes order on the chaos of existence, however, and one cannot do without some system of order. The question Zinnes poses provides its answer: How can one balance art and life, and is there a difference? According to Zinnes there is indeed a difference between the two, and in order to truly experience either, one must balance the two. Art and life are poles of experience, and to Zinnes these poles of experience, if acknowledged and embraced and reconciled, help to create form from the chaos of life. Zinnes said in *Contemporary Authors* (1993):

> Yes, life is loss, but for the writer, there is the joy of the very process of creation. Out of loss, out of experience, sad or joyful, there is always the possibility of creating form. I am no formalist, for each poem, it seems to me, begs its own form, its own music, too. And without music, lyrical, cacophonous, or strangely rooted in prose, there is no poetic line. Therefore the freedom that comes from the initial momentum of word upon word, the outgrowth of the feeling derived from the impulse of the word, from the cumulative tumult of experience lodged in the intense architectonics of memory. There forms the necessary order—becoming, if one is lucky, a singular vision.

Throughout *I Wanted to See Something Flying* Zinnes attempts to reconcile oppositions in order to approach the "singular vision." For instance, in the poem "Saltimbanque," a poem that attempts to deal with the poet's ongoing struggle to understand her relationship to her father, Zinnes writes, "If you are my *Papa* / kiss me. / Rearrange those numbers in my pockets / Scramble them together / To make the sum of ONE // Or shall I live alone with my numbers / *dérangés?*" The striving toward "oneness," the movement (often presented as impossible) toward unity, toward the reconciliation of oppositions, dominates this volume.

It is in her next book that Zinnes fully achieves the first major fusion of her aesthetic and philosophical notions, that she combines her notions of art and verse and prose and the chaos of the postmodern condition and produces the breakthrough volume *Entropisms* (1978). Neither verse nor narrative, this short volume (only forty-one pages) is a collage of seemingly disjunct vignettes that range in subject matter from brief philosophical statements to descriptions of events to conversations between nameless characters. Of this book James Laughlin, editor of New Directions and the publisher of Zinnes's next book, *Ezra Pound and the Visual Arts* (1980), said, "Harriet Zinnes's *Entropisms* are an important new direction in the evolution of the prose poem as a literary form." Poet David Ignatow said, "These are witty disjunctions and they ask little of the reader except that he or she recognize the disjunctive self at work here. They are metaphors in which order is bred from disorder, a subtle assurance to the reader that lapses from linear logic are all to the good in helping one to grasp a disjunctive world as itself a complete whole, playfully at work and self assured." Zinnes opens the book with the following statement:

> I combine the words *entropy, tropism, trope* to assert man's imagination in the face of the absurdity and chaos of our time. If entropy suggests the ever-increasing random "mess" of the physical universe (a Buckminster Fuller definition), and *tropism á la* Nathalie Sarraute, the unspoken, irrational undercurrent in a conversation, and *trope,* the metaphor, then the *entropism* ties it all together, breaking down the aleatoric into a controlled formulation to achieve equilibrium for perception itself. To put it simply: the physical universe is entropic. Man's imagination is antientropic.

The first sentence following the opening statement, "Everything is open and permissible," gives the reader the pivotal statement concerning Zinnes's stance regarding form. In her first three books Zinnes, while attempting to free herself from the constraints of the poetic form, nonetheless writes in forms readily recognizable as verse. In *Entropisms,* however, she has broken free of the constraints of verse. It is a book of pure idea, a book that operates intellectually with no boundaries other than those imposed by the limits of language. This freedom produces some rather startling results, not only through the implications of the juxtapositions of disparate subjects and styles but also through the range of areas of discourse Zinnes sees fit to present. One vignette reads,

> Plangency and, as Baudelaire said of Delacroix, color "that thinks for itself," and a hand and an eye. A hand an eye and plangency and color "that thinks for itself." But the earth is a pigment and the sow pisses.

And another reads,

> The mouth utters curses, and the tongue returns to its next (hidden). Some songs begin in the throat; others

Cover for Zinnes's 1992 book, a collection of poems on the numbers one through twenty

start from the tongue's quick reach above the upper teeth.

The disparity between these two passages is characteristic of the way the book progresses. However random the book may seem at first, as it unfolds, a merciless logic of the nature of chaos and disarray becomes apparent. Each vignette is carefully placed, meticulously arranged so that the reader can generate meaning not only from the individual passages but also from the blank space between the passages. A poetic treatise on the times, *Entropisms* brought Zinnes into the forefront of American letters. Nearly half of the book was published in the prestigious *New Directions* annual.

Entropisms established Zinnes as a significant voice in the New York literary scene. Directly following its publication, she edited and introduced the formidable *Ezra Pound and the Visual Arts*. Her choice to edit Pound's voluminous writings on art was the logical manifestation of Zinnes's ongoing interest in art and her affinity for the work of the mod-

ernists, especially Ezra Pound. A member of the Association of International Art Critics and an influential art critic in her own right, Zinnes combines her passion for arts with her longtime interest in Pound and produces a carefully edited volume that continues to be the primary source of Pound's writings on art. In the "Introduction" Zinnes writes,

> Pound's art criticism . . . is . . . not just occasionally significant in itself but is also of special interest as the continuation by an American writer of a tradition, particularly French, in which a man of letters devotes himself to art as well as to literary criticism. . . .

> It is only recently that an interest in the history of art criticism itself has come into being. An important poet's contribution to that history is of some significance.

These statements about Pound could just as easily be applied to Zinnes herself since her work as a poet is, like Pound's, influenced by her work as an art critic. The cumulation of Zinnes's art criticism will one day be, like Pound's art criticism, seminal to an understanding not only of the art of the poet's times but also to an understanding of her poetry.

A year after the publication of *Ezra Pound and the Visual Arts* Zinnes published *Book of Ten* (1981). She dedicates the book to her husband: "In memory of my physicist-musician husband Irving this little book of numbers." It is a collection of ten poems, each centered on the first ten numbers. Its companion volume, *Book of Twenty* (1992), also dedicated to her late husband, includes the entirety of *Book of Ten* and continues the project through the number twenty. In a prefatory note to *Book of Twenty,* Zinnes writes,

> That one can take any one system, such as perhaps the alphabet, or, as I have now done, numbers one to ten, and contain all systems: that any structure can be used either as starting points to contain multiple even infinite structures: that any one thing is all: that one is many—that the single self is all selves: that one cell is the whole man or woman.

These two books of poems work through her stated objective, continuing the overall project of her poetry—to discover the underlying structure that binds all things together. However, she knows that this unity can never be discovered, if indeed it does exist. The closing poem of the first volume, "TEN," makes this belief clear:

> "Each part, or *cántica,*
> contains 33 cantos
> for a total of 99. If we add
> the first, introductory, canto,

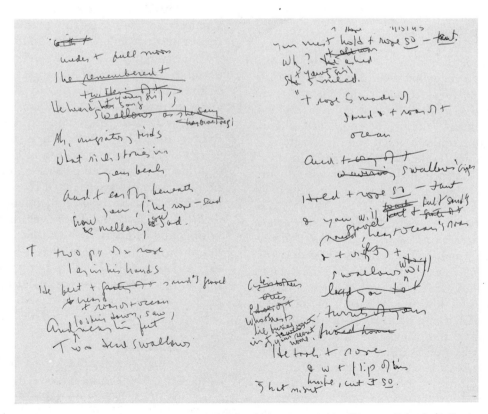

Manuscript for a poem in Zinnes's 1995 collection, My, Haven't the Flowers Been? *(Collection of Harriet Zinnes)*

we obtain a grand total of 100
which is the square of 10;
10 is the perfect number,
for it is composed solely of the square
of the Trinity, plus 1 which represents
the unity of God.

The *Cantos* of Ezra Pound
are over 100.
Unity?
No unity.
Paradise?
No, no paradise

unless it lies
somewhere between
the one eucalyptus pip
he took with him from Rapallo
under guard
and his whispers
to the patients he befriended
in St. Elizabeths
those thirteen years of fire

or in his long silences after.

I whisper too
in my encaged 10
10
Ten times I whisper
10 10 10 10 10 10 10 10 10 10.

The superimposition of a system does not, for Zinnes, mean that order has been achieved, and the goal of science to systematize the cosmos is no more productive of truth than are the metaphysical speculations of religion. Science, like religion and art, is founded upon belief and faith as there is ultimately no verifiable reality, no certitude.

In addition to poetry and criticism, during her career as a writer Zinnes has steadily been writing and publishing fiction. *Lover* (1988) is Zinnes's first short-story collection. The stories are by no means traditional works of fiction, and several of them appeared originally in the avant-garde *New Directions* annuals. With a mastery of craft uncommon to poets writing in the medium of fiction, Zinnes abandons conventional story lines, and instead of writing narratives that follow the predictable pattern of the classic story, Zinnes focuses on the development of characters through the use of highly cadenced, deliberately nonrealistic language. Many of the stories are so linguistically based and lyrically written that they are, in effect, extended prose poems. Set primarily on the East Coast and in Manhattan, the twenty-nine stories that comprise *Lover* deal with the rewards and, more often, the perils of love and sex. Fusing form and content, Zinnes writes of love and sex with a

language that is undulating, rhythmic, and sensual when the mood calls for such language. The climax of the opening of the first story, "Two Roads," is the final paragraph—a four-hundred-word sentence that is reminiscent of Nora's soliloquy in the final chapter of James Joyce's *Ulysses* (1922)—in which the main character, who is going to meet her lover, approaches her lover's home. The story ends not with the main character's arrival but with the anticipation of the arrival. The last word of the story is "longing," a state Zinnes attempts not only to represent in the character but also to create in the reader. The repetition Zinnes uses to such great effect in her poetry finds its place in her prose and creates an incantatory mood, a spellbinding representation not of a story but of a state, a condition of humanity. Zinnes's fiction throughout the collection strives not for the certitude of narrative wholeness but for a tension akin to the tension so many of the lovers in her stories either revel in or suffer through. The stories create the angst and uneasiness which is so characteristic of Zinnes's early poetry, but they do so with lyricism rather than juxtaposition, cadences of prose rather than shards of verse. The intent, however, is the same. Zinnes in her fiction attempts to dislocate the reader, to force the reader into a recognition that all is not as it seems.

Throughout Zinnes's poetry are lines rendered in French, and Zinnes uses her knowledge of French and her love of the poets of that language to produce *Blood and Feathers: Selected Poems of Jacques Prévert* (1993). Zinnes began translating Prévert in the late 1960s, when she was living in Geneva. The book, a bilingual edition of forty-eight poems, was received with much praise by the literary community. Richard Howard, America's premier translator into English from French, says of *Blood and Feathers:* "These versions are as entertaining and as instructive as their originals. They delight without damaging one's sense of a necessary strangeness." Rochelle Lynn Holt writes that the book is "A superior translation of a superb poet by a translator who is also an excellent poet." Of the project Zinnes herself writes in the "Preface,"

As I worked on the poems, I found that it was not the famous word games of Prévert that essentially interested me—though of course there was the delight, and the frustration, of translating them. It was rather the poet "who speaks to others of a palpable world," who paradoxically enough, on occasion, with sentiment attacks the false sentiment, false morality, and virtue of the world that is not real but made up by politicians, rhetoricians, false prophets. Prévert looks at death, suicide, war, at the difficulty of earning a living, at the lies of those who govern, at the powerful who make us all feel so powerless. But the poet looks also at men and women who love, who have dreams, and who simply sit at a table and drink their *café-crème*, their *vin,*

The complexities and absurdities of Prévert attracted Zinnes to his work; Zinnes was drawn as well to Prévert's presentation of the contradictions inherent in the chaotic and often nonsensical world of his poetry.

In her 1995 collection of poetry, *My, Haven't the Flowers Been?,* Zinnes is at the height of her powers of poetic and philosophical thought. Seventy-nine poems categorized into three discrete sections titled "Time," "Simulacrum," and "Mates" comprise the volume. Each section has a distinct character; yet, though the sections differ thematically, they work together to form a unified whole that represents the primary concerns of Zinnes's ongoing project. "Time" is primarily concerned with the relationship between the frozen instant and the notion of a mutable, infinitely divisible eternity; "Simulacrum" deals with the theoretical problems that arise through consideration of aesthetics, metaphysics, and science; and "Mates" ties all these concerns together, recognizing the power and necessity of Eros and asserting that human emotions and the spectrum of the things called love ultimately subsume and overwhelm all other speculative considerations. Central to the collection is the poem "Light and Darkness," found in the last section, "Mates." The last thirteen lines of the poem are indicative of the resolution Zinnes has found for the contradictions of nature:

> It is then I know you know
> that light and darkness are one
> that the cave of light
> is the cave of darkness,
> that the body and the soul are one:
> that god and man are one,
> that the grass and the serpent are one,
> that the terrorist, the assassin
> roam the same earth

as their victims.

> Cruel is this earth.
> Joyous is this earth.
> Only the shudder of love accepts that equation.

Zinnes's work has always tended toward the sensual and the erotic, yet she has continually grappled with the problems of modernist and postmodernist aesthetics and philosophy. In her early work these interests tend to present themselves in opposition to each other, or sometimes to find their resolution in collage and juxtaposition. In *My, Haven't the Flowers Been?,* however, Zinnes has worked out her ideas and has moved beyond both the modern and the postmodern. If the current period, as yet unnamed, is beyond the postmodern, this latest volume of Zinnes's poetry is a notable representative text.

An established figure in American letters, Zinnes continues to produce at an astonishing rate. Her newest volume of short stories, "The Radiant Absurdity of Desire," is currently at press, and she has recently completed a novel as well as a collection of art and literary criticism. Her critical writing continues to appear regularly in leading American journals and papers, as do her poetry and fiction. Zinnes has acknowledged and learned from her literary, philosophic, and artistic roots and, over the course of an increasingly influential career, has moved past categorization through an integration of the many areas of her interests. Rather than operating in the microcosm of letters, Zinnes has drawn from areas as seemingly disparate as theoretical physics, sexuality, aesthetics, literary studies, and art history to produce an unusual brand of contemporary literary art. Having grown to maturity during the age of the modernists, Zinnes was inundated early in her life by theories of disjuncture, fragmentation, and chaos. During the course of her ongoing career she has managed to make sense of the disunity, to intellectually and artistically reconcile the contradictions of our times.

Papers:
Zinnes's papers are held at the Beinecke Library of Yale University; Lockwood Memorial Library of the State University of New York, Buffalo; and the Sweetbriar College Library in Virginia.

Checklist of Further Readings

Allen, Donald, and Warren Tallman, eds. *The Poetics of the New American Poetry*. New York: Grove, 1973.

Altieri, Charles. *Enlarging the Temple: New Directions in American Poetry During the 1960s*. Lewisburg, Pa.: Bucknell University Press, 1979.

Altieri. *Self and Sensibility in Contemporary American Poetry*. New York: Cambridge University Press, 1984.

Baker, Peter. *Obdurate Brilliance: Exteriority and the Modern Long Poem*. Gainesville: University of Florida Press, 1991.

Baker, ed. *Onward: Contemporary Poetry and Poetics*. New York: Peter Lang, 1996.

Bartlett, Lee. *Talking Poetry: Conversations in the Workshop with Contemporary Poets*. Albuquerque: University of New Mexico Press, 1987.

Beach, Christopher. *ABC of Influence: Ezra Pound and the Remaking of American Poetic Tradition*. Berkeley & Los Angeles: University of California Press, 1992.

Bellamy, Joe David, ed. *American Poetry Observed: Poets on Their Work*. Urbana: University of Illinois Press, 1984.

Berke, Roberta Elzey. *Bounds Out of Bounds: A Compass for Recent American and British Poetry*. New York: Oxford University Press, 1981.

Bernstein, Charles. *A Poetics*. Cambridge, Mass.: Harvard University Press, 1992.

Blasing, Mutlu Konuk. *American Poetry: The Rhetoric of Its Forms*. New Haven: Yale University Press, 1987.

Blasing. *Politics and Form in Postmodern Poetry: O'Hara, Bishop, Ashbery, Merrill*. New York: Cambridge University Press, 1995.

Bloom, Harold, ed. *Contemporary Poets*. New York: Chelsea House, 1986.

Boyers, Robert, ed. *Contemporary Poetry in America: Essays and Interviews*. New York: Schocken Books, 1974.

Breslin, James E. B. *From Modern to Contemporary: American Poetry, 1945–1965*. Chicago: University of Chicago Press, 1983.

Breslin. "Poetry: 1945 to the Present," in *Columbia Literary History of the United States,* edited by Emory Elliott and others. New York: Columbia University Press, 1988, pp. 1079–1100.

Breslin, Paul. *The Psycho-Political Muse: American Poetry Since the Fifties*. Chicago: University of Chicago Press, 1987.

Bryan, Sharon, ed. *Where We Stand: Women Poets on Literary Tradition*. New York: Norton, 1993.

Carroll, Paul. *The Poem in Its Skin*. Chicago: Follett, 1968.

Codrescu, Andrei, ed. *American Poetry Since 1970: Up Late*. New York: Four Walls Eight Windows, 1987.

Conte, Joseph M. *Unending Design: The Forms of Postmodern Poetry.* Ithaca, N.Y.: Cornell University Press, 1991.

Damon, Maria. *The Dark End of the Street: Margins in American Vanguard Poetry.* Minneapolis: University of Minnesota Press, 1993.

Davidson, Michael. *Ghostlier Demarcations: Modern Poetry and the Material Word.* Berkeley: University of California Press, 1997.

Davidson. *The San Francisco Renaissance: Poetics and Community at Mid-Century.* Cambridge, U.K.: Cambridge University Press, 1989.

Dembo, L. S. *Conceptions of Reality in Modern American Poetry.* Berkeley: University of California Press, 1966.

Dodd, Elizabeth C. *The Veiled Mirror and the Woman Poet: H. D., Louise Bogan, Elizabeth Bishop, and Louise Glück.* Columbia: University of Missouri Press, 1992.

Doreski, William. *The Modern Voice in American Poetry.* Gainesville: University Press of Florida, 1995.

Duberman, Martin B. *Black Mountain: An Exploration in Community.* Garden City, N.Y.: Doubleday, 1973.

Erkilla, Betsy. *The Wicked Sisters: Women Poets, Literary History and Discord.* New York: Oxford University Press, 1992.

Faas, Ekbert. *Towards a New American Poetics: Essays and Interviews.* Santa Barbara, Cal.: Black Sparrow Press, 1978.

Feirstein, Frederick, ed. *Expansive Poetry: Essays on the New Narrative and the New Formalism.* Santa Cruz, Cal.: Story Line Press, 1989.

Finch, Annie. *The Ghost of Meter: Culture and Prosody in American Free Verse.* Ann Arbor: University of Michigan Press, 1993.

Finch, ed. *A Formal Feeling Comes: Poems in Form by Contemporary Women.* Brownsville, Oreg.: Story Line Press, 1994.

Finkelstein, Norman. *The Utopian Moment in Contemporary American Poetry.* Lewisburg, Pa.: Bucknell University Press, 1988.

Frank, Robert, and Henry Sayre, eds. *The Line in Postmodern Poetry.* Urbana: University of Illinois Press, 1988.

Fredman, Stephen. *The Grounding of American Poetry: Charles Olson and the Emersonian Tradition.* Cambridge & New York: Cambridge University Press, 1993.

Fredman. *Poet's Prose: The Crisis in American Verse,* second edition. Cambridge, U.K.: Cambridge University Press, 1990.

Gardner, Thomas. *Discovering Ourselves in Whitman: The Contemporary American Long Poem.* Urbana & Chicago: University of Illinois Press, 1989.

Géfin, Laszlo K. *Ideogram: History of a Poetic Method.* Austin: University of Texas Press, 1982.

Gelpi, Albert. *A Coherent Splendor: The American Poetic Renaissance, 1910–1950.* New York: Cambridge University Press, 1987.

Gilbert, Roger. *Walks in the World: Representation and Experience in Modern American Poetry*. Princeton, N.J.: Princeton University Press, 1991.

Gioia, Dana. *Can Poetry Matter?: Essays on Poetry and Culture*. St. Paul, Minn.: Graywolf Press, 1992.

Glazier, Loss Pequeño. *Small Press: An Annotated Guide*. Westport, Conn.: Greenwood Press, 1992.

Golding, Alan. *From Outlaw to Classic: Canons in American Poetry*. Madison & London: University of Wisconsin Press, 1995.

Gould, Jean. *Modern American Women Poets*. New York: Dodd, Mead, 1984.

Gray, Richard. *American Poetry of the Twentieth Century*. New York: Longman, 1990.

Hall, Donald. *Death to the Death of Poetry: Essays, Reviews, Notes, Interviews*. Ann Arbor: University of Michigan Press, 1994.

Hamilton, Ian, ed. *The Oxford Companion to Twentieth-Century Poetry*. New York: Oxford University Press, 1994.

Hartley, George. *Textual Politics and the Language Poets*. Bloomington: Indiana University Press, 1989.

Hartman, Charles O. *Free Verse: An Essay on Prosody*. Princeton, N.J.: Princeton University Press, 1980.

Hass, Robert. *Twentieth Century Pleasures: Prose on Poetry*. New York: Ecco Press, 1984.

Heller, Michael. *Conviction's Net of Branches: Essays on the Objectivist Poets and Poetry*. Carbondale & Edwardsville: Southern Illinois University Press, 1985.

Henderson, Stephen, ed. *Understanding the New Black Poetry*. New York: Morrow, 1973.

Hoffman, Daniel, ed. *American Poetry and Poetics*. Garden City, N.Y.: Doubleday, 1962.

Holden, Jonathan. *The Fate of American Poetry*. Athens: University of Georgia Press, 1991.

Holden. *Style and Authenticity in Postmodern Poetry*. Columbia: University of Missouri Press, 1986.

Homberger, Eric. *The Art of the Real: Poetry in England and America Since 1939*. London: Dent, 1977.

Hoover, Paul, ed. *Postmodern American Poetry*. New York: Norton, 1994.

Howard, Richard. *Alone with America: Essays on the Art of Poetry in the United States Since 1950*. New York: Atheneum, 1980.

Howard, ed. *Preferences: 51 American Poets Choose Poems from Their Own Work and from the Past*. New York: Viking, 1974.

Ignatow, David, ed. *Political Poetry*. New York: Chelsea, 1960.

Ingersoll, Earl, Judith Kitchen, and Stan Sanvel Rublin, eds. *The Post-Confessionals: Conversations with American Poets of the Eighties*. Cranford, N.J.: Associated University Presses, 1989.

Jackson, Richard. *Acts of Mind: Conversations with Contemporary Poets*. Tuscaloosa: University of Alabama Press, 1983.

Jackson. *The Dismantling of Time in Contemporary Poetry*. Tuscaloosa: University of Alabama Press, 1988.

Juhasz, Suzanne. *Naked and Fiery Forms: Modern American Poetry by Women*. New York: Harper & Row, 1976.

Kalaidjian, Walter. *Languages of Liberation: The Social Text in Contemporary American Poetry*. New York: Columbia University Press, 1989.

Kalstone, David. *Becoming a Poet: Elizabeth Bishop with Marianne Moore and Robert Lowell*. New York: Farrar, Straus & Giroux, 1989.

Kalstone. *Five Temperaments: Elizabeth Bishop, Robert Lowell, James Merrill, Adrienne Rich, John Ashbery*. New York: Oxford University Press, 1977.

Keller, Lynn. *Forms of Expansion: Recent Long Poems by Women*. Chicago & London: University of Chicago Press, 1997.

Keller. *Re-making It New: Contemporary American Poetry and the Modernist Tradition*. Cambridge, U.K.: Cambridge University Press, 1987.

Keller, and Cristanne Miller, eds. *Feminist Measures: Soundings in Poetry and Theory*. Ann Arbor: University of Michigan Press, 1995.

Kostelanetz, Richard. *The Old Poetries and the New*. Ann Arbor: University of Michigan Press, 1981.

Lacey, Paul A. *The Inner War: Forms and Themes in Recent American Poetry*. Philadelphia: Fortress Press, 1972.

Larrissy, Edward. *Reading Twentieth-Century Poetry: The Language of Gender and Objects*. Oxford: Blackwell, 1990.

Lazer, Hank. *Opposing Poetries*, 2 volumes. Evanston, Ill.: Northwestern University Press, 1996.

Lazer, ed. *What Is a Poet?: Essays from the Eleventh Alabama Symposium on English and American Literature*. Tuscaloosa: University of Alabama Press, 1987.

Leary, Paris, and Robert Kelly, eds. *A Controversy of Poets*. Garden City, N.Y.: Anchor/Doubleday, 1965.

Lehman, David. *The Big Question*. Ann Arbor: University of Michigan Press, 1995.

Lehman. *The Line Forms Here*. Ann Arbor: University of Michigan Press, 1992.

Lehman, ed. *Ecstatic Occasions, Expedient Forms: 65 Leading Contemporary Poets Select and Comment on their Poems*. New York: Macmillan, 1987.

Lensing, George S., and Robert Moran. *Four Poets and the Emotive Imagination: Robert Bly, James Wright, Louis Simpson, and William Stafford*. Baton Rouge: Louisiana State University Press, 1976.

Lepper, Gary M. *A Bibliographical Introduction to Seventy-Five Modern American Authors*. Berkeley, Cal.: Serendipity Books, 1976.

Libby, Anthony. *Mythologies of Nothing: Mystical Death in American Poetry, 1940–1970*. Urbana: University of Illinois Press, 1984.

Lieberman, Laurence. *Unassigned Frequencies: American Poetry in Review, 1964–77*. Urbana: University of Illinois Press, 1977.

Martin, Robert K. *The Homosexual Tradition in American Poetry*. Austin: University of Texas Press, 1979.

Mazzaro, Jerome. *Postmodern American Poetry*. Urbana: University of Illinois Press, 1980.

McClatchy, J. D. *White Paper: On Contemporary American Poetry*. New York: Columbia University Press, 1989.

McClure, Michael. *Scratching the Beat Surface*. San Francisco: North Point Press, 1982.

McCorkle, James. *The Still Performance: Writing, Self, and Interconnection in Five Postmodern American Poets*. Charlottesville: University Press of Virginia, 1989.

McCorkle, ed. *Conversant Essays: Contemporary Poets on Poetry*. Detroit: Wayne State University Press, 1990.

McDowell, Robert, ed. *Poetry After Modernism*. Brownsville, Oreg.: Story Line Press, 1991.

Mersmann, James F. *Out of the Vietnam Vortex: A Study of Poets and Poetry Against the War*. Lawrence: University Press of Kansas, 1974.

Messerli, Douglas, ed. *From the Other Side of the Century: A New American Poetry, 1960–1990*. Los Angeles: Sun & Moon Press, 1994.

Middlebrook, Diane Wood, and Marilyn Yalom, eds. *Coming to Light: American Women Poets in the Twentieth Century*. Ann Arbor: University of Michigan Press, 1985.

Miller, James E. Jr. *The American Quest for a Supreme Fiction: Whitman's Legacy in the Personal Epic*. Chicago: University of Chicago Press, 1979.

Molesworth, Charles. *The Fierce Embrace: A Study of Contemporary American Poetry*. Columbia: University of Missouri Press, 1979.

Moss, Howard, ed. *The Poet's Story*. New York: Macmillan, 1973.

Myers, Jack, and David Wojahn, eds. *A Profile of Twentieth-Century American Poetry*. Carbondale & Edwardsville: Southern Illinois University Press, 1991.

Nelson, Cary. *Our Last First Poets: Vision and History in Contemporary American Poetry*. Urbana & Chicago: University of Illinois Press, 1981.

Nelson. *Repression and Recovery: Modern American Poetry and the Politics of Cultural Memory, 1910–1945*. Madison: University of Wisconsin Press, 1989.

Ossman, David. *The Sullen Art*. New York: Corinth Books, 1967.

Ostriker, Alicia Suskin. *Stealing the Language: The Emergence of Women's Poetry in America*. Boston: Beacon, 1986.

Packard, William, ed. *The Craft of Poetry: Interviews from the New York Quarterly*. Garden City, N.Y.: Doubleday, 1974.

Palmer, Michael, ed. *Code of Signals: Recent Writings in Poetics*. Berkeley, Cal.: North Atlantic Books, 1983.

Parini, Jay, and Brett C. Millier, eds. *The Columbia History of American Poetry*. New York: Columbia University Press, 1993.

Paul, Sherman. *In Search of the Primitive: Rereading David Antin, Jerome Rothenberg, and Gary Snyder*. Baton Rouge: Louisiana State University Press, 1986.

Perelman, Bob. *The Marginalization of Poetry: Language Writing and Literary History*. Princeton, N.J.: Princeton University Press, 1996.

Perelman. *The Trouble with Genius: Reading Pound, Joyce, Stein, and Zukofsky*. Berkeley: University of California Press, 1994.

Perkins, David. *A History of Modern Poetry: Modernism and After*. Cambridge, Mass.: Harvard University Press, 1987.

Perloff, Marjorie. *The Dance of the Intellect: Studies in the Poetry of the Pound Tradition*. Cambridge, U.K.: Cambridge University Press, 1985.

Perloff. *Poetic License: Essays on Modernist and Postmodernist Lyric*. Evanston, Ill.: Northwestern University Press, 1990.

Perloff. *The Poetics of Indeterminacy: Rimbaud to Cage*. Princeton, N.J.: Princeton University Press, 1981.

Perloff. *Radical Artifice: Writing Poetry in the Age of Media*. Chicago: University of Chicago Press, 1991.

Perloff. *Wittgenstein's Ladder: Poetic Language and the Strangeness of the Ordinary*. Chicago: University of Chicago Press, 1996.

Pinsky, Robert. *The Poet and the World*. New York: Ecco Press, 1988.

Pinsky. *The Situation of Poetry: Contemporary Poetry and Its Traditions*. Princeton, N.J.: Princeton University Press, 1976.

Poulin, A. Jr., ed. *Contemporary American Poetry*. Boston: Houghton Mifflin, 1971.

Quartermain, Peter. *Disjunctive Poetics: From Gertrude Stein and Louis Zukofsky to Susan Howe*. Cambridge, U.K.: Cambridge University Press, 1992.

Rasula, Jed. *American Poetry Wax Museum: Reality Effects, 1940–1990*. Urbana, Ill.: National Council of Teachers of English, 1996.

Rasula and Steve McCaffery, eds. *Imagining Language: An Anthology*. Cambridge, Mass.: MIT Press, 1998.

Redmond, Eugene. *Drumvoices: The Mission of Afro-American Poetry: A Critical History*. Garden City, N.Y.: Anchor/Doubleday, 1976.

Reinfeld, Linda. *Language Poetry: Writing as Rescue*. Baton Rouge: Louisiana State University Press, 1992.

Richman, Robert, ed. *The Direction of Poetry: An Anthology of Rhymed and Metered Verse Written in the English Language Since 1975*. Boston: Houghton Mifflin, 1988.

Rosenthal, M. L. *The New Poets*. New York: Oxford University Press, 1967.

Rosenthal and Sally M. Gall. *The Modern Poetic Sequence: The Genius of Modern Poetry*. New York: Oxford University Press, 1983.

Ross, Andrew. *The Failure of Modernism: Symptoms of American Poetry*. New York: Columbia University Press, 1986.

Rothenberg, Jerome, and Pierre Joris, eds. *Poems for the Millennium: The University of California Book of Modern & Postmodern Poetry*, volume 1: *From Fin-de-Siècle to Negritude*. Berkeley & Los Angeles: University of California Press, 1995.

Schultz, Susan M., ed. *The Tribe of John: Ashbery and Contemporary Poetry*. Tuscaloosa: University of Alabama Press, 1995.

Shaw, Robert B., ed. *American Poetry Since 1960: Some Critical Perspectives*. Chester Springs, Pa.: Dufour, 1974.

Shetley, Vernon. *After the Death of Poetry: Poet and Audience in Contemporary America*. Durham, N.C.: Duke University Press, 1993.

Shucard, Alan, Fred Moramarco, and William Sullivan. *Modern American Poetry, 1865–1950*. Boston: Twayne, 1989.

Simpson, Eileen. *Poets in Their Youth: A Memoir*. New York: Random House, 1982.

Smith, Dave. *Local Assays*. Urbana: University of Illinois Press, 1985.

Sorrentino, Gilbert. *Something Said*. San Francisco: North Point Press, 1984.

Spiegelman, Willard. *The Didactic Muse: Scenes of Instruction in Contemporary American Poetry*. Princeton, N.J.: Princeton University Press, 1989.

Steele, Timothy. *Missing Measures: Modern Poetry and the Revolt Against Meter*. Fayetteville: University of Arkansas Press, 1990.

Stepanchev, Stephen. *American Poetry Since 1945: A Critical Survey*. New York: Harper & Row, 1965.

Taggart, John. *Songs of Degrees: Essays on Contemporary Poetry and Poetics*. Tuscaloosa: University of Alabama Press, 1994.

Thurley, Geoffrey. *The American Moment: American Poetry in the Mid-Century*. London: E. Arnold, 1977.

Tytell, John. *Naked Angels: The Lives and Literature of the Beat Generation*. New York: McGraw-Hill, 1976.

Vendler, Helen. *The Music of What Happens*. Cambridge, Mass.: Harvard University Press, 1988.

von Hallberg, Robert. *American Poetry and Culture, 1945–1980*. Cambridge, Mass.: Harvard University Press, 1985.

Young, David, and Stuart Friebert, eds. *A Field Guide to Contemporary Poetry and Poetics*. New York: Longman, 1980.

Contributors

Robert Archambeau ....*Lake Forest College*
Ronald Baughman ....*University of South Carolina*
Robert J. Bertholf...*State University of New York at Buffalo*
George F. Butterick ....*University of Connecticut*
Bruce Campbell ....*University of California, Riverside*
Constance Coiner ....*State University of New York, Binghamton*
Jacques Debrot ....*Harvard University*
Patrick F. Durgin ....*University of Iowa*
Steve Evans...*Brown University*
Edward Halsey Foster...*Stevens Institute of Technology*
Benjamin Friedlander ....*State University of New York, Buffalo*
Elisabeth A. Frost ....*Fordham University at Lincoln Center*
Charla Howard...*Long Beach City College*
Sergei Lobanov-Rostovsky...*Kenyon College*
Elizabeth Losh ....*University of California, Irvine*
Sara Lundquist ....*University of Toledo*
Steven Marks ....*New London, Connecticut*
James McCorkle ....*Geneva, New York*
Susan Marie Powers ....*Woodstock Academy*
Jed Rasula...*Queen's University*
Gary Roberts ....*Brandeis University*
Mark Scroggins ....*Florida Atlantic University*
Rod Smith ....*Washington, D.C.*
Chris Stroffolino ....*Brooklyn, New York*
Ann Vickery...*University of Melbourne*
William Walsh ....*Miami University (Ohio)*
Gabrielle Welford ....*University of Hawaii at Manoa*
Eric Miles Williamson...*San Jose State University*
Melissa Studdard Williamson ....*The City University of New York, Hunter College*

Cumulative Index

Dictionary of Literary Biography, Volumes 1-193
Dictionary of Literary Biography Yearbook, 1980-1997
Dictionary of Literary Biography Documentary Series, Volumes 1-16

Cumulative Index

DLB before number: *Dictionary of Literary Biography,* Volumes 1-193
Y before number: *Dictionary of Literary Biography Yearbook,* 1980-1997
DS before number: *Dictionary of Literary Biography Documentary Series,* Volumes 1-16

C

F

K

O

P

W

X

Y

ISBN 0-7876-1848-9